IRAQ:
GUIDE TO LAW
AND POLICY

ASPEN PUBLISHERS

IRAQ: GUIDE TO LAW AND POLICY

Chibli Mallat
Presidential Professor of Law and
Professor of Middle Eastern Law and Politics
S.J. Quinney College of Law
University of Utah

EU Jean Monnet Professor of European Law
Saint Joseph's University, Lebanon

Wolters Kluwer

Law & Business

AUSTIN   BOSTON   CHICAGO   NEW YORK   THE NETHERLANDS

Aspen Publishers
Attn: Permissions Department
76 Ninth Avenue, 7th Floor
New York, NY 10011-5201

To contact Customer Care, e-mail customer.care@aspenpublishers.com, call 1-800-234-1660, fax 1-800-901-9075, or mail correspondence to:

Aspen Publishers
Attn: Order Department
PO Box 990
Frederick, MD 21705

Printed in the United States of America.

1 2 3 4 5 6 7 8 9 0

ISBN 978-0-7355-8484-6

Library of Congress Cataloging-in-Publication Data

Mallat, Chibli.
   Iraq : guide to law and policy / Chibli Mallat.
      p. cm.
   Includes index.
   ISBN 978-0-7355-8484-6
1. Law—Iraq.   2. Iraq—Politics and government.   I. Title.
KMJ68.M35 2009
349.567—dc22

                                                                    2009040061

About Wolters Kluwer Law & Business

Wolters Kluwer Law & Business is a leading provider of research information and workflow solutions in key specialty areas. The strengths of the individual brands of Aspen Publishers, CCH, Kluwer Law International and Loislaw are aligned within Wolters Kluwer Law & Business to provide comprehensive, in-depth solutions and expert-authored content for the legal, professional and education markets.

CCH was founded in 1913 and has served more than four generations of business professionals and their clients. The CCH products in the Wolters Kluwer Law & Business group are highly regarded electronic and print resources for legal, securities, antitrust and trade regulation, government contracting, banking, pension, payroll, employment and labor, and healthcare reimbursement and compliance professionals.

Aspen Publishers is a leading information provider for attorneys, business professionals and law students. Written by preeminent authorities, Aspen products offer analytical and practical information in a range of specialty practice areas from securities law and intellectual property to mergers and acquisitions and pension/benefits. Aspen's trusted legal education resources provide professors and students with high-quality, up-to-date and effective resources for successful instruction and study in all areas of the law.

Kluwer Law International supplies the global business community with comprehensive English-language international legal information. Legal practitioners, corporate counsel and business executives around the world rely on the Kluwer Law International journals, loose-leafs, books and electronic products for authoritative information in many areas of international legal practice.

Loislaw is a premier provider of digitized legal content to small law firm practitioners of various specializations. Loislaw provides attorneys with the ability to quickly and efficiently find the necessary legal information they need, when and where they need it, by facilitating access to primary law as well as state-specific law, records, forms and treatises.

Wolters Kluwer Law & Business, a unit of Wolters Kluwer, is headquartered in New York and Riverwoods, Illinois. Wolters Kluwer is a leading multinational publisher and information services company.

For the peoples of Iraq and their friends,
May they choose well.

SUMMARY OF CONTENTS

CONTENTS

ACKNOWLEDGMENTS

There is not enough room for the proper acknowledgement of those who worked hard in each of the complex fields at play. This book grew from a seminar on the Iraqi conflict at the SJ Quinney College of Law at the University of Utah in Spring 2008, on the suggestion of Dean Hiram Chodosh, a close friend and visionary colleague. The seminar, relying on the dedication of seven students attending the class, turned into the present work. For each of the following six chapters, there was generally a principal researcher and compiler, and a reviewer: respectively Shanna Francis and James Smith for Chapter 2; Craig Flinders and Isaak Hurst for Chapter 3; Dan Burton and Craig Flinders for Chapter 4; Dan Burton for Chapter 5; Isaak Hurst and Shanna Francis for Chapter 6; Joe Kreidel and James Smith for Chapter 7; Josh Rupp helped coordinate the book, and offered an active assistance at all stages of the research and production, and Ben Lear helped research and edit several chapters. I am most grateful to the intensive commitment of these dedicated students for this project. This book is really their accomplishment much more than mine. I am especially grateful to Nada Chahine and Mary Wheeler, for their help in the final stages of the production.

The book also benefited from the dedication of the Global Think Tank students under the leadership of Artemis Vamianakis, of other colleagues at the University of Utah, and beyond. I am particularly grateful to Hiram Chodosh, again, for delving into some of the details in the book, especially Chapter 4; Professor Deena Hurwitz, from the University of Virginia Law School, William "Spence" Spencer, from the Institute for International Law and Human Rights (previously The Public International Law and Policy Group), Washington, D.C., and his colleagues Julia Pataki and Robin Gary, who have worked closely with Iraqis in support of the rule of law; Dan E. Stigall, then with the U.S. Army JAG Corps, who has published several articles on complex areas of Iraqi law, for Chapter 5; Professor Haider Ali Hamoudi of the University of Pittsburgh, who is bridging the American and Iraqi legal worlds with unprecedented scholarship, for Chapter 3. Haider Hamoudi, Deena Hurwitz, and Dan E. Stigall kindly agreed to review the full version of the book in record time, and I cannot thank them enough for their friendship and scholarly dedication. Although their comments have been invaluable, I am exclusively responsible for the choice of material and its treatment in the book, and for its many imperfections.

At Aspen Publishers, I am grateful to Carol McGeehan's leadership, and to the support of Lynn Churchill, John Devins, Troy Froebe, and their colleagues. I should also acknowledge the genuine inspiration for the course from the highest levels of government in Iraq, starting with the Iraqi ambassador to the UN, Dr. Hamid al-Bayyati, who visited Salt Lake City in Fall 2007.

Reengaging with Iraq. I had learned to appreciate Hamid's dedication when we worked together on Indict, a group we founded together in London in 1996 to bring Saddam Hussein and his close aides to trial for crimes against humanity. When I decided to re-engage with Iraq, Hamid arranged for an invitation from Prime Minister Maliki to discuss some of the issues now presented in this book, and that encouragement made the effort suddenly real to all. This reengagement with Iraq, also helped by another old friendship, that of Iraq's ambassador to the U.S., Samir al-Sumaidaie, unexpectedly intensified when the College of Law at the University of Utah received two significant grants from the U.S. State Department to assist the Government of Iraq in constitutional, legislative, and judicial matters. This led to three working visits to Baghdad in four months to help establish the Global Justice Project: Iraq (www.gjpi.org).

The book had been mostly completed by the time the visits took place, and I have avoided the inclusion of any sensitive or internal documents since the Global Justice Project started. But the visits were exceptional, and the welcome of old friends overwhelming. The list is too long to cite, but I must mention the warm embrace of the Iraqi President Jalal Talibani and his close aides, Dr. Fuad Ma'sum, who sits on the leadership of the Constitutional Review Committee, Deputy Prime Minister Barham Saleh, and Dr. Lateef Rashid, Minister of Water; all dear friends from the days of lead, as well as the president of the Kurdish region Mas'ud al-Barzani and his chief of staff Fuad Hussein; Hiram Chodosh and I were warmly greeted by Prime Minister Nuri al-Maliki, his chief advisor Ambassador Sadiq al-Rikabi, and his chief of staff Dr. Tarek Najm 'Abdallah. Old friendships contacted again in Baghdad include Sayyed Muhammad Bahr al-'Ulum, the distinguished Shi'i scholar and first president of the Iraq Governing Council, who introduced me to the world of Najaf scholarship over two decades ago; Dr. Ahmad Chalabi, a man as extraordinary and courageous as he is controversial, though not controversial to me who shared with Ahmad exalted and difficult moments in opposition to dictatorship, including a few hours spent in jail on the Iranian border in May 1992; the National Security Council advisor Dr. Muwaffaq al-Rubaie; Speaker Dr. Ayad al-Samarra'i and Sheikh Khaled 'Atiyyeh, the Deputy Speaker and author of one of the most remarkable modern compendia of Shi'i law; MPs Dr. Salem al-Jiburi and Dr. Baha' al-A'raji, from the legal committee of the Iraqi Council of Representatives; and several other remarkable MPs of the new Iraq, including the Secretary General of the Fadila party, Sayyed Hashim al-Hashimi, Assyrian leader Yonadam Kanna, Karim al-Ya'qubi, Malhan al-Moguter, former judge Wael al-Fadel, leading female MPs Zahra al-Hashimi and Shatha al-Obosi, Dr. Saleh Mutlak and his distinguished colleagues in the Hiwar bloc and many others met in committees and working groups. I must acknowledge the extraordinary trust and friendship of MP Sheikh Humam Hamoudi, head of the Constitutional Review Committee (CRC), his assistant 'Ali Fadel', and the members of the CRC, MPs Fuad Ma'sum, Dr. Salem al-Jiburi again, MP Abbas Bayyati, MP Dr. Fariad Rawanduz, MP Sayyed 'Ali Allaq, MP 'Alia Nassif, Dr. Mayada Al-Ihtishami, and Dr. Hassan Al-Yasiri, the diligent secretary of the CRC.

I was also warmly welcomed by the country's senior judges: the courageous president of the High Criminal Court, 'Aref al-Chahine, ably assisted by the court director Haithem al-Musawi, the distinguished Shura Council president Ghazi al-Janabi, and the energetic Chief Justice Midhat al-Mahmud, president of the Higher Judicial Council, of the Federal Supreme Court, and of the Court of Cassation. While this book was in the main completed before I went to Baghdad again in October 2008, many passages were reinforced, enlightened, or corrected in view of subsequent work with my Iraqi and Global Justice Project colleagues. Again, I have avoided the inclusion of any material I have been privy to thanks to the extraordinary GJPI work.

Albeit a different type of warmth, I should acknowledge the welcome of Ambassadors Ryan Crocker and Robert Ford, anti-corruption Ambassadors Lawrence Benedict and Joseph Stafford, whose democratic vision and hopes for Iraq have been chiefly translated for me by the U.S. Embassy's Constitutional and Legislative advisor April Powell-Willingham, her deputies Marc Chrétien and Jim Beeby, along with Alan Zangana and an impressive staff devoted to Iraqi democracy and human rights; as well as the Embassy's INL-Rule of Law dedicated colleagues of whom Alex Wong will remain a lasting impression. I cannot emphasize enough the exceptional engagement of April Powell-Willingham with Iraqis. Her humanistic, almost driven view of American commitment, should be a model for a foreign policy still looking for its world bearings beyond *Realpolitik*.

A happy coincidence joined me in Iraq with the two leaders of the UN mission, the Chief of Mission Staffan de Mistura and his deputy Andrew Gilmore. On reflection, this was not a total coincidence, for they represent the best that the United Nations Secretariat has offered to Middle Eastern democrats in the past two decades. Not surprisingly, their staff was also remarkable, and I have closely worked with Sven Spengemann and his colleagues for a better Iraq. It is unusual for a jurist such as myself to get involved in as challenging a milieu as the one prevailing in 2008-2009 Iraq, especially when one is blessed with old and new friendships of this caliber, and a growing unsurpassed expert team around the GJPI that includes Andrew Allen, my former student who has long surpassed his teachers, Joanne Dickow, Jim Holbrook, Ambassador Vincent Battle, Haider Hamoudi, Wayne McCormack, Melissa Waters, Jaye Sitton, Jeff Fischer and Sean Grafton, Muayyad al-Chalabi and Janan Dakak, distinguished Iraqi staff holding the fort in Baghdad in always difficult circumstances, and outstanding colleagues and students at the University of Utah. I do not know of any legal occasion like this one for exploring avenues between Iraqi and like-minded American and other opinion leaders in this way. I must also say how privileged I have been in Utah with the leadership and wide horizons of the University's president, Michael Young, and Governor Jon Huntsman.

Also in the manner of disclosing my interest, I should state that my involvement with Iraq is neither new, nor usual in the traditional scholarly sense. I have worked on Iraq with Iraqis for over 20 years. Ever since brutal turf wars between the Iraqi, Iranian, and Syrian governments in my native Lebanon in the late 1970s, and the intimate link between the Iran-Iraq war and the Israeli invasion in 1982, when the Iraqi ruler engineered the attempted assassination of the Israeli ambassador to London to encourage that ill-conceived invasion, through to my work on the late Muhammad Baqer as-Sadr and the forging of many friendships of Iraqi opposition leaders in London, including Sayyed Mahdi al-Hakim (who was assassinated in the Sudan in April 1988), Iraq has been a constant personal concern as the key to a better, more humane, Middle East. I opposed the war in 2003, but I had long supported efforts to bring Saddam Hussein and his close aides to account: politically by siding with many Iraqi oppositional figures since the brutal death of Mahdi al-Hakim, and helping them within the limited means at my disposal to bring an end to the dictatorship; and judicially by developing human rights tools to bring an end to impunity in Iraq. My personal Iraqi tribulations are uninteresting, and I brook no illusion that they deflected the course of Iraqi history in any meaningful way, but such a long personal commitment to human rights and democracy in Iraq, and to non-violence in the whole region, inevitably colors my views. This *Guide* is very much informed by this commitment, and the reader will find many texts drawn from this close interaction with the country over two decades.

I would also like to thank the following authors and publishers for kindly granting permission to reproduce excerpts of, or illustrations from, the following materials.

Batatu, Hanna, *The Old Social Classes and the Revolutionary Movements of Iraq* 545-557 (1978). Reprinted with permission of Saqi books, with special thanks to André Gaspard.

Brown, Nathan, The Final Draft of the Iraqi Constitution: Analysis and Commentary (Sept. 15, 2005), http://www.carnegieendowment.org. Reprinted with permission of the Carnegie Endowment for International Peace, with special thanks to Nathan Brown.

Caron, David D., *The Reconstruction of Iraq: Dealing with Debt*, 11 U.C. Davis J. Intl. L. & Poly. 123 (2004). Reprinted with permission.

Crane, David, A., *Gallows in Baghdad: International Justice in 2006* (Jan. 3, 2007), http://jurist.law.pitt.edu/forumy/2007/01/gallows-in-baghdad-international.php. Reprinted with permission of Jurist Legal News and Research Services, Inc., with special thanks to Bernard Hibbits

Danner, Mark, *"The Moment Has Come to Get Rid of Saddam,"* El País Minutes Transcript Between President Bush and Spanish Prime Minister Jose Maria Aznar at Crawford, Texas (Nov. 8, 2007), http://www.nybooks.com/

articles/20770. Reprinted with permission of The New York Review of Books.

Dickinson, Laura A., *Abu Ghraib: The Battle over Institutional Culture and Respect for International Law*, in *International Law Stories* 414-416 (John E. Noyes, Laura A. Dickinson & Mark W. Janis eds., 2007). Reprinted with permission of Thomson West, with special thanks to Laura Dickinson.

Dobbins, James, *The UN's Role in Nation-Building: From Congo to Iraq* (2005). Reprinted with permission of the National Book Network, with special thanks to Lauren Skrabala at the Rand Coporation.

Hamoudi, Humam, *My Perceptions on the Iraqi Constitutional Process*, 59 Stan. L. Rev. 1315 (2007). Reprinted with permission from Stanford Law Review.

Kirgis, Frederic L., *International Agreements and the U.S. Law*, ASIL Insights (May 1997), http://www.asil.org/insigh10.cfm#author. Reprinted with permission of the American Society of International Law.

Latif, Ali, Iraq: Status of National Reconciliation (Mar. 2008). Reprinted by permission of the publisher from *Iraq: Status of National Reconciliation*, Ali Latif (Washington, DC; Carnegie Endowment for International Peace, 2008). http://www.carnegieendowment.org/arb/.

Low, Lucinda A., *Enforcement of the Foreign Corrupt Practices Act in the United States: Trends and the Effects of International Standards* 771-776 (PLI Corporate Law and Practice Handbook Series, Apr.-May 2008). This material has been published as a part of *Foreign Corrupt Practice Act 2008: Coping with Heightened Enforcement Risks*, by Lucinda A. Low et al., available at 1-800-260-4754; www.pli.edu © The Practising Law Institute. Reproduced with permission. All rights reserved.

Muir, Richard, *The Iraq-Kuwait Border Dispute: Still a Factor for Instability?*, 35 Asian Aff. 147 (2004), copyright © The Royal Society for Asian Affairs, reprinted by permission of (Taylor & Francis Ltd, http://www.tandf .co.uk/journals) on behalf of The Royal Society for Asian Affairs.

Stigall, Dan, *A Closer Look at Iraqi Property and Tort Law*, 68 La. L. Rev. 776 (2008). Reprinted with permission of the Louisiana Law Review.

World Bank, *Rebuilding Iraq: Economic Reform and Transition*, http://sitere sources.worldbank.org/IRFFI/Resources/CEMEXsum.pdf. With thanks to the International Bank for Reconstruction and Development, The World Bank, which is the source and the copyright holder of the data used.

World Bank, *United Nations/World Bank Joint Iraq Needs Assessment* (Oct. 2003), http://siteresources.worldbank.org/INTIRAQ/Overview/20147568/Joint% 20Needs%20Assessment.pdf. With thanks to the International Bank for Reconstruction and Development, The World Bank, which is the source and the copyright holder of the data used.

NOTE ON SOURCES, SPELLING, AND CITATIONS

The amount of material on Iraq is overwhelming and hard choices had to be made. A search in American and British law journals yielded over 250 entries for articles and notes on Iraq since 2003. There was hardly a tenth that number over the previous 50 years. Over 100 books have been published in the United States only since 2003, from descriptions of military operations to heart-rending accounts of the death of loved ones in often gruesome circumstances. In contrast, perhaps no more than a dozen important books appeared on Iraq in the full course of the 20th century. "Iraq in Books," a remarkable review by Michael Rubin in the *Middle East Quarterly* (Spring 2007) briefly discusses 33 titles since the invasion. The present book has tried to keep up-to-date on that immense production, but preference has been given to reports and discussions focusing on policy-making, with a legal slant. The "Iraq cottage book industry" is expected to grow and surpass the Vietnam literature in years to come. It is not humanly possible to cover it all, let alone to give their due to some remarkable works that range from personal accounts by soldiers and journalists to the book-length recollections of the American presidential envoy and the former Iraqi minister of finance. Access to and dissemination of Iraqi books and studies in Arabic and Kurdish is difficult within Iraq, let alone abroad, although some good books, especially on the Iraqi Constitution, are already available. To the extent I could reach some of these sources, they are mentioned in this book.

Because of the variety of sources, consistency was not practical. Originally exotic Arabic words have become well known, but orthography did not follow. The Ba'th party is found in the book as Baath or Ba'th; Hussein could also be spelled Husayn, Husein, or Husain; Shi'is is the same as Shi'ites, Shiites, Shia, Shi'a; Ayat Allah is the same as Ayatollah, etc. Footnotes are generally omitted, and when they are profuse in the cited text, an additional reference is included to remind the reader of their availability in the original. References to website URLs were current by the end of 2008, but rapid shifts mean sudden lack of availability. With the change of administration in 2009, all White House original sources and texts have for instance suddenly disappeared, so I tried to rely on texts whose lifespan is not as fragile. Ellipses indicate an omission in the documents selected.

IRAQ:
GUIDE TO LAW
AND POLICY

CHAPTER 1

INTRODUCTION: ROADS NOT TAKEN

This book is ambitious. Its objective is to help shape law and policy in Iraq, based on the best available public sources. It dwells in the tradition of case-books common in American law schools, where notes and questions follow excerpts from court decisions, legislation, and law articles. This is a particularly useful method to understand the complex and nuanced facets of the Iraqi conflict because it poses a number of questions rather than pretending to offer set-and-ready solutions. This *Guide* hopes to encourage thinking about the various pressing issues in Iraq based on of the extensive documentation publicly available.

Law and policy in Iraq consist of "roads not taken" when one looks at history and the constant, renewed dilemmas that occur every day on the next forking path: which path is available and why should it be taken, rather than the other beckoning path or paths? "Iraq: The Road Not Taken" is a remarkable article written by Edward Mortimer in the *New York Review of Books* (May 16, 1991) just after the defeat of Saddam Hussein in Kuwait in March 1991, in which he argued that ending the regime would have been a far better option than the hasty pullout of troops. Instead, the victorious coalition forces, camped deep inside Iraq, watched the Iraqi dictator reassert his hold on the country and overpower the immense revolt that had engulfed 14 out of 18 Iraqi provinces. The controversy has endured. The 41st President George Bush and his assistants and allies at the time used the Vietnam argument to maintain their stand against "regime change," namely that the march on Baghdad would have transformed Iraq into a quagmire. The debate was also couched in legal language: the mission of the coalition at the time authorized freeing Kuwait from Iraqi troops, not deposing Saddam Hussein. Mortimer questioned the argument, in part because a massive march onto Baghdad may not have been necessary, since leveling Saddam Hussein's killing field might have been sufficient, in addition to the fact that supporting the revolt had been called for in a statement of the U.S. president on January 15, 1991. There were in fact many possible roads that were taken, before, during, and after the war.

The debate endured in different shapes. Passionate arguments over "regime change" remained central for a full decade after the ouster of

1

Saddam Hussein was rejected in Washington in 1991. It is as ironic as it is tragic that the 43rd president of the United States, and his father's namesake, was the one who activated that road again, opening to history difficult questions that have yet to be answered.

"Roads not taken" are questions of a more pressing nature since Baghdad fell to American forces on April 9, 2003. Between 1991 and 2003, other than the status quo choice generally pursued by successive U.S. administrations — or indeed a slow or more active "normalization" process — there were possibilities that were discussed within and outside policy-making circles. The creation of a "safe haven" zone in the South, like the one in the North, leaving Saddam a mere "mayor of Baghdad" was hotly debated. A formal de-legitimization of the Iraqi dictator and the close group around him could have developed if INDICT, an international NGO that received the formal support of the U.S. and British governments, had succeeded in the establishment of a UN-sanctioned tribunal. A different, more serious, pursuit of the oil-for-food UN regime was also possible with a focus on ordinary Iraqis at the center of the system as requested by the UN rapporteur on human rights at the time on the basis of an early UN Security Council Resolution asking the Iraqi government "to cease repressing its own people." A government in exile could have been set up — indeed in the few weeks preceding the invasion an oppositional government based in Northern Iraq (so not strictly an "exile" government) had been seriously considered. And instead of what turned out to be the dead-ended Weapons of Mass Destruction (WMD) justification, crimes against humanity and the argument for human rights and a democratic government in Baghdad could have constituted the diplomatic battleground for regime change in Iraq. So many roads not taken.

With the collapse of the regime, doors to many more roads were suddenly flung open. This book focuses on the period from 2003 to date with a prospective spirit, rather than dwelling on the previous history, however rich and complex. Every decision, and non-decision, is a matter of law and policy. To distinguish the wheat from the chaff is not easy, but one enhances the quality of the choice by knowledge, reflection, and public debate.

The conflict is passionate and driven for Iraq, the United States, indeed for the rest of the world, and many sacrifices, mostly in Iraqi and American lives, continue daily. Few doubt the central importance of Iraq for the future of the Middle East and for the world at large. Despite a strong competition in the region from bloody and protracted conflicts in Afghanistan, Sudan, Somalia, Israel-Palestine, and Lebanon, Iraq remains a defining issue for the region's future. Grave decisions need to be made at each juncture by concerned parties, and this *Guide* is conceived for both the decision-maker and the concerned citizen, so that they have at hand the documents needed to see more clearly in the surrounding thicket, and some guidance in the shape of introductions, notes, and questions. The policy-maker will find texts and questions that will hopefully help her make the best choice or set of choices. The concerned citizen is offered available data and scholarship to help her understand and take a better-informed position towards her government's policy. All should keep in mind that questions are never neutral, either for their formulation, their addressees, or their timing. There is always a risk in posing the wrong question. In a passage of his lectures on the history of philosophy (1820),

Hegel appropriately cites his colleague Moses Mendelssohn: "A question which I cannot fathom I cannot answer, and is for me as good as no question." (*Gesammelte Werke*, Frankfurt, Suhrkamp ed. 1971, vol. 20, 317).

HOW TO USE THIS BOOK

The casebook method prevails in the work in the form of relevant texts, in full or excerpted, which are introduced and followed by notes and questions inspired by the overarching approach described above: what was the road taken? As importantly, what was the road not taken? Which would have been better? These questions are so close to us in time that the spirit is resolutely prospective. For the policy-maker and the educated citizen alike, documents are presented with remarks and questions that are directed to the future: considering the current state of things, what are the options available? Do they offer a better road forward?

Chapter 2, on history, shortly conveys the main dates and events on the long timeline from Mesopotamia to present-day Iraq. The original chapter consisted at one point of some 450 pages, but publication of the full documents would have been beyond the scope of this book. Some documents were moved to other chapters. Because of space restrictions, this chapter was reduced to a timeline of the most important events with a focus on their lasting importance for the pre-modern period, operating over centuries; the establishment of reference dates in the 20th century within a shorter, decade-long framework; and a more detailed calendar since 2001 for the most salient events every year.

Chapter 3 is about constitutional issues. How did the constitution in Iraq come about? How should it be interpreted? How should the Constitution be amended? What about electoral laws? The chapter is different from those that follow because of the nature of the Iraqi Constitution of 2005. This is a fundamental text not only formally. On its interpretation will depend many roads taken in the country. Four full commentaries on the Iraqi Constitution are included, in addition to the 2004 Transitional Administrative Law (TAL) included as an endnote to the chapter. The TAL immediately preceded the current "permanent" text. These four commentaries, which raise a host of questions about the interpretation of a rich document, are preceded by a section on the making of the Constitution, and followed by an article of one of the Constitution's chief architects on the task ahead. Despite the fact that electoral laws are not usually included in the discussion of a constitution, their importance in the shape-up of Iraq could not be ignored. One section addresses the most important electoral and political parties' laws.

Chapter 4 examines the fledgling rule of law in Iraq in more detail. How does the judiciary perform? What are the meaning of human rights and the rule of law during an insurgency? What about the trial of Saddam Hussein and the grave human rights violations by American soldiers in Abu Ghraib? These are the four main questions addressed in this chapter. Of course, these are also constitutional issues, which go to the very heart of the legal order in Iraq. Partly for convenience, and partly because of received academic tradition, they are considered separately from the Constitution proper, even if, like all legal issues of importance, they are derivatives of the fundamental text.

Chapter 5 is entitled "International law and the UN." What is the role of the United Nations? Since the controversy over the legality of the war launched by the U.S. and its allies in the absence of an express authorization by the Security Council, the organization went through several phases, including the traumatic attack against the UN compound in Iraq on August 19, 2003. This contrasted course is examined critically, as are the most important reports and resolutions in New York and Baghdad. More pointed sections address the border with Kuwait, Iraqi debt and compensation, and the lasting consequences of the oil-for-food regime.

Chapter 6 is on the economy. How to read the economy? Or the rampant corruption? How are international and American departments and agencies assessing it, and how has their public assessment developed since 2003? Oil, of course, is the most important source of revenue for Iraq. What is the state of the oil industry? Should oil contracting be open to foreign investments? What does the controversial draft hydrocarbon law, reproduced here in full, provide in terms of answers? Are other schemes and experiments useful, such as the Alaska Fund? How about water? Why has water-sharing in Iraq not been as controversial as oil? How does federalism deal with both issues? A final section is more general: can the Iraqi economy benefit from leading Iraqi thinkers about the economic system? How are economic transactions perceived under a different legacy, that of the Iraqi Civil Code?

Chapter 7 focuses on security. How should one regard security in Iraq? Are there identifiable strategies in the conflict, namely the "Petraeus" and "Zarqawi" doctrines, and how do they bear on events on the ground? What were the main arguments being debated in America during a presidential campaign over which the Iraqi conflict loomed large? Are the status of forces agreements (SOFAs), common since World War II, adequate? How different are the Strategic Framework Agreement and the SOFA/withdrawal agreement that entered into force in January 2009? Are there alternatives?

Those are some of the questions, supported by documentation, which are found in the various chapters. Issues are inevitably intertwined, but I have avoided intensive cross-referencing and relied on the index for assisting the reader in this regard.

When law and policy are at play, the difference in the audience matters, even if this *Guide* made a genuine effort to reach beyond nationality and political persuasion. The book was originally conceived to help Iraqis familiarize themselves with the immense research triggered by the invasion, and the data available from as diverse open sources as possible in the United States in the shape of books, articles, reports, and expert studies. My approach is the one adopted by Professor Haider Ala Hamoudi in a column published on *Jurist.com* on March 20, 2008:

> Much has been said and written about the fifth anniversary of the Iraq war on television, in the print media, and on the Internet. Most, though certainly not all, of this excess of verbiage tends to be rather polemical, extolling the magnificent successes of the American venture, or decrying it as the worst foreign

policy venture in American history. Sometimes more nuanced analyses are given, but nearly all view the entire affair through the prism of the interests of the United States. To the extent that the Iraqis are discussed, they tend to be externalized and reduced to a passive polity awaiting liberation from an evil dictator, a vengeful lot more concerned about settling old grievances than running the country, or an unfortunate people poorly represented by a venal and corrupt set of politicians who cannot make necessary compromises, ungratefully debating endlessly while American blood and treasure is wasted on them.

A more nuanced approach is indeed needed, and a more purposeful one.

This book hopes to alleviate some misconceptions and enrich the debate, especially between Iraqis and Americans, on the roads not taken, and the better roads to take. Questioning previous roads is useful as a matter of method. Even more useful is to make available different roads, with sets of precise enough questions, so that policy-makers and legislators decide on the best choice.

A pressing question from day one of the invasion has been about the U.S. military withdrawal from Iraq: when and how should U.S. soldiers leave Iraq? With President Barack Obama winning a historic victory in part over the promise to bring American troops home, one hopes the reader will find in the book some fresh approaches to one of the most intractable conflicts of the 21st century.

CHAPTER 2

FROM MESOPOTAMIA TO IRAQ: TIMELINE

Introduction. There are several ways to consider the importance of Iraqi history for a present understanding of the conflict. One is traditional: it is linear and dwells on the important moments from the "cradle of civilization" to the modern period. The other is functional: the important dates in the history of Iraq are chosen for their definition or framing of a current problem or set of problems.

The second approach is more useful for law- and policy-makers, indeed to any concerned citizen who doesn't have the time or the interest in an extensive reading of materials on Iraqi history. In that approach, history operates with the different intensities of trends and events in mind, building on the three different *temps* developed most famously by Fernand Braudel: structural (long, "tectonic" periods); cyclical (medium-term trends); *événementiel* (short-term, event-based periods).

The structural is determined by geography and slow population moves. One example of structural determinations appears in the weight of Iraq's river system throughout history. Iraq has been determined through the ages by its two formidable rivers, and recent problems with Turkey and Syria over the flow of the Euphrates constitute an evident illustration of changes threatening a structural trait. Another example is the formation of religious communities, their rise and disappearance, and the long domination of indigenous or conquering empires. The dwindling and exile of the Jewish community since the 1950s is an example of the former. Until then, it was the oldest continuous community of learning in world history. The threat to the Christian communities in the wake of violence in 2004-2005 is of a similar portent. The collapse of the Ottoman Empire after 400 years of rule over Iraq is an additional example. Such developments represent historical breaks against century-, possibly millennium-long trends.

Braudel identified a second-tier, cyclical rhythm that operates over decades rather than centuries. It is a development mostly of an economic and cultural nature. In the case of the economy of Iraq, the discovery of oil in the 1920s marks a novelty of considerable consequences on modern developments. On the cultural level, after the embrace of Islam in the 7-8th century, the ebb and flow of the Sunni-Shi'i divisions, as well as of the Arab-Kurdish linguistic and national divide, represent cyclical manifestations of conviviality and conflict between these groups operating in this medium-term category.

Political events, Braudel's *temps événementiel*, constitute the third type. They operate in years, sometimes in days. Several events identified here after 2003 are of this type.

The reader is best served by reading the following timeline with the three different rhythms in mind. Such list is, inevitably, arbitrary. It is also insufficient to offer the key to any current problem, but it offers a helpful perspective to assess law and policy against long-term, cyclical, and events-driven developments.

For lack of space, the original documents of this chapter, put together by Shanna Francis, could not be included in this book. Only the timeline is included here, and several chapters provide, each, their own specialized timeline.

TIMELINE

BCE (BEFORE COMMON ERA aka B.C., *BEFORE CHRIST*)

About 9000-7000 BCE

The region of the world located along the Tigris and Euphrates Rivers, historically known as Mesopotamia, and, today, Iraq, was home to some of the world's first-known human fixed settlements as early as 7000 BCE, though evidence of the first inhabitants in the region goes back as far as the end of the last ice age, or 10,000 BCE.

6500-5000

One of the oldest known Neolithic sites in Mesopotamia, a village site, is Jarmo, which was located east of Kirkuk in the foothills of the southern Zagros Mountains in present Kurdish Iraq.

5500-4000

Sedentary agricultural society settles in southern Mesopotamia, relying on the spring floods of the Euphrates to increase its crop yields. These settlers are called proto-Euphrateans or Ubadians after the village of al-'Ubaid, where their earliest remains have been discovered. They are known for their endeavors to drain marshlands so the land could be used for agricultural purposes.

4000

Semites move in from the desert of modern Syria and Arabia.

3500

The oldest document describing the wheel is found in Mesopotamia.

3300

The Sumerians make their way into the Mesopotamian region of the Middle East. Their origin is uncertain, but is believed to be from today's

Turkey. Sumerian civilization is generally viewed as the world's first civilization on account of its literary legacy.

3000 BCE

The first known political congress meets. The Sumerians take the first steps towards reducing the power of the kings by the use of a political assembly.

Around 2800

The king of Kish, Etana, manages to defeat other city-states and unites the region. Later, King Meskiaggasher of Erech takes control of Sumer and extends the kingdom from the Mediterranean Sea to the Zagros Mountains.

Around 2700

King Enmebaragesi becomes the ruler of Sumer, and wins over Elam. He makes Nippur the cultural center of Sumer. King Gilgamesh rules the city Ur (Uruk) with a population of about 50,000. Around 2700, Gilgamesh, king of Uruk, conquers his neighbors and takes control of the region.

About 2550

First Dynasty of Ur is founded by King Mesanepeda after defeating the ruler of Sumer.

2334-2125

Approximate dates of Akkadian Dynasty. The Akkadians adopted much of the Sumerian way of life. Akkadian power was obtained at the hands of Sargon, the great Akkadian military leader. Their language is part of the Semitic language group which includes Hebrew, Arabic, Assyrian, and Babylonian. Semitic peoples dominate the region for centuries.

2316

Akkadians defeat local Sumerians. Defeated Sumerians regain limited control over many of their city-states, such as the city of Ur in 2125.

21st Century

Sumer flourishes under stable leadership.

2000

The Elamites destroy Ur and capture their king.

20th Century

Many wars are waged between the city-states of Sumer.

Around 1900

Semitic tribes, the Amorites, conquer most of Mesopotamia, and establish their kings in Babylon. The Amorites rule Old Babylonia until about 1530 BCE. Their empire encompassed Mesopotamia and regions known today as Syria and Palestine.

1900

Hebrews and Israelites leave Mesopotamia for Palestine, including Abraham. Other Israelites go to Egypt and are enslaved by Ramses II.

1894-1595

Era of the Babylonian Empire.

1792-1750 BCE

Rule of King Hammurabi over the Babylonian Empire. It is during his era that the region, previously called Sumer, becomes known as the land of Babylonia or Babylon. Akkadian becomes the common language as the Sumerian language begins to die out.

Hammurabi is best known for the code of laws he establishes — the Code of Hammurabi — that encompasses 282 laws/articles governing family life, criminal punishment, civil law, ethics, business, prices, trade, and slavery. Hammurabi was the first ruler of the Babylonian empire, and holds the claim of restoring order and justice to the region, and of unifying Mesopotamia/Babylon.

14th Century

During the first half of the fourteenth century BCE, from present-day Turkey, Hittites control an area stretching from the Mediterranean Sea to the Persian Gulf. Their military successes were attributed to their monopoly in iron production and to their use of the chariot. They were eventually defeated in the twelfth century BCE. The Hittites first emerged on history's stage in the Middle East in approximately 1600 BCE, after invading India. Other tribes settled in Iran and in Europe. One group of Hittites allied themselves with the Kassites, a people of unknown origin. Together, they conquered and destroyed Babylon. Their power then waned until it was reasserted in the fourteenth century.

While adopting much of the Sumerian culture and legal and political customs, they differed from previous civilizations by their skills and advances in trade and commerce, which led to an infusion of Mesopotamian thought, political and economic structure, law, and culture into outside regions such as Egypt and Greece. They also modified the legal system, leaving a mass of legal writings as part of their legacy.

1170-612 BCE

Assyrians rule in Mesopotamia. Their basis for power in the region was founded on their advances in metallurgy and other scientific inventions and discoveries.

746-721

A time of internal decay, with six kings — the last being Hoshea.

721

Sargon II takes the title of King of Babylon, and reigns from 721 to 705.

539 BCE

Babylon falls to the Iranians under Cyrus the Great whose general Gobryas takes the city, without a fight, on October 29. Assyria ceases to exist, and Babylonia comes under Persian rule. The Assyrian rulers flee west to Egypt, and the history of "Mesopotamia" ends.

331 BCE

Alexander the Great enters Babylon. Age of Hellenization begins.

227-126

Parthians complete conquest of the Tigris-Euphrates River Valley.

64

Assyria's name is shortened to "Syria" under Roman rule. Mesopotamia is on the periphery of the Roman Empire.

Poorly documented stretch of history starts.

CE (COMMON ERA AKA A.D., *ANNO DOMINI,* YEAR OF THE LORD, BEGINNING OF CHRISTIAN GREGORIAN CALENDAR)

636 CE

Islamic conquest of Iraq. Events in Arabia begin to change rapidly in the sixth century CE when Muhammad, a member of the Hashimite clan of the powerful Quraysh tribe of Mecca, claims prophethood. Islamic forays into Iraq begin during the reign of Abu Bakr. In 634 an army of 18,000 Arab tribesmen, under General Khalid ibn al-Walid, reaches the perimeter of the Euphrates delta, and resistance in the area fails in 636.

680

Battle of Karbala, followed by the slow establishment of the city as a Shi'i shrine. Grandson of Prophet Muhammad is slain by the rival, Damascus-based, Umayyads. Formal division of Muslims between Sunnis and Shi'is.

762

July 30, founding of Baghdad, "the city of peace, *madinat al-salam,*" by the Abbasid dynasty led by Caliph Abu Ja'far al-Mansur, the second Abbasid caliph, replacing Harran as the seat of the caliphal government. Baghdad eclipses Ctesiphon, the capital of the Persian Empire, which was located about 20 miles to the southeast. Ctesiphon had fallen to Muslim control in 637. It is quickly deserted after the foundation of Baghdad. The site of Babylon, which had been deserted since the 2nd century BCE, is situated approximately 55 miles to the south.

The multicultural city of Baghdad was a hub of learning and commerce from about the 8th to the 13th century. The House of Wisdom (*bayt al-hikma*) was an establishment dedicated to the translation of Greek, Middle Persian, and Syriac works. The Barmakids were influential in bringing scholars from the nearby Academy of Gundishapur, facilitating the introduction of Greek and Indian science into the Arabic world. Baghdad was probably the largest city in the world from shortly after its foundation until the 930s. Estimates suggest that the city contained over a million inhabitants at its peak. The period between the 9th and the 13th centuries in Baghdad's history is considered the Golden Age of Arab-Islamic civilization. The city is destroyed by the Mongols in 1258.

765

Death of Ja'far al-Sadeq, sixth Imam of the Shi'is, and founder of Shi'i ('Ja'fari) legal school/doctrine.

8-9th Century

Rise of Sunni legal scholars in Iraq, including eponyms of Hanafi (Abu Hanifa d.767) and Hanbali (Ibn Hanbal d.855) schools.

c.800

Najaf founded. The city soon becomes the principal city of Shi'i learning in the world. Uninterrupted string of top scholars to the present leadership—*marja'iyya*, led by *Ayat Allah* (Ayatollah, highest Shi'i title) 'Ali al-Sistani.

808-819, 836-892

Troubles with the caliphate and relocation of capital to Samarra.

833

Great *Mihna* (or inquisition) under Caliph al-Ma'mun, over the created or uncreated nature of the Qur'an, a religious-legal controversy within the dominant Sunni schools.

945-1055

Loss of the western and easternmost provinces, and political domination by the Iranian Buwayhids or Buyids, a proto-Shi'i dynasty.

965

Iraqi-born Al-Mutanabbi, arguably the greatest poet in Arab history, is killed in a revenge attack by the uncle of a subject of his derogatory verses.

1055-1135

Domination by Seljuk Turks.

1258

Mongol Invasion. Baghdad is sacked by the Mongols under Hulagu Khan. Most of the city's inhabitants are massacred, including the Abbasid Caliph Al Musta'sim, along with large sections of the city.

1401

Baghdad is again sacked by Timur the Lame, or Tamerlane, who was of Turco-Mongol descent. After its capture, about 20,000 of its citizens are massacred. It becomes a provincial capital controlled by Jalayirir until 1411.

1501

Sunnis in Baghdad are massacred by the Safavids, just established in Persia as Shi'i dynasty.

1508 to 1534

Rule by Safavid dynasties.

1534

Baghdad is conquered by the Ottoman Turks under Sultan Sulaiman the Magnificent. The city falls into a long period of decline. The Ottomans maintain Iraq as a Sunni-controlled buffer state called the Principality of

Baghdad. Ottoman rule lasts four centuries during which Iraq constitutes the frontier battleground between Persia and the Ottomans.

1623

The Ottomans lose Baghdad to Shah Abbas of the Safavids, though they regain it in 1632.

1743

Nader Shah attempts to reconcile Sunnis and Shi'is at the 1743 theological Congress in Najaf. He is assassinated in 1747.

1747 to 1831

Iraq is ruled, with short intermissions, by the Mamluk officers of Georgian origin who enjoy local autonomy from Istanbul.

1831

Ottomans dominate Baghdad again and capture the last Mamluk governor. Ottoman hold lasts until World War I.

1869-1872

Enlightened Ottoman governor Midhat Pasha applies Tanzimat reforms to Baghdad. He institutes legal reforms, imports a printing press, builds schools, begins a newspaper, and constructs hospitals. Iraq as province is divided into three governorates: Baghdad, Basra, and Mosul. Midhat implements wide, straight thoroughfares, and establishes the basis of a modern administration. Significant Ottoman architecture is incorporated into the city's landscape.

1908

Sultan Abdulhamid II is deposed.

Revolution of the Young Turks spawns Arab Nationalism in Iraq. While the Young Turks' ideology seeks the imposition of a Turkish identity within the entire Ottoman Empire, a correlated effect is the birth of Pan-Arabism.

First parliamentary elections to Istanbul's *Majlis al-mab'uthan* ("Parliament of the emissaries"). Active participation of Iraqi elected representatives from the three provinces of Mosul, Baghdad, Basra.

1914

November, World War I British occupation of Basra.

1916

May, Sykes-Picot Agreement, a secret understanding made during World War I, between Great Britain and France, with the assent of Russia, for the dismemberment of the Ottoman Empire. The agreement leads to the division of Ottoman Syria, Lebanon, Iraq, and Palestine into respectively French- and British-administered areas.

1917

March, British occupation of Baghdad.

1917

November, British occupation of Mosul.

1920

The San Remo Peace Conference of Allied Powers decides on April 24 to endorse the French and British mandate over the Levant, with Britain holding the mandate in Palestine, Transjordan, and Mesopotamia (renamed Iraq), created out of the Ottoman provinces of Basra, Baghdad, and Mosul; the French are given a mandate over Syria and Lebanon. Mandate for Iraq is formally given to United Kingdom. The terms of the Mandate are also discussed with the U.S., which was not a member of the League. An agreed text is confirmed by the Council of the League of Nations on July 24, 1922, and becomes operational in September 1923.

1920

July-October, Great Iraqi Revolt. Massive national uprising led by the Shi'i religious leaders against British occupation. After its defeat, several leaders go into exile.

1920

November, Sayyid 'Abd al-Rahman al-Kailani forms first Iraqi government.

1921

March, Cairo Conference decides on Prince Faisal bin Husain al-Hashemi as king of Iraq.

1921

August, enthronement of King Faisal in Baghdad.

1922

October 10, first Anglo-Iraqi Treaty ratified by Iraq. The treaty sets out the scope of Britain's involvement in Iraqi affairs.

1924

Anglo-Iraqi Treaty passed by Constituent Assembly.

1925

March, Iraqi government signs Turkish Petroleum Company oil concession.

1925

December, League of Nations decides that Mosul should remain part of Iraq.

1926

January 13, first Anglo-Iraqi Treaty signed.

1927

December, Britain pledges to support Iraqi membership to the League of Nations on condition that it shows "progress" in the intervening period.

1927

British strike oil. First major oil finds are near Kirkuk in Northern Iraq, the largest find in the world so far. Its exploitation is transferred to the Iraq Petroleum Company in 1929, which builds pipelines to Tripoli and Haifa by 1934.

1929

Former Prime Minister's chief of staff Nuri al-Sa'id rises to position of Prime Minister.

1930

June 30, Prime Minister Nuri al-Sa'id signs the new Anglo-Iraqi Treaty promising Iraqi independence. It is ratified on November 16. Iraq gains independence, but must allow the presence of the British Royal Air Force (RAF), grant Britain land and resources, and coordinate foreign policy with Britain for the next 25 years.

1932

October 3, League of Nations ends Mandate and grants formal independence to Iraq. Pan-Arabist groups oppose concessions to Britain stated in the 1930 Anglo-Iraqi Treaty.

1933

August 4-11, hundreds of Iraqi Assyrians are massacred.

1933

September 8, King Faisal dies; King Ghazi succeeds him.

1935

January, official opening of Kirkuk-Mediterranean pipeline.

1936

October, military coup d'état, launched by General Bakr Sidqi and backed by Hikmat Sulaiman who becomes Prime Minister, overthrowing the government of Yasin al-Hashimi, promising social reform and bringing the Ahali group into government.

1937

August 11, Iraq's military leader Bakr Sidqi is assassinated in Mosul after Ahali and nationalist military officers withdraw support on June 19, 1937; Hikmat Sulaiman is overthrown by army and resigns position as Prime Minister. Jamil al-Midfa'i takes over position as Prime Minister but soon alienates the military.

1939

April 4, King Ghazi killed in car accident; succeeded by infant son, Faisal II, under regency of Prince 'Abd al-Ilah.

1941

April 1, second military coup d'état; "Government of National Defense" formed by Rashid 'Ali al-Kailani. The regent flees Baghdad along with other pro-British Iraqi politicians.

1941

May 2, British troops march on Baghdad; collapse and flight of Rashid 'Ali al-Kailani's government.

1941

June 1, civil order breaks down in Baghdad. An extensive pogrom against Jews is carried out (120 to 600 estimated killed, 2,100 injured), with wide-scale looting of their property. The British ambassador, Kinahan Cornwallis, refuses to allow British troops to enter the city until the pogrom, called "Farhud" by the Jews, is over. In the immediate aftermath, British consular authorities receive over 1,000 visa applications from Iraqi Jewish merchants wanting to travel to India. Increase in illegal immigration to Palestine from Iraq.

1943

Iraq declares war on the Axis powers.

1946

June, recurrent strikes and demonstrations that turn violent. On July 3, 1946, 5,000 workers at the Iraq Petroleum Company (IPC) facility in Kirkuk, under the leadership of Communist Party of Iraq activists, go on strike for higher wages.

1946

July 12, Iraqi police try to break up a meeting of striking workers by shooting at the oil workers. Ten Iraqi oil workers are killed and 27 oil workers are wounded in the "Massacre of Gawurpaghi."

1946

November 26, the royal government's new premier, Nuri as-Sa'id, promises free elections, but the leader of the Communist Party of Iraq, Fahd, calls for the overthrow of the monarchy's government and an end to British control of Iraq.

1947

January 18, the government arrests the Communist Party of Iraq leaders Fahd and Zaki Basim. They are court-martialed and executed in February 1949.

1948

January 15, new Anglo-Iraqi Treaty signed at Portsmouth; mass protests in Baghdad against the Portsmouth Treaty — known as *al-Wathba* (the leap); the treaty is finally abandoned.

1948

May, Iraq sends expeditionary force to Palestine.

1949

February, Iraqi army withdraws from Palestine.

1952

February, Iraqi agreement with IPC on 50-50 share of profits.

1952

November-December, demonstrations erupt in Baghdad — known as *al-Intifada* (the uprising).

1953

May 2, King Faisal II enthroned; regency ends.

1955

February, formation of Baghdad Pact that includes Great Britain, Turkey, Iran, Iraq, and Pakistan.

1956

October, Suez Crisis; riots in Baghdad, Mosul, and Najaf.

1958

February 14, formation of United Arab Republic (UAR) by Egypt and Syria; Jordan and Iraq form Arab Union in response.

1958

July 14, beginning of 1958 Revolution. Military coup d'état in Baghdad. A secret organization of 200 Free Officers overthrows the monarchy in a coup acclaimed throughout Iraq. A republic is established with Brigadier 'Abd al-Karim Qasim becoming the prime minister, minister of defense, and commander in chief. Citizens fill the streets hours after the first shots are fired. Parliament is abolished, and the army purged. A People's Court under Colonel Fadhil Abbas Mahdawi is set up to try members of the old regime. King Faisal, Nuri as-Sa'id, and the crown prince of Iraq are killed, together with Deputy Prime Minister Ibrahim Hashim and Defense Minister Sulaiman Tuqan.

1958

September, Agrarian Reform Law is passed.

1959

October, Mustafa Barzani asserts his control of Kurdistan Democratic Party (KDP).

1959

October 7, failed Ba'thist coup attempt on Qasim. Qasim is injured and his driver is killed. Seventy-eight Ba'thists are tried. One of them, Saddam Hussein, is wounded, and escapes to Syria and then Egypt.

1959

December, Iraq withdraws from Baghdad Pact.

1961

June, Kuwaiti independence; Qasim demands its integration into Iraq; Great Britain sends troops to Kuwait, replaced by Arab League force in August.

1961

July, Barzani demands substantial autonomy for Kurdish region.

September, fighting in Kurdistan between Barzani's forces and Iraqi army.

December, Law 80 reclaims unexploited areas of IPC's concession.

1963

February 8, military coup d'état by Ba'thist and Arab nationalist officers; Qasim and colleagues killed.

1963

October-November, splits and confusion in the Ba'th Party.

November, President 'Abd al-Salam 'Arif and military allies eject Ba'thists from power.

1968

July 17, military coup by Arab nationalist and Ba'thist army officers; 'Abd al-Rahman 'Arif sent into exile; Ahmad Hasan al-Bakr becomes president.

1968

July 30, Ba'thist military coup organized by al-Bakr. Non-Ba'thist allies are ousted. Supreme authority passes to the RCC (Revolutionary Command Council) chaired by Ahmad Hasan al-Bakr, secretary-general of the ABSP (Arab Ba'th Socialist Party), who also becomes president and commander in chief of the army. Saddam Hussein, who is already assistant secretary-general of the party, becomes deputy chairman of the RCC in charge of internal security.

1970

March 11, agreement on Kurdistan, granting limited autonomy; Barzani calls cease-fire.

May, land reform measures implemented.

July, new provisional constitution recognizes Kurdish nationalism.

1971

Relations between Iraq and Iran severed.

1972

April, Iraq and USSR sign 15-year Iraq-USSR Treaty of Friendship and Co-operation.

1972

June, IPC nationalized.

1973

July, failed coup attempt by Kazzar; al-Bakr and Saddam Hussein reinforce their hold on the state.

1973

Limited Iraqi participation in war with Israel.

1974

Collapse of March 1970 agreement granting national autonomy for the Kurds from Iraq.

1977

February, 30,000-strong religious procession from Najaf to Karbala; called the Safar *intifada*, it becomes an anti-government Shi'i protest.

1978

October, expulsion of Ayat Allah Khumaini from Najaf, Iraq, where he resides since 1965.

1978

November, Baghdad Summit following Camp David accords marks Iraqi bid for Arab leadership.

1979

Spring, success of Iranian revolution encourages militant Shi'i organizations to launch a more active campaign in Iraq.

1979

July 16, al-Bakr resigns for what Saddam Hussein calls "health problems." Hussein declares himself President. A large purge of the RCC and top Ba'thists follows. Muhyi Rashid, secretary of RCC, is forced to confess and then shot along with his whole family. One-third of the members of the RCC are executed. By August 1, some 500 top-ranking Ba'thists are said to have been executed.

In November, the Kurdistan Democratic Party (KDP) Congress elects Masoud Barzani as chairman and calls for the continuation of the armed struggle inside Iraq.

1980

March, closely controlled elections of National Assembly in Iraq.

1980

April 8, Shi'i religious leader Muhammad Baqer al-Sadr and his sister Bint al-Huda are executed in Baghdad; over 40,000 Shi'is expelled to Iran.

1980

September 22, Saddam Hussein launches full-scale war against Iran. Iraqi forces invade Iranian territory. Commonly called the Iran-Iraq war, it is also the first Persian Gulf War, and the most devastating in the history of the modern Middle East, with an estimated one-million casualties.

1982

June-July, Iran's counteroffensive recaptures most of its territory.

1982

9th Regional Congress of Ba'th Party reasserts Saddam Hussein's absolute control.

1982

Autumn, sudden death of former president Ahmad Hasan al-Bakr.

1984

Iraq re-establishes diplomatic relations with U.S.

1987

Iraqi government campaign against KDP and Patriotic Union of Kurdistan (PUK) in Kurdistan. Reports of chemical warfare attacks on Kurdish villages and guerrilla fighters become more frequent and detailed. Several thousand Kurdish civilians and Iranian soldiers in the area are killed and several thousands more injured.

1988

February, start of large-scale massacres and deportations operation in Kurdistan under Codename *al-Anfal*. March 16, some 5,000 Kurdish civilians killed by poison gas in Halabja.

1988

July, Iran accepts UN cease-fire resolution 678 of previous year; war with Iraq ends.

1990

August 2, Iraq invades and annexes Kuwait; UN imposes total trade embargo and sanctions on Iraq.

1991

January, "Desert Storm" begins: air bombardment of Iraq by U.S.-led allied forces leading to liberation of Kuwait by allied forces in February.

1991

March-April, eruption and crushing of massive uprising in Shi'i south and Kurdish north.

1991

April 3, UNSCR (United Nations Security Council Resolution) 687 demands Iraqi recognition of Kuwait and destruction of all of Iraq's non-conventional weapons, and affirms that economic sanctions would continue until full compliance. Resolution 688, on April 5, calls on Iraqi government to stop oppressing its own people as massive flight of Kurds and Shi'is take place. By June, "safe haven" established in northern Iraq, effectively placing most of Kurdistan under allied protection.

1991

May, first visit of United Nations Special Commission on Disarmament (UNSCOM) weapons inspection team.

1991

October, Iraqi armed forces blockade Kurdistan.

1992

May, election in Kurdish zone results in more or less equal balance between KDP and PUK.

July, Kurdish Regional Government formed by both parties, but, in effect, two parallel administrations are created that run separate areas.

1993

May, UNSC approves demarcation of Iraq-Kuwait border in Kuwait's favor.

1993

June, U.S. launches missile strike on headquarters of Iraq intelligence services in Baghdad in reprisal for Iraqi plot to kill President Bush during his visit to Kuwait.

1993

October-November, Iraqi forces launch campaign against inhabitants of marshes in Southern Iraq and consolidates hold by draining the marshes.

1994

Start of Kurdish civil war between KDP and PUK. Over 3,000 casualties until end of hostilities in 1996.

1994

October-November, Iraqi threats to Kuwait lead to crisis and eventual Iraqi recognition of Kuwait as an independent state.

1994

November 8, UN Report on Human Rights in Iraq is released, considers the rule of Saddam Hussein "probably the worst since World War II."

1996

February, Iraq accepts UNSCR 986 allowing limited Iraqi oil sales for purchase of vital civilian supplies. Beginning of oil-for-food regime.

1996

August, Iraqi government forces enter Kurdish region at invitation of KDP, and help capture Irbil from PUK. Iraqi National Congress, the umbrella group of the Iraqi opposition formed in 1992, loses some 100 members and is forced out of Iraq.

1996

December, Iraqi oil flows again through pipeline to Turkey; Iraq returns to world oil market as a producer.

1998

November, Iraq Liberation Act is passed by U.S. Congress and signed by U.S. President Clinton.

1998

December, "Operation Desert Fox," air bombardment of Iraq by U.S. Air Force and Royal Air Force in retaliation for Iraqi non-cooperation with weapons inspections. Iraq ceases all cooperation.

1999

January-December, weekly attacks by American and British planes on Iraqi forces challenging their right to overfly Iraqi territory in southern and northern no-fly zones.

1999

19 February. Presumed assassination of Ayat Allah Muhammad Sadeq al-Sadr and his two sons.

1999

December, UNSCR 1284 offering to suspend sanctions if Iraq cooperates with weapons inspection regime for 120 days; new weapons inspection agency set up: United Nations Monitoring, Verification and Inspection

Commission (UNMOVIC). Iraq rejects the resolution and refuses to allow UNMOVIC into Iraq until sanctions are lifted.

2000

March, Iraq defies UN ban on civil air flights and organizes flights of pilgrims to Mecca.

September, Baghdad airport reopens. Much-publicized flights arrive from Russia, France, Syria, and other countries.

November, domestic civil flights resume within Iraq.

2000

Summer, Republican Party Platform advocates "regime change" in Iraq.

2001

January, Masoud Barzani (KDP leader) and Jalal Talibani (PUK leader) meet for first time in three years.

2001

February, extensive American and British air strikes against air defense systems around Baghdad.

2001

May-July, U.K. and U.S. try and fail to persuade UNSC to adopt "smart sanctions" resolution.

2001

August, extensive American and British air strikes against air defense systems in southern Iraq.

2001

Iraqi officials consider September 11 attacks as a "lesson for America." Beginning of U.S. mobilization for the removal of the Iraqi regime.

2001

November, UN Security Council Resolution 1382 renews six-month "oil-for-food" arrangement and opens way for possible reform of sanctions regime and return of weapons inspectors.

2002

January, U.S. President George Bush identifies Iraq as part of an "axis of evil."

2002

March, public Iraqi reconciliation with Saudi Arabia at Arab League Summit in Beirut.

2002

June, President Bush and staff finalize war plans against Iraq.

2002

October, U.S. Congress passes resolution authorizing use of military force against Iraq.

2002

November, UN Security Council Resolution 1441 requiring Iraq to re-admit weapons inspectors of UNMOVIC. Iraq accepts.

2003

January, General Jay Garner appointed to head Office of Reconstruction and Humanitarian Assistance (ORHA) for the planned invasion.

2003

February-March, U.S. and U.K. try and fail to obtain UNSCR explicitly authorizing the use of force against Iraq.

2003

March, "Operation Iraqi Freedom" launched by U.S., U.K., and allied forces to overthrow Saddam Hussein and occupy Iraq. In April, Basra, Baghdad, and Mosul fall to allied forces. Saddam Husain flees into hiding.

2003

April 9, fall of Baghdad as Saddam's regime collapses and U.S. forces take control of the city. Several days of severe looting follow.

2003

End of April, Iraqi demonstrators protest American presence in Iraq with street marches in different cities. On two separate occasions, U.S. Marines fire into angry and threatening crowds. Several deaths in Falluja and Mosul.

2003

May, L. Paul Bremer III replaces Jay Garner as chief U.S. authority in Iraq, heading the Coalition Provisional Authority (CPA); "Debaathification" starts with dissolution of Ba'th Party and of Iraq armed forces; UNSCR 1483 grants U.S. and U.K. power to govern Iraq, and ends 13-year sanctions regime.

2003

May, Bush's "end of war" victory speech given from the deck of the USS Lincoln.

2003

July, CPA sets up Iraq Governing Council (IGC) with limited powers; U.S. military command admits it is facing "guerrilla war" in Iraq.

July, Uday and Qusay Husayn are killed by U.S. forces in a firefight at their safehouse in Mosul.

2003

August, UN headquarters in Baghdad blown up, and Ayat Allah Baqir al-Hakim (head of Supreme Council for the Islamic Revolution in Iraq— SCIRI) is assassinated.

2003

October, "No Weapons of Mass Destruction (WMD) Report" released.

2003

October 15, UNSCR 1551 supports creation of Iraqi cabinet and preliminary constitutional committee, makes UN resources available to Iraqi government "upon request," and authorizes a multinational force under unified command.

2003

October, sectarian violence in Baghdad with inter-ethnic violence in Kirkuk.

2003

November, U.S. creates timetable for handover of power to Iraqi government.

2003

December, capture of Saddam Hussein about nine miles from his hometown of Tikrit. He is held in coalition custody, and his capture heralded as a great victory, with hopes that it would break organized political resistance.

2004

March, IGC (Iraqi Governing Council) approves draft provisional constitution (TAL, Law of Administration for the State of Iraq for the Transitional Period).

2004

April-May, fierce fighting between U.S. forces and insurgents in Falluja; in August, U.S. forces fight Mahdi Army in Najaf.

2004

November, U.S. and Iraqi forces attack insurgents in Falluja; widespread destruction.

2005

January, general elections for the transitional national assembly charged with drafting a new constitution; boycotted by Sunni Arabs. United Iraqi Alliance ('Ayat Allah Sistani's Shi'i list') wins overall majority; elections for Kurdish Regional Assembly dominated by KDP and PUK.

2005

April, Ibrahim al-Ja'fari of UIA (United Iraqi Alliance) becomes prime minister and forms government; Jalal Talibani elected by Parliament president of Iraq.

2005

August, constitutional committee presents draft constitution to Parliament which submits it to a referendum. In October, the constitutional referendum approves constitution by 78 percent to 22 percent. Arab Shi'i and Kurdish provinces vote in favor, Arab Sunni provinces against.

2005

October, trial of Saddam Hussein and aides begins.

2005

December, general elections for permanent national assembly, the Council of Representatives (CoR): UIA largest single bloc, but no overall majority. Sunnis boycott election, but less massively than in January.

2006

February, al-'Askariyya mosque in Samarra blown up; sectarian conflict intensifies.

2006

April, Jalal Talibani sworn in as president of Iraq.

2006

May, Nuri al-Maliki of UIA forms new government.

2006

July, British authorities hand over Muthanna province to Iraqi control.

2006

September, Italian forces hand over Dhi Qar province to Iraqi control.

2006

October, National Assembly passes law allowing establishment of provinces.

2006

November, Saddam Hussein sentenced to death by Iraqi High Tribunal. He is executed in December. Death toll of U.S. forces since 2003 reaches 3,000; UN estimates over 100 Iraqi civilians die violently every day.

2007

January, draft law allowing foreign investment and participation in Iraqi oil industry put before Council of Representatives (CoR).

2007

February, "Surge": U.S. sends 28,000 extra troops to Iraq to implement new security plan for Baghdad.

2008

March-April, Maliki Government prevails in fights against "Mahdi army" insurgents in Basra and Baghdad. March Report to the U.S. Congress is released on improved stability and security in Iraq. Security outlook cautious but positive for the first time since 2004.

2008

November, after intense discussions between Iraqi and American governments over the future of U.S. forces in Iraq, adoption by Iraqi CoR of Strategic Framework Agreement and "SOFA/Withdrawal Agreement," which come into effect January 1, 2009.

CONSTITUTIONAL ISSUES

Introduction. This chapter deals with core constitutional issues. Like most other social compacts, the Iraqi Constitution of 2005 comprises:

- a Preamble (Chapter/section 1, "Fundamental Principles")
- a Bill of Rights (Chapter 2, "Rights and Freedoms")
- the main institutions, with federalism as an important characteristic
  Chapter 3, "The Federal Authorities"
  Chapter 4, "Powers of the Federal Authorities"
  Chapter 5, "Authorities of the Regions"
- an amendment process, together with transitional measures
  Chapter 6, "Final and Transitional Guidelines"

Electoral laws are also included in the present chapter. Despite their importance, electoral laws have traditionally remained outside the text of constitutions. In Iraq and elsewhere, they are imperative for civil peace and appropriate representation.

The Iraqi Constitution holds many promises, despite the grave chaos that has prevailed in the country, and the stigma of occupation. In time, if the fledgling democratic experiment succeeds and Iraqi citizens find a peace that preserves their acquired freedom against difficult odds, the Constitution may represent a central landmark in their history. For that, it requires a healthy and consistent deliberation in government and in Iraqi society at large. Public deliberation is key, as is the availability of important texts. The text of the constitutional arrangement that preceded the Iraqi Constitution, the Transitional Administrative Law (TAL), as well as four commentaries, are included in this chapter with this deliberation in mind.

A. A BRIEF HISTORY OF THE CONSTITUTION-MAKING PROCESS[*]

1. THE PERIOD UP TO THE ESTABLISHMENT OF THE IRAQI CONSTITUTION DRAFTING COMMITTEE

1. Following the invasion of Iraq, American and Iraqi officials, as well as members of the international community, attempted to create a framework in which a permanent constitution could be drafted. These attempts proved difficult as conflicting interests were difficult to reconcile.

2. The U.S. administration established the short-lived Office of Reconstruction and Humanitarian Assistance (ORHA) under Jay M. Garner on 20th January, 2003. Garner's intention was to complete the transition to a permanent Iraqi government within four months after first appointing an Iraqi government which would select an Iraqi constitutional convention, which would in turn write a democratic constitution. This plan met with immediate resistance by Iraqis including the Shia Supreme Council for Islamic Revolution in Iraq (SCIRI). On 6th May, the U.S. Administration replaced Garner and OHRA with the Coalition Provisional Authority (CPA) under Paul Bremer.

3. Following Security Council Resolution 1483, the CPA took immediate steps to appoint the Iraqi Governing Council (IGC). While this allowed for some Iraqi involvement in the political process, its membership was heavily slanted towards former exiles.

4. Whereas Bremer wished to appoint a National Conference to assist in the administration of Iraq, Grand Ayatollah Ali al-Sistani demanded an elected body to perform the task and draft a constitution. In the end, the IGC and the CPA reached agreement on a process and timetable for political transition. This

---

[*]Section A partially reproduces a report of the United Nations Assistance Mission for Iraq (UNAMI), Office of Constitutional Support, 3-9 Dec. 2005.

envisaged the election of a Transitional National Assembly (TNA) by 31st May, 2004. Controversially, Bremer envisaged that the TNA would be elected by caucuses in each of Iraq's eighteen governorates. Again Sistani issued a fatwa calling for direct and democratic elections. At the heart of the ensuing debate was the question of the timeframe within which proper elections could be held.

5. The upshot was that the UN was asked to send a delegation under Lakhdar Brahimi to investigate the feasibility of elections. Brahimi went on to recommend that, pending elections around the end of 2004, an interim Iraqi government should be selected in June 2004 to steer the country until the elections.

6. The remaining question that had to be resolved was the drafting of a basic law governing the transitional period. From January to March 2004 a committee of CPA/IGC officials drafted the Law of Administration for the State of Iraq for the Transitional Period (the "TAL"). After intense negotiations, notably on whether other regions than Kurdistan could be formed and on the Kurdish referendum proposal which allowed three governorates to veto the draft constitutional text, the TAL was signed on 8th March 2004. Although there was discussion of amending the TAL, there was no attempt to do so aside from on 15th August 2005 as is set out later in this report. TAL envisaged a time sequence as follows:

a. The first phase of the transitional period would begin with the forma-tion of the sovereign Iraqi Interim Government (IIG) on 30th June 2004. Elections for a democratically elected Transitional National Assembly (TNA) would be held no later than 31st January 2005.

b. The TNA would write or designate a permanent constitution no later than 15th August 2005, which would be presented to the Iraqi people in a general referendum to be held no later than 15th October 2005. The TNA was given the option of applying for a six month extension if by 1st August 2005 it was of the view that it was unable to finish the task on time.

c. If the TNA failed to draft a constitution or if the constitution was defeated in the referendum, the whole process would be repeated in 2006 following elections for a new TNA. If the constitution were approved at the referendum, elections for a permanent government would be held no later than 15th December 2005.

7. It should be noted that the TAL was controversial with many Iraqi commentators who claimed that it was drafted in a back room and in English. As a consequence of the latter, the Arabic translation was ambiguous in parts.

8. On 8th June, the UN SCR 1546 providing that UNAMI should "promote national dialogue and consensus building on the drafting of a national consti-tution among the people of Iraq." On 28th June, the CPA formally ceased to exist and sovereignty was officially transferred to the IIG under Iyad Allawi.

9. The parliamentary elections that took place on 30th January 2005 took place largely without the participation of the Sunni community, for reasons such as intimidation and a boycott following the assault on Fallujah. In the result, a Shia coalition (United Iraqi Alliance: UIA) won 140 of the 275 seats.

The Kurdish Alliance won 75 and Allawi's Iraqiya List won 40. Because of the Sunni boycott this configuration put the Kurdish Alliance and the Shia list in a particularly powerful position unlikely to be repeated. Sunni parties won only 17 seats. This imbalance would have a lasting effect on the constitutional deliberations.

2. THE CONSTITUTION-MAKING PROCESS UNDER THE TAL

10. Although the TAL envisaged a six-month process to write the constitution, in reality the actual time devoted to this task by the TNA is better measured in term of weeks rather than months. The TNA declined to establish a constitution drafting committee or embark upon its task of designating a text until the political bargaining around the establishment of the Iraqi Transitional Government had been completed. Talabani was named president on 6th April and a new government endorsed by the TNA only on 28th April. It was only on 23rd May that the TNA succeeded in finally nominating Sheikh Humam Hammoudi as Chair of the Constitutional Drafting Committee (CDC). However, the CDC still did not immediately begin sitting, and it would take yet longer before it agreed on its modus operandi. By this stage, there would only be six weeks to the 1st August deadline, and some eight weeks to the 15th August deadline.

11. The already shortened time period for drafting the permanent constitution was further complicated by the absence of Sunnis on the CDC (just 3 of the original 55 drafters were Sunnis), which was a function of the low Sunni representation in the TNA.

12. As a result of pressure from the international community, the CDC and the TNA eventually agreed to appoint supplementary Sunni members with equal status and to take decisions by consensus between the three main groups. In was only on 16th June that agreement was finally reached that 15 Sunni Arabs would join the CDC together with an additional 10 Sunni Arab advisors. After investigation by the De-Baathification Commission the Sunni representatives got the go ahead on 30th June to take up their seats which they only did on 5th July. On 19th July Sunni CDC member Mijbil Issa and a CDC adviser were gunned down as they left a restaurant. The Sunni members thereafter boycotted the CDC until 25th July when assurances were given to them that they would be able to contest all issues and that no final decisions had been taken by the CDC.

13. During the period in which Sunni participation was negotiated and was included, the CDC started its work through six subcommittees it had established: General Principles, Human Rights, Structures of Government, Federalism, Constitutional Guarantees, Final Provisions.

14. The CDC was reluctant to report on the work of the subcommittees, including to the [UNAMI Office of Constitutional Support] (OCS), for fear of criticism that its deliberations had been completed prior to Sunni participation. Thus the CDC only began its work in earnest when Sunni participation resumed and the subcommittee reports were only submitted days before the deadline for deciding whether an extension was required.

15. A further fact to consider in assessing how much real time the CDC had to conduct its deliberations was that for several weeks after inception it had neither premises, appropriate security, equipment or staff. As a result of UN assistance, including assisting in negotiations for accommodation with the authorities, it was only in July that the CDC could be said to be in functional existence.

16. Around 8th August the CDC handed over its drafts, and to some degree its responsibility, to an imprecise leadership group called the "Leadership Council" comprising party leaders or a selection of some of them. The CDC thereafter effectively ceased to function except to acknowledge changes to the text agreed upon by unspecified leaders of the UIA and Kurdish Alliance. From this review it appears that the real work of the CDC took place at best between the end of July and the end of the first week of August, although its subcommittees sat for approximately three to four weeks before this.

17. Throughout this period the OCS raised questions about the adequacy of the timeframe, pointing out that a proper constitution-making process required time for effective national dialogue, public participation and deliberations taking into account Iraqi opinion and best practice. However, the members of the Coalition were insistent on maintaining adherence to the timeline and, it should not be underemphasized, that many Iraqi parties were equally insistent. The context in which the Iraqi constitution-making process took place necessarily implicated urgent considerations of achieving national stability or in the case of the Sunnis, their antipathy to any extension of the period in office of the current government overrode their desire and need to engage in further negotiations.

3. THE CONCLUSION OF THE NEGOTIATIONS ON A FINAL TEXT

18. It is important to describe the evolution of the negotiations between mid-August and the finalization (amendment) of the text initially on the 22nd August, then on the 28th August, again on 13th September and finally on 12th October, three days before the referendum.

19. After the CDC resolved that its delegates were not in a position to arrive at the kind of compromises that were required to bring the negotiations to a close, arrangements were made to convene a meeting of political party leaders. This was subsequently called the "Leadership Council." The work of the CDC effectively ended and its six subcommittees ceased to function (in effect they had ceased to function at the end of July, but were re-convened from time to time to reconsider issues referred to them by the CDC). Once the Leadership Council took over the commitment to transparency dwindled and the process became chaotic with multiple drafts emerging.

20. The US Ambassador played a leading role in facilitating these meetings but it is not clear what influence the US Embassy exercised on the substance of the draft other than on human rights questions relevant to its domestic audience (notably gender and the role of religion).

21. The most noticeable amendment to the CDC's draft, when it surfaced on 15th August and again on 22nd August, was the apparently unformed framework for the establishment of regions and the unusual degree of autonomy afforded to them. During this period the OCS and other advisors found it difficult to either comment on the draft or to engage directly with the decision-makers.

22. In addition, the draft was subjected to continuous renegotiation right up until the referendum. This was due, in part, to the imperative of engaging more substantively with the Sunni representatives who had played little role in the formulation of the draft text. It became clear that the draft did not have the support of the Sunni community, and its implications for the referendum required at least some attempt to bring Sunni notables within the consensus. As it happens, this was partially achieved through the negotiation and adoption of a provision which would expressly allow for the review of the constitution after the election of a new, hopefully more representative, parliament in the first four months of 2006.

23. There were, however, other issues which surfaced during this period which emanated from the caucuses of the principal partners to the consensus (such as federal control over water resources).

24. We would note that, during this phase, although the process followed the broad trend of the framework set out in TAL there were deviations from it in several respects, more particularly in regard to the finalization of the draft within the time period, the process by which the TAL was amended and the provision for a sufficient period for national dialogue and debate on the final text prior to the referendum.

NOTES AND QUESTIONS

1. *The security context.* When considering the success or failure of the Iraqi Constitution-making process it is imperative to keep in mind the security context in which the Constitution was drafted. The Iraqi Constitution was written during a time when sectarian violence resulted in 62 deaths a day on average in Iraq. The insurgency had openly declared its opposition to the drafting of a constitution. Any and all members of the Transitional National Assembly (TNA), and particularly the Constitutional Drafting Committee (CDC), were under constant threat of assassination. On July 19, 2005, Mijbil 'Isa, a Sunni member of the CDC, was killed. The tense atmosphere created conditions inimical to negotiation, dialogue, and consensus among the competing sectarian groups represented in the CDC. Was the tight timeline and the TNA's fixation on producing a draft Constitution by August 15 ill-advised? Should the TNA, as authorized by the 2004 Transitional Administrative Law, have extended the deadline by six months for the completion of a draft Constitution? Should the TNA have postponed the drafting of the Constitution until the security situation had significantly improved?

2. *The Shi'ite-Kurdish Political Bargain.* The Iraqi Constitution that emerged from the October 15, 2005 constitutional referendum was largely the product of a Shi'ite-Kurdish political alliance. Since the formation of the Iraqi Transitional Government, it was clear that the dominant Shi'ite United Iraqi Alliance party and the Kurdish Alliance party had entered into agreements that later facilitated constitutional compromises benefiting the two

parties but leaving the Sunnis out. The Sunnis' outsider status was partly of their own making due to their boycott of the January 2005 parliamentary elections. It took five months of intense pressure and negotiations before the TNA acceded to international calls to include unelected Sunnis on the CDC. Shi'i and Kurdish parliamentarians were concerned about involving in the constitution-making process unelected Sunnis who had been associated with the Ba'th and were even possibly sympathetic to the insurgency. Even after their inclusion on the committee the Sunni members were quickly marginalized as their participation became viewed as increasingly obstructionist. Sunni marginalization within the CDC further increased once negotiations of the most difficult constitutional issues were removed from the CDC to the Leadership Council. Consequently, the final draft Constitution that was approved by the TNA two days prior to the constitutional referendum appeared essentially as a consensus between the Shi'ites and the Kurds. Recognizing their under-representation and powerlessness in the TNA and CDC, the predominant Sunni position shifted to expediting the December 15 elections and the formation of a new government. The Sunnis would eventually place their hopes for addressing their constitutional grievances in the amendment process under the Constitutional Review Committee.

3. As one reads the Constitution, the difficult tripartite arrangement needs to be constantly kept in mind. How egalitarian can such a scheme be? How can sectarianism (Shi'i-Sunni) and nationalism (Kurdish-Arab) be accommodated with the principle of individual equality in citizenship? On this difficult issue see Chibli Mallat, Introduction to Middle Eastern Law 171-80 (2007).

4. This UN report raises questions of a historical nature which will bear on the viability of the Constitution and its interpretation for a long time to come: what was the role of the U.S.? Of the UN? How different is the Constitution from the TAL? Could the boycott of the Sunni community have been avoided? Was the electoral law not responsible for the dominance of the exclusive Shi'i list? On the electoral laws, see section C, *infra*.

5. In time, one should expect several readings and notes from participants and close observers of the drafting process. Despite its apparent "neutral" tone, the UN description of constitutional drafting omits some important dimensions, which Professor Haider Ala Hamoudi underlined in a comment to the present section. It was not so much, for instance, UN envoy Lakhdar Brahimi, but the insistence of leading Shi'i Imam Sistani "that resulted in the agreement following which the permanent constitution would be written by a body that was elected." Also, Paragraph 16 of the UN report exaggerates the role of the Leadership Council and the CDC, according to Hamoudi:

> This is not what happened. What happened was the CDC, which had more or less a Shi'i version of the draft, distributed it to the UN and others, and the Leadership Council began to make amendments that the United Iraqi Alliance (UIA) [the "Sistani list," which was the main bloc in Parliament and overwhelmingly Shi'i] didn't think were necessary. Generally the Shi'a and the UIA ignored what the Leadership Council was doing, and didn't think they had to listen to amendments made chiefly by Sunni and Shi'i liberals,

and by the Kurds. Hajem Al Hassani, Ghazi Yawer, Iyad Allawi were the main players. Abdul Aziz al-Hakim and Humam Hamoudi, who had played a central role in the Constitution submitted to the UN, barely attended, and two drafts emerged by the second week of August, one by the UIA, and one by the Leadership Council. In what the Shi'a derisively call the "political kitchen" (*al-matbakh al-siyasi*), everyone sat down and made one draft. The most memorable statement when this started was by the Sadrist representative, who told a Kurdish colleague, "okay Kaka [Sir in Kurdish], one article for you, and the next one for me, and we'll get this done in an hour." Memorable because this was only a slight exaggeration of what ultimately transpired, for they met August 14 and were almost done by August 15.

6. For a good overview of the Constitution, see Faleh Jabar, "The Constitution of Iraq: Religious and Ethnic Relations," published by Minority Rights Group, London, December 2005. It is available at http://www.minorityrights.org/?lid=957. Jabar mentions that as many as 450,000(!) proposals were made to the Drafting Committee. Hopefully, at least some of these will have been preserved for the historical record. See also the important article of two close American observers, Ashley Deeks & Matthew Burton, Iraq's Constitution: A Drafting History, 40 Cornell Int'l L.J. 1-88 (2007).

B. THE CONSTITUTION AND COMMENTARIES

1. PRESENTATION AND GUIDE

The Constitution of Iraq was completed and published by the Iraqi Constitutional Commission on August 25, 2005. The text was slightly amended on September 4, then on October 12. The current text was ratified by referendum on October 15, 2005, when it became effective. It is supposed to become "final" after a long series of provisional constitutions through the 20th century, including the 2004 Transitional Administrative Law (TAL, *Qanun idarat al-dawlat*).* For the text of all the constitutions since the 1925 Basic Law, see www.iraqijudicature.com, under *al-dasatir al-'iraqiyya*. By its own account, the 2005 Constitution is lacking, mostly on federal powers. A key institution at least has yet to be established, the Federation (or Federal, Council, literally the Council of the Union, *majlis al-ittihad*) only adumbrated in Article 65. Considering the centrality of the concept of federalism, a novelty in Iraq and in the region, the emergence of this Council will be decisive for a host of issues, from political representation to oil sharing.

This section includes the full text of the Constitution, with its immediate predecessor the TAL in the endnotes, and interspersed with four full or excerpted commentaries. To facilitate reading and referencing, the text of the Constitution runs in regular text while the comments are provided

---

*The full text of the Transitional Administrative Law (2004) in English can be found at http://www.cpa-iraq.org/government/TAL.html/. It is reproduced in the endnotes to this chapter.

(after each article when available and after a fuller section when appropriate) as insets, indented and in a unique format, in the following order:

- Insets preceded by *CM* for Chibli Mallat, "A Brief Commentary on the Iraqi Constitution." This text was composed in the last week of August 2005, shortly after the text of the Constitution was made public, and sent to several Iraqi leaders. It appears here for the first time, despite its telegraphic style, which was meant to encourage the amendment of the most glaring inconsistencies. Unlike the other three commentaries, which are retrospective, it was conceived as hortatory, with the constitutional drafters in mind as they were revising and smoothing out the text. It has been slightly amended from the original for the purposes of the present chapter.
- Insets preceded by *HAH* for the comments contributed by Haider Ala Hamoudi to this chapter. Professor Hamoudi, who teaches law at the University of Pittsburgh, was very close to, and has spoken extensively with, many of the key drafters of the Iraqi Constitution. He is the author of several law journal articles on Islamic, Iraqi, and U.S. law. See, e.g., Chapter 5 and the recently published *Howling in Mesopotamia* (2008).
- Insets preceded by *NB* for Nathan Brown, "The Final Draft of the Iraqi Constitution: Analysis and Commentary," September 16, 2005, available at http://www.carnegieendowment.org/files/FinalDraftSept16.pdf. Nathan Brown is a professor of political science at George Washington University and the author of *Constitutions in a Non-Constitutional World* (2001) and *The Rule of Law in the Arab World: Courts in Egypt and the Arab States of the Gulf* (1997).
- Insets preceded by *UN* for United Nations Assistance Mission for Iraq, Office of Constitutional Support, "Analysis and Overview of the Text of the Iraqi Constitution," 7-8 December 2005.

An English version of the Constitution by the Associated Press was released on August 28, 2005. Another translation was undertaken by the United Nations and can be found at http://portal.unesco.org/ci/en/files/20704/11332732681iraqi_constitution_en.pdf/iraqi_constitution_en.pdf. The AP version, which is the basis of the Brown commentary, includes 139 Articles, and Brown's text has therefore been annotated in square brackets where necessary to refer to the final version of the article numbers. The final Arabic text consists of 144 Articles. This is because some sections were rearranged into separate articles and some late amendments were made. Below we have used the UN/U.S./UK translation dated January 25, 2006 of the final, current Arabic version. It is available at http://www.uniraq.org/documents/iraqi_constitution.pdf.

In Arabic, the portal of the Iraqi Parliament includes the Constitution and several important laws, http://www.parliament.iq/. Of note is the collective book put together by the Iraq Institute for Strategic Studies, directed by Faleh 'Abd al-Jabbar, *Ma'zaq al-dustur al-'iraqi* (Dilemmas of the Iraqi Constitution) (2006), which includes the three successive drafts of the Constitution in full, along with chapters by several observers and scholars. The Institute also published another collective work on the Constitution, *Muraja'at fil-dustur al-'iraq* (Considerations on the Iraqi Constitution) (2006).

A good resource on the Internet for federalism in Iraq, including Arabic texts, can be found at http://forumfed.org/en/products/books.php#arabicpubs. It is set up by the Canadian Forum of Federations (*forumfed.org*), which runs a constitutional program on Iraq. For Arabic, the website set up by the Higher Judicial Council and the Federal Supreme Court contains indispensable texts and court decisions. See www.iraqijudicature.com.

2. TEXT AND COMMENTARIES

The Preamble[1]

In the name of God, the most merciful, the most compassionate.

> **CM:** Such formulation excludes non-Muslim Iraqis. The oppositional Kefaya movement in Egypt, which is led by Copts and Muslims, successfully rejected a similar formula to introduce its public statements.

We have honored the sons of Adam.

> **CM:** Reference starts with a sexist overtone, Eve not being mentioned. Many more expressive passages in the Qur'an could have been chosen, especially texts on God's predilection for the diversity of peoples and tribes, *shu'ub wa qaba'el* (Qur'an 49:13), and the texts addressing women and men on a par.

> **HAH:** I see the point, though I would render the translation "we have dignified the children of Adam." I've never seen Bani Israel, for example, translated from the Qur'an as anything but "the children of Israel." Also, I prefer "dignify" because it is the verse most commonly used by modern Muslims to defend the notion that Islam respects human rights, on which basis God has dignified man, i.e. conferred on him dignity associated with basic rights. This background is important in so far as the verse is intended to show that the Constitution, human rights and Islam are all part of one grand, comprehensive, system.

We, the people of Mesopotamia, the homeland of the apostles and prophets, resting place of the virtuous imams, cradle of civilization, crafters of writing, and home of numeration. Upon our land the first law made by man was passed, and the oldest pact of just governance was inscribed, and upon our soil the saints and companions of the Prophet prayed, philosophers and scientists theorized, and writers and poets excelled;

> **CM:** Reference to Mesopotamia is positive, but "virtuous" and "holy Imams" connotes preeminence of Shi'is, despite the fact that Imam Abu Hanifa (d.767), like so many other Sunni jurists, was behind the first "Iraqi"

legal school. It is unfortunate that Hammurabi was not mentioned by name.

HAH: The Shi'i bias is more obvious in Arabic. It's *athar,* the "pure." Amongst Shi'is, the Imams and the Household of the Prophet are described as "*al-tayyibin al-tahirin,*" from *tahir,* singular of *tahirin* or *athar.*

Acknowledging God's right over us, and in fulfillment of the call of our homeland and citizens, and in a response to the call of our religious and national leaderships and the determination of our great authorities and of our leaders and politicians, and in the midst of international support from our friends and those who love us, we marched for the first time in our history towards the ballot boxes by the millions, men and women, young and old, on the thirtieth of January 2005, invoking the pains of sectarian oppression inflicted by the autocratic clique and inspired by the tragedies of Iraq's martyrs, Shiite and Sunni, Arabs and Kurds and Turkmen and from all other components of the people, and recollecting the darkness of the ravage of the holy cities and the South in the Sha'abaniyya uprising and burnt by the flames of grief of the mass graves, the marshes, Al-Dujail and others and articulating the sufferings of racial oppression in the massacres of Halabcha, Barzan, Anfal and the Fayli Kurds and inspired by the ordeals of the Turkmen in Bashir and the sufferings of the people of the western region, as is the case in the remaining areas of Iraq where the people suffered from the liquidation of their leaders, symbols, and Sheiks and from the displacement of their skilled individuals and from drying out of its cultural and intellectual wells, so we sought hand in hand and shoulder to shoulder to create our new Iraq, the Iraq of the future, free from sectarianism, racism, complex of regional attachment, discrimination, and exclusion.

CM: Reference to the religious leaders is characteristic of Shi'ism in the Iraqi context because of the special structure of the Shi'i clergy. Noteworthy is the reference to electoral consultation of 2005 as a potentially founding precedent of Iraqi democracy.

Accusations of being infidels, and terrorism did not stop us from marching forward to build a nation of law. Sectarianism and racism have not stopped us from marching together to strengthen our national unity, following the path of peaceful transfer of power, adopting the course of just distribution of resources, and providing equal opportunity for all.

CM: Rejection of sectarianism sounds hollow, considering the recent Iraqi past. Reference to terrorism and *takfir* (accusation of religious "infidelity") may be both overly political and transient for a constitutional text destined to last.

We, the people of Iraq, who have just risen from our stumble, and who are looking with confidence to the future through a republican, federal, democratic, pluralistic system, have resolved with the determination of our men, women, elderly, and youth to respect the rule of law, to establish justice and equality, to cast aside the politics of aggression, to pay attention to women and their rights, the elderly and their concerns, and children and their affairs, to spread the culture of diversity, and to defuse terrorism.

CM: Such reference to a resolve to "pay attention" is not a constitutional concept, despite the expected rhetoric in a Preamble, although English tends to exaggerate the "natural" Arabic flourish of the text.

We, the people of Iraq, of all components and across the spectrum, have taken upon ourselves to decide freely and by choice to unite our future, to take lessons from yesterday for tomorrow, and to enact this permanent Constitution, through the values and ideals of the heavenly messages and the findings of science and man's civilization. The adherence to this Constitution preserves for Iraq its free union of people, of land, and of sovereignty.

CM: To consider the Constitution "permanent" in an express manner will hopefully be unnecessary.

As possible alternatives to this Preamble, reference to non-violence as an essential dimension of political *modus operandi* may be more enticing, as was the case in the Preamble to the TAL. Also some reference to dictatorship as unacceptable mode of government may be couched more positively. The elections of January 30, 2005, considering the large Sunni boycott, may not be appealing enough to all Iraqis.

NB: Some elements of the preamble were a source of controversy: Although the brief narration of the country's history insists on an ancient Iraqi nationality, it still seems tilted toward Shiite and Kurdish interpretations.

Preambles are almost always extremely general and sometimes quite flowery. In the Iraqi case, however, the vague and hortatory language packs a punch, because it refers to the Iraqi union (*ittihad,* the same word used to mean federation in this text) as voluntary — a major Kurdish demand because it can imply a right of secession. Some participants in the drafting process wanted to insert an explicit provision stating that the preamble was legally binding, and indeed such language was included in some earlier drafts. Such a provision is not unknown internationally, but the usual purpose is to encourage the use of the preamble to guide constitutional interpretation. In the end, the provision for an explicitly binding preamble was dropped, although even after August 28, some sought to revive the idea.

Some versions of the AP translation omit an opening invocation, "In the name of God, the Merciful, the Compassionate," a Qur'anic formula that is a standard opening for any official text or speech. A very brief Qur'anic quotation follows the invocation again omitted from the AP translation: "We have honored the children of Adam."

Section One—Fundamental Principles[2]

Article 1:

Amended: The Republic of Iraq is a single federal, independent and fully sovereign state in which the system of government is republican, representative, parliamentary, and democratic, and this Constitution is a guarantor of the unity of Iraq.

(*Previous text:* The Republic of Iraq is a single, independent federal state with full sovereignty. Its system of government is republican, representative, parliamentary and democratic. This Constitution is the guarantor of its unity.)

CM: In Arabic, "representative," *tamthili*, would ring better than "parliamentary," *barlamani*, which is a neologism.

Article 2:

First: Islam is the official religion of the State and is a foundation source of legislation:

CM: "A foundation" instead of "the foundation" harks unnecessarily to the Egyptian debate over Article 2 of the 1980 Constitution. What are the constitutional consequences for Islam being dubbed "the official religion"?

A. No law may be enacted that contradicts the established provisions of Islam.

CM: The definition of "established" is key. Would a person's change of religion be unacceptable? Would a ban on polygamy? How about criminal regulations?

HAH: The real dispute came over the term *hukm* for 'provisions'. I don't know why every translation I have read renders this as "provisions," I think "rulings" is much better. The specific Sunni concern was that a "ruling" could just be something Sistani said, which is a plausible reading. The Shi'i compromise was to add "established" to ruling, and much will turn on what either means. But the retention of *hukm* is important. Compare TAL "the certainties of Islam upon which there is consensus." That clearly includes Sunni thought, the world *mujma' 'alayh* ensures consensus of all Muslims in the Sunni tradition. One wonders whether the final text does not underline the specific role of the Shi'i leadership known as *marja'iyya*.

B. No law may be enacted that contradicts the principles of democracy.
C. No law may be enacted that contradicts the rights and basic freedoms stipulated in this Constitution.

> *CM:* B and C are slightly redundant.
> Alternative formulation suggested:
> Islamic law, together with the laws of the land since Hammurabi, and the principles of democracy as practiced in the law of the most advanced nations, form a privileged reference for this constitution and the laws of Iraq.

Second: This Constitution guarantees the Islamic identity of the majority of the Iraqi people and guarantees the full religious rights to freedom of religious belief and practice of all individuals such as Christians, Yazidis, and Mandean Sabeans.

> *CM:* It is meaningless to guarantee identity, Islamic or otherwise. A constitution can never be presumed to have been conceived for a majority.

Article 3:

Amended: Iraq is a country of multiple nationalities, religions, and sects. It is a founding and active member in the Arab League and is committed to its charter, and it is part of the Islamic world.

(*Previous text:* Iraq is a country of many nationalities, religions and sects, and is a part of the Islamic world, is a founding and active member of the Arab League, and is committed to its covenant.)

> *CM:* All references redundant.

> *HAH:* True, but this Arab League mention was controversial throughout the period.

Article 4:

First: The Arabic language and the Kurdish language are the two official languages of Iraq. The right of Iraqis to educate their children in their mother tongue, such as Turkmen, Syriac, and Armenian shall be guaranteed in government educational institutions in accordance with educational guidelines, or in any other language in private educational institutions.

> *CM:* Text should stop at *Arabic and Kurdish are the two official languages for Iraq*, or better: Arabic and Kurdish are official languages.

Second: The scope of the term "official language" and the means of applying the provisions of this article shall be defined by a law and shall include:

A. Publication of the Official Gazette, in the two languages;
B. Speech, conversation, and expression in official domains, such as the Council of Representatives, the Council of Ministers, courts, and official conferences, in either of the two languages;

C. Recognition and publication of official documents and correspondence in the two languages;

D. Opening schools that teach the two languages, in accordance with the educational guidelines;

E. Use of both languages in any matter enjoined by the principle of equality such as bank notes, passports, and stamps.

CM: All of these details appear redundant in a constitution. [Hereinafter "redundant."]

Amended: Third: The federal and official institutions and agencies in the Kurdistan region shall use both languages.

(*Previous text*—Third: The federal institutions and agencies in the Kurdistan region shall use the Arabic and Kurdish languages.)

Fourth: The Turkomen language and the Syriac language are two other official languages in the administrative units in which they constitute density of population.

Fifth: Each region or governorate may adopt any other local language as an additional official language if the majority of its population so decides in a general referendum.

Article 5:

The law is sovereign. The people are the source of authority and legitimacy, which they shall exercise in a direct, general, secret ballot and through their constitutional institutions.

CM: Good.

Article 6:

Transfer of authority shall be made peacefully through democratic means as stipulated in this Constitution.

CM: As part of the same logic of rule of law, Art. 6 should be fused with Art.5, all in one sentence that comprises rule of law + alternation in power + basic individual rights.

Article 7:

First: Any entity or program that adopts, incites, facilitates, glorifies, promotes, or justifies racism or terrorism or accusations of being an infidel (*takfir*) or ethnic cleansing, especially the Saddamist Ba'ath in Iraq and its symbols, under any name whatsoever, shall be prohibited. Such entities may not be part of the political pluralism in Iraq. This shall be regulated by law.

CM: Saddam Hussein not worth mentioning in a permanent constitution.

> *HAH:* This was a Shi'i compromise, although even then the Sunnis had a problem with it. Originally the ban was going to be on the Ba'ath party itself, "Saddamist Ba'ath" was intended to limit the ban so that people who claimed to be Ba'athis but not in the Saddamist mold could reform that party.

Second: The State shall undertake to combat terrorism in all its forms, and shall work to protect its territories from being a base, pathway, or field for terrorist activities.

> *CM:* Redundant.

Article 8:

Iraq shall observe the principles of good neighborliness, adhere to the principle of non-interference in the internal affairs of other states, seek to settle disputes by peaceful means, establish relations on the basis of mutual interests and reciprocity, and respect its international obligations.

> *CM:* Simplify: Iraq shall respect its international obligations.

Article 9:

First:

A. The Iraqi armed forces and security services will be composed of the components of the Iraqi people with due consideration given to their balance and representation without discrimination or exclusion. They shall be subject to the control of the civilian authority, shall defend Iraq, shall not be used as an instrument to oppress the Iraqi people, shall not interfere in the political affairs, and shall have no role in the transfer of authority.
B. The formation of military militias outside the framework of the armed forces is prohibited.
C. The Iraqi armed forces and their personnel, including military personnel working in the Ministry of Defense or any subordinate departments or organizations, may not stand for election to political office, campaign for candidates, or participate in other activities prohibited by Ministry of Defense regulations. This ban includes the activities of the personnel mentioned above acting in their personal or professional capacities, but shall not infringe upon the right of these personnel to cast their vote in the elections.
D. The Iraqi National Intelligence Service shall collect information, assess threats to national security, and advise the Iraqi government. This Service shall be under civilian control, shall be subject to legislative oversight, and shall operate in accordance with the law and pursuant to the recognized principles of human rights.
E. The Iraqi Government shall respect and implement Iraq's international obligations regarding the non-proliferation, non-development, non-production, and non-use of nuclear, chemical, and biological weapons,

and shall prohibit associated equipment, materiel, technologies, and delivery systems for use in the development, manufacture, production, and use of such weapons.

Second: Military service shall be regulated by law.

> *CM:* Simplify: All security and military personnel and services are subject to the civilian, democratically elected government.

Article 10:

The holy shrines and religious sites in Iraq are religious and civilizational entities. The State is committed to assuring and maintaining their sanctity, and to guaranteeing the free practice of rituals in them.

> *CM:* No need.

> *HAH:* An earlier draft made specific reference to the *marja'iyya* as holy figures, Sunnis were dismayed.

Article 11:

Baghdad is the capital of the Republic of Iraq.

Article 12:

First: The flag, national anthem, and emblem of Iraq shall be regulated by law in a way that symbolizes the components of the Iraqi people.
Second: A law shall regulate honours, official holidays, religious and national occasions and the Hijri and Gregorian calendar.

> *CM:* Either fix in text, or leave out. Reference to "law" in the constitution weakens the natural supremacy of the constitutional text. Since this appears in several places in the Constitution, I refer henceforth to the anomaly hereinafter as "Law . . ." to avoid repetition.

Article 13

First: This Constitution is the preeminent and supreme law in Iraq and shall be binding in all parts of Iraq without exception.
Second: No law that contradicts this Constitution shall be enacted. Any text in any regional constitutions or any other legal text that contradicts this Constitution shall be considered void.

> *NB:* Article 1: Name and Basic Description
>
> A reference to Iraq as an Islamic state, proposed by Islamist members of the drafting committee, was dropped in the final draft of the constitution. In the end, the name of the country is simply the Republic of Iraq, as it has been since the overthrow of the monarchy in 1958.

Article 2: Official Religion and Bases of Legislation

This article attracted the greatest amount of international attention and has widely been termed "contradictory." That characterization probably goes too far, but there are some tensions in the final language that reflect compromises made among the drafters.

- The reference to Islam as the official religion provoked little debate. The provision would certainly make it difficult to object to state funding for religious institutions, Religious instruction in the schools, and use of Islamic symbols in public life — but such practices would have likely continued even if the clause had been omitted.
- The reference to using Islam as a "basic source" of legislation is a compromise between those who wished it to be mentioned as "a source" and those who wanted it to be "the source." The significance of the impact of such phrasing was almost certainly exaggerated in much of the discussions that took place both inside Iraq and internationally. Interestingly, this part of the article does not mention Islamic law, only Islam.
- Potentially more significant is the provision that bars passage of any law that contradicts "the fixed elements of the rulings of Islam." (The translation is my own — less felicitous than the AP reference to the "undisputed rules" but more faithful to the original Arabic.) The formula appears to be an oddly worded compromise between those who wished to make reference to the "fixed elements" (*thawabit*) — which would presumably be very general and fairly few in number, given the diversity of the Islamic heritage — and those who favored protecting "rulings" (*ahkam*), a far more specific — and clearly legal, not only religious — term. It is not clear precisely what the effect of combining these two terms will be. In the short term, the article is likely to have little practical impact. The wording suggests that the provision might only apply to legislation passed after the constitution is adopted (although the opposite interpretation is not implausible either), so that the existing Iraqi legal order is likely to remain intact. The impact on future legislation is completely dependent on who has authority to interpret the article. The primary burden, at least in theory, would seem to fall on the parliament: It is to use Islam as a source for legislation and take care to avoid violating the fixed rulings of the religion. And the parliament is quite likely to be dominated by Islamist parties and influenced informally by leading Shiite clerics. At least at present, such clerics give fairly few specific instructions, but it is clear that when they do so, any government would have difficulty ignoring them (as Paul Bremer discovered). The Supreme Federal Court would probably be called on to play a major interpretive role as well, and the composition of that body is therefore critical for the meaning of Article 2 in the long term. [*HAH:* This is true, but the role of interpreting Article 2's "certain rulings" of Islam may well fall to religious jurists, who can sit on the court. One cannot imagine Islamist Shi'a wanting a secular judge to determine *shari'a* in possible derogation to the *marja'iyya.*]
- The article also prohibits passing laws that violate the principles of democracy and the stipulated rights and freedoms. This provision also gives strong but very uncertain advice to the parliament. In the

long term, it might provide a formula for strengthening some of the fairly weak constitutional provisions for rights. Some Coalition Provisional Authority (CPA) legal documents restored the pre-1958 name "State of Iraq," although this seems to have been only the result of sloppy drafting and has not been retained since the dissolution of the CPA in 2004.

Article 3: Identity

The constitution also describes Iraq in multiethnic terms, as did the Baathist constitutions (although those older documents were less detailed and far less credible). The failure to describe Iraq as an Arab state provoked strong objections from some of the Arab Sunni drafters (and even led to talk of suspending Iraq from the Arab League). Compromise wording (such as describing Iraq as a founding member of the Arab League) was carefully negotiated, partially with the Arab League. While the September 13 draft does not describe Iraq as an Arab country, it does describe Iraq as bound by the Arab League Charter. Since describing Iraq as an Arab state is an entirely symbolic step but binding the country constitutionally to an international document could have real practical implications, it is ironic that the final formula was regarded as a compromise.

Article 4: Official Languages

Kurdish is an official language under the Transitional Administrative Law (TAL, the country's interim constitution), but it is rarely used outside of Iraqi Kurdistan. This article leaves many details to ordinary legislation, but it does attempt to provide some real guarantees that Kurdish will be used as an official language at the national level.

Article 7: Forbidden Political Ideologies and Practices

The ban on *takfir* (accusation of apostasy or religious unbelief) is probably a reference to radical Sunni groups, some of which have declared Shiites apostates. The ban on the "Saddamist Baath" is a concession to Sunnis. Earlier drafts banned even the ideology of the party, seeking to prevent it from emerging under a different name. However, specifying the "Saddamist" Baath leaves open the possibility of establishing a party that claims to be based on Baathist principles prevailing in Syria or in the pre-Saddam Hussein Iraqi branch of the Baath Party.

Article 9: Military and Security

The TAL required the provisions against military intervention in politics.

Article 10: Holy Places

The phrase translated as "holy shrines" by the AP (*'atabat*) is one that I believe is generally used for Shiite religious places. The rest of the article is religiously neutral. An earlier attempt to stipulate respect for senior Shiite religious leaders was not included in the final draft.

Article 12: Symbols

The reference to holidays on the Christian calendar might be taken to imply an oblique official status for Christianity. However, the phrasing could also be taken merely to refer to those holidays that are based on the Gregorian calendar, not those that are generally seen as Christian in nature (such as May Day or all Iraqi national holidays).

Article 13: Supremacy of Constitution

This establishment of the constitution as the supreme law of the country may seem implicit in the very idea of a written constitution, but it was probably made explicit to assure those who feared that Iraqi Kurdistan would claim a right to override constitutional provisions. It may have also been an assurance to those who worried that Article 2 implied that Islamic law would prevail over other sources of law.

UN: Identity issues

Section One enshrines the supremacy of the Constitution, and explicitly indicates that no legal provision (federal or regional) can contradict it. At the same time, as noted, the text explicitly points out that no law that contradicts the "established provisions" of Islam may be enacted. While the inclusion of this clause has generated controversy for the oversight capacity it may reserve for religious over civilian authorities, the same Article indicates that no law may be enacted that contradicts "the principles of democracy," and the "rights and basic freedoms stipulated in this Constitution." It should also be noted that the concept of "established provisions" appears as less prescriptive than the formula "judgments and tenets," which had been incorporated in previous drafts.

The inclusion of those three sets of references in the same Article — unusual in comparative constitutional practice in the Muslim and Arab world — may in principle facilitate a secular interpretation of legislation. We note however that different schools within the Shia and Sunni traditions may have different interpretations of the concept of "established provisions" of Islam. We also note the explicit reference in Article 43 of the Husseini rituals — which belong to the Shia and not the Sunni tradition. In any case, as noted above, it is important to recognize that there is no longer any mention of the Marja'iya in the text itself. Fears that Iraq will follow the path of Iran in establishing a religious state with a wilayat al-faqih appear, at least based on the text, premature. [*HAH:* Nobody who is reasonably knowledgeable about Iraq and its leadership, religious and political, can ignore the power of the *marja'iyya.* The more plausible position is that the mechanisms for review are going to be built in a manner that basically gives the jurists of Najaf the ability to override legislation (through political allies or through jurists on the court determining the "certain rulings" of Islam) when they think it exceeds permissible Islamic boundaries.]

Among the formulations used in comparative Arab constitutionalism, the consideration of Islam as "a" fundamental source of legislation appears as less prescriptive than formulas such as "the fundamental source" or "the only source". Defining Islam as "a fundamental source" both recognizes that Islam is a source of legislation and acknowledges the existence of other sources. It needs to be noted that this provision appears in the same Article as the repugnancy clause described above, which constitutionally links Islam as "a" source of legislation to the general democratic principles and rights and freedoms recorded in Section Two of the text (Rights and Liberties).

Armed forces

As noted, reference to the armed forces and to their control by the civilian authority is included. In accordance with international best practice, the text forbids the armed forces to interfere in the political affairs of the country and to have any role in the transfer of authority. The Constitution, however, does not include reference to parliamentary oversight of external deployment of military forces, which is not included either among the powers of the Council of Representatives as listed in Section Three. Although such a concept could be technically derived from the principle of civilian control of the armed forces, the inclusion of such explicit provision is common in comparative practice.

The Constitution explicitly prohibits the formation of militias outside the framework of the armed forces, but as noted provides for the establishment and organization of regional guards. The interplay between both provisions is not clear. This is likely to generate discrepancies of interpretation in the future. Also, it is not clear from the referred formulation whether the specific prohibition of the formation of militias involves recognition of militias that are already in existence (see further comments in 5.3.7). The text also records that Iraq will fight terrorism and prevent its territories from being used as a base for terrorist activities. We note that this clause in particular needs to be read in the light of the particular context in which the text has been drafted.

Section Two: Rights and Liberties[3]

Chapter One — Rights

CM: The following articles have all a "Western" resonance which the Iraqi founding fathers could have avoided by drawing on the extraordinary legacy of Iraqi law through history.

For instance, instead of Art.14 on equality, which is a simple translation from Western human rights declarations, the Constitution could make use of a saying (*hadith*) of the prophet, "*al-nas sawasiya 'alal-itlaq,*" "people/humans are equal in absolute," which is adapted from the *hadith* "*al-nas sawasiya ka-asnan al-misht,*" "people/humans are equal like the teeth of a comb."

Instead of Art. 15, again a translation from Western texts, Islamic law has a more idiomatic formulation, "*hirmat al-nafs wal-hurriyya wal-mumtalak masuna*," literally "soul, liberty and property are protected."

On the role of the state in the protection of the citizen, Hammurabi's prologue already mentioned the essential role of law in "the protection of the weak."

In criminal law rights, Islamic law has a concise, powerful formula, "*al-asl al-bara'a*," "the principle is innocence," which dispenses with long texts drawn from the Western legal tradition.

Similarly, the Qur'anic verse "*la ikrah fil-din*," "no compulsion in religion," is far more eloquent in Arabic than any Western-style rendering on religious freedom.

For more on the issue of constitutional style and Iraqi legal tradition, the reader is referred to the end of section 4 in this chapter, and to the references cited therein.

First: Civil and Political Rights

Article 14:

Iraqis are equal before the law without discrimination based on gender, race, ethnicity, nationality, origin, color, religion, sect, belief or opinion, or economic or social status.

Article 15:

Every individual has the right to enjoy life, security and liberty. Deprivation or restriction of these rights is prohibited except in accordance with the law and based on a decision issued by a competent judicial authority.

Article 16:

Equal opportunities shall be guaranteed to all Iraqis, and the state shall ensure that the necessary measures to achieve this are taken.

Article 17:

First: Every individual shall have the right to personal privacy so long as it does not contradict the rights of others and public morals.

Second: The sanctity of the homes shall be protected. Homes may not be entered, searched, or violated, except by a judicial decision in accordance with the law.

Article 18:

Amended:
First: Iraqi citizenship is a right for every Iraqi and is the basis of his nationality.
(*Previous text*: First: An Iraqi is any person born to an Iraqi father or mother.)

Amended:

Second: Anyone who is born to an Iraqi father or to an Iraqi mother shall be considered an Iraqi. This shall be regulated by law.

(Previous text: Second: Iraqi nationality is the right of every Iraqi and shall be the basis of his citizenship.)

> *CM:* Wide notion of *jus sanguinis* with laudable application of gender equality principle.

Third:

A. An Iraqi citizen by birth may not have his citizenship withdrawn for any reason. Any person who had his citizenship withdrawn shall have the right to demand its reinstatement. This shall be regulated by a law.
B. Iraqi citizenship shall be withdrawn from naturalized citizens in cases regulated by law.

> *CM:* Law . . .

Fourth: An Iraqi may have multiple citizenships. Everyone who assumes a senior, security or sovereign position must abandon any other acquired citizenship. This shall be regulated by law.

> *CM:* Not necessary — why should a minister be allowed two nationalities and not a person in a "security position"?

Fifth: Iraqi citizenship shall not be granted for the purposes of the policy of population settlement that disrupts the demographic composition of Iraq.

> *CM:* Reference to Palestinian threat — redundant.

> *HAH:* There was also concern that communities would start importing their own kin into Iraq — Kurds from Turkey, Shi'a from Lebanon, Sunnis from Egypt — to boost their numbers.

Sixth: Citizenship provisions shall be regulated by law. The competent courts shall consider the suits arising from those provisions.

> *CM:* Again law . . .

Article 19:

First: The judiciary is independent and no power is above the judiciary except the law.

> *CM:* Awkward: Law superior to judiciary?

Second: There is no crime or punishment except by law. The punishment shall only be for an act that the law considers a crime when perpetrated. A harsher punishment than the applicable punishment at the time of the offense may not be imposed.

CM: Interesting application in the case of Saddam Hussein's arrest, because Paul Bremer had issued an edict suspending the death penalty. Should Saddam [have] benefit[ed]?

Third: Litigation shall be a protected and guaranteed right for all.

Fourth: The right to a defense shall be sacred and guaranteed in all phases of investigation and the trial.

Fifth: The accused is innocent until proven guilty in a fair legal trial. The accused may not be tried for the same crime for a second time after acquittal unless new evidence is produced.

Sixth: Every person shall have the right to be treated with justice in judicial and administrative proceedings.

Seventh: The proceedings of a trial are public unless the court decides to make it secret.

Eighth: Punishment shall be personal.

Ninth: Laws shall not have retroactive effect unless stipulated otherwise. This exclusion shall not include laws on taxes and fees.

Tenth: Criminal laws shall not have retroactive effect, unless it is to the benefit of the accused.

Eleventh: The court shall appoint a lawyer at the expense of the state for an accused of a felony or misdemeanor who does not have a defense lawyer.

Twelfth:

A. Unlawful detention shall be prohibited.
B. Imprisonment or detention shall be prohibited in places not designed for these purposes, pursuant to prison laws covering health and social care, and subject to the authorities of the State.

Thirteenth: The preliminary investigative documents shall be submitted to the competent judge in a period not to exceed twenty-four hours from the time of the arrest of the accused, which may be extended only once and for the same period.

Article 20:

Iraqi citizens, men and women, shall have the right to participate in public affairs and to enjoy political rights including the right to vote, elect, and run for office.

Article 21:

First: No Iraqi shall be surrendered to foreign entities and authorities.

CM: What about legitimate extradition rules?

Second: A law shall regulate the right of political asylum in Iraq. No political refugee shall be surrendered to a foreign entity or returned forcibly to the country from which he fled.

Third: Political asylum shall not be granted to a person accused of committing international or terrorist crimes or to any person who inflicted damage on Iraq.

HAH: It should be noted that this is problematic under international law, if denial of asylum is meant to mean *refoulement*. Professor Cherif Bassiouni has expressed this concern several times — "accused" for Arabic *muttaham* (which isn't exactly accused, but a category in between suspect and accused, close to indicted) is too broad a standard, international law requires a person to be convicted in a court of law. "Inflicted damage" is an even broader category.

Second: Economic, Social and Cultural Liberties

Article 22:

First: Work is a right for all Iraqis in a way that guarantees a dignified life for them.

CM: Redundant.

Second: The law shall regulate the relationship between employees and employers on economic bases and while observing the rules of social justice.

CM: Law . . .

Third: The State shall guarantee the right to form and join unions and professional associations, and this shall be regulated by law.

CM: Awkward. Why *the State*? Suggested alternative formulation: the right to form or join trade-unions and other associations is guaranteed.

Article 23:

First: Private property is protected. The owner shall have the right to benefit, exploit and dispose of private property within the limits of the law.

CM: Law . . .

Second: Expropriation is not permissible except for the purposes of public benefit in return for just compensation, and this shall be regulated by law.

CM: Law . . .

Third:

A. Every Iraqi shall have the right to own property anywhere in Iraq. No others may possess immovable assets, except as exempted by law.

CM: Law . . .

B. Ownership of property for the purposes of demographic change is prohibited.

CM: Again. Fear of Israel-made Palestinian precedent?

Article 24:

The State shall guarantee freedom of movement of Iraqi manpower, goods, and capital between regions and governorates, and this shall be regulated by law.

CM: Law. . . . It is good to guarantee free movement of persons. But what about federalism and the protection of a place like Kurdistan from massive demographic moves from the south?

Article 25:

The State shall guarantee the reform of the Iraqi economy in accordance with modern economic principles to insure the full investment of its resources, diversification of its sources, and the encouragement and development of the private sector.

Article 26:

The State shall guarantee the encouragement of investment in the various sectors, and this shall be regulated by law.

CM: Law . . .

Article 27:

First: Public assets are sacrosanct, and their protection is the duty of each citizen.

CM: Redundant with Art. 23.2.

Second: The provisions related to the preservation of State properties, their management, the conditions for their disposal, and the limits for these assets not to be relinquished shall all be regulated by law.

Article 28:

First: No taxes or fees shall be levied, amended, collected, or exempted, except by law.

Second: Low income earners shall be exempted from taxes in a way that guarantees the preservation of the minimum income required for living. This shall be regulated by law.

Article 29:

First:

A. The family is the foundation of society; the State shall preserve it and its religious, moral, and national values.
B. The State shall guarantee the protection of motherhood, childhood and old age, shall care for children and youth, and shall provide them with the appropriate conditions to develop their talents and abilities.

Second: Children have the right to upbringing, care and education from their parents. Parents have the right to respect and care from their children, especially in times of need, disability, and old age.

Third: Economic exploitation of children in all of its forms shall be prohibited, and the State shall take the necessary measures for their protection.

Fourth: All forms of violence and abuse in the family, school, and society shall be prohibited.

CM: Reference to violence within the family is novel and alluring.

Article 30:

First: The State shall guarantee to the individual and the family—especially children and women—social and health security, the basic requirements for living a free and decent life, and shall secure for them suitable income and appropriate housing.

Second: The State shall guarantee social and health security to Iraqis in cases of old age, sickness, employment disability, homelessness, orphanhood, or unemployment, shall work to protect them from ignorance, fear and poverty, and shall provide them housing and special programs of care and rehabilitation, and this shall be regulated by law.

Article 31:

First: Every citizen has the right to health care. The State shall maintain public health and provide the means of prevention and treatment by building different types of hospitals and health institutions.

Second: Individuals and entities have the right to build hospitals, clinics, or private health care centers under the supervision of the State, and this shall be regulated by law.

Article 32:

The State shall care for the handicapped and those with special needs, and shall ensure their rehabilitation in order to reintegrate them into society, and this shall be regulated by law.

Article 33:

First: Every individual has the right to live in safe environmental conditions.

Second: The State shall undertake the protection and preservation of the environment and its biological diversity.

CM: Reference to environment innovative, but vague.

Article 34:

First: Education is a fundamental factor for the progress of society and is a right guaranteed by the state. Primary education is mandatory and the state guarantees that it shall combat illiteracy.

Second: Free education in all its stages is a right for all Iraqis.

CM: This may be too costly and therefore counterproductive, especially at university level.

Third: The State shall encourage scientific research for peaceful purposes that serve humanity and shall support excellence, creativity, invention, and different aspects of ingenuity.

Fourth: Private and public education shall be guaranteed, and this shall be regulated by law.

CM: Private and community-based (*ahli*)?

Article 35:

Amended: The state shall promote cultural activities and institutions in a manner that befits the civilizational and cultural history of Iraq, and it shall seek to support indigenous Iraqi cultural orientations.

(Previous text merged originally a paragraph in Art. 37.)

Article 36:

Amended: Practicing sports is a right of every Iraqi and the state shall encourage and care for such activities and shall provide for their requirements.

(Previous text originally a paragraph in Art. 38.)

Chapter Two: Liberties

Article 37:

First:

A. The liberty and dignity of man shall be protected.
B. No person may be kept in custody or investigated except according to a judicial decision.

CM: Redundant with previous texts.

C. All forms of psychological and physical torture and inhumane treatment are prohibited. Any confession made under force, threat, or torture shall not be relied on, and the victim shall have the right to seek compensation for material and moral damages incurred in accordance with the law.

CM: Reference to torture and compensation interesting especially in the Iraqi context.

Second: The State shall guarantee protection of the individual from intellectual, political and religious coercion.

CM: Freedom of religion noted, with a proviso on style as per the comment at the beginning of the chapter.

Third: Forced labor, slavery, slave trade, trafficking in women or children, and sex trade shall be prohibited.

Article 38:

The State shall guarantee in a way that does not violate public order and morality:

A. Freedom of expression using all means.
B. Freedom of press, printing, advertisement, media and publication.
C. Freedom of assembly and peaceful demonstration, and this shall be regulated by law.

Article 39:

First: The freedom to form and join associations and political parties shall be guaranteed, and this shall be regulated by law.

CM: Redundant with associations/trade unions.

Second: It is not permissible to force any person to join any party, society, or political entity, or force him to continue his membership in it.

CM: Interesting reference to previous regime practice.

Article 40:

The freedom of communication and correspondence, postal, telegraphic, electronic, and telephonic, shall be guaranteed and may not be monitored, wiretapped, or disclosed except for legal and security necessity and by a judicial decision.

Article 41:

Iraqis are free in their commitment to their personal status according to their religions, sects, beliefs, or choices, and this shall be regulated by law.

CM: Again risk of watering down freedom of religion by subsequent law.

HAH: Later commentaries do not discuss why this is a matter of "rights." It isn't your individual "right" to pick your own family law, as it is to pick your own religion, at most there are three or four choices to select from. So while one commentator said the choice is not "unbounded," it's more than that, it's restricted. So why is this mention of personal status here? The reason is that the Shi'a wanted a mention in the Constitution reflecting their desire to return personal status to be controlled by religious authorities according to sect and there was ample opposition to their saying as much, from secular forces and the United States, and so this was added as a "right" rather than what it really is, a choice of law provision requiring statutory elaboration. This has been a continuing Shi'a effort since the era of the CPA, the Constitution just flags it here for future action.

Article 42:

Each individual shall have the freedom of thought, conscience, and belief.

Article 43:

First: The followers of all religions and sects are free in the:

A. Practice of religious rites, including the Husseini rituals.
B. Management of religious endowments (waqf), their affairs, and their religious institutions, and this shall be regulated by law.

Second: The State shall guarantee freedom of worship and the protection of places of worship.

Article 44:

First: Each Iraqi has freedom of movement, travel, and residence inside and outside Iraq.

Second: No Iraqi may be exiled, displaced, or deprived from returning to the homeland.

Second: No Iraqi may be exiled, displaced, or deprived from returning to the homeland.

Article 45:

First: The State shall seek to strengthen the role of civil society institutions, and to support, develop and preserve their independence in a way that is consistent with peaceful means to achieve their legitimate goals, and this shall be regulated by law.

> *CM:* Reference to "civil society" is novel in constitutions, despite the elastic and imprecise dimension of 'civil society' as a constitutional category.

Second: The State shall seek the advancement of the Iraqi clans and tribes, shall attend to their affairs in a manner that is consistent with religion and the law, and shall uphold their noble human values in a way that contributes to the development of society. The State shall prohibit the tribal traditions that are in contradiction with human rights.

> *CM:* Interesting reference to tribalism and human rights. But "human rights" as concept appears odd here, as it is not defined in the Constitution.

Article 46:

Restricting or limiting the practice of any of the rights or liberties stipulated in this Constitution is prohibited, except by a law or on the basis of a law, and insofar as that limitation or restriction does not violate the essence of the right or freedom.

> *CM:* This is an interesting attempt to entrench basic laws, but the pervasive reference to laws to be passed later is awkward and may defeat the intended purpose.

> *NB:* Chapter Two: Rights and Freedoms
>
> General Comments
>
> Rights and freedoms provisions have grown very extensive in modern constitutions, but many drafting efforts concentrate far more on naming freedoms rather than developing firm structural guarantees to protect them. This criticism can certainly be made of all Arab constitutions, including the current Iraqi draft. In one sense, this is a surprise, because the Iraqi process was dominated by those who felt themselves (with considerable justification) to have been victims of a regime that showed no respect for fundamental human rights. But many of the drafters also clearly anticipated that their political movements will form part of any majority coalition governing Iraq and

therefore left many of the details concerning defining and protecting rights to parliamentary legislation.

The section of the final draft has a friendlier title ("Rights and Free-doms") than intermediate drafts, which spoke of rights, freedoms, and duties. More specifically, there are several noteworthy features:

- Some critical basic freedoms are to be determined by law, a phrasing that many of Iraq's neighbors have turned into gaping loopholes. The same could happen in Iraq, although there are some limiting factors. First, the formula is not used for a portion of the freedoms, implying that they do not depend on implementing legislation. Second, the specific phrasing used to render freedoms dependent on legislation is sometimes a little less open than is the norm in the region—for instance, instead of saying that freedom to form political parties is "to be guaranteed by law," the constitution simply states that the free-dom is "guaranteed" and then adds that this will be "organized by law." Third, there are some structures that might be expected to defend rights, such as the Human Rights Commission and the Supreme Federal Court, although almost no details are given on how these structures will operate. Finally, Article 44 [46] expressly prohibits undermining the essence of a right in the guise of defining it, a formula sometimes adopted in other constitutions to help close the loophole of relying on legislation.

- Article 36 [38] provides surprisingly weak support for the very basic freedoms of expression, the press, public meetings, and peaceful dem-onstration insisting that these rights not be allowed to harm morals and the public order. Almost all restrictions placed by authoritarian govern-ments are justified precisely on such grounds.

- Christian and religious rights activists based in the United States pressed for phrasing religious freedoms in individual terms. In most Middle East-ern constitutions, religious freedom is guaranteed to communities—and indeed, most religious minorities have seemed primarily concerned with communal rights. Communal protections offer little to free-thinkers, atheists, and members of unrecognized groups. The Iraqi con-stitution phrases religious rights in communal rather than individual terms, although Article 40 explicitly places freedom of thought, con-science, and creed on an individual basis.

- The Iraqi constitution explicitly allows women to pass citizenship on to their children, a rare privilege in the region. Earlier drafts had also guaranteed the right of Iraqis who had been stripped of citizenship to reclaim it, while trying to prevent those Jews who fled after the creation of the state of Israel from taking advantage of that privilege. The fact that few Israelis of Iraqi origin are clamoring to return escaped the attention of constitution drafters. The final draft does preserve the general principle but leaves implementation to legislation.

- Strong language on positive economic and social rights in initial drafts was substantially scaled back in the final draft.

- A provision in the TAL protecting cooperation with international civil society organizations was not included in the draft permanent constitution.

- A somewhat sinister-sounding citizen obligation to maintain state secrets and national unity was dropped from the final draft.

Article 39 [41]: Personal Status Law

Middle Eastern states establish an area of law governing "personal status" — chiefly, marriage, divorce, and inheritance. Personal status law almost always is grounded in religion, although many states have attempted to codify and legislate a specific interpretation of religious teachings. In other states, it remains uncodified. In some states (such as Israel and Lebanon), separate personal status courts exist; in others (such as Egypt and Kuwait), personal status issues are adjudicated by a specialized branch of the regular court system.

As opposed to many constitutional controversies that are largely symbolic, the outcomes of debates over personal status are enormously important on a practical level. Iraqis will encounter the law when they are born, die, marry, or divorce.

In the draft constitution, personal status issues are addressed in the chapter on "rights and freedoms," a rather telling choice: For the Shiite religious parties that dominated the drafting process, the issue of personal status law is understood as one of religious freedom. Iraq's current law of personal status — dating back to 1959 — is based on Islamic law, but it is also legislated by the state, administered in the secular court system, and applies uniformly to all Iraqis with the exception of specified non-Muslim communities. In the process of legislating the uniform code of 1959, interpretations from the Islamic legal tradition most favorable to women were generally selected, sometimes quite eclectically. Although subsequent governments have tinkered with the 1959 law, most of its provisions remain intact. [*HAH*: More than tinkered at least in one case, as the original law required distribution of the estate upon death to children to be equal irrespective of sex. The 1963 Amendment returned to the traditional Islamic understanding.] Shiite religious parties objected that the 1959 law did not allow their own community to practice Shiite law; they also found the transfer of authority from religiously trained judges to secular judges tantamount to a state takeover of religious interpretation.

Article 39 [41] does not explicitly overturn the 1959 law, but it could very well require changing very significant parts of it by requiring that Iraqis be free in matters of personal status according to their "religions, sects, beliefs, or choices." At a minimum, this would seem to suggest that Iraqis who wished to be governed by sectarian law could insist that courts honor that choice. It is less clear what other choices might be presented. Freedom of choice over personal status law could not be boundless (in the sense of allowing each individual to write his or her own law); instead Article 39 [41] would seem to require a menu of choices. There is certainly no explicit requirement that a nonsectarian or civil option be offered or that the 1959 law be maintained for those who wish to use it. Neither would such options be barred should the legislature wish to offer them. Thus, the draft constitution would seem to allow (though not require) continuation of the 1959 uniform code of personal status for those who wish to use it.

Article 39 [41] explicitly requires implementing legislation, and writing that legislation will be a very complex task. Several questions must be addressed:

- Although it is clear that individuals must be offered the option of following sectarian law, it is not clear who has the authority to determine content of that law. Will there be an attempt to legislate separate Sunni and Shiite codes? Or will the law be uncodified, left for individual judges to decide on the basis of their training?

- The text refers to the law but says nothing about the courts that apply it. Will the existing court system be used, with judges expected to be ready and able to apply the appropriate law in accordance with the choice of the litigants? Or will separate sectarian courts be constructed? Both models have been used in the modern Arab world, but the trend in the twentieth century was toward unified courts even when there was variation in the law applied. Iraq took the step of unifying its court system in 1959. No Arab country has ever dismantled a unified system once it constructed one.

- If individuals may choose among different codes or laws, what will happen when litigants disagree over the law to be applied? Will "forum shopping" — in which, for instance, a Sunni temporarily becomes Shiite to escape alimony or allow his daughters to inherit a more generous share — be allowed?

It should be noted that it was precisely these sorts of problems that led many Arab states to adopt uniform codes and unified court systems for matters of personal status in the first place. From a religious standpoint, this was state encroachment on religious freedom, but from an official standpoint, a decentralized system seemed chaotic and confusing.

UN: Evaluation

We note that most of the rights and freedoms included in the international conventions are contained in this text. In consonance with analogous provisions in other modern Constitutions, this section also deals with aspects of recognition, protection and promotion of rights. As noted above, civil and political rights are treated extensively and include right to life security and liberty, equal opportunities, privacy, participation in public affairs for men and women, right to vote and be elected, guarantees for fair trial and the right of asylum. The positive obligation to ensure the enjoyment of the rights and liberties is also developed, in particular in the context of economic and social rights. We note that the text presents inconsistencies regarding the subject of rights (for instance, Articles 30/31 present three different subject formulations: "individual and family," "Iraqis" and "every citizen"). While the most used formulation is "all Iraqis," others — "person," "the individual," "every individual" — are also used. Consistency in the use of a single formulation would be recommended.

More specifically, the text leaves the following issues of contention:

Personal Status: The clause that has finally been included in the text prescribes that Iraqis are free in their commitment to their personal status in accordance with their religions, sects, beliefs, or choices. The clause provides that individuals are free to choose, and leaves the issue to further regulation by legislation. In principle, the clause sanctions freedom of choice, which can be positively contrasted to the more restrictive approach used in other Islamic Constitutions. We need to note, however, that this Article has been cited by women's groups as a source of concern, on the basis that the used formulation may be used to sanction the existence of religious courts, and that in reality women in rural areas will not be able to exercise this right.

Limitations Clause: This clause provides that any limitations to rights contained in the text can only be effected by, and cannot violate, the essence of the right or freedom to be limited. The inclusion of this clause needs to be welcomed, particularly as it was not present until the latest version of the draft. However, unlike in analogous provisions in modern Constitutions, the precise formulation used in the text does not contain a requirement of proportionality, nor safeguards against unnecessary and far-reaching limitations (limitations the scope of which go beyond their purpose). This could have also been contained in an additional require-ment that the restriction should only impair the exercise of the rights to the minimum extent.

Right to Freedom of Religion: The text provides for freedom of religious practice and belief. The right is in fact further extended through recogni-tion of freedom of thought and conscience. It needs to be noted, however, that the text does not go as far as to allow for conversion. The reason for this may be that the Koran in fact does not contemplate the right of con-version (apostasy) of a Muslim to other religions. The freedom of religion as recognized in this text thus stops short of allowing freedom of religious choice.

Equality and Women's Rights: The text bestows the right to equality and non-discrimination to Iraqi citizens only. Save for this restriction, the right is relatively of general comprehensive value (e.g. non-discrimination on the basis of sex, sect, religion etc). The formulation could still be improved. We consider that the scope of equality could be expanded to prohibit discrimination on the grounds of disability. We would also recommend that the list prescribing the basis for potential discrimination be left open, by adding a formulation such as "and other similar grounds." This would provide for constitutional protection of equality against all forms of dis-crimination. The additional general equality clause between men and women had been dropped on account of women's representations against a phrase requiring the State to assist in the reconciliation between women's role in the family and in society. An explicit supplementary provision on the equality between men and women can be found in regards to the right to participate in public affairs (i.e. right to vote and be elected).

Right to Asylum and Extradition: The language used in the provision on the right to asylum could be brought in line with international refugee law, particularly with regard to the definitions of asylum and refugee (the text only recognizes political refugees, while the concept of refugee under international law recognizes other categories), and to the "exclusion clause." On the latter, the list of acts which may give rise to exclusion is contained in the 1951 Geneva Convention and must be considered exhaustive (i.e. crime against peace, a war crime, or a crime against humanity, serious non-political crime outside the country of refuge prior to the admission to that country as a refugee). The language used with regard to terrorist crimes and on "damage on Iraq" is ambiguous and should be brought instead under the formulation of "serious non-political crime." As regards the prohibition on extradition of Iraqi citizens, we note that the Section uses ambiguous language by stating that no Iraqi can be surrendered to "foreign entities and authorities."

Freedom of Expression and Freedom of Assembly: The formulation of the Article does not make clear that freedom of expression and freedom of assembly are guaranteed. The text mandates the State to guarantee freedom of expression, freedom of the press and freedom of assembly "in a way that does not violate public order and morality." The text also indicates that "freedom of assembly and peaceful demonstration will be regulated by law." The text does not make it entirely clear whether the mandate for legislative regulation affects only freedom of assembly and demonstration (Article 38C), or whether it also covers freedom of expression and freedom of the press (38A and 38B, respectively).

On the basis of the wording, restrictions to the exercise of these rights could be simply made by law, on the basis of subjective interpretation of the concepts of public order and morality. It is our opinion that the clause contained in the Article should be reformulated to provide for the legal regulation of these rights separately from the guarantee of their protection. The drafting of Article 7 — on banning political parties that fall within certain categories — would be improved if appropriate protection for parties not falling within those categories was provided.

Right to information: We note that the right to access information — which was included in previous drafts — was removed from the final text. Justification was given on the basis that the right is covered by the right to freedom of communication. However, this is not the case. A specific reference to the right to information should therefore be included.

International Treaties on Human Rights ratified by Iraq: Section Two of the Constitution no longer provides that all individuals enjoy the rights contained in the international agreements that Iraq has ratified, provided they do not contradict with the principles of the Constitution. The clause was removed following discussion among the parties after 28th August. Reference to compliance with international treaties and to the role of international law as an interpretative mechanism would be advisable.

Minority issues: Provisions on minorities are dealt with in diverse parts of the Constitution, but need to be read in the light of the provisions included in this Section. Thus, Section One recognizes that Iraq is a country of "multiple nationalities, sects and religions," places the Constitution as the guarantee of the "religious rights of all individuals in the freedom of belief," and commits the State to guaranteeing free religious practice. Unlike in a previous draft of the text, there is no list of explicit groups or communities, and there is no mention of Kurds and Arabs/ Shias/Sunnis as major demographic groups of the country. Regarding component elements of the Iraqi nation, the drafters have opted for an even and neutral formulation relating to a plurality of communities, whilst giving emphasis to the affiliation with the Islamic world and — for the Arab part of the Iraqi population — the Arab nation. [*HAH*: This has always been controversial. Is Iraq "part of the Arab nation," as the Arabs wanted it phrased, or is it just "the Arabs of Iraq," as the Kurds eventually got.]

Protection of minorities' identity is guaranteed through the general provision of freedom of religious practices and freedom of belief (see above), and right of education in the mother tongue within public and private educational institutions. Turkmen and Syriac languages have special status as official languages in the areas in which they are spoken. Additionally, the Constitution contemplates the possibility to make official any other language in the governorates and regions if the population so decides in a general referendum. While possibly generating problems of application in practice, provisions regarding official languages are generally in line with international best practice.

In Section Five, the Constitution sets out the basic principle of local administration, and guarantees the political, administrative and education rights of the different nationalities. However, it does not explicitly mention the modalities of representation of demographic, ethnic and religious composition of the population. Turkmen and Syriac communities are the only ones here specifically indicated.

State of Emergency: The Constitution makes vague reference to the legal framework related to states of emergency. More clarity is essential because the State is entitled to legally restrict the enjoyment of fundamental rights, whether the emergency was caused by human conflict or a natural disaster. International standards set the criteria and requirements for the implementation of exceptional measures by the State when a state of emergency is declared.

The state of emergency can be declared when there is an actual and imminent threat to the life of the nation and the ordinary law of the land is not adequate to deal with the situation. International norms suggest that the measures adopted in this context must be judicially reviewable and be subject to legislative oversight. Finally, the measures must be rationally linked to the objective they seek to achieve and be no more than required to deal with the emergency. Some rights cannot be derogated from. In accordance with international human rights standards, non-derogable rights include the right to life, prohibition of torture and inhuman treatment, prohibition of slavery, the slave trade and servitude, imprisonment due not non-fulfillment of contractual obligations, non-discrimination, recognition of personality before the law, freedom of thought, and the fundamental requirements of due process and fair trial. The state of emergency cannot be invoked to justify violation of international humanitarian law.

The Constitution does not contain a list of non-derogable rights, and fails to indicate with precision when it is that the ratification of the state of emergency at the Council of Representatives needs to take place. Also, constitutions generally provide for parliament to ratify a state of emergency—which has come into effect by declaration of the Executive—after a limited number of days. This reference is absent in the text. What the Constitution does is limit the period of emergency to thirty days, and to provide for the approval of extension by the legislature every time this period is completed. We particularly value the guarantee provided by this legislative oversight, but note that the overall regulation of the state of emergency is problematic.

Section Three: Federal Powers[4]

Article 47:

The federal powers shall consist of the legislative, executive, and judicial powers, and they shall exercise their competencies and tasks on the basis of the principle of separation of powers.

Chapter One: The Legislative Power

Article 48:

The federal legislative power shall consist of the Council of Representatives and the Federation Council.

First: The Council of Representatives

Article 49:

First: The Council of Representatives shall consist of a number of members, at a ratio of one seat per 100,000 Iraqi persons representing the entire Iraqi people. They shall be elected through a direct secret general ballot. The representation of all components of the people shall be upheld in it.

Second: A candidate to the Council of Representatives must be a fully qualified Iraqi.

Third: A law shall regulate the requirements for the candidate, the voter, and all that is related to the elections.

Fourth: The elections law shall aim to achieve a percentage of representation for women of not less than one-quarter of the members of the Council of Representatives.

CM: Women's quota is a remarkable sign of maturity.

HAH: It should be noted that this provision got watered down by the first electoral law, which runs by national list rather than by region. It means there is no real independence or stature for the list members, each either follows the party line or is removed from the list at the next election. Still, the willingness, even of Islamic parties, to have women actively involved is notable.

Fifth: The Council of Representatives shall promulgate a law dealing with the replacement of its members on resignation, dismissal, or death.

Sixth: It is not permissible to combine membership in the Council of Representatives with any work or other official position.

CM: Including sitting as minister!

Article 50:

Each member of the Council of Representatives shall take the following constitutional oath before the Council prior to assuming his duties:

"I swear by God Almighty to carry out my legal duties and responsibilities with devotion and integrity and preserve the independence and sovereignty of Iraq, and safeguard the interests of its people, and ensure the safety of its land, sky, water, wealth, and federal democratic system, and I shall endeavor to protect public and private liberties, the independence of the judiciary, and pledge to implement legislation faithfully and neutrally. God is my witness."

> *CM:* This oath summarizes basic rights better than many articles in the constitution.

Article 51:

The Council of Representatives shall establish its bylaws to regulate its work.

Article 52:

First: The Council of Representatives shall decide, by a two-thirds majority, the authenticity of membership of its member within thirty days from the date of filing an objection.

> *CM:* Courts should preferably determine challenges to electoral proceedings, as in the next paragraph.

Second: The decision of the Council of Representatives may be appealed before the Federal Supreme Court within thirty days from the date of its issuance.

Article 53:

First: Sessions of the Council of Representatives shall be public unless, for reasons of necessity, the Council decides otherwise.

> *CM:* And televised?

Second: Minutes of the sessions shall be published by means considered appropriate by the Council.

> *CM:* Verbatim recording may be preferable.

Article 54:

The President of the Republic shall call upon the Council of Representatives to convene by a presidential decree within fifteen days from the date of the ratification of the general election results. Its eldest member shall chair the first session to elect the speaker of the Council and his two deputies. This period may not be extended by more than the aforementioned period.

> *CM:* Lebanese and other Arab misuses of presidential power offer unfortunate precedents that explain express bars on extended periods, but such precision should be redundant for a normal democracy.

Article 55:

The Council of Representatives shall elect in its first session its speaker, then his first deputy and second deputy, by an absolute majority of the total number of the Council members by direct secret ballot.

> *CM:* Is absolute majority for election of speaker the simple majority of members present *after* quorum or an absolute one, i.e., majority plus one? Clarification of majorities and quorum would be helpful throughout the Constitution.

Article 56:

First: The electoral term of the Council of Representatives shall be four calendar years, starting with its first session and ending with the conclusion of the fourth year.

Second: The new Council of Representatives shall be elected forty-five days before the conclusion of the preceding electoral term.

> *CM:* Date fixed exactly at 45 days? This is arguably better than a minimal and maximal period, but "calendar" may prove controversial.

Article 57:

The Council of Representatives shall have one annual term, with two legislative sessions, lasting eight months. The bylaws shall define the method to convene the sessions. The session in which the general budget is being presented shall not end until approval of the budget.

> *CM:* Better define budgetary session and possible priority over other legislative bills? What does *not end* mean?

Article 58:

First: The President of the Republic, the Prime Minister, the Speaker of the Council of Representatives, or fifty members of the Council of Representatives may call the Council to an extraordinary session. The session shall be restricted to the topics that necessitated the call for the session.

Second: The legislative session of the Council of Representatives may be extended for no more than 30 days to complete the tasks that require the extension, based on a request from the President of the Republic, the Prime Minister, the Speaker of the Council, or fifty members of the Council of Representatives.

Article 59:

First: The Council of Representatives quorum shall be achieved by an absolute majority of its members.

Second: Decisions in the sessions of the Council of Representatives shall be made by a simple majority after quorum is achieved, unless otherwise stipulated.

> *CM:* Is this also the case with majority in Art. 55 for the election of the Speaker?

Article 60:

First: Draft laws shall be presented by the President of the Republic and the Council of Ministers.

Second: Proposed laws shall be presented by ten members of the Council of Representatives or by one of its specialized committees.

Article 61:

The Council of Representatives shall be competent in the following:

First: Enacting federal laws.

Second: Monitoring the performance of the executive authority.

Third: Electing the President of the Republic.

Fourth: Regulating the ratification process of international treaties and agreements by a law, to be enacted by a two-thirds majority of the members of the Council of Representatives.

> *CM:* Two-thirds too high.

Fifth: Approving the appointment of the following:

A. The President and members of the Federal Court of Cassation, the Chief Public Prosecutor, and the President of Judicial Oversight Commission by an absolute majority, based on a proposal from the Higher Juridical Council.

> *CM:* Heavy machinery.

B. Ambassadors and those with special grades, based on a proposal from the Council of Ministers.

> *CM:* Idem.

C. The Iraqi Army Chief of Staff, his assistants, those of the rank of division commander and above, and the director of the intelligence service, based on a proposal from the Council of Ministers.

> *CM:* Head of army and of intelligence oversight is sufficient.

Sixth:

A. Questioning the President of the Republic, based on a petition with cause, by an absolute majority of the members of the Council of Representatives.

CM: "Questioning"?

B. Relieving the President of the Republic by an absolute majority of the Council of Representatives after being convicted by the Federal Supreme Court in one of the following cases:
   1. Perjury of the constitutional oath.
   2. Violating the Constitution.
   3. High treason.

Seventh:

A. A member of the Council of Representatives may direct questions to the Prime Minister and the Ministers on any subject within their specialty and each of them shall answer the members' questions. Only the member who has asked the question shall have the right to comment on the answer.
B. At least twenty-five members of the Council of Representatives may raise a general issue for discussion in order to inquire about a policy and the performance of the Council of Ministers or one of the Ministries and it shall be submitted to the Speaker of the Council of Representatives, and the Prime Minister or the Ministers shall specify a date to come before the Council of Representatives to discuss it.

CM: Should there be limitations on the time frame? E.g., a week after presentation of issue to the Speaker?

C. A member of the Council of Representatives, with the agreement of twenty-five members, may direct an inquiry to the Prime Minister or the Ministers to call them to account on the issues within their authority. The debate shall not be held on the inquiry except after at least seven days from the date of submission of the inquiry.

Eighth:

A. The Council of Representatives may withdraw confidence from one of the Ministers by an absolute majority and he shall be considered resigned from the date of the decision of withdrawal of confidence. A vote of no confidence in a Minister may not be held except upon his request or on the basis of a request signed by fifty members after the Minister has appeared for questioning before the Council. The Council shall not issue its decision regarding the request except after at least seven days from the date of its submission.

B.

1. The President of the Republic may submit a request to the Council of Representatives to withdraw confidence from the Prime Minister.
2. The Council of Representatives may withdraw confidence from the Prime Minister based on the request of one-fifth of its members. This request shall not be submitted except after an inquiry directed at the Prime Minister and after at least seven days from the date of submitting the request.
3. The Council of Representatives may decide to withdraw confidence from the Prime Minister by an absolute majority of the number of its members.

C. The Government is deemed resigned in case of withdrawal of confidence from the Prime Minister.
D. In case of a vote of withdrawal of confidence in the Council of Ministers as a whole, the Prime Minister and the Ministers continue in their positions to run everyday business for a period not to exceed thirty days until a new Council of Ministers is formed in accordance with the provisions of Article 76 of this Constitution.
E. The Council of Representatives may question independent commission heads in accordance with the same procedures related to the Ministers. The Council shall have the right to relieve them by absolute majority.

Ninth:

A. To consent to the declaration of war and the state of emergency by a two-thirds majority based on a joint request from the President of the Republic and the Prime Minister.
B. The state of emergency shall be declared for a period of thirty days, which can be extended after approval each time.
C. The Prime Minister shall be delegated the necessary powers which enable him to manage the affairs of the country during the period of the declaration of war and the state of emergency. These powers shall be regulated by a law in a way that does not contradict the Constitution.
D. The Prime Minister shall present to the Council of Representatives the measures taken and the results during the period of the declaration of war and the state of emergency within 15 days from the date of its end.

CM: What a long article!

Article 62:

First: The Council of Ministers shall submit the draft general budget bill and the closing account to the Council of Representatives for approval.

Second: The Council of Representatives may conduct transfers between the sections and chapters of the general budget and reduce the total of its sums, and it may suggest to the Council of Ministers that they increase the total expenses, when necessary.

Article 63:

First: A law shall regulate the rights and privileges of the speaker of the Council of Representatives, his two deputies, and the members of the Council of Representatives.

CM: Should the Speaker be treated differently from a normal parliamentarian?

Second:

A. A member of the Council of Representatives shall enjoy immunity for statements made while the Council is in session, and the member may not be prosecuted before the courts for such.
B. A Council of Representatives member may not be placed under arrest during the legislative term of the Council of Representatives, unless the member is accused of a felony and the Council of Representatives members consent by an absolute majority to lift his immunity or if he is caught *in flagrante delicto* in the commission of a felony.
C. A Council of Representatives member may not be arrested after the legislative term of the Council of Representatives, unless the member is accused of a felony and with the consent of the speaker of the Council of Representatives to lift his immunity or if he is caught *in flagrante delicto* in the commission of a felony.

Article 64:

First: The Council of Representatives may be dissolved by an absolute majority of the number of its members, or upon the request of one-third of its members by the Prime Minister with the consent of the President of the Republic. The Council shall not be dissolved during the period in which the Prime Minister is being questioned.

Second: Upon the dissolution of the Council of Representatives, the President of the Republic shall call for general elections in the country within a period not to exceed sixty days from the date of its dissolution. The Council of Ministers in this case is deemed resigned and continues to run everyday business.

Second: The Federation Council

Article 65:

A legislative council shall be established named the "Federation Council," to include representatives from the regions and the governorates that are not organized in a region.

A law, enacted by a two-thirds majority of the members of the Council of Representatives, shall regulate the formation of the Federation Council, its membership conditions, its competencies, and all that is connected with it.

CM: This must be regulated by the Constitution, not by an ordinary law. The Constitution should also specify the Federation Council powers and competence. The mode of election of Federation Council members is crucial, and numbers are key. This also requires defining regional and federal problems (See, infra, how do territorial units for the Federation Council and Regions interact? And Baghdad?) It may be necessary to specify in the Constitution that the Federation Council is established to strengthen the voice of the regions and provinces in the center.

Chapter Two: The Executive Power

Article 66:

The federal executive power shall consist of the President of the Republic and the Council of Ministers and shall exercise its powers in accordance with the Constitution and the law.

First: The President of the Republic

Article 67:

The President of the Republic is the Head of the State and a symbol of the unity of the country and represents the sovereignty of the country. He shall guarantee the commitment to the Constitution and the preservation of Iraq's independence, sovereignty, unity, and the safety of its territories, in accordance with the provisions of the Constitution.

Article 68: A nominee to the Presidency of the Republic must be:

First: An Iraqi by birth, born to Iraqi parents.
Second: Fully qualified and must be over forty years of age.
Third: Of good reputation and political experience, known for his integrity, uprightness, fairness, and loyalty to the homeland.
Fourth: Free of any conviction of a crime involving moral turpitude.

CM: Art. 68.1 is bizarre. If one parent is not Iraqi, is a candidate barred from running for the presidency? 68.3 and 68.4 are redundant in a Constitution.

Article 69:

First: The provisions for nomination to the office of the President of the Republic shall be regulated by law.
Second: The provisions for nomination to the office of one or more Vice Presidents of the Republic shall be regulated by law.

Article 70:

First: The Council of Representatives shall elect a President of the Republic from among the candidates by a two-thirds majority of the number of its members.

Second: If none of the candidates receive the required majority vote then the two candidates who received the highest number of votes shall compete and the one who receives the majority of votes in the second election shall be declared President.

CM: Should the president be elected by parliament ? How about direct elections by the people?

Article 71:

The President shall take the constitutional oath before the Council of Representatives according to the language stipulated in Article 50 of the Constitution.

Article 72:

First: The President of the Republic's term in office shall be limited to four years. He may be re-elected for a second time only.
Second:

A. The President of the Republic's term in office shall end with the end of the term of the Council of Representatives.
B. The President of the Republic shall continue to exercise his duties until after the end of the election and the meeting of the new Council of Representatives, provided that a new President of the Republic is elected within thirty days from the date of its first convening.
C. In case the position of the President of the Republic becomes vacant for any reason, a new President shall be elected to complete the remaining period of the President's term.

CM: Term limit on presidency is excellent. It may also be useful for prime minister, MPs and other high elected officials.

Article 73:

The President of the Republic shall assume the following powers:

A. To issue a special pardon on the recommendation of the Prime Minister, except for anything concerning a private claim and for those who have been convicted of committing international crimes, terrorism, or financial and administrative corruption.

CM: Why specify crimes?

B. To ratify international treaties and agreements after the approval by the Council of Representatives. Such international treaties and agreements are considered ratified after fifteen days from the date of receipt by the President.

CM: Can he veto?

HAH: This issue is very much part of the review process. The Sunnis want stronger presidential authority, right now the president seems fairly ceremonial, which is how the Shi'a prefer it.

C. To ratify and issue the laws enacted by the Council of Representatives. Such laws are considered ratified after fifteen days from the date of receipt by the President.

CM: Veto?

D. To call the elected Council of Representatives to convene during a period not to exceed fifteen days from the date of approval of the election results and in the other cases stipulated in the Constitution.
E. To award medals and decorations on the recommendation of the Prime Minister in accordance with the law.
F. To accredit ambassadors.
G. To issue Presidential decrees.
H. To ratify death sentences issued by the competent courts.
I. To perform the duty of the High Command of the armed forces for ceremonial and honorary purposes.
J. To exercise any other presidential powers stipulated in this Constitution.

Article 74:

A law shall fix the salary and the allowances of the President of the Republic.

Article 75:

First: The President of the Republic shall have the right to submit his resignation in writing to the Speaker of the Council of Representatives, and it shall be considered effective after seven days from the date of its submission to the Council of Representatives.

Second: The Vice President shall replace the President in case of his absence.

Third: The Vice President shall replace the President of the Republic in the event that the post of the President becomes vacant for any reason whatsoever. The Council of Representatives must elect a new President within a period not to exceed thirty days from the date of the vacancy.

Fourth: In case the post of the President of the Republic becomes vacant, the Speaker of the Council of Representatives shall replace the President of the Republic in case he does not have a Vice President, on the condition that a new

President is elected during a period not to exceed thirty days from the date of the vacancy and in accordance with the provisions of this Constitution.

Second: Council of Ministers

Article 76:

First: The President of the Republic shall charge the nominee of the largest Council of Representatives bloc with the formation of the Council of Ministers within fifteen days from the date of the election of the President of the Republic.

CM: Definition of parliamentary majority? This is too general and might give excessive margin of manipulation to the president. What if largest bloc not part of the overall majority in parliament?

Second: The Prime Minister-designate shall undertake the naming of the members of his Council of Ministers within a period not to exceed thirty days from the date of his designation.

Third: If the Prime Minister-designate fails to form the Council of Ministers during the period specified in clause "Second," the President of the Republic shall charge a new nominee for the post of Prime Minister within fifteen days.

Fourth: The Prime Minister-designate shall present the names of his members of the Council of Ministers and the ministerial program to the Council of Representatives. He is deemed to have gained its confidence upon the approval, by an absolute majority of the Council of Representatives, of the individual Ministers and the ministerial program.

Fifth: The President of the Republic shall charge another nominee to form the Council of Ministers within fifteen days in case the Council of Ministers did not win the vote of confidence.

Article 77:

First: The conditions for assuming the post of the Prime Minister shall be the same as those for the President of the Republic, provided that he has a college degree or its equivalent and is over thirty-five years of age.

Second: The conditions for assuming the post of Minister shall be the same as those for members of the Council of Representatives, provided that he holds a college degree or its equivalent.

Article 78:

The Prime Minister is the direct executive authority responsible for the general policy of the State and the commander-in-chief of the armed forces. He directs the Council of Ministers, presides over its meetings, and has the right to dismiss the Ministers, with the consent of the Council of Representatives.

CM: "Consent" of CoR?

Article 79:

The Prime Minister and members of the Council of Ministers shall take the constitutional oath before the Council of Representatives according to the language stipulated in Article 50 of the Constitution.

Article 80:

The Council of Ministers shall exercise the following powers:

First: To plan and execute the general policy and general plans of the State and oversee the work of the ministries and departments not associated with a ministry.

Second: To propose bills.

Third: To issue rules, instructions and decisions for the purpose of implementing the law.

Fourth: To prepare the draft of the general budget, the closing account, and the development plans.

Fifth: To recommend to the Council of Representatives that it approve the appointment of undersecretaries, ambassadors, state senior officials, the Chief of Staff of the Armed Forces and his deputies, division commanders or higher, the Director of the National Intelligence Service, and heads of security institutions.

Sixth: To negotiate and sign international agreements and treaties, or designate any person to do so.

Article 81:

First: The President of the Republic shall take up the office of the Prime Minister in the event the post becomes vacant for any reason whatsoever.

Second: If the event mentioned in "First" of this Article occurs, the President shall charge another nominee to form the Council of Ministers within a period not to exceed fifteen days in accordance with the provisions of Article 76 of this Constitution.

Article 82:

A law shall regulate the salaries and allowances of the Prime Minister and Ministers, and anyone of their grade.

Article 83:

The responsibility of the Prime Minister and the Ministers before the Council of Representatives is of a joint and personal nature.

Article 84:

First: A law shall regulate the work and define the duties and authorities of the security institutions and the National Intelligence Service, which shall operate in accordance with the principles of human rights and shall be subject to the oversight of the Council of Representatives.

Second: The National Intelligence Service shall be attached to the Council of Ministers.

> *CM:* See supra Art. 9 on subordination of agencies and military (coercive force) to judiciary and to executive power—details provided here may be unnecessary.

Article 85:

The Council of Ministers shall establish internal bylaws to organize the work therein.

Article 86:

A law shall regulate the formation of ministries, their functions, and their specializations, and the authorities of the minister.

Chapter Three: The Judicial Authority[5]

> *CM:* Generally in this chapter, it would be useful to clarify the structure and hierarchy of courts so as to prevent competition and conflict between them. Also the recourse of the citizen to judicial protection for his and her basic rights must be ensured and made paramount over the recourse to the judiciary of any other institution.

Article 87:

The judicial power is independent. The courts, in their various types and levels, shall assume this power and issue decisions in accordance with the law.

Article 88:

Judges are independent, and there is no authority over them except that of the law. No power shall have the right to interfere in the judiciary and the affairs of justice.

Article 89:

The federal judicial power is comprised of the Higher Juridical Council, the Federal Supreme Court, the Federal Court of Cassation, the Public Prosecution Department, the Judiciary Oversight Commission, and other federal courts that are regulated in accordance with the law.

First: Higher Juridical [Judicial] Council

Article 90:

The Higher Juridical Council shall oversee the affairs of the judicial committees. The law shall specify the method of its establishment, its authorities, and the rules of its operation.

Article 91:

The Higher Juridical Council shall exercise the following authorities:

First: To manage the affairs of the judiciary and supervise the federal judiciary.

Second: To nominate the Chief Justice and members of the Federal Court of Cassation, the Chief Public Prosecutor, and the Chief Justice of the Judiciary Oversight Commission, and to present those nominations to the Council of Representatives to approve their appointment.

CM: This is a powerful role. What about the Federal Supreme Court? Is it wise to have a body above it?

Third: To propose the draft of the annual budget of the federal judicial authority, and to present it to the Council of Representatives for approval.

Second: Federal Supreme Court

Article 92:

First: The Federal Supreme Court is an independent judicial body, financially and administratively.

Second: The Federal Supreme Court shall be made up of a number of judges, experts in Islamic jurisprudence, and legal scholars, whose number, the method of their selection, and the work of the Court shall be determined by a law enacted by a two-thirds majority of the members of the Council of Representatives.

Article 93:

The Federal Supreme Court shall have jurisdiction over the following:

First: Overseeing the constitutionality of laws and regulations in effect.

Second: Interpreting the provisions of the Constitution.

Third: Settling matters that arise from the application of the federal laws, decisions, regulations, instructions, and procedures issued by the federal authority. The law shall guarantee the right of direct appeal to the Court to the Council of Ministers, those concerned individuals, and others.

Fourth: Settling disputes that arise between the federal government and the governments of the regions and governorates, municipalities, and local administrations.

Fifth: Settling disputes that arise between the governments of the regions and governments of the governorates.

Sixth: Settling accusations directed against the President, the Prime Minister and the Ministers, and this shall be regulated by law.

Seventh: Ratifying the final results of the general elections for membership in the Council of Representatives.

Eighth:

    A. Settling competency disputes between the federal judiciary and the judicial institutions of the regions and governorates that are not organized in a region.

    B. Settling competency disputes between judicial institutions of the regions or governorates that are not organized in a region.

Article 94:

Decisions of the Federal Supreme Court are final and binding for all authorities.

Third: General Provisions

Article 95:

The establishment of special or extraordinary courts is prohibited.

Article 96:

The law shall regulate the establishment of courts, their types, levels, and jurisdiction, and the method of appointing and the terms of service of judges and public prosecutors, their discipline, and their retirement.

Article 97:

Judges may not be removed except in cases specified by law. Such law will determine the particular provisions related to them and shall regulate their disciplinary measures.

Article 98:

A judge or public prosecutor is prohibited from the following:

First: Combining a judicial position with legislative and executive positions and any other employment.

Second: Joining any party or political organization or performing any political activity.

Article 99:

A law shall regulate the military judiciary and shall specify the jurisdiction of military courts, which are limited to crimes of a military nature committed by members of the armed forces and security forces, and within the limits established by law.

CM: Military courts may contradict the no special courts disposition of Art. 95.

Article 100:

It is prohibited to stipulate in the law the immunity from appeal for any administrative action or decision.

Article 101:

A State Council may be established, specialized in functions of the administrative judiciary, issuing opinions, drafting, and representing the State and various public commissions before the courts except those exempted by law.

Chapter Four: Independent Commissions

Article 102:

The High Commission for Human Rights, the Independent Electoral Commission, and the Commission on Public Integrity are considered independent commissions subject to monitoring by the Council of Representatives, and their functions shall be regulated by law.

> *CM:* More is needed on the common, basic organization and functions of these bodies. See also comment under Art. 108.

Article 103:

First: The Central Bank of Iraq, the Board of Supreme Audit, the Communication and Media Commission, and the Endowment Commissions are financially and administratively independent institutions and the work of each of these institutions shall be regulated by law.

Second: The Central Bank of Iraq is responsible before the Council of Representatives. The Board of Supreme Audit and the Communication and Media Commission shall be attached to the Council of Representatives.

Third: The Endowment Commissions shall be attached to the Council of Ministers.

Article 104:

A commission named The Martyrs' Foundation shall be established and attached to the Council of Ministers, and its functions and competencies shall be regulated by law.

Article 105:

A public commission shall be established to guarantee the rights of the regions and governorates that are not organized in a region to ensure their fair participation in managing the various state federal institutions, missions, fellowships, delegations, and regional and international conferences. The commission shall be comprised of representatives of the federal government and representatives of the regions and governorates that are not organized in a region, and shall be regulated by a law.

Article 106:

A public commission shall be established by a law to audit and appropriate federal revenues. The commission shall be comprised of experts from the federal government, the regions, the governorates, and its representatives, and shall assume the following responsibilities:

First: To verify the fair distribution of grants, aid, and international loans pursuant to the entitlement of the regions and governorates that are not organized in a region.

Second: To verify the ideal use and division of the federal financial resources.

Third: To guarantee transparency and justice in appropriating funds to the governments of the regions and governorates that are not organized in a region in accordance with the established percentages.

Article 107:

A council named the Federal Public Service Council shall be established and shall regulate the affairs of the federal public service, including appointments and promotions, and its formation and competencies shall be regulated by law.

Article 108:

Other independent commissions may be established by law, according to need and necessity.

CM: All these bodies are interesting and novel in Iraq. But do they have a place in the Constitution? The text provides a mixture of substance and institutions, with substantive powers not clearly allocated in a separation of powers scheme. The risk is to diminish the democratic legitimacy of these commissions and put them in conflict with judicial decisions.

Section Four: Powers of the Federal Government

Article 109:

The federal authorities shall preserve the unity, integrity, independence, and sovereignty of Iraq and its federal democratic system.

CM: Who exactly are the federal authorities?

Article 110:

The federal government shall have exclusive authorities in the following matters:

First: Formulating foreign policy and diplomatic representation; negotiating, signing, and ratifying international treaties and agreements; negotiating, signing, and ratifying debt policies and formulating foreign sovereign economic and trade policy.

Second: Formulating and executing national security policy, including establishing and managing armed forces to secure the protection and guarantee the security of Iraq's borders and to defend Iraq.

Third: Formulating fiscal and customs policy; issuing currency; regulating commercial policy across regional and governorate boundaries in Iraq; drawing up the national budget of the State; formulating monetary policy; and establishing and administering a central bank.

Fourth: Regulating standards, weights, and measures.

Fifth: Regulating issues of citizenship, naturalization, residency, and the right to apply for political asylum.

Sixth: Regulating the policies of broadcast frequencies and mail.

Seventh: Drawing up the general and investment budget bill.

Eighth: Planning policies relating to water sources from outside Iraq and guaranteeing the rate of water flow to Iraq and its just distribution inside Iraq in accordance with international laws and conventions.

Ninth: General population statistics and census.

CM: Good. Oil should be added here, and not as separate item, for it is no less important than water in Iraq.

Article 111:

Oil and gas are owned by all the people of Iraq in all the regions and governorates.

Article 112:

First: The federal government, with the producing governorates and regional governments, shall undertake the management of oil and gas extracted from present fields, provided that it distributes its revenues in a fair manner in proportion to the population distribution in all parts of the country, specifying an allotment for a specified period for the damaged regions which were unjustly deprived of them by the former regime, and the regions that were damaged afterwards in a way that ensures balanced development in different areas of the country, and this shall be regulated by a law.

Second: The federal government, with the producing regional and governorate governments, shall together formulate the necessary strategic policies to develop the oil and gas wealth in a way that achieves the highest benefit to the Iraqi people using the most advanced techniques of the market principles and encouraging investment.

CM: Subsidiarity may be a better principle to enshrine than this belabored text. The subsidiarity principle, which was developed in European Union constitutionalism, means that a "higher" institution (here the federal government) should withhold taking a decision in a matter which is more efficiently addressed by a "lower" one (the regions, the governorates, and so on.)

Article 113:

Antiquities, archeological sites, cultural buildings, manuscripts, and coins shall be considered national treasures under the jurisdiction of the federal authorities, and shall be managed in cooperation with the regions and governorates, and this shall be regulated by law.

Article 114:

The following competencies shall be shared between the federal authorities and regional authorities:

First: To manage customs, in coordination with the governments of the regions and governorates that are not organized in a region, and this shall be regulated by a law.

Second: To regulate the main sources of electric energy and its distribution.

Third: To formulate environmental policy to ensure the protection of the environment from pollution and to preserve its cleanliness, in cooperation with the regions and governorates that are not organized in a region.

Fourth: To formulate development and general planning policies.
Fifth: To formulate public health policy, in cooperation with the regions and governorates that are not organized in a region.

Sixth: To formulate the public educational and instructional policy, in consultation with the regions and governorates that are not organized in a region.

Seventh: To formulate and regulate the internal water resources policy in a way that guarantees their just distribution, and this shall be regulated by a law.

Article 115:

All powers not stipulated in the exclusive powers of the federal government belong to the authorities of the regions and governorates that are not organized in a region. With regard to other powers shared between the federal government and the regional government, priority shall be given to the law of the regions and governorates not organized in a region in case of dispute.

NB: Chapter Three: The Federal Authorities
Part One: The Legislative Authority
Council of Representatives

Article 49 [47]: Elections

The article gives little guidance on how an election law should be written. The transitional parliament is currently working on a draft; the electoral system adopted could have a strong impact on the nature of the parliament elected. It is currently anticipated that the transitional parliament will design a system that departs from the one used for the elections of January 30, 2005 (in which the entire country formed a single electoral district and seats were allotted to each list in accordance with its share of the national vote). Instead, each province will be allocated seats in accordance with its population (although no accurate census figures exist), and proportional representation will be used within each province.

Article 52 [50]: Membership

The requirement that electoral disputes be resolved in 30 days may be a response to an Egyptian problem — in Egypt, complaints are investigated by the courts but referred to the parliament for final decision. The parliament has very often simply ignored a court finding. Assigning parliamentary decisions in election disputes to be appealed to the Federal Supreme Court would be considered a violation of separation of powers in many Arab states but is probably a healthy move.

Article 58 [55]: Sessions

The provisions for meetings of the Assembly seem unnecessarily detailed for a constitutional document, especially one that is relatively difficult to amend.

Article 61 [58]: Responsibilities

The article sets a high bar (two-thirds parliamentary majority) for a law governing the approval of treaties. This requirement will likely to give the opposition a voice in the matter (unless the governing coalition controls more than two-thirds of the parliament). This provision is likely to be tested almost immediately, since UN Security Council Resolution 1546 allows the presence of the multinational force only until the completion of the transition. In other words, unless other arrangements are made, the legal basis for the coalition forces will be removed the moment the first cabinet meets under the constitution (which is when the constitution comes into full effect and the transitional process is completed). Although some device might be found to extend the mandate of coalition forces for a short period, the permanent Iraqi government is likely to wish to negotiate an arrangement itself rather than rely on a Security Council resolution. Indeed, the United States will also likely wish to negotiate the status of its forces and bases. It should be noted that the September 13 draft differs slightly from the August 28 draft in this respect. The September 13 draft makes clear that the two-thirds majority is required for approval of the law that specifies the procedure for ratifying treaties. It lays down no other conditions for approval of treaties (though Article 70 requires parliamentary and presidential approval). The August 28 draft left some ambiguity on this score, leading some (including me) to conclude that the two-thirds requirement applied to the treaties themselves. This was apparently an erroneous reading, but it does seem unusual for a constitution to refer such a matter to legislation. If the attitude of the transitional parliament is a good indication, the parliament is likely to take its responsibility regarding treaties quite seriously: In May 2005, when the foreign minister in the transitional government reported to the Security Council that Iraq favored a continuation of the mandate of the multinational force, he was greeted with a storm of criticisms from some deputies who claimed that he had violated the TAL's provisions for a parliamentary role in approving international agreements. Allowing the parliament a role in senior appointments — especially in the military, judicial, diplomatic, and intelligence realms — is a marked departure from the norm in the Arab world.

Allowing the interpellation of the president is an odd innovation because the president is not politically responsible to the parliament once elected. He is only accountable to the parliament if he violates the constitution or his oath or commits treason. But the matter is not of tremendous importance, because the president is not likely to be a powerful figure.

Requiring an absolute majority rather than a simple majority to withdraw confidence from a minister is a high bar, although it should be noted that an absolute majority is also required to grant confidence to a minister under Article 76 [73].

The parliament can withdraw confidence from individual ministers, a step likely to wreak havoc on a coalition government.

What the AP translates as "independent associations" are really governmental bodies mentioned in Articles 102-108 [101-105]. Making their heads responsible to parliament will diminish their independence, although much about these bodies is simply unspecified.

Article 62 [59]: Budget

This article seems to give the parliament great authority over the budget, especially when combined with Article 28, which requires that taxes be imposed by law. But it may be difficult for the parliament to make much use of its authority, because there is no requirement that the budget be presented in sufficient time to review it. This might be corrected by legislation. But there is also no provision forcing the cabinet to resign if it fails to submit (or obtain approval) of a budget. And because any cabinet will have the support of a majority of the parliament, a full confrontation between the two is unlikely.

Article 64 [61]: Dissolution and New Elections

The parliament may dissolve itself, but there is no provision forcing the dissolution of parliament if it fails to approve a cabinet.

Council of the Union

Article 65 [62]: Formation and Duties of the Council

A second parliamentary chamber was originally proposed to allow some representation for the subnational units of the Iraqi state (the regions and provinces). In the end, however, the purpose, prerogatives, duties, procedures, and selection of the Council of the Union have simply been omitted, with the details to be filled in by legislative act of the Council of Representatives. It is absolutely extraordinary for the Council of the Union — an independent chamber of parliament — to be formed by a law written by the other house. In essence, this gives one chamber of parliament absolute authority over the other. This is presumably an effect of the hurried drafting process.

Another odd aspect of the Council of the Union is that Article 133 delays the effect of any provision for the Council of the Union until after the second round of parliamentary elections following promulgation of the constitution. This may be to encourage the parliament writing the legislation to take a longer-term (and not a jealous) view when designing the mechanisms for selecting the body as well as its authorities.

Part Two: The Executive Authority
The President

Article 69 [66]: Nomination and Deputies

It is also extraordinary to have all details concerning presidential deputies determined by law.

Article 72 [69]: Presidential Term

By having the president's term end with that of the parliament (or with the first meeting of the new parliament), the newly seated deputies will be forced to make election of a new president one of their very first agenda items — especially since the new president must charge the candidate chosen by the parliamentary majority with forming a cabinet. It is unclear why the drafters chose this arrangement. There is no need for the president's term to end with the parliament's if the office is ceremonial and not political.

Article 73 [70]: Authorities

Although the president must approve laws and treaties, this requirement seems to be designed to be a mere formality rather than a potential presidential veto. However, a very literal reading of the constitution might allow the president to block a law by refusing to sign it.

The Cabinet

Article 76 [73]: Formation of the Cabinet

The article here is written in an unnecessarily confusing way to cover cases in which the cabinet is formed after new elections as well as cases in which it is not. I think the Arabic here could be better translated as: "The president of the Republic charges the nominee of the largest parliamentary bloc with forming the Cabinet within fifteen days from the date of the first meeting of the Council of Representatives, except for the case stipulated in Article 69(2)(b) of this constitution in which case he shall charged within fifteen days from the date of the election of the President of the Republic."

Put more simply, the president has 15 days to name a candidate for prime minister. That candidate must be the nominee of the largest parliamentary bloc. (There is apparently no requirement that the prime minister — or any of the ministers — be a member of parliament.)

Should the first candidate fail, the president is free in his selection of a second choice. Ministers have to be approved individually, but if any one of them does obtain parliamentary approval, the cabinet as a whole is considered not to have the confidence of parliament. This provision, combined with the short deadline for obtaining a parliamentary vote of confidence, may make assembling a cabinet a rushed affair.

Especially because Iraqi cabinets are likely to be coalitions (either formally in the sense of multiparty governments or effectively in the sense that the only kind of electoral list likely to gain a majority of parliamentarians will itself be a coalition), forming a government will be difficult.

Article 81[78]: Succession

Having the president serve as prime minister on an acting basis is very unusual — generally a deputy prime minister would assume such duties. In a parliamentary system, in which the prime minister is responsible to the parliament, it seems odd to give the post even temporarily to a president who lies beyond parliamentary oversight.

Article 84 [81]: Security Services

Placing the security services under parliamentary oversight and having them operate in accordance with law are welcome innovations. However, a strict reading of Chapter Four — on the duties of the various levels of government — would leave little room for involvement of the central government in matters of internal security.

Part Three: The Judiciary

Articles 87 and 88 [90 and 91]: Supreme Judicial Council

Most advocates of judicial independence in the Arab world have focused their energies on creating autonomous judicial councils and giving them oversight over most judicial work (such as hiring, assignments, promotions, and budgets).

The constitution does little to create an autonomous judicial council; it merely defers to legislation on the matter. The current legislative basis for the judicial council — initiated under the U.S.-led Coalition Provisional Authority — does provide for considerable autonomy. The senior leadership of the Iraqi judiciary has emerged as an effective advocate for continued autonomy, although the constitution's silence on the issue might lead some judges to be nervous.

The constitution does little to protect the autonomy of the judicial council, but it does award it considerable jurisdiction in judicial affairs. The Iraqi judicial council will have wide authority by regional standards, although a few of its competencies are vaguely defined.

Articles 89 through 91 [92-94]: Supreme Federal Court

The Supreme Federal Court will be a potentially powerful structure, so it is surprising how many details concerning its composition, structure, and operation are deferred to legislation.

The TAL provided for a Supreme Federal Court to handle constitutional disputes as well as those arising between different levels of government. Earlier drafts of the permanent constitution separated these two functions. With an already existing court of cassation — the supreme court for most ordinary cases — Iraq was to have a wealth of high courts. In the final draft the constitutional jurisdiction of the Supreme Federal Court was restored. Many of the most sensitive issues involving federalism and the constitution could easily wind up in this court. It generally takes some time for such courts to establish themselves (with some exceptions), so any critical role may only develop over time.

But there are some remarkable features about this court. First, its composition is left to legislation by a supermajority — although this is not surprising given the potentially critical nature of the body. Second, experts in Islamic jurisprudence are eligible for seats the court. It seems unlikely that any senior Shiite clerics will want to serve, however; most would consider it beneath their dignity. But other clerics might serve. Because the legislation must pass by a two-thirds majority, it is unlikely that the structure will resemble the Iranian Council of Guardians. But some representation of religious figures on the court is quite possible. Finally, the court is assigned some ancillary responsibilities — such as certifying election results — that grant it a status of a symbol of sovereignty over the state.

One legal gap left by the constitution is the role of the current Supreme Federal Court, a body that was recently formed under the provisions of the TAL. Will that court continue operating until the new law is approved? Or will it expire with the TAL? Normally it might be expected that legal and judicial structures would continue until specifically replaced, but in this case, the Supreme Federal Court is given very significant responsibilities; it might not be seen as appropriate to assign them to a caretaker body.

And of course the current court would not have the legitimacy gained from being formed in accordance with a law passed by a two-thirds majority under the permanent constitution.

Articles 92 and 96 [95 and 99]: Exceptional and Military Courts

Barring exceptional courts and preventing trials of civilians in military courts are welcome steps given the common abuse of such mechanisms by authoritarian governments in the Middle East.

Article 100 [97]: Judicial Review of Administrative Acts

Political leaders in many different systems have tinkered with the jurisdiction of the courts to avoid losing control over certain kinds of cases. In the Arab world, some governments have tried to remove administrative actions from judicial oversight. This article is designed to prevent such a step.

Article 101 [98]: State Council

Iraq has an administrative court system; in civil law countries, such courts generally have jurisdiction over cases in which the state is a party. The constitution allows — but does not require — the establishment of a "council of state," which generally combines the administrative courts with advisory functions in legislative drafting. The system was designed first in France and has spread to some other countries; in the Arab world the influential Egyptian system constructed a council of state in 1946. The council of state has no obvious common law counterpart. It is generally regarded as a device for ensuring that official bodies operate within the law and that a court system has the ability to review and overturn administrative acts (rather than merely order compensation for injured parties).

Part Four: Independent Associations
General Comments

What are called "Independent Associations" in the AP translations are probably better termed "Independent Agencies" or "Autonomous Bodies."

They are very much official and governmental but are designed to operate independently of the three branches of government. It has become far more common to establish such bodies in constitutional terms in recent years to govern those areas in order to insulate them from political pressures. This makes moderate use of the device, extending them to three areas (human rights, elections, and integrity). These bodies will not be wholly new, but it is my impression that only the elections commission has played a significant role. Almost all the autonomy that these bodies will enjoy under the constitution must be established by statute.

The constitution also mentions some other independent bodies with a less significant potential for independence: the central bank, the financial oversight bureau, the media and communications organization, and the bureaus for religious endowments. These are again preexisting organizations. All but the last are to operate under the parliament. Religious endowments — which are administered by a ministry in most Arab states (including preinvasion Iraq) — are attached to the cabinet. There are now separate Sunni and Shiite bureaus, a division that was made in the early days of the CPA. That decision now seems enshrined by the constitution's use of the plural to refer to these bureaus. The current Iraqi cabinet has begun to treat the bureaus as subject to its direct jurisdiction already, most notably by dismissing the director of the Sunni bureau.

Finally, some new agencies are envisioned: for example, martyrs (presumably to assist families of victims of the various waves of violence that Iraqi society has suffered from), and the civil service (awkwardly if accurately translated by the AP as the "federal public service council." On federalism, the constitution actually establishes two separate bodies. One is to assist the subnational units (provinces and regions) in international representation; the other to "monitor and allocate" the revenues of the central government. Both bodies include representatives from the various levels of government and how they operate could determine whether the Iraqi political system tends more toward federalism or confederalism (a looser kind of association in which constituent parts retain considerably more autonomy and many attributes of sovereignty).

Chapter Four: Powers of the Federal Authorities
General Comments

By regional standards, the list of those areas that are exclusively the responsibility of the central government is remarkably short. In most Arab countries, the central government focuses much of its resources and attention on defense and foreign affairs, internal security, education, economic infrastructure, and health; it is also frequently concerned with supplies of basic commodities. In the draft constitution, only defense and foreign affairs are exclusively assigned to the central government. (And even the monopoly on foreign affairs is undermined by Article 102, discussed above, as well as by the very unusual sharing of responsibility for administering customs and the provisions of Article 117, in the following chapter, allowing for regional and provincial representation in Iraqi diplomatic missions). Education, infrastructure, and health are to be shared between the central government and the subnational units.

It is true that an ambitious central government would have some tools to expand its authority. First, some of the division of responsibilities explicitly requires implementing legislation; the rest implicitly require it. Second, it might be possible to use some of the general language (such as the authority to regulate trade between regions and provinces) very expansively. But Article 111 [115] allocates any unspecified authority to the regional and provincial governments and also adds that in all disputes priority should be given to regional law. And Article 117 [121] in the following chapter allows regional law to trump federal law in areas designated for joint responsibility. Such provisions may cause Iraq to lurch in a confederal direction, especially if the Federal Supreme Court emerges as a powerful body even mildly friendly to the regions. Constitutional provisions for oil resources are fraught with ambiguity and potential conflict. Article 108 [111], covering petroleum and gas, awards ownership to "all the people of Iraq" but then rushes to add "in each of the regions and provinces." It is unclear whether the latter phrase is intended to ensure that the benefits are distributed equally throughout the country or instead shared with the subnational units. Article 109 [112] does not clarify matters. It first distinguishes between existing oil fields and new ones. Although the central government must coordinate with subnational units for both new and old fields, only the benefits from older fields must be distributed nationally "on the basis of the population distribution in all areas of the country." The distribution of revenues from new fields is not specified, although there is a reference to "market principles" implying perhaps a degree of privatization.

Article 107 [110] allows the government the right to set fiscal policy. At least one enthusiast for Kurdish independence has argued that this implies no central government authority to levy taxes. I find that interpretation implausible in the extreme. In Article 107 [110] and elsewhere a taxation authority is implied. Indeed, the term used for "fiscal policy" (*siyasa maliyya*) would be taken to include taxation in any Arab country; it is, after all, the Ministry of Finance (*wizarat al-maliyya*) that oversees taxation in Arab states. [*HAH:* The commentators seem more exercised about taxation than the drafters. Nobody pays taxes in any of these oil economies, I don't think the government considers taxes as a significant source of revenue.]

As for oil, the text remains ambiguous, and this has resulted in an important controversy between the Kurds and the central government concerning Kurdish ability to sign exploration contracts in the Kurdish region. The issue of oil belonging to all and distributed among all Iraqis is, however, not controversial. All agree on that. See Chapter 6 [of the Constitution].

UN: Evaluation

We might assess this chapter in general as providing for a weak Prime Minister, a strong President, and insufficient detail on the interaction between the two:

Legislature

In spite of the general validity of the parliamentary model proposed by the Constitution, the text includes a number of provisions that are not consistent with international best practice. This is particularly significant as regards the constitutional articulate on the Upper House: the Federation Council. Specifically, it is unusual in comparative constitutionalism that its establishment and functions be defined by law. In its provisions on legislative powers, the Constitution should provide reference to a future role of the Federation Council, and to the fact that the provisions that will be regulated by law (powers of the Federation Council) should have the same status as constitutional provisions regulating functions of the Council of Representatives. This by itself generates legal problems.

The absence of further constitutional development results into the Federation Council finding itself precluded from having an effective legislative role, or any role whatsoever. It is important for the Constitution to specify outright what will be the function of the second chamber, specially its role in the legislative process. This should not be left to be determined by law.

It is legally problematic for one body given full legislative powers on the federal field, to give this constitutionally-mandated power to another body. We find it highly unlikely that the first chamber will be motivated to pass a law renouncing part of its powers to a second chamber.

Moreover, we note that the timeframe for enactment of that law is not clear. On the one hand, Article 65 provides for a law to regulate the Federation Council's formation, function and membership conditions. On the other, Article 136 indicates that application of the provisions of the articles related to the Federation Council shall be postponed until the Council of Representatives' second electoral term after the Constitution comes into force.

In general, then, a major point of the model of Upper House included in the initial working documents — regional representation — is reflected in the final text. The constitutional status of the chamber, however, has been diminished, which may result in the downgrading of an institution that could give coherence to the territorial structure of the system as a whole.

Interaction Legislature — Executive

We also find inconsistencies with international best practice as regards the institutional interaction between the executive and the legislative organs of government. We notice that only the Lower Chamber — and not both chambers, as in most federal systems — plays a role in the election of the President of the Republic. It also appears unusual to constitutionally require the nomination as Prime Minister of the nominee of the largest group represented in parliament. While in practice the nominee of the group with more representatives in parliament tends to be the strongest candidate, it is possible sometimes to have a minority government — a Prime Minister who only commands a minority group in parliament but who can form a government with programmatic support from other groups. To encompass this possibility, this section could refer to the requirement of holding the support of a majority of members.

The text, we note, does not allow the Prime Minister-designate to have a second attempt at forming a cabinet if a first proposal is not accepted by the Council of Representatives. [*HAH:* True, but this doesn't happen in practice. They secure the necessary permissions before the vote, and the whole thing is done by consensus among the major players. This would only be an issue if the major alliances started to fragment.] We consider that the text could soften this restriction by providing for more flexibility, for example, allowing the same Prime Minister-designate an extension of the time to form a cabinet. Such degree of flexibility is not unusual in comparative practice.

Also, procedures for withdrawal of confidence of members of the Executive are inconsistent with international best practice. The Constitution provides for the Council of Representatives to withdraw confidence from members of the Council of Ministers on an individual basis, which de facto eliminates the principle of collegiality of the Council and weakens the position of the Prime Minister vis-à-vis the legislature. The Prime Minister cannot dismiss members of the cabinet. This is a very unusual limitation, which weakens the office of the Prime Minister substantially.

We also note that the Prime Minister needs the support of the President of the Republic to propose the dissolution of the Council, and that the final decision is taken by the Council of Representatives itself, with no final word of the Executive on the issue. It is uncommon practice in parliamentary systems to subject the Prime Minister's right of initiative for dissolution of parliament to the consent of the Head of State, and to give parliament the initiative and/or final word on its own dissolution.

The President of the Republic is conferred the power to introduce legislative bills, as is the Prime Minister. However, the Constitution offers no indication of whether the President and Prime Minister can act independently in the exercise of this power. This could be assumed from Article 79 (which includes this power in the list of powers of the Council of Ministers — not the Prime Minister), but should be clarified (as the capacity of introducing bills is not included in the list of powers of the President). On the other hand, the text provides the President with decree-making powers, but does not offer further detail.

We note that the President's term is closely linked to that of the Council of Representatives, which contributes to making its role more political. This by itself need not be a negative feature, except for the fact that — combined with the institutional weakness of the Prime Minister — it may facilitate tensions between the two branches of the Executive.

The Constitution provides the Council of Representatives the capacity to hold secret sessions if so desires, with no particular reference to limitations in this practice, either in regards to quorum for putting the issue to vote or to a maximum time period for such session.

We also point out that, unlike in the provisions regulating the exercise of executive powers, the Constitution does not explicitly mandate legislative powers to be exercised "in accordance with the Constitution." Although such circumstance could be derived from the rest of the text, an explicit formulation would improve the coherence of the text.

We also note that the text specifies a ratio of representation of citizens at the Council of Representatives (one representative per 100,000 Iraqis), which by itself may be too directive. At the same time, the principle for elections enshrined in that Article, which refers to "direct" and "secret" elections, could be complemented with an explicit reference to universal and competitive elections. We particularly encouraged a direct injunction that the system yield an accurate proportional share of power in accordance with the vote.

The text includes no reference to voters' eligibility criteria. It does provide a specific requirement that no less than one quarter of the seats at the Council of Representatives shall be allocated to women. While not referring to any similar arrangement for the future Federation Council or any executive office, this provision needs to be valued as a positive development, especially because it is not subject to any time limitation (previous drafts had limited the validity of this arrangement to the first two parliamentary terms).

Independent Commissions

The text includes references to the civil service and establishes a Federal Public Service Council, aimed at regulating its affairs, in particular as regards appointment to the civil service. The text *however* makes no mention of the independence of the administration and the civil service, and there is no constitutional mandate for this body to preserve it. Unlike in the provision on composition of the armed forces, there is no reference in the text to representation of all groups of society in the civil service, as it is common in post-conflict Constitutions. It is also part of best practice to include reference to ethical standards applicable to the administration, and the establishment of a code of conduct for civil servants.

As indicated, the Constitution also establishes other independent commissions — including the electoral commission — but in most cases fails to define their mandate and leaves details to regulation by law. The Constitution prescribes that Heads of the independent commissions can be dismissed by absolute majority by the Council of Representatives. This prescription compromises the independence of these bodies in a substantial way. The Human Rights Commission is constitutionally subject to "monitoring" by the Council of Representatives. While an interpretation of this term based on the concept of reporting would not be problematic, other interpretations could also challenge the independence of the Commission.

Article 102(2) makes the Central Bank accountable to the Council of Representatives. In comparative constitutionalism, it is very unusual for a Central Bank to be accountable to parliament. Article 105 includes an Audit and Appropriations Commission, but it is not clear how this institution is related to the Board of Supreme Audit included in Article 102. The merging of audit and appropriations functions, on the other hand, appears as problematic.

In general, we believe that further constitutional protection of the independence of these commissions would have been advisable, together with a more precise definition of their mandate and composition. As structures for addressing needs that are very likely to arise in the future, the establishment of an Oil and Gas Commission and a Law Review Commission could have also been considered.

Judiciary

In regards to provisions on judicial authority, we find an absence of clear organization of the judicial system as a whole. There is a lack of articulation of the distinction between the federal legal structure and the regional legal structure, and reference to regional courts is extremely vague. The text provides courts the right to have secret proceedings, which is uncommon in modern constitutionalism.

Reference to independence of the judiciary is not found in the Chapter on the Judiciary, but in the Bill of Rights (a relocation of Article 19 is advised). Article 96 provides that judges may not be removed "except in cases specified by law." This threatens judicial independence. The Constitution makes no reference to judicial tenure or qualifications.

The text fails to offer sufficient clarity on membership of key judicial institutions. The text indicates that the initiative for nomination of the Chief Justice and the Federal Court of Cassation, the Chief Public Prosecutor and the Chief Justice of the Judiciary Oversight Commission, lays in the High Judicial Council. There is however no constitutional reference to membership of the High Judicial Council, other than the indirect provision that bodies composing the Federal Judicial Authority are regulated in accordance with the law. The significance of the High Judicial Council in the regulation of the judiciary — it has the power to nominate members of all federal courts — except the Federal Supreme Court — and to present the draft of the annual budget of the Federal Judiciary Authority — would thus require further constitutional definition.

Particularly problematic is the absence of further reference regarding composition of the Federal Supreme Court, to be regulated by law. Especially important is the lack of definition on the appointment of experts in Islamic Law that are to be part of the Court. Also, there is no explicit indication of whether the jurisdiction of the Court is original or appellate. Article 92(1) — jurisdiction of the Federal Supreme Court over the oversight of the constitutionality of laws — might be intended to make clear that its jurisdiction is not anticipatory, but no further reference is included. Guidelines should be outlined on whether and when the Federal Supreme Court should act as a court of first instance. We note that the constitutional provision regulating access to the Federal Supreme Court is not clear. Article 92(3) lists possible litigants, followed by "and others." "Others" should be specified.

Finally, we want to point out that — in the light of the constitutionally assigned functions of the Federal Supreme Court — the text offers no clarity on the specific role of the Court of Cassation, including whether it is a court of first instance or of appellate jurisdiction. Further definition is recommended.

Distribution of powers: Overall schema

The Constitution establishes a system of regional autonomy based on the status currently enjoyed by the Kurdish autonomous region. Constructing a system for the entire country based on this level of autonomy as a one-step process can have negative consequences. In fact, the model assumes that the high degree of autonomy granted to Kurdistan based on its de facto autonomy, should serve as the basis for a federal system with each federal unit enjoying these powers. The way this is recognized in the Constitution, such option provides for an exclusive list of powers of the federal government — only areas where regional authority would not be pre-eminent — that does not include all the powers that are necessary for a stable functioning of the State.

The list of shared competences is limited, and concurrency in the exercise of those shared competences is not really existent, as the regional overriding capacity provided for by the Constitution makes this concurrency unbalanced, at best. As noted, residual powers are automatically assigned to the regions. It needs to be noted that in order to increase the number of exclusive powers of the central government via amendment of the Constitution, the text requires — beyond the rigid amendment procedures themselves — consent of the regional legislative authority and referendum in the region. This makes this option almost impossible in practice.

Article 120.2 provides for a regional right to amend national legislation in case of contradiction between regional and national legislation in areas outside the exclusive powers of the federal government. The interpretation of whether there is contradiction is in hands of the regional authorities. This provision, in fact, risks an uneven application of national law throughout the country. On the other hand, since the concept of "shared powers" is not explicitly used in that provision, it could be implied that the central government has the authority to legislate beyond its areas of exclusive and shared powers. This would be a positive development, but it needs to be confirmed, as the outline of the general schema indicates otherwise. The overriding capacity of regional legislation would still not be challenged.

Even in areas of regional jurisdiction or shared jurisdiction between regions and central government, a strong case can be made that there is need for pre-eminence of national legislation in cases where national legislation is necessary in respect of a matter that a single region cannot deal with effectively (e.g. interstate waters, international air traffic, contagious animal diseases). The current provisions do not allow for such option. [*HAH:* I cannot imagine that the Kurds would allow such a provision to pass — i.e. the central government to strip it from autonomy if the central government determined that the region wasn't handling something effectively.]

It seems that the state/central government would have no powers to intervene in a region that financially or administratively collapses or which is the subject of a natural disaster. A state of emergency does not empower the central government to act outside the framework established in the Constitution.

The text does not provide for the transfer of a flexible number of powers to different regions in accordance with their willingness or capacity to administer some specific powers and not others (there is no option for a statute specifying which powers can be assumed). The proposed model does not give the federal legislature (or any other body) the possibility of assessing whether a region has the capacity of administering the powers that are to be transferred, and sets no objective conditions (e.g. stability, resources) for the guaranteeing of such autonomy. A mechanism of capacity assessment and a schema for transfer of powers in accordance with that level of capacity would be advisable. [*HAH:* In this vein it is important to note that many of the Shi'a request a separate region, and they have no incentive to cut down on the autonomy for the regions as a result, nor do the Kurds. The proposal for such a mechanism is unrealistic.]

We note that the text allows for delegation of powers between governorate and federal levels of government, but surprisingly does not allow for delegation between the regional and the federal level. The possibility of delegation between the federation and individual governorates is conditioned by the requirement of consent by both levels. It is thus conceivable that a governorate could decline to assume all constitutionally available powers. This option appears unlikely in the light of the current political debate. As it stands, the current provision may have the unintended consequence of legislative inaction in important areas due to lack of governorate capacity, unless the central government is delegated the powers to intervene.

As it currently stands, the model requires that each governorate or group of governorates assume in one step the same powers that Kurdistan currently enjoys in order to become region. Technically, they have nothing or everything. We note that it is possible to construe Article 119 on regional Constitutions as allowing for a region to assume lesser powers, but this interpretation flies in the face of the outright grant of all regional powers in the Article.

Distribution of powers: Key areas

The two lists of powers currently included in the constitutional text — exclusive and shared — do not include the power of taxation, which by default, is assigned to the regions. We note that the text does assign fiscal "policy" to the national level, but when we sought to make explicit that this included taxation, we were informed that it did not and that it was not intended to. The central government, therefore, cannot raise and collect taxes in regions once they are established. This is problematic. Also, stronger indication of borrowing powers to the federal level would provide more extensive powers to that level.

Natural resources are effectively to be managed by the region (they are not in the exclusive federal list of powers, and to the extent that current resources are jointly managed it is the region which will be pre-eminent). The Constitution grants ownership of oil and gas resources to the people of Iraq and assigns the management of existing oil and gas reserves, including the distribution of revenues, jointly to the federal government and the producing governorate/region. However, by default, all regions would have exclusive rights over new oil and gas ventures. Even in relation to current oil fields, there are no details on mechanisms for shared management, other than leaving the issue to regulation by law. The Constitution does not consider possible options such as the creation of a national oil company, or the consideration of a central fund for oil revenues. Article 111 fails to define the concept of "damaged regions" and the "set period" during which special compensation in the distribution of oil and gas revenues is to be provided.

The text deals with the key area of water management in a manner that elicited criticism even from sections of the Shia leadership. It lists the planning of "policies" relating to the distribution of external water sources as one of the exclusive powers of the federal government, and internal water sources are left to shared legal regulation, thus providing regions with the capacity to override national legislation in this area. Problems may yet arise on the question of how this policy making power is to be exercised and enforced, as well as on defining the difference between internal and external water sources. Nonetheless, the introduction of a clearer federal responsibility to see to the fair distribution of these water sources in the very late amendment is an improvement.

The formulation of environmental and planning policies is also included in the list of shared powers, when these areas would require federal exclusive jurisdiction, or at least federal overriding capacity.

We note that there is no general central government policing power, or the power to establish a federal police service, which would normally be essential, especially in the context of separate regional police forces. On the contrary, as noted in our comments to Section One, provisions regarding establishment and organization of internal security services allow for the establishment of "regional guards" by each region. This provision accommodates the existing concerns of specific constituencies, but at the same time encourages the creation of regional armed forces, which is a development not conducive to security and stability.

Sections Four and Five do not make reference to legislation regulating the exercise and protection of rights. Likewise, we find no mention of the level of government responsible for implementation and incorporation of international law. In both cases, an explicit indication of federal jurisdiction is strongly advised.

Section Five: Powers of the Regions[6]

Chapter One: Regions

Article 116:

The federal system in the Republic of Iraq is made up of a decentralized capital, regions, and governorates, as well as local administrations.

Article 117:

First: This Constitution, upon coming into force, shall recognize the region of Kurdistan, along with its existing authorities, as a federal region.

Second: This Constitution shall affirm new regions established in accordance with its provisions.

Article 118:

The Council of Representatives shall enact, in a period not to exceed six months from the date of its first session, a law that defines the executive procedures to form regions, by a simple majority of the members present.

Article 119:

One or more governorates shall have the right to organize into a region based on a request to be voted on in a referendum submitted in one of the following two methods:

A. A request by one-third of the council members of each governorate intending to form a region.
B. A request by one-tenth of the voters in each of the governorates intending to form a region.

Article 120:

Each region shall adopt a constitution of its own that defines the structure of powers of the region, its authorities, and the mechanisms for exercising such authorities, provided that it does not contradict this Constitution.

Article 121:

First: The regional powers shall have the right to exercise executive, legislative, and judicial powers in accordance with this Constitution, except for those authorities stipulated in the exclusive authorities of the federal government.

CM: Is there a right for the citizen to appeal from a regional court of cassation to the Federal Supreme Court?

HAH: It is worth pointing out how terribly confusing the provisions concerning judicial authority are. It is unclear who has the right to interpret what.

Second: In case of a contradiction between regional and national legislation in respect to a matter outside the exclusive authorities of the federal government, the regional power shall have the right to amend the application of the national legislation within that region.

Third: Regions and governorates shall be allocated an equitable share of the national revenues sufficient to discharge their responsibilities and duties, but having regard to their resources, needs, and the percentage of their population.

Fourth: Offices for the regions and governorates shall be established in embassies and diplomatic missions, in order to follow cultural, social, and developmental affairs.

Fifth: The regional government shall be responsible for all the administrative requirements of the region, particularly the establishment and organization of the internal security forces for the region such as police, security forces, and guards of the region.

Chapter Two: Governates That Are Not Incorporated in a Region

Article 122:

First: The governorates shall be made up of number of districts, sub-districts and villages.

Second: Governorates that are not incorporated in a region shall be granted broad administrative and financial authorities to enable them to manage their affairs in accordance with the principle of decentralized administration, and this shall be regulated by law.

Third: The governor, who is elected by the Governorate Council, is deemed the highest executive official in the governorate to practice his powers authorized by the Council.

Fourth: A law shall regulate the election of the Governorate Council, the governor, and their powers.

Fifth: The Governorate Council shall not be subject to the control or supervision of any ministry or any institution not linked to a ministry. The Governorate Council shall have independent finances.

Article 123:

Powers exercised by the federal government can be delegated to the governorates or vice versa, with the consent of both governments, and this shall be regulated by law.

***

CM: What about the relation between the regions and the Federation Council?

***

Chapter Three: The Capital

Article 124:

First: Baghdad in its municipal borders is the capital of the Republic of Iraq and shall constitute, in its administrative borders, the governorate of Baghdad.
Second: This shall be regulated by a law.
Third: The capital may not merge with a region.

***

CM: Is there a representation of Baghdad in the Federation Council?

***

Chapter Four: The Local Administrations

Article 125:

This Constitution shall guarantee the administrative, political, cultural, and educational rights of the various nationalities, such as Turkomen, Chaldeans, Assyrians, and all other constituents, and this shall be regulated by law.

***

CM: Redundant, since the Constitution should naturally protect individuals and communities.

***

NB: Chapter Five: Authorities of the Regions
    General Comments

While the title of this chapter refers only to regions, in fact this chapter covers other levels of government.
The draft constitution confirms the arrangement first designed in the TAL of three levels of Iraqi federalism: central government, regional

governments, and provincial governments. The one existing regional government — Kurdistan — is confirmed (Article 113 [117]). Other regions may also be formed. Although the process for forming these regions will be governed by a federal law, the constitution stresses that such a law will be passed by a simple parliamentary majority (Article 114 [118]) within six months of the parliament's first meeting. Given the experience with deadlines in the drafting of the constitution, it might be considered mildly surprising that a new deadline has been created — although the result of failing to meet the date is not specified. More significant than the deadline, however, is that Article 115 [119] provides that the initiative for forming a region can come from a purely local initiative (either from provincial councils or directly from the people) and be approved by a referendum. It is also to be approved by a referendum (implicitly of the people in the prospective region), suggesting that after the parliament passes the relevant law, all power over establishing regions shall pass out of the hands of the central government. It is difficult to imagine a more favorable set of constitutional provisions for creation of a southern region (the main potential region under discussion).

Article 116 [120]: Regional Constitutions

Each region will be responsible for writing its own constitution; as I understand it, the process has already begun for the Kurdish region.

Article 117 [121]: Responsibilities of the Regions

Allowing the regions complete responsibility for internal security will likely turn existing militias into regional security forces. Indeed, Kurdish leaders claim that their militias have already made this transformation. A similar development could easily occur if a southern region is created.

Article 118 [122]: Provincial Government

Placing provincial councils outside the purview of any ministry of the central government is unusual for the Middle East (indeed, several countries have an oddly named "Ministry of Local Government" as part of their central government).

Article 120 [124]: Capital

Baghdad is converted into a province, but it is explicitly barred from joining one of the regions.

Article 121 [125]: Local Administration

It is not clear why the rights of various ethnic minorities are mentioned in this chapter unless it is to imply that the communities are to be viewed as administrative units as well as ethnic categories. Indeed, unspecified administrative rights are mentioned. The purpose might also be to placate those non-Kurds who live in Kurdistan, a region with geographical boundaries but still formed for a specific ethnic group.

UN: SECTION FIVE: POWERS OF THE REGIONS

Governorates and regions

In a context where the governorate is the instance of decentralization in all parts of the country except Kurdistan, there is almost nothing said on governorate structures and powers, and what is said is, in fact, contradictory. The text is not clear regarding the right of governorates that are not incorporated into a region to assume non-exclusive national powers. While Article 121(2) grants them "broad administrative and financial authorities" to enable them "to manage its affairs in accordance with the principle of decentralized administration," Article 114 does in fact assign "all powers not stipulated in the exclusive authorities of the federal government" to the regions "and governorates that are not organized in a region." Different articles, then, provide contradictory assessments of the exact nature of the governorates that do not incorporate themselves into a region. It is therefore not clear whether governorates are entitled to legislative powers or not.

The inclusion of the clause mandating the Council of Representatives to enact legislation defining "the executive procedures to form regions" was aimed at delaying the actual configuration of the territorial distribution of powers until the new parliament was elected. However, this provision needs to be considered together with the constitutional provision outlining the governorates' right to organize into a region (which include right of initiative and referendum as means of ratification). Thus, it is not clear what is exactly to be enacted by legislation, and whether the notion of "executive procedures" (as opposed to "legislative procedures") provides for a role for the Council of Representatives in assessing whether a region can or cannot come into being, on the basis of its legislative and executive capacity. The introduction of that legal requirement does not amount to a requirement that the Council can limit those powers, set conditions for their transfer, or determine the manner in which such conditions could be established. This seems to fly in the face of the normal approach to such devolution, which would recognize that the taking of substantive powers from the central government is a bilateral, not unilateral act. The term "executive procedures" was intended to be confined to administrative or executive procedures, and not to the imposition of substantive conditionalities relating to competence or desirability.

Unlike in previous drafts, there is no limitation in the number of governorates that can form a region. This can ultimately lead to a federation with a very small number of ethnically homogeneous regions, which is a development conducive to instability. Also, the status of the capital is left unclear. The Constitution indicates that the governorate of Baghdad "may not merge into a region," but does not say whether it can turn into one. This precision would be especially important if regions and governorates are not entitled to the same powers.

The existence of a fixed, final federal structure of the country finds itself challenged by the constitutional lack of a closed model on region formation, which may result in a federation subject to change on a rolling basis, with the subsequent destabilizing effects. A model of formation of regions with defined timelines is recommended in order to prevent continuous change in the overall structure.

We note that the regions shall establish their own judicial authorities including, it appears, the judicial authority over the constitutionality and validity of regional laws (save for those that are already in effect) and be the final judicial authority in respect of all legal disputes in the region, save for those that arise from the application of the few federal laws applicable in a region. Article 92(1) can possibly be interpreted to imply that the Federal Supreme Court has constitutional jurisdiction over regional laws but this is not clear. At the least there is no appeal from a regional court to the federal courts. We note that judicial and related matters such as criminal and civil procedure are not in the exclusive or shared powers of the federal government. The federal judiciary will have only the "boundary drawing competency" to determine whether a dispute falls within its jurisdiction or not (Article 92(8)). The two judicial and legal systems are separated. It is not clear whether there is a unified apex court in terms of appeals from the regional courts.

The Constitution is largely silent on the structures and modalities of government in the regions, which gives the regions a free hand in designing their systems of government. The text is also silent on institutional structures for local government (the only reference on this regard — mandate for minority representation — would be better placed in the Bill of Rights section). Even minimal requirements of accountability or specific uniform democratic electoral norms are absent from the text. At the least, regional Constitutions and authorities should remain subject to the Section on Fundamental Principles and Rights and Duties in the Constitution.

We note that there is an absence in the general structure of institutions that would integrate regions into the central government. Such institutions are normally a critical feature of allowing regions to collaborate in the task of managing the country, and also in integrating regions into the task of national government. This is *particularly* relevant given the inclusion of a shared list of powers. The consideration of an institutional forum for federal-regional intergovernmental relations and inter-regional consultations is advised. Countries such as Canada are currently contemplating the introduction of such institutions, and they are central elements of the design of federations such as South Africa and Germany.

Section Six: Final and Transitional Provisions[7]

Chapter One: Final Provisions

Article 126:

First: The President of the Republic and the Council of the Ministers collectively, or one-fifth of the Council of Representatives members, may propose to amend the Constitution.

Second: The fundamental principles mentioned in Section One and the rights and liberties mentioned in Section Two of the Constitution may not be amended except after two successive electoral terms, with the approval of two-thirds of the members of the Council of Representatives, the approval of the people in a general referendum, and the ratification by the President of the Republic within seven days.

Third: Other articles not stipulated in clause "Second" of this Article may not be amended, except with the approval of two-thirds of the members of the Council of Representatives, the approval of the people in a general referendum, and the ratification by the President of the Republic within seven days.

CM: What if the President refuses to ratify after the whole process is completed?

Fourth: Articles of the Constitution may not be amended if such amendment takes away from the powers of the regions that are not within the exclusive powers of the federal authorities, except by the approval of the legislative authority of the concerned region and the approval of the majority of its citizens in a general referendum.

Fifth:

A. An amendment is considered ratified by the President of the Republic after the expiration of the period stipulated in clauses "Second" and "Third" of this Article, in case he does not ratify it.
B. An amendment shall enter into force on the date of its publication in the Official Gazette.

CM: Amendment process unduly complicated.

Article 127:

The President of the Republic, the Prime Minister, members of the Council of Ministers, the Speaker of the Council of Representatives, his two Deputies, members of the Council of Representatives, members of the Judicial Authority, and people of special grades may not use their influence to buy or rent any state properties, to rent or sell any of their assets to the state, to sue the state for these assets, or to conclude a contract with the state under the pretense of being building contractors, suppliers, or concessionaires.

CM: Nice but implementable?

Article 128:

The laws and judicial judgments shall be issued in the name of the people.

Article 129:

Laws shall be published in the Official Gazette and shall take effect on the date of their publication, unless stipulated otherwise.

Article 130:

Existing laws shall remain in force, unless annulled or amended in accordance with the provisions of this Constitution.

Article 131:

Every referendum mentioned in this Constitution is deemed successful with the approval of the majority of the voters unless otherwise stipulated.

Chapter Two: Transitional Provisions

Article 132:

First: The State shall guarantee care for the families of the martyrs, political prisoners, and victims of the oppressive practices of the defunct dictatorial regime.

Second: The State shall guarantee compensation to the families of the martyrs and the injured as a result of terrorist acts.

Third: A law shall regulate matters mentioned in clauses "First" and "Second" of this Article.

CM: Law . . .

Article 133:

The Council of Representatives shall adopt in its first session the bylaws of the Transitional National Assembly until it adopts its own bylaws.

Article 134:

The Iraqi High Tribunal shall continue its duties as an independent judicial body, in examining the crimes of the defunct dictatorial regime and its symbols. The Council of Representatives shall have the right to dissolve it by law after the completion of its work.

Article 135:

First: The High Commission for De-Ba'athification shall continue its functions as an independent commission, in coordination with the judicial authority and the executive institutions within the framework of the laws regulating its functions. The Commission shall be attached to the Council of Representatives.

Second: The Council of Representatives shall have the right to dissolve this Commission by an absolute majority after the completion of its function.

Third: A nominee to the positions of the President of the Republic, the Prime Minister, the members of the Council of Ministers, the Speaker, the members of the Council of Representatives, the President, members of the Federation Council, their counterparts in the regions, or members of the judicial commissions and other positions covered by de-Ba'athification statutes pursuant to the law may not be subject to the provisions of de-Ba'athification.

> *CM:* An important provision to deal with Iraq's authoritarian history.

> *HAH:* There is an important twist that has gone undiscussed in the commentaries. Nobody knows what this provision means. Looking at the Arabic, the first word *yushtarat* seems to mean "it is a condition that," and the last phrase is not "is not subject to" but "is not included under," making it even more confusing. Is it a disqualification from seeking office in the first place or an immunity granting provision? There has been a public debate about this, although translations seem to favor the latter interpretation.

Fourth: The conditions stated in clause "Third" of this Article shall remain in force unless the Commission stated in item "First" of this Article is dissolved.

> *CM:* Obscure.

Fifth *(Added by amendment)*: Mere membership in the dissolved Ba'ath party shall not be considered a sufficient basis for referral to court, and a member shall enjoy equality before the law and protection unless covered by the provisions of De-Ba'athification and the directives issued according to it.

Sixth *(Added by amendment)*: The Council of Representatives shall form a parliamentary committee from among its members to monitor and review the executive procedures of the Higher Commission for De-Ba'athification and state institutions to guarantee justice, objectivity, and transparency and to examine their consistency with the laws. The committee's decisions shall be subject to the approval of the Council of Representatives.

Article 136:

First: The Property Claims Commission shall continue its functions as an independent commission in coordination with the judicial authority and the executive institutions in accordance with the law. The Property Claims Commission shall be attached to the Council of Representatives.

Second: The Council of Representatives shall have the right to dissolve the Commission by a two-thirds majority vote of its members.

Article 137:

Application of the provisions of the articles related to the Federation Council, wherever it may be cited in this Constitution, shall be postponed until the Council of Representatives issues a decision by a two-thirds majority vote in its second electoral term that is held after this Constitution comes into force.

> *CM:* Bizarre, underlines uncertainty for the projected Federation Council.

Article 138:

First: The expression "the Presidency Council" shall replace the expression "the President of the Republic" wherever the latter is mentioned in this Constitution. The provisions related to the President of the Republic shall be reactivated one successive term after this Constitution comes into force.

CM: Awkward, transforms presidency into a semi-collective triumvirate.

Second:

A. The Council of Representatives shall elect the President of the State and two Vice Presidents who shall form a Council called the "Presidency Council," which shall be elected by one list and with a two-thirds majority.
B. The provisions to remove the President of the Republic present in this Constitution shall apply to the President and members of the Presidency Council.
C. The Council of Representatives may remove a member of the Presidency Council with a three-fourths majority of the number of its members for reasons of incompetence and dishonesty.
D. In the event of a vacant seat in the Presidency Council, the Council of Representatives shall elect a replacement by a two-thirds majority vote of its members.

Third: Members of the Presidency Council shall be subject to the same conditions as a member of the Council of Representatives and must:

A. Be over forty years of age.
B. Enjoy good reputation, integrity and uprightness.
C. Have quit the dissolved (Ba'ath) Party ten years prior to its fall, in case he was a member of it.
D. Have not participated in suppressing the 1991 and Al-Anfal uprisings. He must not have committed a crime against the Iraqi people.

Fourth: The Presidency Council shall issue its decisions unanimously and any member may delegate to one of the two other members to take his place.

CM: Unanimity might make decisions difficult to reach.

Fifth:

A. Legislation and decisions enacted by the Council of Representatives shall be forwarded to the Presidency Council for their unanimous approval and for its issuance within ten days from the date of delivery to the Presidency Council, except the stipulations of Articles 118 and 119 that pertain to the formation of regions.
B. In the event the Presidency Council does not approve, legislation and decisions shall be sent back to the Council of Representatives to reexamine the disputed issues and to vote on them by the majority of its

members and then shall be sent for the second time to the Presidency Council for approval.

C. In the event the Presidency Council does not approve the legislation and decisions for the second time within ten days of receipt, the legislation and decisions are sent back to the Council of Representatives, which has the right to adopt it by three-fifths majority of its members, which may not be challenged, and the legislation or decision shall be considered ratified.

Sixth: The Presidency Council shall exercise the powers of the President of the Republic stipulated in this Constitution.

Article 139:

The Prime Minister shall have two deputies in the first electoral term.

Article 140:

First: The executive authority shall undertake the necessary steps to complete the implementation of the requirements of all subparagraphs of Article 58 of the Transitional Administrative Law.

Second: The responsibility placed upon the executive branch of the Iraqi Transitional Government stipulated in Article 58 of the Transitional Administrative Law shall extend and continue to the executive authority elected in accordance with this Constitution, provided that it accomplishes completely (normalization and census and concludes with a referendum in Kirkuk and other disputed territories to determine the will of their citizens), by a date not to exceed the 31st of December 2007.

Article 141:

Legislation enacted in the region of Kurdistan since 1992 shall remain in force, and decisions issued by the government of the region of Kurdistan, including court decisions and contracts, shall be considered valid unless they are amended or annulled pursuant to the laws of the region of Kurdistan by the competent entity in the region, provided that they do not contradict with the Constitution.

CM: Who decides whether they contradict the constitution?

Article 142 *(Added by amendment)*:

First: The Council of Representatives shall form at the beginning of its work a committee from its members representing the principal components of the Iraqi society with the mission of presenting to the Council of Representatives, within a period not to exceed four months, a report that contains recommendations of the necessary amendments that could be made to the Constitution, and the committee shall be dissolved after a decision is made regarding its proposals.

Second: The proposed amendments shall be presented to the Council of Representatives all at once for a vote upon them, and shall be deemed approved with the agreement of the absolute majority of the members of the Council.

Third: The articles amended by the Council of Representatives pursuant to item "Second" of this Article shall be presented to the people for voting on them in a referendum within a period not exceeding two months from the date of their approval by the Council of Representatives.

Fourth: The referendum on the amended Articles shall be successful if approved by the majority of the voters, and if not rejected by two-thirds of the voters in three or more governorates.

Fifth: Article 126 of the Constitution (concerning amending the Constitution) shall be suspended, and shall return into force after the amendments stipulated in this Article have been decided upon.

Article 143:

The Transitional Administrative Law and its Annex shall be annulled on the seating of the new government, except for the stipulations of Article 53(A) and Article 58 of the Transitional Administrative Law.

Article 144:

This Constitution shall come into force after the approval of the people thereon in a general referendum, its publication in the Official Gazette, and the seating of the government that is formed pursuant to this Constitution.

NB: Chapter Six: Final and Transitional Guidelines
General Comments

The drafters have taken some care to specify transitional provisions that will allow for institutional and legal continuity in the presidency, the parliament, and some other bodies.

Article 122 [126]: Constitutional Amendments

It will be fairly difficult to amend the Iraqi constitution. All amendments must be supported by a two-thirds majority of parliament and a popular majority in a referendum. The first two chapters cannot be amended until two parliamentary terms have been completed. And the consent of regional parliaments and a majority of the population of a region is necessary before regional powers are diminished. This last provision might provoke dispute if a regional parliament claimed its rights were being diminished by a proposed amendment but the national parliament claimed otherwise.

Article 126 [130]: Continuing Validity of Existing Legislation

Implicitly the body of legislation issued by decree by the CPA continues in effect until modified, because it is currently treated as valid Iraqi legislation. One could make an argument otherwise based on Article 138 [143]

(which repeals the TAL, a document that affirmed the continuing validity of CPA orders). But a more gradual path seems likely; indeed, a committee within the Ministry of Justice has been reviewing CPA legislation and has recently recommended the repeal or amendment of some measures.

Articles 130 [134] and 131 [135]: Supreme Iraqi Criminal Court and De-Baathification Commission

Two controversial structures — the tribunal for trying those who committed grave offenses under the Baathist regime and the De-Baathification Commission — are affirmed; the second requires an absolute majority of parliamentarians (not a simple majority) to abolish.

Article 134 [138]: Presidency Council

The TAL provides for a three-person presidency council rather than a single president. That system will be retained for the first parliamentary session elected under the draft constitution (the wording seems to suggest that the presidency council will continue to operate throughout the first parliament's term).

Article 136 [140]: Kirkuk, Other Disputed Areas, and the TAL

Kirkuk and provincial boundaries have been a major issue of dispute since the drafting of the TAL. Although the TAL did not resolve the issue, it did establish some mechanisms for resolution. None of those mechanisms has been implemented however. The draft constitution affirms those mechanisms and places responsibility in the hands of the executive, implicitly bypassing the parliament. By stressing the continued applicability of "all sections" of Article 58 of the TAL, the constitution creates a mild legal paradox: One of those sections requires the transitional presidency council to recommend mechanisms for changing provincial boundaries in the permanent constitution and specifies some steps for developing such recommendations if the members are unable to agree. The presidency council has neither made recommendations nor set in motion the stipulated alternatives. As a result, the draft constitution affirms a text that has already been violated by the failure to develop recommendations for the permanent constitution.

More significant, Article 136 [140] represents a compromise. Kurdish leaders wished to have the provisions of the TAL's Article 58 implemented before the constitution was adopted, believing that this would further Kurdish claims to Kirkuk. They are probably correct in their political judgment, because Article 58 requires counteracting the population movements implemented by the Baath regime and might result in a Kurdish majority there, depending on how it is implemented. The Kurdish leadership finally gave way in not insisting on immediate implementation, but they gained a promise that it would be implemented expeditiously.

Some guidance is given on how to resolve the status of Kirkuk, but none is given on how to resolve disputes over provincial boundaries and the matter is likely to prove quite contentious.

Article 138 [143]: Voiding the TAL

The abolition of the TAL might be considered implicit by the adoption of a new constitution, but this article makes the step explicit. The two TAL provisions that remain in force are Article 58 (discussed above) and Article 53(a), which recognizes the government of the Kurdish region.

Article 139 [144]: Effective Date of the Constitution

This article was omitted from the AP translation. My translation of the final article is: "This constitution is to be considered effective after the people approve it in the general referendum, it is published in the Official Gazette, and the government [here meaning cabinet] is formed in accordance with its provisions."

UN: SECTION SIX: FINAL AND TRANSITIONAL PROVISIONS

Evaluation
Amendment procedures

In response to the argument that the Constitution will be a flexible document that can be adaptable to the future needs of the country, it needs to be noted that the procedure for constitutional amendment included in the text is unusually rigid and highly unpractical (we refer herewith to the amendment procedure outlined in Article 125, and not to the ad hoc procedure for a four month constitutional review envisaged by Article 142). This degree of rigidity is particularly true in what refers to fundamental principles (Section One). Thus, the procedure requires two successive electoral terms, 2/3 approval from the Council of Representatives, national referendum and ratification of the President of the Republic. Amendment of other parts of the Constitution requires the same degree of majority, referendum and presidential ratification, but no need for two successive electoral terms. The amendment provisions for Section One appear as particularly rigid in the light of comparative constitutionalism, since in practice require an eight-year period for a modification to be put in place.
On the other hand, we note that this rigid amendment procedure also applies to the Bill of Rights section of the text, which is usually the most protected chapter in post-conflict Constitutions. This is in consonance with international best practice.
A particular anomaly in the described procedures is the absent role of the Federation Council. It is common practice in federal models that the chamber of regional representation at the federal level is entitled a role in the amendment process. This is not contemplated in the text. We notice, in any case, that the last-minute amendment providing for a Constitutional Review Committee addresses some of these issues in light of the particular need for engagement with the Sunni community in the post-October 15th scenario.

Presidency Council

This section describes the particular legislative interaction between the Council of Representatives and the Presidency Council, which are to operate during the first term after ratification of the Constitution. This interaction provides for the Presidency Council to propose amendments to legislation, but ultimately gives the Council of Representatives the capacity to pass legislation without the consent of the Presidency Council, on second reading and by a 3/5th majority. In the consideration that the Presidency Council does in the interim period institutionally play the legislative role of a second chamber, the characteristics of this interaction are in consonance with international best practices.

Two Deputy Prime Ministers will be designated in the first electoral cycle. These provisions seem not to change the substance of the structure of government as it is only a transitional provision. The consideration of transitional provisions in regards to the structure of government, on the other hand, finds no parallel in the judicial sphere, where transitional provisions are notably absent.

Kirkuk

The Articles regarding Kirkuk are potentially divisive. It is notable that Article 53C of TAL contemplated that Kirkuk would be regarded as a separate governorate incapable (as with Baghdad) of merging with other governorates. The provisions in the Constitution regarding Kirkuk, however, envisage that Kirkuk may now accede to Kurdistan. In this context, these provisions in part tilt the balance of power in favor of Kurdistan. In particular, we note that the text provides a specific date upon which a consensus needs to be achieved and a referendum held (31st December 2007). The drafters have thus opted for providing a specific date for the resolution of the problem within the framework of Article 58 of TAL, but not Article 53. While Article 58 is perpetuated by the constitutional text understandably because it provides a consensual process solution to the problem, the reference to the referendum and its date may contribute to an immediate impetus for demographic engineering and suspect voter registration (an astonishing 220,000 new voters were added to the registration list before the October 15th referendum). This is likely to increase tension in the region.

C. ELECTORAL AND POLITICAL PARTIES LAWS

Introduction. The Constitution of 2005 has a few interspersed clauses that bear on the electoral system when it comes to universal suffrage. Alongside the general democratic/republican principle that the people elect their government, it establishes for the Council of Representatives a ratio of 1 deputy for each 100,000 inhabitants. Other than the quota for women set at one-fourth of Parliament, this is the only instance where popular electoral representation is addressed in the text. It is left for laws to flesh out the details of the elections.

The Iraqi text is not unusual, and constitutions generally leave it to the executive and legislative branches to pass the necessary legislation, and to the courts to ensure that votes are not diluted by discriminatory laws, or tampered with after they are cast. Beyond the question whether a high level of generality should be retained as constitutional practice when it comes to such a crucial matter as popular representation, many issues remain unresolved in Iraq. The following section presents the main legislation that affects the conduct of elections in Iraq: the law establishing the Independent High Electoral Commission of Iraq; Election Law 16 of 2005, enacted by the Transitional National Assembly, under which the 2005-2009 Parliament was elected; and the law organizing political parties. I am grateful to Jaye Sitton for the precisions and clarifications she provided for this section.

1. LAW OF THE INDEPENDENT HIGH ELECTORAL COMMISSION

LAW OF THE INDEPENDENT HIGH ELECTORAL COMMISSION

Enacted 18 September 2007*

Pursuant to the provisions of Article 61 and Item 3 of Article 73 and Article 102 of the Constitution, the following law was passed

Section 1

Article 1

1) This Law abolishes the Coalition Provisional Authority (CPA) Order Number 92 of 31/5/2004 from the day this law and all regulations and instructions issued according to it enter into force.

2) This law establishes a body named The Independent High Electoral Commission.

Section 2

Article 2

The Independent High Electoral Commission is a professional, governmental, independent, neutral and autonomous body, subject to the supervision of the Council of Representatives, and shall have the authority to

1. Promulgate rules and adopted principles for federal, regional and local elections and referenda throughout Iraq to ensure their implementation in a just and transparent manner.

2. Oversee all various federal and regional elections and referenda, and in provinces that are not organized into a region.

3. Declare, organize and conduct all various federal and local elections and referenda in the provinces that are not organized into a region referred to in the Constitution, throughout Iraq.

4. The Regional Electoral Body, in coordination and collaboration with the National Office, shall be in charge of administration, conduct and

---

* Available at http://www.gjpi.org/library/primary/statutes/.

organization of regional and local elections in that particular region or governorate under the supervision of the Independent High Electoral Commission.

Section 3 The Commission's Organization

Article 3

1) The Independent High Electoral Commission shall consist of:
    a. The Board of Commissioners
    b. The Electoral Administration

2) The Board of Commissioners

- shall consist of nine members, at least two of whom must be law professionals, selected by majority vote of the Council of Representatives upon their nomination by a committee composed of members of the Council of Representatives and must have expertise and experience in elections and must be known for their competence, integrity and independence taking into consideration women representation).
- Candidates for the membership of the Board of Commissioners must fulfill the following:
  1. Must be an Iraqi citizen residing permanently in Iraq.
  2. Must have at least a first university degree.
  3. Must not be less than thirty five years old.
  4. Must be of good behaviour.
  5. Must be competent and experienced in the field of administrative work.
  6. Must be politically independent.
  7. Must not be covered by the De-Ba'thification law, and must not have enriched himself on the account of public money or committed a crime against the Iraqi people or be affiliated to a repressive apparatus.
  8. Must not have been convicted of a dishonorable crime.

3) a) The Board shall elect at its first meeting from amongst it members, with a majority of five members, a President and a Vice President, a Rapporteur and a non-voting Chief Electoral Officer.

b) The term of office for the President shall be one year renewable by a majority vote of at least five members.

c) The President is the Commission's legal representative and, accordingly, shall represent it before others.

d) The President or who is acting on his behalf shall perform the following functions:

    1. Manage the regulatory and administrative work of the Board.

    2. Prepare the meeting agenda, conduct and preside over them including a meeting requested by at least four members of the Board.

    3. Any other functions designated by the Board.

4) The Board of Commissioners shall take an oath of office before the Higher Juridical Council with the following wording:

I swear by Almighty God to perform my legal and professional duties with honesty, dedication and devotion, and work to accomplish the functions designated to me independently and neutrally. God is Witness to what I am saying.

5) The Board meeting shall hold with an absolute majority of its members and it shall take its decisions with a majority of members present. In case there is a tie of votes then the option for which the President votes shall prevail, unless otherwise stipulated by the law.

Section 4 Functions of the Commission

Article 4

The Commission shall perform the following functions:

1. Establish and update voter registry in collaboration with the Governorate and Regional Electoral Offices.

2. Regulate the registration and certification of political entities for the purpose of contesting elections.

3. Regulate and certify candidate lists for elections.

4. Accredit election observers and political entity agents and media representatives.

5. Adjudicate all electoral complaints and appeals, and its decisions can be appealed before a competent judicial electoral panel.

6. Certify tally procedures.

7. Declare and certify final results of elections and referenda with the exception of the results of the Council of Representatives elections which shall be certified by the Federal Supreme Court.

8. Set regulations and instructions preserving fair electoral process.

9. Certification of the structure of the Electoral Administration and the appointments in senior posts.

10. Set financial policy for the Commission.

Section 5 Electoral Administration

Article 5

a) The Electoral Administration shall be made up of the National Office and Electoral Offices in the regions and governorates according to a structure to be suggested by the Chief Electoral Officer/Head of Electoral Administration and ratified by the Board of Commissioners. The Chief Electoral Officer shall be in charge of Electoral Administration and represent it before the Board of Commissioners and organize its works and ensure their good performance.

b) It shall be responsible for the implementation of regulations and decisions passed by the Board of Commissioners, and management of all activities of operational, executive and procedural nature at the national and regional levels.

c) Senior posts at the National Office from Deputy Chief Electoral Officer and directors of divisions in the Office shall be nominated by the Executive Administration and ratified by the Board with a majority of five votes out of eight. As for the Governorate and Regional Electoral Offices' managers, five candidates shall be nominated by members of the Council of Representatives from those regions or governorates, and one of them shall be selected and ratified by the Board of Commissioners by a majority vote of at least five of its members.

d) The heads and members of the Electoral Offices shall be responsible for the performance of their functions before the Chief Electoral Officer, who has the right to hold them accountable and suggest the replacement of any of them who neglects his duties with the same mechanism stipulated in item c.

Section 6 Replacement of Members

Article 6

Membership in the Board of Commissioners shall be terminated for one of the following reasons:

1. If the member's resignation is accepted by the Board of Commissioners in accordance with internal regulations.

2. If the member dies or becomes incapacitated.

3. If a member of the Board of Commissioners is convicted of a dishonoring crime.

4. If the recommendation by a majority of five members of the Board of Commissioners for the removal of one of its members for violating the code of conduct is ratified by a simple majority of the Council of Representatives.

5. The Council of Representatives may relieve the Board of Commissioners of its post in its entirety or in part by an absolute majority vote after violation of a law is proven against them.

6. If it is proven that the information supplied by the member while assuming his post is incorrect.

7. If the seat of any of the members of the Board of Commissioners is vacant for any of the reasons mentioned in Article 6 of this section, he shall be replaced by another member selected with the same mechanism stipulated in Article 3 item 2 a.

Section 7 The Rights of the Members

Article 7

1. The members of the Board of Commissioners shall enjoy the privileges of the rank of Under-Secretary of a ministry for a renewable period of five years.

2. The Board of Commissioners may grant its employees allocations not exceeding those granted to the employees of the Council of Ministers.

3. Members of the Board of Commissioners may not be appointed into a public post, with the exemption of academic posts, for three years after the end of their work as commissioners.

4. Commissioners shall be entitled to a pension of 80% of their salaries, after the end of their post, except in case of dismissal, resignation, or conviction of a crime related to their work. The provisions of this item shall apply to former commissioners.

5. The Council of Ministers must appoint those who have contracts with the former IECI at the National Office and the Governorate Electoral Offices

into governmental departments according to their qualifications and in consistence with the applicable procedures.

6. The same treatment stipulated in item 3 of this Article will be applied to the former Board of Commissioners.

Section 8 Complaints

Article 8

1) The Board has exclusive jurisdiction with respect to the civil enforcement of its own procedures and regulations. The Board must refer a criminal case to appropriate authorities if it finds evidence of criminal misconduct relating to the integrity of the electoral process.

2) Except as provided by the IHEC law, the Board has an exclusive jurisdiction to resolve disputes arising out of the preparation for and execution of national, regional and governorate elections, and may delegate jurisdiction to resolve disputes in the first instance to the Electoral Administration.

3) The Court of Cassation shall form a committee of three non full time judges to look into the appeals referred to it by the Board of Commissioners or submitted to the judicial authority by those directly affected by the Board decisions.

4) Decisions of the Board may be appealed only to the Electoral Judicial Panel.

5) Board decisions shall be published in three daily newspapers for a period of at least three days both in Arabic and Kurdish. Appeals against such decisions must be submitted by the concerned political entity within three days starting from the last day of the publication of the decision. Such appeals may be submitted to the National Office or any Electoral Office in the regions and governorates.

6) The Electoral Judicial Panel must decide on an appeal within ten days of its referral by the Board of Commissioners.

7) Decisions by the Electoral Judicial Panel are final and cannot be appealed in all cases.

8) Upon its formation, the Judicial Appeals Panel shall establish appeal procedures before it against the decisions of the Board of Commissioners without violating what is mentioned in this law. This shall be exempted from the applicable amended civil procedural law No. 83 of 1969 and other procedural laws.

Section 9 Final Provisions

Article 9

1. The Independent Electoral Commission shall continue its work until the formation of the Independent High Electoral Commission according to this law. The Board of Commissioners shall be selected within 60 days as of the date of approval of this law.

2. A committee shall be established in the Council of Representatives to follow up the formation of the Board of Commissioners of the Independent High Electoral Commission.

3. The Commission must seek the assistance of international experts in the electoral field from the United Nations at the stages of preparation and conduct of election and referenda.

4. The Commission shall have an independent annual budget prepared according to the basis and customary rules, proposed by the Board of Commissioners in consultation with the Ministry of Finance and shall be approved by the Council of Representatives and incorporated into the general budget for the state.

5. The Governorate and Regional Electoral Offices shall be linked with the Regional Electoral Body.

6. The Board of Commissioners shall make a by-law for the Commission.

7. Employees of the Independent Electoral Commission, with the exception of the commissioners, shall chose between taking retirement or being appointed to public posts, in accordance with their functional grades.

8. The Board of Commissioners must publish its decisions in both Arabic and Kurdish within 24 hours in a way it determines without prejudice to item 4 of Article 9 of this law.

9. Quarterly reports must be prepared and submitted to the Council of Representatives.

10. Representation of the components of the Iraqi society shall be put into consideration in the formation of the Independent High Electoral Commission in accordance with the rules and regulations.

11. The Chairman of the Board of Commissioners shall have the powers of a minister in terms of official communication with the ministries and other governmental departments.

12. The Independent High Electoral Commission shall adopt the general population census officially conducted by the Federal government.

13. This law shall enter into force from the date its approval and shall be published in the National Gazette.

Reasons for the Law

As the transitional period mentioned in the Law of Administration for the State of Iraq for the Transitional Period has ended with the ratification of the permanent constitution in a general referendum, and certification of the results of the Council of Representatives' elections;

As the law establishing the Independent Electoral Commission of Iraq (the Coalition Provisional Authority (CPA) Order Number 92 of 2004) ended with the end of the transitional period;

And because of the need for a new law which will regulate the functions of the Commission pursuant to Article 102 of the constitution;

This law has been passed.

2. LAW 16 OF 2005: THE COUNCIL OF REPRESENTATIVES ELECTION LAW

LAW 16 OF 2005: THE COUNCIL OF REPRESENTATIVES ELECTION LAW

Published in the Iraqi Official Gazette on September 15, 2005
Unofficial translation by the U.S. Embassy's Office of Constitutional and
Legislative Affairs*

Chapter One
Application of the Law

Article 1

This law applies to the following:

1. Election of a House of Representatives.

2. Election of the National Assembly in the case where item (E) of Article 61 of TAL is implemented.

3. Elections of the national parliaments of the regions, governorate councils and local councils, unless otherwise provided by law.

Chapter Two
The Right to Vote

Article 2

Elections shall be held by public process, direct voting and secret ballot.

Article 3

The voter must be:

1. An Iraqi citizen.

2. Legally competent.

3. 18 years old, in the month in which elections are held.

4. Registered to vote in accordance with the procedures established by the Independent Electoral Commission of Iraq.

Article 4

1. Voting shall be conducted in one day.

2. Voting may be postponed in one or more districts if the security situation requires it.

Article 5

The date of the elections will be determined by a presidential decree and it shall be announced through all of the media 60 days before the date of holding the elections.

Chapter Three
The Right to Be a Candidate

Article 6

A candidate must be a voter, in addition to the following:

1. Must be no less than thirty years old of age.

---

*Available at http://www.gjpi.org/library/primary/statutes/.

2. Must not be covered by the Deba'thification law.
3. He must not have enriched himself illegally at the expense of the state or public funds.
4. He must not have been convicted of a crime that violates honor and must be known for his good conduct.
5. He must have at least a high school certificate or its equivalent.
6. He must not be a member of the armed forces upon nomination.

Article 7

Nominees shall be subjected to the approval of the Independent Electoral Commission of Iraq.

Article 8

A qualified nominee can be a candidate in any district he wants.

Article 9

Candidacy shall be through the closed list method, but a candidate may contest as an individual.

Article 10

The number of nominees in a list must not be less than three and not more than the number of seats allotted to the election district.

Article 11

At least one woman must be among the first three nominees on the list and at least two women must be among the first six nominees on the list and so on until the end of the list.

Article 12

Seats allotted to an entity or coalition shall be awarded to candidates in accordance with the order of the names on the list.

Article 13

Seats shall be awarded to candidates and not political entities. No political entity may withdraw from a candidate the seat awarded to him.

Article 14

First: If a member of the House loses his seat for any reason he shall be replaced by the next candidate on the list according to the order on the list.

Second: If the vacant seat belonged to a woman, it is not necessary that the woman be replaced by a woman unless not doing so would affect the percentage of women's representation.

Third: If the vacant seat belongs to a political entity composed of one person or an entity that has no more candidates, the seat shall be allotted to another candidate from another political entity that obtained the minimum number of votes specified for obtaining a seat, otherwise, the seat shall remain vacant.

Chapter Four
Electoral districts

Article 15

First: The House of Representatives shall be composed of 275 members, 230 seats shall be distributed to the electoral districts and 45 of them shall be distributed as compensatory seats.

Second: Each governorate is one electoral district in accordance with official borders and shall be allotted a number of seats proportional to the number of registered voters in the governorate in accordance with the elections of January 30, 2005 "based on the public distribution list."

Article 16

Seats allotted to electoral districts shall be allocated to entities through the system of proportional representation and in accordance with the following procedures:

1. The total number of valid votes in the district shall be divided by the number of seats allotted to the district to obtain "the election quota."
2. The total number of votes obtained by each entity shall be divided by "the election quota" to determine the number of the seats to be allocated to each entity.
3. The remaining seats shall be allocated by the method of the largest remainders.

Article 17

The compensatory seats shall be distributed as follows:

1. The total number of valid votes in Iraq shall be divided by the number of the seats in the House of Representatives, to obtain the "national average."
2. The total number of votes obtained by each entity shall be divided by the "national average" to determine the number of seats allotted to it.
3. Compensatory seats shall first be allocated to entities which did not obtain representation in the election districts, but that obtained at least the national average of votes.
4. The remaining seats shall be distributed to the entities that have been allocated seats in the electoral districts based on ratio of the number of its votes to the total votes.

Article 18

Political entities shall present lists of its nominees for occupying the compensatory seats.

Article 19

Iraqis outside of Iraq shall vote in polling centres designated by the Independent Electoral Commission of Iraq and the votes will be counted on the national level.

Chapter Five
Media campaign

Article 20

The election campaign shall be free in accordance with provisions of this law, and candidates may commence their campaigns from the date of nomination and continue to the day immediately preceding the date designated for holding the election.

Article 21

Organizing electoral meetings in any building occupied by ministries and various government offices shall be prohibited.

Article 22

The use of any official government emblem in meetings, advertisements or electoral leaflets and in all types of written and drawn materials that are used in the electoral media campaign shall be prohibited.

Article 23

Local authorities and government employees may not conduct the media campaign for the interest of any candidate.

Article 24

Defaming any candidate or inciting sectarianism, religious bigotry, tribalism or regionalism among the citizens during the political campaign is prohibited.

Article 25

Presenting gifts, donations or any other assistance or promises thereof by any candidate for the purpose of influencing the voters shall be prohibited.

Article 26

Publishing or posting or placing of any advertisement or leaflet or poster including pictures, photographs or writing is prohibited, except at locations for such purposes designated by the local council and municipalities.

Chapter Six
Election Offences

Article 27

Any of the following acts committed by any person constitutes an electoral offence:

- a. Voting more than once.
- b. Impersonating, or using the name of another person for the purpose of voting.
- c. Nominating oneself in more than one district or on more than one list.
- d. Carrying a firearm, or any other instrument that threatens security in any polling centre on the day of the election.

e. Entering an election or tally centre by force to influence the election process or to inflict harm on any of the election officials.

f. Impeding the freedom of election or hampering the election process.

g. Tampering with any of the voting boxes, counting sheets or ballots or stealing any of these boxes, sheets or ballots or destroying them or conducting any act with the intention of affecting the integrity of and secrecy of the election.

h. Committing any prohibited act stipulated in Chapter Five of this law.

Chapter Seven
Final Provisions

Article 28

Order No. 96 of year 2004 "the elections law" is repealed.

Article 29

The Independent Electoral Commission of Iraq has the right to issue regulations and instructions necessary for the implementation of this law.

Article 30

This law shall enter in force as of the date of its issuance and shall be published in the official gazette.

Reasons for the Law

The existing Election Law number (96) of the year 2004 was enacted by the Transitional Coalition Authority in a historical period with its special circumstances. The goal of the law was to establish a National Assembly whose principal task was to prepare a draft constitution. The Law was based on a system which considered Iraq as one electoral district. This system was suitable in its time.

3. POLITICAL PARTIES LAW

COALITION PROVISIONAL AUTHORITY ORDER NUMBER 97
POLITICAL PARTIES AND ENTITIES LAW

CPA/ORD/7 June 2004/97*

Pursuant to my authority as Administrator of the Coalition Provisional Authority (CPA), and under the laws and usages of war, and consistent with relevant U.N. Security Council resolutions, including Resolution 1483 (2003), and Resolution 1511 (2003);

Reaffirming the right of the Iraqi people, as recognized in Resolutions 1483 and 1511, to freely determine their own political future;

Noting that the Law of Administration for the State of Iraq for the Transitional Period (the "TAL") provides for the Iraqi people to choose their government through genuine and credible elections to be held by the end of December 2004 if possible and, in any event, no later than 31 January 2005;

---

* Available at http://www.cpa-iraq.org/regulations/20040615_CPAORD_97_Political_Parties_and_Entities_Law.pdf.

Determined to achieve the transitional goals of the TAL, including the drafting and ratification of a permanent constitution, and the establishment of an elected government under that constitution;

Underscoring the need for international cooperation to achieve these goals and the essential role to be played by the United Nations and other internationally recognized experts in electoral administration;

Committed to establishing an impartial and internationally recognized body of Iraqi professionals and expert advisors to coordinate and oversee genuine and credible elections in Iraq;

Having consulted extensively with the representatives of the United Nations and benefited from their consultations with the Governing Council and a broad cross section of Iraqis, I hereby promulgate the following:

Section 1
Purpose

This Order forms part of the legal framework for genuine and credible elections that fairly reflects Iraq's rich diversity of political thought by encouraging and impartially regulating the development of vibrant political entities across Iraq.

Section 2
Recognition of Political Entities

1) A "political entity" means an organization, including a political party, of eligible voters who voluntarily associate on the basis of common ideas, interests or views, for the purpose of articulating interests, obtaining influence and having their representatives elected to public office, so long as that organization of eligible voters is officially certified as a political entity by the Independent Electoral Commission of Iraq ("Commission"). A "political entity" also means an individual person who intends to stand for election to public office, so long as the individual person is officially certified as a political entity by the Commission.

2) The Commission shall establish regulations that govern the certification and decertification of political entities. Such regulations shall include the total number of eligible voters — as measured by signatures, personal marks, or other identifiable means — required for certification as a political entity, provided that the total number of eligible voters required for certification of organizations or individual persons shall not exceed 500.

Section 3
Status and Treatment of Political Entities

1) Each political entity, except certified individuals, shall become, upon certification, a distinct legal entity in Iraq, unless it already had such status.

2) As distinct legal entities, political entities shall be capable of owning, leasing or having legal tenure of property, entering into contracts, and conducting transactions. Political entities shall enjoy any additional legal entitlement or protection provided by the Commission through regulations, rules, procedures, and decisions.

3) All political entities, including certified individual persons, are equal before the law, and shall be treated equally at all times by all levels of government in Iraq.

4) No organization or group of individuals may offer candidates for elections in Iraq unless certified as a political entity by the Commission. No individual person may stand for election in Iraq unless certified as a political entity by the Commission.

Section 4
Recognition of Common Principles

1) Political entities will be bound by regulations, rules, procedures, and decisions promulgated by the Commission.

2) The Commission will duly establish actions and omissions that are electoral offenses and subject to sanction. Sanction for electoral offenses may include, without limitation, injunction, financial penalty, public notice, certification suspension and decertification. Such offenses and sanctions shall be in addition to criminal offenses set forth in Iraqi law.

3) The following principles shall apply to all political entities in Iraq and shall be incorporated into and implemented by the Commission's regulations governing political entities:

a) No political entity may have or be associated with an armed force, militia or residual element as defined in CPA Order No. 91, Regulation of Armed Forces and Militias within Iraq (CPA/ORD/June 2004/91);

b) No political entity may be directly or indirectly financed by any armed force, militia, or residual element;

c) No political entity may put forth any candidate who fails to meet the applicable legal criteria;

d) Political entities must abide by all laws and regulations in Iraq, including public meeting ordinances, prohibitions on incitement to violence, hate speech, intimidation, and support for, the practice of and the use of terrorism;

e) Political entities must operate pursuant to the code of conduct that will be promulgated by the Commission — such code must include, among other things, the requirements in Section 4(3)(d) of this Order;

f) Political entities other than individuals certified as political entities must promulgate a statute to govern their organization and operation, including the method or process for selecting leaders and candidates, and this statute must be available to any member of the public upon request;

g) Political entities, to compete freely and openly in an election, are free to form coalitions to aggregate interests, and to build a campaign for candidates around coalitions of such interests; and

h) Political entities must strive, to the extent possible, to achieve full transparency in all financial dealings. In this regard, the Commission may issue regulations with respect to financial disclosure.

4) The Commission retains full discretion to define mechanisms for enforcing its regulations against any political entity.

Section 5
Modification and Further Regulation

All further matters regarding the regulation and certification of political entities lie with the Commission exclusively.

Section 6
Inconsistent Legislation

Any provision of Iraqi law that is inconsistent with this Order is hereby suspended to the extent of such inconsistency.

Section 7
Effective Date

The present Order shall enter into force upon the date of signature.

NOTES AND QUESTIONS

1. The Independent Electoral Commission law, passed by the CPA as Order 92, has now been replaced with very similar legislation (except for the transitional nature of the original text, and the fact that the Board of Commissioners no longer includes an *ex officio* international community member), establishing the Independent High Electoral Commission (IHEC) (*Qanun al-mufawwadiyya al-'ulya al-mustaqilla lil-intikhabat*, enacted 18 September 2007, Arabic text at http://www.parliament.iq/Iraqi_Council_ of_Representatives.php?name=articles_ajsdyawqwqdjasdba46s7a98das6 dasda7das4da6sd8asdsawewqeqw465e4qweq4wq6e4qw8eqwe4qw6eqwe4 sadkj&ffile=showdetails&sid=666).

2. On their own, these three laws tell only part of the story. Major differences distinguish the first parliamentary elections in January 2005 from the second parliamentary elections that were carried out in December 2005. The Electoral Law promulgated as CPA Order 96 was replaced with the Elections Law, No. 16 (2005), adopted by the Transitional National Assembly in September 2005. The December 2005 elections treated each province as a single electoral district as opposed to the January 2005 elections in which the entire country composed a single district. Additionally, in the December 2005 elections most parliamentary seats were divided up among the provinces according to voting population and those seats were awarded to the parties in proportion to the number of votes won. There were also 45 additional national seats up for grabs in the December 2005 elections. The main beneficiaries of these changes were the Sunnis. While these changes only modestly affected individual electoral outcomes, they significantly aided Sunni representation in the National Assembly by dampening the effect of high voter turnout rates in Shi'i- and Kurdish-dominated provinces. By increasing Sunni representation in the National Assembly and presumably forcing the prime minister to build a broader coalition to form a government, were these electoral changes likely to improve the political situation in Iraq or did they simply cement the sectarian divisions within the Iraqi government even more? Has the change from national list to district-based lists led to more consensual and inclusive politics in Iraq?

3. Will it remain for next elections to lead to more inclusive politics, considering the tainted nature of the recent election's emergence under occupation? How should it be improved? What is the relation between the Constitution and these laws? Could they be challenged constitutionally? A new "political parties and organizations law" was under discussion in the summer of 2008 and remains a subject of considerable interest.

4. How does one secure sectarian and national representation electorally? When Ayatollah Sistani originally requested one-person one-vote, the United List he sponsored turned out to be heavily sectarian. Could that have been prevented? By a quota system, as for women? By any other device? Can federalism assist?

5. The Independent High Electoral Commission of Iraq (IHEC) is the body in charge of elections in Iraq. It is supported actively by the UN mission (www.uniraq.org), as well as by the U.S.-led Coalition, which has provided the bulk of the security in the elections carried out since 2003. Several elections are planned for 2009, starting with the elections on January 31 of the councils in the governorates, except for the governorate around the disputed city of Kirkuk, and the three governorates organized in the Kurdish Region. The law governing these elections was therefore entitled "the Law of Governorates not organized into a Region." See for relevant texts the IHEC website, in Arabic (http://www.ihec.iq/Arabic/legislation.aspx) and in English (http://www.ihec.iq/content/ file/cor_laws/cor_law_36_2008_elections_law_en.pdf). The most important feature of the local elections was the governorate as a unit (elections were carried out in 14 of the 18 governorates), and the open list system, which allows for voters to pick and choose from within the lists, thereby ensuring a larger choice, but also watering down party-provided lists.

D. REVISING THE CONSTITUTION

Introduction. Four years after the Constitution was passed by referendum, major gaps remain, and the committee in charge of amendments has been working intermittently to address inconsistencies and gaps. The Committee is chaired by Sheikh Humam Hamoudi, who was also the president of the drafting committee when it produced the "final" text in July 2005. The following text provides some of the responses of the Committee to criticism, as well as the high expectations for the revisions expected.

A VIEW FROM THE CONSTITUTIONAL REVIEW COMMITTEE CHAIRMAN

Humam Hamoudi, My Perceptions on the Iraqi Constitutional Process

59 Stanford Law Review 1315-1320 (2007)

We Iraqis are a people plagued by massacres, random killing, bombs, and fiery statements — all targeting the democratic and constitutional processes.

According to my appraisal, the reason behind this is that we are swimming against the current of a backward region, which still lives in the era of early centuries where people are governed not by democracy and constitutions but by single families, parties, or individuals. We experience the crisis of our political reality in the nonexistence of democratic constitutions and elected regimes.

It was a difficult and historic birth for this new Iraq Constitution. This infant has bravely faced violent, wicked threats to its existence. With its bright, lovely face, it has challenged death, overlooking the dark smoke, bombed cars, and dark-red blood encircling us everywhere. To make matters worse, the proposed burial of this innocent constitution (the birth of dawn) has been carrying a lovely title and beautiful cover: to face and resist the occupation. By committing this crime, the wicked desire of the people of the region collaborate to murder the newborn constitution. But success will disclose the corruption and awkwardness of their regimes.

The powers of the region have used their oil revenues to tempt some pens and brains, who, instead of supporting this huge step and the new infant, attempt to deform it. These paid pens and brains call for giving up democracy; they favor authoritarian regimes and an untenable course. They pretend that the region would not accept the democracy, whilst the truth is that the rulers are the ones who are resistant to modern state democracy. Freedom, justice, equality, and participation in government are natural rights evolving with man; they are not to be granted or denied by an individual ruler.

This is what I understand concerning the birth of the constitution in Iraq and the challenges ahead.

The Charge of Nonparticipation of the Sunnis

Some mention that the problem with the Iraq Constitution lies in the nonparticipation of the Iraqi Sunnis. Let me address this charge, and then deal with the main attitudes and points of disagreements therewith.

First, were the Sunnis excluded? Or did they themselves decide not to take part, although there was an open opportunity for participation?

Obviously, and in a few words, the Sunni leadership made a political decision to reject the offer to participate, despite many requests and appeals for them to take part. It is worth mentioning that Sayed Al-Sistani — before the formation of the Iraqi United Alliance (IUA) — had sent delegations to the Iraqi Islamic Party and the (secular) Al-Iraqia list, calling upon them to join a broad, nonsectarian, national alliance to establish a founding assembly in charge of writing the constitution. But the two parties refused this invitation. Moreover, the Iraqi Islamic Party (Sunni) refused to join the national assembly. Thus, all doors were open to the Sunnis and others, but they insisted on remaining outside the train.

Only once the train began to move did they make the decision to participate. With neither electoral nor official representation, they boarded the train, some of them reserving front seats. I maintained documentation concerning their participation — active sometimes and obstructive at other times — in all committees involved with writing the constitution. Some of the Sunnis' opinions were taken into account, and their rights were maintained. But this doesn't mean that the majority is bound to consider all that is demanded by the minority; this would be adverse to democracy. I hereby challenge those who allege that the Sunnis were not given adequate opportunity by the committee to participate in writing the constitution.

Questions Addressed in the Iraqi Constitutional Process

The questions that constituted the core disputes among the Iraqi political blocs were as follows:

1) The new Iraq: shall it be one Iraq or an Iraq divided into states and provinces? A central Iraqi government or a federalist one?
2) The system of power in the new Iraq: shall it be parliamentary, presidential, or both?
3) Does the democratic system in Iraq grant one voice for every person, or shall it be a sectarian-conciliatory system?

These were the core disagreements representing the key political trends and the mode, nature, and management of power in the new Iraq.

1) *Shall it be one Iraq or an Iraq divided into states and provinces? A central Iraqi government or a federalist one?*

The administrative system of power in Iraq for over one thousand years was based on provinces and states. When the Islamic Army entered Iraq, Welayat was divided into the states of Basrah and Kofah. At the end of the Ottoman Era, it was divided into the states of Basrah, Baghdad, and Mosul. Then came the British occupation, which created a system of central power; this so-called "National Power" traced the same course for over a half century. This mode of power caused continuous infighting in Iraq, both in the north and south, political instability, and ethnic and sectarian oppression and injustice. Hence, the inclination of the elected elites and the majority of the people was to return to a system of states and provinces to get rid of the central system which caused disaster and instability.

It is worth mentioning that the Shi'a have so far outlined, via the statements of their religious references (Marajeahum) and politicians, that the power system doesn't weigh much for them. This is based on the fact that they represent the absolute (numerical) majority, and that they would lose nothing, regardless of the mode of the power system (federal or central), provided that all Iraqis get equal opportunities in their choices on equal footing. The system should be open to all Iraqis, whether it be a system of federalism or centralized power. Discrimination in terms of this right brings oppression, invites condemnation, and causes problems.

Since the Kurds decided to adopt federalism after a long struggle, then federalism, according to the equality principle, is a right to which all are entitled, unless they refuse it.

The outcome of these issues? Iraq is a unified country — an Iraq of states, not one central state. This outcome is rejected by a minority of Iraqis, as well as all neighboring countries and the Arab homeland.

They claim that federalism will lead to the breakup of Iraq! Then the question turns into a debate of intentions. The constitution does not bind federalism as an administrative system in Iraq; it only binds decentralization and gives the right to turn to federalism, once the provinces and governorates choose to do so with the participation of half of the population. If this occurs, this means that there is a strong, genuine determination and a definite desire for this transformation.

What certifies the unity of Iraq is that the oil and gas are owned by the Iraqi people and equally shared by all Iraqi individuals, regardless of the place of extraction and production. This concession encourages all governorates and provinces to maintain their linkage with the center and the federal government; this was stipulated in the constitution.

2) *The new Iraq: shall it be parliamentary, presidential, or both?*

In the light of the dictatorship experience under central power, which brought about a furious aversion to centralization and presidential systems because all matters are maintained in the custody of one president, the need has emerged to assign the same to the custody of the cabinet and prime minister, and to ensure that key decisions are enacted, controlled, and ratified by the Parliament—the representatives of people.

On the other side, there was an opinion that favored presidential power, to join Iraq under a strong presidency, directly elected by the Iraqi people and vested with broad powers to sustain the past situation and to realize the unity of Iraq.

The plurality opinion in Iraq was to get rid of the fancy of a single leader. Fear of a return to dictatorship made the most accepted view one that insisted on a parliamentary system. Although it heavily prejudices the Shi'a, it is still more feasible for Iraq and for all.

3) *Does the democratic system in Iraq grant one voice for every person, or shall it be a sectarian-conciliatory system?*

This question is still unsettled for some groups: they deny and curse sectarianism, but they simultaneously claim sectarian dues and a share in conciliation; the latter was emphasized in the constitution, along with the participation principle, representation of all components in all fields—legislation, implementation, recruitment, the army, and the judiciary—and the right of equal citizenship for all individuals. The constitution sets out guarantees to provide for participation and the equality of opportunities.

The constitution is based on the principle of individual citizenship, not on sects or ethnicity. It simultaneously asserts the intellectual, religious, and ethnic plurality of the Iraqi people and secures equality; it does not confine any positions in the state to a certain religion or sect, as is the case in many of the regions' constitutions.

The endeavor of the region, the Arabs in particular, aims at deviating from democracy—which is based on there being a voice for each person—and turning to a sectarian-conciliatory system (ethnic or sectarian), as it is in Lebanon. Therefore, some call, behind closed doors, for Taif—for an Iraq in which power is shared on a sectarian basis, as in Lebanon. This request is denied in the media by the Sunnis and all Iraqis, but it is called for in political discussions behind closed doors, and it is called for by the very same parties to safeguard the interests of the minority.

This crisis should be addressed by the Constitution Review Committee (CRC).

Questions that Remain to be Addressed in the Iraqi Constitutional Process

There are a set of detailed issues, beyond the basic or fundamental, still to be discussed:

1) Iraq's Arab identity: some are reluctant to impose an Arab identity on Iraq, as an Arab identity is sometimes thought to cause oppression against minorities and other components. This problem was addressed skillfully, but the national Arab community still asks for more.
2) The meaning of Iraqi nationality and the entitlements that should come with it.
3) The representation of component groups in the Iraqi army, and mechanisms to achieve such representation.
4) Personal status: whether there is a diversity of laws and systems for different sects, or whether a single law dominates all Iraqis.
5) Powers of provinces: how disagreements should be resolved, and how powers should be shared and defined between the states and the federal government.
6) Constitutional oversight of laws: whether decisions are consequential or precedential, as in the difference between the European (French) and American approaches.
7) Oil and gas: the extent and scope of the provinces' powers in terms of production and extraction policies.

Many of these questions might constitute points of disagreement, but they can be addressed and settled under agreed-upon laws. Thus, they cannot be considered endless problems.

In addition to answering such questions, the CRC has been tasked with a broader opportunity for discussion and dialogue. To reach these goals, it was divided into three subcommittees: the first is a political one that deals with suitable issues and proposes answers to them, such as was mentioned at the beginning of this Essay. (For example, what kind of a new Iraq do we want?) The second subcommittee is a supplementary one, which looks to supplement some aspects of the constitution, like the Federation Council and the Judicial Power. The third is a drafting subcommittee for rereading the constitution and unifying its terms, in case of any differences.

Conclusion

There is a political insistence from the U.S. government, conciliating the Arab governments and others, on the necessity of amending the constitution. In fact, there is a kind of illusion, adopted by some experts interested in the Iraqi dossier who are unfamiliar with the Iraqi situation and its daily contingencies, that the amendment of the constitution would put an end to the dissension in Iraq. To me, this is only an illusion fancied by its followers. The conflict in Iraq is an ideological, power-related one. The infidel (Takfiri) factions are rejecting the constitution in full — and even the idea of writing a constitution — as they argue that a constitution is dispensable.

The Saddamists and the remains of Saddam's Ba'ath party, backed by the Arabs, are against democracy in all forms, and the people are beyond their agenda. As was stated by an emir in the Arab region, they want Shura (consultative) representation and not a democracy of minority and majority. They are unfortunately favoring the awkward line and a return to a premodern state era. This will by no means happen, for the people, who have tasted the flavor of freedom following a century of oppression, will not recess to the humiliation of dictatorship, even if democracy entails considerable sacrifice. That is my reading of what is going on in Iraq, and Allah remains the best insider.

NOTES AND QUESTIONS

1. In a comment on this text, Professor Haider Ala Hamoudi, who is the nephew of Sheikh Humam, cast doubt on the disinterest of Shi'is in federalism on account of their majoritarian status: "The Shi'a care for federalism, because they have long lived in marginalized status, and constant oppression looms large in their theological teachings. Despite the demography, they worry about a Sunni return to power. If that were not true, it would be hard to understand see why 'Abd al-'Aziz al-Hakim, who leads the party to which Dr. Humam Hamoudi belongs, is pushing so hard for a Shi'i federal region." Does federalism also protect the majority? See Reidar Visser & Gareth Stansfield eds., An Iraq of Its Regions? Cornerstones of a Federal Democracy (2007) (a collection of useful articles on Iraqi federalism).

2. *Islamic law.* Note throughout the commentaries, and in the article by the chief Iraqi constitutional drafter, the sparsity of references to Islamic law. More important for the constituents was the prominence of Islamic jurists, especially those formed in the traditional Shi'i schools known as the *marja'iyya*, and the debate over their formal inclusion in the judiciary or in the higher political apparatus of the State, as in the Iranian Constitution. The result of the controversy was inconclusive, and it will be important to see how reference to Islamic law develops in practice, both in Parliament and in the courts. So far, the decisions of the Federal Supreme Court (see next chapter) have not addressed that issue in any noticeable manner. Iraq will no doubt constitute an additional terrain for a worldwide controversy on the place of Islamic law as reference, dominant or subsidiary, in the elaboration and interpretation of the Constitution and other laws.

3. *Style.* In March 2005, when work on the "final" Iraq Constitution was about to start, the author of this book received an official invitation from the Iraqi government to help with the drafting process. The invitation was conveyed by Professor Hasan Chalabi, a prominent Iraqi legal scholar during the long opposition to the rule of the Ba'th. Because the Cedar Revolution was in full motion in Beirut, this participation in a remarkable experience was not

possible, but a lecture, chaired at the American University of Beirut by Chalabi, was contributed to the debate on March 16. The lecture was entitled "*al fiqh fi tahaddiyat al-qanun* (Islamic law (*fiqh*) before the challenge of positive law (*qanun*))," and published in the daily *al-Nahar* on April 24, 2005. A retrospective 2006 talk at a conference on the Iraqi Constitution at the University of Pennsylvania School of Law underlined the missed occasion to take the Islamic legal tradition seriously:

> . . . Second problem. Pluralism and Islamic law. Iraqi constituents have missed the one major challenge which the world put to them: reconciling world constitutionalism and universal human rights with the Islamic legal tradition. Under the chairmanship of Hasan Chalabi, the most respected jurist of Iraq, who presides over the Islamic University in Lebanon, I suggested the need to take Islamic law seriously as the drafting process was engaged. Taking Islamic law seriously is premised on two elements: scholarship and humanism. Humanism means that any bill of rights, whether Islamic or not, must subscribe to the basic values shared on the planet. This includes the refusal of compulsion, even in religion, and the equality between men and women. Scholarship means hard work. All kinds of Islamic congresses have failed to transcend an obscurantist interpretation. . . . Obscurantism is a direct function of laziness, which gets manifested in circuitous and obsessive shortcomings. You dismiss the issue, either through general clauses, e.g. in endless discussion whether Islamic law is *a* source or *the* source of legislation; or, as in the Afghani and Iraqi constitutions, you juxtapose Western-style bills of rights and Islamic law, and brazenly proclaim that we respect everything. Well, laziness and ignorance will not work. What we need is a paradigmatic shift: take Islamic law seriously, and, as in the Ottoman Majalla, work hard on classical sources and style, also making sure that Islamic law becomes Iraqi law, I mean law that non-Muslims can identify with. Iraqi law for all Iraqis, Middle Eastern law in the region. . . . [M]ake Islamic law universal law, which it is no less capable of being than French or American law.

Mallat, Pluralism and the Iraqi Constitution: Critical Issues for All of Us, *Jurist.com*, October 12, 2006. At least no one doubts that, unlike the previous Transitional Administrative Law, the Iraqi Constitution was drafted in Arabic.

4. *Constitutional Revision.* By postponing resolution of many of the most difficult disputes facing the Iraqi government and people, the Constitution might have merely formulated those disputes in constitutional language instead of actually addressing them. Still, constitutional revision through amendment procedures provided for in the Constitution in conjunction with the Constitution Review Committee appear to be the only means available for resolving the remaining issues and challenges facing Iraq. In this regard, many observers have expressed their doubts that the CRC will be able to actually promulgate constitutional amendments. The procedural requirements for constitutional amendments in the text of the constitution set an unusually high bar. They require two-thirds approval from the Council of Representatives, approval in a national referendum, and ratification by the President. In addition to the stiff procedural requirements, the same political and sectarian dynamics that imperiled the constitution-making process make significant revisions to the constitutional text fraught with hurdles,

especially when one considers that the revision process was designed to give the major parties veto power over any proposed constitutional changes. Do the political reality in Iraq and the necessity of consensus among all the major parties make the prospect of constitutional revision as a means of addressing Iraq's remaining issues illusory? Is Humam Hamoudi right when he says that constitutional revision is besides the point, "a kind of illusion" when it comes to dealing with the fundamental problems that continue to beset Iraq? Should politics always trump law?

ENDNOTES: THE 2004 TRANSITIONAL ADMINISTRATIVE LAW (TAL)

1. TAL, Preamble: The people of Iraq, striving to reclaim their freedom, which was usurped by the previous tyrannical regime, rejecting violence and coercion in all their forms, and particularly when used as instruments of governance, have determined that they shall hereafter remain a free people governed under the rule of law.

These people, affirming today their respect for international law, especially having been amongst the founders of the United Nations, working to reclaim their legitimate place among nations, have endeavored at the same time to preserve the unity of their homeland in a spirit of fraternity and solidarity in order to draw the features of the future new Iraq, and to establish the mechanisms aiming, amongst other aims, to erase the effects of racist and sectarian policies and practices.

This Law is now established to govern the affairs of Iraq during the transitional period until a duly elected government, operating under a permanent and legitimate constitution achieving full democracy, shall come into being.

2. Article 1.

(A) This Law shall be called the "Law of Administration for the State of Iraq for the Transitional Period," and the phrase "this Law" wherever it appears in this legislation shall mean the "Law of Administration for the State of Iraq for the Transitional Period."

(B) Gender-specific language shall apply equally to male and female.

(C) The Preamble to this Law is an integral part of this Law.

Article 2.

(A) The term "transitional period" shall refer to the period beginning on 30 June 2004 and lasting until the formation of an elected Iraqi government pursuant to a permanent constitution as set forth in this Law, which in any case shall be no later than 31 December 2005, unless the provisions of Article 61 are applied.

(B) The transitional period shall consist of two phases.

(1) The first phase shall begin with the formation of a fully sovereign Iraqi Interim Government that takes power on 30 June 2004. This government shall be constituted in accordance with a process of extensive deliberations and consultations with cross-sections of the Iraqi people conducted by the Governing Council and the Coalition Provisional Authority and possibly in consultation with the United Nations. This government shall exercise authority in accordance with this Law, including the fundamental principles and rights specified herein, and with an annex that shall be agreed upon and issued before the beginning of the transitional period and that shall be an integral part of this Law.

(2) The second phase shall begin after the formation of the Iraqi Transitional Government, which will take place after elections for the National Assembly have been held as stipulated in this Law, provided that, if possible, these elections are not delayed beyond 31 December 2004, and, in any event, beyond 31 January 2005. This second phase shall end upon the formation of an Iraqi government pursuant to a permanent constitution.

Article 3.

(A) This Law is the Supreme Law of the land and shall be binding in all parts of Iraq without exception. No amendment to this Law may be made except by a three-fourths majority of the members of the National Assembly and the unanimous approval of the Presidency Council. Likewise, no amendment may be made that could abridge in any way the rights of the Iraqi people cited in Chapter Two; extend the transitional period beyond the timeframe cited in this Law; delay the holding of elections to a new assembly; reduce the powers of the regions or governorates; or affect Islam, or any other religions or sects and their rites.

(B) Any legal provision that conflicts with this Law is null and void.

(C) This Law shall cease to have effect upon the formation of an elected government pursuant to a permanent constitution.

Article 4.

The system of government in Iraq shall be republican, federal, democratic, and pluralistic, and powers shall be shared between the federal government and the regional governments, governorates, municipalities, and local administrations. The federal system shall be based upon geographic and historical realities and the separation of powers, and not upon origin, race, ethnicity, nationality, or confession.

Article 5.

The Iraqi Armed Forces shall be subject to the civilian control of the Iraqi Transitional Government, in accordance with the contents of Chapters Three and Five of this Law.

Article 6.

The Iraqi Transitional Government shall take effective steps to end the vestiges of the oppressive acts of the previous regime arising from forced displacement, deprivation of citizenship, expropriation of financial assets and property, and dismissal from government employment for political, racial, or sectarian reasons.

Article 7.

(A) Islam is the official religion of the State and is to be considered a source of legislation. No law that contradicts the universally agreed tenets of Islam, the principles of democracy, or the rights cited in Chapter Two of this Law may be enacted during the transitional period. This Law respects the Islamic identity of the majority of the Iraqi people and guarantees the full religious rights of all individuals to freedom of religious belief and practice.

(B) Iraq is a country of many nationalities, and the Arab people in Iraq are an inseparable part of the Arab nation.

Article 8.

The flag, anthem, and emblem of the State shall be fixed by law.

Article 9.

The Arabic language and the Kurdish language are the two official languages of Iraq. The right of Iraqis to educate their children in their mother tongue, such as Turcoman, Syriac, or Armenian, in government educational institutions in accordance with educational guidelines, or in any other language in private educational institutions, shall be guaranteed. The scope of the term "official language" and the means of applying the provisions of this Article shall be defined by law and shall include:

(1) Publication of the official gazette, in the two languages;

(2) Speech and expression in official settings, such as the National Assembly, the Council of Ministers, courts, and official conferences, in either of the two languages;

(3) Recognition and publication of official documents and correspondence in the two languages;

(4) Opening schools that teach in the two languages, in accordance with educational guidelines;

(5) Use of both languages in any other settings enjoined by the principle of equality (such as bank notes, passports, and stamps);

Use of both languages in the federal institutions and agencies in the Kurdistan region.

3. CHAPTER TWO — FUNDAMENTAL RIGHTS

Article 10.

As an expression of the free will and sovereignty of the Iraqi people, their representatives shall form the governmental structures of the State of Iraq. The Iraqi Transitional Government and the governments of the regions, governorates, municipalities, and local administrations shall respect the rights of the Iraqi people, including those rights cited in this Chapter.

Article 11.

(A) Anyone who carries Iraqi nationality shall be deemed an Iraqi citizen. His citizenship shall grant him all the rights and duties stipulated in this Law and shall be the basis of his relation to the homeland and the State.

(B) No Iraqi may have his Iraqi citizenship withdrawn or be exiled unless he is a naturalized citizen who, in his application for citizenship, as established in a court of law, made material falsifications on the basis of which citizenship was granted.

(C) Each Iraqi shall have the right to carry more than one citizenship. Any Iraqi whose citizenship was withdrawn because he acquired another citizenship shall be deemed an Iraqi.

(D) Any Iraqi whose Iraqi citizenship was withdrawn for political, religious, racial, or sectarian reasons has the right to reclaim his Iraqi citizenship.

(E) Decision Number 666 (1980) of the dissolved Revolutionary Command Council is annulled, and anyone whose citizenship was withdrawn on the basis of this decree shall be deemed an Iraqi.

(F) The National Assembly must issue laws pertaining to citizenship and naturalization consistent with the provisions of this Law.

(G) The Courts shall examine all disputes arising from the application of the provisions relating to citizenship.

Article 12.

All Iraqis are equal in their rights without regard to gender, sect, opinion, belief, nationality, religion, or origin, and they are equal before the law. Discrimination against an Iraqi citizen on the basis of his gender, nationality, religion, or origin is prohibited. Everyone has the right to life, liberty, and the security of his person. No one may be deprived of his life or liberty, except in accordance with legal procedures. All are equal before the courts.

Article 13.

(A) Public and private freedoms shall be protected.

(B) The right of free expression shall be protected.

(C) The right of free peaceable assembly and the right to join associations freely, as well as the right to form and join unions and political parties freely, in accordance with the law, shall be guaranteed.

(D) Each Iraqi has the right of free movement in all parts of Iraq and the right to travel abroad and return freely.

(E) Each Iraqi has the right to demonstrate and strike peaceably in accordance with the law.

(F) Each Iraqi has the right to freedom of thought, conscience, and religious belief and practice. Coercion in such matters shall be prohibited.

(G) Slavery, the slave trade, forced labor, and involuntary servitude with or without pay, shall be forbidden.

(H) Each Iraqi has the right to privacy.

Article 14.

The individual has the right to security, education, health care, and social security. The Iraqi State and its governmental units, including the federal government, the regions, governorates, municipalities, and local administrations, within the limits of their resources and with due regard to other vital needs, shall strive to provide prosperity and employment opportunities to the people.

Article 15.

(A) No civil law shall have retroactive effect unless the law so stipulates. There shall be neither a crime, nor punishment, except by law in effect at the time the crime is committed.

(B) Police, investigators, or other governmental authorities may not violate the sanctity of private residences, whether these authorities belong to the federal or regional governments, governorates, municipalities, or local administrations, unless a judge or investigating magistrate has issued a search warrant in accordance with applicable law on the basis of information provided by a sworn individual who knew that bearing false witness would render him liable to punishment. Extreme exigent circumstances, as determined by a court of competent jurisdiction, may justify a warrantless search, but such exigencies shall be narrowly construed. In the event that a warrantless search is carried out in the absence of an extreme exigent circumstance, the evidence so seized, and any other evidence found derivatively from such search, shall be inadmissible in connection with a criminal charge, unless the court determines that the person who carried out the warrantless search believed reasonably and in good faith that the search was in accordance with the law.

(C) No one may be unlawfully arrested or detained, and no one may be detained by reason of political or religious beliefs.

(D) All persons shall be guaranteed the right to a fair and public hearing by an independent and impartial tribunal, regardless of whether the proceeding is civil or criminal. Notice of the proceeding and its legal basis must be provided to the accused without delay.

(E) The accused is innocent until proven guilty pursuant to law, and he likewise has the right to engage independent and competent counsel, to remain silent in response to questions addressed to him with no compulsion to testify for any reason, to participate in preparing his defense, and to summon and examine witnesses or to ask the judge to do so. At the time a person is arrested, he must be notified of these rights.

(F) The right to a fair, speedy, and open trial shall be guaranteed.

(G) Every person deprived of his liberty by arrest or detention shall have the right of recourse to a court to determine the legality of his arrest or detention without delay and to order his release if this occurred in an illegal manner.

(H) After being found innocent of a charge, an accused may not be tried once again on the same charge.

(I) Civilians may not be tried before a military tribunal. Special or exceptional courts may not be established.

(J) Torture in all its forms, physical or mental, shall be prohibited under all circumstances, as shall be cruel, inhuman, or degrading treatment. No confession made under compulsion, torture, or threat thereof shall be relied upon or admitted into evidence for any reason in any proceeding, whether criminal or otherwise.

Article 16.

(A) Public property is sacrosanct, and its protection is the duty of every citizen.

(B) The right to private property shall be protected, and no one may be prevented from disposing of his property except within the limits of law. No one shall be deprived of his property except by eminent domain, in circumstances and in the manner set forth in law, and on condition that he is paid just and timely compensation.

(C) Each Iraqi citizen shall have the full and unfettered right to own real property in all parts of Iraq without restriction.

Article 17.

It shall not be permitted to possess, bear, buy, or sell arms except on licensure issued in accordance with the law.

Article 18.

There shall be no taxation or fee except by law.

Article 19.

No political refugee who has been granted asylum pursuant to applicable law may be surrendered or returned forcibly to the country from which he fled.

Article 20.

(A) Every Iraqi who fulfills the conditions stipulated in the electoral law has the right to stand for election and cast his ballot secretly in free, open, fair, competitive, and periodic elections.

(B) No Iraqi may be discriminated against for purposes of voting in elections on the basis of gender, religion, sect, race, belief, ethnic origin, language, wealth, or literacy.

Article 21.

Neither the Iraqi Transitional Government nor the governments and administrations of the regions, governorates, and municipalities, nor local administrations may interfere with the right of the Iraqi people to develop the institutions of civil society, whether in cooperation with international civil society organizations or otherwise.

Article 22.

If, in the course of his work, an official of any government office, whether in the federal government, the regional governments, the governorate and municipal administrations, or the local administrations, deprives an individual or a group of the rights guaranteed by this Law or any other Iraqi laws in force, this individual or group shall have the right to maintain a cause of action against that employee to seek compensation for the damages caused by such deprivation, to vindicate his rights, and to seek any other legal measure. If the court decides that the official had acted with a sufficient degree of good faith and in the belief that his actions were consistent with the law, then he is not required to pay compensation.

Article 23.

The enumeration of the foregoing rights must not be interpreted to mean that they are the only rights enjoyed by the Iraqi people. They enjoy all the rights that befit a free people possessed of their human dignity, including the rights stipulated in international treaties and agreements, other instruments of international law that Iraq has signed and to which it has acceded, and others that are deemed binding upon it, and in the law of nations. Non-Iraqis within Iraq shall enjoy all human rights not inconsistent with their status as non-citizens.

4. CHAPTER THREE—THE IRAQI TRANSITION GOVERNMENT

Article 24.

(A) The Iraqi Transitional Government, which is also referred to in this Law as the federal government, shall consist of the National Assembly; the Presidency Council; the Council of Ministers, including the Prime Minister; and the judicial authority.

(B) The three authorities, legislative, executive, and judicial, shall be separate and independent of one another.

(C) No official or employee of the Iraqi Transitional Government shall enjoy immunity for criminal acts committed while in office.

Article 25.

The Iraqi Transitional Government shall have exclusive competence in the following matters:

(A) Formulating foreign policy and diplomatic representation; negotiating, signing, and ratifying international treaties and agreements; formulating foreign economic and trade policy and sovereign debt policies;

(B) Formulating and executing national security policy, including creating and maintaining armed forces to secure, protect, and guarantee the security of the country's borders and to defend Iraq;

(C) Formulating fiscal policy, issuing currency, regulating customs, regulating commercial policy across regional and governorate boundaries in Iraq, drawing up the national budget of the State, formulating monetary policy, and establishing and administering a central bank;

(D) Regulating weights and measures and formulating a general policy on wages;

(E) Managing the natural resources of Iraq, which belongs to all the people of all the regions and governorates of Iraq, in consultation with the governments of the regions and the administrations of the governorates, and distributing the revenues resulting from their sale through the national budget in an equitable manner proportional to the distribution of population throughout the country, and with due regard for areas that were unjustly deprived of these revenues by the previous regime, for dealing with their situations in a positive way, for their needs, and for the degree of development of the different areas of the country;

(F) Regulating Iraqi citizenship, immigration, and asylum; and

(G) Regulating telecommunications policy.

Article 26.

(A) Except as otherwise provided in this Law, the laws in force in Iraq on 30 June 2004 shall remain in effect unless and until rescinded or amended by the Iraqi Transitional Government in accordance with this Law.

(B) Legislation issued by the federal legislative authority shall supersede any other legislation issued by any other legislative authority in the event that they contradict each other, except as provided in Article 54(B).

(C) The laws, regulations, orders, and directives issued by the Coalition Provisional Authority pursuant to its authority under international law shall remain in force until rescinded or amended by legislation duly enacted and having the force of law.

Article 27.

(A) The Iraqi Armed Forces shall consist of the active and reserve units, and elements thereof. The purpose of these forces is the defense of Iraq.

(B) Armed forces and militias not under the command structure of the Iraqi Transitional Government are prohibited, except as provided by federal law.

(C) The Iraqi Armed Forces and its personnel, including military personnel working in the Ministry of Defense or any offices or organizations subordinate to it, may not stand for election to political office, campaign for candidates, or participate in other activities forbidden by Ministry of Defense regulations. This ban encompasses the activities of the personnel mentioned above acting in their personal or official capacities. Nothing in this Article shall infringe upon the right of these personnel to vote in elections.

(D) The Iraqi Intelligence Service shall collect information, assess threats to national security, and advise the Iraqi government. This Service shall be under civilian control, shall be subject to legislative oversight, and shall operate pursuant to law and in accordance with recognized principles of human rights.

(E) The Iraqi Transitional Government shall respect and implement Iraq's international obligations regarding the non-proliferation, non-development, non-production, and non-use of nuclear, chemical, and biological weapons, and associated equipment, materiel, technologies, and delivery systems for use in the development, manufacture, production, and use of such weapons.

Article 28.

(A) Members of the National Assembly; the Presidency Council; the Council of Ministers, including the Prime Minister; and judges and justices of the courts may not be appointed to any other position in or out of government. Any member of the National Assembly who becomes a member of the Presidency Council or Council of Ministers shall be deemed to have resigned his membership in the National Assembly.

(B) In no event may a member of the armed forces be a member of the National Assembly, minister, Prime Minister, or member of the Presidency Council unless the individual has resigned his commission or rank, or retired from duty at least eighteen months prior to serving.

Article 29.

Upon the assumption of full authority by the Iraqi Interim Government in accordance with Article 2(B)(1), above, the Coalition Provisional Authority shall be dissolved and the work of the Governing Council shall come to an end.

CHAPTER FOUR—THE TRANSITIONAL LEGISLATIVE AUTHORITY

Article 30.

(A) During the transitional period, the State of Iraq shall have a legislative authority known as the National Assembly. Its principal mission shall be to legislate and exercise oversight over the work of the executive authority.

(B) Laws shall be issued in the name of the people of Iraq. Laws, regulations, and directives related to them shall be published in the official gazette and shall take effect as of the date of their publication, unless they stipulate otherwise.

(C) The National Assembly shall be elected in accordance with an electoral law and a political parties law. The electoral law shall aim to achieve the goal of having women constitute no less than one-quarter of the members of the National Assembly and of having fair representation for all communities in Iraq, including the Turcomans, Chaldo-Assyrians, and others.

(D) Elections for the National Assembly shall take place by 31 December 2004 if possible, and in any case no later than by 31 January 2005.

Article 31.

(A) The National Assembly shall consist of 275 members. It shall enact a law dealing with the replacement of its members in the event of resignation, removal, or death.

(B) A nominee to the National Assembly must fulfill the following conditions:

(1) He shall be an Iraqi no less than 30 years of age.

(2) He shall not have been a member of the dissolved Ba'ath Party with the rank of Division Member or higher, unless exempted pursuant to the applicable legal rules.

(3) If he was once a member of the dissolved Ba'ath Party with the rank of Full Member, he shall be required to sign a document renouncing the Ba'ath Party and disavowing all of his past links with it before becoming eligible to be a candidate, as well as to swear that he no longer has any dealings or connection with Ba'ath Party organizations. If it is established in court that he lied or fabricated on this score, he shall lose his seat in the National Assembly.

(4) He shall not have been a member of the former agencies of repression and shall not have contributed to or participated in the persecution of citizens.

(5) He shall not have enriched himself in an illegitimate manner at the expense of the homeland and public finance.

(6) He shall not have been convicted of a crime involving moral turpitude and shall have a good reputation.

(7) He shall have at least a secondary school diploma, or equivalent.

(8) He shall not be a member of the armed forces at the time of his nomination.

Article 32.

(A) The National Assembly shall draw up its own internal procedures, and it shall sit in public session unless circumstances require otherwise, consistent with its internal procedures. The first session of the Assembly shall be chaired by its oldest member.

(B) The National Assembly shall elect, from its own members, a president and two deputy presidents of the National Assembly. The president of the National Assembly shall be the individual who receives the greatest number of votes for that office; the first deputy president the next highest; and the second deputy president the next. The president of the National Assembly may vote on an issue, but may not participate in the debates, unless he temporarily steps out of the chair immediately prior to addressing the issue.

(C) A bill shall not be voted upon by the National Assembly unless it has been read twice at a regular session of the Assembly, on condition that at least two days intervene between the two readings, and after the bill has been placed on the agenda of the session at least four days prior to the vote.

Article 33.

(A) Meetings of the National Assembly shall be public, and transcripts of its meetings shall be recorded and published. The vote of every member of the National Assembly shall be recorded and made public. Decisions in the National Assembly shall be taken by simple majority unless this Law stipulates otherwise.

(B) The National Assembly must examine bills proposed by the Council of Ministers, including budget bills.

(C) Only the Council of Ministers shall have the right to present a proposed national budget. The National Assembly has the right to reallocate proposed spending and to reduce the total amounts in the general budget. It also has the right to propose an increase in the overall amount of expenditures to the Council of Ministers if necessary.

(D) Members of the National Assembly shall have the right to propose bills, consistent with the internal procedures that are drawn up by the Assembly.

(E) The Iraqi Armed Forces may not be dispatched outside Iraq even for the purpose of defending against foreign aggression except with the approval of the National Assembly and upon the request of the Presidency Council.

(F) Only the National Assembly shall have the power to ratify international treaties and agreements.

(G) The oversight function performed by the National Assembly and its committees shall include the right of interpellation of executive officials, including members of the Presidency Council, the Council of Ministers, including the Prime Minister, and any less senior official of the executive authority. This shall encompass the right to investigate, request information, and issue subpoenas for persons to appear before them.

Article 34.

Each member of the National Assembly shall enjoy immunity for statements made while the Assembly is in session, and the member may not be sued before the courts for such. A member may not be placed under arrest during a session of the National Assembly, unless the member is accused of a crime and the National Assembly agrees to lift his immunity or if he is caught *in flagrante delicto* in the commission of a felony.

CHAPTER FIVE—THE TRANSITIONAL EXECUTIVE AUTHORITY

Article 35.

The executive authority during the transitional period shall consist of the Presidency Council, the Council of Ministers, and its presiding Prime Minister.

Article 36.

(A) The National Assembly shall elect a President of the State and two Deputies. They shall form the Presidency Council, the function of which will be to represent the sovereignty of Iraq and oversee the higher affairs of the country. The election of the Presidency Council shall take place on the basis of a single list and by a two-thirds majority of the members' votes. The National Assembly has the power to remove any member of the Presidency Council of the State for incompetence or lack of integrity by a three-fourths majority of its members' votes. In the event of a vacancy in the Presidency Council, the National Assembly shall, by a vote of two-thirds of its members, elect a replacement to fill the vacancy.

(B) It is a prerequisite for a member of the Presidency Council to fulfill the same conditions as the members of the National Assembly, with the following observations:

(1) He must be at least forty years of age.

(2) He must possess a good reputation, integrity, and rectitude.

(3) If he was a member of the dissolved Ba'ath Party, he must have left the dissolved Party at least ten years before its fall.

(4) He must not have participated in repressing the *intifada* of 1991 or the Anfal campaign and must not have committed a crime against the Iraqi people.

(C) The Presidency Council shall take its decisions unanimously, and its members may not deputize others as proxies.

Article 37.

The Presidency Council may veto any legislation passed by the National Assembly, on condition that this be done within fifteen days after the Presidency Council is notified by the president of the National Assembly of the passage of such legislation. In the event of a veto, the legislation shall be returned to the National Assembly, which has the right to pass the legislation again by a two-thirds majority not subject to veto within a period not to exceed thirty days.

Article 38.

(A) The Presidency Council shall name a Prime Minister unanimously, as well as the members of the Council of Ministers upon the recommendation of the Prime Minister. The Prime Minister and Council of Ministers shall then seek to obtain a vote of confidence by simple majority from the National Assembly prior to commencing their work as a government. The Presidency Council must agree on a candidate for the post of Prime Minister within two weeks. In the event that it fails to do so, the responsibility of naming the Prime Minister reverts to the National Assembly. In that event, the National Assembly must confirm the nomination by a two-thirds majority. If the Prime Minister is unable to nominate his Council of Ministers within one month, the Presidency Council shall name another Prime Minister.

(B) The qualifications for Prime Minister must be the same as for the members of the Presidency Council except that his age must not be less than 35 years upon his taking office.

Article 39.

(A) The Council of Ministers shall, with the approval of the Presidency Council, appoint representatives to negotiate the conclusion of international treaties and agreements. The Presidency Council shall recommend passage of a law by the National Assembly to ratify such treaties and agreements.

(B) The Presidency Council shall carry out the function of commander-in-chief of the Iraqi Armed Forces only for ceremonial and protocol purposes. It shall have no command authority. It shall have the right to be briefed, to inquire, and to advise. Operationally, national command authority on military matters shall flow from the Prime Minister to the Minister of Defense to the military chain of command of the Iraqi Armed Forces.

(C) The Presidency Council shall, as more fully set forth in Chapter Six, below, appoint, upon recommendation of the Higher Juridical Council, the Presiding Judge and members of the Federal Supreme Court.

(D) The Council of Ministers shall appoint the Director-General of the Iraqi National Intelligence Service, as well as officers of the Iraqi Armed Forces at the rank of general or above. Such appointments shall be subject to confirmation by the National Assembly by simple majority of those of its members present.

Article 40.

(A) The Prime Minister and the ministers shall be responsible before the National Assembly, and this Assembly shall have the right to withdraw its confidence either in the Prime Minister or in the ministers collectively or individually. In the event that confidence in the Prime Minister is withdrawn, the entire Council of Ministers shall be dissolved, and Article 40(B), below, shall become operative.

(B) In the event of a vote of no confidence with respect to the entire Council of Ministers, the Prime Minister and Council of Ministers shall remain in office to carry out their functions for a period not to exceed thirty days, until the formation of a new Council of Ministers, consistent with Article 38, above.

Article 41.

The Prime Minister shall have day-to-day responsibility for the management of the government, and he may dismiss ministers with the approval of an simple majority of the National Assembly. The Presidency Council may, upon the recommendation of the Commission on Public Integrity after the exercise of due process, dismiss the Prime Minister or the ministers.

Article 42.

The Council of Ministers shall draw up rules of procedure for its work and issue the regulations and directives necessary to enforce the laws. It also has the right to propose bills to the National Assembly. Each ministry has the right, within its competence, to nominate deputy ministers, ambassadors, and other employees of special grade. After the Council of Ministers approves these nominations, they shall be submitted to the Presidency Council for ratification. All decisions of the Council of Ministers shall be taken by simple majority of those of its members present.

5. CHAPTER SIX — THE FEDERAL JUDICIAL AUTHORITY

Article 43.

(A) The judiciary is independent, and it shall in no way be administered by the executive authority, including the Ministry of Justice. The judiciary shall enjoy exclusive competence to determine the innocence or guilt of the accused pursuant to law, without interference from the legislative or executive authorities.

(B) All judges sitting in their respective courts as of 1 July 2004 will continue in office there-after, unless removed from office pursuant to this Law.

(C) The National Assembly shall establish an independent and adequate budget for the judiciary.

(D) Federal courts shall adjudicate matters that arise from the application of federal laws. The establishment of these courts shall be within the exclusive competence of the federal government. The establishment of these courts in the regions shall be in consultation with the presidents of the judicial councils in the regions, and priority in appointing or transferring judges to these courts shall be given to judges resident in the region.

Article 44.

(A) A court called the Federal Supreme Court shall be constituted by law in Iraq.

(B) The jurisdiction of the Federal Supreme Court shall be as follows:

(1) Original and exclusive jurisdiction in legal proceedings between the Iraqi Tran-sitional Government and the regional governments, governorate and municipal admin-istrations, and local administrations.

(2) Original and exclusive jurisdiction, on the basis of a complaint from a claimant or a referral from another court, to review claims that a law, regulation, or directive issued by the federal or regional governments, the governorate or municipal administrations, or local administrations is inconsistent with this Law.

(3) Ordinary appellate jurisdiction of the Federal Supreme Court shall be defined by federal law.

(C) Should the Federal Supreme Court rule that a challenged law, regulation, directive, or measure is inconsistent with this Law, it shall be deemed null and void.

(D) The Federal Supreme Court shall create and publish regulations regarding the procedures required to bring claims and to permit attorneys to practice before it. It shall take its decisions by simple majority, except decisions with regard to the proceedings stipulated in Article 44(B)(1), which must be by a two-thirds majority. Decisions shall be binding. The Court shall have full powers to enforce its decisions, including the power to issue citations for contempt of court and the measures that flow from this.

(E) The Federal Supreme Court shall consist of nine members. The Higher Juridical Council shall, in consultation with the regional judicial councils, initially nominate no less than eighteen and up to twenty-seven individuals to fill the initial vacancies in the aforementioned Court. It will follow the same procedure thereafter, nominating three members for each subsequent vacancy that occurs by reason of death, resignation, or removal. The Presidency Council shall appoint the members of this Court and name one of them as its Presiding Judge. In the event an appointment is rejected, the Higher Juridical Council shall nominate a new group of three candidates.

Article 45.

A Higher Juridical Council shall be established and assume the role of the Council of Judges. The Higher Juridical Council shall supervise the federal judiciary and shall administer its budget. This Council shall be composed of the Presiding Judge of the Federal Supreme Court, the presiding judge and deputy presiding judges of the federal Court of Cassation, the presiding judges of the federal Courts of Appeal, and the presiding judge and two deputy presiding judges of each regional court of cassation. The Presiding Judge of the Federal Supreme Court shall preside over the Higher Juridical Council. In his absence, the presiding judge of the federal Court of Cassation shall preside over the Council.

Article 46.

(A) The federal judicial branch shall include existing courts outside the Kurdistan region, including courts of first instance; the Central Criminal Court of Iraq; Courts of Appeal; and the Court of Cassation, which shall be the court of last resort except as provided in Article 44 of this Law. Additional federal courts may be established by law. The appointment of judges for these courts shall be made by the Higher Juridical Council. This Law preserves the qualifications necessary for the appointment of judges, as defined by law.

(B) The decisions of regional and local courts, including the courts of the Kurdistan region, shall be final, but shall be subject to review by the federal judiciary if they conflict with this Law or any federal law. Procedures for such review shall be defined by law.

Article 47.

No judge or member of the Higher Juridical Council may be removed unless he is convicted of a crime involving moral turpitude or corruption or suffers permanent incapacity. Removal shall be on the recommendation of the Higher Juridical Council, by a decision of the Council of Ministers, and with the approval of the Presidency Council. Removal shall be executed immediately after issuance of this approval. A judge who has been accused of such a crime as cited above shall be suspended from his work in the judiciary until such time as the case arising from what is cited in this Article is adjudicated. No judge may have his salary reduced or suspended for any reason during his period of service.

CHAPTER SEVEN—THE SPECIAL TRIBUNAL AND NATIONAL COMMISSIONS

Article 48.

(A) The statute establishing the Iraqi Special Tribunal issued on 10 December 2003 is confirmed. That statute exclusively defines its jurisdiction and procedures, notwithstanding the provisions of this Law.

(B) No other court shall have jurisdiction to examine cases within the competence of the Iraqi Special Tribunal, except to the extent provided by its founding statute.

(C) The judges of the Iraqi Special Tribunal shall be appointed in accordance with the provisions of its founding statute.

Article 49.

(A) The establishment of national commissions such as the Commission on Public Integrity, the Iraqi Property Claims Commission, and the Higher National De-Ba'athification Commission is confirmed, as is the establishment of commissions formed after this Law has gone into effect. The members of these national commissions shall continue to serve after this Law has gone into effect, taking into account the contents of Article 51, below.

(B) The method of appointment to the national commissions shall be in accordance with law.

Article 50.

The Iraqi Transitional Government shall establish a National Commission for Human Rights for the purpose of executing the commitments relative to the rights set forth in this Law and to examine complaints pertaining to violations of human rights. The Commission shall be established in accordance with the Paris Principles issued by the United Nations on the responsibilities of national institutions. This Commission shall include an Office of the Ombudsman to inquire into complaints. This office shall have the power to investigate, on its own initiative or on the basis of a complaint submitted to it, any allegation that the conduct of the governmental authorities is arbitrary or contrary to law.

Article 51.

No member of the Iraqi Special Tribunal or of any commission established by the federal government may be employed in any other capacity in or out of government. This prohibition is valid without limitation, whether it be within the executive, legislative, or judicial authority of the Iraqi Transitional Government. Members of the Special Tribunal may, however, suspend their employment in other agencies while they serve on the aforementioned Tribunal.

6. CHAPTER EIGHT—REGIONS, GOVERNORATES, AND MUNICIPALITIES

Article 52.

The design of the federal system in Iraq shall be established in such a way as to prevent the concentration of power in the federal government that allowed the continuation of decades of tyranny and oppression under the previous regime. This system shall encourage the exercise of local authority by local officials in every region and governorate, thereby creating a united Iraq in which every citizen actively participates in governmental affairs, secure in his rights and free of domination.

Article 53.

(A) The Kurdistan Regional Government is recognized as the official government of the territories that were administered by the that government on 19 March 2003 in the governorates of Dohuk, Arbil, Sulaimaniya, Kirkuk, Diyala and Neneveh. The term "Kurdistan Regional Government" shall refer to the Kurdistan National Assembly, the Kurdistan Council of Ministers, and the regional judicial authority in the Kurdistan region.

(B) The boundaries of the eighteen governorates shall remain without change during the transitional period.

(C) Any group of no more than three governorates outside the Kurdistan region, with the exception of Baghdad and Kirkuk, shall have the right to form regions from amongst themselves. The mechanisms for forming such regions may be proposed by the Iraqi Interim Government, and shall be presented and considered by the elected National Assembly for enactment into law. In addition to being approved by the National Assembly, any legislation proposing the formation of a particular region must be approved in a referendum of the people of the relevant governorates.

(D) This Law shall guarantee the administrative, cultural, and political rights of the Turcomans, Chaldo-Assyrians, and all other citizens.

Article 54.

(A) The Kurdistan Regional Government shall continue to perform its current functions throughout the transitional period, except with regard to those issues which fall within the exclusive competence of the federal government as specified in this Law. Financing for these functions shall come from the federal government, consistent with current practice and in accordance with Article 25(E) of this Law. The Kurdistan Regional Government shall retain regional control over police forces and internal security, and it will have the right to impose taxes and fees within the Kurdistan region.

(B) With regard to the application of federal laws in the Kurdistan region, the Kurdistan National Assembly shall be permitted to amend the application of any such law within the Kurdistan region, but only to the extent that this relates to matters that are not within the provisions of Articles 25 and 43(D) of this Law and that fall within the exclusive competence of the federal government.

Article 55.

(A) Each governorate shall have the right to form a Governorate Council, name a Governor, and form municipal and local councils. No member of any regional government, governor, or member of any governorate, municipal, or local council may be dismissed by the federal government or any official thereof, except upon conviction of a crime by a court of competent jurisdiction as provided by law. No regional government may dismiss a Governor or member or members of any governorate, municipal, or local council. No Governor or member of any Governorate, municipal, or local council shall be subject to the control of the federal government except to the extent that the matter relates to the competences set forth in Articles 25 and 43(D), above.

(B) Each Governor and member of each Governorate Council who holds office as of 1 July 2004, in accordance with the law on local government that shall be issued, shall remain in place until such time as free, direct, and full elections, conducted pursuant to law, are held, or, unless, prior to that time, he voluntarily gives up his position, is removed upon his conviction for a crime involving moral turpitude or related to corruption, or upon being stricken with permanent incapacity, or is dismissed in accordance with the law cited above. When a governor, mayor, or member of a council is dismissed, the relevant council may receive applications from any eligible resident of the governorate to fill the position. Eligibility requirements shall be the same as those set forth in Article 31 for membership in the National Assembly. The new candidate must receive a majority vote of the council to assume the vacant seat.

Article 56.

(A) The Governorate Councils shall assist the federal government in the coordination of federal ministry operations within the governorate, including the review of annual ministry plans and budgets with regard to activities in the governorate. Governorate Councils shall be funded from the general budget of the State, and these Councils shall also have the authority to increase their revenues independently by imposing taxes and fees; to organize the operations of the Governorate administration; to initiate and implement province-level projects alone or in partnership with international, and non-governmental organizations; and to conduct other activities insofar as is consistent with federal laws.

(B) The *Qada'* and *Nahiya* councils and other relevant councils shall assist in the performance of federal responsibilities and the delivery of public services by reviewing local ministry plans in the afore-mentioned places; ensuring that they respond properly to local needs and interests; identifying local budgetary requirements through the national budgeting procedures; and collecting and retaining local revenues, taxes, and fees; organizing the operations of the local administration; initiating and implementing local projects alone or in conjunction with international, and non-governmental organizations; and conducting other activities consistent with applicable law.

(C) Where practicable, the federal government shall take measures to devolve additional functions to local, governorate, and regional administrations, in a methodical way. Regional units and governorate administrations, including the Kurdistan Regional Government, shall be organized on the basis of the principle of de-centralization and the devolution of authorities to municipal and local governments.

Article 57.

(A) All authorities not exclusively reserved to the Iraqi Transitional Government may be exercised by the regional governments and governorates as soon as possible following the establishment of appropriate governmental institutions.

(B) Elections for Governorate Councils throughout Iraq and for the Kurdistan National Assembly shall be held at the same time as the elections for the National Assembly, no later than 31 January 2005.

Article 58.

(A) The Iraqi Transitional Government, and especially the Iraqi Property Claims Commission and other relevant bodies, shall act expeditiously to take measures to remedy the injustice caused by the previous regime's practices in altering the demographic character of certain regions, including Kirkuk, by deporting and expelling individuals from their places of residence, forcing migration in and out of the region, settling individuals alien to the region, depriving the inhabitants of work, and correcting nationality. To remedy this injustice, the Iraqi Transitional Government shall take the following steps:

(1) With regard to residents who were deported, expelled, or who emigrated; it shall, in accordance with the statute of the Iraqi Property Claims Commission and other measures within the law, within a reasonable period of time, restore the residents to their homes and property, or, where this is unfeasible, shall provide just compensation.

(2) With regard to the individuals newly introduced to specific regions and territories, it shall act in accordance with Article 10 of the Iraqi Property Claims Commission statute to ensure that such individuals may be resettled, may receive compensation from the State, may receive new land from the State near their residence in the governorate from which they came, or may receive compensation for the cost of moving to such areas.

(3) With regard to persons deprived of employment or other means of support in order to force migration out of their regions and territories, it shall promote new employment opportunities in the regions and territories.

(4) With regard to nationality correction, it shall repeal all relevant decrees and shall permit affected persons the right to determine their own national identity and ethnic affiliation free from coercion and duress.

(B) The previous regime also manipulated and changed administrative boundaries for political ends. The Presidency Council of the Iraqi Transitional Government shall make recommendations to the National Assembly on remedying these unjust changes in the permanent constitution. In the event the Presidency Council is unable to agree unanimously on a set of recommendations, it shall unanimously appoint a neutral arbitrator to examine the issue and make recommendations. In the event the Presidency Council is unable to agree on an arbitrator, it shall request the Secretary General of the United Nations to appoint a distinguished international person to be the arbitrator.

(C) The permanent resolution of disputed territories, including Kirkuk, shall be deferred until after these measures are completed, a fair and transparent census has been conducted and the permanent constitution has been ratified. This resolution shall be consistent with the principle of justice, taking into account the will of the people of those territories.

7. CHAPTER NINE — THE TRANSITIONAL PERIOD

Article 59.

(A) The permanent constitution shall contain guarantees to ensure that the Iraqi Armed Forces are never again used to terrorize or oppress the people of Iraq.

(B) Consistent with Iraq's status as a sovereign state, and with its desire to join other nations in helping to maintain peace and security and fight terrorism during the transitional period, the Iraqi Armed Forces will be a principal partner in the multi-national force operating in Iraq under unified command pursuant to the provisions of United Nations Security Council Resolution 1511 (2003) and any subsequent relevant resolutions. This arrangement shall last until the ratification of a permanent constitution and the election of a new government pursuant to that new constitution.

(C) Upon its assumption of authority, and consistent with Iraq's status as a sovereign state, the elected Iraqi Transitional Government shall have the authority to conclude binding international agreements regarding the activities of the multi-national force operating in Iraq under unified command pursuant to the terms of United Nations Security Council Resolution 1511 (2003), and any subsequent relevant United Nations Security Council resolutions. Nothing in this Law shall affect rights and obligations under these agreements, or under United Nations Security

Council Resolution 1511 (2003), and any subsequent relevant United Nations Security Council resolutions, which will govern the multi-national force's activities pending the entry into force of these agreements.

Article 60.

The National Assembly shall write a draft of the permanent constitution of Iraq. This Assembly shall carry out this responsibility in part by encouraging debate on the constitution through regular general public meetings in all parts of Iraq and through the media, and receiving proposals from the citizens of Iraq as it writes the constitution.

Article 61.

(A) The National Assembly shall write the draft of the permanent constitution by no later than 15 August 2005.

(B) The draft permanent constitution shall be presented to the Iraqi people for approval in a general referendum to be held no later than 15 October 2005. In the period leading up to the referendum, the draft constitution shall be published and widely distributed to encourage a public debate about it among the people.

(C) The general referendum will be successful and the draft constitution ratified if a majority of the voters in Iraq approve and if two-thirds of the voters in three or more governorates do not reject it.

(D) If the permanent constitution is approved in the referendum, elections for a permanent government shall be held no later than 15 December 2005 and the new government shall assume office no later than 31 December 2005.

(E) If the referendum rejects the draft permanent constitution, the National Assembly shall be dissolved. Elections for a new National Assembly shall be held no later than 15 December 2005. The new National Assembly and new Iraqi Transitional Government shall then assume office no later than 31 December 2005, and shall continue to operate under this Law, except that the final deadlines for preparing a new draft may be changed to make it possible to draft a permanent constitution within a period not to exceed one year. The new National Assembly shall be entrusted with writing another draft permanent constitution.

(F) If necessary, the president of the National Assembly, with the agreement of a majority of the members' votes, may certify to the Presidency Council no later than 1 August 2005 that there is a need for additional time to complete the writing of the draft constitution. The Presidency Council shall then extend the deadline for writing the draft constitution for only six months. This deadline may not be extended again.

(G) If the National Assembly does not complete writing the draft permanent constitution by 15 August 2005 and does not request extension of the deadline in Article 61(F) above, the provisions of Article 61(E), above, shall be applied.

Article 62.

This law shall remain in effect until the permanent constitution is issued and the new Iraqi government is formed in accordance with it.

JUDICIARY AND THE RULE OF LAW

Introduction. With the fall of Baghdad on April 9, 2003, Iraq entered a period of domestic instability that was increasingly marked by violence.

Among the casualties was the hope for the rapid emergence of an independent judiciary. Iraq's path to security, human rights, the rule of law, and the development of a free, secure private transactions economy depend in large part on the independence, integrity, and effectiveness of its judicial system. This was true from day one of Iraq's occupation; it is no less true half a decade hence. The search for so-called "political reconciliation" is meaningless if the violence exercised outside the monopoly of the state is not brought back to the state's exclusive fold.

After an uncertain first year, where the main preoccupation was the arrest of former leaders, collapse of law and order accelerated in April 2004, reaching a peak in Spring 2005, and continued through most of 2005-2006. In 2007, against rising domestic American pressure to withdraw from Iraq, a "surge" in troops was ordered by President Bush. Decline in violence ensued, but the verdict is still out on its long-term effectiveness (see Chapter 7 on security). Success depends in large part upon the strengthening of the Iraqi judiciary in its primary role: to secure peaceful interaction between the citizens through the rule of law.

Judges were prime targets for insurgents. Over 40 judges and hundreds of policemen on active duty or waiting in line to be recruited have been killed in targeted attacks since 2005. The Chief Justice himself, Midhat al-Mahmud, lost close members of his family in an attempt on his life. Without this stark perspective, which may be unique in modern history, the following analysis makes little sense. This story is also that of immense courage by judges, lawmakers, and the people of Iraq.

A. THE COLLAPSE OF LAW AND ORDER

In the very first week of the occupation, the looting of the Baghdad Museum, and of a large number of ministries and other administrative buildings, was an ominous signal of lawlessness. Other serious cases included the resort to violence by U.S. troops against demonstrations in Falluja in late April 2003, and the impunity of the murderers of Shi'i religious leader 'Abd al Majid al-Khu'i in Najaf on 10 April 2003.

1. "DAS LOOT"

ANNE-MARIE SLAUGHTER, DAS LOOT
_____

N.Y. Times, Mar. 16, 2008

In April 2003, just after American troops secured Baghdad, Iraqis looted the Iraqi national museum. American soldiers nearby made no effort to stop them, much less provide a guard. . . .

This failure was simply a "matter of priorities," according to Gen. Richard Myers, chairman of the Joint Chiefs of Staff. Defense Secretary Donald Rumsfeld thought it was a "stretch" to attribute the theft and destruction of priceless Mesopotamian artifacts to "any defect in the war plan."

Our government knew how to destroy but not how to build. We had toppled a regime, and in coming months we would dismantle Saddam Hussein's bureaucracy and disband his army. But we did so with absolutely no understanding of how to build a liberal democracy, or even a stable, rights-regarding government with broad popular support.

. . . Protecting the symbols of a common and proud heritage is Democracy Building 101 — at least for anyone who understood anything about Iraqi history and culture.

Americans are still living with the aftermath of this ignorance, and we will be for decades to come. In 2003 and 2004, experts debated whether it would take one year or three to rebuild Iraq. Now we debate whether it will take 10 to 15 years or whether it can be done at all.

Those broken and stolen statues from the museum are the enduring symbols of what has gone so wrong. They were easy to smash, so hard to repair.

NOTES AND QUESTIONS

1. In one of the plans for the post-Saddam era, prepared by Tom Warrick, State Department Future of Iraq Project coordinator, the Baghdad museum was specifically designated as an important site for protection. The plan became one of the victims of U.S. inter-departmental wrangling.

   "Stuff happens!" Defense Secretary Rumsfeld exclaimed at a Pentagon briefing on April 11, 2003, when asked about the looting. "But in terms of what's going on in that country, it is a fundamental misunderstanding to see those images over, and over, and over again, of some boy walking out with a vase and say, 'Oh, my goodness, you didn't have a plan.' That's nonsense. They know what they're doing, and they're doing a terrific job. And it's untidy, and freedom's untidy, and free people are free to make mistakes and commit crimes and do bad things. They're also free to live their lives and do wonderful things, and that's what's going to happen here.

   Thomas Ricks, Fiasco 136 (2006). If the Defense Secretary's argument about "the freedom to commit crimes" is questionable, how about his attempt to minimize the importance of the museum looting from the larger perspective of the new era of freedom after Saddam Hussein's brutal reign over three decades? More problematic is the question of what to do about the sudden outburst immediately after the capture of Baghdad: if the U.S. army had orders to shoot looters, how would human casualties have appeared to Iraqis and to the world in comparison to the brutality of the regime just removed?

2. It took several months for the effects of "shock and awe" to subside and for the insurgency to take root. More than the museum looting, precursors of the structural deficiency in the rule of law were apparent in two events leading to violent deaths north and south of Baghdad, in the Sunni-dominant city of Falluja and in the Shi'i Holy City of Najaf.

3. A determined effort was made by Americans and Iraqis to find the Museum's stolen artifacts, with a measure of success. See by a central protagonist of this recovery, Matthew Bogdanos, *Thieves of Baghdad* (2005).

4. By the end of April 2003, news came of demonstrations in Falluja. On April 29, Al-Jazeera television station reported that in response to a call from the Imams in the city's mosques, a group of Iraqis came out to protest for the removal of American forces from Iraq, and that the Americans fired on the protesters, killing ten and wounding seven.

2. VIOLENT RESPONSE: THE U.S. ARMY IN AL-FALLUJA

Violent Response: The U.S. Army in al-Falluja

Human Rights Watch report, June 2003

Since the government of Saddam Hussein was overthrown in mid-April, U.S. forces have encountered hostility in some quarters, and increasing armed resistance from individuals or small groups, particularly in central Iraq. One site of continued armed clashes is the mid-sized desert city of al-Falluja, sixty kilometers (thirty-five miles) west of Baghdad.

Al-Falluja had been spared the ground war in March and April 2003, but had come under air bombardment. Local resentment was evident from the day U.S. soldiers from the 82nd Airborne Division arrived in al-Falluja, on April 23. The key turning point came five days later, on April 28, when a demonstration calling for the soldiers to leave turned violent. According to protesters, U.S. soldiers fired on them without provocation, killing seventeen people and wounding more than seventy. According to the U.S. military, the soldiers returned precision fire on gunmen in the crowd who were shooting at them.

At a protest in town two days later, a U.S. military convoy opened fire killing three persons and wounding another sixteen. Again the military said it had come under armed attack, which the protesters denied. That same night, grenades were thrown into a U.S. base in al-Falluja, injuring seven U.S. soldiers. An attack a month later, on May 28, killed two U.S. soldiers and wounded nine. This and other attacks in late May and early June killed four U.S. soldiers and wounded twenty-one.

This report documents these first two violent incidents of April 28 and 30, the facts of which continue to be deeply contested by both sides. The conclusions of Human Rights Watch's investigation challenge some of the assertions made by the U.S. military. Significantly, Human Rights Watch did not find conclusive evidence of bullet damage on the school where U.S. soldiers were based during the first incident, placing into serious question the assertion that they had come under fire from individuals in the crowd. In contrast, the buildings across the street facing the school had extensive evidence of multi-caliber bullet impacts that were wider and more sustained than would have been caused by the "precision fire" with which the soldiers maintain they responded, leading to the civilian casualties that day. Witness testimony and ballistics evidence suggest that U.S. troops responded with excessive force to a perceived threat.

In the second incident on April 30, protesters admitted throwing rocks, and one broke the window of a U.S. military vehicle, injuring a soldier. But there was no clear evidence of shooting from the crowd, again suggesting that U.S. forces responded with disproportionate force.

While none of the Iraqi interviewees said there had been shooting at U.S. soldiers in either incident, and despite the lack of conclusive ballistics and other concrete evidence indicating otherwise, it is possible that agents provocateurs in the crowds did fire at U.S. troops. Soldiers from the 82nd Airborne Division alleged that rounds were whipping over their heads; in military terms, they had come under "effective fire." For reasons described in this report, and as attacks on U.S. soldiers since April 28 show, al-Falluja was a hostile place for U.S. troops.

The report also highlights some of the difficulties of putting a powerful combat force in a law enforcement role. The paratroopers of the 82nd Airborne had come straight from battle, having suffered casualties. Regardless of the possible responsibility of the individuals involved in the shooting that led to the killing of up to twenty and wounding of scores of others, one conclusion is inescapable. U.S. military and political authorities who placed combat-ready soldiers in the highly volatile environment of al-Falluja without adequate law enforcement training, translators, and crowd control devices followed a recipe for disaster. They entered a town that had to some extent been traumatized by the air campaign, and they apparently had not adapted to the post-conflict role of policing, crowd-control and community relations they were required to perform. The soldiers and commanders of the 82nd Airborne in al-Falluja lacked some of the key tools for an effective law enforcement mission. Notably, they had no teargas or other forms of non-lethal crowd control, although riot control gear had reportedly been given to other units heading north. In addition, the commanders told Human Rights Watch that they lacked enough translators, and thus the ability to communicate effectively with the community they were now policing.

Under international humanitarian law, the United States, as the occupying power in Iraq, has the obligation to restore and ensure public order and safety, in conformity with international human rights standards. When engaged in law enforcement functions, such as crowd control, law enforcement standards should govern their response. The United Nations Basic Principles on the Use of Force and Firearms, by Law Enforcement Officials applies to all those who exercise police powers, particularly the powers of arrest and detention, including soldiers when they are acting in this capacity. Law enforcement officials may use lethal force only "when strictly unavoidable in order to protect life." When doing so, they must: act with restraint and in proportion to the seriousness of the offence and the legitimate objective to be achieved; minimize injury; and respect and preserve human life.

Human Rights Watch's findings of excessive use of force by U.S. troops point to the need for a full, independent and impartial investigation of the al-Falluja incidents by U.S. authorities. Such an investigation should aim to determine the full circumstances that led to the killing of as many as twenty Iraqi civilians in these two incidents, and to hold accountable anyone found to have violated international humanitarian law. Human Rights Watch's own findings are not a substitute for a full independent and impartial investigation, which would have access to classified evidence, such as communications between U.S. commanders, debriefings of the soldiers involved and other intelligence sources. An investigation should also focus on the possible role of provocateurs within the crowd, in order to determine their responsibilities in the incidents.

NOTES AND QUESTIONS

1. How could the U.S. army provide for law enforcement without changing its character of "fighting force"? In the absence of an Iraqi transitional government, which could have provided a first line of responsibility, one option was offered by the Democratic Iraq Initiative (DII), launched in late December 2002: deploy human rights monitors in a way similar to the "embedded" journalists. Neither the U.S. government nor established human rights organizations followed up, despite the expressed interest in the DII proposal by senior Defense Department officials and Amnesty International's secretary-general. The original DII statement called for "the immediate resignation of Saddam Hussein, whose rule over three decades has been a nightmare for Iraq and the Arab world, [a]s the only way to avoid more violence and build the rule of democracy in Baghdad." It also called "for the stationing across Iraq of human rights monitors from the United Nations and the Arab League, to oversee the peaceful transition of power in the country." (See Khaled Yacoub Oweis, Arab Intellectuals Seek Saddam Resignation, *Reuters.com*, Jan. 2, 2003.) In a letter to the President of the Security Council on February 11, Amnesty International's Secretary-General Irene Khan formally called for the stationing of human rights monitors in Iraq: "Human rights monitors in Iraq would make a significant contribution to the protection of human rights not only in the current circumstances but also in any future scenario. . . . Their mandate should cover human rights abuses in Iraqi territory by any party, and their reports should provide the United Nations system with authoritative information on the human rights situation and advice on remedial action." On DII, see also Chapter 5 on international law, on alternatives to war, and the full dossier that is available at http://mallat.com/articles/iraq%20DII.htm.

2. A more natural route was the imposition of a military curfew in restless zones like Baghdad and Falluja. The curfew was to be used effectively by the Iraqi government after 2005:

   > Millions of Iraqis had headed to the polls in January 2005 for the country's first democratic election in decades. In Baghdad, in the Kurdish north, and in the Shiite south, the day was a stunning triumph. Men and women waved ink-stained fingers to show that they had voted. There was far less violence than expected, largely because American and Iraqi troops put most cities under a three-day curfew, preventing vehicular traffic and searching pedestrians at random checkpoints. One Iraqi remarked to me that American soldiers should have done the same thing when they arrived in April 2003.

   Rajiv Chandrasekaran, Imperial Life in the Emerald City 335 (2006).

3. As the symbol of the rising Sunni insurgency, Falluja would dominate the news for another two years. In the aftermath of a gruesome display of joy upon the assassination of four Blackwater "contractors" on March 31, 2004,

a massive assault was launched to retake the city. It ended in a compromise which left a large number of insurgents active inside Falluja. In November and December 2004, Americans fought for six weeks, with the political assent of the Iraqi transitional government, to take over Falluja again. For an in-depth account of the battle, see Bing West, No True Glory: A Frontline Account of the Battle for Fallujah (2005). On the "security contractors" in Iraq, see Jeremy Scahill, Blackwater (2007), and Chapter 7 about immunity from Iraqi criminal law.

4. Perhaps one of the most atrocious and underestimated events of the early failure of the rule of law occurred in Najaf, just one day after American troops took Baghdad in 2003, on April 10, with the assassination of 'Abdel-Majid Khoei (Khu'i) by supporters of Muqtada Sadr.

3. "A MURDER IN THE MOSQUE AND BEYOND"

CHIBLI MALLAT, A MURDER IN THE MOSQUE AND BEYOND

The Daily Star (Beirut, Lebanon), Aug. 15, 2003

Perhaps not since the assassination of Archbishop Thomas Becket in Canterbury Cathedral in 1170 did history record a similar event. On April 10, 2003, the day after Iraq was freed from the rule of deposed dictator Saddam Hussein, Sayyed Abdel-Majid al-Khoei, the son of the late Grand Ayatollah Abu al-Qassem al-Khoei, was stabbed to death in the Sahn Sharif—the mosque of Imam Ali in Najaf and the holiest shrine in Shiite Islam. According to witnesses, his assassins then dragged his corpse for five hundred yards into the street.

Becket's murder was immortalized in T.S. Eliot's play *Murder in the Cathedral*. Khoei's murder in Ali's mosque conjured up fresher, more pressing Iraqi memories: On July 14, 1958, the entire royal family of Iraq was killed. The following day, Prime Minister Nuri al-Said, the strongman of the regime, was discovered wearing a woman's disguise by a crowd and set upon. His body was cut to pieces, and what was left of it dragged through the streets of Baghdad.

Iraqis have a word for this ugly practice: *sahl*. All those who suffered at the hands of Saddam Hussein and his colleagues agreed that *sahl* would not occur again. Yet Khoei's killing took place in the same abhorrent way. Three people were eventually arrested, but all have since been released. Those who committed the crime remain at large, with impunity remaining the hallmark of the new Iraq. Eyewitness accounts point to people close to the young cleric Muqtada al-Sadr, whose father Ayatollah Mohammed Sadeq al-Sadr and two brothers were killed in 1999 in a car accident widely believed to have been engineered by the Baath regime. The assassination of Khoei was more troubling since Shiite clerics, including those in post-revolutionary Iran, have shied away from killing their colleagues since 1909, when an Iranian cleric, Ayatollah Fadlallah Nuri, was hanged in a murky scheme in which other clerics took part.

I hope Muqtada Sadr has nothing to do with Khoei's *sahl*, as he has insistently repeated since April 10. For Sadr to remove that black cloud hanging over his head, however, he needs to clear his name in the face of many concordant accounts suggesting that his close supporters caused Khoei's death (nor have recent accusations that Sadr is intimidating Najafi clerics been reassuring). This will happen only when a full and serious judicial investigation is carried out, preferably by Iraqis under international supervision.

In the dark days when we stood by the Iraqi opposition, one unfailing premise was, in Eliot's words, that such "sordid particulars" as the murder in the mosque "would not prevent the eternal design to appear," and that impunity in Iraq would cease. I spoke to an American audience in Washington soon after the killing of Mohammed Sadeq Sadr, and supported accountability for his murder and those of countless others by Saddam Hussein's brutal system. It is one of the great indignities of the US that it turned its back on the relentless suffering of Iraqis during former President Bill Clinton's eight years in power. Now that the policy has been reversed and Saddam Hussein is gone, those practices attached to his name cannot be allowed to continue. Peace can only be restored if justice is enforced, otherwise the Saddamist system of impunity will persist, and all talk of democracy and stability will remain empty.

A judicial investigation into Khoei's killing remains the most pressing task of Iraq's governing council, whether in memory of the late Ayatollahs Mohammed Baqer al-Sadr and Mohammed Sadeq Sadr, or to reaffirm the respect for human life accepted since 1909 by the archbishops of Shiite Islam.

Sahl should never again go unpunished.

NOTES AND QUESTIONS

1. An earlier version of the article was published in Arabic in the Lebanese daily *al-Nahar* on April 23, 2003. Despite ample evidence of his responsibility, Muqtada Sadr was not investigated after the assassination of Khu'i until much later. But the assassination closed the door to Sadr's co-option onto the Iraq Governing Council, the first Iraqi government, because it was made impossible by Sadr's association with the murder of Khu'i. Resentment towards the former exile Iraqis in government, and the mounting criticism leveled against him for Khu'i's death, led Sadr to increase his nationalist appeal and act with impunity. For more on Sadr, see Patrick Cockburn, *Muqtada* (2008).

2. An arrest warrant was eventually issued by investigative judge Ra'ed Juhi in August 2003, but no arrest was made, despite Paul Bremer's and leading Iraqis' support for it. See Bremer, My Year in Iraq 129-131 (2006). Far worse than *sahl*, which was associated with the killing of the Hashemite family and Nuri Sa'id in 1958, violence in Iraq reached magnitude and depths rarely seen in modern times, from torture in Abu Ghraib to crimes against humanity that took the lives of tens of thousands of Iraqi civilians. Would the arrest of Muqtada Sadr in April 2003 have hindered those acting with seeming impunity? Would a curfew preventing looting in Baghdad have forced a different imprint on the occupation? Would dealing with the first Falluja demonstrations in the way the U.S. police or the national guard confronts riotous

demonstrations in Los Angeles or Washington D.C. have prevented the descent into the Iraqi spiral of unpunished violence?

3. Consider whether the much-vaunted policy of national reconciliation, underlined in the next article, squares with ending impunity.

4. NATIONAL RECONCILIATION?

ALI LATIF, IRAQ: THE STATUS OF NATIONAL RECONCILIATION

Arab Reform Bulletin, March 2008, Volume 6, Issue 2*

National reconciliation has been a top priority for all concerned with aiding Iraq's path toward economic and political stability. But what exactly does it mean in the Iraqi context? Since the end of the war, several distinct and sometimes competing issues have developed, requiring meaningful dialogue among all sections of Iraq's population. The first is the administration of justice for the crimes of the Baath regime, which has not been fully addressed despite Saddam Hussein's much publicized trial and execution. The balance between meaningful justice to victims and post-war stability has yet to be struck.

The post-war picture laid bare three communities with seemingly divergent visions about their own future and that of their country. The Kurds, mindful of many years of persecution, were set on cementing their autonomy and looked toward possible independence. The previously marginalized and repressed Shi'a looked to assert their majority status and prevent a return to minority rule. The Sunna, largely in denial of the new Iraq, looked on in dread and feared retribution by the Shi'a and Kurds, a contingency that would invariably lead to the breakup of the country. Added to this are previously simmering but dormant tensions between the tribal and the urban, the religious and secular, and rich and poor that have evolved across as well as within ethnic fault-lines.

Given this complex picture, a national reconciliation initiative amidst a brutal insurgency and escalating sectarian conflict was never going to be easy. Prime Minister Maliki's National Reconciliation Framework, launched in June 2006, attempted to address issues such as the de-Baathification law, disarmament of the militias, and reform of public institutions. The twenty-four point plan was right in addressing issues across all levels of Iraqi society from the political elite to the grass-roots in order to forge genuine national reconciliation. Two years on, however, even in a much improved security context, progress has been fitful and disjointed. The National Unity Government, designed to bring all factions into the fold, fell victim to walkouts from various parties, leaving only the United Iraqi Alliance and Kurdish parties.

Nevertheless the Iraqi parliament, despite the disputes and scarce attendance, has managed to pass several vital pieces of legislation that will aid the process of national reconciliation; namely those of de-Baathification and the national budget. The recent impasse in legislation on provincial powers is certainly a setback, but the current lack of consensus should not take away

---

*Available at http://www.carnegieendowment.org/files/Latif-march2008.pdf.

from the fact that parliament is still the venue for this debate and the ultimate vehicle for national reconciliation.

While the political process in Baghdad has been frustratingly slow, reconciliation amongst the political elite is at an acceptable level. This top-down approach, however, has failed to initiate reconciliation at the lower levels. Ordinary Iraqis faced with daily hardships feel far removed from the political elite in the Green Zone. Ministries and public bodies still function largely as they did during the previous regime, with patronage networks that now run along ethnic rather than Baath party lines. The numerous cases of sectarian bias from the police and army have further eroded public trust.

The altered composition of the previously mixed areas in and around Baghdad has been the most visible breakdown in communal relations. Despite the dramatic decrease in violence, people are reluctant to return to their homes, fearing they will find them occupied and wary of turning to authorities that run along sectarian lines. The situation of refugees is of grave concern, incubating resentment that will add to the difficulty of national reconciliation. The decision of tribes in central Iraq to stand against al-Qaeda and work with U.S. forces has greatly assisted in improving security. These armed militias, however, are less cooperative with the Iraqi army and government, raising concerns about their future within the Iraqi state. Similarly, the ceasefire declared by Shi'i leader Muqtada al-Sadr has allowed Iraqi and U.S. forces to target the rogue elements of the Mahdi Army. But the issue of the Mahdi Army itself, as well as of other militias, remains unresolved — as illustrated by the collective sigh of relief that followed al-Sadr's recent decision to extend his ceasefire.

In addressing the major challenges to national reconciliation that persist beneath the more-visible political agreements in Baghdad, the judiciary will have a pivotal role. A robust and independent judiciary that has the necessary legal framework and law enforcement partners will be in the best position to address sources of sectarian and ethnic tension in public institutions, disputes over property, and the dismantling of the militias.

NOTES AND QUESTIONS

1. Is national reconciliation possible without an amnesty law? How can amnesty be reconciled with ending impunity? Can the judiciary have a "pivotal role," as suggested at the end of this article? Can an amnesty fall short of releasing those leading figures of the former regime still being tried before the High Criminal Court? See section C. below on the Tribunal.

2. Reform of the judiciary is easier said than done. It is a bland understatement that the judiciary under Saddam Hussein did not work well. Transitional solutions were necessary, but they were hard to apply in a situation of occupation, with no indigenous government and a disbanded army. Still, the rule of law can only be built on and by an independent and effective judiciary. The next sections look at the multiple layers of difficulties, and the choices available, from the overhauling of the hollow shell of the judiciary under Saddam Hussein to the Special Tribunal set up to judge him and his associates for crimes against humanity.

B. REFORMING THE JUDICIARY

1. THE IRAQI JUDICIARY: AN OVERVIEW

More than any other place on earth, Iraq has an unusually deep legal tradition that can be documented back to the second millennium before Christ. Arguably the first court record preserved by humankind ever is that of the Nippur Homicide trial. Defendant is Nin-Dada, the wife of Lu-Inana, who was killed by a number of other male defendants. They told Nin-Dada they had committed the murder. "Nin-Dada, opened not her mouth, covered it up." Was she also guilty? The few lines of the surviving clay tablet tell a story of the state acting as plaintiff, a judicial process with possibly an appeal going to an assembly of sages/judges in Nippur, and a defendant whose argument is made in court. The majority of those who argue in court consider her guilty. But one soldier and one gardener "took the floor and stated: 'Did Nin-Dada in fact kill her husband? What did the woman do that she put to death?'" The Assembly of Nippur, the court, saw otherwise: "She heard that her husband had been killed, so why did she keep silent about him? It is she who killed her husband; her guilt is greater than the men who killed him." They were all "given up to be killed. Verdict of the Assembly of Nippur." The text of the judgment can be found in Nicholas Postgate, Early Mesopotamia 278 (1992). The decision was originally published and discussed by Thorkild Jakobsen, *An Ancient Mesopotamian Trial for Homicide*, in Studia Biblica et Orientalia III: Oriens Antiquus 130-150 (1959).

From the trial of Nin-Dada to the trial of Saddam Hussein, the history of the Iraqi judiciary is understandably patchy. During the Islamic classical age, the role of the *qadi* (judge) was central to society, but we have no actual cases extant from Iraq, although remarkable progress has been made in the past 20 years, especially over decisions rendered during the Ottoman Empire and now even earlier. See Mallat, Introduction to Middle Eastern Law 61-89 (2007). In Iraq, work is developing on case law from the 19th-century Ottoman registers which should shed important light on a crucial period that sees the passage from a single *qadi* court to a system of appeal eventually ending in the Court of Cassation in Istanbul.

The British occupation during World War I, then the American occupation in 2003, constitute landmark moments for the Iraqi legal system. The Constitution of 2005 establishes a number of judicial institutions in a special section on "the judicial authority" (Arts. 87-101), including most prominently the "Higher Juridical [Judicial] Council, the Federal Supreme Court, the Federal Court of Cassation, the Public Prosecution Department, the Judiciary Oversight Commission, and other federal courts that are regulated in accordance with the law" (Art. 90); in addition to the State Council (*majlis al-shura*, the higher administrative court, to be eventually renamed *majlis al-dawla*, Art. 101) and the courts established in the region, so far only in Kurdistan. Articles 87 and 88 emphatically underline the independence of the judiciary (Art. 87) and of the judges (Art. 88).

In the context of 20th-century legal history, two characteristics of the judicial system should be underlined. The first is the wish to separate the judiciary to the largest extent possible from the executive branch, especially the Minister of Justice. The second is the superimposition over a largely civil law system—institutions and concepts drawn from the U.S. experience, especially the U.S. Supreme Court. Such hallmarks of criminal law (the investigative judge, who has no equivalent in the Anglo-American system), and of adminisrative law (the Higher Judicial Council, which appoints and manages most of the judiciary, and the State Council, which acts as the higher administrative court, as well as the main technical drafter of laws for the government) remain well-entrenched, but they sit uneasily with a different judicial framework drawn from the U.S. experience. The Federal Supreme Court, an important new institution, sits normally at the apex of the judiciary, but its role as final appellate court as well as its relation with the Higher Judicial Council remains ill-defined.

2. TARGETING JUDGES

The next excerpt serves as a reminder of the most difficult dimension in the pursuit of justice in Iraq: the security of judges.

JEFFREY GETTLEMAN, THE STRUGGLE FOR IRAQ: KILLINGS, ASSASSINATIONS TEAR INTO IRAQ'S EDUCATED CLASS

N.Y. Times, Feb. 7, 2004

A couple of weeks ago, Dr. Mayah, a 53-year-old political scientist and human rights advocate . . . became one of hundreds of intellectuals and mid-level administrators who Iraqi officials say have been assassinated since May in a widening campaign against Iraq's professional class.

. . . [B]y silencing urban professionals, said Brig. Gen. Mark Kimmitt, a spokesman for the occupation forces, the guerrillas are waging war on Iraq's fledgling institutions and progress itself. The dead include doctors, lawyers and judges.

. . . American and Iraqi officials say there is no tally of all the professionals assassinated. But Lt. Akmad Mahmoud, of the Baghdad police, said there had been "hundreds" of professionals killed in Baghdad.

Mr. Saadi, the Baghdad city council member who works closely with the police, estimated the number at from 500 to 1,000.

In Mosul, Yousef Khorshid, an investigative judge, and Adel al-Haddidi, head of the local lawyer's association, were killed in drive-by shootings in December. The same car was seen by witnesses in both cases.

. . . "We had a pledge, to live together and die together," Khalid, the professor's brother, said as he started to cry. What hurts most, he said, is that after all the years his brother secretly worked for democracy in Iraq, its arrival was just around the corner.

"These people are not just assassinating our brothers," he said. "They are assassinating our future."

3. STRUCTURE OF THE COURTS

The two charts below, prepared respectively by Andrew Allen and Dan Burton for this book, provide two perspectives on the court system in Iraq:

Figure 4.1   Judiciary Chart: Overall Structure, Andrew Allen

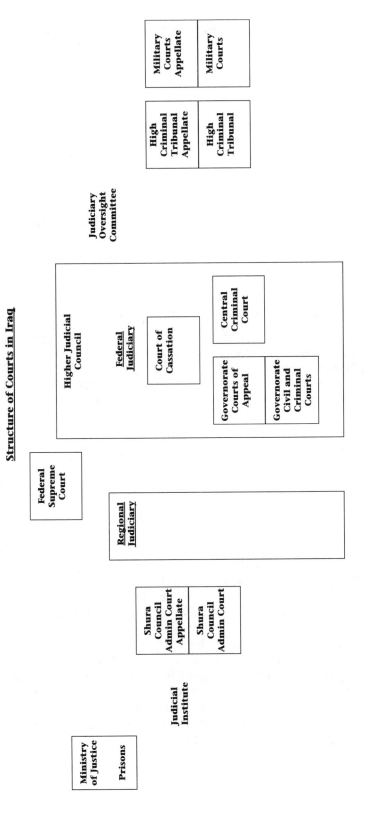

Structure of Courts in Iraq

Figure 4.2 Judiciary Chart: Governorate and Federal Courts, Dan Burton

At Governorate Level (*muhafaza*)

Civil Courts	Criminal Courts
General: Courts of first instance, (*bidaya*)	General: Investigative judges (*tahqiq*) ↓ Felony courts (*jinayat*)
Specialised: Personal status courts (*ahwal shakhsiyya*) Labor courts (*'amal*) Customs courts (*jamarik*)	Specialised: Juvenile courts (*ahdath*) Appeal courts
Appeal Courts	

At Central (Federal, *markazi, ittihadi*) Level

Central Criminal Court (*al-mahkama al-markaziyya lil-jinayat*)
State Council (*majlis al-shura*, two levels)
High Criminal Court (*al-mahkama al-jina'iyya al-'ulya*, two levels)
Court of Cassation (*mahkamat al-tamyiz*)
Federal Supreme Court (*al-mahkama al-ittihadiyya al-'ulya*)

NOTES AND QUESTIONS

1. The uncertainty in these charts reflects an unsettled situation and a fuzzy institutional hierarchy. More work is needed to appreciate the Federal Supreme Court's exact role under the Constitution vis-à-vis the rest of the system. Like other countries in the Middle East, the choice is between a U.S.-style court (and possibly lower courts) having a right to be heard on constitutional violations by the Federal Supreme Court; or with a French-style Conseil Constitutionnel system, which limits the right to be heard on constitutional violations to a restricted number of officials. See Mallat, Introduction to Middle Eastern Law 207-210 (2007). Which should Iraq follow?

2. Noteworthy in the above charts is the so-called Council of State [or State Shura Council] (*majlis al-shura*), which adds another judicial layer to an already complicated and unruly structure. While the Council of State adheres to the French and Egyptian legacy, would it not be simpler to keep the system unified jurisdictionally, and establish a specialized chamber in the Court of Appeals and the Court of Cassation to adjudicate administrative cases?

3. The Iraqi system is a hybrid, or a multiple of hybrids. Family (or personal status) courts follow traditional Islamic law, but the structure of the judiciary is most reminiscent of the French system as it jelled in the early 20th century, and was carried over by Egypt and most Arab jurisdictions, including Iraq. This French-Egyptian hybridization meant a series of top courts and institutions, of which the Court of Cassation and the Higher Judicial Council (HJC) are the most important. The Court of Cassation sits at the apex of civil, commercial, family, and criminal courts. The HJC follows the French and Arab court management model, and operates as a parallel decision-maker, with a heavy input by the top executive through the Minister of Justice, while Iraq is trying hard to sever the link between the two, adding to the hybridization. One lingering problem is that the Ministry of Justice under the former regime dominated the judiciary. As a matter of law, all ministries, and the Cabinet as a whole, used to be under the absolute control of the Revolutionary Command Council, which could issue decrees at will under the rule of Saddam Hussein, its official head for almost three decades. What are the roles of the Minister of Justice, and executive power in general, to be under the new regime?

4. A further layer of hybridization results from the formal espousal by the Constitution of federalism. This adds to the system an important court, the Federal Supreme Court (FSC). See Chapter 3, the comments under Arts. 92-94 of the Iraqi Constituion. The FSC has started working, and its decisions can now be found at https://www.iraqijudicature.com. But there is confusion over the respective competence of the higher judicial institutions of Iraq, especially the Court of Cassation, the Higher Judicial Council, and the FSC. One present danger is the multiplication of courts and the inevitable competition between them. A single judicial body at the top is needed to cement the rule of law. Is that to vest in the FSC? In the Court of Cassation? What about the Ministry of Justice, and the HJC?

5. While these overarching issues are central to the reform of the judiciary at the top, no less important is the prosaic dimension at the bottom. This is especially important for the access of the citizen to justice. There are no comprehensive and reliable reports on that crucial dimension, even though an effort is under way by the Higher Judicial Council to compile the necessary statistics. The reality, by any reliable account, is stark, and hundreds, more likely thousands, of detainees languish in U.S. and Iraqi prisons without a proper trial. A generation at least is needed to get things right.

6. The following chart, by jurist Zuhair al-Maliki, handed out to participants in a legal seminar held on October 22, 2007, usefully describes the criminal process:

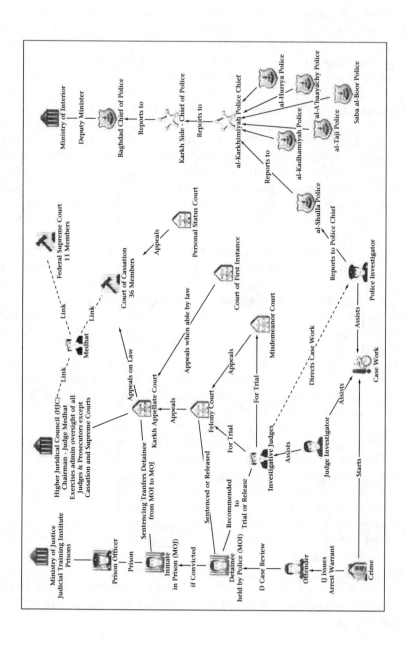

7. A judiciary is as good as the judges who form it, and judges in the former regime were undermined by their necessary, open allegiance to the Ba'ath party. The basic level of judicial recruitment follows a French model. After four years of law school, a competitive exam to become a judge is carried out amongst willing graduates. Successful candidates undertake two to three years of training in a special judicial institute, then are assigned a position in one of the first instance courts in the Republic. They then progress through the system, until eventually reaching a position on the Court of Cassation, the highest court in the republic for civil and criminal cases. The career of a judge—advancement, promotion, discipline—is determined by the Higher Judicial Council. A parallel system is followed for the administrative courts. Recruitment for higher levels of courts, especially in the court of appeals, is also possible for lawyers with over ten years in practice. The retirement age is 63, and has been occasionally extended, generally by a decision of the Council of Ministers.

8. In *Global Justice Reform: A Comparative Methodology* (2005), Hiram Chodosh underlined the common problem in judicial reforms the world over as one where the people's adhesion and support for the system remain outside the purview of the analysis. In so many reports and proposals, one is left "wondering whether anyone has focused on the society's hunger for judicial decision-making and process in Iraq's special context." (Chodosh, in a comment on this chapter.) A judiciary is as good as the sense of the people that it serves justice. How can that be assessed in Iraq? Should the government take the lead? NGOs? The judiciary itself?

9. The next sections feature the United Nations' Basic Principles on the Independence of the Judiciary, a table summarizing the American Bar Association 2006 findings on the state of the Iraqi judiciary, in addition to the "Miranda warning," a memo from a legal advisor to the U.S. Embassy on the specific deficiencies relating to U.S. policy regarding the rule of law in Iraq.

4. "U.N. BASIC PRINCIPLES ON THE INDEPENDENCE OF THE JUDICIARY"

U.N. Basic Principles on the Independence of the Judiciary

Adopted by the Seventh United Nations Congress on the Prevention of Crime and the Treatment of Offenders held at Milan from 26 August to 6 September 1985 and endorsed by General Assembly resolutions 40/32 of 29 November 1985 and 40/146 of 13 December 1985

Whereas in the Charter of the United Nations the peoples of the world affirm, inter alia, their determination to establish conditions under which justice can be maintained to achieve international co-operation in promoting and encouraging respect for human rights and fundamental freedoms without any discrimination,

Whereas the Universal Declaration of Human Rights enshrines in particular the principles of equality before the law, of the presumption of innocence and of the right to a fair and public hearing by a competent, independent and impartial tribunal established by law,

Whereas the International Covenants on Economic, Social and Cultural Rights and on Civil and Political Rights both guarantee the exercise of those rights, and in addition, the Covenant on Civil and Political Rights further guarantees the right to be tried without undue delay,

Whereas frequently there still exists a gap between the vision underlying those principles and the actual situation,

Whereas the organization and administration of justice in every country should be inspired by those principles, and efforts should be undertaken to translate them fully into reality,

Whereas rules concerning the exercise of judicial office should aim at enabling judges to act in accordance with those principles,

Whereas judges are charged with the ultimate decision over life, freedoms, rights, duties and property of citizens,

Whereas the Sixth United Nations Congress on the Prevention of Crime and the Treatment of Offenders, by its resolution 16, called upon the Committee on Crime Prevention and Control to include among its priorities the elaboration of guidelines relating to the independence of judges and the selection, professional training and status of judges and prosecutors,

Whereas it is, therefore, appropriate that consideration be first given to the role of judges in relation to the system of justice and to the importance of their selection, training and conduct,

The following basic principles, formulated to assist Member States in their task of securing and promoting the independence of the judiciary should be taken into account and respected by Governments within the framework of their national legislation and practice and be brought to the attention of judges, lawyers, members of the executive and the legislature and the public in general. The principles have been formulated principally with professional judges in mind, but they apply equally, as appropriate, to lay judges, where they exist.

Independence of the Judiciary

1. The independence of the judiciary shall be guaranteed by the State and enshrined in the Constitution or the law of the country. It is the duty of all governmental and other institutions to respect and observe the independence of the judiciary.
2. The judiciary shall decide matters before them impartially, on the basis of facts and in accordance with the law, without any restrictions, improper influences, inducements, pressures, threats or interferences, direct or indirect, from any quarter or for any reason.
3. The judiciary shall have jurisdiction over all issues of a judicial nature and shall have exclusive authority to decide whether an issue submitted for its decision is within its competence as defined by law.
4. There shall not be any inappropriate or unwarranted interference with the judicial process, nor shall judicial decisions by the courts be subject to revision. This principle is without prejudice to judicial review or to mitigation or commutation by competent authorities of sentences imposed by the judiciary, in accordance with the law.

5. Everyone shall have the right to be tried by ordinary courts or tribunals using established legal procedures. Tribunals that do not use the duly established procedures of the legal process shall not be created to displace the jurisdiction belonging to the ordinary courts or judicial tribunals.

6. The principle of the independence of the judiciary entitles and requires the judiciary to ensure that judicial proceedings are conducted fairly and that the rights of the parties are respected.

7. It is the duty of each Member State to provide adequate resources to enable the judiciary to properly perform its functions.

Freedom of Expression and Association

8. In accordance with the Universal Declaration of Human Rights, members of the judiciary are like other citizens entitled to freedom of expression, belief, association and assembly; provided, however, that in exercising such rights, judges shall always conduct themselves in such a manner as to preserve the dignity of their office and the impartiality and independence of the judiciary.

9. Judges shall be free to form and join associations of judges or other organizations to represent their interests, to promote their professional training and to protect their judicial independence.

Qualifications, Selection and Training

10. Persons selected for judicial office shall be individuals of integrity and ability with appropriate training or qualifications in law. Any method of judicial selection shall safeguard against judicial appointments for improper motives. In the selection of judges, there shall be no discrimination against a person on the grounds of race, colour, sex, religion, political or other opinion, national or social origin, property, birth or status, except that a requirement, that a candidate for judicial office must be a national of the country concerned, shall not be considered discriminatory.

Conditions of Service and Tenure

11. The term of office of judges, their independence, security, adequate remuneration, conditions of service, pensions and the age of retirement shall be adequately secured by law.

12. Judges, whether appointed or elected, shall have guaranteed tenure until a mandatory retirement age or the expiry of their term of office, where such exists.

13. Promotion of judges, wherever such a system exists, should be based on objective factors, in particular ability, integrity and experience.

14. The assignment of cases to judges within the court to which they belong is an internal matter of judicial administration.

Professional Secrecy and Immunity

15. The judiciary shall be bound by professional secrecy with regard to their deliberations and to confidential information acquired in the

course of their duties other than in public proceedings, and shall not be compelled to testify on such matters.

16. Without prejudice to any disciplinary procedure or to any right of appeal or to compensation from the State, in accordance with national law, judges should enjoy personal immunity from civil suits for monetary damages for improper acts or omissions in the exercise of their judicial functions.

Discipline, Suspension and Removal

17. A charge or complaint made against a judge in his/her judicial and professional capacity shall be processed expeditiously and fairly under an appropriate procedure. The judge shall have the right to a fair hearing. The examination of the matter at its initial stage shall be kept confidential, unless otherwise requested by the judge.

18. Judges shall be subject to suspension or removal only for reasons of incapacity or behaviour that renders them unfit to discharge their duties.

19. All disciplinary, suspension or removal proceedings shall be determined in accordance with established standards of judicial conduct.

20. Decisions in disciplinary, suspension or removal proceedings should be subject to an independent review. This principle may not apply to the decisions of the highest court and those of the legislature in impeachment or similar proceedings.

NOTES AND QUESTIONS

1. The UN document offers a standard list of conditions for an independent judiciary. A superficial reading of the previous document describing the formal structure of the judiciary would suggest that 20th-century Iraq was fitting, at least on paper, the main conditions for rule of law under an independent judiciary. Of course it did not, and one needs to pay attention to the warning in the UN document of the "gap between the vision underlying those principles and the actual situation." There is no dearth of testimonies to that gap in the new Iraq.

2. In July 2006, the American Bar Association, in conjunction with the ongoing Rule of Law Initiative through the Iraq Legal Development Project, issued a Judicial Reform Index, which "draws upon a diverse pool of information that describes [Iraq's] legal system." ABA Report, at www.abanet.org/rol/publications/jri-iraq-2006.pdf. The study found positive improvements in seven of thirty areas of assessment, negative results in twelve, and neutral response in the other eleven. Summarizing the findings, the study found a dichotomy that saw improvements and reforms in areas of legal reform of the judiciary's role and structure but failure in factors related to how the courts operate day-to-day. The neutral factors were generally areas where Iraqi judges had made strides but an assessment could not be shown because how well the reforms were put into practice remained to be seen. Two prominent areas where substantive

and long-term results were "yet to be seen" concern the lack of balanced gender, ethnic, and religious representation in the courts and the inadequacy of court buildings.

The table of correlations produced by the ABA lists "30 factors":

5. "MEASURING" THE JUDICIARY

STATE OF THE JUDICIARY: THE JUDICIAL REFORM INDEX FOR IRAQ, 2006

The American Bar Association

Judicial Reform Index Factors		Correlation 2006
I. Quality, Education, and Diversity		
Factor 1	Judicial Qualification and Preparation	Positive
Factor 2	Selection/Appointment Process	Neutral
Factor 3	Continuing Legal Education	Negative
Factor 4	Minority and Gender Representation	Negative
II. Judicial Powers		
Factor 5	Judicial Review of Legislation	Positive
Factor 6	Judicial Oversight of Administrative Practice	Positive
Factor 7	Judicial Jurisdiction over Civil Liberties	Neutral
Factor 8	System of Appellate Review	Positive
Factor 9	Contempt/Subpoena/Enforcement	Negative
III. Financial Resources		
Factor 10	Budgetary Input	Positive
Factor 11	Adequacy of Judicial Salaries	Positive
Factor 12	Judicial Buildings	Negative
Factor 13	Judicial Security	Negative
IV. Structural Safeguards		
Factor 14	Guaranteed Tenure	Positive
Factor 15	Objective Judicial Advancement Criteria	Neutral
Factor 16	Judicial Immunity for Official Actions	Neutral
Factor 17	Removal and Discipline of Judges	Neutral

Factor 18	Case Assignment	Negative
Factor 19	Judicial Associations	Neutral
V. Accountability and Transparency		
Factor 20	Judicial Decisions and Improper Influence	Neutral
Factor 21	Code of Ethics	Neutral
Factor 22	Judicial Conduct Complaint Process	Negative
Factor 23	Public and Media Access to Proceedings	Neutral
Factor 24	Publication of Judicial Decision	Negative
Factor 25	Maintenance of Trial Records	Neutral
VI. Efficiency		
Factor 26	Court Support Staff	Negative
Factor 27	Judicial Positions	Neutral
Factor 28	Case Filing and Tracking Systems	Negative
Factor 29	Computers and Office Equipment	Negative
Factor 30	Distribution and Indexing of Current Law	Negative

NOTES AND QUESTIONS

1. The table above is part of a long study that includes useful data on the judiciary and the main problems it continues to face. It identified the security of judges, their qualifications and continued legal training, and the representation of minorities, including women, as areas of particular concern. Since 2006, the security situation has improved, although judges and other law enforcement officials continue to remain a principal target of the insurgents. In the table above, factor 2, on the selection process, and factor 3, continuing legal education, have improved. Factor 4, on representation, is less clear. There is a genuine effort to recruit women, but women in the upper echelons are almost non-existent, and the best Kurdish judges remain in Kurdish Iraq, where the question of the larger interaction between them and the rest of the judiciary is in question. In the criminal process, especially the one that deals with "terrorists," the elected Sunni leadership complains about the lack of Sunni representation in the *parquet* (investigative judges and prosecutors), and the subservience of the current criminal judges to the executive, especially the Prime Minister's office and the Ministry of the Interior, both firmly entrenched since 2005 in the Shi'i community.

2. On judicial powers, factors 5 to 9 in the table above, a more recent general assessment appears in the following text:

> The third dimension [for concern] is the build up of the judiciary. In addition to the federal judicial dimension, especially in the context of the go-it-alone of

the Kurdish judiciary so far, there is the problem of coherence of the rule of law in the central judicial institutions, specifically the Higher Judicial Council, the Federal Supreme Court, and the Court of Cassation. By luck, they are all under the banner of one president, Chief Justice Midhat al-Mahmud. The question is whether this felicitous alignment is personal, or institutional, and if the latter, what the situation of other satellite and quite important courts stands with regard to that coherence: the Shura Council, the highest administrative court; the High Criminal Tribunal, which condemned Saddam Hussein to death and continues to judge the leaders of the prior regime; and the military courts. One can see how daunting the work is to secure judicial independence, and an effective judiciary.

Mallat, *Legal Developments and Constitutional Structures in Iraq*, 31:1 Michigan International Lawyer 5 (2009).

3. Each of the items identified by the ABA table can be turned into a question, or a series of questions, for the enhancement of the rule of law. What makes a judge's salary adequate? How effective is implementation? What do safety and security mean for the judge, but also for the litigants, be they victims and sometimes perpetrators? Approval by the Council of Representatives weakens the independence of the judiciary in setting and controlling its budget, especially since the government is in charge of preparing the budget. Are there ways to lessen this dependence on the political branches?

4. Clarifying rule of law, court hierarchy, and ultimate judicial decision-making is necessary for any country. But Iraq has immense difficulties of its own obtaining from the tragic security situation, and the weight offered by the "advisory" role of the U.S. government. A leaked 2008 Memo from Manuel Miranda, legislative advisor to the U.S. Embassy in Iraq, underlines the importance of that additional layer.

6. "A MIRANDA WARNING"

LETTER FROM MANUEL MIRANDA TO U.S. AMBASSADOR RYAN CROCKER

To: Ambassador Ryan Crocker
From: Manuel Miranda, Office of Legislative Statecraft
Date: February 5, 2008
Re: Departure Assessment of Embassy Baghdad

Introduction

As I prepare to sign out after a year with the State Department, I feel it my last duty to offer you my assessment of what I observed. Please accept this assessment in that spirit. The presence of so many Section 3161 temporary direct hires in various areas of expertise in the Embassy is a unique opportunity for the evaluation and oversight of the Foreign Service and the State Department's bureaucracy and competence, whether it is a Service at War or Peace.

We all have opinions. If there is any doubt of the sincerity of mine, I am ready to share to list the names of those scores of other 3161's who share it, each from the vantage point of their areas of expertise and particular experience in the Embassy.

I have kept my observations to the areas that I have most directly observed as Senior Advisor for Legislative Framework in the Iraq Reconstruction Management Office and the Embassy's Rule of Law community, and as Director of the Office for Legislative Statecraft in the Political Section. I apply to this assessment my background as a former counsel to the Senate Majority Leader and as a student of legal institutions, and, as importantly, as a lawyer with 12 years experience in sovereign government negotiations, comparative and international law, and the legal framework and conditions needed for foreign direct investment in energy infrastructure and domestic economic progress and stability in developing democracies.

Nothing in this assessment is intended to be critical of General Petraeus, his leadership, his staff, the efforts of the Coalition forces in Iraq, or the success of the security component of the "Surge" initiative, now one year old. Nothing in this assessment is intended to cast doubt on the diplomatic strengths of the Foreign Service in Iraq. Nothing in this assessment should be read as critical of the hundreds of civilian men and women, of all ages and backgrounds, who work in Iraq tirelessly and at great personal sacrifice of their careers and family lives, and the many at lower levels of internal management who support us. Although my assessment is limited to certain areas of expertise, it is applicable Embassy-wide.

I should point out that I support America's mission in Iraq, while fully recognizing our many errors over time. I support the President's policy that ignores the historic stereotypes of the Middle East and offers the region a culture of liberty protected by responsible government and the rule of law. I support a long-term American military presence in Iraqi bases, welcomed by the overwhelming majority of Iraqis and a democratically-elected government, as a means of bringing peace and stability to the region, as we did in Europe and the Far East. History may recognize this end as singularly worthy of the sacrifice that America's sons and daughters have made. I believe, however, that the potential for this peace requires the progress of Iraqi society and the confidence of the Iraqi people in their government.

That civilian progress, and the Pax Americana, will not be achieved with the Foreign Service and the State Department's bureaucracy at the helm of America's number one policy consideration. You are simply not up to the task, and many of you will readily and honestly admit it. I believe that a better job can be done. It is simply that we have brought to Iraq the worst of America—our bureaucrats—and failed to apply, as President Roosevelt once did, the high-caliber leadership class and intellectual talent, whose rallying has defined all of America's finest hours.

Summary

America's success in Iraq requires pacifying the country and assisting its government to inspire the confidence of Iraq's people. America can be confident that the former task is in good hands, but the latter effort will fail if we continue to rely on the State Department and the Foreign Service to lead or manage our civilian support efforts. As we did with the military Surge, America and Iraq would be well served by retaining our diplomats to do the work of diplomacy, but putting the effort to stand up the GOI in more competent hands. This is especially true in the areas of legislative reform and the rule of law. But it is also true in other areas.

At stake, as a whole, is not only the success of the mission, the lives of Americans and the future of a country for which we must now bear some responsibility, but also hundreds of millions of taxpayer dollars being wasted and poorly managed.

General Assessment

After a year at the Embassy, it is my general assessment that the State Department and the Foreign Service is not competent to do the job that they have undertaken in Iraq. It is not that the men and women of the Foreign Service and other State Department bureaus are not intelligent and hard-working, it is simply that they are not equipped to handle the job that the State Department has undertaken. Apart from the remarkable achievements of Coalition forces in the pacification of Iraq, the few civilian accomplishments that we are presently lauding, including the debathification law and the staffing of PRT's are a thin reed. It was regrettable to see the President recently grab on to it.

The purpose of the Surge, now one year old, was to pacify Iraq to allow the GOI to stand up. The State Department has not done its part coincident with the Commanding General's effort. This is not the fault of intelligent and hard working individuals skilled at the functions of the "normal embassy." The problem is institutional. The State Department bureaucracy is not equipped to handle the urgency of America's Iraq investment in blood and taxpayer funds. You lack the "fierce urgency of now."

Foreign Service officers, with ludicrously little management experience by any standard other than your own, are not equipped to manage programs, hundreds of millions in funds, and expert human capital assets needed to assist the Government of Iraq to stand up. It is apparent that, other than diplomacy, your only expertise is your own bureaucracy, which inherently makes State Department personnel unable to think outside the box or beyond the paths they have previously taken.

Inadequate Management Profile

As managers, the Embassy's leaders may be talented regionalists and diplomats, but they do not have the leadership profiles or management experience called for by the nation's high sacrifice of blood and treasure. It has been impossible, at any time this year, to believe that the pacification and standing up of Iraq is America's No. 1 policy consideration by observing the leadership of the U.S. Embassy, the State Department's negligent manner of making decisions, or the management priorities and changing goal posts of the State Department and Embassy leadership.

In particular, neither the State Department nor its Foreign Service is competent to manage and lead personnel who have been hired and brought to Iraq as experts, or to synchronize expertise, funds, and programs to support the GOI. As managers, the Embassy's leaders do not have the leadership profiles or management experience required by the nation's high sacrifice of blood and treasure.

The American people would be scandalized to know that, throughout the Winter, Spring and Summer of 2007, even while our Congress debated the Iraq question and whether to commit more troops and more funds, the Embassy was largely consumed in successive internal reorganizations with contradictory management and policy goals. In some cases, administrative and management goals that occupied our time reflected the urgencies and priorities that could only originate in Foggy Bottom and far-removed from the reality or urgencies on the ground. The fact that over 80 people sit in Washington, second-guessing and delaying the work of the Embassy, many who have [never] been to Baghdad, is an embarrassment alone.

Likewise, the State Department's culture of delay and indecision, natural to any bureaucracy, is out of sync with the urgency felt by the American people and the Congress in furthering America's interests in Iraq. The delay in staffing the Commanding General's Ministerial Performance initiative (from May to the present) would be considered grossly negligent if not willful in any environment.

I would venture to say that if the management of the Embassy and the State Department's Iraq operation were judged by rules that govern business judgment and asset waste in the private sector, the delays, indecision, and reorganizations over the past year, would be considered willfully negligent if not criminal. In light of the nation's sacrifice, what we have seen this past year in the Embassy is incomprehensible.

Most emblematic of the State Department's weakness in basic management was its decision to dismantle and cannibalize the Iraq Reconstruction Management Office rather than to strengthen it and to fix its problems, among them inadequate management by Foreign Service officers placed at the helm. The fact that this massive reorganization was undertaken at the critical time that it did, and even while the Commanding General was requesting greater civilian support of the GOI has to join the list of fatal errors that we have made, this time under the State Department's ledger.

The Embassy is also severely encumbered by the Foreign Service's built-in attention deficit disorder, with personnel and new leaders rotating out within a year or less. Incumbent in this constant personnel change is a startling failure to manage and retrieve information. The Embassy is consequently in a constant state of revisiting the same ground without the ability to retrieve information of past work and decisions. This misleads new personnel at senior levels into the illusion of accomplishment and progress. This illusionary process of "changing goal posts," as one senior official put it, helps to explain why so few goals are scored by us on those benchmarks codified by Congress, the President, or by the GOI itself.

Most notable, there is a near complete lack of strategic forethought or synchronization between Embassy staffing and program initiatives and funding. This is also true of PRTs. Only the military takes seriously the Joint Campaign and its metrics of achievement, while State Department leaders use it only when advantageous.

Overall, the lack of coordination and leadership in key areas (including Rule of Law activity, PRT's, and others), upon which the Special Inspector General for Iraq Reconstruction has repeatedly commented, is real and pervasive. The waste of taxpayer funds resulting from such mismanagement is something that only a deeply entrenched bureaucracy with a unionized attitude, like the Foreign Service and Main State, could find acceptable.

False Premises

This past year, the State Department and the Embassy has been led by two misguided premises: first, the obsessive aim that the Embassy be turned into a "normal embassy" and, second, that the State Department cannot be faulted for things that the GOI is not doing, i.e. "the Iraqis need to do this themselves."

The impulse to transform the Embassy into a "normal embassy" displays most starkly the State Department bureaucracy's endemic problems, including inflexibility and the inability to understand alternative management principles, use expertise and funds in any manner outside the State Department's normal experience, the inability to respond to the urgency of America's presence in Iraq, and the inclination to make excuses and blame the Embassy's failures on others.

The impact of the obsession to establish a normal embassy was most vivid this Spring as four contradictory administrative initiatives took up the time of the Embassy's leaders and senior consultant's: the sunset of the Iraq Reconstruction Management Office and the establishment of its successor, the staffing limitations imposed by the publication and application of Main State's Kennedy Report, the Embassy's preparation for the move to the New Embassy Compound, and the Commanding General's call for a civilian Surge.

At the keystone moment that America's leaders and people were pained over the debate of our continued national sacrifice, the Baghdad Embassy was doing a bureaucratic imitation of the Keystone Cops, counting chairs and desks and reviewing decisions over and over again.

The second mantra, that political success in Iraq depends entirely on Iraqis, amounts to little more than excuse-making by people who cannot imagine alternative paths and who are limited by their own limited experience in government and economic development.

The Foreign Service's gripping culture of excused inaction is also framed and exacerbated by the paralyzing question of the "buy in" of Iraqi officials in some of the areas in which they most need, and that we can offer, assistance. The obvious reality that nothing can happen without Iraqi support is over-used as an excuse by bureaucrats who simply do not have the ability of conceiving or executing scenarios of institution-building assistance that does not comport with their past experience and over-cautious diplomatic instincts.

Simply put, Foreign Service officers are not equipped to manage process-oriented assistance programs and yet we have put into their hands hundreds of millions of dollars. Any American graduate school study group could do better.

The excuse-making tendency of the Foreign Service is most evident in the areas of meeting Legislative Benchmarks and Rule of Law objectives, which I address in Specific Assessments below.

In this excuse-making culture, the State Department has been an albatross around the neck of the Coalition command, whose leaders and personnel have a leadership profile radically opposite to the State Department's. Among other things, the State Department has failed to assist Coalition initiatives by delaying or failing to supply the civilian expertise needed in a thoughtful and timely manner and also delaying decisions on funding and staffing vital to GOI (and our) success.

One example of excuse-making, is blaming the failure to accomplish the 18 benchmarks on regional history, the hostility of Iraq's neighbors, and on the GOI. It will be interesting if Congress will allow the State Department to slide by any deeper oversight than that in March as they did in September. In ordinary time, I have seen oversight and accomplishment reviews distracted by Embassy reports on what appears to be achievement, without ever any focus or evaluation of what we are failing to do.

Information Flow and Management

Another cavity in the Foreign Service culture is in the flow and management of information in both a greater and lesser degree.

In the greater degree of importance, the Foreign Service culture has created a situation where important information is kept from vital decision-makers. In my year in Baghdad, I have seen the Embassy intentionally keep information from:

The White House and relevant policy-making agencies.

The State Department in Washington (because "we cannot trust that they will not leak to the press"), and

The Commanding General (because "we do not wash our dirty laundry in public").

I have also witnessed a relentless culture of information-hoarding within the Embassy. The dysfunctional failure to communicate and share information is beyond anything that can be imagined under any circumstances. It is endemic of a bureaucracy that is far beyond its pale of competence and experience.

Needless to say, I have also witnessed the failure to coordinate and communicate with allies and international organizations.

In the lesser degree, despite the countless and deeply-researched written products created by the Embassy over 5 years, and by contractors who are paid millions of dollars for the work product, the Embassy has no system in place to retrieve vital information about Iraq, its government and laws, and past experiences and decisions. In light of the turnover in personnel, this lack of management forethought is an expensive negligence.

Embassy (and Coalition) personnel are in a constant state of information-gathering that relies mostly on luck and personality, and is always retaking the same ground. One of the most commonly heard phrases in the Embassy has to be "I had no idea that document existed," or "I did not know that was done."

Curiously, a memo was circulated asking us to store all administrative correspondence concerning the New Embassy Compound. No similar attempt at archiving important documents has been organized and documents are often being discarded for lack of interest or outlet. More importantly, previous work product is generally unavailable as a resource in almost all areas of expertise. Similarly, there has been no attempt to coordinate and collect translations, often being produced several times.

This problem could be easily solved with dedicated staffing. The significance of our work in Iraq would suggest that the State Department might need to think outside its box on an information management system that any medium-sized law firm would have.

Specific Assessments

Legislative Benchmarks

All experience in Rule of Law development in new democracies through the last sixty years points to the need to apply significant resources to law-making and law-making institutions. Law-making, except for a few isolated instances of interest in particular legislative reforms pertaining to the judiciary, has not been a focal point of the Baghdad Embassy's massive and expensive Rule of Law effort. While a few contractors have in the past made a few contributions in developing Parliament offices, these activities have been far removed from the Embassy.

Despite the political primacy of legislative reform to the success of the GOI and America's investment, since CPA there has been no concerted effort in the Embassy to support legislative reform in any manner, let alone a qualified and concerted manner.

I was hired to lead an office as close as the Embassy has come to such an effort, approved by the Iraq Reconstruction Management Office in October 2006. After countless re-approvals in the course of a year, at my departure the office, which the Embassy has listed as a Rule of Law accomplishment, is still not fully functional or funded.

Again, the failure lies in the State Department and Foreign Service's inability to think outside its box. The Embassy has disguised its failure by blaming the Iraqis for failing to make progress. "They have to do it themselves." The experience of our own government is completely contrary to this mantra.

If any 100 or 100,000 Washingtonians were gathered and told that an Energy Bill or any Bill should be left to the American Congress or the American government to do, — that they should do it themselves, — and the result would be uproarious laughter. Legislative practice, i.e. lobbying, is entirely devoted to making sure that legislators have the information and resources they need to pass laws desired on a timely basis. In the case of Iraq, America is not lacking in talented legal minds.

Only American bureaucrats, without practical legal or business experience, who spend their careers abroad, could fail to understand the role of legislative practice in our own country, or the need for a concerted, professional support effort in our Embassy in Baghdad. We do this for Electricity and other vital sectors. Such an effort would focus on law-making institutions as well as quality legal product and their adoption. Instead, we have a normal political section approach that merely reports on legislative progress and makes amateur attempts at offering input.

It is for good reason that one Minister forcefully asked that he no longer be sent Embassy political officers to speak about legislation, and would only meet with a credentialed lawyer.

For example, the Iraqi State Council is the most legitimate institution in the Iraqi law-making process. Yet from 2003 through 2007, not a single American dollar was spent to develop the capacity of that institution to process legislation in a timely fashion. Even while Congress imposed legislative bench-marks this past year, the Embassy and Main State delayed funds approved for the assistance of this and other vital Iraqi legislative offices. One reason for this is that you simply do not know better.

The lack of such a focus has serious consequences. You, Mr. Ambassador, were at post for several months before you asked for a briefing on the State Council's role. The immediate past Political Section head was one month from her departure before she requested a similar briefing.

In short, despite millions of dollars spent on assisting the GOI's capacity in many less or equally crucial areas, the contributions of the Embassy in achiev-ing Iraq's legislative agenda of over 60 constitutionally required reforms and Congress's own legislative benchmarks for success has been negligible or ham-fisted.

An example is the Embassy's history with the draft oil law(s). Any experi-enced international lawyer could have judged in 15 seconds or less that the draft that your predecessor checked off as if done, was one in which Iraqis were not invested. This has repeated itself again and again.

Our approach has assumed that Iraqi lawyers, who work on drafts after politicians have their say, are ignorant and careless. As a result, GOI officials involved in legislation have been justified in dismissing our political demands.

Rule of Law

In addition to carving out any focus on law-making, our Rule of Law effort in Iraq has mostly ignored legal culture institutions that address underlying requirements for the very success of the rule of law, such as the confidence of citizens, a preventive rather than punitive program against corruption, and the qualifications of the legal profession.

As Aswad Al-Minshidi, the president of the Iraq Bar put in a letter to President Bush: "America's Rule of Law effort in Iraq has focused almost entirely on training police, building prisons, and supporting prosecutions. This is understandable. These areas are important to security but they represent a policeman's and prosecutor's definition of what Rule of Law means. This is definition is limited to law enforcement. . . . [O]ur legal culture is in need of assistance and America's millions of dollars have done little to assist our institutions. . . . If you think that "implanting" the Rule of Law in Iraq is limited to your current Rule of Law efforts, then you are receiving poor advice. . . ."

With a few exceptions by the military and a few other recent efforts, we have ignored the Iraqi Bar, the 26 law schools and the development of the culture beyond the areas associated with arrest and prosecution. This has been extraordinarily short sighted, and is explained only in part by the fact that we have left our Rule of Law efforts to be led by assistant U.S attorneys with very narrow past experience.

This failure is accented by the little relative cost of any effort in these areas as compared to the hundreds of millions America has spent on assisting with police, prosecution and prisons. A legal comparativist scholar will someday document the opportunities we had and lost to enhance the legal culture of Iraq.

Conclusion

Two *Washington Post* articles caught my attention this past year. One reported on a memo of yours noting that the Embassy was staffed with young and inexperienced people. Presumably you were referring to the Foreign Service personnel at the Embassy and not to the experienced experts still at the Embassy at the time in larger numbers than now. A more recent article, reported on the rebellion of the Foreign Service to serve in Iraq. Both articles disguise a false premise.

America's success in Iraq will not be had with older or more Foreign Service officers doing the little that the Foreign Service is competent to do. The last thing that we need in Baghdad is more Foreign Service officers. We need experts, experienced human capital managers, and leaders who can think outside the box to synchronize staffing, funding, and urgent needs.

In addition, you should [know] that there are no lack of other Americans who are willing to come to Iraq. At the Embassy today, there are Americans who have foregone incomes five times greater than what they make now and who put aside careers to serve. If I thought the State Department were competent, I would have been glad to sign on for more than a year. Recruitment is not your problem. Your system of staffing is. The State Department would do the nation a service if it admits that it is not equipped to the job you have undertaken. Our Congress has an obligation to give you the oversight our national sacrifice demands. We are now living our latest error.

As a graduate of Georgetown's School of Foreign Service, I was proud last year when I swore in at the State Department. By the middle of 2007 that changed. I was ashamed for my country. I repeat, however, that my observations are not that you all are anything but wonderful Americans, it is that you are doing a job for which you are not prepared as a bureaucracy or as leaders.

The American and Iraqi people deserve better.

NOTES AND QUESTIONS

1. Miranda's warning identifies two major problems in the way the U.S. Embassy works. One is ignorance of the legislative situation in Iraq, focusing on the need to support "the Shura Council"; the other external assistance. What is the role of the Shura Council? How is it composed? What is the nature of the referral to the Council? Is it as important as Miranda suggests?

2. In the ABA report, reference was made to the State Consultative Council (see above under "Factor 5"). This is the same institution, and it is particularly confusing for lawyers trained in the Western tradition. In fact, the State/Shura Council operates as a clearing house for legislation, and is common to a number of Arab jurisdictions that were influenced by France,

where the Conseil d'Etat originally had a dual function: that of a court of last resort for administrative cases, that is, cases where the government or one of its agencies or branches was a party, and as a legal drafting advisor to the government on legislation. The latter function is what Miranda has in mind. The concept is totally alien to common law jurisdictions, which would find anathema to the separation of powers principles a body that works both as a court and as a legislative advisor to government.

3. The more fundamental questions: is a Shura/State Council useful in its present contradictory shape? Would it be at all useful? If expertise is needed to draft legislation, why shouldn't the Ministry of Justice provide it, and in case of Parliament, experts assigned to the legislators, usually vesting in the Legislative Drafting Committee of Parliament?

4. At the center of the Miranda memo lies the role of the Embassy and, more generally, the U.S. government's place in assisting the GOI in its efforts to establish rule of law in Iraq. "Letting the Iraqis do it," Miranda says, is not an option. It is like asking a group of non-expert Americans to draft an energy law. They are simply not equipped to do it. But is the parallel fair? Surely the U.S. Embassy knows that it is not individual Iraqis who can, or should, do the work, but their elected bodies: Parliament, and the executive branch. Since the official dismantlement of the CPA in June 2005, there is no legal authority for the Americans (or any coalition government) to issue or veto laws and regulations undertaken or approved by the Iraqi authorities. In practice, things are more complex: the Americans continue to exercise significant influence through the military, and they have both the expertise and the funds to advise on legislation. The Iraqi Bar and the 26 law schools may be an appropriate relay, but even worse than the judiciary, these are institutions that need years if not decades to establish themselves as proper legal conduits. Meanwhile, is there any other way but to hobble along? If hobbling along is inevitable, what is the proper order of priorities?

C. THE TRIAL OF SADDAM HUSSEIN

1. TIMELINE

The following timeline is adapted from National Public Radio, Timeline: Saddam's Violent Road to Execution, available at http://www.npr.org/templates/story/story.php?storyId=4961744.

Dec. 13, 2003
Saddam is captured by U.S. forces at 8:30 P.M. in the town of Adwar, 10 miles south of Tikrit. He was hiding in a specially prepared "spider hole."

December 2003
War Crimes Tribunal. The U.S.-appointed government, the Iraqi Governing Council, establishes the Iraqi Special Tribunal to prosecute war crimes committed during Saddam's rule. The law calls for Iraqi judges to hear

cases presented by Iraqi lawyers, with international experts serving only as advisers.

June 30, 2004

The U.S. symbolically hands Saddam over to Iraqi authorities, but maintains physical custody of the deposed leader. The legal transfer means that Saddam is no longer a prisoner of war. He is now a criminal defendant whose treatment is governed by Iraqi law. The change in status gives him the right to legal representation.

July 17, 2005

Charges Filed. The Iraqi tribunal, still under U.S.-installed Iraqi Governing Council jurisdiction, announces that it has filed charges against Saddam in the Dujail case. Iraqi law requires the court to announce the start date for a trial within 45 days of the filing of charges.

Aug. 8, 2005

Saddam fires his 1,500-member Arab and Western legal defense team. He retains Iraqi attorney Khalil al-Dulaimi. (Saddam's mostly Arab legal team included volunteers from the United States, France, Jordan, Iraq, and Libya.)

Oct. 19, 2005

A defiant Saddam Hussein pleads innocent to charges of murder and torture and questions the legitimacy of the court.

Dec. 22, 2005

Saddam Hussein repeats accusations that he'd been beaten and tortured in U.S. custody.

Feb. 1, 2006

Saddam Hussein's trial resumes in Baghdad, but neither the main defendant nor his attorneys are present. The deposed Iraqi leader and his lawyers say the newly appointed judge is biased against Saddam.

Feb. 13, 2006

The chief judge forces Saddam Hussein and his seven co-defendants to attend their trial. Saddam and his half brother Barzan Ibrahim respond to their appearance in court with shouts of "Down with Bush!"

February 28, 2006

Prosecution lawyers presented a document approving death sentences against 148 Dujail residents, with a signature they said was Saddam's — the most direct evidence yet against him.

June 21, 2006

Men wearing police uniforms abduct and kill Saddam's principal defense lawyer, Khamis Al-Obeidi — the third member of the defense team member to be killed.

Aug. 21, 2006

A Second Trial. The second Saddam trial begins in Baghdad. He is charged with genocide, stemming from a gas attack on a Kurdish village during the infamous Anfal campaign of the late 1980s. Saddam and six co-defendants are accused of orchestrating the killings of tens of thousands of Iraqi Kurds.

Sept. 20, 2006

The chief judge presiding over Saddam's second trial is removed by the Iraqi cabinet after declaring in a court session that Hussein was "no dictator."

Nov. 5, 2006

Death Sentence. Saddam and two co-defendants are sentenced to death for his first trial, covering the deaths of 148 Shiite Muslims in the town of Dujail. He is found guilty of war crimes and crimes against humanity, including murder.

Dec. 26, 2006

Hanging Ordered. Iraq's highest appeals court upholds the death sentence for Saddam from his trial for the 1982 killing of 148 Shiites in the city of Dujail. The chief appeals court judge says Saddam must be hanged within 30 days.

Dec. 30, 2006

Execution. Saddam Hussein hanged. Trial continues with other accused.

2. A GALLOWS IN BAGHDAD: INTERNATIONAL JUSTICE IN 2006

DAVID CRANE, A GALLOWS IN BAGHDAD: INTERNATIONAL JUSTICE IN 2006

Jurist.com, Jan. 3, 2007*

A trapdoor in Baghdad swung open on December 30, 2006, dropping to his death the convicted and condemned war criminal Saddam Hussein. In some sense, with this execution, the end of mankind's bloodiest century ended. During the 20th century, it is estimated that 215 million human beings perished, 135 million at the hands of their own governments. The likes of Hussein were a scourge upon that century. Importantly, this sad and tragic chapter in history was closed not by force but by the law. The trial of Hussein for the Dujail massacre was rough justice, but justice nonetheless. Is this a harbinger for the 21st century? Will the standard be that the law will bring down tyrants or will it be something else? The record is mixed, the way uncertain indeed, yet the year 2006 augurs well for the future of the rule of law. How so?

Slobodan Milosevic died in custody, under indictment and on trial for war crimes and crimes against humanity. With his death, ended the long and drawn out agony of a trial that showed the world the monster that he was. This trial exposed the strengths and weaknesses of international criminal law. From this years-long trial will come lessons learned that will assist the advancement of the practice. The world faced down the butcher of the Balkans, the first head of state to be tried for war crimes and crimes against humanity.

---

* Available at http://jurist.law.pitt.edu/forumy/2007/01/gallows-in-baghdad-international.php.

Charles Taylor, the first head of state in Africa indicted for war crimes, was handed over by an African head of state to an African based international tribunal via an African country for war crimes and crimes against humanity. As his helicopter touched down at the tribunal's compound in Sierra Leone, a country he personally destroyed, thousands of Sierra Leoneans cheered in the hills surrounding the compound. As he entered the court room several days later to be arraigned on those war crimes and crimes against humanity, Africans came to know that their lives mattered and that cynical African leaders could no longer take for granted their power. The beast of impunity was leashed in West Africa, and perhaps, over time, the continent.

Augusto Pinochet died a disgraced outlaw in his own country that he kept in utter terror for decades. Chileans sent a powerful signal to their government and to all of South America that the old ways of absolute power are no longer acceptable. His passing reflects the end of centralized power in a dictatorial regime, bolstering the concept of good governance in Chile and within Latin America.

Saddam Hussein was tried, convicted, and executed by an American-backed Iraqi court set up to prosecute his regime for the deaths of his own people. Though the process followed Iraqi criminal law, the specter of justice delivered so swiftly by the Iraqis will always be an asterisk next to this court from an international point of view. As he was led to the gallows, the manner of his execution also showed the indignity by which he died as political partisans shouted insults. In some sense that execution was a final reflection of the sloppy mix of law and politics that floated around that Iraqi court. History will tell whether justice was done. All in all, the law prevailed.

Yet there are wrinkles related to international criminal justice in 2006:

Darfur is the festering and fetid wound that exposes the cynical politics that surrounds international criminal justice. With the limited successes at the end of the last century and the beginning of the 21st century, Darfur reminds us that the path of justice is rocky, strewn with practical and political obstacles that highlight the reality of how politics plays out along with justice at the international level.

In the former Yugoslavia, Messrs. Karadzic and Mladic continue to hide behind the protection of the Serbs [Karadzic was arrested in July 2008 and flown to be tried in the Hague], in some way hiding in plain sight. Their continued freedom will keep the tragedy of the Balkans an open chapter in a sad book of agony and horror. Without their handover for trial at The Hague, that tribunal's work will be incomplete. Closure and reconciliation continues to be fleeting for the victims.

The world's superpower, the United States, has stepped away from its responsibility of conducting its military operations in accordance with international standards and this administration is openly attacking the international criminal law regime set up by the Rome Statute. Without the moral leadership of the United States the global effort to face down impunity and international terror will continue to struggle. Only through the rule of law can this so-called ideological struggle against these terrorists be successful.

International justice is as much a political act as it is a legal process. The legal act can only take place after the political one is complete, which can be awkward and unsure to say the least. Darfur is just such an example, as well as Charles Taylor's sanctioned exile for three years. However, the international community is putting together a political framework which may allow the condition for justice to take place for the victims in Darfur; and the international community finally moved efficiently in March of 2006 to hand over Charles Taylor to the Special Court for Sierra Leone as the political atmosphere cleared for that to happen. He awaits trial in this spring, the first African head of state ever to be indicted for violating international humanitarian law.

Despite this, mankind, in general, recognizes that impunity must be faced down wherever it rears its ugly head, of that I am now convinced. Nothing that civilization has done related to atrocity has been precise, yet today we tend not to look the other way, but to act. Historians will look at the beginning years of this century, particularly 2006, with mixed feelings on how the international community dealt with atrocity. All in all, with the benefit of 20/20 hindsight, it will either be the beginning of a new dawn for international humanitarian law or a more bleak future. Only time will tell. Regardless, 2006 will be looked on as a watershed year in the evolution of justice at the international level.

NOTES AND QUESTIONS

1. David Crane, the former Prosecutor in the Special Court for Sierra Leone (SCSL) who teaches at Syracuse University, put the execution of Saddam Hussein in the larger context of the end of impunity for dictators responsible for mass crime in their countries and regions. During Saddam Hussein's trial, the former president of Liberia Charles Taylor was arrested and extradited to The Netherlands to stand trial before the SCSL. Two major differences are striking in Saddam Hussein and Charles Taylor's respective trials: Saddam was tried in Baghdad by an Iraqi court, while Taylor, like Milosevic, was tried in The Netherlands by a UN-established court. Which offered better justice?

2. From the outset, following the model of the ICTY and ICTR, and the ICC, the SCSL rejected the death penalty. Taylor does not risk being executed. Was it possible to imagine any other result but the death penalty for Saddam Hussein and his aides being tried in Iraq? The author recalls a preparatory meeting for the tribunal in Amsterdam in 2004, where the senior Iraqi judges in attendance were adamant at keeping the death penalty. Would the continued suspension of the death penalty, which Paul Bremer decreed in 2004, have affected the overall trust in the rule of law in Iraq? What would have been the effect on the vaunted process of "reconciliation"?

3. Excerpts from the decision of the Court of Appeals in the Dujail trial follow, which confirmed the death sentence against Saddam Hussein on appeal from the trial court within the same court structure. Both are part of the Supreme [or High] Iraqi Criminal Tribunal (*al-mahkama al-jina'iyya al-'iraqiyya al-'ulya*, established by Law 10, 2005. The full English text of Law 10 is available at http://www.ictj.org/static/MENA/Iraq/iraq.statute. engtrans.pdf). The two decisions are available in full, non-official

translations. For the trial court decision that sentenced Saddam Hussein to death on November 5, 2006, see http://law.case.edu/saddamtrial/dujail/opinion.asp.

4. For the full translation of the appellate, final decision, rendered on December 26, 2006 under the presidency of Aarif Abed Al-Razaq Al-Shaheen, see http://law.case.edu/saddamtrial/ content.asp?id=88. A more thorough translation of the dispositive parts of the Court of Appeals' decision is provided by Issam Saliba, Foreign Law Specialist for the Middle East and North African Arab States at the U.S. Congress Law Library, available at http://www.loc.gov/law/help/hussein/appellate.html. The appellate decision summarizes the prior proceedings, concludes that the appeal was timely filed, and then affirms the verdict against Saddam Hussein. Excerpts follow.

3. DEATH SENTENCE FOR SADDAM HUSSEIN: EXCERPTS FROM THE APPELLATE DECISION

It has been found that, the evidence relied upon by the trial court to issue its guilty verdict against Saddam Hussein al-Majid in his capacity as having had been at the time of the incident and from July 8, 1982 to January 16, 1989, President of the Republic, Supreme Commander of the Military forces and Chairman of the Revolutionary Command Council, and had the legislative and executive powers in his hand; in addition to the video and audio recordings that show the accused addressing the residents of al-Dujail, stating that those who fired at him are 2 or 3 and no more than 10; and the contents of his statements during the preliminary and judicial investigation, and the orders he issued to those in charge of the security agencies reporting directly to him; in addition to the hundreds of official documents in the file the convicted acknowledged they are authentic; in addition to his issuing an order to compensate the owners of the orchards that had been destroyed; therefore the convicted is responsible for the systematic and widespread attack against the civilian population of the town of al-Dujail that occurred with his knowledge; thus, the intent to commit intentional murder as a crime against humanity is realized; the physical element consisting of the criminal behavior (the act of killing), the criminal result consisting of the death of the victims from among the inhabitants of al-Dujail, and the causal connection between that behavior have all been realized; and whereas the law defines crimes against humanity as any of the acts specified in article (12) of Law No. 10 of 2005 when committed as a part of a systematic or widespread attack, with the knowledge of the attack, against any group of the civilian population; therefore most of these crimes could occur as a result of a state action or policy carried out by actors who possess official authority or otherwise; but it is clear that if such crimes were committed or directed against civilian inhabitants they should be the result of a state policy carried out by actors who have official authority, or the result of the policy of actors who do not have official authority; and whereas the convicted Saddam Hussein had official authority as he held the position of former President of the Republic, and he directed his crimes against the civilian inhabitants of al-Dujail population for the purpose of killing them; therefore he had the intent to kill and thus he is responsible for these crimes as crimes against humanity, and the objections invoked by his attorneys are rejected.

The convicted cannot hide behind the legitimacy because the basic purpose of the principle of legitimacy is to identify the one who is responsible for the act, and the one who commits the crime of abusing his authority cannot claim that he is not aware of his act.

Order Number (48) of December 10, 2003, issued by the Administrator of the Coalition Provisional Authority which granted the Governing Council the authority to establish a special Iraqi tribunal with jurisdiction to try Iraqis or persons residing in Iraq accused of committing genocide, crimes against humanity and war crimes, or of violating specific Iraqi laws, was issued in conformity with UN Security Council resolutions Number (1843, 1500, 1511) of 2003; the government derived its authority to enact such a law from the UN Security Council resolutions that gave the successor government the authority to enact the laws and regulations relating to the situation of the Iraqi people; thus the establishment of the tribunal and the issuing of its statute was done legally, and its legitimacy was not adversely affected by the manner by which the law was drafted, and the tribunal was established and became, under the law, independent of all other Iraqi tribunals and independent of any Iraqi government agencies.

On March 8, 2004, the Iraqi Constitution was issued and among other things, it established a road map for the creation of an Iraqi tribunal, and it confirmed the creation of the law of the special Iraqi tribunal on June 28, 2004; and after the end of the occupation of Iraq and the formation of a full sovereign Iraqi government and its receiving the authority to govern in accordance with the provisions of the Constitution and the Security Council resolutions and its remaining in power until May 3, 2005; and during its time in office it financed, supported and allowed the tribunal to function, and indeed the judges of the tribunal were appointed and a separate budget was allocated to allow it to function; and on May 3, 2005, the interim Iraqi government elected by more than 60% of the Iraqi people replaced the interim government; and the powers of the government were described in the Constitution; and it was recognized as a government with full sovereignty and it continued to finance the tribunal until a permanent Iraqi government assumed power on May 20, 2006, and a new law for the Tribunal was issued as Law number (10) of 2005 and the Tribunal was named the Iraqi High Tribunal.

The law was issued by a government elected by 78% of the Iraqi people and in a national referendum and it is therefore a legitimate tribunal and any objections to this effect are rejected. As to the objection based on the immunity of officials we say the immunity is the practical immunity which comes for the purpose of the position; it is not possible for any person to claim that he committed crimes and that his actions are outside the reach of the law; the immunity is limited to the time in the position and does not continue thereafter, and it is tied in its existence and non-existence to the position, and it is not given to the benefit of a person who clings to the position, but it is given for the benefit of society.

The immunity does not violate part two of the international criminal law and the constitution; no state has the right to give its officials immunity from prosecution for crimes against humanity and genocide, and if immunity constitutes a means to avoid prosecution this principle has disappeared after World War II and immunity has no more effect. The establishment of criminal courts is nothing but a sign of the end of the immunity principle and since the law of the tribunal permits the trying of any person accused of committing a crime irrespective of his official position even if the person were president or member of the government or its council because his position does not protect him from punishment or constitute a mitigating circumstance, and whereas the law of the tribunal contains penalty provisions, therefore the claim of immunity of head of state or that the act was committed by the accused in his official capacity does not constitute an acceptable defense or a reason to reduce the sentence, and therefore the immunity does not prevent the tribunal from using its jurisdiction to try those persons for the crimes they committed and over which it has jurisdiction, and therefore the immunity must be a cause to increase the sentence and not to reduce it, because whoever enjoys immunity normally has the power to influence a great number of people which increases the seriousness of the losses and damages resulting from the crimes.

The head of state is responsible internationally for the crimes he commits against the international community because it is not logical or just to punish the subordinates who carry out illegal orders issued by the president and his assistants and spare the president who ordered and planned the commission of these crimes and he is therefore considered a gang chief and not a head of state who respects the law and therefore the supreme president is to be considered responsible for the crimes committed by his subordinates not only on the basis of his knowledge of those crimes but for his negligence in not obtaining such knowledge; and the non-action is considered equal to a positive action in light of article (13/1) of the Third Geneva Convention of 1949 which provides that any illegal action or abstention on the part of the authority which causes death or exposes the safety of prisoners of war to danger is prohibited and constitutes a serious violation of this convention.

The responsibility of leaders and presidents for crimes committed by those who are under their command is a responsibility for acts committed by subordinates under his command and authority provided the said leader knew that his forces are committing or about to commit any of these crimes; thus it considered the high government position occupied by the accused itself as an aggravating circumstance because he is supposed to know what is happening and because he exploited his position by the commission of the crimes.

Besides, the failure of a leader or a person to take all reasonable and necessary precautions within his authority to prevent the commission of those crimes exposes him to legal accountability. Furthermore the overlooking of crimes is considered as a sign to his subordinates to continue the commission of his crimes without fear of punishment; the principle dictates an obligation on the leader to prevent his subordinates from committing international crimes, and his responsibility is proven irrespective of the intent to admit whenever he fails willfully or negligently to prevent their commission.

The act of the subordinate should be considered unlawful because it neglects the interests under his protection and confers on them illegitimacy, and does not comply with what the domestic criminal law stipulates; a subordinate is a human being who possesses the faculties of awareness and understanding and is not a tool that executes without thinking the orders he receives; rather he has the obligation of examining the orders and abstaining from carrying them out unless they are in compliance with the rules of the law; the subordinate is one of the persons of law who has equal standing as his superior and is required to discharge all the duties that the law imposes on him; his responsibility to uphold these duties is direct and therefore the immunity defense is also rejected.

As to the defense of non-retroactive application of criminal law we say that criminal legislation normally does not apply retroactively in the field of criminal law, and this is called the principle of non-applicability of the criminal law to the past and means that the effects of criminal law does not reach into the past but apply to the facts that took place after its enactment; this principle has been adopted by the Iraqi Criminal Code Number (111) of 1969 and was referred to in article (2/F1) but article (1/Second) of the law of the Tribunal made the law applicable to the crimes committed between 7/17/1968, and 5/1/2003, as provided for in Law Number (1) of 2003 and Law Number (10) of 2005; the said two laws did not violate this principle because these crimes are provided for in articles (11, 12, 13, and 14) and have also been provided for since the 1950s of the past century and were included in international treaties; the crime of genocide was stipulated in the international treaties of 1948, ratified by Iraq on 1/20/1959, therefore the ratification of the treaties is considered as a part of the Iraqi law and Iraq is obligated by their provisions which were stipulated in paragraphs one and two of the law of the tribunal and they are therefore in effect and Iraq is obligated to comply with them by virtue of its explicit ratification of them.

As to article (12) of the law of the tribunal concerning crimes against humanity, despite the fact that their original source is international customary law since there is no international treaty that regulates their provisions and provides explicitly for them, the international customary law and the international practice are settled on considering these crimes as international crimes, and because Iraq is a part of the international community, it is also committed to them pursuant to the United Nations Charter.

As to article (13) concerning war crimes which represent the serious violations of the Geneva Conventions of 1949, Iraq ratified them on 2/12/1956, and Iraq is therefore bound by them, and they are considered a part of its laws, therefore those committing these crimes shall be accountable; furthermore Iraq ratified the international treaties concerning civil and political rights approved by the General Assembly of the United Nations on December 16, 1966, to which Iraq acceded by Law Number (193) of 1970, and which became effective on March 23 1976; therefore, and pursuant to the principles of justice, no criminal can avoid punishment on the basis of this principle because the legal principles were given for the welfare of society and not the welfare of the criminal.

The legal rule is not eternal but can expire and be replaced by another rule; therefore, the provisions of criminality can not have retroactive effects; and the criteria of the non-retroactivity of the law goes back to the time before the

Roman system in accordance with the same criteria which determine the scope of the legitimacy principle on the basis that the non-retroactivity is considered a logical result of the legitimacy principle; therefore the principle of criminality can not have a retroactive effect.

Based on the foregoing if a provision in an international treaty or agreement criminalizes a specific act, the application of this provision to acts committed prior to its enactment does not mean that the provision has been applied retroactively, because this provision was preceded by an international custom that makes the act illegitimate, and the provision did not do anything other than record the substance of the prior custom under which the act was committed; therefore the principle of the legality of crimes and punishment is compatible with the principles of justice because it is among the principles adopted in all the legal systems including international criminal law; therefore the defense based on the non-retroactivity of the law is also rejected.

As to the defense based on the principle of applying the lesser penalty, this court is of the view that when the law is amended in the period between the commission of the criminal act attributed to the accused and the time the verdict is issued against him the lesser of the penalties shall apply to the accused, and the only restriction on the court against the application of the death penalty is the Coalition Provisional Authority's order Number (7/F3) issued during the period of the occupation of Iraq by the Coalition Provisional Authority, and the purpose of this principle as provided for in article (2) of the Iraqi Criminal Code Number (111) of 1969, is to give the accused the opportunity [to benefit] from the value judgment of the society, and since Order Number (7/F3) of the Coalition Provisional Authority was not the product of the Iraqi Legislative authority and did not reflect the standards of the public opinion but reflected the necessity that the coalition used in light of the power granted to it in accordance with the occupation law in its capacity as the provisional caretaker of the actual situation in Iraq, and did not have any sovereignty over the occupied region, and therefore the coalition authority was as a separate authority, and in accordance with established international laws the Iraqi High Tribunal is not bound to apply the [coalition's] decisions or its law, and the Coalition Provisional Authority's order which suspended the death penalty was simply and at best a temporary action imposed by a temporary authority and can not be considered as a law issued prior to the verdict and by which the death penalty is eliminated as an option of judicial decisions, and pursuant to international law the death penalty is a legitimate penalty that also exists in the Iraqi present law and is among the penalties allowed for felonies and was in force prior to the formation of the government in 1919, and chapter 5, part one provided for the death penalty. And the Iraqi Law continued to apply the death penalty without any changes as with respect to the present case.

In addition the Iraqi people has the legal and moral right to establish an entity to try the leading personalities in the former regime, and if the Iraqi High Tribunal is to accomplish the objectives for which it was established its decisions shall be compatible with the international standards of justice and in accordance with international law; as to the death penalty, it is a legitimate penalty existing in Iraqi law and conforms to the accepted international law if applied in accordance with the International Convention for Civil and Political

Rights and to which Iraq has been a party since January 25, 1971, and there is a universal consensus that war crimes, genocide and crimes against humanity are among the most serious violations of the law, and because of their seriousness these crimes go far beyond the simplest of the requirements of the International Convention for Civil and Political Rights which says that the death penalty shall not be used as a penalty except for crimes that are considered very dangerous according to law; therefore in a domestic trial for commission of these crimes the sentence of death is considered a legitimate penalty allowed under both domestic and international law, and therefore this defense is also rejected.

As to the other defenses the accused were given what is sufficient to conduct a just trial against him, he was informed promptly of the nature of the crimes filed against him, he was given enough time to prepare his defense and received legal assistance from those whom he personally chose, and was given the opportunity to defend himself with the help of his lawyer consultants, and was given the opportunity to examine the prosecution and defense witnesses, and he used his right to defend himself fully, and was not forced to say anything he did not want to say; therefore the objections he raised to this effect are also rejected.

NOTES AND QUESTIONS

1. Despite all the travails and risks, the Iraqi High Criminal Court succeeded in producing two detailed, argued decisions. Points of law dominate the text of the Appeals' decision. How does the Court of Appeals respond to the criticism about non-retroactivity of criminal law? To the immunity of a former head of state? To the relationship between domestic and international law? To the *respondeat superior* argument? To its own legitimacy and the legitimacy of the Iraqi government? To the relevance of the laws of war? To the formal legal occupation of Iraq as a bar to justice? How does the quality of the decision compare with other tribunals dealing with crimes against humanity?

2. Was the evidence in the Dujail trial compelling? For details, see trial court decision that sentenced Saddam Hussein to death on November 5, 2006, cited above. Why was Dujail chosen, with 148 victims, as opposed to the more dramatic Anfal operation carried out against the Kurds in 1987-1988, where over 100,000 victims are reported to have died, including 5,000 in the gassing of the village of Halabja? Were the victims of Halabja deprived of a trial that would shed light on their ordeal? Why did the putting down of the southern and northern rebellion in April 1991, where thousands of people were also killed, not provide the grounds for the case against Hussein? Would there have been a responsibility for the coalition troops at the time, mainly the French and the Americans who did not assist the population despite their proximity on the ground? Could Saddam Hussein have also been prosecuted for starting the war against Iran in September 1980?

3. From the outset, the High Criminal Court was conceived as a special tribunal within the system. The Court continues its work, but has decided not to enlarge its docket. At the end of 2008, trial was continuing for ten defendants, all high officials from the Old Regime. The Court was

planning to complete its work in 2010. Its legacy, like the Hindawi Court in the early 1960s, will no doubt constitute a decisive moment ("a Grotian moment" as described by Michael Scharf, also the co-author, with Michael Newton, of *Enemy of the State: The Trial and Execution of Saddam Hussein* (2008). For a systematic criticism by one of Hussein's family lawyers, see Abdul-Haq Al-Ani, *The Trial of Saddam Hussein* (2008).) If the quality of its decisions remains as high as the one produced in Appeals in the Dujail trial, the negative track record of the Hindawi court might give way to a record which will shape positively the rule of law in Iraq, and make a strong impact in a Middle East region plagued with dictatorship, occupation, and concomitant crimes against humanity.

4. ON SADDAM HUSSEIN'S EXECUTION

CHIBLI MALLAT, PASSION AND LAW IN IRAQ: REFLECTIONS ON
SADDAM HUSSEIN'S EXECUTION

Jurist.com, Jan. 7, 2007*

Passion runs high in Iraq, even by the standards of a Middle East where the Arab-Israeli conflict has been an emotional hotbed for almost a century. Every issue seems to befuddle rational action. The hanging of Saddam Hussein is the latest and perhaps strongest instance of Iraqi passion violently trumping reason and humanity.

In twenty years of academic and political involvement in matters Iraqi, I have learnt the dangers of passions over Iraq, and not only amongst Iraqis. Those have affected anyone who has dealt with the country. It is palpable in the United States nowadays, where Iraq hardly leaves the limelight of front page news, but it was also true in the considerable struggle within the US government between the State and Defense Departments in the run-up to and aftermath of the March-April 2003 invasion, not to mention the CIA's dogged support for its own candidates in a determination that borders on the irrational. Successive episodes since at least 1995 show the depth of passionate struggle over Iraq, within the US government, in ways unwarranted by traditional bureaucratic rivalry.

Nor did passion spare the UN: oil-for-food money consistently trumped any attempt to sway successive secretary-generals on the side of Iraqi human rights, and the period of direct UN involvement in Spring and early Summer 2004 was no less passionate, whether in the appointment and then brutal death of Sergio de Mello, or the heavy hand of his successor, Lakhdar Ibrahimi, who got embroiled with a fierce battle between contenders to the prime ministership in ways for which Iraq suffers to date.

Passion over Iraq was not only American. In the 1990s, an extremely passionate argument developed between the late Edward Said and Kenaan Makkiyye, famous for authoring the *Republic of Fear* under the pseudonym Samir al-Khalil. Having then friendly ties to both, and not quite understanding

---

*Available at http://jurist.law.pitt.edu/forumy/2007/01/passion-and-law-in-iraq-reflections-on.php.

the reasons why they should be so strongly opposed to each another considering their common inclination to denounce dictatorship and injustice, I tried to deflect the passion in their exchanges, which split the Arab intellectual community. I failed. Working with the Iraqi opposition leadership, I could see how passionate the animosity between its better protagonists despite their common goal of bringing Saddam Hussein's rule to an end. It proved extremely difficult to put together a working opposition, let alone a working government after their return to Baghdad in 2003.

So I wasn't surprised at the amount of passion which the trial and execution of Saddam Hussein triggered, and the conflicting, excessive reactions before and since. Nor was the ugly end surprising, embroiled as the execution was in Iraqi bloody politics, with relatives of Muhammad Sadeq al-Sadr and Muhammad Baqer al-Sadr, respectable religious figures whom Saddam had assassinated in 1999 and in 1980, wanting to have a last jibe at a clearly unrepentant assassin. At least Saddam was buried in his village, but one may wonder how many people will die in the battle over his sepulcher.

Passion and controversy will continue to run high. The trial is over for Saddam, but not for Ammar Bandar and Barzan Takriti, both now on death row. And in the middle of passion, few people noticed that the Appeals' Court of the Iraq High Tribunal sentenced on 26 December a third person to death, Taha Yasin Ramadan. The Court held that the lower court's life sentence was too lenient, reversed it, and remanded his case for harsher sentencing to conform with its judgment. As the Anfal trial proceeds, with "Chemical Ali" standing in the dock for the killing of thousands of Kurdish Iraqis, passion will continue, this time of an ethnic-nationalist nature as opposed to the sectarian passion one has witnessed so far all the way to the gallows.

I know from experience that the rule of law is often sacrificed in the tide of passion. One should try nonetheless, and hold on to one's ideals and beliefs in adverse moments.

It is time to stay the hand of the executioner. Being for or against the death penalty is a strong personal choice, one that arouses great passion the world over. I have chosen to be against it, with no exception. That includes Saddam Hussein, who, of all mass murderers on earth since the end of the Second World War, probably deserved it most. This is not a mere personal conclusion about Saddam's rule. In the 1990s Max van der Stoel was in charge of the human rights file as UN Special Rapporteur for Iraq. He concluded in one of his reports that the exactions of Saddam Hussein's government were the worst since World War II. Still, no death penalty means no death penalty, and examples abound on the wisdom of its abolition, from the wide revulsion at the execution of Nicolae Ceaucescu and his wife in 1989 — a sad blot on Eastern Europe's non-violent revolution — all the way back to the French Revolution. History would have kept a better place to "the Incorruptible," Maximilien Robespierre, had he been consistent with his declared opposition to the death penalty. Instead, he turned into the architect of Terror, which claimed through judicial means thousands of innocents, after leaving his beliefs at the door of Louis XVI's trial in December 1792. "Louis must die," Robespierre said, "so that the Nation can live." Surely France did not need Louis to die, nor will Iraq owe its survival to the execution of Saddam Hussein.

These are times that grip one's conscience. Maybe I could have saved Saddam Hussein, when colleagues on the then-Iraqi Governing Council asked me to sit on the Court. But I couldn't join the Court: there was a conflict of interest because I had helped establish Indict in 1996, whose mission was to bring Saddam and other mass murderers to trial. It was also difficult to contemplate living in Baghdad through what turned out to be an unprecedented butchery of witnesses, defense lawyers, and judges. But I made the case as strongly as I could that Iraq would be better served by an appropriately monitored "reality camera" for the rest of Saddam's life, rather than his execution, at a meeting held in Amsterdam in preparation of the Tribunal. I also made the argument that when Saddam Hussein was arrested, the death penalty had been frozen by the "occupation forces" in an order issued by Paul Bremer, and that a harsher penalty could not be meted on him without undermining basic principles of criminal law.

Before the first decision was issued last November 5, I worked for the court to be moved abroad. Afterwards in a *Jurist* column I urged that the appeal of the verdict be moved outside Iraq, and I even looked for jurisdictions where the death penalty was not officially banned to make the possibility more accept-able to Iraqis. I also made the argument that the Iraqi constitution, no less, required the president to sign the death warrant for Saddam. Why should the Prime Minister end up doing so against an explicit Article 70 vesting that essential responsibility in the president?

Only in a place not overrun with high human emotions, as Iraq is, can one avoid the contradictions between law and a reality gripped by passion. In Saddam's death, I can see the fate of so many Middle Eastern dictators and their families. When Saddam was arrested and filmed coming out from the spider-hole, Libyan dictator Qaddafi stayed mesmerized hours on end before the television set. Since then, his international policy has somewhat changed, though not his brutal home practice, and one knows that Saddam's copycat rulers in the Middle East will be shaken by his brutal demise. And so they should. What has Saddam Hussein achieved? His whole family, including wives and daughters, lives in exile and in fear of being surrendered to the Iraqi government when it stabilizes. Saddam Hussein killed his two sons-in-law, along with a grandchild. His two sons, and another grandson, were killed in a battle where they were doomed. He was removed from a hole, his head full of lice, to be incarcerated for two years while continuing to fan the flames of death and killings. His trial was the occasion of so many unnecessary deaths: almost a dozen people were killed in direct connection with the trial, including witnesses and families of witnesses and judges, and three defense lawyers, including two innocent souls assigned to him by the tribunal and one who served by his own choice. For what? Does any of his family or supporters believe that it was worth it? Wouldn't Saddam and his family, and so many others, be still alive had he relinquished power in March 2003 and gone into exile? More importantly, will those lesser figures than Saddam who rule the Middle East end up differently as hatred in society, their clinging to power for life, and the resulting spiral of death, turn them into increasingly harsh despots?

What struck me most this past week is the contrast in the death of two former presidents. I could not stop thinking of Gerald Ford and Saddam Hussein's deaths, and the way their respective publics dealt with them.

What explains the chasm between the controversies swirling in America in the last week of 2006, one about the pardon by Gerald Ford to Richard Nixon, the other about the way Saddam Hussein was put to death? What is it that makes us in the 21st century appear to be living on different planets?

D. THE SHADOW OF ABU GHRAIB

1. TIMELINE 2003-2007

The following timeline is adapted from "Abuse at Abu Ghraib," available at http://www.cbsnews.com/elements/2004/05/07/iraq/timeline616248.shtml.

Spring 2003

The International Committee of the Red Cross first warns U.S. officials that prisoners in Iraq are being abused by U.S. troops, according to the group's director. It continues giving verbal and written reports through November, including detailed allegations of mistreatment at Abu Ghraib.

Aug. 31–Sept. 9

Maj. Gen. Geoffrey Miller, who runs the military prison for terror suspects at Guantanamo Bay, Cuba, conducts an inquiry on interrogation and detention procedures in Iraq. He suggests that prison guards can help set conditions for the interrogation of prisoners.

Nov. 5

Maj. Gen. Donald Ryder, the Army's provost marshal, submits his "Report on Detention and Corrections in Iraq." According to a later report by Maj. Gen. Antonio Taguba, Ryder finds the 800th Military Police Brigade is "understrength" and "did not receive corrections-specific training."

Jan. 14, 2004

According to the Pentagon, a soldier reports suspected abuse at Abu Ghraib to his superiors. The *New Yorker* magazine identifies the whistleblower as Spc. Joseph Darby, saying he slipped an anonymous note under an officer's door after receiving a CD of photos showing naked detainees.

Jan. 16

At a CENTCOM briefing, Army Brig. Gen. Mark Kimmitt tells reporters about the allegations and announces an investigation that's in its "early stages."

Jan. 18

A guard leader and a company commander at the prison are suspended from their duties.

Jan. 19

Lt. General Ricardo Sanchez orders a separate administrative investigation into the 800th Military Police Brigade.

Jan. 24

U.S. administrator L. Paul Bremer first hears of the Abu Ghraib abuse allegations, according to his spokesman, Dan Senor. Senor says he does not know when Bremer first saw the photos of abusive acts.

January 2004

Janis Karpinski, commander of the 800th Military Police Brigade, is quietly suspended from her position as commander of U.S.-run prisons in Iraq and is placed under investigation.

Jan. 31

Taguba begins an administrative investigation of procedures at Abu Ghraib.

January–February

President Bush becomes aware of the charges during this time period, according to White House spokesman Scott McClellan, although the spokesman has not pinpointed a date. Defense Secretary Donald H. Rumsfeld tells Bush of the charges, McClellan says.

February

The Army inspector general begins a review of U.S. detention facilities throughout Iraq and Afghanistan.

February

The international Red Cross submits a 24-page report to U.S. authorities describing prisoner abuse at Abu Ghraib, including the deaths of unarmed prisoners who'd been shot from watchtowers. The ICRC's director says the report summarizes information given to U.S. authorities in 2003.

March

Lt. Gen. James R. Helmly, the chief of the Army Reserve, starts an assessment of training for his MPs and military intelligence personnel.

Mar. 12

Taguba presents his report to his commanders. He finds blatant and sadistic abuse by U.S. military police and perhaps others. He also agrees with Ryder's opinion that guards should not play any role in the interrogation of prisoners.

Mar. 15

The criminal investigation of the Abu Ghraib case is completed, according to a timeline given by Pentagon spokesman Larry Di Rita.

Mar. 20

Criminal charges are filed against six military police officers as a result of the abuse investigation. In total the Army says 17 soldiers in Iraq, including a brigadier general, have been removed from duty following charges of mistreating Iraqi prisoners.

Apr. 23

The military opens an investigation dealing directly with the role of military intelligence officials in prisoner operations.

Apr. 28

The abuse scandal erupts when "60 Minutes II" broadcasts photos of prisoner mistreatment at Abu Ghraib. Aides to the president say Mr. Bush later chastises Defense Secretary Donald Rumsfeld for failing to tell him about the pictures until after they aired.

Apr. 30

The military announces Miller has been put in charge of U.S.-run prisons in Iraq.

May 6

President Bush apologizes for the abuse at Abu Ghraib, saying he is "sorry for the humiliation suffered by the Iraqi prisoners and the humiliation suffered by their families." He says the images have made Americans "sick to their stomach."

May 7

In testimony before the Senate Armed Services Committee, Rumsfeld apologizes to Iraqis abused by U.S. troops. He says, "As secretary of defense, I am accountable for them and I take full responsibility."

May 19

Spc. Jeremy Sivits, who took some of the photos at Abu Ghraib, pleads guilty to four abuse charges. He receives the maximum penalty: one year in prison, reduction in rank and a bad conduct discharge. Earlier, three other accused soldiers appeared for arraignment, and deferred their pleas.

Aug. 24

A report by an independent panel of civilian defense experts says soldiers running Abu Ghraib are mainly to blame for the inmate abuses, but fault also lies with the most senior officials, including Donald Rumsfeld. "There was chaos at Abu Ghraib," says the head of the commission.

Aug. 25

Army investigators say 27 members of an intelligence unit either requested or condoned abuses of Iraqi detainees. Their report makes a distinction between the small group of rogue guards tied to the Abu Ghraib abuse photos, and wider use of abusive techniques during interrogations there.

Dec. 1

The Pentagon confirms that a confidential report prepared for the Army's command in Baghdad in December 2003 said a joint CIA-military team hunting for Saddam Hussein had mistreated and possibly physically abused some of their detainees. It is not said which U.S. commanders saw the report.

Jan. 14, 2005

Army Spc. Charles Graner Jr., the reputed ringleader of a band of rogue guards at Abu Ghraib, is convicted of conspiracy, assault, maltreating prisoners, dereliction of duty and committing indecent acts. He faces up to 17½ years behind bars upon sentencing.

Jan. 15

A military jury sentences Army Spc. Charles Graner Jr. to 10 years behind bars. The panel needed less than five hours to reach its verdict.

May 2

Army Pfc. Lynndie England pleads guilty to charges arising from her role in the Abu Ghraib prison abuse scandal. She enters her pleas to two counts of conspiracy to maltreat prisoners, four counts of maltreating prisoners and one count of committing an indecent act.

May 6

A judge throws out England's guilty plea, saying it is not clear she knew her actions were wrong. This follows testimony from Pvt. Charles Graner, in which he said the abuse photos were meant as a training aid. In her plea, England said they were taken for amusement.

Sept. 26

England is convicted by a military jury of five male Army officers of one count of conspiracy, four counts of maltreating detainees and one count of committing an indecent act. She is acquitted on a second conspiracy count. She faces a maximum of 10 years in prison.

Sept. 27

England is sentenced to three years in prison.

Mar. 21, 2006

Military jury finds Army dog handler Sgt. Michael J. Smith, 24, guilty of abusing detainees at Abu Ghraib prison by terrifying them with a military dog, allegedly for his own amusement. Smith was found guilty of six of 13 counts. He had faced the stiffest potential sentence of any soldier charged so far in the scandal if convicted on all counts.

Mar. 22

A military judge sentences Army dog handler Sgt. Michael J. Smith, 24, to six months behind bars for using his snarling canine to torment prisoners at Abu Ghraib.

June 2

A military jury sentences Army dog handler Sergeant Santos Cardona to 90 days hard labor without confinement and a reduction in rank. On June 1, the soldier was convicted of dereliction of duty and unlawfully threatening a detainee with his dog. He is the 11th soldier convicted of crimes stemming from the abuse of inmates at the prison.

Jan. 30, 2007

The only U.S. military officer charged with a crime in the Abu Ghraib scandal will be court-martialed on eight charges, including cruelty and maltreatment of prisoners, the Army said. Lt. Col. Steven Lee Jordan, 50, arraigned in Washington.

Aug. 28

Jordan was acquitted of all charges related to prisoner mistreatment and received a reprimand for disobeying an order not to discuss a 2004 investigation into the allegations.

2. CRITICISM BY HUMAN RIGHTS ORGANIZATIONS

"No Blood, No Foul" (Summary and Recommendations)

Human Rights Watch report, July 2006

I pulled the guy out [an E6 interrogator, and said]: "I looked—I looked this stuff up and this is not the way it's supposed to be," you know? He was like, "This is the directive we had. You need to go ahead and drop this, sergeant." You know, and he outranked me. "Drop this sergeant," [he said]. It was repeatedly emphasized to me that this was not a wise course of action to pursue. . . . It was blown off, but it was a little more stern: "You don't want to take this inquiry anywhere else," kind of thing. "You should definitely drop this; this is not something you wanna do to yourself."

—U.S. Army M.P. Sergeant stationed at Forward Operating Base Tiger, al Qaim, Iraq, in 2003, describing his efforts to complain about detainee abuse.

I was very annoyed with them because they were saying things like we didn't have to abide by the Geneva Conventions, because these people weren't POWs. . . . [T]hey're enemy combatants, they're not POWs, and so we can do all this stuff to them and so forth. . . . It just went against everything we learned at Huachuca.

—Military Intelligence Interrogator attached to a secretive task force stationed at Camp Nama, at Baghdad airport in Iraq, describing a briefing by military lawyers in early 2004 after soldiers raised concerns about abusive interrogation methods.

U.S. forces have [at the time of publication] been deployed in Iraq for over three years. During this time, tens of thousands of Iraqis have been arrested, detained, and interrogated by U.S. personnel. Many of the detainees—held at Forward Operating Bases (FOBs) or at central detention centers such as Abu Ghraib prison, Camp Cropper, and Camp Bucca—have been interrogated by personnel from U.S. Military Intelligence (MI) or the Central Intelligence Agency (CIA). While some detainees have been insurgents, others have been innocent civilians caught up in U.S. military operations, in the wrong place at the wrong time.

There is mounting evidence to show that many detainees have been abused. The Abu Ghraib scandal, which broke in April 2004, brought the issue of detainee abuse to the world's attention, but it is now clear that the scope of the problem is far broader than was known at the time. Since 2003, Human Rights Watch has reviewed hundreds of credible allegations of serious mistreatment and torture of detainees in U.S. custody. Alleged abuses have taken place in locations all over Iraq, in both FOBs and centralized facilities, and have involved CIA agents, military interrogators, MP guards, and ordinary combat soldiers. Abuses have also been alleged in detention facilities in Afghanistan and at Guantanamo Bay, where smaller numbers of detainees are held. In many cases, it has taken years for abuses to come to light.

This report is based largely on firsthand accounts by U.S. military personnel stationed in Iraq, and describes abuses that took place in three separate locations in Iraq in 2003-2005. Many of the accounts are from soldiers who witnessed and in some cases participated in the abuses. . . .

In all three locations, soldiers witnessed seriously abusive treatment and interrogation of detainees, including beatings, psychological torture of varying kinds, and other physical torture and mistreatment. At Camp Nama, for instance, detainees were regularly stripped naked, subjected to sleep deprivation and extreme cold, placed in painful stress positions, and beaten. At FOB Tiger, they were held without food or water for over 24 hours at a time, in temperatures sometimes exceeding 135 degrees Fahrenheit, and then taken into interrogations where they were beaten and subjected to threats. At Mosul, detainees were regularly subject to extreme sleep deprivation, exposure to extreme cold, forced exercises, and were threatened with military guard dogs.

In all three locations, the abuses appear to have been part of a regularized process of detainee abuse — "standard operating procedure," in the words of some of the soldiers.

The accounts . . . provide compelling new evidence that detainee abuse was an established and apparently authorized part of the detention and interrogation processes in Iraq for much of 2003-2005. The accounts also suggest that U.S. military personnel who felt the practices were wrong and illegal have faced significant obstacles at every turn when they attempted to report or expose the abuses.

One military interrogator, cited at the beginning of this report, described to Human Rights Watch what happened when he and other colleagues complained about abuses to the colonel on duty: "a team of two JAG officers, JAG lawyers, came and gave us a couple hours slide show on why this is necessary, why this is legal, they're enemy combatants, they're not POWs, and so we can do all this stuff to them and so forth." After that presentation, the interrogator said, the abuses continued, but he and the others who were unhappy with the situation felt that they had nowhere else to turn. As far as he knew, no other reporting mechanism existed. "That was it, case closed," he explained. "There was nobody else to talk to."

Many of the soldiers who have spoken with Human Rights Watch about detainee abuse have voiced anger at the way their concerns and complaints were dismissed, and said that they decided to speak publicly because they were concerned about the systemic problems that made reporting abuse so difficult. . . .

The military and the Bush Administration appear to be in denial. Both have consistently portrayed abuse cases from Iraq as exceptional and perpetrators as lone and independent actors — "rotten apples" — despite evidence that Military Intelligence officers and higher-echelon military and civilian leaders knew about or may even have authorized abusive techniques that were used against detainees. Such sweeping denials, and the military's general failure to place any blame on leadership for abuses that occurred, have hindered candid assessments about the detainee abuse problem.

Take, for example, the role of U.S. Military Intelligence (MI) in formulating and executing interrogation and detention policy in Iraq. There are clear indications that MI battalions systematized the use of abusive techniques in Iraq in 2003 and 2004, and that MI interrogators — including officers — are implicated in the widespread abuses that occurred during that time. As detailed in this report, internal military documents and soldiers' own accounts show that MI interrogators were using abusive tactics through much of 2003-2005; and that for much of this time these tactics were authorized by officers up the chain of command. Yet to date, no military intelligence officers who have served in Iraq have been charged with any criminal acts, either as a principal or under the doctrine of command responsibility. The few courts-martial that have occurred in relation to detainee abuse in Iraq have primarily involved military police, most of whom have claimed in courts-martial that they were ordered or authorized by military intelligence interrogators to use the tactics they were charged with.

Notably, Gen. Barbara Fast, the chief of military intelligence in Iraq during the period of the most serious abuses — late 2003 through 2004 — has since been promoted for her work in Iraq. She is now the commander of the Army Intelligence Center, the U.S. Army's interrogation school at Fort Huachuca, Arizona.

CIA personnel have also gone unpunished. Several homicide cases, involving detainees who died while being interrogated by the CIA, were referred to the Department of Justice for prosecution in 2004 and 2005, yet to date not one CIA agent has been charged. Human Rights Watch has repeatedly urged Justice Department officials to move forward with the investigation and prosecution of civilian personnel implicated in abuses, but as of June 2006 only a single civilian contractor had been indicted, for a case from Afghanistan. And there are others who have escaped investigation as well — for instance, military Judge Advocate Generals, Special Forces personnel, and civilian leadership in the Department of Defense.

Human Rights Watch is aware that U.S. forces in Iraq are fighting armed groups who themselves have shown little willingness to abide by international humanitarian law. As Human Rights Watch has detailed in previous reports, Iraqi insurgent groups routinely violate international humanitarian law, carrying out abductions and attacks against civilians and humanitarian aid workers, and detonating hundreds of bombs in bazaars, mosques, and other civilian areas. Human Rights Watch has previously stated that those responsible for violations, including the leaders of these groups, should, if captured, be investigated and prosecuted for violations of Iraqi law and the laws of war.

But the activities of these groups are no excuse for U.S. violations. Abuses by one party to a conflict, no matter how egregious, do not justify violations by the other side. This is a fundamental principle of international humanitarian law.

Recommendations

The U.S. government has refused to acknowledge the systemic nature of the problem of detainee abuse in Iraq since 2003, and done little to address the underlying problems that have led to abuse.

It is time for the Bush Administration to admit that there has been no real accountability for detainee abuses. It is time for military and CIA leaders to acknowledge that serious and systemic abuse has occurred, and recognize the weakness of their internal reporting procedures. It is time for the U.S. Congress to get serious about oversight on these issues, and work to ensure that systemic flaws are corrected and that criminal conduct is adequately investigated and punished, both now and in the future.

Human Rights Watch makes the following recommendations:

- Congress should appoint an independent bipartisan commission to investigate the scope of current and past detainee abuses, identify the involvement of military and civilian officials in authorizing and allowing abusive interrogation techniques, and determine why military and civilian leaders who are implicated in abuse have not been held accountable.
- Congress should also re-open hearings on detention abuse issues, to address the same issues as above.
- Congress should push the President to appoint independent prosecutors — in the military and Justice Department — to investigate and prosecute detainee abuse cases, focusing not only on abusive interrogators and guards, but also on military and civilian leaders who authorized or condoned abuse.
- The U.S. military and CIA should identify institutional flaws that make it difficult for personnel to complain about illegal conduct and report crimes and abuses being committed by personnel, and remedy those flaws.
- The Secretary of Defense should appoint a panel of high-level members of the various Judge Advocate General Corps to consider reforms in the criminal justice system of the U.S. military, to increase the power and independence of military criminal investigators, and to remove institutional obstacles that make it difficult for personnel to report abuse.
- The Attorney-General should work with the Secretary of Defense, the National Director of Intelligence and the Director of the Central Intelligence Agency to revise procedures and protocols for investigating and prosecuting cases of abuse by non-military personnel.

3. CRITICISM UNDER INTERNATIONAL LAW

LAURA A. DICKINSON, ABU GHRAIB: THE BATTLE OVER INSTITUTIONAL CULTURE
AND RESPECT FOR INTERNATIONAL LAW

International Law Stories, John E. Noyes et al. eds., 414-416 (2007)

Violations of International Law

The acts committed at Abu Ghraib, as reported by the media [for the first time in April of 2004] and in the subsequent administration reports and congressional hearings, likely constituted serious violations of international law. The Convention Against Torture and Cruel, Inhuman and Degrading Treatment defines torture as "any act by which severe pain or suffering, whether physical or mental, is intentionally inflicted on a person for such purposes as obtaining from him or a third person information or a confession" when "inflicted by or at the instigation of or with the consent or acquiescence of a public official or other person acting in an official capacity." A very strong case could be made that many of the abuses committed at Abu Ghraib — including the reported sodomizing of a detainee with a broomstick and threatening detainees with electric shocks in order to set "conditions for favorable interrogation"—constituted torture. And while the Torture Convention does not define cruel, inhuman or degrading treatment, it is unquestionable that virtually all of the acts alleged would qualify as cruel treatment as interpreted by the many courts that have addressed the issue. Moreover, the Convention admits of no exceptions to the ban on torture even in times of war or national emergency, and obligates all states parties to criminalize torture and extradite or prosecute those suspected of committing torture. At the time of the conflict in Iraq, the United States had ratified the Torture Convention and had enacted domestic legislation criminalizing the practice.

Similarly, a strong case could be made that the acts in question constituted violations of the Geneva Conventions. Unlike Guantanamo Naval Base, where the applicability of the Geneva Conventions was subject to debate, U.S. officials did not dispute—at least not in public—the authority of the treaty regimes over activities in Iraq. Under the Conventions, "grave breaches" include "torture or inhuman treatment . . . , willfully causing great suffering and serious injury to body or health," and such acts are relatively defined as war crimes. The 1949 Geneva Convention Relative to the Protection of Civilian Persons in Time of War also contains numerous additional provisions prohibiting cruel and inhumane treatment. As with the Torture Convention, the United States has ratified the Geneva Conventions and enacted domestic legislation conferring jurisdiction on U.S. courts to criminally punish offenders. The Uniform Code of Military Justice (UCMJ) confers jurisdiction on military courts to try and punish uniformed personnel for engaging in acts that would constitute war crimes. In addition, the War Crimes Act gives jurisdiction to U.S. courts to criminally punish anyone who has committed war crimes overseas, and the Military Extraterritorial Jurisdiction Act extends the jurisdiction of federal courts to prosecute civilians working with the Armed Forces for violations of the UCMJ and other federal criminal law.

Some scholars have argued that the acts at Abu Ghraib also constitute crimes against humanity. While the Statute of the International Criminal Court (ICC) defines and prohibits such crimes, neither the United States nor Iraq has ratified this treaty. The ICC is therefore unavailable as an enforcement mechanism for such abuses. Yet such crimes are generally established as a matter of customary international law dating back to the Nuremberg tribunals, and might be enforced domestically or in a suit in a third-party state under principles of universal jurisdiction.

Accountability

. . . Thus, although the military trials of some of the low-ranking military police reservists produced evidence that higher-ranked military and civilian personnel had ordered the abuse, and strongly suggested that more evidence might exist, these higher-ranked military and civilian personnel have not faced trial. . . . Moreover, only one military intelligence soldier . . . has been convicted. Perhaps just as troubling, those convicted have received light sentences. Of the forty who have been sentenced to jail time, fewer than ten have served more than a year. . . .

While transnational criminal prosecution in a third-party state under principles of universal jurisdiction remains a possibility, the prospect of such suits is slim. For example, although a group of Abu Ghraib victims filed an action for war crimes in Germany under that country's universal jurisdiction statute, the statute requires approval from the chief German prosecutor before jurisdiction can be exercised, and the prosecutor has declined to move forward with the case, most likely because of its politically sensitive nature.

Conclusion

. . . The broader lesson is that, because international law relies in part on institutional internalization, we must take account of the ways in which weakening that institutional commitment can create the conditions where abuses can occur. But we must also recognize that, if a culture of internalization is nurtured over a long period of time, it can respond and reclaim a role for international law going forward. As the Army's response to the My Lai massacres indicates, revulsion concerning abuses such as those committed at Abu Ghraib can themselves inspire a new generation committed to preventing such abuses in the future. Institutional culture, it turns out, is a key site where battles over international law are fought, and Abu Ghraib has already become an iconic touchstone in that crucial, though sometimes invisible, internal struggle.

NOTES AND QUESTIONS

1. The Abu Ghraib timeline suggests that prosecutions did take place, but only a dozen trials were conducted, with the heaviest sentence standing at ten years. Is that sufficient? Could the Abu Ghraib abuses have been prevented? How? Under what law?

2. Human Rights Watch recommended a full Congressional investigation, along with a number of reviews within the administration. Two official reports were conducted, the Schlesinger and Taguba Reports. The Schlesinger Report was released on August 24, 2004, full text available at http://news.bbc.co.uk/nol/shared/bsp/hi/pdfs/24_08_04_abughraibreport.pdf. It made radical suggestions, including "the need" for the United States "to redefine its approach to customary and treaty international humanitarian law," at 90. Earlier that year, the Taguba Report, which was originally secret but was cited by Seymour Hersh in a *New Yorker* article in May 2004, had made several findings and recommendations to improve detention and interrogation techniques, deeming it "essential to establish the conditions with the resources and personnel required to prevent future occurrences of detainee abuse." AR 15-6 Report, known as the Taguba Report, available at www.npr.org/iraq/2004/prison_abuse_report.pdf, at 51. Together with Guantanamo, Abu Ghraib has been a major focus of a world debate on detention conditions and interrogation tools, and a consistent issue of contention within the U.S. See, e.g., Philippe Sands, *Torture Team: Rumsfeld's Memo and the Betrayal of American Values* (2008).

3. Are there remedies under international law, as suggested in the Dickinson article? Under Iraqi law? Under American law? Elsewhere? Note the

difficulty of bringing a case under "universal jurisdiction laws," as in Germany. Can one be confident that abuses do not continue in Abu Ghraib and other detention places in Iraq? By U.S. troops? By Iraqis? With the formal devolving of authority to the Iraqi government since June 2005, has all Coalition responsibility for Abu Ghraib and similar detention centers passed onto Iraqis?

E. CONCLUSION: A PERSPECTIVE FROM THE IRAQI BENCH

1. PRESENTATION

On October 2004, Medhat al Mahmood (Midhat al-Mahmud), the Iraqi senior judge who presently heads the Federal Supreme Court, the Higher Judicial Council, and the Court of Cassation (in Iraq, Mahmud is addressed in English as "Chief Justice," a title which does not appear in the Constitution, but underlines his preeminence amongst his peers as the head of three top judicial institutions), offered at a conference in Amman a vision of the "Judicial system of Iraq" which presented a historical vision of the judiciary. The paper covered the series of laws organizing the judiciary since Ottoman rule where decisions of the Iraqi courts could be brought up to Istanbul for cassation, through to the reestablishment of the Higher Judicial Council in CPA Order 35.

The paper shows the Chief Justice's concern for the independence of the judiciary both from foreign rule and executive diktat. He has harsh words alike for British rule and for the dominance of Saddam Hussein, through the Minister of Justice, over the judiciary. In the text of the paper published in Arabic on the High Judicial Council website (http://www.iraqijudicature.com), the following remarks show the vision he has for the independence of the Iraqi judiciary.

2. VIEW OF THE CHIEF JUSTICE

MIDHAT AL-MAHMUD, INDEPENDENCE OF THE JUDICIARY AND THE ROLE OF THE PERMANENT CONSTITUTION IN ITS PROTECTION (*'ISTIQLAL AL-QADA' WA DAWR AL-DUSTUR AL-DA'EM FI HIMAYATIH'*)

http://www.iraqijudicature.com

For an independent judicial power to fulfill its mission, the elected National Assembly in the new Iraq must include in the permanent Constitution texts that guarantee the independence of the judiciary, its independence as a separate power from the legislative and executive branches. It is not sufficient to produce general texts as was the case in previous constitutions. Principles needed for judicial independence must be developed, including:

1. Establishment of the principle of judicial independence and the autonomous work of judicial power within the judiciary's field of expertise,

alongside legislative and executive powers. Judicial power constitutes with them the pillars of a modern nation. On that basis, the judiciary has an exclusive general power in adjudicating all conflicts between natural and corporate persons, including the government, while respecting relevant international treaties.

2.   The judiciary is the only institution in charge of managing the issues relevant to judges, public prosecutors, and associated judicial agencies. Neither the legislative nor executive powers may intervene in its affairs in any way whatsoever. Any such intervention is subject to legal prosecution.

3.   The judicial institution comprises the judicial apparatus, which includes courts, the public prosecution office, the judicial oversight council [the Higher Judicial Council], and the judicial institute for the training of judges, public prosecutors and auxiliaries, in addition to the protection agencies and related services.

4.   The head of the judicial power is directly linked to the president, as the symbol representing the State, so as to confirm the independence of the judiciary from the legislative and executive powers.

5.   Judicial power has an independent moral personality, financial and administrative independence, and a separate budget which it coordinates with the relevant financial agencies. The budget is presented directly to the president for his ratification, thereby confirming judicial independence from legislative and executive powers, and preventing the budget from being used as a means of pressure on judicial power and as a way to influence it and limit its work or independence.

6.   Judicial power is solely responsible for the determining and securing due process in courts and judicial agencies for the adjudication of disputes and related tasks.

7.   Decisions of courts and relevant judicial agencies are binding and executory. Any person preventing their execution is liable to be prosecuted.

8.   The appointment of judges and prosecutors is the exclusive responsibility of judicial power. Legislative and executive powers may not interfere in these appointments.

9.   Judicial power, represented by the [Higher] Judicial Council, is solely in charge of managing the affairs of judges and public prosecutors, starting with their appointment through promotion, transfer, guarantee and stability in their positions, salaries and benefits, disciplinary measures, criminal responsibility [i.e., removal of immunity from the delinquent judge], continuous education, freedom of expression, membership in and formation of professional and economic associations.

10. Judicial power is committed to establishing a law that organizes the affairs of judges, public prosecutors and auxiliaries. Judges and prosecutors will enjoy full independence in carrying out their duties in accordance with the law. Their promotion will be based on their abilities without attention to gender, community or ethnicity. Financial resources will be secured, as will protection against vengeance, threats, or criticism for their discharging their duties, by way of threats and the wrongful use of the media. They will remain accountable for faulty professional

behavior before a higher judicial body. They will receive enough compensation upon retirement, or upon death for their families, so that members of the judiciary will not need to get this security by illegal means.

11. Amendment of constitutional texts regarding judicial power will not be carried out with a majority of less than two thirds of the National Assembly members, so that the Constitution provide the assured guarantee of protecting judicial independence and enabling it to fulfill its calling for the consolidation of the rule of law, the protection of human rights and freedoms, and securing justice in society.

NOTES AND QUESTIONS

1. This text was probably written in 2003 or 2004. How much was the Chief Justice's vision fulfilled? In the 2005 Constitution? In the laws? In practice?

2. How can the "direct link" to the president (literally, head of state in the Arabic original) ensure the independence of the judiciary ?

3. Judicial independence from the executive is not easy to secure, in Iraq or elsewhere. How will members of the political branches be prosecuted when using their influence with judges? How does one stop the infamous telephone call? Indeed how does one know about it in the first place? And even if the principle is separation of powers, can the public prosecutors be independent from the Ministry of Justice, which provides the security and other services without which it is difficult to imagine them operating?

INTERNATIONAL LAW
AND THE UNITED NATIONS

Introduction. This chapter addresses international law issues mostly relevant to Iraq after 2003. The United Nations' "seal of legitimacy," as former UN Secretary General Kofi Annan underlined time and again, is essential to the international rule of law. The debate on the exact relevance of the organization remains as active nowadays as it was in 2003, when U.S. President George W. Bush's "coalition of the willing" was developed to bypass the UN. One question looming over the international order takes the shape of the usefulness of a "league of democracies," mainly Western, to prevent countries perceived to be authoritarian, chiefly Russia and China, from using their veto power in New York. The debate, however, is inevitably global. The EU's "soft power" strategy, with complications arising from the permanent UN membership of France and Britain, and the history of the Transatlantic relation and NATO, have turned Iraq into a defining international issue for the whole planet. For a fresh account by an Italian international relations expert, see

Vittorio Emanuele Parsi, *The Inevitable Alliance: Europe and the United States Beyond Iraq* (2007).

Iraq, in the midst of this unique international maelstrom, is trying to survive three decades of continuous wars. Iraqis have been subjected to massive violence since the devastating Iran-Iraq war between 1980 and 1988, through to the Kuwait invasion and a decade and a half of unprecedented isolation between 1990 and 2003, the 2003 invasion, and the armed resistance, civil war and ethnic cleansing that reached its height in 2005-2006. Civilian casualties have been massive, while the economic costs spiraled. Chris Hedges & Laila al-Arian, *Collateral Damage, America's War Against Iraqi Civilians* (2008), underlines the former; Joseph Stiglitz & Linda Bilmes, *The Three Trillion Dollar War* (2008), the latter. Human rights and economic issues are dealt with in more detail in Chapters 4 and 6. International law as it bears on boundaries, the unprecedented food-for-oil regime, and a massive debt, is discussed in this chapter, against the immense shadow cast by the UN troubled history over Iraq.

A. TIMELINE OF POST-INVASION UN SECURITY COUNCIL RESOLUTIONS ON IRAQ 2003–2008

Introduction. Summaries of UN Resolutions can be found in the Iraq Analysis Group's study at http://www.iraqanalysis.org/info/343, current until the end of 2007. The UN site (www.un.org/Docs/sc) includes all resolutions and is reliably updated. Asterisks (*) in the table below denote resolutions whose text are included in this chapter. See also the chronological table on Iraqi earlier history in Chapter 2, and modern chronologies by Henry E. Mattox, *A Chronology of United States-Iraqi Relations 1920-2006* (2008), and Appendix 2 for a list of the 57 Security Council Resolutions between 1974 and 2006, at 173-174. The Center for Arab Unity, based in Beirut, published a massive compilation of documents related to the conflict, *Markaz dirasat al-wahda al-'arabiyya, Al-harb 'alal-'iraq 1990-2005* (The War on Iraq 1990-2005) (2007).

Date	Summary
March 19, 2003	**Beginning of "Operation Iraqi Freedom."**
March 28, 2003	**UN Security Council Resolution 1472.** • Authorized administration of oil-for-food programme for the next 45 days. • Authorized Secretary-General to establish alternate locations for delivery of humanitarian supplies and equipment, and proceed with its work after a review and re-prioritization of contracts. • Provided additional flexibility for funding certain changes in Programme activities necessitated by the invasion.

Date	Summary
April 9, 2003	**Baghdad falls to Multi-National Force.**
April 21, 2003	**Establishment by the U.S. of the Coalition Provisional Authority.**
April 24, 2003	**UN Security Council Resolution 1476.** • Extended certain provisions of UN Security Council Resolutions until June 3, 2003.
May 1, 2003	**From the deck of the USS Abraham Lincoln, U.S. President George W. Bush announces the end of major combat operations in Iraq.**
May 22, 2003	**UN Security Council Resolution 1483.*** • Lifted non-military sanctions. • Formally recognized the Coalition Provisional Authority and called on it to improve security and stability. • Called for the provision of opportunities for Iraqis to determine their political future. • Created the position of UN Secretary General's Special Representative to Iraq. • Provided for termination of oil-for-food programme and the transfer of its assets to a new Development Fund for Iraq. • Froze Iraqi government assets in member states and provided for their transfer to the Development Fund for Iraq.
May, 2003	**Sergio Vieira de Mello appointed UN Secretary General's Special Representative for Iraq.**
July 3, 2003	**UN Security Council Resolution 1490.** • Set the date for the disbanding of the UN Iraq-Kuwait Observer Mission (UNIKOM) as the 6 October 2003. • Terminated the demilitarized zone between Iraq and Kuwait effective October 6, 2003.
July 13, 2003	**Establishment of the Iraqi Governing Council.**
August 14, 2003	**UN Security Council Resolution 1500.*** • Welcomed the creation of Governing Council. • Established UN Assistance Mission for Iraq (UNAMI), as suggested by the Secretary General's report of July 17, 2003.
August 19, 2003	**First Canal Hotel bombing. UN Special Representative Sergio Vieira de Mello is among those killed.**
September 22, 2003	**Second Canal Hotel bombing.**

Date	Summary
October 12, 2003	**Ross Mountain appointed Acting Special Representative pending the appointment of a new Special Representative.**
October 16, 2003	**UN Security Council Resolution 1511.*** • Condemned the attacks on the UN headquarters in Baghdad and other terrorist attacks and recognized the situation in Iraq as a "threat to international peace and security." • Mandated that the UN "strengthen its vital role in Iraq," "as circumstances permit." • Reiterated the "temporary nature" of the CPA and the steps taken towards Iraqi self-government, and invited the Iraqi Governing Council to develop a timetable for the drafting of a constitution and elections; requested progress reports on these efforts from the CPA. • Authorized a multinational security force. This mandate to be reviewed within a year, and to expire on transfer of power to an Iraqi government. • Encouraged member states to contribute both to the multinational security force and towards Iraqi reconstruction efforts.
October 30, 2003	**Non-Iraqi UN staff are evacuated from Baghdad.**
November 21, 2003	**Oil-for-Food Program officially terminated.**
November 24, 2003	**UN Security Council Resolution 1518.** • Established a committee to locate money belonging to the former regime, and transfer it to the Development Fund for Iraq. (This work had formerly been undertaken by the "661 committee" which had been a part of the oil-for-food program, and which had ceased to exist on November 22.)
January 27, 2004	**UN Secretary-General Kofi Annan announces that a UN team led by Lakhdar Brahimi will return to Iraq to assess the possibility for direct elections.**
April 21, 2004	**UN Security Council Resolution 1538.** • Established a high-level inquiry to investigate oil-for-food kickbacks.
June 8, 2004	**UN Security Council Resolution 1546.** • Endorsed the formation of the interim government, the end of the occupation and the planned January 2005 elections.

Date	Summary
	• Directed the UN Assistance Mission to play a leading role in the upcoming elections and to otherwise support the Iraqi Interim Government. • Renewed the mandate for the multinational force pursuant to letters from Iraqi Prime Minister Ayad Allawi and U.S. Secretary of State Colin Powell.
June 28, 2004	**Coalition Provisional Authority succeeded by Iraqi Interim Government.**
July 14, 2004	**Ashraf Jehangir Qazi appointed UN Secretary General's Special Representative for Iraq.**
August 12, 2004	**UN Security Council Resolution 1557.** • Extended the mandate of the UN Assistance Mission for Iraq for twelve months.
January 30, 2005	**Election of transitional Iraqi National Assembly.**
May 3, 2005	**Iraqi Interim Government succeeded by Iraqi Transitional Government**
August 11, 2005	**UN Security Council Resolution 1619.** • Extended the mandate of the UN Assistance Mission for Iraq for twelve months.
October 15, 2005	**New Iraqi constitution is approved by a national referendum.**
November 8, 2005	**UN Security Council Resolution 1637.** • Extended the mandate of the multinational force until December, 2006, subject to review by Iraqi government prior to June 15, 2006. • Extended current arrangements for the depositing into the Development Fund for Iraq of proceeds from petroleum product export sales until December 2006, also subject to review by Iraqi government prior to June 15, 2006.
December 15, 2005	**Election of permanent Iraqi National Assembly.**
May 20, 2006	**Iraqi Transitional Government succeeded by permanent Government of Iraq.**
August 10, 2006	**UN Security Council Resolution 1700.** • Renewed mandate of the UN Assistance Mission for Iraq.
November 28, 2006	**UN Security Council Resolution 1723.** • Extended the mandate of the multinational force until the end of 2007.
January 1, 2007	**Ban Ki-Moon replaces Kofi Annan as Secretary General of the United Nations.**

Date	Summary
June 29, 2007	**UN Security Council Resolution 1762.** • Terminated the operation of UN weapons inspections teams and IAEA in Iraq. • Transferred funds held to finance WMD inspections to Development Fund for Iraq.
August 10, 2007	**UN Security Council Resolution 1770.*** • Renewed mandate of the UN Assistance Mission for Iraq and expanded it to include economic, human rights, and legal reform, as well as the reconstructive role it had taken previously.
September 11, 2007	**Staffan de Mistura appointed UN Secretary General's Special Representative for Iraq.**
December 18, 2007	**UN Security Council Resolution 1790.** • Extended the mandate of the multinational force until the end of 2008.
August 7, 2008	**UN Security Council Resolution 1830.** • Extended the mandate of the multinational force until the end of 2009.
December 22, 2008	**UN Security Council Resolution 1859.*** • Extended the Development Fund for Iraq arrangements until end 2009. • Accepted the request of the Government of Iraq to review all UNSC resolutions since 661 (1990) with a view to fully restore the sovereignty of the country as it was before the invasion of Kuwait.

B. OCCUPATION AND THE COALITION PROVISIONAL AUTHORITY (MARCH 2003–JUNE 28, 2004)

Introduction. Even before the invasion of Iraq, a passionate discussion amongst American political leaders and Iraqi oppositional figures had been taking place since at least 1991 over the best way to end the dictatorship in Iraq. Part of the complex dialogue was UN Security Council Resolution 688 (April 5, 1991), which "[c]ondemns the repression of the Iraqi civilian population in many parts of Iraq, including most recently in Kurdish populated areas, the consequences of which threaten international peace and security in the region; [and d]emands that Iraq, as a contribution to remove the threat to international peace and security in the region, immediately end this repression."

Nearer the invasion, which started on March 19, 2003, the idea of an oppositional government developed. U.S. government officials, headed by Zalmay Khalilzad, then USG special coordinator with the Iraqi opposition, met with some of its leaders in November 2002 in Northern Iraq. The idea of an oppositional government stalled over resistance from Sunni participants. Would such a government—not technically in exile, as it was to be established on Iraqi territory known as "the Safe Haven"—have constituted an alternative to occupation? Could it have been considered as a form of belated implementation of UNSCR 688 by providing an alternative to the authority of the central Baghdad government led by Saddam Hussein, and by securing a recognized repression-free zone in a significant part of Iraq?

Alternatives to war were sought at the highest level in the region, and in Washington. The following minutes, released four years after the event, suggest the skeptical readiness of the American president to avoid the war in the event of Saddam Hussein's departure. It also underlines a clear objective, the removal of Hussein's regime, rather than the declared WMD-removal policy.

1. THE MARCH TO WAR

THE *PAÍS* MINUTES

El País, Sept. 26, 2007*

Transcript of a meeting between President George W. Bush and Spanish Prime Minister José María Aznar at Crawford, Texas, on February 22, 2003.

President Bush: We're in favor of obtaining a second resolution in the Security Council and we'd like to do it quickly. We'd like to announce it on Monday or Tuesday [February 24, 2003].

Prime Minister Aznar: Better on Tuesday, after the meeting of the European Union's General Affairs Council. It's important to maintain the momentum achieved by the resolution of the European Union summit [in Brussels, on Monday, February 17]. We'd prefer to wait until Tuesday.

PB: It could be Monday afternoon, taking the time zone differences into account. In any case, next week. We're looking at a resolution drafted in such a way that it doesn't contain mandatory elements, that doesn't mention the use of force, and that states that Saddam Hussein has been incapable of fulfilling his obligations. That kind of resolution can be voted for by lots of people. It would be similar to the one passed during Kosovo [on June 10, 1999].

PMA: Would it be presented to the Security Council before and independently of a parallel declaration?

Condoleezza Rice: In fact there won't be a parallel declaration. We're thinking about a resolution that would be as simple as possible, without too many details on compliance that Saddam could use as [an excuse to stall via] phases

---

*Available at http://www.nybooks.com/articles/20770. Original Spanish publication: http://www.elpais.com/articulo/espana/Llego/momento/deshacerse/Sadam/elpepunac/20070926 elpepinac_1/Tes.

and consequently fail to meet. We're talking with Blix [the UN chief inspector] and others on his team, to get ideas that can help introduce the resolution.

PB: Saddam Hussein won't change and he'll continue playing games. The time has come to get rid of him. That's it. As for me, I'll try from now on to use a rhetoric that's as subtle as can be while we're seeking approval of the resolution. If anyone vetoes [Russia, China, and France together with the U.S. and the UK have veto power in the Security Council, being permanent members], we'll go. Saddam Hussein isn't disarming. We have to catch him right now. Until now we've shown an incredible amount of patience. There are two weeks left. In two weeks we'll be militarily ready. I think we'll get the second resolution. In the Security Council we have the three Africans [Cameroon, Angola, and Guinea], the Chileans, the Mexicans. I'll talk to all of them, also Putin, naturally. We'll be in Baghdad by the end of March. There's a 15 percent chance that at that point Saddam Hussein will be dead or will have fled. But those possibilities don't exist until we've shown our resolve. The Egyptians are talking to Saddam Hussein. It seems that he's indicated that he's willing to go into exile if they let him take $1 billion and all the information that he wants about the weapons of mass destruction. [Muammar] Gaddafi has told Berlusconi that Saddam Hussein wants to go. Mubarak tells us that in those circumstances there are many possibilities that he'll be assassinated. We'd like to act with the mandate of the United Nations. If we act militarily, we'll do it with great precision and focus very closely on our objectives. We'll decimate the loyal troops and the regular army will know quickly what it's about. We've sent a very clear message to Saddam's generals: we'll treat them as war criminals. We know that they've accumulated a huge amount of dynamite to blow up the bridges and other infrastructure, and blow up the oil wells. We've planned to occupy those wells very quickly. The Saudis will also help us by putting as much oil as necessary on the market. We're developing a very strong humanitarian aid package. We can win without destruction. We're already putting into effect a post-Saddam Iraq, and I believe there's a good basis for a better future. Iraq has a good bureaucracy and a civil society that's relatively strong. It could be organized into a federation. Meanwhile, we're doing all we can to attend to the political needs of our friends and allies.

PMA: It's very important to [be able to] count on a resolution. It isn't the same to act with it as without it. It would be very convenient to count on a majority in the Security Council that would support that resolution. In fact, having a majority is more important than anyone casting a veto. We think the content of the resolution should state, among other things, that Saddam Hussein has lost his opportunity.

PB: Yes, of course. That would be better than to make a reference to "all means necessary" [referring to the standard UN resolution that authorizes the use of "all means necessary"].

PMA: Saddam Hussein hasn't cooperated, he hasn't disarmed, we should make a summary of his breaches and send a more elaborate message. That would, for example, allow Mexico to make a move [he refers to changing its position, opposed to the second resolution, that Aznar heard personally from President Vicente Fox on Friday, February 21 during a travel stop he made in Mexico City].

PB: The resolution will be tailored to help you as best it can. I don't care much about the content.

PMA: We'll send you some texts.

PB: We don't have any text. Just one condition: that Saddam Hussein disarms. We can't allow Saddam Hussein to stall until summer. After all, he's had four months already in this last phase, and that's more than sufficient time to disarm.

PMA: That text would help us sponsor it and be its coauthors, and convince many people to sponsor it.

PB: Perfect.

PMA: Next Wednesday [February 26] I'll meet with Chirac. The resolution will have started to circulate by then.

PB: That seems good to me. Chirac knows the reality perfectly. His intelligence services have explained it to him. The Arabs are sending Chirac a very clear message: Saddam Hussein should go. The problem is that Chirac thinks he's Mister Arab, and in reality he's making life impossible for them. But I don't want any rivalry with Chirac. We have different points of view, but I would want that to be all. Give him my best regards. Really! The less he feels that rivalry exists between us, the better for all of us.

PMA: How will the resolution and the inspectors' report be combined?

Condoleezza Rice: Actually there won't be a report on February 28, the inspectors will present a written report on March 1, and their appearance before the Security Council won't happen until March 6 or 7 of 2003. We don't expect much from that report. As with the previous ones, it will be six of one and half a dozen of the other. I have the impression that Blix will now be more negative than before about the Iraqis' intentions. After the inspectors have appeared before the Council we should anticipate the vote on the resolution taking place one week later. Meanwhile, the Iraqis will try to explain that they're meeting their obligations. It's neither true nor sufficient, even if they announce the destruction of some missiles.

PB: This is like Chinese water torture. We have to put an end to it.

PMA: I agree, but it would be good to be able to count on as many people as possible. Have a little patience.

PB: My patience has run out. I won't go beyond mid-March.

PMA: I'm not asking you to have indefinite patience. Simply that you do everything possible so that everything comes together.

PB: Countries like Mexico, Chile, Angola, and Cameroon have to know that what's at stake is the United States' security and acting with a sense of friendship toward us. [Chilean President Ricardo] Lagos has to know that the Free Trade Agreement with Chile is pending Senate confirmation, and that a negative attitude on this issue could jeopardize that ratification. Angola is receiving funds from the Millennium Account that could also be compromised if they don't show a positive attitude. And Putin must know that his attitude is jeopardizing the relations of Russia and the United States.

PMA: Tony [Blair] would like to extend to the 14th.

PB: I prefer the 10th. This is like good cop, bad cop. I don't mind being the bad cop and that Blair be the good one.

PMA: Is it true that there's a possibility of Saddam Hussein going into exile?

PB: Yes, that possibility exists. Even that he gets assassinated.

PMA: An exile with some guarantee?

PB: No guarantee. He's a thief, a terrorist, a war criminal. Compared to Saddam, Milosevic would be a Mother Teresa. When we go in, we'll uncover many more crimes and we'll take him to the International Court of Justice in The Hague. Saddam Hussein believes he's already gotten away. He thinks France and Germany have stopped holding him to his responsibilities. He also thinks that the protests of last week [Saturday, February 15] protect him. And he thinks I'm much weakened. But the people around him know that things are different. They know his future is in exile or in a coffin. That's why it's so important to keep the pressure on him. Gaddafi tells us indirectly that this is the only thing that can finish him. Saddam Hussein's sole strategy is to stall, stall, and stall.

PMA: In reality, the biggest success would be to win the game without firing a single shot while going into Baghdad.

PB: For me it would be the perfect solution. I don't want the war. I know what wars are like. I know the destruction and the death that comes with them. I am the one who has to comfort the mothers and the widows of the dead. Of course, for us that would be the best solution. Besides, it would save us $50 billion.

PMA: We need your help with our public opinion.

PB: We'll do everything we can. On Wednesday I'll talk about the situation in the Middle East, and propose a new peace framework that you know, and about the weapons of mass destruction, the benefits of a free society, and I'll place the history of Iraq in a wider context. Maybe that's of help to you.

PMA: What we are doing is a very profound change for Spain and the Spaniards. We're changing the politics that the country has followed over the last two hundred years.

PB: I am just as much guided by a historic sense of responsibility as you are. When some years from now History judges us, I don't want people to ask themselves why Bush, or Aznar, or Blair didn't face their responsibilities. In the end, what people want is to enjoy freedom. Not long ago, in Romania, I was reminded of the example of Ceaucescu: it took just one woman to call him a liar for the whole repressive system to come down. That's the unstoppable power of freedom. I am convinced that I'll get that resolution.

PMA: That would be the best.

PB: I made the decision to go to the Security Council. In spite of the disagreements within my administration, I told my people that we should work with our friends. It would be wonderful to have a second resolution.

PMA: The only thing that worries me about you is your optimism.

PB: I am an optimist, because I believe that I'm right. I'm at peace with myself. It's up to us to face a serious threat to peace. It annoys me to no end to contemplate the insensitivity of the Europeans toward the suffering Saddam Hussein inflicts on the Iraqis. Perhaps because he's dark, far away, and a Muslim, many Europeans think that everything is fine with him. I won't forget what [former NATO Secretary General, the Spaniard Javier] Solana once asked me: why we Americans think the Europeans are anti-Semites and incapable of facing their responsibilities. That defensive attitude is terrible. I have to admit that I have a splendid relationship with Kofi Annan.

PMA: He shares your ethical concerns.

PB: The more the Europeans attack me, the stronger I am in the United States.

PMA: We will have to make your strength compatible with the support of the Europeans.

NOTES AND QUESTIONS

1. *Exile for Saddam?* Weeks before the meeting at Crawford, the author of this book was involved in the launch of the Democratic Iraq Initiative as an alternative to war. The idea was formed in late December 2002 in Beirut with Roland Tomb, Selim Mouzannar, Elias Khoury, and Michael Young. Khoury, a celebrated novelist and journalist, drafted a text that was

published in *al-Nahar*, the leading Arab newspaper, and in *The Daily Star*, the leading newspaper in English, on February 1, 2003. The Democratic Iraq Initiative (DII), as it developed, called for Hussein's resignation and the marshalling of Arab opinion towards that goal. On DII, see http://www.mallat.com/iraq%20DII.htm; and see Chapter 4 for the second leg of DII: the concept of "human rights monitors' deployment" in the transitional period following Saddam Hussein's eviction. The initiative was embraced by a large number of personalities from the Arab world, including a significant group in Bahrain that called for the resignation of Hussein to avoid the occupation of Iraq. Two years after the invasion, news came of the late president of the United Arab Emirates Zayed ibn Nahayan working unsuccessfully within the Arab League to call for the resignation of the Iraqi dictator. Would such a call from the Arab League, assuming it materialized, have made any difference? How close were the various initiatives to the discussion between the U.S. president and the Spanish Prime Minister as revealed in the *País* minutes?

2. *Draft SCR on warless transition to democracy.* At a meeting in Washington on March 5, 2003, the author of this book discussed the implementation of DII with then-Deputy Secretary of Defense Paul Wolfowitz and suggested that the option be included in any additional UN Security Council resolution the U.S. might seek. Wolfowitz was sympathetic and supported the initiative, but he voiced his doubts that major European nations would go along with such a scheme. Following the meeting, on the basis of the four points articulated by Wolfowitz and reproduced in the Executive Summary below, a UNSC draft Resolution was prepared to implement the DII concept:

ALTERNATIVE TO WAR DRAFT UN SC RESOLUTION
Source: http://www.mallat.com/iraq%20DII.htm, circulated first week of March 2003

[Executive Summary: "Democratic Iraq Resolution"

1. End of dictatorship: deployment of Human Rights Monitors, with the support and protection of available international forces, to enforce human rights in all the territory of Iraq.
2. Government of Iraq to accept the Resolution and give way to international forces and human rights monitors within 48 hours in zones further defined geographically. (see paras 4, 5, 12 and 13)
3. Acceleration of WMD destruction and establishment of Commission of Enquiry.
4. Reconstruction.

Disclaimer: this Draft resolution was prepared with colleagues at the Human Rights Clinic of the Yale Law School, but the responsibility for its content can in no way be ascribed to any of them or to the Clinic. Particular thanks go to Paul Kahn, Deena Hurwitz, and Greg Khalil for its timely redaction. Through the DII network, it has circulated in major Western capitals, and at UN headquarters.]

The Security Council,
Gravely concerned by the escalating tensions in Iraq and its environs, and the serious consequences war promises for international peace and security,

Mindful of its solemn mission under the United Nations Charter at once to prevent armed conflict wherever possible and to promote and protect all persons' fundamental human rights,

Reaffirming that protecting the fundamental human rights of all persons represents the only way to ensure international peace and security, and to prevent armed conflict,

Recalling all its previous relevant resolutions, in particular its resolutions 661 (1990) of 6 August 1990, 678 (1990) of 29 November 1990, 686 (1991) of 2 March 1991, 687 (1991) of 3 April 1991, 688 (1991) of 5 April 1991, 707 (1991) of 15 August 1991, 715 (1991) of 11 October 1991, 986 (1995) of 14 April 1995, 1284 (1999) of 17 December 1999, and 1382 (2001) of 29 November 2001 and its intention to fully implement all these resolutions,

Recalling in particular its resolution 1441 (2002) of 8 November 2002 and its intention to fully implement it,

Recognizing the grave and increasing threat that the present government of Iraq's non-compliance with Council resolutions, proliferation of weapons of mass destruction and long-range missiles, and gross violations of the fundamental human rights poses to international peace and security,

Noting the significant material breaches, over the course of two decades, of international law and order by the government of Iraq under its present leadership, principally but not exclusively through:

- the aggression against the Islamic Republic of Iran on 22 September 1980
- the repeated use of chemical weapons against its own people and against Iran, notably in the city of Halabja and other Kurdish cities
- the occupation of Kuwait until its forceful eviction by international force,
- "the worst record on human rights since the second World War" amongst the governments of the world, as underlined in the reports of the UN Special Rapporteur on Iraq, such record continuing to date without the government of Iraq ceasing or desisting as requested by this Council in its Resolution 688 of 5 April 1991,
- the occupation of Kuwait until its forceful eviction by international force, the wanton destruction of life and property in Iran, Kuwait, and Iraq, notably in the draining of the Arab Marshes and the forceful displacement of its population,
- the unprovoked attacks against civilian targets across the Middle East and Europe, including the missile attacks against Israeli civilians and the attempt to assassinate the former president of the USA,

All the above amounting to severe breaches of international law and order,

Recalling the Security Council's previous determinations that the government of Iraq has failed to disarm and protect fundamental human rights and has thus failed to adequately comply with Security Council resolutions, in particular resolution 1441 (2002) of 8 November 2002, which found Iraq in material breach of resolution 1382 (2001) of 29 November 2001,

Recalling Iraq's obligations to disclose fully all weapons of mass destruction in its possession and to account for all such weapons previously disposed of or destroyed, and to provide immediate, unconditional and unfettered access to all locations, documentation and personnel in Iraq deemed relevant by United Nations inspection personnel, consistent with the privileges and immunities accorded those personnel under the Charter of the United Nations, as well as previous Security Council resolutions on the inspection regime in Iraq, including resolution 1441 (2002) of 8 November 2002,

Recalling in particular recent reports to the Security Council by UNMOVIC and IAEA revealing that the government of Iraq has not fully cooperated with United Nations weapons inspectors deployed pursuant to Security Council Resolution 1382 (2001) of 29 November 2001 and Resolution 1441 (2002) of 8 November 2002,

Deploring the government of Iraq's refusal to provide immediate, unconditional and unrestricted access to UNMOVIC and IAEA weapons inspectors as mandated by Security Council Resolution 1441 (2002) of 8 November 2002, and its continued obstruction of efforts by the UNMOVIC and the IAEA to discharge their monitoring, inspection and verification duties pursuant to Security Council Resolution 1441 (2002) of 8 November 2002,

Deploring Iraq's proliferation of weapons of mass destruction, at the direct and serious expense of both the humanitarian needs of its own people and regional stability and security,

Deploring further the government of Iraq's failure to comply with its commitments pursuant to resolution 688 (1991) of 5 April 1991 to end repression of its civilian population and to provide access by international humanitarian organizations to all those in need of assistance in Iraq as well as its commitments pursuant to resolution 687 (1991) of 3 April 1991 with regard to terrorism, and resolutions 686 (1991) of 2 March 1991, 687 (1991) of 3 April 1991, and 1284 (1999) of 17 December 1999 to return or cooperate in accounting for Kuwaiti and third country nationals wrongfully detained by Iraq,

Lamenting the government of Iraq's use of weapons of mass destruction against civilian populations within its own sphere of control, in gross violation of both the United Nations Universal Declaration of Human Rights and international conventions concerning weapons of mass destruction, including the 1925 Geneva Protocol for the Prohibition of the Use in War of Asphyxiating, Poisonous or Other Gases, and of Bacteriological Methods of Warfare, ratified by Iraq on 8 September 1931,

Further recalling paragraph 13 of resolution 1441 (2002) of 8 November 2002, also decided under Chapter VII of its Charter powers, which authorizes "serious consequences" in the event that Iraq materially breaches the terms the Council set forth in that resolution,

Reaffirming its strong commitment to the territorial integrity of Iraq, Kuwait, and neighboring nations,

Emphasizing that, for the maintenance of international peace and security and for the good of humanity, particularly the civilian population of Iraq, armed conflict must be avoided if at all possible,

Acting under Chapter VII of the Charter of the United Nations, the Security Council

1. *Decides* that Iraq is in further material breach of resolution 1441 (2002) of 8 November 2002, and of resolution 688 (1991) of 5 April 1991, in addition to all previously cited resolutions, and that the Council must therefore ensure compliance with its previous resolutions mandating the eradication of all Iraqi weapons of mass destruction and protection of the fundamental human rights of all persons within Iraq,

2. *Expands* the mandates and budgets of UNMOVIC and IAEA to support a number of inspectors adequate to accelerate and complete the disarmament process through intensified weapons inspections, and to establish national and regional support offices in Iraq for use by inspection teams for that purpose,

such activities to also provide a model for the preparation and organisation of a Weapons of Mass Destruction Free-Zone across the Middle East as mandated by resolution 687 (3 April 1991)

3. *Declares* the territory of Iraq a "Human Rights Zone" (HRZ), to be administered by United Nations personnel under the authority of the Security Council with the support and assistance of specialised Non-Governmental Organisations,

4. *Directs* the Secretary-General to designate, with the assistance and support of the available forces of permanent members of the Security Council, such sub-Human Rights Zones (HRZs) as necessary for the immediate withdrawal of all Iraqi military and security personnel within the terms specified in paragraphs 12 and 13, and the deployment of human rights monitors under the protection of international forces in accordance with paragraph 5, of the present Resolution,

5. *Directs* the Office of the UN High Commissioner for Human Rights (OHCHR) to establish a national office in Iraq, with regional offices in established HRZs, to monitor and report on all human rights abuses, civil and political, within Iraq, such that all persons working for or affiliated with or protected by the new OHCHR-administered Iraqi human rights office be accorded the privileges and immunities described for United Nations personnel in the Charter of the United Nations and all other relevant international conventions,

6. *Prohibits* any interference with the establishment of HRZs or with the work or privileges and immunities of personnel, or with Iraqi citizens' travel to and from HRZs,

7. *Authorizes* the delivery of food and other humanitarian aid to individuals in established HRZs, to be distributed by OHCHR and UNDP personnel to persons under the authority of the Security Council and under the protection of United Nations security forces,

8. *Commands* the government of Iraq to withdraw immediately all military forces from duly designated HRZs, and to disband all security forces in all HRZs without exception,

9. *Authorizes* the deployment of armed forces to secure designated HRZs in order to facilitate the administration of UN human rights initiatives, and to protect all UN personnel and Iraqi civilians in such areas,

10. *Emphasizes* that the government of Iraq shall not take or threaten hostile acts against any representative or personnel of the United Nations or the IAEA or of any Member State taking action to uphold any Council Resolution, or any persons or family members or coworkers of persons aiding any United Nations or Member Statement personnel in the execution of this or other Security Council resolutions,

11. *Directs* the Secretary-General to establish a Commission of Enquiry into the severe breaches of international law and international humanitarian law carried out by the government of Iraq,

12. *Requests* that the Secretary-General immediately notify Iraq of this resolution, which is binding on Iraq; demands that the government of Iraq signal full and unconditional acceptance of all terms of this resolution within 24 hours of its passage by way of certified letter to the United Nations; demands immediate, unconditional and active cooperation with all UN-affiliated personnel,

13. *Authorizes* the use of any means necessary to enforce this resolution, should the government of Iraq fail to disband all of its security apparatus and personnel in all the territory of Iraq and to withdraw all military and

security forces completely from the required HRZs within 24 hours of its acceptance of this resolution,

14. *Requests* all Member States to give full support to UN personnel in the
discharge of their mandates under this resolution,

15. *Determines* that failure by the government Iraq to accept fully all of
the terms of this resolution, any obstruction, interference or opposition by
Iraq to the weapons inspection or humanitarian initiatives outlined here, or
any further material breach of previous Security Council resolutions, all of
which remain in force, will result in Iraq's disarmament by any means necessary,
including the use of force,

16. *Resolves further* that, notwithstanding any initial acceptance by the government of Iraq of this resolution and its terms, any subsequent obstruction,
interference or opposition by Iraq to the weapons inspection or humanitarian
initiatives outlined here shall constitute further material breach of the government of Iraq's obligations under this and other relevant resolutions,

17. *Resolves* that the Council remain seized of this matter, . . .

NOTES AND QUESTIONS

1. How realistic was the appeal of transforming Iraq into a "Human Rights
   Zone"? In the fog of the imminent invasion, a multitude of actors mobilized
   to develop their own concept of an alternative to all out war. Defenders of the
   status quo coalesced behind the head of the UN Inspectors' team, Swedish
   diplomat Hans Blix. A detailed account was provided by Blix in *Disarming Iraq*
   (2004), and more recently by the Chilean ambassador to the UN, Heraldo
   Muñoz, *A Solitary War* (2008). With the argument of the Weapons of Mass
   Destruction dominating the UN debate, while the clear objective of the U.S.
   administration was the removal of Saddam Hussein, a game of diplomatic
   shadows ensued. For a light reading on a serious issue, see the contradictory
   quotes of the main protagonists in Christopher Cerf & Victor Navasky,
   Mission Accomplished! Or How We Won the War in Iraq: The Experts Speak (2008).

   The following contemporaneous accounts from the *New York Times*
   underline the complex diplomacy at play. One question to bear in mind:
   when an international crisis intensifies, how much can individual actors,
   NGO militants, even government officials and bureaucrats, hold off the
   march to war?

DAVID E. SANGER & WARREN HOGE, THREATS AND RESPONSES: DIPLOMACY; BUSH AND 2 ALLIES SEEM SET FOR WAR TO DEPOSE HUSSEIN

N.Y. Times, Mar. 17, 2003[*]

President Bush and the leaders of Britain and Spain issued an ultimatum to
the United Nations Security Council today, declaring that the diplomatic
effort to win support for disarming Iraq would end on Monday. They made
it clear that they were ready to start a war to depose Saddam Hussein, with or
without the endorsement of the United Nations.

. . .

---

[*]Available at http://query.nytimes.com/gst/fullpage.html?res=9C03E2DA1731F934A25750C
0A9659C8B63&sec=&spon=&pagewanted=1.

But Mr. Bush made it clear today that to his mind, the outcome at the United Nations made little difference, and that military action would begin soon.

"Tomorrow is the day that will determine whether diplomacy can work," he said today, his voice rising and his jaw clenched as he punched the air with his fist. He added: "Saddam Hussein can leave the country if he's interested in peace. You see, the decision is his to make, and it's been his to make all along on whether or not there's the use of military."

But in private, administration officials said they had no doubt what it meant: war without the sanction of the Security Council.

Senior administration officials said that if the three leaders determined by late Monday that the resolution was doomed, it was likely that they would withdraw it. . . .

Mr. Hussein did not respond directly to the ultimatum today, but late on Saturday he placed one of his sons and three other aides in charge of the defense of the nation.

Felicity Barringer, Threats and Responses: Security Council; Eclipsed by Events; U.N. Officials Wonder About the Past and Ponder the Future

N.Y. Times, Mar. 18, 2003[*]

Diplomats and United Nations officials changed their tenses today, speaking less about what was going to happen and more often and more ruefully about what might have been.

. . . With th[e] war seeming imminent, the thin bubble in which the United Nations has existed for the past month, where the topics of discussion were the pursuit of peace, or the meaning of Security Council resolutions on Iraq or the work program of the weapons inspectors, finally disintegrated. . . .

Indeed, there was already talk of the next issue: the United Nations' role in providing assistance and endorsing, in the words of the joint American-British-Spanish declaration from the Azores, "an appropriate post-conflict administration for Iraq."

The French ambassador did not openly complain, preferring to declare victory.

"They have realized that the majority in the Council is against and oppose a resolution authorizing the use of force," said the envoy, Jean-Marc de la Sablière.

There was clear unease here over some American statements in recent days. United Nations officials with memories of exactly what the Security Council did and did not do during earlier crises gritted their teeth at the remark made Sunday by President Bush: "Remember Rwanda or Kosovo — the U.N. didn't do its job."

A report in July 2000 by an independent international panel emphasized that it was the United States that had prevented the Security Council from sending peacekeepers to Rwanda once the 1994 massacres had begun.

---

*Available at http://query.nytimes.com/gst/fullpage.html?res=9E03E5D71431F93BA25750C 0A9659C8B63&sec=&spon=&pagewanted=2.

EDITORIAL, WAR IN THE RUINS OF DIPLOMACY

N.Y. Times, Mar. 18, 2003[*]

America is on its way to war. President Bush has told Saddam Hussein to depart or face attack. For Mr. Hussein, getting rid of weapons of mass destruction is no longer an option. Diplomacy has been dismissed. Arms inspectors, journalists and other civilians have been advised to leave Iraq.

Now that logic is playing out in a war waged without the compulsion of necessity, the endorsement of the United Nations or the company of traditional allies. . . .

This war crowns a period of terrible diplomatic failure, Washington's worst in at least a generation. The Bush administration now presides over unprecedented American military might. What it risks squandering is not America's power, but an essential part of its glory. . . .

The American-sponsored Security Council resolution that was withdrawn yesterday had firm support from only four of the council's 15 members and was opposed by major European powers like France, Germany and Russia. Even the few leaders who have stuck with the Bush administration, like Tony Blair of Britain and José María Aznar of Spain, have done so in the face of broad domestic opposition, which has left them and their parties politically damaged.

There is no ignoring the role of Baghdad's game of cooperation without content in this diplomatic debacle. And France, in its zest for standing up to Washington, succeeded mainly in sending all the wrong signals to Baghdad. . . .

The result is a war for a legitimate international goal against an execrable tyranny, but one fought almost alone. At a time when America most needs the world to see its actions in the best possible light, they will probably be seen in the worst. This result was neither foreordained nor inevitable.

2. *Legality of war.* Was the war "legal"? The general position of international law scholars points to the war's illegality. This is based on the failure to secure an express authorization from the UN Security Council after the acceptance by the Government of Iraq of the deployment of UN inspectors to verify WMD presence in Iraq. See Muege Guersoy Soekmen, *World Tribunal on Iraq: Making the Case Against War* (2008), especially the preface by Richard Falk. Among the most articulate arguments defending the legitimacy of the invasion was the opinion of British Attorney General, Lord Peter Goldsmith, released to the House of Commons on March 17, 2003. The argument is based on the continuous breach of former SC resolutions, especially Security Council Resolution 687 (April 3, 1991), which established the terms of the ceasefire for the first (or more accurately second) Gulf War. The fuller opinion, dated March 7, was more nuanced. It was leaked two years later. See "Full Text: Leaked Summary of Advice," available at http://news.bbc.co.uk/2/hi/uk_news/politics/2857347.stm/.

---

[*]Available at http://query.nytimes.com/gst/fullpage.html?res=9C01EFDA1431F93BA25750C0 A9659C8B63&scp=20&sq=Iraq+resolution&st=nyt.

**Statement of British Attorney General, Peter Goldsmith, on the legality
of the war, 17 March 2003**
Source: http://news.bbc.co.uk/2/hi/uk_news/politics/2857347.stm

. . . All of these resolutions were adopted under Chapter VII of the UN
Charter which allows the use of force for the express purpose of restoring
international peace and security:

1. In resolution 678 the Security Council authorised force against Iraq, to eject
it from Kuwait and to restore peace and security in the area.

2. In resolution 687, which set out the ceasefire conditions after Operation
Desert Storm, the Security Council imposed continuing obligations on Iraq
to eliminate its weapons of mass destruction in order to restore international
peace and security in the area.

Resolution 687 suspended but did not terminate the authority to use force
under resolution 678.

3. A material breach of resolution 687 revives the authority to use force under
resolution 678.

4. In resolution 1441 the Security Council determined that Iraq has been and
remains in material breach of resolution 687, because it has not fully complied
with its obligations to disarm under that resolution.

5. The Security Council in resolution 1441 gave Iraq "a final opportunity to
comply with its disarmament obligations" and warned Iraq of the "serious
consequences" if it did not.

6. The Security Council also decided in resolution 1441 that, if Iraq failed at any
time to comply with and cooperate fully in the implementation of resolution
1441, that would constitute a further material breach.

7. It is plain that Iraq has failed so to comply and therefore Iraq was at the time
of resolution 1441 and continues to be in material breach.

8. Thus, the authority to use force under resolution 678 has revived and so
continues today.

9. Resolution 1441 would in terms have provided that a further decision of
the Security Council to sanction force was required if that had been
intended.

Thus, all that resolution 1441 requires is reporting to and discussion by the
Security Council of Iraq's failures, but not an express further decision to autho-
rise force.

I have lodged a copy of this answer, together with resolutions 678, 687 and
1441 in the Library of both Houses.

3. Can the war be ratified retroactively, by way of the various statements by
the Iraqi government, including Iraqi Prime Minister Ayad Allawi's letter
to the President of Security Council that was attached to UN Resolution
1546? How about UN Resolutions during and subsequent to the war, starting with UNSCR 1472 (March 28, 2003)? Or even Resolution 1483 (May
2003) which develops in great detail the role of the UN in post-Saddam
Iraq? Do elections carried out to appoint a democratic government matter?
Does the continuation of foreign military troops taint the legitimacy of
any subsequent government? Would the full or partial departure of foreign
troops remove these question marks? See also Chapter 7 on U.S.-Iraqi
security arrangements adopted in 2008.

2. FIRST RESPONSE: RESOLUTION 1483

United Nations Security Council Resolution 1483 (2003)

Adopted by the Security Council at its 4761st meeting, on 22 May 2003

The Security Council,

Recalling all its previous relevant resolutions,

Reaffirming the sovereignty and territorial integrity of Iraq,

Reaffirming also the importance of the disarmament of Iraqi weapons of mass destruction and of eventual confirmation of the disarmament of Iraq,

Stressing the right of the Iraqi people freely to determine their own political future and control their own natural resources, *welcoming* the commitment of all parties concerned to support the creation of an environment in which they may do so as soon as possible, and *expressing* resolve that the day when Iraqis govern themselves must come quickly,

Encouraging efforts by the people of Iraq to form a representative government based on the rule of law that affords equal rights and justice to all Iraqi citizens without regard to ethnicity, religion, or gender, and, in this connection, *recalls* resolution 1325 (2000) of 31 October 2000,

Welcoming the first steps of the Iraqi people in this regard, and *noting* in this connection the 15 April 2003 Nasiriyah statement and the 28 April 2003 Baghdad statement,

Resolved that the United Nations should play a vital role in humanitarian relief, the reconstruction of Iraq, and the restoration and establishment of national and local institutions for representative governance,

Noting the statement of 12 April 2003 by the Ministers of Finance and Central Bank Governors of the Group of Seven Industrialized Nations in which the members recognized the need for a multilateral effort to help rebuild and develop Iraq and for the need for assistance from the International Monetary Fund and the World Bank in these efforts,

Welcoming also the resumption of humanitarian assistance and the continuing efforts of the Secretary-General and the specialized agencies to provide food and medicine to the people of Iraq,

. . .

Affirming the need for accountability for crimes and atrocities committed by the previous Iraqi regime,

Stressing the need for respect for the archaeological, historical, cultural, and religious heritage of Iraq, and for the continued protection of archaeological, historical, cultural, and religious sites, museums, libraries, and monuments,

Noting the letter of 8 May 2003 from the Permanent Representatives of the United States of America and the United Kingdom of Great Britain and Northern Ireland to the President of the Security Council (S/2003/538) and recognizing the specific authorities, responsibilities, and obligations under applicable international law of these states as occupying powers under unified command (the "Authority"),

Noting further that other States that are not occupying powers are working now or in the future may work under the Authority,

Welcoming further the willingness of Member States to contribute to stability and security in Iraq by contributing personnel, equipment, and other resources under the Authority,

. . .

Determining that the situation in Iraq, although improved, continues to constitute a threat to international peace and security,

Acting under Chapter VII of the Charter of the United Nations,

1. *Appeals* to Member States and concerned organizations to assist the people of Iraq in their efforts to reform their institutions and rebuild their country, and to contribute to conditions of stability and security in Iraq in accordance with this resolution;

2. *Calls upon* all Member States in a position to do so to respond immediately to the humanitarian appeals of the United Nations and other international organizations for Iraq and to help meet the humanitarian and other needs of the Iraqi people by providing food, medical supplies, and resources necessary for reconstruction and rehabilitation of Iraq's economic infrastructure;

3. *Appeals* to Member States to deny safe haven to those members of the previous Iraqi regime who are alleged to be responsible for crimes and atrocities and to support actions to bring them to justice;

4. *Calls upon* the Authority, consistent with the Charter of the United Nations and other relevant international law, to promote the welfare of the Iraqi people through the effective administration of the territory, including in particular working towards the restoration of conditions of security and stability and the creation of conditions in which the Iraqi people can freely determine their own political future;

5. *Calls upon* all concerned to comply fully with their obligations under international law including in particular the Geneva Conventions of 1949 and the Hague Regulations of 1907;

. . .

7. *Decides* that all Member States shall take appropriate steps to facilitate the safe return to Iraqi institutions of Iraqi cultural property and other items of archaeological, historical, cultural, rare scientific, and religious importance illegally removed from the Iraq National Museum, the National Library, and other locations in Iraq since the adoption of resolution 661 (1990) of 6 August 1990, including by establishing a prohibition on trade in or transfer of such items and items with respect to which reasonable suspicion exists that they have been illegally removed, and *calls upon* the United Nations Educational, Scientific, and Cultural Organization, Interpol, and other international organizations, as appropriate, to assist in the implementation of this paragraph;

8. *Requests* the Secretary-General to appoint a Special Representative for Iraq whose independent responsibilities shall involve reporting regularly to the Council on his activities under this resolution, coordinating activities of the United Nations in post-conflict processes in Iraq, coordinating among United Nations and international agencies engaged in humanitarian

assistance and reconstruction activities in Iraq, and, in coordination with the Authority, assisting the people of Iraq through:

(a) coordinating humanitarian and reconstruction assistance by United Nations agencies and between United Nations agencies and non-governmental organizations;

(b) promoting the safe, orderly, and voluntary return of refugees and displaced persons;

(c) working intensively with the Authority, the people of Iraq, and others concerned to advance efforts to restore and establish national and local institutions for representative governance, including by working together to facilitate a process leading to an internationally recognized, representative government of Iraq;

(d) facilitating the reconstruction of key infrastructure, in cooperation with other international organizations;

(e) promoting economic reconstruction and the conditions for sustainable development, including through coordination with national and regional organizations, as appropriate, civil society, donors, and the international financial institutions;

(f) encouraging international efforts to contribute to basic civilian administration functions;

(g) promoting the protection of human rights;

(h) encouraging international efforts to rebuild the capacity of the Iraqi civilian police force; and

(i) encouraging international efforts to promote legal and judicial reform;

9. *Supports* the formation, by the people of Iraq with the help of the Authority and working with the Special Representative, of an Iraqi interim administration as a transitional administration run by Iraqis, until an internationally recognized, representative government is established by the people of Iraq and assumes the responsibilities of the Authority;

10. *Decides* that, with the exception of prohibitions related to the sale or supply to Iraq of arms and related materiel other than those arms and related materiel required by the Authority to serve the purposes of this and other related resolutions, all prohibitions related to trade with Iraq and the provision of financial or economic resources to Iraq established by resolution 661 (1990) and subsequent relevant resolutions, including resolution 778 (1992) of 2 October 1992, shall no longer apply;

11. *Reaffirms* that Iraq must meet its disarmament obligations, *encourages* the United Kingdom of Great Britain and Northern Ireland and the United States of America to keep the Council informed of their activities in this regard, and *underlines* the intention of the Council to revisit the mandates of the United Nations Monitoring, Verification, and Inspection Commission and the International Atomic Energy Agency as set forth in resolutions 687 (1991) of 3 April 1991, 1284 (1999) of 17 December 1999, and 1441 (2002) of 8 November 2002;

12. *Notes* the establishment of a Development Fund for Iraq to be held by the Central Bank of Iraq and to be audited by independent public accountants

approved by the International Advisory and Monitoring Board of the Development Fund for Iraq and looks forward to the early meeting of that International Advisory and Monitoring Board, whose members shall include duly qualified representatives of the Secretary-General, of the Managing Director of the International Monetary Fund, of the Director-General of the Arab Fund for Social and Economic Development, and of the President of the World Bank;

13. *Notes further* that the funds in the Development Fund for Iraq shall be disbursed at the direction of the Authority, in consultation with the Iraqi interim administration, for the purposes set out in paragraph 14 below;

14. *Underlines* that the Development Fund for Iraq shall be used in a transparent manner to meet the humanitarian needs of the Iraqi people, for the economic reconstruction and repair of Iraq's infrastructure, for the continued disarmament of Iraq, and for the costs of Iraqi civilian administration, and for other purposes benefiting the people of Iraq;

15. *Calls upon* the international financial institutions to assist the people of Iraq in the reconstruction and development of their economy and to facilitate assistance by the broader donor community, and *welcomes* the readiness of creditors, including those of the Paris Club, to seek a solution to Iraq's sovereign debt problems;

16. *Requests* also that the Secretary-General, in coordination with the Authority, continue the exercise of his responsibilities under Security Council resolution 1472 (2003) of 28 March 2003 and 1476 (2003) of 24 April 2003, for a period of six months following the adoption of this resolution, and terminate within this time period, in the most cost effective manner, the ongoing operations of the "Oil-for-Food" Programme (the "Programme"), both at headquarters level and in the field, transferring responsibility for the administration of any remaining activity under the Programme to the Authority, including by taking the following necessary measures:

(a) to facilitate as soon as possible the shipment and authenticated delivery of priority civilian goods as identified by the Secretary-General and representatives designated by him, in coordination with the Authority and the Iraqi interim administration, under approved and funded contracts previously concluded by the previous Government of Iraq, for the humanitarian relief of the people of Iraq, including, as necessary, negotiating adjustments in the terms or conditions of these contracts and respective letters of credit as set forth in paragraph 4 (d) of resolution 1472 (2003);

(b) to review, in light of changed circumstances, in coordination with the Authority and the Iraqi interim administration, the relative utility of each approved and funded contract with a view to determining whether such contracts contain items required to meet the needs of the people of Iraq both now and during reconstruction, and to postpone action on those contracts determined to be of questionable utility and the respective letters of credit until an internationally recognized, representative government of Iraq is in a position to make its own determination as to whether such contracts shall be fulfilled;

(c) to provide the Security Council within 21 days following the adoption of this resolution, for the Security Council's review and consideration, an estimated operating budget based on funds already set aside in the account established pursuant to paragraph 8 (d) of resolution 986 (1995) of 14 April 1995, . . .

(e) to fulfil all remaining obligations related to the termination of the Programme, including negotiating, in the most cost effective manner, any necessary settlement payments, which shall be made from the escrow accounts established pursuant to paragraphs 8 (a) and 8 (b) of resolution 986 (1995), with those parties that previously have entered into contractual obligations with the Secretary-General under the Programme, and to determine, in coordination with the Authority and the Iraqi interim administration, the future status of contracts undertaken by the United Nations and related United Nations agencies under the accounts established pursuant to paragraphs 8 (b) and 8 (d) of resolution 986 (1995);

(f) to provide the Security Council, 30 days prior to the termination of the Programme, with a comprehensive strategy developed in close coordination with the Authority and the Iraqi interim administration that would lead to the delivery of all relevant documentation and the transfer of all operational responsibility of the Programme to the Authority;

17. *Requests further* that the Secretary-General transfer as soon as possible to the Development Fund for Iraq 1 billion United States dollars from unencumbered funds in the accounts established pursuant to paragraphs 8 (a) and 8 (b) of resolution 986 (1995), restore Government of Iraq funds that were provided by Member States to the Secretary-General as requested in paragraph 1 of resolution 778 (1992), and *decides* that, after deducting all relevant United Nations expenses associated with the shipment of authorized contracts and costs to the Programme outlined in paragraph 16 (c) above, including residual obligations, all surplus funds in the escrow accounts established pursuant to paragraphs 8 (a), 8 (b), 8 (d), and 8 (f) of resolution 986 (1995) shall be transferred at the earliest possible time to the Development Fund for Iraq;

18. *Decides* to terminate effective on the adoption of this resolution the functions related to the observation and monitoring activities undertaken by the Secretary-General under the Programme, including the monitoring of the export of petroleum and petroleum products from Iraq;

. . .

20. *Decides* that all export sales of petroleum, petroleum products, and natural gas from Iraq following the date of the adoption of this resolution shall be made consistent with prevailing international market best practices, to be audited by independent public accountants reporting to the International Advisory and Monitoring Board referred to in paragraph 12 above in order to ensure transparency, and *decides further* that, except as provided in paragraph 21 below, all proceeds from such sales shall be deposited into the Development Fund for Iraq until such time as an internationally recognized, representative government of Iraq is properly constituted;

21. *Decides further* that 5 per cent of the proceeds referred to in paragraph 20 above shall be deposited into the Compensation Fund established in accordance with resolution 687 (1991) and subsequent relevant resolutions and

that, unless an internationally recognized, representative government of Iraq and the Governing Council of the United Nations Compensation Commission, in the exercise of its authority over methods of ensuring that payments are made into the Compensation Fund, decide otherwise, this requirement shall be binding on a properly constituted, internationally recognized, representative government of Iraq and any successor thereto;

22. *Noting* the relevance of the establishment of an internationally recognized, representative government of Iraq and the desirability of prompt completion of the restructuring of Iraq's debt as referred to in paragraph 15 above, further *decides* that, until December 31, 2007, unless the Council decides otherwise, petroleum, petroleum products, and natural gas originating in Iraq shall be immune, until title passes to the initial purchaser from legal proceedings against them and not be subject to any form of attachment, garnishment, or execution, and that all States shall take any steps that may be necessary under their respective domestic legal systems to assure this protection, and that proceeds and obligations arising from sales thereof, as well as the Development Fund for Iraq, shall enjoy privileges and immunities equivalent to those enjoyed by the United Nations except that the abovementioned privileges and immunities will not apply with respect to any legal proceeding in which recourse to such proceeds or obligations is necessary to satisfy liability for damages assessed in connection with an ecological accident, including an oil spill, that occurs after the date of adoption of this resolution;

23. *Decides* that all Member States in which there are:

(a) funds or other financial assets or economic resources of the previous Government of Iraq or its state bodies, corporations, or agencies, located outside Iraq as of the date of this resolution, or

(b) funds or other financial assets or economic resources that have been removed from Iraq, or acquired, by Saddam Hussein or other senior officials of the former Iraqi regime and their immediate family members, including entities owned or controlled, directly or indirectly, by them or by persons acting on their behalf or at their direction,

shall freeze without delay those funds or other financial assets or economic resources and, unless these funds or other financial assets or economic resources are themselves the subject of a prior judicial, administrative, or arbitral lien or judgment, immediately shall cause their transfer to the Development Fund for Iraq, it being understood that, unless otherwise addressed, claims made by private individuals or non-government entities on those transferred funds or other financial assets may be presented to the internationally recognized, representative government of Iraq; and *decides further* that all such funds or other financial assets or economic resources shall enjoy the same privileges, immunities, and protections as provided under paragraph 22;

24. *Requests* the Secretary-General to report to the Council at regular intervals on the work of the Special Representative with respect to the implementation of this resolution and on the work of the International Advisory and Monitoring Board and *encourages* the United Kingdom of Great Britain and Northern Ireland and the United States of America to inform the Council at regular intervals of their efforts under this resolution;

25. *Decides* to review the implementation of this resolution within twelve months of adoption and to consider further steps that might be necessary;

26. *Calls upon* Member States and international and regional organizations to contribute to the implementation of this resolution;

27. *Decides* to remain seized of this matter.

NOTES AND QUESTIONS

1. *A Military Administration.* Why did the U.S. have a general (Jay Garner) represent it on the ground upon ending the Saddam Hussein regime? Why was L. Paul Bremer then entrusted with running the CPA, rather than an Iraqi Provisional Government? Why didn't the U.S. government turn national power directly over to a transitional government made up of Iraqis, especially the Iraqi Governing Council when it was finally formed in July 2003? Jay Garner never wrote up memoirs, as did his successor. Contrary to Bremer's hands-on policy, Garner preferred a low-key type of administration, with a genuine belief that Iraqis should be in charge. "Garner, for his part, was not anticipating that he would be taking on the political and physical reconstruction of Iraq, and he was hoping to find a partner among the Iraqis." Michael Gordon & Bernard Trainor, Cobra II 534 (2007). In a meeting in Baghdad in December 2004, Jalal Talibani confirmed to the author of this book the insistence of Garner since his arrival in Baghdad on April 20, 2003 to see the Iraqis immediately form a transitional government, and the quarrels amongst the former exiles as a major reason preventing the emergence of an Iraqi government.

2. *ORHA to CPA.* Although National Security Presidential Directive (NSPD) 24, issued on January 20, 2003, was never released, converging news stories show it to have assigned Garner the task to assist, rather than lead, governmental affairs in Iraq. The official organization's name, ORHA, Organization for Reconstruction and Humanitarian Assistance, betrayed that initial caution. There was no mention of political leadership for ORHA, and the concept of "Assistance" translated in the appointment of advisors in key ministries to ensure a smoother transition for the Iraqis. NSPD 24 was also important because it vested authority with the Department of Defense, rather than the State Department. See on Garner, by his "executive assistant," Colonel Kim Olson USAF (Ret.), Iraq and Back: Inside the War to Win the Peace 16-17 (2006), on ORHA's threefold mission, reconstruction of physical infrastructure, humanitarian assistance, and "set[tting] up an environment that would encourage democracy to flourish." The Coalition Provisional Authority was from the outset a different legal entity, as its name indicates, and L. Paul Bremer III was appointed as "presidential envoy," heightening his profile and authority, and weakening Iraqi self-determination. The most striking dimension of Bremer's memoirs, *My Year in Iraq* (2006), is the constant insistence, at all levels in Washington, that he should surrender power as soon as possible to Iraqis — against his own determination to keep the matters in his hands. The personality contrast between Bremer and Garner is remarkable, as is their assessment of the mission assigned. In the process, the Iraqi Governing Council was undermined by

the stigma of occupation. After a relatively calm period, overbearing U.S. occupation, magnified by Bremer's assertion of a high profile and combined with UN persistent meddling, prevented the transition to Iraqi self-government from operating the affairs of the country until the elections two years later. Was the delay inevitable? Did it betray differences of personalities, or of conflicting agencies and institutions?

3. *Occupation.* Noah Feldman, who advised the CPA on legal and constitutional matters in the early period, relates the following story. At a meeting in May 2003 at the Iraqi Bar Association, it turned out that the president of the bar was a Ba'thist. Under the rule of the Bar Association, he had the right to preside, and could not be denied this privilege without the cumbersome dismissal by a large majority of his colleagues, and the holding of new elections: "I've got an answer," Noah Feldman explains, "but I am not sure the crowd is going to like it. 'Judge [to the US judge, Donald Campbell, who was presiding over the meeting], I recommend that you tell him that under the international law of occupation, the CPA is authorized to take all measures to restore public life and order, and that pursuant to the authority vested in you by Ambassador Bremer, you have removed him.'" Noah Feldman, What We Owe Iraq 54-55 (2004). The judge agreed, and fired the president of the bar who picked up his papers and left. "It's over. International law has done its work. But what work was that? By citing Article 43 of the Annex to the Hague Convention of 1907, which requires the occupying power to 'take all measures in its power to restore *l'ordre et la vie publics,* while respecting, unless absolutely prevented, the laws in force in the country,' Judge Campbell has proffered a legal justification for superseding the Iraqi Lawyers Law." Id., at 55.

The stigma of occupation as a formal legal regime loomed large over Iraq, and it is not clear why this legal form was chosen, when, unlike Japan or Germany after World War II, the population by and large, and especially within the major Kurdish and Shi'i constituencies in the country, welcomed the end of a uniquely oppressive regime. Was there a legal alternative to "occupation"? Could another legal regime have been conceived? Would a Security Council Resolution authorizing expressly the use of force to remove Saddam from power have given way to a legal format other than occupation? Would the Afghanistan or Kosovo precedents have worked more appropriately? See also on the stigma of occupation and the realities of direct rule when the legal logic of occupation sets in, Patrick Cockburn, *The Occupation, War and Resistance in Iraq* (2006); Jonathan Steele, *Defeat, Why America and Britain Lost Iraq* (2008).

4. *Re-Integration into the International Community.* UN Security Council Resolution 1483 recognized the Coalition Provisional Authority as the governing entity in Iraq and acknowledged that it would take time to establish a representative government. Nevertheless, it called for "an Iraqi interim administration as a transitional administration run by Iraqis." *Paragraph 9.* It revoked the international sanctions against Iraq enacted in the wake of the First Gulf War, with the exception of arms sales not authorized by the CPA, *Paragraph 10,* but stressed Iraq's continuing obligation to divest itself of any weapons of mass destruction under previous UN resolutions. *Paragraph 11.*

5. *The end of Oil-for-Food.* The United Nations had permitted Iraq to use revenue from its sale of petroleum products in order to purchase humanitarian aid for its citizens. Resolution 1483 provided for the termination of this program. In the future, Iraq's petroleum revenues would be funneled into a new Development Fund for Iraq. This fund was administered by the CPA (and, later, the Iraqi government), and overseen by the International Advisory and Monitoring Board of the Development Fund for Iraq. Resolution 1483 called for the Development Fund to be disbursed in a "transparent" manner. However, the CPA would find the accounting requirements of the Development Fund far less strenuous than those imposed on international aid, including that received from the United States. Later audits of the fund by KPMG and the U.S. government's Special Inspector General for Iraq Reconstruction found major issues with the manner in which these funds had been disbursed. The Development Fund for Iraq continues to function, but oversight of the fund has been gradually transferred to Iraq's own Committee of Financial Experts.

4. *United Nations Compensation Commission.* In the wake of the First Gulf War, UN Security Council Resolution 687 required Iraq to pay compensation to Kuwait for damages inflicted during Iraq's invasion of that country. Compensation payments were to be overseen by the United Nations Compensation Commission.

> On [August 15, 1991], the Security Council adopted resolution 706 (1991), which authorized the import by Member States of oil products originating from Iraq for a six-month period, up to a value of US$1.6 billion, in order to finance the United Nations operations mandated by resolution 687 (1991), including the UN Compensation Commission.
>
> Iraq, however, failed to take advantage of the resolution and ad hoc arrangements became necessary to ensure that the Commission could carry forward its work. These arrangements provided for the Commission's access to an amount advanced from the Working Capital Fund of the United Nations, to reimbursable voluntary contributions from Governments prior to and in accordance with resolution 778 (1992) and to the proceeds of Iraqi oil sold after the invasion of Kuwait that had since been frozen by various Governments.
>
> Early in 1995, new attempts were made to persuade Iraq to accept a scheme that would allow it to sell oil for humanitarian purposes. On 14 April of that year, the Security Council adopted resolution 986 that provided for thirty per cent of the proceeds of such sales to be allocated to the Compensation Fund. However, it was to be twenty months before the scheme came into effect during which time the Commission operated with restricted financing. Ultimately, however, in December 1996, the "oil-for-food" scheme envisaged in resolution 986 (1995) was finally launched and the Commission began to receive thirty per cent of the proceeds of Iraq's oil sales (reduced to 25 per cent pursuant to Security Council resolution 1330 (2000)) thereby permitting the Commission to continue its operations uninterrupted and, more importantly, to begin to make regular compensation payments to successful claimants. (Source: UN Compensation Commission website, at http://www2.unog.ch/uncc/introduc.htm, visited May 2007.)

Resolution 1483 effectively reduced the amount of Iraq's obligation to the Compensation Commission from 25 percent of its petroleum exports to 5 percent. See paragraph 21 of Resolution 1483 above. The current

Government of Iraq continues to make payments to the United Nations Compensation Commission. How fair is such an arrangement? For additional discussion of the topic of compensation, see section D.2 below.

3. FROM DEBACLE TO RENEWED INVOLVEMENT: THE UN ASSISTANCE MISSION TO IRAQ

On July 17, 2003, and pursuant to paragraph 24 of Security Council resolution 1483 (2003), the UN Secretary-General, released a lengthy report which looked forward to a growing role for the organization despite the lingering misgivings by Iraqis and Americans over the past role of the UN secretariat in support of "appeasement" with Saddam Hussein. Full Report available at http://daccessdds.un.org/doc/UNDOC/GEN/N03/430/63/PDF/N0343063.pdf. In the Report, he "endorse[d] the approach taken by [my] Special Representative, which is based on the twin principles of inclusiveness and empowerment of the Iraqi people, and has capacity-building as its natural corollary." A month later, the Special Representative, Brazilian diplomat Sergio Vieira de Mello, who had been appointed on May 27, was killed with several other UN personnel in a massive bomb attack against the UN compound in Baghdad.

The UN promptly retreated from Iraq, but work by the World Bank and other international agencies continued. In January 2004, the UN Secretariat engaged again, eventually sending a new Special Representative, Algerian diplomat Lakhdar Ibrahimi. The following documents underline the difficult, seesaw engagement of the UN in Iraq.

FRESH UN RETREAT FROM IRAQ

BBC, Sept. 25, 2003[*]

The United Nations says it is cutting back its operations in Iraq amid a deteriorating security situation in the country. "Today there remain 42 in Baghdad and 44 in the north of the country, and those numbers can be expected to shrink over the next few days," said Fred Eckhard, a spokesman for UN Secretary General Kofi Annan. . . .

Some 600 international staff were stationed in Iraq before the bomb attack on the UN's Baghdad offices last month, which killed 22 people, including the chief UN envoy, Sergio Vieira de Mello. . . .

Blow for Bush

The reaction in Washington has been a combination of disappointment and sympathy with the UN's plight, says the BBC's David Bamford. The decision is a blow to United States' claims that the security situation in Iraq is under control, and is likely to undermine efforts by US President George W Bush to increase the UN role in Iraqi reconstruction. . . .

Second Bombing

The UN had already scaled back its operation in the country after the suicide attack on its headquarters on 19 August, in which 22 people were killed.

---

[*]Available at http://globalpolicy.igc.org/security/issues/iraq/after/2003/0925retreat.htm.

Where it had around 650 international staff, the blast saw that figure scaled back to about 100.

Most international organisations working in Iraq have been on high alert since the bombing. On Monday, a vehicle exploded at a police checkpoint near the UN headquarters in Baghdad, killing the bomber and an Iraqi police officer, and injuring at least 12 others.

The BBC's Greg Barrow says the latest decision was widely expected after a UN committee examining security in Iraq recommended to Mr Annan that all international staff should be pulled out.

United Nations Security Council Resolution 1500 (2003)

Adopted by the Security Council at its 4808th meeting, on 14 August 2003

The Security Council,

Recalling all its previous relevant resolutions, in particular resolution 1483 (2003) of 22 May 2003,

Reaffirming the sovereignty and territorial integrity of Iraq,

Reaffirming also the vital role for the United Nations in Iraq which was set out in relevant paragraphs of resolution 1483 (2003),

Having considered the report of the Secretary-General of 15 July 2003 (S/2003/715),

1. *Welcomes* the establishment of the broadly representative Governing Council of Iraq on 13 July 2003, as an important step towards the formation by the people of Iraq of an internationally recognized, representative government that will exercise the sovereignty of Iraq;

2. *Decides* to establish the United Nations Assistance Mission for Iraq to support the Secretary-General in the fulfilment of his mandate under resolution 1483 in accordance with the structure and responsibilities set out in his report of 15 July 2003, for an initial period of twelve months;

3. *Decides* to remain seized of this matter.

United Nations Security Council Resolution 1511 (2003)

Adopted by the Security Council at its 4844th meeting, on 16 October 2003

The Security Council,

Reaffirming its previous resolutions on Iraq, including resolution 1483 (2003) of 22 May 2003 and 1500 (2003) of 14 August 2003, and on threats to peace and security caused by terrorist acts, including resolution 1373 (2001) of 28 September 2001, and other relevant resolutions,

. . .

Welcoming the decision of the Governing Council of Iraq to form a preparatory constitutional committee to prepare for a constitutional conference that will draft a constitution to embody the aspirations of the Iraqi people, and *urging* it to complete this process quickly,

Affirming that the terrorist bombings of the Embassy of Jordan on 7 August 2003, of the United Nations headquarters in Baghdad on 19 August 2003, of the Imam Ali Mosque in Najaf on 29 August 2003, and of the Embassy of Turkey on 14 October 2003, and the murder of a Spanish diplomat on 9 October 2003 are attacks on the people of Iraq, the United Nations, and the international community, and *deploring* the assassination of Dr. Akila al-Hashimi, who died on 25 September 2003, as an attack directed against the future of Iraq,

. . .

Determining that the situation in Iraq, although improved, continues to constitute a threat to international peace and security,

Acting under Chapter VII of the Charter of the United Nations,

1. *Reaffirms* the sovereignty and territorial integrity of Iraq, and *underscores*, in that context, the temporary nature of the exercise by the Coalition Provisional Authority (Authority) of the specific responsibilities, authorities, and obligations under applicable international law recognized and set forth in resolution 1483 (2003), which will cease when an internationally recognized, representative government established by the people of Iraq is sworn in and assumes the responsibilities of the Authority, inter alia through steps envisaged in paragraphs 4 through 7 and 10 below;

2. *Welcomes* the positive response of the international community, in fora such as the Arab League, the Organization of the Islamic Conference, the United Nations General Assembly, and the United Nations Educational, Scientific and Cultural Organization, to the establishment of the broadly representative Governing Council as an important step towards an internationally recognized, representative government;

3. *Supports* the Governing Council's efforts to mobilize the people of Iraq, including by the appointment of a cabinet of ministers and a preparatory constitutional committee to lead a process in which the Iraqi people will progressively take control of their own affairs;

4. *Determines* that the Governing Council and its ministers are the principal bodies of the Iraqi interim administration, which, without prejudice to its further evolution, embodies the sovereignty of the State of Iraq during the transitional period until an internationally recognized, representative government is established and assumes the responsibilities of the Authority;

5. *Affirms* that the administration of Iraq will be progressively undertaken by the evolving structures of the Iraqi interim administration;

6. *Calls upon* the Authority, in this context, to return governing responsibilities and authorities to the people of Iraq as soon as practicable and *requests* the Authority, in cooperation as appropriate with the Governing Council and the Secretary-General, to report to the Council on the progress being made;

7. *Invites* the Governing Council to provide to the Security Council, for its review, no later than 15 December 2003, in cooperation with the Authority and, as circumstances permit, the Special Representative of the Secretary-General, a timetable and a programme for the drafting of a new constitution for Iraq and for the holding of democratic elections under that constitution;

8. *Resolves* that the United Nations, acting through the Secretary-General, his Special Representative, and the United Nations Assistance Mission in Iraq, should strengthen its vital role in Iraq, including by providing humanitarian relief, promoting the economic reconstruction of and conditions for sustainable development in Iraq, and advancing efforts to restore and establish national and local institutions for representative government;

9. *Requests* that, as circumstances permit, the Secretary-General pursue the course of action outlined in paragraphs 98 and 99 of the report of the Secretary-General of 17 July 2003 (S/2003/715);

10. *Takes note* of the intention of the Governing Council to hold a constitutional conference and, recognizing that the convening of the conference will be a milestone in the movement to the full exercise of sovereignty, *calls for* its preparation through national dialogue and consensus-building as soon as practicable and *requests* the Special Representative of the Secretary-General, at the time of the convening of the conference or, as circumstances permit, to lend the unique expertise of the United Nations to the Iraqi people in this process of political transition, including the establishment of electoral processes;

11. *Requests* the Secretary-General to ensure that the resources of the United Nations and associated organizations are available, if requested by the Iraqi Governing Council and, as circumstances permit, to assist in furtherance of the programme provided by the Governing Council in paragraph 7 above, and encourages other organizations with expertise in this area to support the Iraqi Governing Council, if requested;

12. *Requests* the Secretary-General to report to the Security Council on his responsibilities under this resolution and the development and implementation of a timetable and programme under paragraph 7 above;

13. *Determines* that the provision of security and stability is essential to the successful completion of the political process as outlined in paragraph 7 above and to the ability of the United Nations to contribute effectively to that process and the implementation of resolution 1483 (2003), and *authorizes* a multinational force under unified command to take all necessary measures to contribute to the maintenance of security and stability in Iraq, including for the purpose of ensuring necessary conditions for the implementation of the timetable and programme as well as to contribute to the security of the United Nations Assistance Mission for Iraq, the Governing Council of Iraq and other institutions of the Iraqi interim administration, and key humanitarian and economic infrastructure;

14. *Urges* Member States to contribute assistance under this United Nations mandate, including military forces, to the multinational force referred to in paragraph 13 above;

15. *Decides* that the Council shall review the requirements and mission of the multinational force referred to in paragraph 13 above not later than one year from the date of this resolution, and that in any case the mandate of the force shall expire upon the completion of the political process as described in paragraphs 4 through 7 and 10 above, and *expresses* readiness to consider on that occasion any future need for the continuation of the multinational force, taking into account the views of an internationally recognized, representative government of Iraq;

16. *Emphasizes* the importance of establishing effective Iraqi police and security forces in maintaining law, order, and security and combating terrorism consistent with paragraph 4 of resolution 1483 (2003), and *calls upon* Member States and international and regional organizations to contribute to the training and equipping of Iraqi police and security forces;

17. *Expresses* deep sympathy and condolences for the personal losses suffered by the Iraqi people and by the United Nations and the families of those United Nations personnel and other innocent victims who were killed or injured in these tragic attacks;

18. *Unequivocally condemns* the terrorist bombings of the Embassy of Jordan on 7 August 2003, of the United Nations headquarters in Baghdad on 19 August 2003, and of the Imam Ali Mosque in Najaf on 29 August 2003, and of the Embassy of Turkey on 14 October 2003, the murder of a Spanish diplomat on 9 October 2003, and the assassination of Dr. Akila al-Hashimi, who died on 25 September 2003, and *emphasizes* that those responsible must be brought to justice;

19. *Calls upon* Member States to prevent the transit of terrorists to Iraq, arms for terrorists, and financing that would support terrorists, and *emphasizes* the importance of strengthening the cooperation of the countries of the region, particularly neighbours of Iraq, in this regard;

20. *Appeals* to Member States and the international financial institutions to strengthen their efforts to assist the people of Iraq in the reconstruction and development of their economy, and *urges* those institutions to take immediate steps to provide their full range of loans and other financial assistance to Iraq, working with the Governing Council and appropriate Iraqi ministries;

21. *Urges* Member States and international and regional organizations to support the Iraq reconstruction effort initiated at the 24 June 2003 United Nations Technical Consultations, including through substantial pledges at the 23-24 October 2003 International Donors Conference in Madrid;

22. *Calls upon* Member States and concerned organizations to help meet the needs of the Iraqi people by providing resources necessary for the rehabilitation and reconstruction of Iraq's economic infrastructure;

23. *Emphasizes* that the International Advisory and Monitoring Board (IAMB) referred to in paragraph 12 of resolution 1483 (2003) should be established as a priority, and *reiterates* that the Development Fund for Iraq shall be used in a transparent manner as set out in paragraph 14 of resolution 1483 (2003);

24. *Reminds* all Member States of their obligations under paragraphs 19 and 23 of resolution 1483 (2003) in particular the obligation to immediately cause the transfer of funds, other financial assets and economic resources to the Development Fund for Iraq for the benefit of the Iraqi people;

25. *Requests* that the United States, on behalf of the multinational force as outlined in paragraph 13 above, report to the Security Council on the efforts and progress of this force as appropriate and not less than every six months;

26. *Decides* to remain seized of the matter.

UNITED NATIONS/WORLD BANK JOINT IRAQ NEEDS ASSESSMENT, OCTOBER 2003

http://siteresources.worldbank.org/IRFFI/Resources/
Joint+Needs+Assessment.pdf

Executive summary

Background and Process

i. This Joint Iraq Needs Assessment was prepared by staff from the United Nations (UN) and the World Bank Group; International Monetary Fund (IMF) staff prepared a macroeconomic assessment. The Needs Assessment covers fourteen priority sectors and three cross-cutting themes, as agreed among the international community at the Technical Reconstruction Meeting held in New York on June 24, 2003. In addition to Iraqi expertise, the work benefited from significant inputs by the Coalition Provisional Authority (CPA), several non-governmental organizations (NGOs), and a number of experts from the European Commission, Australia, Japan, and countries of the European Union.

ii. The Assessment is based on the best possible data available at the time. However, overall security and travel constraints, the tragic events and subsequent repercussions of the bombing of the UN Headquarters in Baghdad, the lack of primary sources and significant time constraints all made systematic data collection extremely difficult. It also interrupted ongoing and planned consultations with Iraqi officials and civil society stakeholders that were considered critical for ensuring Iraqi ownership of the Assessment's findings. To adjust partially for this, Bank and UN staff held intensive discussions on the draft Assessment, and in particular the investment and policy priorities contained therein, with Iraqi representatives in Dubai during the week of September 21, 2003. In addition, IMF staff discussed issues related to macroeconomic policies for 2004, and in particular the draft 2004 budget. Discussions were also held separately on some of the sector assessments in Amman, Jordan. Finally, a meeting to present the findings in the draft Assessment was held with the Core Group (European Union, United Arab Emirates, United States, and Japan) on October 2, 2003, in Madrid.

iii. The purpose of this Needs Assessment is to inform the Donor Reconstruction Conference scheduled for October 23-24, 2003, of the current status and priority reconstruction and rehabilitation needs in each sector, focusing on the most urgent requirements for 2004 and indicative reconstruction needs for the period 2005-2007. In addition, this report strives to put the sector assessments in their proper context, highlighting the need for a sustainable approach to reconstruction and development, and outlining a number of policy reform options. Overall investment needs along with a discussion of absorptive capacity are provided in the final chapter.

NOTES AND QUESTIONS

1. *"Iraqi Expertise."* Some Iraqi officials took issue with the Assessment's claim to have delved on "Iraqi expertise." Ali A. Allawi, later to serve as Minister of Finance in the Iraqi Transitional Government, maintains that "Iraqi ministers were barely consulted on this." Ali A. Allawi, The Occupation of Iraq: Winning the War, Losing the Peace 198 (2007).

2. *The Madrid Conference.* The Joint Iraq Needs Assessment concluded that Iraqi reconstruction would cost a total of $35.8 billion through 2007. A donor conference was held in Madrid on October 23-24, 2003, where a variety of nations and transnational organizations pledged to make donations towards Iraqi reconstruction.

   The donors included:

   • United States: $18.4 billion, contained in a supplementary spending bill approved by Congress a few days after the conference ended (the legislation also included $1.2 billion for Afghanistan and $200 million for Liberia);

- Japan: $1.5 billion in grants in 2004, plus $3.5 billion in loans in 2005-2007;
- World Bank: $3 billion to $5 billion in loans over the next five years;
- International Monetary Fund: $2.5 billion to $4.25 billion in loans over three years;
- European Union: $812 million in 2004;
- Kuwait: $500 million;
- Spain: $300 million through 2007;
- South Korea: $200 million through 2007;
- United Arab Emirates: $215 million;
- China: $24.2 million;
- Slovakia: $290,000.

Many countries, including France, Germany, and Russia — which pledged no new funds — promised to cooperate with the U.S.-led effort to reduce Iraq's large debt burden. Some countries also donated products or services in lieu of money: Bulgaria and Egypt offered technical assistance; Iran donated electricity, gas supplies, and oil export facilities; Vietnam donated rice; and Sri Lanka gave 100 tons of tea. See Esther Pan, *Backgrounder: Iraq: Madrid Donor Conference*, Council on Foreign Relations, available at http://www.cfr.org/publication/7682/#1.

3. ***Administration of International Humanitarian Aid.*** The vast majority of the reconstruction aid pledged at the Madrid conference came from countries with close ties with the United States that were willing to allow the Coalition Provisional Authority to administer the funds directly. Other donors, however, insisted on international oversight for the funds they contributed. Thus was born the International Reconstruction Fund Facility for Iraq. By the end of February 2008, the IRFFI had received just over $1.8 billion in donations. This money is allocated between two funds: one administered by the United Nations Development Group, and another administered by the World Bank. The World Bank fund is generally distributed to Iraqi government ministries, while the UNDG fund is distributed to various United Nations agencies for use in Iraq.

4. Late in December 2003, the UN announced its intention to expand its international staff in Iraq. A highly visible opportunity for an expanded UN role came the following month, when Grand Ayatollah Ali al-Sistani objected to the CPA's intention to select a constitutional assembly by a system of regional caucuses rather than by direct elections. Sistani intimated that he would abide by the decision of a UN team, which arrived in Iraq in early February under the leadership of Lakhdar Brahimi, Special Advisor on Iraq to the UN Secretary General. The team recommended against direct elections at that time, but later that year assisted in laying the groundwork for nationwide elections. Brahimi himself played a role in the formation of the Iraqi Interim Government. See *Letter dated 7 June 2004 from the Secretary General to the President of the Security Council*, available at http://www.undemocracy.com/S-2004-461.pdf.

5. The author of this work was meanwhile involved in an attempt to accelerate the passage of sovereignty to Iraqis. In December 2003, then in February 2004, he visited Baghdad to encourage the Iraqi Governing Council to assert

full sovereignty immediately. He opposed interference, especially by the United Nations, in the formation of the Iraqi government. The following op-ed in the *New York Times* reflected this position:

Chibli Mallat, Note to the U.N.: Hands Off Iraqi Politics
N.Y. Times, Jan. 19, 2004

When members of the Iraqi Governing Council and L. Paul Bremer III, the American administrator in Baghdad, open talks at the United Nations today, nothing short of the future of the region will be at stake. Having come under increasing pressure over its plan to form an Iraqi government without direct elections, the United States is counting on greater United Nations involvement both to help ease the resistance and secure a lasting democracy.

Beyond the involvement of additional stakeholders like France and Germany, can a more determined role on the part of the United Nations trans-late into government-building? Considering the organization's dismal record of silence during Saddam Hussein's 30 years of totalitarian rule, I'm not so sure.

Having visited Iraq last month to meet with the leadership there, I think the better solution already lies within the nation's borders. To spend a day at the 25-member Iraqi Governing Council headquarters is to learn what all honest people in the Arab world already admit: the most representative of all govern-ments in the Middle East sits in Baghdad. With all its shortcomings and contra-dictions, the council covers the fullest possible spectrum of Iraqi society, from the Islamists to the Communists, and all the strands in between, including Shiites, Sunnis, Kurds, Turkmens and Christians.

The continued disagreements in the United Nations over the justification for overthrowing Saddam Hussein and problems with securing postwar peace mask the one major achievement in the new Iraq: within the governing council and outside, freedom reigns supreme. It may sometimes look or sound messy to the rest of the world, but a fledgling democracy often does.

In a heartening sign, no one in Iraq, no matter what side of the debate he is on, is afraid to speak his mind. At the Baghdad airport, for example, an Iraqi employee expressed to me his regret that Saddam Hussein had been caught, and his hope that resistance will survive his arrest.

On the other hand, when I asked Dr. Ibrahim Bahr al-Uloum, Iraq's interim oil minister, about criticism by Baathists within his ministry for his close ties to the United States, he shrugged off the possibility of silencing them. This is especially remarkable, given he had lost several family members to Saddam Hussein's repression.

During my trip, I visited the Bahr al-Uloum home in Najaf, where some 50 tribal leaders from the Middle Euphrates Valley sang of their attachment to Iraq, Shiism and national unity from the mountain to the marsh. The family's patriarch, Sheikh Muhammad Bahr al-Uloum, a member of the governing council and an old friend, is optimistic about Iraq's future. But Sheikh Uloum, who like many struggled for decades against Saddam Hussein's dicta-torship, is also upset at what he perceives as mismanagement of his country by the United States. More than eight months after the passing of the ancien régime, the scene is of intermittent electricity and phone service, no airport service and surreal lines for gas in a country with the second largest oil reserves.

But security, despite newspaper headlines, is a fleeting concern. After all, armed resistance to the new democratic order has no chance of success against the new spirit of freedom if basic services are restored, and if the national political process takes root. This is clearly the dual challenge ahead, and Iraqis rightly feel they are in the best position to run their country.

The way forward, then, is simple. The 10 members of the governing council whom I met with agree on this: the council, as a national unity government, should be unconditionally recognized as in charge of Iraq's destiny, with the support of the United States-led coalition and whoever else wishes to join in a democratic course of reconstruction.

As such, the council would be deemed the official interim government of Iraq — making the United States plan to select a national assembly by July 1 unnecessary. The council would be empowered to draft a constitution and set the parameters for what a new government would look like and when and how it would be elected. In the long term, this would consolidate the whole process of democracy — something Iraqis both in and outside the council want.

Strengthening the power of Iraqis over their own affairs can come with the proviso that any contender who furthers his own political agenda by violent means should be punished by either being banned from a leadership post or being brought to trial by an international court for those crimes. Human rights monitors, supported by the United Nations or the coalition, should be deployed to further ensure international commitment to the cause of democracy and nonviolence.

Today's meeting at the United Nations provides the perfect opportunity to focus the future of Iraq in the right direction: inward. When I met in Baghdad with Naseer Chaderji, a liberal Sunni Arab who sits on the governing council, he voiced skepticism of of the United States' reaction to a request for an acceleration of Iraqi self-governance. While Paul Bremer was a good listener, Mr. Chaderji explained, he was not following suggestions made by Iraqi leaders.

But after discussing the issue with other council members — including Ahmad Chalabi and Ibrahim Jafari, an Islamist Dawa leader — as well as with American officials committed to Middle East democracy, including Paul Wolfowitz, I am more hopeful. I sense that Iraqis and Americans are far more in agreement on the country's future than the controversies there suggest. Now that the most dictatorial system in the region has been undone, the rest of the world owes Iraq's long-ignored victims a commitment to their national unity government.

6. Despite the emphasis of all major figures in the U.S. administration to pass the torch of government to Iraqis, the acceleration of sovereignty was opposed by Bremer. In March and April 2004, the security situation deteriorated dramatically. In June, as sovereignty was finally surrendered to a new Iraqi government, headed by Ayad Allawi, openly favored by the CIA and Brahimi (who failed however to have his preferred candidate, Sunni veteran politician Adnan Pachachi, accede to the presidency), the Governing Council collapsed in profound disagreement. Would matters have been different if the Governing Council had been empowered in 2003 to simply act as fully sovereign, transitional government?

C. THE UN AND THE "SOVEREIGN" GOVERNMENT OF IRAQ (JUNE 28, 2004–MAY 3, 2005)

Introduction. Finally, in late June 2004, formal sovereignty was passed on to the Iraqis. The Interim Government was formed, and Bremer went home on

June 28, closing the CPA chapter in Iraqi history. The stigma of occupation, and the insurgency, fuelled by sectarianism, continued. The UN Security Council promptly acknowledged the new legal situation. Drawing on United Nations Security Council Resolution 1546 (2004), a string of UN resolutions emphasized the role of UNAMI in assisting the Government of Iraq on a wide range of tasks. The most precise language came in Resolution 1770.

UNITED NATIONS SECURITY COUNCIL RESOLUTION 1770 (2007)

Adopted by the Security Council at its 5729th meeting, on 10 August 2007

The Security Council,

Recalling all its previous relevant resolutions on Iraq, in particular 1500 (2003) of 14 August 2003, 1546 (2004) of 8 June 2004, 1557 (2004) of 12 August 2004, 1619 (2005) of 11 August 2005 and 1700 (2006) of 10 August 2006,

Reaffirming the independence, sovereignty, unity and territorial integrity of Iraq,

Emphasizing the importance of the stability and security of Iraq for the people of Iraq, the region, and the international community,

Acknowledging that a democratically elected and constitutionally based Government of Iraq is now in place,

Underscoring the need for all communities in Iraq to reject sectarianism, participate in the political process, and engage in an inclusive political dialogue and national reconciliation for the sake of Iraq's political stability and unity,

Reaffirming the importance of the United Nations, in particular the United Nations Assistance Mission for Iraq (UNAMI), in supporting the efforts of the Iraqi people and Government to strengthen institutions for representative government, promote political dialogue and national reconciliation, engage neighbouring countries, assist vulnerable groups, including refugees and internally displaced persons, and promote the protection of human rights and judicial and legal reform,

Expressing concern for the humanitarian issues confronting the Iraqi people and stressing the need for a coordinated response and adequate resources to address these issues,

Underscoring the sovereignty of the Government of Iraq and reaffirming that all parties should take all feasible steps to ensure the protection of affected civilians, and should create conditions conducive to the voluntary, safe, dignified, and sustainable return of refugees and internally displaced persons,

Urging all those concerned as set forth in international humanitarian law, including the Geneva Conventions and the Hague Regulations, to allow full unimpeded access by humanitarian personnel to all people in need of assistance, and to make available, as far as possible, all necessary facilities for their operations, and to promote the safety, security and freedom of movement of humanitarian personnel and United Nations and its associated personnel and their assets,

Welcoming the formal launch of the International Compact with Iraq on 3 May 2007 as well as the expanded Neighbours Conference on 4 May 2007 and resultant working groups, and underscoring the importance of continued regional and international support for Iraq's development,

Acknowledging with appreciation past contributions by Member States to the United Nations Assistance Mission for Iraq (UNAMI) and recalling the need for UNAMI to have the necessary resources to fulfil its mission,

Welcoming the letter of 6 August 2007 from the Minister for Foreign Affairs of Iraq to the Secretary-General (S/2007/481, annex), expressing the view of the Government of Iraq requesting the United Nations Assistance Mission for Iraq (UNAMI) to assist Iraqi efforts to build a productive and prosperous nation at peace with itself and its neighbours,

1. *Decides* to extend the mandate of UNAMI for another period of twelve months from the date of this resolution;

2. *Decides further* that, as circumstances permit, the Special Representative of the Secretary-General and UNAMI, at the request of the Government of Iraq, shall:

(a) Advise, support, and assist:

(i) The Government and people of Iraq on advancing their inclusive, political dialogue and national reconciliation;

(ii) The Government of Iraq and the Independent High Electoral Commission on the development of processes for holding elections and referendums;

(iii) The Government of Iraq and the Council of Representatives on Constitutional review and the implementation of constitutional provisions, as well as on the development of processes acceptable to the Government of Iraq to resolve disputed internal boundaries;

(iv) The Government of Iraq on facilitating regional dialogue, including on issues of border security, energy, and refugees;

(v) The Government of Iraq at an appropriate time and in connection with progress on reconciliation efforts, on planning, funding and implementing reintegration programmes for former members of illegal armed groups;

(vi) The Government of Iraq on initial planning for the conduct of a comprehensive census;

(b) Promote, support, and facilitate, in coordination with the Government of Iraq:

(i) The coordination and delivery of humanitarian assistance and the safe, orderly, and voluntary return, as appropriate, of refugees and displaced persons;

(ii) The implementation of the International Compact with Iraq, including coordination with donors and international financial institutions;

(iii) The coordination and implementation of programmes to improve Iraq's capacity to provide essential services for its people and continue active donor coordination of critical reconstruction and assistance programmes through the International Reconstruction Fund Facility for Iraq (IRFFI);

(iv) Economic reform, capacity-building and the conditions for sustainable development, including through coordination with national and regional organizations and, as appropriate, civil society, donors, and international financial institutions;

(v) The development of effective civil, social and essential services, including through training and conferences in Iraq when possible;

(vi) The contributions of United Nations agencies, funds, and programmes to the objectives outlined in this resolution under a unified leadership of the Secretary-General through his Special Representative for Iraq;

(c) And also promote the protection of human rights and judicial and legal reform in order to strengthen the rule of law in Iraq;

3. *Recognizes* the important role of the Multi-National Force Iraq (MNF-I) in supporting UNAMI, including security and logistical support, and further recognizes that security is essential for UNAMI to carry out its work on behalf of the people of Iraq;

4. *Calls on* Member States to continue providing UNAMI with the necessary financial, logistical and security resources and support to fulfil its mission;

5. *Expresses its intention* to review the mandate of UNAMI in twelve months or sooner, if requested by the Government of Iraq;

6. *Requests* the Secretary-General to report to the Council within three months from the date of this resolution on UNAMI operations in Iraq, and on a quarterly basis thereafter on the progress made towards the fulfilment of all UNAMI's responsibilities; and

7. *Decides* to remain seized of the matter.

NOTES AND QUESTIONS

1. Several domestic developments followed the passage to Iraqi sovereignty, including a new government, elections in January 2005, elections again in December 2005 after the ratification of the "permanent" Constitution in August and its confirmation by referendum in October. The Constitution replaced the Transitional Administrative Law, which the Iraqi Governing Council had passed in April 2004. See for these constitutional-political developments Chapters 3 and 4. The UN continued to remain active, but the descent into civil war in 2005 and 2006 dealt a heavy blow to normal, secure life on the streets of Baghdad. By the summer of 2007, the insurgency seemed to be gaining the upper hand, but a combined "surge" of U.S. troops, decided against the recommendations of the U.S. Congress-established bipartisan Iraq Study Group, and the strengthening of Iraqi capabilities, seemed to offer a new chance for normalcy. These developments are essentially of a security nature. They are discussed in Chapter 7. With the improvement of the situation, the UN role also increased.

2. In a report to the Security Council, Secretary General Ban Ki-Moon described the additional responsibilities imposed by Resolution 1770.

66. I welcome the new mandate given to the United Nations under resolution 1770 (2007) as it increases United Nations assistance in the promotion of stability in Iraq. In particular, the mandate expands the role of the United

Nations in advancing national dialogue and reconciliation, and calls for specific action in promoting the constructive engagement of neighboring countries. Additionally, the United Nations role in coordinating and providing humanitarian, as well as reconstruction and development assistance, especially through the International Compact with Iraq, is underscored in the resolution. The high-level meeting I co-hosted with Prime Minister al-Maliki on 22 September reinforced support for the United Nations role in these important areas. The United Nations will also continue its strong role in providing electoral and constitutional support to the Government of Iraq and promoting the protection of human rights, among other items.

Report of the Secretary-General pursuant to paragraph 6 of resolution 1770 (2007), 15 October 2007, paragraph 66.

3. In April 2008, a full report of the UNSG on the situation in Iraq was released. Excerpts follow.

Report of the Secretary-General pursuant to paragraph 6 of resolution 1770 (2007)

April 22, 2008

. . . II. Summary of Key Political and Security Developments in Iraq

3. Despite some improvements in the security situation, the Government of Iraq continues to face formidable challenges to reaching a national consensus on how to share power and resources; however, efforts were made at reconciliation through legislation. On 12 January 2008 the Justice and Accountability Law was adopted by the Council of Representatives, replacing earlier debaathification policies. On 13 February the Council of Representatives passed a package of laws: the Law on Governorates not Organized into a Region, the General Amnesty Law and the 2008 Budget. This package represented a compromise between the interests of three parliamentary blocks: the Kurdistan Alliance, the United Iraqi Alliance, and Tawafuq. Efforts to persuade Tawafuq to rejoin the Cabinet are continuing as part of a wider attempt to restructure the Government.

4. The growing Sahwa movement, composed of local alliances of tribal sheikhs that have been instrumental in providing neighbourhood-level security in Anbar province and other formerly restive areas, established the "Awakening Conference" at a meeting in Ramadi on 13 February, publicly announcing its transformation from a tribal grouping to a political bloc with aspirations for participating in Governorate Councils and the next general legislative elections. Despite their relative success and growing numbers, Sahwa Council forces, which currently number over 90,000 nationwide, temporarily withdrew their support of the multinational force in Iraq and the Iraqi Security Forces in Diyala and Babil. Fraying relations between the Government of Iraq and tribal elements in Anbar province caused a spike in violence in this area. Tensions were also reported between the Sahwas and the Iraqi Islamic Party. Slightly more than 10,000 Sahwas have now been transferred into the regular security forces.

5. On 17 February the five-month-old stabilization pact between the Sadrist Movement and the Islamic Supreme Council of Iraq expired, and on 22 February, Moqtada al-Sadr extended the freeze on military activities by the Mahdi Army. The Prime Minister's Office, the multinational force in Iraq and UNAMI publicly welcomed the announcement as a boost to security and national unity in Iraq. However, on 24 March the Government announced an operation to pursue criminal elements in Basra. This led to six days of intense fighting between the Government and armed groups, including the elements of the Mahdi Army, in many parts of the country until agreement was reached to stop the violence, by which time, according to several sources, over 700 people had been killed. The security situation in Basra and Baghdad had eased since this agreement. Military and police are continuing operations to seize militia assets in both cities and the resistance from militias has been minimal and short-lived. On 5 April, the Iraqi President, Prime Minister and the heads of political blocs in Parliament issued a 15-point statement calling on all parties and political blocs to dissolve their militias immediately and hand in their weapons. The statement did not mention any militias by name.

6. Security arrangements by the Government of Iraq supported by the multinational force are believed to have prevented mass casualty attacks during Ashura and Arba'in festivities in Baghdad, Karbala and Najaf. There was a decrease in violent incidents compared to previous years and an apparent increase in the public turnout. According to the provincial governor, 2 million visitors gathered in Karbala alone.

Regional Developments Pertaining to Iraq

7. The Government of Iraq continued to strengthen ties with neighbouring countries. For the first time in the modern political history of Iraq and the Islamic Republic of Iran, the Iranian President, Mahmoud Ahmadinejad, visited Baghdad on 2 and 3 March 2008. He met with the President, Jalal Talabani, the Prime Minister, Nuri Kamel al-Maliki, and others, primarily to discuss economic and development cooperation.

8. On 7 March, President Talabani was the first democratically elected Iraqi Head of State to visit Turkey. The two-day visit focused on closer economic cooperation and efforts to confront Kurdish Workers' Party (PKK) elements. Days earlier, Turkish armed forces had withdrawn from northern Iraqi territory after a week-long cross-border ground operation against PKK armed elements based inside Iraqi territory.

9. On 28 February, a delegation from the League of Arab States concluded a three-day visit to Baghdad to discuss national reconciliation with Iraqi officials as well as political and tribal leaders. Efforts to encourage the Governments of Arab States to open embassies in Iraq continued, and on 11 and 12 March, Iraq hosted the 13th Meeting of the Arab Inter-Parliamentary Union Conference in Arbil. On 24 March, Bahrain announced its decision to reopen its embassy in Iraq and appoint an ambassador. Preliminary assessments between the Government of Iraq and other Arab States on their representation in Baghdad are reportedly under way. On 30 March, Iraq participated in the Arab League Summit in Damascus. The Government of Iraq reportedly expressed its reservations with certain sections of the final communiqué related to Iraq.

10. On 20 January 2008, the Minister for Foreign Affairs of Iraq, Hoshyar Zebari, publicly emphasized the importance of holding expanded meetings with neighbouring countries at the ministerial level and the affiliated working groups. In his view, the regional mechanism has proved to be effective for the situation in Iraq. On 2 and 3 March, a second round of meetings on regional dialogue between Iraq and its neighbours got under way with a meeting of the Working Group on Energy in Istanbul. On 18 March the Working Group on Refugees met in Amman, co-chaired by Jordan and Iraq. The Syrian Arab Republic hosted a meeting of the Working Group on Security and Border Control on 13 April in Damascus. Participation in the meetings was more inclusive in terms of regional representation than in previous ones.

11. Efforts to organize a fourth round of direct talks on Iraqi security issues between the United States of America and the Islamic Republic of Iran at the technical level remained unfulfilled. The Iraqi Government announced in March that in the future it would take responsibility for setting the dates for such meetings to avoid delays.

III. Activities of the United Nations Assistance Mission for Iraq
Political Activities

12. My Special Representative and other senior UNAMI officials have continued to engage with a wide range of Iraqi political figures, both in Government and in Parliament, as well as diplomatic and military officials based in Baghdad, on various aspects of the UNAMI expanded mandate. He also explored ways to further the prospects for national reconciliation and political dialogue.

13. On 5 March 2008, my Special Representative travelled to Turkey for discussions with senior officials at the Foreign Ministry. Their talks covered the role of the United Nations in facilitating national reconciliation and regional dialogue, including in the context of northern Iraq.

14. On 11 March my Special Representative visited Najaf and held extensive meetings with Grand Ayatollah Ali al-Sistani, Grand Ayatollah al-Hakim, Ayatollah Muhammad al-Yacoubi, the Governor of Najaf and other religious leaders and political figures, including representatives of the Sadrist Trend. The meetings focused on provincial elections, national reconciliation, government performance and the need to provide assistance to Iraq's vulnerable communities, especially internally displaced persons. UNAMI intends to carry out more frequent visits to Najaf to maintain close contacts with key interlocutors.

15. My Special Representative chaired the first comprehensive anti-corruption conference for Iraq on 17 and 18 March 2008. He also attended a Government of Iraq national political reconciliation conference in Baghdad on 18 March 2008. Despite an initial desire to participate, the Sadrist Trend and Tawafuq decided to boycott the conference to signal their dissatisfaction with how negotiations for their return to the Iraqi cabinet were proceeding.

16. As part of its programme to expand United Nations outreach throughout the country, UNAMI has started deploying national Governorate Liaison Officers to each governorate of Iraq to help the Mission better understand the political, economic, social and security conditions in all areas of Iraq

by liaising with local authorities and political parties and providing feedback to UNAMI. Moreover, this process would assist in designing programmatic responses that are most suited to particular Iraqi governorates. In March, UNAMI deployed its first nine Governorate Liaison Officers in Muthanna, Baghdad, Karbala, Najaf, Qadisiyah, Hilla, Nasariyah, Salahaddin and Wassit governorates. It is currently in the process of selecting candidates from the remaining governorates. . . .

Disputed Internal Boundaries

18. Pursuant to its mandate under paragraph 2 of resolution 1770 (2007) to help resolve disputed internal boundaries, UNAMI has prioritized activity on this issue, especially in northern Iraq. The Mission has sought to take advantage of the agreed six-month delay in implementing article 140 of the Constitution after its expiry on 31 December 2007 by facilitating dialogue on relatively non-contentious areas to begin with in order to build confidence and momentum among the parties, and to identify principles that could be used as part of a common approach to tackle the more disputed territories, including the city of Kirkuk.

19. In January 2008 UNAMI put together a dedicated team of political, electoral, human rights and constitutional officers to consider the multiple dimensions of this complex and sensitive issue. The team has systematically compiled source material, liaised with the Article 140 Committee and closely analysed its recommendations, and conducted interviews with Iraqi interlocutors across the political and ethnic spectrum. Since January 2008, a series of field visits have been carried out by UNAMI to establish contacts with local stakeholders and gather detailed districtlevel information in Kirkuk, Mosul, Tikrit and Arbil.

20. Mission efforts have focused on a number of initial areas that may offer the possibility for an early resolution by the Iraqi authorities. In early April my Special Representative and senior UNAMI officials led teams to these locations in order to hear the views of local leaders on the ground and consult with them on confidence-building measures that could be taken by the respective communities. Based on these visits, UNAMI will provide technical assistance and recommendations to the Iraqi authorities involved in the decision-making process.

Regional Dialogue

21. UNAMI participated as an observer in the meetings of the three technical working groups, held in Istanbul, Amman and Damascus, and pertaining to regional dialogue between Iraq and its neighbours in March and April. The Mission also attended several preparatory meetings in Baghdad and Amman with Iraqi diplomatic counterparts and experts. . . .

Electoral Activities

23. UNAMI continues to work closely with the Independent High Electoral Commission of Iraq to ensure that it attains a state of readiness to conduct future election events that are seen as credible and accepted by the Iraqi people. Possible election activities in 2008 could include a nationwide voter

registration update exercise, referendum on the formation of regions, a referendum on a new constitution and governorate elections.

24. UNAMI has enhanced its efforts to support the Commission in preparations for a voter registration update exercise scheduled to take place in June. Critical elements in this regard were the development of a comprehensive budget and the finalization of a provisional voter list based on the public distribution system database. UNAMI helped to design a selection process involving 130,000 individual applications for 6,500 voter registration staff, who have yet to be trained and deployed. My Special Representative visited the Commission in late March 2008 to familiarize himself with the selection process of the staff for some 550 voter registration centres located in all Iraq governorates.

25. On 14 February 2008, my Special Representative announced at a press conference with top leaders of the Council of Representatives in Baghdad that UNAMI would assist with a professional and transparent selection process for the directors of eight governorate electoral offices where there had been no consensus among the political parties on possible candidates. An application drive was launched the same day on Iraqi radio and in all leading newspapers. Pre-screened candidates were submitted by my Special Representative to the Council of Representatives in a subsequent press conference on 2 April.

26. Priority was given to developing vital electoral legislation. UNAMI has provided assistance to both the election commission and the Government of Iraq on developing a new election system to better reflect the wishes of the Iraqi people and better accommodate women, internally displaced persons and minority groups. The Government of Iraq drafting has so far limited internally displaced person voting to places of origin. Discussions and working sessions with all political blocs and special interest groups consumed much of the Mission's activities in March and are planned throughout April, as UNAMI tries to forge political consensus on key elements of a law. . . .

Constitutional Support Activities

28. The Council of Representatives has extended the mandate of the Constitutional Review Committee until the end of the current legislative term in June 2008. On 5 April, the Political Council for National Security called for expediting the process of constitutional amendments. The Committee has indicated that it plans to refer issues upon which it is unable to reach consensus to the Presidency Council, the Prime Minister and his deputies, and the Speaker of the Council of Representatives and his deputies. The UNAMI Office of Constitutional Support will continue to provide advice and assistance to the Constitutional Review Committee as it seeks to finalize its proposals.

29. During the reporting period, the UNAMI Office of Constitutional Support provided advice and assistance to the Council of Representatives on constitutionally mandated legislation, particularly on the Law on Governorates not Organized into Regions (Provincial Powers Law). This included responding to a request by Deputy Speaker Sheikh Khaled al-Attiya to provide a technical brief on the scope and application of the principle of administrative decentralization as it relates to Iraq's governorates. UNAMI also continued its role as the co-chair of the international legislative round table, an informal

mechanism developed jointly by the Office of Constitutional Support, the European Commission, the United Kingdom Embassy and the United States Embassy aimed at coordinating international community efforts to facilitate assistance to the Iraqi Government on Council of Representatives legislation. Round-table discussions during the reported period were held on disputed internal boundaries, the Provincial Powers Law and the legal framework for upcoming provincial elections.

30. On 8 March 2008, UNAMI and the United Nations Office for Project Services completed a one-week study tour to Northern Ireland for members of the Constitutional Review Committee and other parliamentarians covering the full range of Iraq's political blocs. Funding was provided by the European Union. The study tour gave Iraqi parliamentarians the opportunity to engage in direct dialogue with counterparts who had participated in the Northern Ireland peace process and to explore how power-sharing can be part of an institutional framework to support the political settlement of sectarian conflict. UNAMI plans to provide its good offices to bring this experience to bear in future multi-party dialogues on divisive constitutional issues in Iraq.

Humanitarian Assistance, Reconstruction and Development

48. As of 31 March 2008, the total contributions to the United Nations Development Group Iraq Trust Fund, one of the two funds of the International Reconstruction Fund Facility for Iraq, equalled $1.33 billion. A total of 141 projects and joint programme projects valued at $1.11 billion were approved as of 31 March 2008 for funding under the Trust Fund. Continuing the significant progress in implementation, commitments worth cumulatively $840 million (76 per cent of approved funding) have been entered into and $727 million (65 per cent of approved funding) have been disbursed as of the end of February. Monthly financial updates are made available on the International Reconstruction Fund Facility for Iraq website (www.irffi.org). Contributions in the first quarter to the United Nations Development Group Iraq Trust Fund included: $27,795,000 from the European Union, and $1,466,000 from the Government of Finland.

Human Rights Activities

49. On 15 March 2008 UNAMI launched its twelfth human rights report, covering the period from July to December 2007. The report acknowledges the substantive comments on the draft report received from the Kurdistan regional government authorities and the multinational force in Iraq. The report addressed serious human rights concerns with respect to the Government of Iraq, the Kurdistan regional government and the multinational force in Iraq and included recommendations aimed at introducing improvements in the human rights situation. UNAMI also welcomed the decision of the Government of Iraq to ratify the United Nations Convention against Torture, as well as its invitation to the Special Representative of the Secretary-General for Children and Armed Conflict to visit Iraq. Preparations by government officials for a visit by the United Nations Special Rapporteur on Torture are also under way. The decision by the Government to allow public reporting on its human rights activities was another positive development.

50. Despite improvements in the general security situation, towards the end of 2007 suicide bombings, car bombs and other attacks continued with devastating consequences for civilians. The reduction in security incidents in Baghdad and other locations was also accompanied by a deterioration of the security situation elsewhere, including Mosul and Diyala. Religious and ethnic minorities and other vulnerable groups were victims of violent attacks, as were women in so-called "honour crimes." Armed groups also carried out assassinations of government or state officials, religious figures, professional groups and law enforcement personnel. There were also numerous incidents involving intimidation, abduction, torture and extrajudicial killings.

Operational, Logistic and Security Issues

55. Following a period of improvements in security, the first quarter of 2008 witnessed a slow but steady increase in violent incidents from January to March. This was not a result of any one specific event, but rather due to the faltering of some key elements underlying security gains in late 2007 against a background of limited political progress. These trends are not irreversible but it will require significant political effort to press forward, given that military efforts alone have not achieved the desired results.

56. As noted in the last quarterly report in December 2007, tensions in the south have been simmering for many months. The various Shia militia factions routinely launch attacks against each other's interests and periodically engage in open conflict lasting several days, or even weeks, before Iraqi Security Forces and the multinational force in Iraq intervene. In February there were numerous public demonstrations against the political and security leadership in Basra. In late March the Government of Iraq launched a new offensive against criminal and militia elements in Basra, which sparked widespread fighting not only in that city but other southern cities and Baghdad as well. The Iraqi Security Forces have conducted operations targeting Jaysh al-Mahdi in Nassiriyah, al-Amarah, al-Kut and Hillah, thus escalating the level of violence in these cities. Najaf and Karbala also suffered explosive attacks in the last week of March, which is highly unusual for these two cities. The incidence of indirect fire attacks on Basra air station rose steadily throughout the quarter, with 48 attacks from January to March. This upward trend in indirect fire attacks is expected as long as factional fighting in Basra persists.

57. In Baghdad the year began on an optimistic note. Sectarian violence appeared much reduced and the number of high-profile attacks had dwindled to such an extent that weeks would go by without a single vehicle bomb or other form of mass casualty attack. However, incidents of roadside bomb attacks against Iraqi Security Forces and multinational forces in particular grew steadily throughout February. By March, the number of daily attacks involving explosive devices, including grenades, rose to averages of between 30 and 40. The security situation in Baghdad continues to limit the daily activities of UNAMI. The indirect fire attacks aimed at the International Zone throughout the quarter was minimal until the last week of March, when fighting between Iraqi Security Forces and Jaysh al-Mahdi in the south prompted a dramatic increase in indirect fire attacks against the military and government facilities in Baghdad, as well as the International Zone. Between 23 and 31 March,

there were 47 separate indirect fire barrages consisting of 149 rounds of 122-mm and 107-mm rockets and at least three devastating 240-mm rockets. These attacks caused four deaths, injured another 15 people and inflicted significant damage to housing and office facilities in the International Zone. Among these casualties, one United Nations contractor was killed and two were injured from the direct impact of a 240-mm rocket at the United Nations accommodation camp later in March. By way of comparison, based on information from multiple sources, there were less than a dozen attacks on the International Zone in the six months prior to 23 March.

58. While the security situation in the Kurdistan region of Iraq has remained consistently stable, military operations in Mosul have forced hostile actors to relocate to the region leading to an unusual level of activity. For example, the Palace Hotel in Sulaymaniyah was attacked by a vehicle bomb on 10 March, the first in the province in over a year. The driver of the vehicle and one hotel security guard were killed; of the 32 injured, most had superficial wounds. The Kurdish security authorities were able to effectively manage the situation. In addition, they also uncovered a further two vehicle bomb devices in the region during the first quarter of this year.

59. Nationally, the average number of recorded incidents of violence has slowly climbed during this reporting period. From highs of over 200 per day last summer, the figure had dropped to averages below 80 during the last quarter of 2007. That figure now averages around 130, without calculating the hundreds of exchanges of fire that have occurred in the south during the last week of March. More disturbing is the renewed propensity for mass-casualty attacks using suicide vests and vehicle bombs, particularly in Baghdad. This trend is believed to be the result of re-engagement by specialized insurgent groups, such as the Islamic State of Iraq, who claim affiliation with Al-Qaida in Iraq. . . .

IV. Observations

65. While some initial steps towards national reconciliation in Iraq have begun, more needs to be done to help Iraqi communities resolve fundamental issues that divide them. Once again I urge influential figures and political parties to publicly reinforce the need for—and to personally work towards—political dialogue, compromise and recognition that Iraq's future depends on its leaders pursuing the Iraqi national interest, rather than individual, party, ethnic or sectarian interests.

66. It is a matter of deep concern that in a country with such vast potential wealth from natural resources, large sections of the population are living in poverty and insecurity. In this regard, I believe that agreement on a hydrocarbon law which enables the sharing of the country's natural resources in a fair and transparent manner could be enormously beneficial, and I call on Iraq's political leadership and Parliament to work together in the country's interest and pass such a law. However, to maximize the reconciliation potential of this law, it will almost certainly need to be accompanied—or swiftly followed—by a broader national compact on powersharing in the country. The decision of the Constitutional Review Committee to redouble its efforts offers an important opportunity to resolve long-standing disputes between Iraqi communities.

67. I believe that the holding of credible governorate elections later this year, as mandated by recent legislation, could in the long run serve to underpin the legitimacy of democratic governance. In order to ensure that credible electoral events are held on time in 2008, it is essential that Iraqi leaders meet a number of prerequisites. In this regard, I call on Iraq's Council of Representatives to urgently pass a governorate elections law, and urge the Government of Iraq to provide all material assistance to the Independent High Electoral Commission in order to conduct these elections as smoothly, transparently and fairly as possible. I also call upon Iraq's political blocs to respect, and to do their utmost to protect, the independence of Independent High Electoral Commission from political interference so that election results can be credible and broadly accepted.

68. The United Nations welcomed the extension of the freeze on military activities of the Mahdi Army, announced by Moqtada al-Sadr on 22 February 2008, as a positive step. Similarly, the end of the fighting in Basra and other places at the end of March was made possible by compromise and agreement. I urge all concerned to do everything possible to maintain the current decrease in violent conflict and to avoid any provocative acts that could serve to undermine it. . . .

71. The regional dialogue process is an essential part of efforts by the international community to restore stability and security in Iraq. I urge Member States to seize the opportunity presented by the third expanded meeting of foreign ministers of neighbouring States of Iraq in Kuwait on 22 April 2008 to lend ready support to the regional dialogue process. It is no less important for Iraq to articulate clearly what direction it would like regional cooperation to take. The Conference could give an important impulse for reinvigorating the regional working group meetings, whose potential for coordinated work in joint technical projects has not been fully utilized. It is important for Iraq and its neighbours to focus their efforts on achieving more tangible outcomes at these meetings and ensure proper follow-up.

72. I welcome the positive step taken by Bahrain to commit to reopening an embassy in Baghdad and I look forward to other Arab States among Iraq's neighbours following suit. In this regard, I would also welcome further steps by the Government of Iraq to encourage this development. I would also urge Iraq's neighbours to do their utmost to strengthen border security by doing more to prevent fighters from crossing into Iraq and closing off the supply of weapons, money and training to armed groups that are destabilizing the country.

73. I was concerned by reports indicating that the parties involved in the recent fighting in Basra and other places had committed human rights abuses. I urge those involved to respect their legal obligations under international humanitarian law, which applies both to States and to non-State actors, to minimize harm to civilians. Every effort should be made to avoid excessive or indiscriminate force. Under no circumstances should civilians be used intentionally as human shields in order to deter attacks from enemy combatants, and all captured combatants should be treated in accordance with the laws of war. All those involved should do their utmost to address the humanitarian consequences of the recent fighting, provide access

to humanitarian workers, and facilitate the delivery of crucial supplies of medicines, foodstuffs, drinking water, fuel and other critical items to hospitals and the civilian population.

74. I am pleased to note that UNAMI, with full support from Headquarters, has continued to move forward in expanding its activities in line with its mandate as revised in Security Council resolution 1770 (2007). It has shown creativity and determination in its efforts to find new ways to support the people and Government of Iraq. I would like to take this opportunity to thank my Special Representative for Iraq, Staffan de Mistura, for his steadfast leadership and strong commitment in meeting the United Nations mandate in Iraq. I would also like to thank the UNAMI national and international staff, as well as the personnel of United Nations agencies, funds and programmes, for their tireless efforts under very challenging conditions.

NOTES AND QUESTIONS

1. Note in the Report the propensity of the UN to please all parties, domestic, regional and international. Considering the fluid situation in New York, with re-alignments and politicking operating as a matter of course, this is expected. But is it effective in all situations? Can the UN always dispense with moral judgment by putting all parties on the same level? Many Iraqis remember the cooperation of the former UN Secretary General Kofi Annan with Saddam Hussein, and the notorious expression of his readiness "to do business with him." How does such legacy reflect on UN authority and efficiency on the ground?
2. Constitutional and security-related issues dominate the daily business of governments and international organizations. Related, but of a different technical nature, are difficult areas of contention, some with deep historical roots, such as boundaries, debt, and, in the case of Iraq, the Oil-for-Food legal regime.

D. ROLES FOR THE UN?

1. THE KUWAIT-IRAQ BORDER

The occupation of Kuwait by the government of Saddam Hussein in August 1990 was the most dramatic manifestation of Iraqi discontent with its Southern border. It was not the first one. From 1958 until he was killed in a coup in 1963, Iraqi president 'Abd al-Karim Qasem was bent on having "the Iraqi province returned." See Charles Tripp, A History of Iraq 165-167 (2002). While one of the first actions of the new Iraqi government in 1963 was the recognition of the border with Kuwait, the absence of a serious ratification process by a freely elected Assembly kept the issue between the two countries a sore point in their relations.

RICHARD MUIR, THE IRAQ-KUWAIT BORDER DISPUTE:
STILL A FACTOR FOR INSTABILITY?

35:2 Asian Affairs 147-161 (July 2004)

From soon after Iraq's independence in 1932 until Saddam Hussein was removed in April 2003 the border between Iraq and Kuwait was a source of actual or potential instability. Successive Iraqi leaders, under the Hashemite monarchy and then under the military and Ba'athist regimes, sought control of strategic parts of Kuwaiti territory and, at times, of the whole Emirate. Invading Kuwait in August 1990, Saddam Hussein reflected an old ambition: "the Iraqi belief that Kuwait is part of Iraq and its 19th province is unshakeable."

Once the coalition had ejected Saddam from Kuwait in March 1991, a United Nations (UN) mission spent two years demarcating the border, with the result enshrined in Resolution 833 of May 1993. Although Iraq reluctantly accepted the Resolution a year later, the Council remained suspicious of Saddam's intentions. It kept in place the 25 km wide demilitarized zone and the 3000 strong UN Observer Mission it had set up when the fighting ended in 1991. The US/UK "No Fly Zone" over southern Iraq added to the disincentives to any further challenge.

With the overthrow of Saddam in April 2003 the "No Fly Zone" came to an end and the Security Council voted to withdraw the Observer Mission. The border, closed for 12 years, re-opened in November 2003. Iraq has since been preoccupied with urgent internal matters as the Sunni groups who controlled Iraq in one form or another from independence to Saddam's fall come to terms with the Shi'a majority and with the Kurds who have developed their own autonomous area.

Whether the Iraq-Kuwait border will again become a major international issue remains to be seen. Iraq's past as part of the Ottoman Empire and the claim to Kuwait as its 19th province are remembered in Iraq and the wider Arab world. For many Iraqis across the political and sectarian spectrum the UN demarcation of 1994 was forced on Iraq in defeat and failed adequately to deal with Iraq's practical need for unfettered access to the sea. For Kuwaitis, on the other hand, the UN demarcation did no more than validate their state's independence and its border with Iraq established as long ago as 1913; they see no case for territorial concessions to Iraq. The Kuwaiti Government now plans to develop a large new port and free zone on the offshore islands on their side of the border.

. . .

What is the outlook now, with Saddam gone and the protective measures removed? There were always two distinct Iraqi ambitions: one to absorb Kuwait in total into Iraq; the other to secure enough territory to give Iraq sovereignty over both shores of the [Khor Abdalla, or Khawr 'Abd Allah] Channel from Umm Qasr to the sea. The first ambition was cherished by the Hashemites, the Sunni elite and the Ba'athist strong men who succeeded them. All saw themselves as heirs of Ottoman Iraq, despised the Al Sabah and envied their wealth. The claim on Kuwait provided useful distraction from internal challenges. If Iraq can now become stable and democratic and rebuild its economy, its leaders should have no more reason to revive these old claims than Germany has to claim Alsace or modern Turkey to claim the Eastern province of Saudi Arabia.

The issue of Umm Qasr and its access to the sea is less easily dismissed. Saddam Hussein's incompetence in defeat after 1991. [In protest, Hussein had withdrawn Iraqi officials from the UN mission demarcating the borders] meant that Iraq had no effective voice in the UN demarcation. Arguments on practical grounds for adjusting the border where it meets the Khor Abdalla and runs down it to the sea were never heard. Had the Iraqis chosen to put them forward they might well have been ignored. The UN work was based on the 1932 and 1963 Agreements supplemented by available documentation — there was no place in this post-invasion process for Iraqi special pleading. Even today Kuwait remains adamantly and understandably opposed to any reopening of the demarcation in Security Council Resolution 833. But, in other circumstances, Iraq's case might have got a fuller hearing on the basis of practical need for expansion of Umm Qasr if not on the historical record.

The vision of [British colonial officials] Pelly and Curzon of a large deep-water port in the Khor Abdalla has not gone away. Umm Qasr and Basra are likely to prove too small for the needs of a reconstructed and flourishing Iraq. The Shatt Al Arab is even more congested today. Kuwait's ports further down the coast are crowded. Both shores of the Khor Abdalla remain undeveloped. With the threat from Iraq lifted, Kuwait is shaping plans for a major port and free zone on Bubiyan and Warba Islands.

Such a development could provide a new hub for shipping at the top of the Gulf — serving Iraq, northern Saudi Arabia, Iran and even the former Soviet republics to the north. It could become an important plank in a modern relationship between the independent sovereign states of Iraq and Kuwait. But Iraq will need first to find stability and Kuwait develop confidence that future governments of Iraq will no longer have designs on Kuwait. Under such circumstances a new port in Kuwaiti territory serving a potentially rich conomic hinterland could be the key to permanent resolution of this old quarrel.

NOTES AND QUESTIONS

1. The imposition of the borderline by the UN in the wake of the 1990-1991 Gulf War did not solve the boundaries problem. Should the border dispute be reopened now that Iraq has conducted free national elections for the first time in its history?

2. Muir notes the absence of an Iraqi voice in the UN demarcation of 1991. Even if Hussein had not withdrawn Iraqi representatives from the process, there remains the question whether a representative Iraqi government would — or should — consider itself bound by any territorial commitments entered into by the Hussein regime. As Harry Brown points out,

> Although the Iraq-Kuwait boundary is now well defined, it is of concern that Iraq [under Hussein] has been reluctant to accept the boundaries it has agreed to in the past with both Kuwait and Iran, and, at times when it has accepted one of these boundaries, it has rejected the other.

Harry Brown, *The Iraq-Kuwait Boundary Dispute: Historical Background and the U.N. Decisions of 1992 and 1993*, IBRU Boundary and Security Bulletin, 66-80 (Oct. 1994).

2. ODIOUS DEBT

Former Minister of Finance Ali Allawi underlines in the following text a long-standing problem: Iraqis have been bearing since 1981 the brunt of an immense debt. Two additional texts, from 1995 and 2004, trace some of the problems associated with "the odious debt."

> Within a few weeks of the formation of the Cabinet, it became clear that the CPA was not prepared to relinquish control over key aspects of the Iraqi economy. This was not only the case in the area of international economic cooperation but also in terms of a proprietary interest in certain sectors which the USA had considered priority areas. For example, in the matter of the resolution of Iraq's debt, the CPA entered into a series of binding agreements with investment banks and lawyers, and acknowledged the legitimacy of Saddam-era debts. Neither the Central Bank nor the Ministry of Finance was judged competent enough to question the conclusions of the US Treasury. The CPA adopted a particular path for debt restructuring that might not have been freely chosen by a sovereign Iraqi government. The governor of the Central Bank, for example, had been a leading member of the Jubilee Fund initiative which called for repudiation of "odious debt," that is, debt incurred by dictatorships and tyrannies for wars and internal repression. His views were not sought when the debt-restructuring plan was being developed.

Ali A. Allawi, The Occupation of Iraq: Winning the War, Losing the Peace 201 (2007).

CHIBLI MALLAT, A CRITICAL NOTE ON COMPENSATION:
THE VIEW FROM IRAQ

Commercial Law in the Middle East, Hilary Lewis Ruttley &
Chibli Mallat eds., 381-387 (1995)

The United Nations Compensation Commission is governed under international law by a number of resolutions of the Security Council. In the wake of a recommendation to the Secretary-General to prepare a report to that effect, and the effective publishing of this Report on May 2, 1991, the Commission started a life of its own, with some 20 decisions of the Governing Council, published to date, that have started a new chapter in the international law of compensation.

    ... [S]ome estimates have put the liability of Iraq under the scheme to $100 billion dollars, which, if Iraq were to pay $5 billion every year, would not be exhausted before twenty years. This is the hard situation, independently from foreign debt and interest thereon accumulated before the war, which itself is a staggering estimate of up to $200 billion, perhaps even $300 billion if one includes the liability to Iran which was established, following the Iran-Iraq Ceasefire Resolution — Resolution 598 — in a formal way by the former Secretary-General, Mr. Perez de Cuellar.

From the premise of the dilemma posed by the pattern of the old order established by Resolution 687 [which made no distinction between the Iraqi government and the Iraqi people — ED.], and the counterpattern inaugurated by Resolution 688 [which did recognize the existence of various peoples within Iraq — ED.], we can draw a different perspective on the issue of compensation as is presently being shaped in international law. This dilemma has been sustained in a remarkably interwoven fashion through the various resolutions relating to compensation.

Since Resolution 687 followed a logic which was illustrated by the absence of a single mention of the Iraqi people in the eleven resolutions preceding it, it itself repeated the elements foreshadowed by Resolution 674 which "remind[ed] Iraq that under international law it is liable for any loss, damage or injury arising in regard to Kuwait and third States, and their nationals and corporations, as a result of the invasion and illegal occupation of Kuwait by Iraq."

Following from this explicit programme, the mechanism of compensation was adumbrated in the Ceasefire Resolution. Under para. 16 of Resolution 687, Iraq was held "liable, under international law, for any direct loss, damage, including environmental damage and the depletion of natural resources, or injury to foreign Governments, nationals and corporations, as a result of Iraq's unlawful invasion and occupation of Kuwait."

By insisting on the concepts of "Iraq" and of "foreign," a crucial subject was missing, which was the "people" or the citizens of Iraq, who were ignored as victims of their government's behavior and were being asked to foot the bill. Under classic international law, of course, there is no possibility to make such a distinction. In the meantime however, Resolution 688 has been adopted, which brings up the missing (and arguably elusive) subject of the peoples of Iraq, and pits them, in international law, against the incumbent Iraqi government. Since then, on the subject of compensation and on other subjects, international law is trapped in the dilemma.

The logic of 687 continued its bureaucratic grinding with the unfolding of the Geneva Gulf Claims Compensation Commission. Whilst ignoring the various laws passed by Iraq on the writing-off of its foreign debt, and the measures initiated to blunt sanctions, the Security Council decided "to create a fund to pay compensation for claims that fall within the scope of paragraph 16 . . . and to establish a Commission that will administer the fund."

The establishment, and beginning of the Commission's work, was accompanied by a number of technical problems which come under the heading of "due process."

A first problem resembles a precedent set by the Iran-US claims tribunal, which seems to play itself out again in the case of Iraq: some 1400 claims against US corporations were frustrated for lack of jurisdictional competence of the tribunal, which decided that the wording of the Algiers accord did not allow claims of one government against nationals of the other, although Iran could bring counterclaims against any corporations only if these corporations initiated an action against it.

This in our case means lack of balance and reciprocity, as Iraq cannot bring to the jurisdiction of the Geneva Compensation Fund proceedings against foreign nationals, states and countries, which may have benefited — through frustrated contracts etc. — from the invasion.

More crucially for due process, the position of Iraq against the claims initiated by foreign parties is not that of a defendant. Iraq has, in effect, a right to some hearing by the Commission, but a proper voice is not allowed under the present procedure to process claims. Whilst this lack of due process is now dormant because of the isolation of the present government, it may be revived if the circumstances of isolation change. As in the case of the Iran-US claims tribunal, imbalance stems from the weak political position of a pariah government, even if this consideration never surfaces as a *de jure* argument.

Whatever the unsatisfactory situation of due process, the fact remains that there are little or no funds to service the work of the Commission, and the clear rejection by the Security Council to dedicate some of the "frozen Iraqi assets" held outside the country under Resolution 660, has meant that the logic could not be practically fulfilled. The refusal to use frozen Iraqi assets to pay into the compensation fund was acknowledged by the Secretary-General in unequivocal terms in his report on the establishment of the Commission pursuant to para. 19 of Resolution 687:

> Iraq has officially notified the UN of its acceptance of the provisions of the resolution . . . it follows from paragraph 19 of resolution 687 (1991) that the method envisaged by the Security Council for the financing of the Fund is a contribution to Iraq based on a percentage of the value of its exports determined in accordance with the mechanism referred to in paragraph 13 above [i.e., the Fund's Governing Council's criteria in assessing the rate and rhythm of Iraqi compensation]. It also follows from the resolution that the Security Council did not envisage using "foreign assets" of Iraq held in third countries for the financing of the Fund.

In practice, this means that very few payments have been made yet, since Iraqi monies which would replenish the Fund are dependent on either the unfreezing of assets — and even then, they seem to be outside the reach of the Fund — or the sale of Iraqi oil. The irony is that the huge machinery of the Commission has been funded, in part, by a limited release by the US government of some assets following Resolution 778, and from loans to the Commission by Middle Eastern governments which should in theory be net beneficiaries of compensation.

The question of the funding of the Commission's work, and more importantly, of the funds it is designed to allocate has meanwhile been made more complicated by the assertion of the other logic of international law started in 688, which is at work, as regards compensation, in Resolutions 705 and 706, 712, and 778.

These resolutions belong to the other logic of international law, in that the exclusivity attached to dealing with the incumbent Iraqi government is being breached by a legal mechanism in which the proceeds of oil sales are earmarked for the purposes of spending which are under international control at all stages, and which are essentially dedicated to the distribution of humanitarian aid, by the UN, directly to the Iraqi people. To the extent that the Iraqi government has refused that principle, such distribution was blocked, and so was the one-third earmarking off the oil sales proceeds to the Compensation Fund.

Resolution 706 illustrates this dimension in plain language. Whilst reiterating its dedication to Resolution 688 "and in particular the importance which the Council attaches to Iraq allowing unhindered access by international humanitarian organizations to all those in need of assistance in all parts of Iraq," and after repeating its concerns for "the serious nutritional and health situation of the Iraqi civilian population," and "the proposal of oil sales by Iraq to finance the purchase of foodstuffs, medicines and materials and supplies for essential civilian needs for the purpose of providing humanitarian relief," the Security Council stated its conviction "of the need for equitable distribution of humanitarian relief to all segments of the Iraqi civilian population through effective monitoring and transparency." The Security Council thus resolved to dedicate up to USD 1.6 billion to the escrow account which would fund, in part, the compensation account of the Geneva commission.

The important word here is "in part," as the logic of Resolution 688 (i.e. the distinction between Iraqi government and Iraqi people), found its way to the Resolution by introducing a factor of competition over the source of funds (Iraqi oil exports) from the vantage point of the way the money ought to be distributed (foreign claimants as against Iraqi civilians). This was labeled in Resolution 706(1)(c) "a scheme for the purchase of foodstuffs, medicines and materials and supplies for essential civilian needs . . . , in particular health related materials, all of which to be labeled to the extent possible as being supplied under this scheme, and for all feasible and appropriate United Nations monitoring and supervision for the purpose of assuring their equitable distribution to meet humanitarian needs in all regions of Iraq and to all categories of the Iraqi civilian population, as well as all feasible and appropriate management relevant for this purpose, such as United Nations' role to be available if desired for humanitarian assistance from other sources."

UN food monitoring and supervising is the direct legacy of 688 separating the peoples from Iraq from the incumbent Iraqi government. This eplains why the Iraqi government, alleging — and this is not incorrect, but considering the arms control regime, trivial — breach of sovereignty, has not yet accepted 706, and refuses to sell oil. The introduction of the 688 other logic has also affected directly the compensation scheme, by, so far, starving the Commission from the funds it needs both to operate and to compensate.

Resolution 778 (2 Oct. 1992) has reinforced the dilemma. Whilst reiterating what was unthinkable two years earlier the now familiar distinction between "Iraq" and the "Iraqi civilian population," it tried to bring some money into the escrow account established by Resolution 706 and 712, by allowing states to transfer to the Fund up to USD 200 million of "proceeds of sale of Iraq petroleum . . . paid for by or on behalf of the purchaser on or after 6 August 1990," as well as to sell oil belonging to Iraq which happens to be under the control of these states, at fair market value, and transferring the monies to the escrow account.

These are limited amounts, and some have trickled down to the UN since through a complex matching scheme devised by the US government. But the more decisive legal dimension appears in the priorities established by the mandate of the Security Council to the Secretary-General for the processing of the money. The Secretary-General is asked "to ascertain the costs of UN activities concerning the elimination of weapons of mass destruction, the provision of humanitarian relief in Iraq, and the other UN operations specified in paragraphs 2 and 3 of Res. 706 (1991) [i.e., humanitarian aid and various activities of the UN on boundaries, elimination of weaponry, and compensation]" and to transfer to the Compensation fund one third of such proceeds, whilst "taking into account any preference expressed by States transferring or contributing funds as to the allocation of such funds among these purposes."

There resides the great dilemma in which the Fund is increasingly finding itself, as the unusual norm comes to replace the traditional one under which Resolution 687 was created. From the moment the people of Iraq were raised, under international law, to the status of victims, their claims for compensation start to compete with other, foreign, victims of the same unlawful behavior of the incumbent Iraqi government.

The question, in practice, is to establish an order of priorities between Iraqi claimants and foreign claimants, in the same way that the work of the Commission has been to establish a chain of priorities among the foreign claimants, and in which small claims come first.

So far as I know, the inclusion of Iraqi civilians of victims has not taken place yet in any serious discussion, but one can see traces of it in a passing remark by Hazel Fox in a discussion of the compensation issue:

> The position of Iraqi civilians who claim to have suffered personal injuries or loss of property from excesses of coalition military operations remains a delicate matter. Whilst guidelines may exclude the issue from the UN Commission's competence, politically some measure acknowledging Iraqi civilians' entitlement to equal humanitarian treatment may be advisable.

Although this argument could probably be enhanced by the establishment of an overall responsibility of the Iraqi rulers that includes the victimization of their own peoples, it underlines the problem of the necessary inclusion of Iraqi civilians in any compensation scheme. There is no equivalent of the Commission for the Iraqis, even if there are resolutions which establish the principles of unhampered aid to the Iraqi people, and even if, as a matter of practice, whether the various Memoranda arranged between the Iraqi government and the UN, or as a fact of life in those outside the control of Baghdad and known as safe havens, international money is already finding its way to Iraq.

From a strictly legal point of view, it could be argued that what the Commission for reparations does is totally severed from other humanitarian aid, and that no necessary legal contention should occur. This is partly comforted by Resolution 706, where a clear one-third of the oil sales goes to the escrow account. But passage of time and the remaining two-thirds under this resolution have transformed the theoretical dilemma into a real one. There is need for a more comprehensive discussion involving both foreign and Iraqi claimants for wrongful behaviour of the incumbent Iraqi government, thus allowing the consolidation of these claims according to a chain of priorities which is yet to be defined.

David D. Caron, The Reconstruction of Iraq: Dealing with Debt

U.C. Davis Journal of International Law and Policy 123-143 (Fall 2009)

II. Understanding Iraq's Debt

To understand Iraq's debt is to appreciate the power and madness of Saddam Hussein.

. . .

Presently the Iraq's debt is often introduced solely in tabular summaries that strip away the context. The following description seeks to put back into the numbers an appreciation of their source. My purpose here is not to offer an exact statement of Iraq's debt in many categories or to various countries. Rather, it is to provide a fairly accurate sense of the major elements of Iraq's debt, their sources and status. In thinking about Iraq's debt in this way, an important starting point is that it had virtually no foreign debt before its war with Iran in 1980. Since then, debt has built up in four stages: The Iran-Iraq War from 1980 to 1988, the Iraqi Invasion and Occupation of Kuwait from 1990 to 1991, the U.N. Sanctions Period from 1991 to 2003, and the Iraq War and reconstruction effort from 2003 to the present. The following sections examine each of these periods considering the debt often discussed, the debt usually overlooked, and the debt forgiven. Table 2 summarizes this discussion.

A. The Iran-Iraq War: 1980 to 1988

The Iran-Iraq War is largely unappreciated in the United States and the world. Iran in 1979 had taken U.S. nationals hostage, ignored the judgment of the International Court of Justice that they be released, and in general, seemed a threat to regional stability and therefore U.S. interests. When the war broke out between Iraq and Iran in 1980, Iran's attempts to invoke the U.N. Charter in response to Iraq's aggression fell on deaf ears. Iran's own actions had made itself an outlaw in the eyes of the world community and its effort to now invoke the very machinery it had flaunted was not successful. As a result, the world seemingly passed over a war that raged from 1980 to 1988 and involved a tremendous loss of life.

The Iran-Iraq War was Saddam Hussein's war. Hussein attended a conference of unaligned nations in Cuba in September of 1979. While there, he and his Ambassador to the United Nations, Salah Omar al-Ali, met with the new Minister of Foreign Affairs for the then-new Islamic Republic of Iran to discuss, among other things, the dispute between the two nations over the Shatt-al-Arab waterway between the two nations. The Iraqi Ambassador is reported to recall with surprise the especially agreeable tone that the Iranian representatives brought to the meeting. Later as Hussein and al-Ali sat in a garden alone, al-Ali's perception that a peaceful resolution of the issue might follow was crushed. Mark Bowden reports al-Ali's version of the exchange:

> "Well, Salah, I see you are thinking of something," Saddam said. "What are you thinking about?"
>
> "I am thinking about the meeting we just had, Mr. President. I am very happy, I'm very happy that these small problems will be solved. I'm so happy that they

took advantage of this chance to meet with you and not one of your ministers, because with you being here we can avoid another problem with them. We are neighbors. We are poor people. We don't need another war. We need to rebuild our countries, not tear them down."

Saddam was silent for a moment, drawing thoughtfully on his cigar. "Salah, how long have you been a diplomat now?" he asked.

"About ten years."

"Do you realize, Salah, how much you have changed?"

"How, Mr. President?"

"How should we solve our problems with Iran? Iran took our lands. They are controlling the Shatt-al-Arab, our big river. How can meetings and discussions solve a problem like this? Do you know why they decided to meet with us here, Salah? They are weak is why they are talking with us. If they were strong there would be no need to talk. So this gives us an opportunity, an opportunity that only comes along once in a century. We have an opportunity here to recapture our territories and regain control of our river."

That was when al-Ali realized that Saddam had just been playing with the Iranians, and that Iraq was going to go to war. Saddam had no interest in diplomacy. . . . Within a year the Iran-Iraq war began.

It ended horrifically, eight years later, with hundreds of thousands of Iranians and Iraqis dead. To a visitor in Baghdad the year after the war ended, it seemed that every other man on the street was missing a limb. The country had been devastated. The war had cost Iraq billions. . . .

The significance of the Iran-Iraq War for the Iraqi economy and for Iraq's debt situation today cannot be overstated. That war generated at least three categories of debt or obligations: (1) external public debt, (2) external private debt, and (3) possible liability for damages suffered by Iran.

First, Iraq's external public debt increased as Iraq borrowed from other nations to finance the war. Indeed, almost all present estimates of Iraq's external public debt find their origin in the period of the Iran-Iraq War. As to the amount of this debt, the Secretary General of the United Nations wrote in 1991 that:

> Iraq's total external debt and obligations have been reported by the Government of Iraq at $42,097 million as of 31 December 1990. However, the exact figure of Iraq's external indebtedness can only be ascertained following discussions between Iraq and its creditors. To estimate debt servicing requirements it is assumed that Iraq reschedules its debts at standard Paris Club terms.

Other accounts of the debt are greater. Lawrence Freedman and Efraim Karsh write: "[I]t increasingly became evident that Iraq had emerged from the war a crippled nation. From a prosperous country with some $35 billion in foreign exchange reserve in 1980, Iraq had been reduced to dire economic straits, with $80 billion in foreign debt and shattered economic infrastructure."

The situation with Iraq's external private debt, i.e. foreign debts of Iraqi residents, is more difficult to estimate. The magnitude of this debt is unclear, but it is thought to be small inasmuch as the Iraqi economy was essentially controlled by the state and, whatever private economy there was, it tended to be small in scale particularly in the international realm. However, the government's dominant presence in the private economy did serve to increase Iraq's external public debt in a second way. In particular, Iraq's external public debt also increased as Iraq's ability to purchase foreign goods and services diminished during the war. Iraq began to default on contractual payments due and commenced renegotiating the terms of contracts for payment. The payment period was no longer the previous customary period of at most three months, but in some cases as long as forty eight months. In essence, the sellers had begun to provide financing for Iraq's purchases.

This external public debt situation in Iraq at the end of the Iran-Iraq War was examined as a part of the U.N. Compensation Commission's ("UNCC") consideration of claims arising out of Iraq's later illegal invasion and occupation of Kuwait ("the Gulf War"). The jurisdiction of the UNCC extended to claims arising out of the invasion and occupation. Some claimants who had either lent monies to Iraq during the Iran-Iraq War or sold goods or services to Iraq during that period argued that but for the Gulf War, they would have received payments on their outstanding debts. For the UNCC, these claims led it to interpret a jurisdictional limitation included in Security Council Resolution 687, the basic constitutive instrument for the Commission. In particular, a panel of the Commission noted that the jurisdictional grant in Resolution 687 to decide claims arising directly out of Iraq's illegal invasion and occupation of Kuwait was explicitly to be "without prejudice to the debts and obligations of Iraq arising prior to 2 August 1990" (hereinafter referred to as the "arising prior to" clause). The Panel found "the object and purpose of the Security Council's insertion of the 'arising prior to' clause was to exclude from the jurisdiction of the Commission Iraq's old debt." Consequently, such "old debt" was not addressed through the UNCC process and remains an outstanding element of today's discussion.

If this tremendous external public debt is often raised and discussed today as an area for possible debt relief, the possible debt only rarely discussed is Iraq's potential liability to Iran. Although the Iran-Iraq War arguably involved violations of applicable law by both sides, it appears that Iraq was the initial aggressor and on balance, Iraq would be liable to Iran for damages arising from the war. The size of this possible debt is unknown, although one State department official stated to me that Iran has stated on occasion that the amount owing to it was on the order of $100 billion.

B. Iraq's Invasion and Occupation of Kuwait: 1990 to 1991

. . .

The Gulf War resulted in two new possible categories of debt. One has been addressed in significant part and the other has been, as a practical matter, forgiven.

First, Iraq in Security Council Resolution 687 was declared liable for damages arising from its illegal invasion and occupation of Kuwait. Paragraph sixteen of the Resolution provides:

> Reaffirms that Iraq, without prejudice to the debts and obligations of Iraq arising prior to 2 August 1990, which will be addressed through the normal

mechanisms, is liable under international law for any direct loss, damage, including environmental damage and the depletion of natural resources, or injury to foreign Governments, nationals and corporations, as a result of Iraq's unlawful invasion and occupation of Kuwait.

The task of resolving the claims expected was given to the UNCC. The docket in terms of both the number of claims and the aggregate amount sought is staggering: some 2.5 million claims from over eighty nations for an amount in excess of 250 billion U.S. dollars. The UNCC has resolved all but 45,000 of these claims awarding compensation in total of 48 billion dollars and administering the payment of 18 billion of that amount. Although the remaining 45,000 claims represent primarily specially authorized late filed claims for individual damage, they also include some 27 claims for damage to the environment, health and safety of the region that in total seek in excess of 69 billion U.S. dollars. The status of the UNCC's docket as of May 2004 is summarized in Table 1.

TABLE 1. Status of UNCC Claims Processing as of May 7, 2004

No. of claims left to be re- solved	Compensation sought by claims left to be resolved (US$ approx.)	No. of claims resolved	Compen- sation sought by claims resolved (US$)	No. of resolved claims awarded compen- sation	Compensation awarded (US$)	US$ paid
44,270	82,620,139,000	2,604,482	265,992,097,839	1,507,374	48,170,438,256	18,395,310,375

It is important to note that the UNCC in resolving 2,604,482 claims awarded compensation only as to 1,507,374 claims. In part, this reduction in the number of claims represents an important function the UNCC has played in both identifying unsubstantiated claims and reducing the amount of damages sought by particular claims. In part, it also reflect jurisdictional decisions excluding certain claims from the purview of the Commission on grounds such as "the arising prior to" clause mentioned above. The important point to note is that exclusion from the jurisdiction of the UNCC does not extinguish these claims, but rather shift these claims to different legal fora or to later possible diplomatic discussions.

The second category of debt created by Iraq's invasion and occupation of Kuwait was the cost of the Coalition's military operations to end Iraq's occupation of Kuwait. The total cost of the Gulf War to the Coalition's lead armed force, the United States, was estimated to be in the range of at least seventy billion dollars. As an international legal matter, such costs represented a potential debt of Iraq. However, for two reasons this debt has as a practical matter been forgiven. First, at least ninety percent of the costs incurred by the United States were reimbursed by several other States, principally Saudi Arabia, Kuwait, Japan, Germany and Korea, thereby spreading the costs of the Gulf War over a larger group of States. Second, the costs of the Coalition's military operations are specifically excluded from the jurisdiction of the UNCC. Again, exclusion from the jurisdiction of the UNCC does not extinguish the possible liability of Iraq for these amounts, but it does make their recovery in a practical sense quite unlikely. Indeed, I am not aware of any effort before or after the 2003 Iraq War to recover such costs from Iraq.

C. The U.N. Sanctions Period: 1991 to 2003

From the end of the Gulf War until the commencement of the 2003 Iraq War, Iraq was subject to one of the most extensive sanction regimes of modern times. Even though recent revelations point to substantial gaps in that regime, it nonetheless was sufficiently strict that a significant amount of attention in the second half of the 1990s was directed at avoiding undue imposition of suffering on the Iraqi people and developing, as they were called at the time, smart sanctions. A curious consequence of this sanction regime's isolation of Iraq was that it prevented Iraq from assuming further external debt.

Particularly interesting from the vantage point of a new Iraq seeking to confront its past, Iraq may have incurred a significant amount of internal debt during the sanctions period. In particular, during the sanctions period, Kurdish lands and property were seized in the Northern Iraq and there were extensive human rights violations against the Shiite population in Southern Iraq.

D. The Iraq War and Subsequent Reconstruction Efforts: 2003 to the Present

The most striking thing concerning the debt associated with the 2003 Iraq War is the sharp contrast of that debt with the debt arising out of the 1991 Gulf War. There were very significant costs incurred principally by the United States and, to a lesser degree, by the United Kingdom in conducting the 2003 war. Indeed, the United States alone is reported to have spent upwards of $150 billion on the conduct of the 2003 Iraq War and that number is expected to grow. As in the Gulf War, there has been no claim against Iraq for these costs. But unlike the Gulf War, there is no group of states stepping forward to reimburse any of the costs of the United States or its allies.

At the same time, the Hussein era, the U.N sanctions regime and the conduct of 2003 Iraq War have all left Iraq desperately in need of reconstruction so as to provide it stability as it rebuilds itself politically and socially. It is clear that Iraq needs assistance in some form. The challenge of approaching Iraq's debt as a part of the challenge of reconstructing Iraq is discussed in the next Part.

TABLE 2. Iraq's Debt: The Discussed, the Overlooked and the Forgiven

Category of Debt	Often Discussed Debt (US dollars)	Usually Overlooked Debt (US dollars)	Forgiven Debt (US dollars)

The Iran — Iraq War (1980 to 1988)

External Public Debt	This amount is often described to be about 125 billion. It is with the addition of interest since 1991 that the figure of 125 billion is reached.	—	This category of debt was the focus of former Secretary of State Baker's mission to seek partial debt forgiveness both within and outside of the "Paris Club."
External Private Debt	—	Difficult to estimate, but thought to be low.	—
Possible Claims of Iran	—	Unknown, but as much as 100 Billion.	—

The Gulf War (1990 to 1991)

Cost of Coalition Military Operations	—	—	Approx 70 billion incurred by the US, reimbursed in large part by Saudi Arabia, Kuwait, Japan, Germany and Korea.
Claims for Damage Arising out of the Invasion and Occupation of Kuwait	48 billion has been awarded, with 30 billion of that amount unpaid as of May 2004. Some 45,000 claims seeking in excess of 80 billion remain unresolved — much of this amount relates to environmental damage.	—	The issue of interest owing on amounts awarded has been deferred by the UNCC and ultimately may be excluded from the jurisdiction of the UNCC making recovery unlikely.

The UN Sanctions Period (1991 to 2003)

The presence of the sanctions prevented Iraq from assuming further external debt. Internally, further debt of Iraq may have arisen. Kurdish property was seized in the Northern Iraq and there were extensive human rights violations against the Shiite population in Southern Iraq.	—	—	—

The Iraq War and Reconstruction (2003 to present)

Cost of Coalition Military Operations	—	—	Approx. 150 billion as of late 2004 incurred by the US.
Reconstruction	—	Certain costs such as cleanup of armaments apparently not yet discussed.	CPA and World Bank 2003 estimates were similar at 70 billion over 5 years.
Claims for Damage Arising out of Military Operations	—	Unknown, partly built into cost of reconstruction.	—

III. Approaching Iraq's Debt

[M]any nations are desperately poor and require foreign assistance. Given the limited political will to provide such assistance, a common response is that such countries receive only a portion of what is needed and that it is received in some mix of loans and grants. In the case of Iraq prior to the war, the Administration testifying to Congress pointed to Iraq's wealth and the unlikely need for U.S. or any external funding of reconstruction. Since the war, the Administration has pointed instead to Iraq's debt, the need for U.S. assistance in the form of grants and not loans, and to the importance of all creditor nations providing debt relief to Iraq through debt forgiveness. Iraq has been argued by the Administration to occupy a special position relative to other countries in need of assistance in that it is crucial that its transition to an elected government succeed, and that the chances of such success will be enhanced through a rapid reconstruction.

At the outset, it is important to recognize that the tie between debt forgiveness and reconstruction is not as clear as it appears at first blush. As already stated, reconstruction may be funded from both domestic and foreign sources. A heavy external debt thus siphons off monies, regardless of their source, otherwise possibly available for reconstruction and thus impedes the rebuilding effort. But the strength of that conclusion depends in part on the relative amounts involved, particularly the amount of foreign debt, and the amount of domestic revenue possibly available. Unlike most other states calling for assistance, Iraq is a country with oil that will in time bring in a steady stream of revenue. In this sense, Iraq in theory could deal with its debt at some distant future date if there was a moratorium on debt repayment rather than on debt forgiveness. But there are two other important aspects to Iraq's debt picture. First, in the eyes of many Iraqis, there is a sense that this debt not only should be forgiven, but rather that it is, in the main, void *ab initio* given the illegitimacy of President Hussein's regime (encapsulated in the notion of "odious debt"). Second, it is important, given the unilateral nature of the U.S. entry into Iraq to the perceived legitimacy of the presence of U.S. forces in Iraq, that there not be a sense of self-dealing and self-enrichment by the U.S. during its presence in Iraq.

Considering all this, one can perceive four aspects, whether they are officially articulated or not, to U.S.'s basic strategy thus far in approaching Iraq's debt:

1. Place a moratorium on debt repayment,
2. Seek forgiveness of the debt that is discussed,
3. Do not discuss the debt that is usually overlooked, and
4. Do not distinguish between the relatives merits of different pools of debt.

Let us briefly review all four aspects of this strategy. First, a moratorium on Iraq's debt was gained in large measure through Security Council resolutions granting, for example, Iraqi petroleum product immunity from legal proceedings. Second, the forgiveness of Iraqi debt held generally by creditor states was sought by a tour of such nations in late 2003 and early 2004 by former U.S. Secretary of State James Baker. Such debt forgiveness is not without precedent; indeed two-thirds of Yugoslavia's external foreign debt was forgiven following its breakup and descent into violence. Secretary Baker visiting individual members of the Paris Club, particularly France and Russia, was able to secure pledges of support for debt reduction. But such negotiations may have hidden costs or tradeoffs. The Russian government was reported to link other issues, for instance, resumption of an oil contract in Iraq, to such willingness. Four Arab creditor nations of Iraq, not members of the Paris Club, were also reported willing to enter into negotiations on substantial debt reduction. But this was conditioned on restoration of Iraq's sovereignty and, particularly in the case of

Kuwait, acceptance that Iraq's liability would not be waived for damages resulting from Iraq's 1990 invasion of Kuwait. Less obviously, forgiveness (in effect) of Iraq's debt for the 1990 Gulf War has been sought through efforts primarily by Iraqi nationals to close down the UNCC and bring its remaining work to an end. Although this would not entail a formal termination of such claims, it would close down the primary mechanism by which they might be resolved and satisfied. Although the UNCC has been allowed to complete its work, the percentage of the Iraqi oil revenues that are directed to the satisfaction of UNCC awards for damages arising out of the 1991 Gulf War was reduced in 2003 from twenty to five percent, thus greatly extending the payment schedule for such awards. Third, there has been no mention of Iraq's potential debt for its aggression against Iran in the 1980 to 1988 Iran-Iraq war. This is not suggesting that the task of raising Iran's possible claim somehow belongs to the United States. It does not. However, it should be recognized that, even absent Iran's pressing of the claim, this matter will continue to occupy a prominent spot in Iraqi-Iranian relations. Fourth and last, there is little apparent distinction by the Administration as to the relative merits of various aspects of Iraq's debt. The U.S. ultimately supported the continuation of the UNCC, albeit with a reduced contribution from Iraqi oil revenue, which probably recognized some greater priority to those claims rather than the older Iran-Iraq war debt. In contrast, Iraqi groups and commentators in several nations have called for a sharp distinction between odious debts and other debts.

IV. Concluding Observations

Iraq after the 2003 war stands apart from previous examples of reconstruction. Like Germany after World War II, Iraq has the capacity to generate domestic revenue and a treasury facing substantial pre-war debt. Unlike Germany, Iraq does not possess the same homogenous social fabric upon which the new Iraq is to be constructed. Rather, Iraq, like Afghanistan, must reconstruct its physical infrastructure at the same time as it seeks to construct its political and social identity as a state. Unlike Afghanistan, Iraq possesses the oil reserves that will provide in time for Iraq's continued growth. The issue for Iraq is how to undertake such multifaceted economic and political reconstruction while addressing a complicated and substantial debt situation in this transition period.

What we know of Iraq's debt is that although it has several components and that different portions of it are pursued more actively than other parts, it stems in large part from the time of the Iran-Iraq War. In Table 2, this article describes these various components in their respective context.

In reviewing that debt and the U.S. Administration's approach to forgiving portions of that debt, two observations seem particularly important in closing. First, the Administration does not, at least openly, appear to acknowledge that the past is not entirely separable from the future, and that the repayment of some categories of the debt actually furthers the goal of reconstruction. For example, resolution of claims regarding Iraq's debt to nations in the region for its invasion of Kuwait in 1990 would go far to reconstructing the health of the greater region. Indeed, such monies often go to actual physical reconstruction. A specific and crucial example is the UNCC's treatment of environmental claims by States in the region. Although these claims probably constitute one of the largest clusters of potential Iraqi debt remaining before the UNCC, it is also true that under UNCC practice, the funds awarded would actually be required to remediate the damaged environment, thereby enhancing the reconstruction and environmental health of a highly integrated region. Second and related, although it may be politically difficult to undertake debt differentiation given the range and variety of creditors, it is appropriate at the final negotiations that distinctions be drawn between the various categories of debt. These distinctions should be drawn between state and private holders of debt, and between commercial debt and debt which arose out of violations of international law in Iraq's use of force in the region. I would argue that such distinctions will help clarify that some categories of debt are less susceptible to forgiveness and would in fact, if repaid, contribute to the reconstruction of the region.

As noted, Secretary Baker's tour seeking debt forgiveness, although partially successful, also met with the objections that (1) other countries also merited such debt relief, and (2) Iraq did not occupy a special position in this regard. In June 2004, President Jacques Chirac of France, for example, reportedly remarked to President George Bush in response to a question concerning debt relief for Iraq that "It would be unfair to treat Iraq more generously than the world's poorest nations." Although pledges were gained from foreign leaders regarding debt relief, both such relief and the delivery of pledged aid have been slow. Ironically, as this article goes to publication, the drive to gain relief for Iraq will probably spur initiatives long sought for debt relief in general. The Editors of the *New York Times* recently wrote:

> [T]he United States is simply proposing to cancel the debts of the world's 30 poorest countries, and Britain has joined in. . . . One motivation for President Bush's efforts in this area is that he wants the world to greatly reduce Iraq's debt.

As the Editors of the *Christian Science Monitor* observe, "The widespread forgiveness of much of Iraq's debt has set an example of what the US can do when it musters its political will." Amidst all the reasons for the military action in Iraq, global debt relief was never mentioned. It may be the most significant unintended beneficial consequence of that action.

NOTES AND QUESTIONS

1. The Government of Iraq continues to make payments to the United Nations Compensation Commission; of the total award amount of $52.4 billion, Iraq had paid approximately $23.4 billion in mid-2008, according the UNCC (*Status of Processing and Payment of Claims*, available at http://www2.unog.ch/uncc/status.htm). Over $80 billion remain outstanding, according to the article of Caron above, albeit claims by governments, as opposed to the claims by individuals and corporations. Iraq's external debt was said to stand in 2004 at $120 billion. Christina Ochoa, *From Odious Debt to Odious Finance: Avoiding the Externalities of a Functional Odious Debt Doctrine*, 49 Harv. Int'l L.J. 109, 119 (2008). Dozens of billions of dollars can be

added, depending on how far back the computation goes. "Despotism" or "dictatorship" appears as one precondition for the debt to be "odious," and Saddam Hussein's dictatorship can be traced back to August 1968 (the Ba'th Party coming to power) or 1979 (Saddam becoming president and absolute leader by an internal purge). Governments are in principle successors to commitments contracted by their predecessors under international law, but the "odious debt" exception has been traced back to Aristotle. Ochoa, at 112. If the central argument for the liberation of Iraq was the welfare of the Iraqis, why should they continue to pay for debts contracted by the dictatorship?

2. Even before Saddam Hussein was removed from power, some authors expressed concern with the legal theories underlying the UN resolutions mandating compensation. Mallat's 1995 article is a case in point. While the UN Geneva Compensation Commission has completed compensation for the private claims during the occupation of Kuwait, governmental debt, especially to the Arab Gulf countries, remains outstanding. If the larger picture needs to be accounted for, the matter becomes even more complex. What about the oil-for-food arrangements, of which a sizeable portion went to the Compensation Commission? What of compensation for the victims of the Iran-Iraq war, launched by Saddam Hussein in 1980, especially since "the liability to Iran which was established, following the Iran-Iraq Cease-fire Resolution—Resolution 598—in a formal way by the former Secretary-General, Mr. Perez de Cuellar"? Could the Iraqi government claim part of the "odious debt" already paid back? What mechanisms are available to extricate the current government from the debt? Legal? Diplomatic?

3. SORTING OUT OIL-FOR-FOOD

Oil for food has become a term of art in international diplomacy and law. It refers to a complicated, phased arrangement, which started soon after the war over Kuwait was over. The proposal for oil-for-food had come originally from the International Committee for a Free Iraq, which acted partly as pressure group, partly as international think tank from 1991 to 1993. On the ICFI, see Mallat, Voices of Opposition: The International Committee for a Free Iraq, in E. Goldberg, R. Kasaba & J. Migdal eds., Rules and Rights in the Middle East: Democracy, Law and Society 174-187 (1993).

NOTES AND QUESTIONS

1. One of the problems Iraqis faced was the strict sanctions regime, established by Resolution 678 soon after Saddam Hussein's invasion of Kuwait in August. UNSCR 661 on August 6, 1990, then UNSCR 678 on November 28, 1990, banned most trade with Iraq except for humanitarian staples, essentially food and medicine. The sanctions regime remained after the war, and threatened Iraqis with starvation. The ICFI developed the concept of "food for oil," that is the sale of oil under international control so that the proceeds are not used by the Iraqi government to buy weapons, and get effectively disbursed for the benefit of the Iraqi population. The concept

found its way to the UN, and in August 1991, the first "Food-for-Oil" UNSC Resolution was adopted. It allowed Iraq to sell up to $1.6 billion of its oil. The proceeds were to be deposited into an UN administered escrow account, to be used to buy humanitarian supplies for Iraq, compensate Kuwait for war damages, and reimburse the WMD inspection commission (UNSCOM) for its costs. The Iraqi government refused to implement it. Five years later, following Resolution 986 (April 14, 1995), the Iraqi government started implementing parts of the oil-for-food scheme following a detailed Memorandum of Agreement with the UN Secretariat (May 20, 1996). Against the original ICFI proposal, all Resolutions also included compensation to the non-Iraqi victims of the Kuwait war. The oil-for-food arrangement was eventually distorted by wide-range corruption. See "the Volcker Report," posted with all documents of the investigation available at www.iic-offp.org; and Jeffrey A. Meyer & Mark G. Califano, *Good Intentions Corrupted: The Oil-for-Food Scandal and the Threat to the UN* (2006).

2. In the wake of the scandal, few people were tried, despite a long list of names disclosed in and around the investigation, including the former UN Secretary General, Boutros Ghali; Kojo Annan, the son of the former UNSG Kofi Annan, Benon Sivan, the top UN manager, and scores of high-profile institutions like France's bank Paribas and political personalities in Russia, France, and the Arab world. Could the Iraqis recoup some of their money, at least for the corruption? Under the spirit of the original food-for-oil proposal, would other liabilities be adjudicated? Under national or international jurisdiction? Civil or criminal? Should the UN be requested to clean up its own act?

3. Some cases found their way to U.S. courts:

ENFORCEMENT OF THE FOREIGN CORRUPT PRACTICES ACT IN THE UNITED STATES: TRENDS AND THE EFFECTS OF INTERNATIONAL STANDARDS
Practicing Law Institute: Corporate Law and Practice Handbook Series,
April-May, 2008, 771-776

International Law Advisory
Recent Oil-for-Food Program Cases Show the Government's Willingness to Pursue "Improper" Payments Outside the FCPA's Antibribery Provisions, Call Attention to Foreign Enforcement

In recent months the Department of Justice (DoJ) and the Securities and Exchange Commission (SEC) have continued to bring enforcement actions and seek substantial fines against companies accused of making improper payments in the course of their involvement with the United Nations' Oil-for-Food Program ("OFFP") and the Government of Iraq. Among other things, these actions illustrate the utility of the accounting provisions of the FCPA in reaching payments that fall outside the scope of the Act's antibribery provisions, but violate other laws, such as OFAC-administered sanctions and general fraud statutes. They reflect continued inter-agency and, indeed, intergovernmental cross-border, cooperation in prosecuting cases. Several of the cases also illustrate the tendency of investigations that begin with one type of payment focus to turn up other issues — in this case, FCPA antibribery issues.

The theory of prosecution in these cases is consistent with the government's past position in FCPA cases regarding "qualitative accuracy" of the books and records and internal control requirements.

Background to the Oil-for-Food Program

The United Nations Security Council established the OFFP pursuant to Resolution 986, entering into an implementing memorandum of understanding with Iraq in 1996 as part of a larger sanctions program imposed against it in the wake of the 1991 Gulf War. This regime generally prohibited UN member states from transacting in Iraqi goods and commodities, but instituted the OFFP to allow certain civilian goods to enter the country on humanitarian grounds, funded by Iraqi oil sales.

Under the Program, the Iraqi government had to devote proceeds from the oil sales to purchase certain enumerated civilian products. The terms allowed the Iraqi government, through its State Oil Marketing Organization (SOMO) to award "allocations" of oil to purchasers, which would pay into an UN-administered escrow account to be used solely for humanitarian purposes in Iraq; payments to any other accounts were explicitly prohibited. The Iraqi government used its allocations authority to extract payments from would-be purchasers, variously called "surcharges," "commissions," "consultancy payments," and "sales fees." The sanctions, and the OFFP, ceased in 2003. The next year, Secretary General Kofi Annan established the Independent Inquiry Committee (IIC) to investigate reports of wide-scale corruption involving the OFFP. The UN Security Council endorsed the IIC in Resolution 1538 (2004), and called for the full cooperation of all member states.

In tandem with and pursuant to the IIC's investigation, which ended in December 2006, numerous countries, including the United States, Australia and the United Kingdom, began their own investigations into corruption surrounding the OFFP involving their nationals.

The United States now has brought roughly a dozen cases under the FCPA for making improper kickback payments under OFFP contracts. In keeping with its practice since its first OFFP case against a major public corporation, brought against El Paso Corporation in February 2007, the US Government has not cited the antibribery provisions of the FCPA, as the payments went not to a "foreign official," but rather the Government of Iraq. (In fact, as discussed further below, the payments initially were directed to several Iraqi government officials' private accounts, but were then transferred to the Iraqi treasury.) Settlement in these cases reflects a range of penalties, from a high of $30 million in the *Chevron* case to a low of $4.65 million in *Textron*.

Chevron

In November 2007, the SEC agreed with Chevron Corporation to settle charges that Chevron inaccurately entered payments into its books and records in violation of the FCPA's antibribery provisions. The settlement resolved the SEC's allegations that Chevron engaged in 36 transactions from April 2001-May 2002 involving payment of US$20 million to third parties for their shares of Iraqi oil allocations, despite knowing or having reason to know that the accompanying "surcharges" — additional payments above the market price — were destined for the Government of Iraq, outside of the OFFP account.

Although Chevron had instituted a compliance policy specifically addressing the OFFP surcharge issue, the SEC found that Chevron failed adequately to implement it or police it with a system of internal controls. The company's policy prohibited such charges, requiring management to scrutinize and approve all transactions company traders proposed involving Iraqi petroleum. The SEC found that Management failed to thoroughly review these transactions, however, in one case green-lighting a purchase from a company with no known assets, operations or experience.

Chevron further failed to implement sufficiently the financial controls in its compliance policy — even with information that higher per-barrel prices of oil purchased from its sellers followed reports of Iraq's surcharge demands in the fall of 2000. Despite the jump in prices, Chevron management regularly allowed its traders to proceed with Iraqi oil purchases.

The SEC's civil action charged that Chevron failed to accurately characterize the surcharges it paid on OFFP purchases as payments to the Iraqi government, instead describing these simply as "premiums," in violation of the FCPA's requirement that US issuers keep accurate books, accounts and records. Because the surcharges ended up in Iraq government coffers, the antibribery provisions presumably did not apply.

Chevron ultimately consented to a permanent injunction from future violations of the accounting provisions and agreed to disgorge $25,000,000 in profits. This amount was to be divided between the US Attorney for the Southern District of New York and the New York District Attorney. In addition, it also agreed to a civil penalty of $3,000,000 for the accounting violations and a penalty of $2,000,000 to be paid to the Office of Foreign Assets Control for its violation of OFAC regulations. As part of this package settlement, Chevron also entered into a non-prosecution agreement with the DOJ, which had alleged wire fraud as the basis of its criminal theory. The level of these fines should make companies aware that the FCPA's books and records provisions can result in fines that far exceed the amount of penalties US companies would pay for solely for an underlying violation of US sanctions laws.

Ingersoll-Rand

A similar deployment of the FCPA's accounting provisions occurred when the SEC in October 2007 brought charges against Ingersoll-Rand ("Ingersoll") accusing it of failing to take action upon notice that several of its foreign subsidiaries had been paying kickbacks to the Iraqi government. The SEC found that Ingersoll, either itself, through its subsidiaries or third parties, authorized kickbacks in the form of hidden "after sales service fees" ("ASSFs") in contracts it with the Iraqi government and submitted to the "661 Committee" charged with managing the OFFP. Frequently these ASSFs involved no actual after-sale services. Further, these payments were made knowingly in violation of the OFFP and US law. By not classifying these payments accurately in "reasonable detail," or as "unlawful kickbacks" to the Iraqi regime, the SEC found that Ingersoll did not accurately detail its accounts.

The DoJ as well as the SEC also brought charges against Ingersoll-Rand for the conduct of an Italian subsidiary, Ingersoll-Rand Italiana SpA ("IR Italiana"). DoJ alleged that IR Italiana conspired to violate the FCPA's books and records provisions by paying some $20,000 in travel and entertainment expenses for eight Iraqi officials for a training visit to the company's facilities. Six of the officials, however, were strictly on vacation, and attended to no business during their stay. IR italiana conspired to conceal these payments on its books and records, resulting in Ingersoll Rand making false statements in its own financial accounts.

Like Chevron, Ingersoll faced no FCPA bribery charges for these payments. With respect to the OFFP payments, the anti-bribery provisions presumably did not apply due to the fact that the payments went to the Iraqi government. For the travel and entertainment expenses, however, the absence of antibribery charges requires another explanation, perhaps of a jurisdictional nature due to the lack of a nexus of the sponsorship activity carried out on behalf of the foreign subsidiary to the United States.

Ingersoll consented to a three-year non-prosecution agreement and a $2.5 million criminal penalty with the DoJ; the company settled with the SEC for over $4 million, split between profit disgorgement and civil penalties. The OFFP side of this case closely models that of *Textron*, settled last August with SEC for $3.5 million and the DoJ for $1.15 million, for similar use of ASSF-labeled kickbacks by a fifth-tier French subsidiary.

Flowserve

More recently, the government settled FCPA accounting and internal controls violation charges with Flowserve Corporation, a maker of large-scale water pumps, for entering into contracts containing ASSFs, in a manner similar to those described above with respect to Ingersoll. The SEC's complaint alleged that two of Flowserve's foreign subsidiaries, one in France and one in the Netherlands, entered into a total of twenty contracts providing for kickbacks amounting to some $820,246. Ultimately, $604,651 of this amount actually was paid, while $173,758 was outstanding at the time of the 2003 US invasion of Iraq. The DoJ focused only on French subsidiary's contracts (comprising nineteen of the twenty) charging that Flowserve had conspired to violate the US wire fraud statutes and the FCPA's books and records provisions.

The SEC found that Flowserve's French subsidiary, Flowserve Pompes, created two different covers to conceal these payments. One involved the creation of records showing payments to a Jordanian agent for installation services and commissions when no such services were ever in fact rendered, and the other, in its contract reimbursement requests to the UN, marking up the unit price of its equipment to cover the ASSF payments. Flowserve Pompes also signed a letter with the Iraq government committing to pay the 10% ASSFs. Flowserve's Dutch subsidiary, Flowserve B.V. entered into only one contract involving a kickback, termed a "special project discount," that was passed through an agent to the Iraqi-government-owned South Gas Company with which the contract was made.

Flowserve consented to the entry of final judgment enjoining it from violating the internal controls or books and records provisions of the FCPA, as well as ordering it to pay a civil penalty of $3,000,000. In addition, it agreed to disgorge approximately $3,500,000 million in profits and pre-judgment interest. Further, under a deferred prosecution agreement with the DoJ, Flowserve agreed to pay a $4,000,000 criminal penalty in respect of an asserted conspiracy to commit wire fraud and criminal books and records violations involving the French subsidiary's alleged violations, as to which the DoJ filed a criminal information against that subsidiary, Flowserve Pompes. Flowserve B.V., the Dutch subsidiary, will also enter into a criminal disposition with the Dutch Public Prosecution.

FCPA Accounting Provisions Reach Non-Official/Non-Governmental Payments

Enforcement actions employing the accounting provisions as an independent ground to reach improper payments, especially those not constituting bribery under the FCPA, are not limited to the OFFP context. In *Schnitzer Steel*, for instance, the government brought criminal charges under the books and records provisions for payments made to managers of privately owned steel mills in China and South Korea, accusing Schnitzer and its subsidiaries as falsely describing the payments as "refunds," "rebates," "sales commissions," or "commission to the customer." These charges accompanied allegations that Schnitzer had also violated the antibribery provisions by paying managers at state-owned scrap metal customers.

These accounting provisions of the FCPA have also been applied to payments that were not commercial bribes or direct or indirect payments to a government, but which fell afoul of US sanctions law. In the *Chiquita* settlement, for example, the DOJ and SEC brought charges under the books and records provisions charging that a Chiquita subsidiary, with knowledge of senior management, misleadingly termed extortion payments it made to the United Self-Defense Forces of Columbia ("AUC")—a Foreign Terrorist Organization and a Specially-Designated Global Terrorist with which business transactions are prohibited—as charges for "security payments," "security services," or "security." Where the government believes there is fraud or deliberate violations of law, these cases show it will not hesitate to bring criminal accounting charges.

From the bribery side, what is most interesting is the fact that in two of the OFFP cases—*Chevron* and *El Paso*—the payments were initially paid to individual Iraqi officials, though subsequently paid over to the government. The lack of FCPA antibribery charges presumably reflects the fact that the companies, in making the payments, intended to pay a fee to the government and not to improperly influence any individual actors. The fact that the government is systematically extracting payments in return for allocating benefits to all users of a system did not prevent the accounting charges.

. . .

Developments in Foreign OFFP Enforcement

Other nations have also stepped up OFFP enforcement actions, some in conjunction with the United States. The Dutch specialty chemical company Akzo Nobel, for instance, recently avoided criminal charges in the US for kickbacks of $280,000 allegedly paid to the Iraqi Government by its Dutch-based subsidiaries through various middlemen it described as agents or consultants to facilitate its OFFP contracts. The DoJ reached a non-prosecution agreement with the company with the condition that it would pay a criminal fine of 381,000 Euros to the Dutch Public Prosecutor, or forfeit $800,000 to the US Treasury if it failed to do so.

The SEC, meanwhile, settled with Akzo Nobel for a civil penalty of $750,000, in addition to $2.2 million in disgorgement of profits, charging that Akzo Nobel had been reckless in failing to know that their subsidiaries engaged in this conduct, and for having a defective system of internal controls. Beyond issuing securities in the US market, Akzo Nobel had no ties to the United States. Akzo Nobel ceased its registration with the SEC during the course of the investigation.

In the UK, the Serious Fraud Office in December 2007 requested the pharmaceutical manufacturers AstraZeneca, Eli Lilly and GlaxoSmithKline, as well as other drug companies, to provide documents pertaining to their participation in the program. The investigation is said to be one of the SFO's largest, estimated to cost some 22 million British Pounds. It is unclear what the SFO will find, but the reported scale of the request and the size of the requested companies suggests that much could be swept up in its wake.

In Australia, the Securities and Investments Commission recently initiated charges against six former managers of the Australian Wheat Board that had steered the Board's OFFP business. They are charged with failing to act with "due diligence" and with failing to act in "good faith and for a proper purpose." Due to a shorter statute of limitations, the Commission is proceeding with these cases prior to possible criminal charges. The civil charges carry potential fines of $150,000 each, with each defendant facing from seven to seventeen counts.

Though less recently, India too has been embroiled in the OFFP scandal. A government investigation ending in August 2006 found that India's former foreign minister, Natwar Singh, had requested oil allocations from Iraqi president Saddam Hussein, setting up transactions similar to those in which El Paso and Chevron had engaged — paying per barrel surcharges to an intermediary that later went to the Iraqi government — and that eventually inured to the benefit of close associates, though not necessarily Mr. Singh himself.

Some of these cases may result in challenges to the prosecution on the ground of the asserted legality of the surcharges under Iraqi law. This was not a defense to the US cases, given US sanctions prohibitions on dealings with the Iraqi government.

Iraq Continues to Provide Grist for the Anti-Corruption Mill

In addition to OFFP actions in the US and overseas, Iraq itself continues to provide fodder for a number of enforcement actions, arising out of Iraqi reconstruction efforts. By the end of 2007, US authorities had brought some 50 prosecutions relating to business activity in Iraq, most arising out of Special Inspector General for Iraqi Reconstruction (SIGIR) investigations, and many for bribery and associated conspiracy, fraud, money laundering and corruption charges. Only one completed Iraqi reconstruction case so far, *United States v. Salam*, has involved the FCPA. Nevertheless, the momentum of assertive prosecution of the statute shows no sign of abating, and has proved adaptable to a wide variety of improper payments that the antibribery provisions do not cover. Just as the Oil-for-Food Program investigations began with investigations into individuals and then moved on to encompass large corporations, so may the efforts of SIGIR and other US authorities investigating activities in Iraq. Perhaps now more than ever, companies, whether with ties to Iraq or not, must be sure that their accounting descriptions encompass all relevant and material aspects of a payment, and that they have stringent internal control systems in place for not only FCPA but sanctions compliance as well.

4. Note the link with corruption, especially under the U.S. Foreign Corrupt Practices Act, in the cases above. What mechanisms, if any, are there within the UN? In other countries?

5. *On "the larger picture."* The history of UN and Iraq, probably more than any country on earth, is inextricably linked. Sections important to this relationship are more conveniently included in other chapters. For more on human rights violations in Abu Ghraib, especially from the point of view of international responsibility, see Chapter 4 on the judiciary. A military role

for the UN is discussed in Chapter 7 on security. Considering the imbroglio in Iraq, both regional and international, the "UN" and "international law" are categories which are ever expansive, and responsibility is bound to expand with them. Specific subject matters such as boundaries, debt, and compensation cannot be addressed without keeping in mind the complex and often imprecise realm of international law, and the unwieldy nature and history of UN institutions, especially the Security Council and the Secretariat. Individual corruption is real, some would say inevitable, and it is to the credit of the UN Secretariat that a full Security Council Resolution was devoted to the oil-for-food scandal, and the need for a full enquiry (UNSCR 1538, April 21, 2004). The main embezzler, a Turkish national, remains at large, but the UN people on the ground offered genuine sacrifices, epitomized in the death of UN envoy Sergio Vieira de Mello in August 2003.

6. *A new chapter? The International Compact for Iraq.* In May 2007, a new international initiative was launched in the Egyptian resort of Sharm al-Sheikh, which included the major countries and international players. It was called the International Compact for Iraq (ICI), with a follow-up in Sweden in May 2008. In its official welcome to the initiative, the Swedish Foreign Ministry explained the objectives of the ICI: "The somewhat improved security situation, Security Council Resolution 1770 from August 2007 and the augmented involvement of the UN, under the new head of the UN Assistance Mission for Iraq (UNAMI), Swedish-Italian Staffan de Mistura, have created new conditions for a deeper involvement in Iraq. The implementation of the ICI, as the only existing framework for international involvement in the development of Iraq, can help move the process of reconciliation and development in the country forward." (Available at http://www.sweden.gov.se/sb/d/10081/a/102186/.) The ICI provides for benchmarks and reviews, although monitoring is by nature elusive. See the dedicated, but not well updated, ICI website available at www.iraqcompact.org/.

7. *A new chapter? UNSCR 1859.* At the end of 2008, the UN Security Council passed Resolution 1859 (Dec. 22, 2008). Its most important dispositive clause appears in paragraph 5, which states that the Security Council.

> *Decides* to review resolutions pertaining specifically to Iraq, beginning with the adoption of resolution 661 (1990), and in that regard *requests* the Secretary-General to report, after consultations with Iraq, on facts relevant to consideration by the Council of actions necessary for Iraq to achieve international standing equal to that which it held prior to the adoption of such resolutions.

The clause seeks to remove the adverse effects of all the previous Security Council resolutions since the invasion of Kuwait in August 1990, in order to restore the fullest possible sovereignty to the country. If applied, it would close the long UN chapter on Iraq. What would the "application" of this clause entail?

ECONOMIC ISSUES:
OIL AND WATER

Whether the . . . regime will stand out historically hinges, in the long run, upon its ability to contribute, in a creative manner, to the process of nation-state building that the 1920 Revolt had set afoot. This will involve, sooner or later, the necessity of binding the peasants to the townsmen and the Shi'is to the Sunnis; and creating mutually advantageous relations between the Kurds and the Arabs; and, at the same time, raising qualitatively the standard of living and level of culture of the mass of Iraqis — all of which presupposes, before anything else, the ability to channel into agricultural and industrial development the wealth that oil generates instead of largely dissipating it, as in past years, in unproductive consumption. . . . Oil payments have, by their immensity, really solved for Iraq the problem of "primitive accumulation": the regime does not have to extract out of the people the economic surplus needed to develop the country. At bottom the question is one of elaborating the institutions and building the skills that could employ the huge oil revenues in a socially effectual way.

These are tasks that are too great for any party acting singly, or simultaneously engaged in combating civil strife, and can be accomplished only if the country's principal political forces pull together and work hand-in-hand for the good of their people.

Hanna Batatu, on the then ruling Ba'th
The Old Social Classes and the Revolutionary Movements of Iraq,
Princeton, 1978 rpt Saqi, London 2004, 1133-1134

Introduction. Depending on the sources, Iraq has between 110 and 115 billion barrels in proven oil reserves, an estimated 200-300 billion in estimated additional reserves, and is least explored of all leading oil producers. Oil represents between 60 and 70 percent of Iraq's annual GDP, 80 to 90 percent of the Government of Iraq (GoI) budget revenue, and 90 to 98 percent of Iraq's export revenue. With oil reserves comparable to Saudi Arabia's and better than Iran's, Iraq is destined to play an increasingly important role in fulfilling the world's energy needs.

The other strategic resource of the country is water. Iraq is blessed since the dawn of recorded history with the Tigris and the Euphrates flowing through the land. But as a downstream country, modern Iraq is at the mercy of Turkey and Syria for its water sources.

This chapter will examine basic economic issues that are inextricably linked to Iraq's future in both its water and oil programs. Documents have been chosen to reflect the immense expertise bearing on Iraq since 2003. The chapter will also consider a specifically Iraqi approach to the economy in the prism of Islamic law by one of its leading jurists, against the overall framework of legislation under the Iraqi Civil Code of 1953.

In a recent article, Michael Ross made the point that

> oil wealth often wreaks havoc on a country's economy and politics, makes it easier for insurgents to fund their rebellions, and aggravates ethnic grievances. Today, with violence falling in general, oil-producing states make up a growing fraction of the world's conflict-ridden countries. They now host about a third of the world's civil wars, both large and small, up from one-fifth in 1992. According to some, the U.S.-led invasion of Iraq shows that oil breeds conflict between countries, but the more widespread problem is that it breeds conflict within them.

Blood Barrels: Why Oil Wealth Fuels Conflict, 87 Foreign Affairs 2-8 (2008). This is certainly true in Iraq, as it is with all so-called "rentier states" in the Gulf. The question is, how can the "oil curse," otherwise known as "Dutch disease," which has contributed to destroying Iraq over the last 50 years, be countered with the benefits one would expect? No doubt, diversification is key, both in terms of production of new values, including petroleum-related products, and in terms of distribution. Does the 2007 hydrocarbon draft law, deadlocked to date, make such a promise? What else is needed on governmental level? Can an Alaska or Norway-style program be useful for Iraq to transform the oil curse into a blessing? Can Islamic law classical categories, whether Islamic Sadr-style or Civil Code-based help?

A. OIL

OIL IN IRAQ: TIMELINE

For an outstanding global appreciation of oil as key to twentieth-century history, see Daniel Yergin, *The Prize: The Epic Quest for Oil, Money, and Power* (1991). The following timeline on Iraq is adapted from the book and other sources.

1908

Oil discovery in Iran spurs the hunt for oil in three adjacent Ottoman Empire provinces corresponding to modern Iraq: Mosul, Baghdad and Basra. Foreign geologists visit disguised as archeologists.

1911

The Turkish Petroleum Company (TPC) is established to explore for oil in Mosul; TPC represents a consortium of British, German and Dutch interests.

1911

Winston Churchill, Britain's First Lord of Admiralty, declares oil to be of paramount importance to the Imperial Navy. Churchill is schooled in the strategic importance of oil by Shell founder Marcus Samuel.

1913

Churchill sends an expedition to assess oil potential in the region. Britain signs a secret pact with the Sheikh of Kuwait, who pledges Britain exclusive oil rights. Kuwait becomes a British protectorate in 1914.

Pre-WWI

Competing oil interests vie for dominance in Mesopotamia with the British eventually winning control of TPC. Ownership consists of Anglo-Persian Oil Co (predecessor to BP): 47.5%, Royal Dutch Shell: 22.5%, Deutsche Bank: 25%, and financier Calouste Gulbenkian ("Mr. Five Percent"): 5%.

ca 1917

British official control of Persian and Mesopotamia oil is a "first-class British War aim."

1918

Ottoman Empire defeated in World War I; British forces occupy oil-rich Mosul, bring Kurdish populated areas under British rule.

1919-20

Post war Franco-British arrangements establish the British Mandate over Iraq.

1919-24

After numerous agreements, WWI victors divvy up TPC. Precursors of BP, Shell, French Total and a U.S. syndicate split the lion's share with 23.75% each, British receive extra royalties in the deal.

1923

Britain, exercising its mandate, pressures Iraq to forego its right to 20% of TPC, voiding a 1920 agreement. The TPC dispute drags through international arbitration for decades and is still officially unresolved.

1925

TPC concludes an oil concession agreement with Iraq. The agreement, to be in effect for 75 years, stipulates that TPC would be and remain a British company registered in Great Britain.

1925

Turkey reluctantly accepts the League of Nations–brokered "Brussels Line" as the Boundary between Iraq and Turkey, marking an end to Ankara's attempts to regain control over Mosul province.

1927-29

Discovery of oil north of Kirkuk, opening the second major new field in the Middle East since the 1908 discovery in Iran. The find is immense—16 billion barrels. TPC becomes Iraq Petroleum Company (IPC). British government becomes reluctant to abandon control over Iraq.

1928

"The Red Line Agreement" establishes a British/French/US oil cartel in the ME, under IPC, that spans Iraq, the Saudi peninsula and Turkey; only Kuwait is excluded as a British preserve.

1931

IPC concession is renegotiated—extended 70 years in exchange for pipelines, payments and loans.

1934

Pipelines completed to Tripoli and Haifa.

1938

Oil is discovered in Saudi Arabia.

1938

IPC wins concessions in southern Iraq forming wholly-owned Basra Petroleum Corporation (BPC).

1948

The Red Line Agreement is scrapped paving the way for U.S. solo investment in Saudi Arabia; IPC's reach is reduced but its monopolistic hold on Iraq is secure. Its monopoly power is used to restrict production (thereby boosting crude prices) resulting in limited growth of Iraq's oil industry and infrastructure.

1952

New agreements boost Iraq's royalties to 50%.

1958

Iraqi Revolution; King Faisal II is killed in the coup.

1961

Revolutionary government led by General Qasem nationalizes 99.5% of concession areas, leaving only producing oil fields in IPC's control.

1961

Kuwait gains independence from Britain. Qasem threatens to invade.

1971-73

Ba'athists, in power since 1968, nationalize remaining oil interests under the Iraq National Oil Company.

1970s

National control of oil assets and high crude prices result in a period of relative prosperity for Iraq.

1979

Saddam, strongman of the regime since the early 1970s, assumes the presidency.

1980s

Iran/Iraq War and low crude oil prices hamper oil industry growth and development.

1990s

Invasion of Iraq/"Second" Gulf War and sanctions cripple oil industry.

1996

UN "Oil-for-Food" program starts; 60% of Iraqis rely on this program for food.

2003

U.S.-led Coalition invades Iraq; Saddam's regime falls. End of Oil-for-Food regime.

2005

Iraqis adopt a new constitution, declaring oil property of all Iraqis.

2007

A hydrocarbon law is drafted under Article 111 of the Constitution.

1. INTERNATIONAL PERSPECTIVES

Abundant natural and human resources enabled Iraq to attain the status of a middle-income country in the 1970s. The country developed good infrastructure and well-performing education and healthcare systems, but the oppressive political atmosphere stifled a skilled and creative workforce and culture. Income per capita rose to over US$3,600 in the early 1980s. Since that time, successive wars and a repressive, state-dominated economic system have undermined growth and development and debilitated basic infrastructure and social services for Iraq's 27 million people. International trade sanctions imposed in 1991 have also taken a toll on the economy. Despite the country's rich resource endowment, Iraq's human development indicators deteriorated steadily over two decades. In 2003, GDP per capita declined by another 30 percent to $480.

The following two texts, respectively an assessment of the World Bank at the time of worsening security in 2004-2006 and a 2008 IMF study, underline the lop-sided state of the Iraqi economy, and the continued heavy reliance on oil.

(a) The World Bank (2006)

REBUILDING IRAQ: ECONOMIC REFORM AND TRANSITION

World Bank, Economic and Social Development Unit, Middle East Department, Middle East and North Africa Region, Feb. 1, 2006[*]

Abstract

This report focuses on the main cross-cutting issues of Iraq's transition and aims to support the Iraqi Government in strengthening its policymaking capacity by laying out the policy options available and discussing tradeoffs under each option. The key themes of the report are reconstruction and job creation; reform of the pricing system; managing oil revenues; and strengthening safety nets. Underpinning this complex agenda are the overarching issues in public sector governance.

Executive Summary

Iraq has a rich and diverse resource base — third largest oil reserves in the world, abundant water, and a national labor force of more than 7 million people — much larger than any member country of the Gulf Cooperation Council (GCC). In one decade this combination of resources could help the country regain the middle-income status it enjoyed earlier. To do this, Iraq will need to make three transitions: from conflict to post-conflict rehabilitation, from a closed, state-dominated economy to a growth-oriented, market-driven economy, and from extreme dependence on oil to a diversified economy. The report lays out some of the policy options to accomplish this transformation.

Recent Developments and Reforms to Date

Oil production and exports have yet to reach the prewar levels, and non-oil sectors remain sluggish. High unemployment, poverty, and weak social protection systems are dominant in people's minds, threatening the fragile democracy. Violence and crime have increased substantially since late 2003, hampering reconstruction and undermining public sector governance. Losses

---

[*]Available at http://www-wds.worldbank.org:80/servlet/main?menuPK=64187510&pagePK= 64193027&piPK=64187937&theSitePK=523679&entityID=000090341_20060222100550.

to social capital have been massive. Success in recovery will depend on how quickly a social consensus emerges on reform priorities and tradeoffs. That consensus is essential. Cross-country analysis shows that countries developing a cohesive and consistent reform strategy outperform in terms of GDP per capita those unable to develop such a consensus by about 50 percent within the first post-conflict decade.

The incidence of absolute poverty is estimated at 8-10 percent, and a further 12-15 percent of the population is vulnerable to falling into absolute poverty. Both monetary and non-monetary aspects of poverty have worsened dramatically in recent decades. Several population groups are especially vulnerable: unemployed youth, demobilized soldiers and militia, war victims with disabilities, and internally displaced persons, refugees, and returnees.

There was some early progress on policy and institutional reforms in public finance, trade, the business climate, and the financial system in 2003–04. Reforms sought to remove price distortions, increase competitiveness, and enhance economic efficiency. Iraq is also reintegrating into the international financial system: in 2004 it adopted an IMF-supported stabilization program, negotiated a highly concessional debt rescheduling, gained access to IDA resources, and submitted a request for full WTO membership. However, severe problems remain. Social indicators are at levels of low income countries. Access to infrastructure services is high — almost universal connection to the national electricity grid and 81 percent access to improved water sources — but the quality of these services had declined sharply in the past decade. In 2004, only 15 percent of households had a stable electricity supply, and a mere 20 percent had safe and stable drinking water.

In October 2004 the Government announced its National Development Strategy (NDS) for reconstruction and reform. The NDS was welcomed by the international donor community, but it needs more specific sectoral strategies and it needs to be further developed into an actionable agenda.

Key Challenges Ahead

Iraq's first need is speedy progress in addressing the most critical condition for economic recovery: security. Beyond security, Iraq's reconstruction strategy is shaped by three main objectives: (a) creating enough productive jobs; (b) rebuilding public services accountable and responsive to citizens' needs such as power, water, roads, schools, and hospitals; and (c) ensuring that vulnerable social groups have access to vital services.

Realizing this vision calls for three main policy instruments: (a) reforming incentive systems to support faster, more efficient growth in private sector jobs; (b) establishing strong formal safety nets, protecting the poor and the vulnerable as prices are freed; and (c) installing accountable and transparent management of oil and other public resources.

Jobs and Reconstruction

Iraq's labor force is growing rapidly (at 2.4 percent a year) and will continue to do so in the medium term. Iraq has one of the highest unemployment rates in the region — close to 30 percent, almost twice the MENA average. More than half of young urban males are unemployed. Iraq also has very high underemployment (over 23 percent), while its female labor participation is a mere 19 percent—low even by MENA standards. Reconstruction should expand the demand for labor substantially.

Iraqi policymakers face a choice on the relative roles of the public and private sector in job creation. A simulation analysis conducted for this report suggests that a strategy reliant on public sector reconstruction without enabling the private sector will run out of steam on jobs and growth within 5-8 years. This simulation demonstrates clearly that there exists urgency to a private sector development strategy now.

Women's labor force participation has been shown to positively contribute to development. Research from other MENA countries show that while the public sector has been the key employer of female labor, in the private sector, women face higher barriers to employment than men. Labor market strategies should also seek to eliminate these barriers.

Strong job creation requires simultaneous improvement of institutions underlying the markets for capital (investment climate) and labor (active labor market policies). . . .

Managing Oil Revenues

Iraq faces a choice between redistributing its oil revenue directly to the people and managing it well through the central budget for overall development impact. In the short-term, oil production and exports remain heavily constrained by rundown facilities and sabotage. Over the medium to long-term, however, Iraq's oil export revenues can rise dramatically—provided that oil production recovers strongly.

The economic performance of oil exporters is often inferior to that of resource-poor countries. This is often explained by the influence of oil wealth on governance and by the harmful real exchange rate effects on the non-oil sector (the Dutch disease). Volatility of oil export revenues may hamper the prospects of Iraq's reconstruction program, since volatility increases uncertainty, leads to wasteful public investment in times of boom and depresses investment when oil prices are low. These effects may combine to undermine economic diversification and growth.

Expenditure smoothing is the key to avoiding the transmission of oil price volatility to the economy. Investment levels should fluctuate substantially less than the price of oil. The Government needs to determine a sustainable level of capital and current spending based on whether the higher revenue flow is temporary or permanent and whether the expected (financial and social) returns justify the expenditure. Given poverty and high unemployment, the Iraqi Government will find it hard to withstand the pressures to spend and invest. Fiscal policy and institutions can help the government maintain a more stable investment strategy. The quality of investment matters as much as the quantity: oil windfalls have often produced huge inefficient projects—"white elephants."

To address volatility, a number of oil-exporting countries have combined mechanisms to accumulate foreign reserves during periods of high revenues with fiscal rules for spending these funds. Others have introduced state oil funds from which an annual transfer is made to meet the needs of the non-oil deficit in the budget. It is important to distinguish between (a) savings funds, which ensure that future generations benefit from the oil wealth even after the oil deposits are depleted; and (b) stabilization funds, achieve expenditure smoothing as discussed earlier. In Iraq, the benefits of a savings fund or a fiscal rule appear to be limited, since the rates of return on investment in the depleted physical and human capital are likely to be vastly superior to returns realized from the stock of financial assets that such a fund could hold overseas. Stabilization, on the other hand, is a legitimate concern; it can be most effectively achieved if pursued within a unified budget framework. Hence a stabilization fund can be virtual, and primarily ensure that each investment project, once started, can be completed.

Given the importance of oil revenues in the Iraqi economy, good governance in their management is crucial. Transparency is needed in the flow of budgetary funds, as well as for the accounts of the Development Fund for Iraq and for the national oil company once it is created. Minimal standards include transparency of the oil sector finances, independent, credible, and transparent audits, and the involvement of civil society.

Reducing Poverty and Vulnerability

Iraq faces a choice between considerably broadening and strengthening its formal safety nets or continuing reliance on untargeted subsidy schemes and subsidized services. The choice is imminent since large segments of Iraq's population face unprecedented social and economic risks.

A first priority is to undertake comprehensive household expenditure surveys to identify the Iraqi poor; these surveys are starting. The next step is to design formal safety nets and finance them in a sustainable fashion.

Apart from the universal food safety net (PDS), social protection consists of a collection of program interventions and providers, including direct assistance from families, private and charity assistance, and government programs. Private and non-governmental safety nets (zakat, waqf) likely account for the majority of social protection. The government-sponsored system has been weakened by wars and sanctions, and the cash benefits currently paid are modest, reaching fewer than 15 percent of the needy. None of these transfers is based on a consistent definition of need, and leakages to the less needy are highly possible. State-sponsored disability care institutions have been severely damaged and have inadequate supplies, while the number of their beneficiaries is small.

Simulations conducted for this study suggest that the Iraqi pension system is financially unsustainable despite the fact that it covers a small share of the population. It is also inefficient and inequitable. Only part of these problems stems from the emergency pension policy put in place in 2003. To a large extent the problems are structural and must be addressed under any circumstances:

- The dual structure of the Iraqi pension system leads to inequality and excessive administrative cost and restrains the efficient allocation of labor.
- The system is unaffordable due to very high benefits—close to 100 percent of the last salary for the average full-career worker.

- Benefit formulas and eligibility conditions distort labor supply and savings decisions and generate adverse distributional transfers (i.e., from low- to high-income workers).
- Current financing mechanisms can impose large costs on employers and discourage job creation.

These structural problems reduce incentives to diversify the sources of savings for retirement, particularly among middle- and high-income workers. In addition, they limit the coverage in the private sector, which is already unacceptably low. Employers systematically underreport the number of employees to remain below the minimum at which pension enrollment becomes mandatory. Finally, the governance structure and administrative capacity of the pension system are a cause of concern. The pension system staff needs skills to design and implement necessary reforms, and then to properly manage the reformed pension fund. Modernization is also called for with regards to information and payment systems.

Strengthening Governance and Public Management

Issues of public management and governance are at the forefront of Iraq's reform agenda for many years. The most immediate challenge is to build a legitimate state and ensure the security and the basic rights and freedoms of Iraqi citizens. Equally pressing is to determine the size and scope of the Government and the appropriate division of responsibilities between ministries and different levels of government. Other pressing questions: How should financial and human resources be organized and optimally deployed? And how can Iraq ensure public sector integrity? The new Iraqi constitution is likely to address many of these issues.

The main fiscal policy issue appears to be strengthening the budgetary framework and anchoring it in a medium-term context. In light of Iraq's large reconstruction needs and uncertain environment, a flexible medium term fiscal framework is the optimal way to manage oil revenues.

Twenty years ago, the budget system in Iraq was fairly efficient and robust. Elements of this system remain, but are hampered by poor security, difficulties in communication, and nontransparent recording of subsidies. In certain areas, for example reporting of fiscal data, the system appears to have deteriorated further since the war. This has degraded the Government's ability to allocate resources effectively and to track spending and outcomes. Urgent reforms are needed to address the fragmentation of the budget, inadequate reporting of revenues and expenditures, and weak accountability. The new Financial Management Law (2004) established principles for strengthening the budget process. However, the law does not itself provide a complete picture of the fiscal architecture required to rebuild the budget as the primary policy instrument; this requires further political and administrative decisions on the appropriate roles for various institutions.

A fundamental problem is budget fragmentation. There are several parallel spending plans but virtually no coordination in their preparation or execution. Improving the coverage of the budget so that it incorporates all significant government revenues and expenditures, and improving its transparency, are critical. It is also important to ensure that all donor aid is brought within the budget. The roles of the Ministry of Finance and Ministry of Planning in preparing the budgets for capital and recurrent expenditures need to be unified within a medium-term expenditure framework. Institutions need to be strengthened in all areas of the budget cycle and in some cases (e.g., internal audit and the parliamentary budget and finance committee) new institutions need to be developed from a rudimentary base. New skills are needed, ranging from treasury operations to debt management to financial auditing. Clearly such reforms will take many years to design and implement though a useful start has been made in some of the key areas.

Public procurement is a closely related area in which reform is urgently needed. The process of reforming the public procurement environment will be challenging, because long-established procedures in the ministries and state-owned enterprises are likely to generate inertia and resistance to change. A major training effort and supporting leadership will be critical. The lack of adequate procurement audit practices, the absence of a code of ethics for procurement officers, and the widespread culture of bribe-taking constitute additional challenges. Strengthening records management requirements and practices for procurement is badly needed. The most urgent action needed from Government is to clarify the legal framework for public procurement and enact the needed legal and regulatory instruments, either by deciding to enforce the new Public Procurement Law through issuance of adequate regulations, or to prepare and enact an entirely new law and suitable regulations. The establishment of an adequately staffed procurement policy body, to be primarily endowed with formulating the regulations and preparing the standard documents which are so badly needed is therefore a very high priority.

Rebuilding Iraq's civil service hinges on making changes in how its employees are organized, including: (1) the statutory basis under which civil servants function; (2) the scope and comprehensiveness of the civil service; (3) its management; (4) the composition of categories and grades; (5) salary structure and benefits; (6) recruitment and promotion; (7) disciplinary procedures and termination; and (8) the boundary between the political and administrative spheres. These issues call for an early attention; also, the gender differences in all these areas should be addressed.

Several CPA directives addressed various aspects of civil service reform, but the record of implementation was uneven. One of the most urgent steps is to create two units with responsibility for human resource management throughout the civil service: one within the executive branch, focusing on human resource management and policy issue; the other with some degree of constitutional independence, overseeing compliance with human resource guidelines and providing an appellate function. In the near term it is of paramount importance that robust payroll and human resource controls be put in place to provide an accurate picture of the civil service and to avoid the pilferage of government resources. New human resource laws and regulations are needed, to enhance meritocracy and protect workers from harassment and discrimination. Modern human resource practices are needed, as well as stronger capacity of line ministries and departments to manage their staff.

Eventually, issues of organizational structure and appropriate staffing levels will require attention.

Intergovernmental fiscal relations require careful consideration as Iraq prepares its Constitution. As with most MENA countries, Iraq is a unitary country with a dominant central government and weak local governments. Three northern governorates are run by the Kurdish regional government and are de facto autonomous. The other 15 governorates are administrative units with no control over revenues and expenditures. The CPA efforts to strengthen local governments in order to prepare the ground for a democratic federation did not build on the existing governance structures and therefore did not live up to expectations. Newly created local councils often lacked basic skills and have found it difficult to exercise authority over departments of central government ministries, which remain in control of service delivery. A confusing patchwork of legislation and practice emerged.

There are no technical answers to the question of how Iraq will proceed with decentralization: this is typically determined by political imperatives. Decentralized governance can accommodate diverse populations and maintain national unity; empower people to support democratization; and improve the efficiency of service delivery. The new Iraqi constitution will need to address three vital questions: Should Iraq be a federal or unitary country? Should decentralization be symmetrical or asymmetrical (equal autonomy for all subnational units or greater autonomy to certain areas)? And how will national revenues be shared?

A second layer of questions revolves around the assignment of responsibilities for each level of government. The guiding principle would be to give responsibilities for public services to the level of government that can discharge them most effectively. The determination of appropriate budget transfer mechanisms and local tax bases would follow. Given the predominance of oil revenue, intergovernmental transfers will remain the main source of financing for local governments. If they are responsible for delivering public services, they must be able to finance them. Finally, institutional arrangements developed, to define accountability and incentive frameworks for each level of government.

Corruption is widely perceived to be significant in Iraq. To combat it, the Government launched several initiatives: the independent Inspector Generals within individual Iraqi ministries, the new Commission on Public Integrity, and the revival of an existing Supreme Board of Audit (SBA). The Inspector Generals were authorized to perform a variety of functions, including auditing all records and activities of the ministry; conducting administrative investigations against any ministry official, including the minister; auditing the economy, efficiency, and effectiveness of the ministry's operations; and reviewing any ministry systems for measuring performance. The Commission on Public Integrity was charged with the criminal investigation of corruption cases and violations of the code of conduct. However, these new institutions have not yet taken root, and their impact is uncertain at this stage. To succeed in anticorruption efforts, Iraq must: (a) strengthen its legal and regulatory framework; (b) develop strong accountability institutions; (c) support prevention within individual agencies; and (d) enhance public opinion and awareness.

(b) The International Monetary Fund (2008)

Iraq continues to experience difficult conditions, but the IMF says its economy has improved over the past two years, and that a new arrangement with the Fund will help the war-shattered economy move toward sustainable growth. The tone is resolutely upbeat, "provided the security situation continues to improve."

ERIK DE VRIJER, UDO KOCK & DAVID GRIGORIAN, IRAQ MAKES PROGRESS ON ECONOMIC FRONT

IMF Middle East and Central Asia Department, Feb. 13, 2008[*]

Iraq made significant progress under an IMF Stand-By Arrangement approved in December 2005. On December 19, 2007, the IMF's Executive Board approved a new Stand-By Arrangement for Iraq. The decision to continue supporting Iraq's economy recognizes the significant progress the country made under the first program. In light of Iraq's strong international reserves position, the authorities will treat the new arrangement as precautionary, which means that they do not intend to draw these resources.

But the IMF noted that much remains to be done to put Iraq on a path to sustainable growth. The main objectives of the new program, which will run through March 2009, are to maintain macroeconomic stability, facilitate higher investment and output in the oil sector, and advance structural reforms and institution building.

Progress Under First Program

Inflation, which spiked at 65 percent at end-2006, was sharply reduced with a policy package that included exchange rate appreciation, monetary tightening, and fiscal discipline. These policies, together with measures to reduce fuel shortages that resulted in declining black market fuel prices, limited the increase in consumer prices to less than 5 percent during 2007. Core inflation, which excludes fuel and transportation prices, fell to about 12 percent from 32 percent in 2006.

Because of security conditions, however, the implementation of the public investment program fell short of budget plans, and oil output and economic activity in general did not expand as much as was hoped. Before oil exports through the northern pipeline to Turkey resumed in the last quarter of 2007, oil production hovered around 2 million barrels per day (mbpd) (see Chart 1).

The shortfall in oil production was offset by higher world market prices (see Chart 2). Iraq's international reserves position has continued to strengthen, allowing the country to repay in advance the full amount outstanding from a 2004 loan under the IMF's Emergency Post-Conflict Assistance, which preceded the first Stand-By Arrangement.

---

*Available at http://www.imf.org/external/pubs/ft/survey/so/2008/CAR021308B.htm.

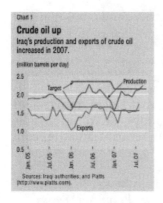

Chart 1

Crude oil up

Iraq's production and exports of crude oil increased in 2007.

(million barrels per day)

Sources: Iraqi authorities; and Platts (http://www.platts.com).

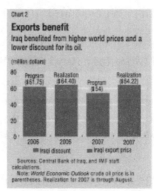

Chart 2

Exports benefit

Iraq benefited from higher world prices and a lower discount for its oil.

(million dollars)

Sources: Central Bank of Iraq; and IMF staff calculations.
Note: World Economic Outlook crude oil price is in parentheses. Realization for 2007 is through August.

Chart 3

Banking limited

Iraq's deposit base and loan portfolio are smaller than in other countries in the region.

(percent of GDP, 2006)

Sources: IMF, International Financial Statistics and staff calculations; Iraqi authorities.

Aside from improving macroeconomic stability, Iraq also made progress on structural reforms. The authorities significantly increased the initially very low domestic official fuel prices to levels that are in line with those in the region's other oil-exporting countries. Direct subsidies on fuel products, which amounted to almost 13 percent of GDP in 2004, were eliminated in 2007, except for a small subsidy on kerosene. This has released much-needed resources for reconstruction and reduced the incentives for smuggling fuel products out of the country. Other achievements include amending the new pension law to make the pension system fiscally sustainable and modernizing the payments system.

Aiming for Stability

Maintaining macroeconomic stability remains a key objective of the authorities' program for 2008. The Central Bank of Iraq will gear its monetary and exchange rate policies toward achieving this objective. Fiscal policy will help contain inflation by keeping current spending, notably the wage and pension bill, in check to limit pressure on Iraq's small non-oil economy. The envisaged increase in government investment, in view of its high import content, should have only a limited impact on inflation.

In light of Iraq's large reconstruction needs, the government has prepared an ambitious investment program for 2008. It is taking steps to speed up projects that could not be undertaken in previous years, in particular to rebuild infrastructure and improve the provision of electricity, water and sanitation, education, and health care. Provided that further security improvements allow execution of the public investment program and a return to a more normal functioning of the economy, economic activity outside the oil sector should pick up.

The authorities' program will also focus on the oil sector and the need for higher investment to raise output and for greater transparency. Raising oil production will be crucial to provide the resources needed for reconstruction over the medium term. Projects to increase production and export capacity in the south and better protect the northern export pipeline are either under way or planned. With continued exports through the north, oil production is projected to increase to 2.2 mbpd in 2008, helping to boost economic growth overall to about 7 percent.

Following the installation of a metering system in the Basra export terminal, metering systems in other ports and oil installations are also being put in place. During 2008, an all-Iraqi Committee of Financial Experts will prepare to take over the audit oversight role of the Development Fund for Iraq, through which all oil revenues are channeled, from the International Advisory Board, which has performed this role since December 2003.

Under the new program, restructuring Iraq's banking sector will be a major challenge. The sector is dominated by state-owned commercial banks, which account for 90 percent of the banking sector's total assets (70 percent for Rafidain and Rasheed banks alone). The banks lack expertise in commercial banking and market finance. There is very little extension of credit to the private sector, and the banks' asset composition is heavily tilted toward government securities.

Compared with other banks in the region, Iraqi banks' deposit base and loan portfolio are small. Most banks lack the expertise to assess risks and, thus, few offer loans with maturities of more than one year. As a result, financial intermediation is weak (see Chart 3). Banks' total loan portfolio at end-2006 was only $2.2 billion (4 percent of GDP), mostly in the form of overdrafts. Total deposits stood at $12.9 billion (26 percent of GDP).

Under the program, financial and operational audits of the two largest banks will be undertaken and a restructuring program adopted, with IMF and World Bank technical assistance. Other structural reforms include modernizing public financial management and strengthening the accounting and reporting framework of the Central Bank of Iraq.

Outlook Hinges on Security

Iraq's medium-term outlook is favorable, provided security continues to improve. The sustainability of its external debt situation would, however, still require the third and final tranche of Paris Club debt rescheduling (worth 20 percent in net present value terms) planned for end-2008 and further progress in reaching debt reduction agreements with Iraq's other creditors. Disbursement of the last Paris Club tranche is contingent on good performance under the new Stand-By Arrangement.

Although much remains to be done, Iraq has registered a number of successes. Significant progress was made in stabilizing the macroeconomic environment and in advancing the structural reform agenda. The 2008 program will focus on similar objectives to capitalize on the momentum achieved by the first program and, in particular, to help the economy begin growing again. Continued progress, however, will depend on the success of efforts to stabilize the security situation and strengthen political consensus.

2. AN IRAQI PERSPECTIVE

Oil as a "Dutch disease," that is, the focus on one lucrative sector that dwarfs all other economic sectors, and corruption as a plague to economic activity, are two structural flaws that continue in post-Saddam Iraq to which insecurity and violence add a particularly tragic component. On oil and corruption, contrast the reading in the last section of the World Bank report with the assessment of the former Minister of Finance, Dr. Ali Allawi, who described several areas of corruption in the oil industry: (1) the lack of metering in oil exports, leading to smuggling through trucks in the North, ships in the South through the

Gulf, and extortion at each occasion; (2) the subsidies, inherited from the previous regime, eating up to 15 percent of the Iraqi budget, and encouraging further smuggling to neighboring countries where Iraqi oil products were resold at several times their price in Iraq; (3) subsidies from the state to various business sectors, like bakeries and fishing, which the recipients would resell at grossly inflated profits; (4) an "abysmal state of control systems throughout the chain of storing, moving, distributing, recording and accounting for oil product," with discrepancies up to 50 percent of the products shipped; (5) absence of punishment of the smuggling rackets, which in turn emboldened them and made them more sophisticated; and (6) "kickbacks on fuel purchases and transport contract that went to senior officials at the Ministry of Oil to the theft of imported and domestic fuel products by smuggling gangs and to the illegal export of crude and fuel oil. . . . The size of the oil racket might have reached $4 billion — in an economy the GDP of which was about $30 billion by 2005." Ali A. Allawi, The Occupation of Iraq — Winning the War, Losing the Peace 356-361 (2007).

NOTES AND QUESTIONS

1. According to the IMF report, metering has steadily developed. It is less certain that the other problems associated with the overbearing weight of the oil in the Iraqi economy are being effectively addressed. Is there a scale of priorities which can be envisaged for economic reforms considering the ebb and flow of oil price and revenues, both internationally and from the Iraqi government's point of view?

2. The economy does not exist in a void. What specific legal reforms could be undertaken to improve production and distribution? How can unemployment and underemployment be tackled? Why is the female workforce lowest in the region, according to the World Bank, despite the relatively high level of educated women in Iraq?

3. U.S. PERSPECTIVES

The role of the U.S. in Iraqi nation-building is unprecedented in the history of Iraq and the region. Parallels with Japan and Germany after World War II are inevitably raised, but the differences may be more important than the similarities. A major problem in the early period of the occupation may have been the fierce infighting over Iraq between the various American governmental departments and agencies, notably the Defense Department, the State Department, and the CIA. The following reports, from 2006 to 2008, show both the intensity of continued expertise on Iraq in the U.S., including at government level, and a relative smoothing out of the decision-making process in Washington, at least with regard to assessing and assisting the Iraqi economy.

(a) SIGIR—Special Inspector General for Iraq Reconstruction

The first document is from SIGIR, the Special Inspector General for Iraq Reconstruction. Each quarter, SIGIR releases a Report to Congress to summarize key findings on progress of Iraq reconstruction efforts. The following documents, the most interesting amongst over 46 figures, graphs, and charts, were published in the April 2008 Quarterly Report. The full SIGIR Report can be found at http://www.sigir.mil/.

Figure 1.1

FIVE YEARS OF U.S. RECONSTRUCTION FUNDING
$ Billions

Source: SIGIR, *Quarterly and Semiannual Reports to the United States Congress*, March 2004–January 2008; USAID, Response to SIGIR Data Call, (4/8/2008); GRD, Response to SIGIR Data Call (4/2/2008); Treasury, Response to SIGIR Data Call (4/3/2008); USTDA, Response to SIGIR Data Call (4/3/2008); DoS Response to SIGIR Data Call (4/5/2007); WHS, Response to SIGIR Data Call, (4/1/2008); DFAS Response to SIGIR Data Call (4/10/2008); DoS, *Iraq Weekly Status* (3/26/2008); ITAO, Response to SIGIR Data Call (1/4/2008); GRD, Response to SIGIR Data Call (4/3/2008); USAID, Response to SIGIR Data Call (4/14/2008); ITAO, *Essential Indicators Report* (3/27/2008); MNC-I, Response to SIGIR Data Call (4/9/2008)

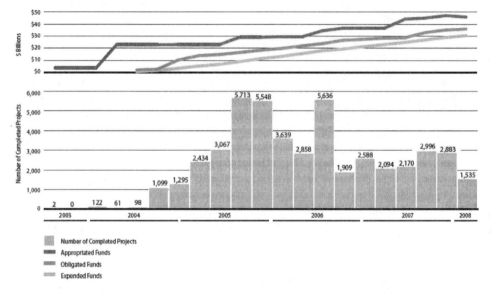

Note: Financial data includes obligations and expenditures from the IRRF 1, IRRF 2, ISFF, ESF, CERP, and INL fund types.
Project data includes projects from the IRRF 2, ISFF, ESF, and CERP.

Figure 1.2

FIVE YEARS OF IRAQI SECURITY FUNDING
$ Billions
Source: SIGIR, *Quarterly and Semiannual Reports to the United States Congress*, March 2004–January 2008; MNSTC-I, Response to SIGIR Data Call (4/17/2008); DoS, *Iraq Weekly Status Report* (3/26/2008); ITAO, Response to SIGIR Data Call (1/4/2008); GRD, Response to SIGIR Data Call (4/3/2008); USAID, Response to SIGIR Data Call (4/14/2008); ITAO, *Essential Indicators Report* (3/27/2008); MNC-I, Response to SIGIR Data Call (4/9/2008)

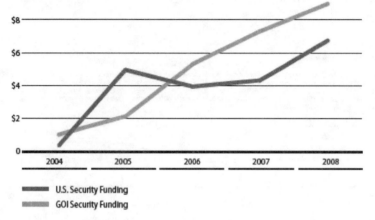

▬▬▬ U.S. Security Funding
▬▬▬ GOI Security Funding

Note: Includes expenditures from the IRRF 2, ISFF, ESF, and CERP. See Appendix D for a sector cross-reference to Security.

Figure 1.3

FIVE YEARS OF IRAQI OIL REVENUE
Millions of Barrels per Day (MBPD), Dollars per Barrel, $ Billions
Source: DoS, *Iraq Weekly Status*, (1/5/2006), (1/4/2006), (4/2/2008); ITAO, *Monthly Import, Production and Export Spreadsheet* (April 2008); U.S. Energy Information Administration, "World Crude Oil Prices: OPEC Average," (4/11/2008)

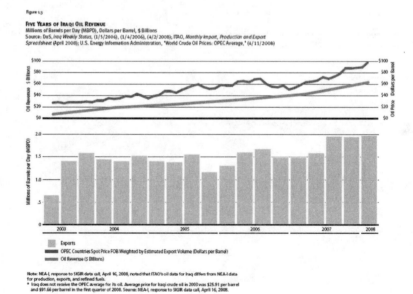

▢ Exports
▬▬▬ OPEC Countries Spot Price FOB Weighted by Estimated Export Volume (Dollars per Barrel)
▬▬▬ Oil Revenue ($ Billions)

Note: NEA-I response to SIGIR data call, April 16, 2008, noted that ITAO's oil data for Iraq differs from NEA-I data for production, exports, and refined fuels.
* Iraq does not receive the OPEC average for its oil. Average price for Iraqi crude oil in 2003 was $25.91 per barrel and $91.66 per barrel in the first quarter of 2008. Source: NEA-I, response to SIGIR data call, April 16, 2008.

Figure 1.4

IRAQI TROOP TRAINING AND AUTHORIZATIONS
Sources: DoD, *Measuring Security and Stability in Iraq*, July 2005, October 2005, February 2006, May 2006, August 2006, November 2006, March 2007, June 2007, September 2007, December 2007, and March 2008; Testimony of General David H. Petraeus (4/8/2008)

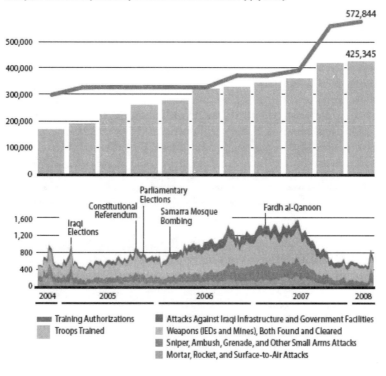

Figure 2.26

PROVINCES TRANSFERRED TO PROVINCIAL IRAQI CONTROL
Source: Multi-National Force-Iraq, Provincial Iraqi Control, www.mnf-iraq.com (1/17/2008)

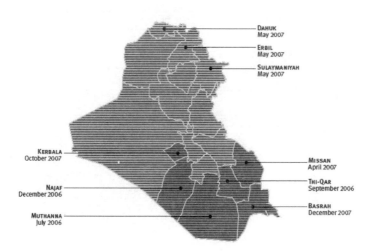

Figure 2.36

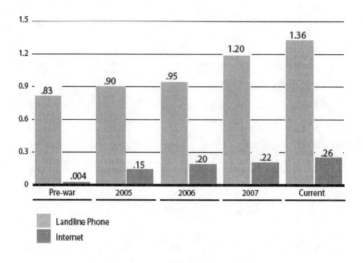

INTERNET AND PHONE USAGE IN IRAQ
Millions of Subscribers
Source: ITAO, Response to SIGIR Data Call (4/3/2008)

Figure 2.41

LOCATION OF MAJOR CRIMES COURTS (MCCs)
Source: DoD, *Measuring Security and Stability in Iraq*, March 2008

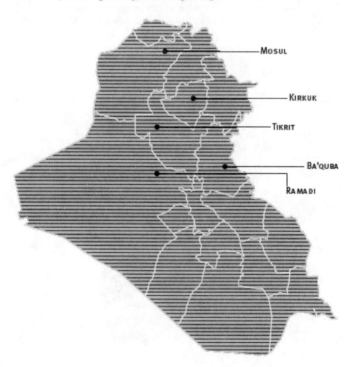

(b) U.S. Department of Energy (2007)

The U.S. Department of Energy releases comprehensive and detailed assessments of oil fields worldwide. The following is a report on Iraq from August 2007.

ENERGY INFORMATION ADMINISTRATION (EIA) BRIEF: IRAQ

---

http://www.eia.doe.gov/emeu/cabs/Iraq/Background.html

> *"Experts agree that Iraq may be one of the few places left where vast reserves, known and unknown, have barely been exploited"*

Iraq has the world's third largest proven petroleum reserves and some of the lowest extraction costs, although just a fraction of its known fields are in development. According to the March 2007, review by the International Monetary Fund (IMF), in 2006, crude oil export revenues represented around 60 percent of GDP and 89 percent of government revenues. In 2006, the U.S Department of Energy's Energy Information Administration (EIA) reported that Iraq was the world's 15th biggest oil producer and Iraq meets approximately 94 percent of its energy needs with petroleum. Iraq's use of abundant natural gas resources and hydropower is limited. According to the findings of the December 2006, Iraq Study Group (ISG), led by former Secretary of State James A. Baker and former Congressman Lee H. Hamilton, the stabilization of Iraq is highly correlated with Iraq's economic success or failure, which in the medium-term is highly dependent on its hydrocarbons industry.

Oil

After more than a decade of sanctions and two Gulf Wars, Iraq's oil infrastructure needs modernization and investment. Despite a large reconstruction effort (including Iraq Relief and Reconstruction Fund (IRRF) support of $1.72 billion), the industry has not been able to meet hydrocarbon production and export targets since 2004. According to the January 2007 Special Inspector General for Iraq Reconstruction (SIGIR) report, Iraq's petroleum sector faces technical challenges in procuring, transporting and storing crude and refined products, as well as managing pricing controls and imports, fighting smuggling and corruption, improving budget execution, and managing sustainability of operations. Oil production has not recovered to pre-war levels, and parliament and cabinet officials are working to map out investment and ownership rights that will help move the industry forward.

Another challenge to Iraq's development of the oil sector is that resources are not evenly divided across sectarian-demographic lines. Most known hydrocarbon resources are concentrated in the Shiite areas of the south and the ethnically Kurdish north, with few resources in control of the Sunni minority.

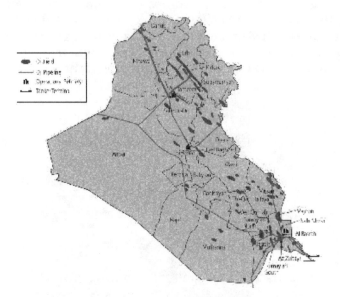

Gas and Oil Resources by Governorate

(Source: SIGIR)

For this reason a legal framework for investment in the hydrocarbon sector remains a main policy objective.

According to reports by various U.S. government agencies, multilateral institutions and other international organizations, long-term Iraq reconstruction costs could reach $100 billion or higher, of which it is estimated that more than a third will go to the oil, gas and electricity sectors. In addition, the World Bank estimates that at least $1 billion in additional revenues needs to be committed annually to the oil industry just to sustain current production.

Oil Reserves

According to the *Oil and Gas Journal*, Iraq's proven oil reserves are 115 billion barrels, although these statistics have not been revised since 2001 and are largely based on 2-D seismic data from nearly three decades ago. Over the past two years, multinational companies, at the request of the Government of Iraq (GoI), have reexamined seismic data and conducted comprehensive surveys of Iraq's hydrocarbons reserves in locations throughout the country. Geologists and consultants have estimated that relatively unexplored territory in the western and southern deserts may contain an estimated additional 45 to 100 billion barrels (bbls) of recoverable oil. While internal Iraqi estimates have ranged into the hundreds of billions of barrels of additional oil, the seismic data under review by a host of international firms seem to be pointing to more conservative, but significant, increases. Iraq has the lowest reserve to production ratio of the major oil-producing countries.

The majority of the known oil and gas reserves in Iraq form a belt that runs along the eastern edge of the country. According to the GoI, Iraq has around 9 fields that are considered "super giants" (over 5 billion bbls reserves) as well as 22 known "giant" fields (over 1 billion bbls). According to independent consultants, the cluster of super-giant fields of southeastern Iraq forms the largest known concentration of such fields in the world and accounts for 70 to 80 percent of the country's proven oil reserves. An estimated 20 percent of oil reserves are in the north of Iraq, near Kirkuk, Mosul and Khanaqin. Control over rights to reserves is a source of controversy between the ethnic Kurds and other groups in the area.

The Western Desert is of interest to oil prospectors as well as to the sectarian groups occupying these areas where there is no active oil production. Minor oil formations beneath western territory have been known of for decades, but little has been done in the way of development. Much of this area is just now undergoing exploration, although it belongs to same geological formation as part of the Saudi Arabian deposits. According to an Egyptian news source from February, 2007, a test well at the Akkas field in the Al-Anbar province is flowing at rates equivalent to larger fields elsewhere in Iraq.

Oil Production

In 2006, Iraq's upstream crude oil production under the control of the regional state-owned oil companies averaged 2.0 million barrels per day (bbl/d), down from around 2.6 million bbl/d of production and a nameplate capacity of 2.8 to 3.0 million bbl/d in pre-invasion January 2003. Estimates of

Iraq's current production levels vary and metering systems have been put in place at Basrah to improve export accounting.

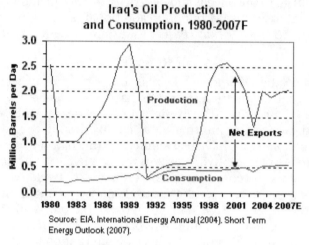

Iraq's Oil Production and Consumption, 1980-2007F

Source: EIA. International Energy Annual (2004). Short Term Energy Outlook (2007).

Note: Production includes crude oil, lease condensate, natural gas liquids, ethanol and refinery gain.

According to 2007 report from the U.S. Government Accountability Office (GAO), the Energy Information Administration (EIA), State Department and GoI reported differences in daily production volumes ranging between 100,000 to 300,000 bbl/d. While EIA reported significantly lower average daily production numbers than the State Department, annual averages only differed by approximately 100,000 bbl/d. Some analysts suggest that differences could be accounted for by oil smuggling, although discrepancies could arise from differing methods used to measure production (e.g. estimating re-injection at the well-head).

Historically, two-thirds of production came from the southern fields and the remainder from the north-central fields near Kirkuk. At present, the majority of Iraqi oil production comes from just three giant fields: North and South Rumaila and Kirkuk. The Rumaila fields, operated by Iraqi parastatal South Oil Company, along with a ring of nearly a dozen smaller fields, including Subha, Luhais, West Qurna and Az-Zubair, have been producing 1.5 to 1.9 million bbl/d; close to pre-war levels. Conversely, average production at Kirkuk and the northern fields of around 200,000 bbl/d is only a fraction of the pre-war peak of around 680,000 bbl/d, due to reservoir damage from gas and water injection as well as shut-in export routes. In May 2007, the Iraq Ministry of Oil (MoO) reported that total production from the northern fields was 206,000 bbl/d, all of which went to domestic consumption.

The table below represents reported installed oil production capacity in Iraq, all of which is not online. Effective capacity, or actual production, is subject to change based on the security situation.

Usable Oil Production Capacity in Iraq			
	Estimated Current Capacity (2007E)	Estimated Pre-War Capacity (2003E)	Est. Reserves
Southern Fields	(bbl/d)	(bbl/d)	(billion bbl)
Rumaila North	500,000	500,000	10
Rumaila South	800,000	800,000	7
West Qurna	180,000	250,000	15-21
Az-Zubair	230,000	230,000	5
Missan (inc. Buzurgan, Jabal Faqi, Abu Ghraib)	100,000	100,000	3
Majnoon	50,000	50,000	20
Luhais	50,000	50,000	2
Southern Sub Total (million bbl/d)	1.9	2.0	
Northern Fields*			
Kirkuk	250000 [600,000 - 700,000]	700,000	10
Bai Hassan	[50,00 - 100,000]	125,000	2
Jambur	[75,000]	75,000	1
Khabbaz	[25,000]	30,000	<1
Ajil	[25,000]	25,000	<1
East Baghdad	0	50,000	8
Ain Zalah/Butmah	[10,000]	10,000	<1
Sufiya (other minor fields)	10,000	10,000	<1
Northern Sub Total (million bbl/d)	0.3	1.0	
Totals (million bbl/d)	2.2	3.0	

Source: EIA, ITAO, Media Reports, Government of Iraq Ministry of Oil

* Most production shut-in due to limited export routes/limited refining capacity.

Amounts in brackets are estimates of production that could potentially come online if export/domestic refining became available.

Currently, the MoO has central control over oil and gas production and development in all but the Kurdish territory through its two operating entities, the North (NOC) and South Oil Companies (SOC). According to the North Oil Company's website, their concession and jurisdiction extends from the Turkish borders in the north to 32.5 degrees latitude (about 100 miles south of Baghdad), and from Iranian borders in the east to Syrian and Jordanian borders in the west. The company's geographical operation area spans the following governorates: Tamim (Kirkuk), Nineveh, Irbil, Baghdad, Diyala and part of Babil to Hilla and Wasit to Kut. The remainder falls under the jurisdiction of the SOC, and though smaller in geographical size, includes the majority of proven reserves.

Petroleum Legislation

Passage and implementation of Iraq's Hydrocarbon Law, which was first presented to upper house of Parliament for review on February 27, 2007, is central to the development of the Iraq's oil and gas industry, and Iraq's economy overall. The draft law focuses on upstream development and lays out the conditions for investment and international participation in the sector. The law also details a governance model which includes the proposed re-establishment of the umbrella operations company that was the Iraq National Oil Company (INOC) and a central regulatory body, such as a Federal

Oil and Gas Council, to review contracts. The original draft law laid out a proposed plan for domestic control of oil and gas fields and a framework for revenue sharing among governorates. Initially, four annexes to the law proposed which fields would be centrally managed and which fields would be under local/regional control, and thus opened to foreign investment at the governorate's discretion. Annexes I and II, which listed currently producing, partially developed or mothballed fields included some 93 percent of proven reserves. Annex III, listing the "undeveloped" fields, and Annex IV, listing 65 exploration blocks, were to fall under regional development authorities. Upstream development privileges based on the aforementioned thresholds are the subject of ongoing negotiations. Following discussions between cabinet members, parliament and other groups in July 2007, the annexes are reported to have been removed from the current version draft law and will be considered at a later date by the yet-to-be-established regulatory body.

| Iraq Draft Oil Law - Field Classification | | |
| I | II | III |
In Production	Near Production	Undeveloped
Abu Ghraib	Alan	Abu Khaimah
Amara	Ibrahim	Samawa
Buzurgan	Qasab	Ahdab
Fuqua (Jabal Faqi)	Najmah	Badrah
Halfaya*	Jawan	Dhafriyah
West Qurna*	Sarjoun	Akkas
Majnoon*	Demir Dagh	Buhaira
Ain Zalah	Makhmour	Chemchemal
(West) Butmah	Qara Chauq	Chia Surkh
Qaiyarah	Himrin (Hamrin)	Gilabat
Sufiya	Kor Moor	Injanah
Az-Zubair (Shuaiba,	Ismail	Khashm
Rafidhiyah, Safwan)*	Judaida	Al-Ahmar
Tuba	Jeria Pika	Qamarim
North Rumaila*	Mansuriyah	Djailia
South Rumaila*	Nahrawan	Kumait
Luhais	Nau Dauman	East Rafidain
Subba	Tal Ghazal	Gharraf
Nahr Umar* (Bin Umar)	Huwaiza	Rafidain
Ajil	Noor	Al-Nasariya
Balad	Rifai	Khanuqa
Tikrit	Jraishan	Khashab
East Baghdad*	Rachi (Raki)	Pulkhana (Bulkhana)
Naft Khanah	Ratawi	Kifl
Bai Hassan	Siba	Marjan
Jambur		West Kifl
Khabbaz		Taq Taq
Kirkuk (Avanah, Baba,		
Khurmala)*		
Source: Media Reports, Global Insight, IHS, DOE estimates		
* Super Giant defined as having 5 billion barrels or more of reserves		

Certain internal groups and some members of the expatriate Iraqi community have voiced reservations about the role of foreign oil companies in Iraq's upstream oil and gas sector. Such groups claim that de facto "denationalization" would make Iraq the only major oil producing country in the region to allow foreign control in upstream operations, and at generous terms. The Kurds also oppose widening central control over planning, upstream development and revenue distribution. The Kurdish Oil and Gas Minister Ashti Hawrami has called for the reclassification of several field in the Annexes, particularly "boundary fields" with unclear borders or fields that have been contracted to or negotiated with foreign companies, including Kor Mor, Demir Dagh, and Taq Taq. It was reported in late June 2007 that the GoI and the Kurds had come to an agreement on the revenue sharing portion of the law, considered an important step forward for the passage of the bill. Following Ministry approval in early July 2007, parliament is expected to consider the law in an amended form in the fall 2007.

Upstream Development Plans

The MoO has announced a goal of 6 million bbl/d of sustainable production by the end of the decade, stating that between $25 and $75 billion in investment is needed to get Iraq's sector producing at such levels. The southern fields intended for development in the immediate term for export are West Qurna, Halfaya, Majnoon and Nahr (Bin) Umar. Experts suggest that these fields could produce an additional 2 million bbl/d in the medium-time frame with moderate investment. In the north, further development at a number of fields, including Bai Hassan, Jambur, Khabbaz, Ajil, Ain Zalah, Butma and others may depend on the final status of Kirkuk (Tamim) and settlement of Kurdish claims on the Nineveh governorate (Mosul). A referendum is scheduled to take place in late 2007.

Despite the lack of agreement over the national law governing investment in hydrocarbons, the Kurdistan Regional Government (KRG) has a signed a half-dozen oil production sharing, development and exploration contracts with several small foreign firms. In June 2007, the KRG announced an offering of 40 additional exploration blocks during the summer of 2007. In addition, more than a dozen contracts signed by the central government with international companies during Saddam Hussein's regime are being renegotiated or may come under review when Iraq's oil law and investment framework is in place. . . .

Refining

Refinery operations, with antiquated infrastructure, are often disrupted by thievery, employee intimidation, and sabotage to feeder pipelines, lack of feedstock, and unreliable power supply. The fuel mix, including high levels of heavy fuel oil, does not reflect the current demand mix. The sector has not been able to meet domestic demand for refined products like gasoline, kerosene, LPG and diesel for the generators that supplement electric power since 2003, and shortages are reported. In 2006, Iraq's petroleum product consumption was approximately 545,000 bbl/d.

According to the *Oil and Gas Journal*, Iraq's total installed refinery capacity is 597,500 bbl/d. Iraq has four major refineries with an installed/nominal capacity of approximately 570,000 bbl/day. Since 2003, these facilities and their related infrastructure (pipelines, external power supply) have been subject to attacks and repeated disruptions.

The main refineries include:

Daura:

The 110,000-bbl/d capacity facility just outside Baghdad, primarily supplies refined products to Iraq's capital and is considered central to supply security in the capital. It is Iraq's oldest refinery, and is a frequent target of sabotage. According to the MoO, Daura will be expanded to 240,000 bbl/d and will be able to meet Baghdad's short-term fuel requirements. A $110 million-contract was initially signed by the Hydrocarbon Supply of Texas and Czech-based ProKop in 2005, although progress has been inhibited by the security situation and rising costs.

Baiji:

Iraq's two largest sister refineries in north-central Iraq (with 310,000 bbl/d capacity) is a point of sectarian contention as the facility currently processes crude from the northern fields, but is located in nominally non-Kurdish territory. In January 2007, Iraqi Deputy Prime Minister Barham Saleh reported to Parliament that the country is losing $1.5 billion annually from attacks and theft at Baiji. The facility has been subject to repeated disruptions and power loss, and generally operates at around 75 percent capacity. The January 2007 SIGIR report indicated that at least some of the oil storage facilities were under "insurgent control" as of December 2006.

Basrah:

The 150,000-bbl/day capacity facility located near the port lacks independent power generation and wastewater treatment.

Other sources report that Iraq's refining capacity also includes several minor plants (called "topping plants"), which produce 10,000 bbl/d or less each. According to the U.S. Department of State's Iraq Reconstruction Management Office (IRMO)/Iraq Transition Assistance Office (ITAO) reports, these facilities (including Mosul-Qaiyarah, Kirkuk, Khanaqin, K3-Haditha, Muftiah, Najaf, Maysan, and Nassiriyah-Samawah) primarily produce asphalt and low-grade kerosene and diesel. Some of these smaller facilities have been reportedly "cannibalized" for spare parts for the larger refineries.

Investment in New Refining Capacity

In order to alleviate shortages, the GoI has initiated a $4-billion plan to attract investment in the downstream operations and raise refinery capacity by around 1 million bbl/d. Timetables for new additions are uncertain due to security and financing roadblocks. . . .

Since 2003, the only new facility to come on-stream is a 10,000-bbl/d reconstruction fund-financed facility in the southern city of Najaf, completed in October, 2006. However, the refinery remains generally inactive due to limited storage facilities and inability to secure transport lines. The 20,000-bbl/d partially completed refinery at Bazyan (Sulaymaniyah) is expected to come online in late 2007.

Refined Products

According to the IMF and independent reporting, subsidies have contributed to local supply shortages and an international black market trade with

Iran and Turkey. As part of their IMF program, the GoI is slowly reducing subsidies on refined products, as seen in the table below:

Oil Exports

Iraq's ability to increase exports and ensure reliable domestic supply is limited, primarily in the north, because of reported sabotage to pipeline infrastructure and other installations. Total installed export capacity is around 3.5 million bbl/d, although effective capacity is lower. Iraq's inability to secure crude pipelines in the north has meant that exports are generally routed through the southern port of Basrah. According to IRMO/ITAO, crude oil exports have fallen from a post-war high of around 2.0 million bbl/d in 2004, to an average of 1.5 million bbl/d in 2006. However, there is some marginal improvement recently mainly due to the intermittent ability to export crude through a northern pipeline, and improved loading capabilities in Basrah. In June 2007, Iraq issued its first tender in almost six months to sell Kirkuk oil. Iraq's oil exports are under the domain of the Iraqi parastatal State Oil Marketing Organization (SOMO). The majority of oil exports go to refineries in Asia, including China and India.

Iraqi's Estimated Exports by Destination (Q1 2007)

Source: ITAO, MEED, Energy Intel

A lack of continuous refining operations has forced the GoI to import light fuels, relying heavily on deals brokered by the USG and the MoO with neighboring countries including Turkey, Iran, Syria and Kuwait. According to SOMO, in May 2006, imports of refined products totaled nearly 160,000 bbl/d. Before the war, Iraq was a large exporter of petroleum products and crude. However, according to the IMF, imports have cost the GoI close to $2.5 billion annually since 2004. In early 2007, the GoI liberalized the fuel import market and now relies on private importers of refined products to meet local demand.

In January 2007, Turkey temporarily stopped exporting refined products to Iraq due to political disagreements over Iraqi Kurdistan and outstanding debt for earlier fuel imports. In addition, Iraq now receives imports from Syria at the Iraqi border city of Al-Hasaka, and transports the fuel in state-owned trucks to the northern part of the country. In June 2007, the GoI announced plans to import an additional estimated 15,000 bbl/d of gas oil, 17,000 bbl/d of gasoline, and 7,700 bbl/d of kerosene from Kuwait.

Pipelines and Supply Security

Iraq's 4,350-mile network of pipelines remains a target of sabotage. According to the Institute for the Analysis of Global Security (IAGS), between April 2003 and May 2007, there were over 400 attacks on Iraqi energy infrastructure. Due to security issues, much of the pipeline infrastructure is offline.

In the north, the major international crude oil pipeline is the 1.1 million-bbl/d capacity Kirkuk-Ceyhan (Iraq-Turkey) pipeline. This pipeline and its 480,000-bbl/day sister-installation have been subject to repeated attacks and function intermittently, particularly in the Baiji-Fatha area. The KRG is reportedly considering building another pipeline that avoids unfortified areas. The inability to export oil through this pipeline has severely limited exports from the northern fields.

The 200,000–300,000 bbl/d Iraq-Syria-Lebanon Pipeline (ISLP) has been closed and the Iraqi portion reported unusable since 2003. The initial capacity of the pipeline was approximately 700,000 bbl/d, with potential to expand to 1.4 million bbl/d. Although discussions were held between Iraqi and Syrian government officials, no timetable has been set up to repair or reopen this line. The pipeline runs across the Western Desert, by the Akkas field. Also, the 1.65 million bbl/d Iraq Pipeline to Saudi Arabia (IPSA) has been closed since 1991. There are no plans to reopen this line.

In the south, in June 2007, it was reported that Iraq is planning to build a 500,000-bbl/d crude pipeline from Haditha to Jordan's port of Aqaba, but the project is in the very early stages of discussion. In March 2007, it was reported that Iraq and Iran agreed to build a 200,000-bbl/d pipeline to transport crude from Basrah to Abadan in return for increased liquefied gas shipments. The project was first discussed in 2005.

Domestic Pipelines

The 120-mile set of eight parallel pipelines connecting north-central Baiji and Daura (Baghdad) installations are frequent targets of attack. The four Baiji feedstock pipelines from Kirkuk are also frequently out of commission. The 1.4 million-bbl/d reversible "Strategic Pipeline," which pre-war connected the northern fields through a pumping station at Haditha, to Rumaila and the storage facilities at Fao in the south, could optimize export options, particularly for the Kurds, but is mothballed due to non-functioning pumping stations and general deterioration.

Ports

Lack of functioning pipelines in the north has meant that nearly all exports have passed through the southern ports since 2003, primarily Basrah. The Al-Basrah Oil Terminal (formerly Mina al-Bakr) has the capacity to load around 82,000 bbl/hour and support Very Large Crude Carriers. There are five smaller ports on the Persian Gulf, all functioning at less than full capacity, including the Khor Al Amaya terminal. Installation of a metering system beginning January 2007, is expected to improve oil accounting.

Overland Routes for Export and Import

Production from the larger northern fields is mostly shut in due to lack of functioning pipelines. However, overland routes are used to export limited amounts of crude from small fields bordering Syria. Other exports via overland routes are limited because they require passing through territory where rule of law is lacking, and truck drivers have been targeted by insurgents. These overland routes include passage to Saudi Arabia, Syria and Jordan.

Natural Gas Reserves and Production

According to the *Oil and Gas Journal*, Iraq's proven natural gas reserves are 112 trillion cubic feet (Tcf). Probable reserves have been estimated at closer to 275-300 Tcf and work is currently underway by several IOCs and independents to accurately update hydrocarbon reserve numbers. Iraq's proven gas reserves are the tenth largest in the world, and two-thirds of resources are associated with oil fields including, Kirkuk, as well as the southern Nahr (Bin) Umar, Majnoon, Halfaya, Nassiriya, the Rumaila fields, West Qurna, and Az-Zubair. Just under 20 percent of known gas reserves are non-associated; around 10 percent is salt "dome" gas. The majority of non-associated reserves are concentrated in several fields in the North including: Ajil, Bai Hassan, Jambur, Chemchemal, Kor Mor, Khashm Al-Ahmar, and Al-Mansuriyah.

According to the EIA's International Energy Annual report, natural gas production in Iraq has steadily declined over the past decade-and-a-half, reportedly due to an associated fall in oil production and deterioration of gas processing facilities. In 2005, dry natural gas production was approximately 87 billion cubic feet (Bcf); down from 215 Bcf in 1989. In late 2006, the MoO reported that natural gas production in was averaging 900 million cubic feet (MMcf/d) in the south (associated) and 490 MMcf/d in the north (non-associated) — including 375 MMcf/d of non- at the northern fields of Ajil and Jambur.

The MoO also reports that approximately 60 percent of associated natural gas production is flared due to a lack of sufficient infrastructure to utilize it for consumption and export. Significant volumes of gas are also reinjected to enhance oil recovery efforts. According to the January 2007 SIGIR report, approximately $4-billion worth of natural gas is flared or reinjected into wells.

Upstream Development

The non-associated gas fields reportedly slated for priority development are mostly in the northern governorates near Kirkuk, including: Al-Mansuriyah and the nearby Khashem-al Ahmer and Jaria Pika, Kor Mor, Akkas, Chemchemal and Siba. According to the MoO, these fields have approximately 10 Tcf of reserves combined and could produce between 900 and 1000 MMcf/d for possible export and around 400 MMcf/d for domestic use. It is also been reported that the GoI plans to capture more associated gas at Rumaila and Az-Zubair within five to ten years. In 2004, Shell began work on a domestic master gas plan for Iraq on a cost-free basis. Results have not been publicly released at this time.

Along with petroleum contracts, several Saddam Hussein-era production sharing agreements and development contracts are reportedly up for review and renegotiation. The KRG is the first to move ahead with development of gas fields within their semi-autonomous territories. As in the petroleum sector, the KRG has exercised significant autonomy over the development of natural gas resources, including a reported deal in April 2007, with Royal Dutch Shell and Turkey's parastatal Turkish Petroleum Corporation (TPAO) to develop

Al-Mansuriyah. The GoI is also believed to have entered into talks with the Korea National Oil Company (KNOC) to discuss upstream gas development in April 2007. According to media reports, the following natural gas projects are moving ahead in Iraq:

Iraq's Natural Gas Development Projects

Status	Field	Location	Partners	Country	Estimated Production Capacity	Reserves (TCF)	Type	Notes
MOU	Kor Mor	KRG (Sulaymaniyah)	Dana Gas Crescent Petroleum	UAE	150-200 MMcf/d/d (Phase I) 300 MMcf/d/d (Phase II)	1.4	Non-Associated Gas-condensate	-Develop, develop process, transport gas (2008) -Will feed a development called "Kurdistan Gas City"
	Chemchemal	KRG (Sulaymaniyah)	Dana Gas Crescent Petroleum	UAE	NA	2.2	Non-Associated Gas-condensate	-Will evaluate for development. -Australia-based Woodside's contract expired in November, 2006.
	Siba, Misan (Buzurgan Jabal Faqi, Abu Ghraib)	South (Misan)	Gulfsands Petroleum	USA	46,000 b/d NGL 338 MMcf/d gas (Misan) 126 MMcf/d gas (Siba)	Siba: 3.1 Misan:1.7	Misan: Associated Gas, Siba: non-associated	-Signed 2005, 5-year implementation (including gas gathering system, NGL gathering plant and transmission pipelines). Not in implementation yet.
Unclear	Mansuriyah	North (Diyala)	Royal Dutch Shell Botas TPAO Tekfen	UK Netherlands Turkey	330 MMcf/d	4.1	Non-Associated Gas-condensate	-Reportedly interested in building an export pipeline from Kirkuk to Ceyhan.
	Akkas	Western Desert (Al-Anbar)	NA	NA	NA	2.1	Non-Associated Gas-condensate	-Several IOCs reported to be interested in developing.

Source: Media Reports, Global Insight, IHS, APS Market Review, USG

In May 2007, the MoO claimed a large natural gas discovery near Nineveh, to the West of Al-Qa'em with further extensions to the Iraqi-Saudi border. A ministry official reported that "the field would produce 100,000-bbl/d" of gas and condensate and that the European Union has expressed interest in developing the field, known as Ukash.

In 2001, the GoI reported a find of 2.1 Tcf of non-associated gas near Akkas field, in the central province/Western Desert, but it is not yet under development. According to recent press reports, there is interest by Shell Oil in developing this field as a source of income for the Sunni-majority governorates. IOCs have also proposed development for export to Syria. In May 2007, it was reported that the Syrian-based Euro-Arab Mashreq Gas Project is considering a link from the Akkas field to the Arab Gas Pipeline (AGP) currently under construction in Syria. The AGP will feed the European gas supply network by way of Turkey. In September 2004, Iraq agreed to join the $1.2-billion, 351-Bcf/year Arab Gas Pipeline project linking Egypt, Jordan, Syria and Lebanon, but progress has been delayed.

Gas Processing & Domestic Pipelines

The gas processing facilities, particularly in the South, have reportedly deteriorated since 2003. Prior to the war, the southern infrastructure included nine gathering stations with a processing capacity of 1.5 day Bcf/d, all of which was intended for export. The associated dry gas gathered from the North and South Rumaila and Az-Zubair fields was piped to a 575-MMcf/d natural gas liquids (NGL) fractionation plant in Az-Zubair and a 100-MMcf/d processing plant in Basra. At Khor al-Jubair there is a 17.5-million-cubic-foot LPG storage tank farm and loading terminals. Iraq also has a major domestic natural gas pipeline in the south with capacity of to deliver 240 MMcf/d of associated gas to Baghdad from the West Qurna field.

Gas processing facilities in the north currently gather supply from Kirkuk, Bai Hassan and Jambur for domestic consumption, including LPG. The system is designed to supply LPG to Baghdad and other cities, as well as dry gas and sulfur to power stations and industrial plants.

Potential Exports

Prior to the 1990-1991 Gulf War, Iraq exported raw natural gas to Kuwait. The gas came from Rumaila through a 105-mile, 400-MMcf/d pipeline to Kuwait's central processing center at Ahmadi. Talks have been in progress since 2005 that would export 35 MMcf/d, rising to 200 MMcf/d, but a final deal is subject to passage of Iraq's Petroleum Law. In 2007, the MoO announced an agreement to fund a feasibility study on the revival of the mothballed pipeline. The Kuwait Foreign Petroleum Exploration Company (KUFOEC) is reported to be interested in developing Iraqi gas in the south, but no deals have been signed. The GoI continues to discuss northern export routes through Turkey, including linking up to the Azeri-Turkish Baku-Tbilisi-Erzerum (BTE) line, the planned Nabucco (Iran-Europe) pipeline, or the ongoing Arab Gas Pipeline project. The idea of gas exports remains controversial due to the amount of idle and sub-optimally-fired electricity generation capacity in Iraq — much a result of a lack of adequate gas feedstock.

Electricity

Rehabilitation of the electricity sector is a major component of the Iraq reconstruction efforts. Iraq's power infrastructure is ageing and in need of rehabilitation; many power plants are over two decades old and affected by decades of sanctions and war. Since 2003, more than $4.24 billion of U.S. Iraq Relief and Reconstruction Fund (IRRF) money has been allocated to investment in the sector.

In 2006, Iraq's average domestic electricity generation capacity was reported to be approximately 4000 MW. This represents approximately 50 percent of average demand, and on average was below prewar levels of 4500 MW and USG/GoI reconstruction goals of 6000 MW. In the first three months of 2007, generation capacity fell slightly due to security and feedstock supply issues, although sustainable generation capacity is expected to surpass pre-war level during summer 2007. Electricity imports are around 200 to 300 MW daily.

Electric Power Generation (MW)				
Pre-war	2006			
Average Generation	Average Generation	Peak Generation[*]	Average Demand	Peak Demand[*]
4,500	4,063	4,855	7,482	9,299
2007 (Q1)				TBD
Average Generation	Peak Generation[**]	Average Demand	Peak Demand[**]	Generation Goal
3,832	4,159	8,533	8,893	6,000
*August 2006				
** February 2007				
Source: SIGIR, Iraq Ministry of Energy, IRMO/ITAO				

The MoE reports that Iraq has around eight steam generation plants, 20 gas-powered facilities and six main hydroelectric plants with an intended capacity of 11,120 MW, though much is in disrepair. Reportedly, 40 percent of existing infrastructure is thermal (diesel, HFO, crude-fired), 22 percent is hydropower and 38 percent is gas-powered.

Power Supply & Challenges to Reconstruction

In 2006, the amount of power from the national grid supplied to areas outside of Baghdad averaged 12 to 14 hours per day, while the average daily hours of power in the capital remained low at 6.5 hours per day. In 2007, average power in the capital has reportedly increased to around eight hours. However, a lack of equitable power generation throughout the country is compounded by the security situation. Power transmission and distribution infrastructure, particularly around the capital, is frequently targeted, amounting to approximately 1000 MW lost per day. As of January 2007, some 80 transmission towers between Baiji and Baghdad alone were reported destroyed by sabotage, preventing power imports from the north. It is estimated that another 1500 MW is lost per day due to shortages of fuel and water supply for hydropower.

A resistance to power sharing, primarily in the south, has contributed to the country's power inequity. Reportedly, provincial authorities are fighting the central authorities in the distribution and rationing of supplies to almost seven million consumers in Baghdad. In the long-term, the GoI aims to reduce Baghdad's dependency on power sharing by extending generation capacity in and around the capital. The GoI is also pursuing opportunities to link grids with neighboring countries including Jordan and Saudi Arabia. In the north, the KRG has accused Baghdad publicly of "turning off the lights" in retaliation for political moves. The KRG's regional 10-year Master Electricity Plan calls for increasing hydropower and thermal capacity annually but expects to remain dependent on imports from abroad from Turkey, Syria and Iran and the national grid at least through 2015.

Growing Cost of Reconstruction

The World Bank estimates that an additional $20 to $25 billion is needed to ensure reliable electricity supply and increase available capacity to approximately 24,000 MW by 2015. Unfortunately, according to the January 2007 SIGIR report, the GoI Operation and Maintenance (O&M) budgets are reportedly too low to support all of the existing installations, in addition to new capacity. The April SIGIR report noted that "O&M allocations by the GoI continue to limit the sustainability of U.S. funded projects as responsibility is transferred to Iraqi operators." However, the electricity ministry is believed to have started issuing independent tenders to bring in private investment to support development. The USG program formally ends in September 2007.

The World Bank recently approved two loans for the electricity sector (only the fourth such loan in 30 years): A $40-million Emergency Hydropower Project at Dokan and Derbandikhan (KRG) in December 2006, and a

US$124-million loan for the Emergency Electricity Reconstruction Project for Hartha (Units 2&3, doubling capacity to 800 MW), in March 2007.

(c) The Iraq Study Group Report

On March 15, 2006, the U.S. Congress supported the creation of the bipartisan Iraq Study Group to review the situation in Iraq and propose strategies for the way forward. The group, which consisted of ten members, was co-chaired by James Baker, a former Secretary of State (Republican), and Lee Hamilton, former Democratic Congressman and president of the Woodrow Wilson Center in Washington. The report was released on December 6, 2005. It contains the Group's findings and proposals for improving security, strengthening the new government, rebuilding the economy and infrastructure, and maintaining stability in the region. The following excerpts deal with the economy and oil policy.

JAMES A. BAKER III & LEE H. HAMILTON (CO-CHAIRS),
THE IRAQ STUDY GROUP REPORT

http://www.usip.org/isg/iraq_study_group_report/report/1206/index.html

Economics

There has been some economic progress in Iraq, and Iraq has tremendous potential for growth. But economic development is hobbled by insecurity, corruption, lack of investment, dilapidated infrastructure, and uncertainty. As one U.S. official observed to us, Iraq's economy has been badly shocked and is dysfunctional after suffering decades of problems: Iraq had a police state economy in the 1970's, a war economy in the 1980's, and a sanctions economy in the 1990's. Immediate and long-term growth depends predominantly on the oil sector.

Economic Performance

There are some encouraging signs. Currency reserves are stable and growing at $12 billion. Consumer imports of computers, cell phones, and other appliances have increased dramatically. New businesses are opening, and construction is moving forward in secure areas. Because of Iraq's ample oil reserves, water resources, and fertile lands, significant growth is possible if violence is reduced and the capacity of government improves. For example, wheat yields increased more than 40 percent in Kurdistan during this past year.

The Iraqi Government has also made progress in meeting benchmarks set by the International Monetary Fund. Most prominently, subsidies have been reduced—for instance, the price per liter of gas has increased from 1.7 cents to 23 cents (a figure far closer to regional prices). However, energy and good subsidies generally remain a burden, costing Iraq $11 billion per year.

Despite the positive signs, many leading economic indicators are negative. Instated of meeting a target of 10 percent, growth in Iraq is at roughly 4 percent this year. Inflation is above 50 percent. Unemployment estimates range widely from 20 to 60 percent. The investment climate is bleak, with foreign direct investment under 1 percent of GDP. Too many Iraqis do not see tangible improvements in their daily economic situation.

The Politics of Oil

The politics of oil has the potential to further damage the country's already fragile efforts to create a unified central government. The Iraqi Constitution leaves the door open for regions to take the lead in developing new oil resources. Article 108 states that "oil and gas are the ownership of all the peoples of Iraq in all the regions and governorates," while Article 109 tasks the federal government with "the management of oil and gas extracted from current fields." This language has led to contention over what constitutes a "new" or and "existing" resources, a question that has profound ramifications for the ultimate control of future oil revenue.

Senior members of Iraq's oil industry argue that a national oil company could reduce political tensions by centralizing revenues and reducing regional or local claims to a percentage of the revenue derived from production. However, regional leaders are suspicious and resist this proposal, affirming the rights of local communities to have direct access to the inflow of oil revenue. Kurdish leaders have been particularly aggressive asserting independent control of their oil assets, signing and implementing investment deals with foreign oil companies in northern Iraq. Shia politicians are also reported to be negotiating oil investments contracts with foreign companies.

There are proposals to redistribute a portion of oil revenues directly to the population on a per capita basis. These proposals have the potential to give all Iraqi citizens a stake in the nation's chief natural resource, but it would take time to develop a fair distribution system. Oil revenues have been incorporated into state budget projection for the next several years. There is no institution in Iraq at present that could properly implement such a distribution system. It would take substantial time to establish, and would have to be based on well-developed state census and income tax system, which Iraq currently lacks.

NOTES AND QUESTIONS

1. This last suggestion, redistributing a portion of oil revenues to Iraqi citizens on a per capita basis, has been put forward ever since Iraq was freed from Ba'athist rule. Several neighboring oil countries save a portion of the oil revenues in an investment fund (now called "sovereign fund"), with which Kuwait had experimented with for the past three decades. These funds, also available in the case of the UAE, tend to be opaque. A more transparent model is offered by the State of Alaska. See presentation and discussion below at A.3.e.

2. Considering the importance of Iraq to the United States, detailed monitoring of the economy is constantly carried out. A sample of the weekly State Department report on Iraq follows.

(d) U.S. State Department

U.S. DEPARTMENT OF STATE, BUREAU OF NEAR EASTERN AFFAIRS

Weekly Report on Iraq, May 28, 2008

Economic & Government Capacity Update

Iraq Inflation Rises Slightly in April: According to the GOI's April Consumer Price Index, year-on-year core inflation (which excludes "fuel and electricity" and "transport and communications" prices) rose to 15.9% in April, up from 12.1% in March. At the same time, year-on-year headline inflation fell slightly, from 5.8% in March to 5.5% in April. Global food price pressures were much more apparent in April than previous months—food prices increased 13.6% for the month. . . .

Crude Oil Update:
Price averages in world markets closed with the following prices:

- Basrah Light at $119.718/barrel
- Dated Brent at $127.894/barrel
- WTI Cushing at $130.098/barrel
- Oman/Dubai at $124.438/barrel

Revenue estimates:

- 2006: $31.3 Billion
- 2007: $41.0 Billion
- 2008: $27.3 Billion (ytd)

GOI Repairs Baghdad Pipelines: Repair teams have begun work on pipeline infrastructure in an attempt to connect the Baiji oil refinery to Baghdad. These repairs will allow for the distribution of more refined products to the Iraqi people and increase the volume of crude oil available for refinement. These pipelines will allow crude oil to move from the north to Doura refinery in Baghdad, increasing the supply of refined products to the capital. The increased crude to Doura will enable the refinery to operate near capacity and meet the needs of its increased capacity expected in the future.

GOI Replaces Oil Officials: The GOI has made strategic changes in the state-owned oil companies in southern Iraq. It has replaced the head of the South Oil Company, the South Gas Company, and the Iraqi Oil Tankers Company. Anonymous local officials claim that the GOI made these moves in an attempt to weaken the Fadhila party, a powerful Shia faction. The officials also say that the replacements are tied to Prime Minister Maliki's Dawa Party. The moves have not been limited to the oil sector, as the head of the Basrah airport has also been replaced. Fadhila formally withdrew from the United Iraqi Alliance, a coalition of Shia parties, in 2006 when its request for the Ministry of Oil was denied. It has, however, maintained considerable influence in the South. The Basrah Provincial Council is protesting the changes, saying it was not consulted prior to the moves.

GOI Funding World Food Programme Support: The GOI is providing funds to the World Food Programme (WFP) to aid the organization's outreach to displaced Iraqis. The GOI has provided $40 million in funding to the WFP for a program, begun in early 2008, that focuses on 1.2 million Iraqis displaced within Iraq and in neighboring Syria. The portion of the program focused on those displaced in Iraq is now 85% funded. Many displaced Iraqis that cannot take part in the government's food distribution program because they are not currently living in the area where they registered will be able to take part in the WFP initiative.

GOI Ministries to Collaborate on Planning: The GOI Ministries of Oil and Electricity have agreed to conduct joint expert level strategic planning workshops. The sessions will provide an opportunity for ministry staff to tackle "real life" obstacles by working together to overcome stumbling blocks to essential services energy project implementation. The joint workshop will address specific requests from the ministries, provide hands-on mentoring support on actual business cases and resolve problems that hinder budget execution. This workshop is a first step toward collaborative energy planning between the two ministries.

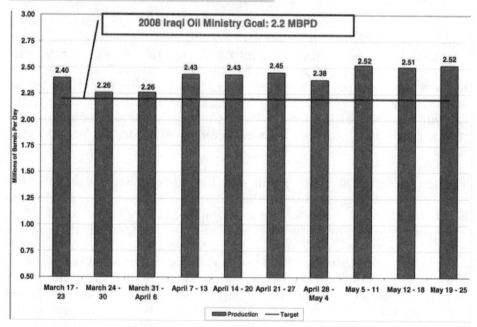

ECONOMIC – Crude Oil Production

ECONOMIC – Crude Oil Export

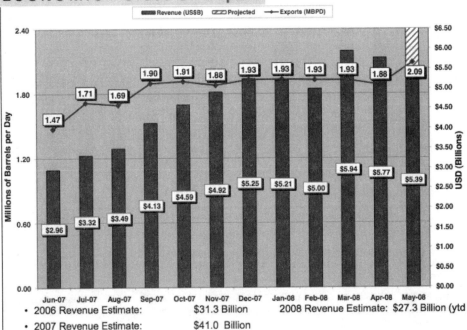

- 2006 Revenue Estimate: $31.3 Billion   2008 Revenue Estimate: $27.3 Billion (ytd
- 2007 Revenue Estimate: $41.0 Billion

ECONOMIC – Total Critical Refined Product Supplies

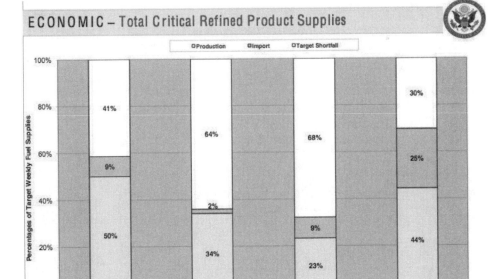

Note: This is a daily average for May 19 – 25

- Diesel: 14.7 ML supply of 24.5 ML target   • Gasoline: 9.0 ML supply of 26.8 ML target
- Kerosene: 3.4 ML supply of 14.6 ML target   • LPG: 3,830 tons supply of 5,100 tons target

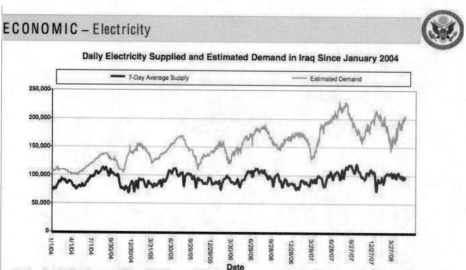

ECONOMIC – Electricity

Daily Electricity Supplied and Estimated Demand in Iraq Since January 2004

- Daily electricity demand May 20-26 was 5% above the same period last year. Daily supply from the grid was 14% above the year-earlier period and met 48% of demand, compared with 43% for the year-earlier period.

- For May 20-26, average hours of power from the grid after meeting demand from essential services were Baghdad: 7.1 and national 10.0. Year-ago levels were Baghdad 3.6 and national 9.3.

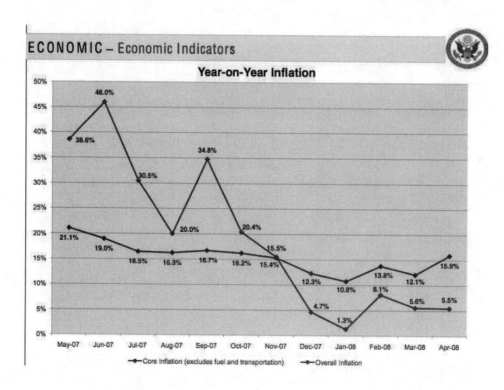

ECONOMIC – Economic Indicators

Year-on-Year Inflation

ECONOMIC – Economic Indicators

Economic Indicator	This Week	Last Week	Last Month	Last Year
Iraqi Commercial Bond Sales				
Price (USD)	$73.10	$70.78	$70.44	$62.82
Yield	8.67%	9.00%	9.04%	10.16%
Central Bank's USD Currency Auction				
USD Sold	$73,322,000	$88,844,000	$100,056,190	$66,957,492
NID Exchange Rate	$1,199	$1,200	$1,204	$1,254.00
Total Employed by USG Programs				
	132,169	132,169	117,699	N/A

ECONOMIC – Iraq Relief and Reconstruction Fund (IRRF) 1 and 2

Sector\Status (Millions of USD)	Allocated	Un-allocated	Committed Last Week	Committed Current	Committed Change	Obligated Last Week	Obligated Current	Obligated Change	Disbursed Last Week	Disbursed Current	Disbursed Change
Security and Law	$4,967	$11	$4,946	$4,946	$0	$4,946	$4,946	$0	$4,864	$4,864	$0
Justice and Civil Society	$2,304	$15	$2,262	$2,262	$0	$2,257	$2,256	$0	$2,171	$2,171	$0
Electricity Sector	$4,188	$25	$4,069	$4,068	-$1	$4,055	$4,054	-$1	$3,837	$3,844	$7
Oil Infrastructure	$1,718	$7	$1,601	$1,601	$0	$1,597	$1,600	$3	$1,576	$1,579	$3
Water and Sanitation	$2,062	$23	$1,978	$1,973	-$6	$1,947	$1,946	$0	$1,809	$1,811	$2
Transportation and Comm\	$462	$2	$458	$458	$0	$458	$458	$0	$412	$412	$0
Roads, Bridges and Const\	$324	$4	$317	$315	-$2	$317	$315	-$2	$252	$252	$0
Health Care	$810	$9	$787	$787	$0	$777	$777	$0	$733	$733	$0
Private Sector Development	$838	$1	$820	$820	$0	$820	$820	$0	$814	$814	$0
Edu\, Refugees, Human Rights	$460	$0	$431	$431	$0	$431	$431	$0	$407	$407	$0
Admin Expense (USAID,DoS)	$220	$0	$218	$218	$0	$218	$218	$0	$208	$208	$0
Total IRRF II	$18,352	$97	$17,887	$17,879	-$8	$17,821	$17,821	$0	$17,081	$17,094	$12
IRRF II Non-Construction	-	-	$7,959	$7,960	$0	$7,945	$7,945	$0	$7,725	$7,727	$1
IRRF II Construction	-	-	$9,408	$9,399	-$9	$9,357	$9,356	$0	$8,839	$8,850	$11
IRRF II Overhead	-	-	$520	$520	$0	$520	$520	$0	$517	$517	$0
Total IRRF I	$2,475	$0	$2,291	$2,291	$0	$2,232	$2,232	$0	$2,139	$2,139	$0
Grand Total IRRF I & II	$20,827	$97	$20,178	$20,170	-$8	$20,053	$20,053	$0	$19,220	$19,233	$12

(e) The Alaskan Permanent Fund Dividend

ADAPTED FROM THE ALASKA PERMANENT FUND CORPORATION

www.apfc.org

The Permanent Fund was established through a constitutional amendment approved by Alaska voters in 1976 after oil was discovered on the North Slope. The constitutional amendment and its supporting statutes set aside at least 25 percent of certain mineral revenues paid to the state for deposit into a public savings account to be invested for the benefit of the current and all future generations of Alaskans. Anyone who has lived in the state for over a year gets the dividend. It was, arguably, the most farsighted public policy decision Alaskans have made since statehood.

Why did Alaskans create the Fund?

During construction of the Trans-Alaska Pipeline in the 1970s, oil companies flooded state coffers with money paid for leases to explore and secure drilling rights. The Legislature spent all $900 million of that initial lease money within a few years. Alaskans realized that they were about to receive a great deal more money from oil when the pipeline was complete. They wished to better safeguard the robust income forthcoming from the pipeline, but the state constitution did not allow for dedicated funds. So Alaskans voted in 1976 to amend the constitution to put at least 25% of the oil money into a dedicated fund: the Permanent Fund. This would save money for future generations, which would no longer have oil as a source of income. In 1976 Governor Hammond proposed a constitutional amendment to create the Fund. The 9th Alaska Legislature modified the governor's legislation and placed it as a ballot proposition in the 1976 General Election. It passed by a margin of two to one.

What is the purpose of the Permanent Fund?

The 1976 state law establishing the Permanent Fund (AS 37.13), states that the Fund was created:

1. to provide a means of conserving a portion of the state's revenue from mineral resources to benefit all generations of Alaskans
2. to maintain safety of principal while maximizing total return
3. to be a savings device managed to allow maximum use of disposable income for purposes designated by law

How is the Fund invested?

The Board's goal is to earn slightly better-than-average rates of return with slightly below-average levels of risk. To accomplish this, it adheres to the Prudent Expert Rule to manage a well-diversified portfolio. The asset allocation includes domestic and foreign stocks, bonds, domestic real estate and REITs [Real Estate Investment Trusts], private equity, absolute return and public infrastructure investments.

How big is the Permanent Fund?

The Fund stood at $37.8 billion as of the end of the 2007 fiscal year, on June 30, 2007. This figure can fluctuate up or down with market movements, but trends upward over time. Check this site's home page [apfc.org] for the Fund's daily updated total market value. The Alaska Permanent Fund is among the largest investment funds in the world. In the U.S., the Fund is larger than any endowment fund, private foundation, or union pension trust.

What happens to Fund income?

The Legislature decides how Fund income is used. To date, the Legislature has:

- inflation-proofed Fund principal
- paid dividends to qualified applicants
- made special appropriations to the principal
- paid for some Fund-related state expenses

Are some Fund investment classes too risky?

Stocks are the most volatile asset class and are high risk in the short run. But for long-run investors like the Permanent Fund, there's actually a greater risk to be out of the stock market than to be in it. The long-term trend of stock prices is more steeply upward than that of other asset classes. Stocks advance in 6 out of every 10 years, in 72% of all 5-year periods and in 77% of all 10-year periods. One study looked at the 62-year period from 1926 through 1987. It showed that if an investor had been out of the stock market only during the 50 best market months (which would be only 7% of the total months in the 744-month time span), total return for the 62 years would have been zero, rather than more than 10% compounded annually had she stayed the duration. The Fund is now also invested in alternative investments, private equities, hedge funds and public infrastructure. Gradual exposure to these classes will be in keeping with how the Fund has started out in stocks ... dedicating just a small percentage of the Fund's total value as Trustees gain knowledge and experience investing in a new asset class.

Could there be no dividend in some years?

Yes. The Alaska Constitution states that the Fund's principal cannot be spent. The dividend can only be paid from Fund earnings. If the earnings reserve is zero or negative on June 30, no money can be paid out. APFC Trustees are proposing a better method for determining Fund annual payout that would require a change to the constitution through a vote of the people. The Percent of Market Value (POMV) payout method would remove the distinction between principal and earnings, treating the Permanent Fund as one pot of money. Five percent of the Fund's total market value could be paid out each year.

How's the Fund doing and why is it successful?

The Fund has earned about 10% annualized total rate of return over the long run (10.34% as of March 2007). This is in excess of its post-inflation targeted rates of return during this time frame. It is successful because:

- It keeps a diversified asset allocation.
- It was created by a Constitutional amendment.
- The APFC, which manages the Fund, receives legislative oversight.
- The dividend program keeps the Fund in the public eye.

- The Fund has sound management practices, including performance oversight of managers.
- The Fund is not used as an economic development bank.

How the PFD amount is calculated each year

1. Add Fund Statutory Net Income from the current plus the previous four fiscal years.
2. Multiply by 21%
3. Divide by 2
4. Subtract prior year obligations, expenses and PFD program operations
5. Divide by the number of eligible applicants

26 Years of Dividends

2007 $1654.00	1998 $1540.88	1989 $873.16
2006 $1106.96	1997 $1296.54	1988 $826.93
2005 $845.76	1996 $1130.68	1987 $708.19
2004 $919.84	1995 $990.30	1986 $556.26
2003 $1107.56	1994 $983.90	1985 $404.00
2002 $1540.76	1993 $949.46	1984 $331.29
2001 $1850.28	1992 $915.84	1983 $386.15
2000 $1963.86	1991 $931.34	1982 $1000.00
1999 $1769.84	1990 $952.63	

4. THE IRAQ HYDROCARBON DRAFT LAW (2007)[*]

Preamble

WHEREAS the Republic of Iraq has entered a new era after the adoption of the Constitution in 2005;

WHEREAS, Article 111 of the said Constitution declares that Oil and Gas are owned by all the people of Iraq in all the Regions and Governorates;

WHEREAS, Articles 110, 112, 114 and 115, seen in the light of Article 111, broadly define the authorities and responsibilities of the Federal, Regional and Governorate Authorities including those in the Petroleum sector;

WHEREAS, the Iraq Republic is endowed with rich Oil and Gas resources, a great portion of which is already discovered and ready for Development whilst more Petroleum resources are yet to be discovered;

---

[*]This section includes the most "authoritative" version of the full Iraqi draft law on hydrocarbons (February 15, 2007), without annexes. The four annexes were controversial from the outset. They divide the fields into "fields in production" (Annex 1), "fields that are close to production" (Annex 2), "fields that are not near production and could be open to competition from international oil companies and the Iraqi National Oil Company" (Annex 3), and "exploration blocks" (Annex 4). Several other drafts are "in circulation." A very useful site on Iraqi oil can be found at www.iraqoilforum.com.

WHEREAS, Iraq's Production capacity during the last decades has been low and at great disparity with its exceptionally rich Oil and Gas resources;

WHEREAS, the Iraqi people find themselves at the crossroad to a new and more prosperous future which will require quick and substantial funding of reconstruction and modernization projects;

WHEREAS revenues from Oil and Gas represent the most important basis for redeveloping the country in general and the Iraqi economy, in particular on sustainable and robust basis in a planned and coordinated manner that takes into consideration the objectives of the Constitution, including the unity of the Iraq Republic, the exhaustible nature of Petroleum resources, the need for preserving the environment;

To help the Iraqi Ministry Of Oil focus on its main duties of creating policies, planning, and supervision, while achieving the necessary upgrading to enhance operational quality, the oil activities operated solely by the Ministry of Oil have to be transferred to technical and commercial entities and institutions including an independent Iraq National Oil Company, to provide authorities to the Regions and Producing Governorates;

WHEREAS, the rehabilitation and further development of the Petroleum industry will be enhanced by the participation of international and national investors of recognized technical, managerial and operational skills as well as robust capital resources to help upgrade and develop national expertise and efficiency in the Petroleum sector;

WHEREAS, the national private industry directly and indirectly related to the Petroleum sector are in need of proactive encouragement and support to play a prominent role in the development of the sector;

WHEREAS, the positive interplay between the Federal and Regional authorities requires appropriate legislative and institutional framework conditions to ensure efficient co-ordination;

WHEREAS, the introduction of a variety of national and international players in the development of the Petroleum sector calls for clear legislative, institutional and operational framework conditions to ensure co-ordination and efficiency between the relevant Iraqi authorities and the commercial players as well as among these players;

WHEREAS, the development of the petroleum sector must be closely coordinated and harmonized with the development of the society and the national economy in a manner that maintains sustainable development for the economy and the environment and in the long term decreases dependence on Oil and Gas revenues;

WHEREAS, the conditions for regulating the Petroleum sector are of great importance to the whole nation as well as to all Investors in the sector, there is a need for a clear, fair, transparent and efficient system of governance that inspires confidence, efficiency and co-operation among all participants in the petroleum sector, including governmental authorities at Federal, Regional and Governorate level, and among national and international actors;

THEREFORE THIS LAW IS ENACTED:

Chapter I: Fundamental Provisions

Article 1: Ownership of Petroleum Resources

Oil and gas are owned by all the people of Iraq in all the Regions and Governorates.

Article 2: Scope of Application

(a) This law applies to Petroleum Operations in all the territory of the Republic of Iraq, including the soil and subsoil on land, as well as inland waters and territorial waters.

(b) The scope of this Law excludes the refining of Petroleum, its industrial utilization as well as the storage, transport, and distribution of Petroleum Products.

Article 3: Purpose

(a) This law establishes the regime for the management of Petroleum Operations in the Republic of Iraq, taking into account the existing international treaties between the Republic of Iraq and other countries on Crude Oil transportation.

(b) The law aims to build upon existing co-operation between the relevant Ministries in the Federal Government administration, in addition to building a base for coordination and discussions among the Federal, Regional, and Producing Governorates' authorities.

Article 4: Definitions

For the purposes of this law, the following terms and expressions shall have the meaning indicated as follows, unless the context in which they are used requires a different meaning:

1. "Discovery": the first Petroleum encountered in a Reservoir by drilling that is recoverable at the surface by conventional petroleum industry methods;
2. "Commercial Discovery": a Discovery which has been deemed to be commercial for Development purposes by the holder of Exploration and Production;
3. "Region": the Kurdistan Region or any other Region created in Iraq after issuing this law according to the Constitution of Iraq;
4. "Good Oilfield Practices": all those practices related to Petroleum Operations that are generally accepted by the international petroleum industry as good, safe, environmentally friendly, economic and efficient in exploring for and producing Petroleum;
5. "Good Pipeline Practices": all those practices related to transportation by pipelines including the design, construction, commissioning,

maintenance, operation and decommissioning of pipelines that are generally accepted in the international petroleum industry as good, safe, environmentally friendly, economic and efficient in transporting Petroleum;

6. "Production": the extraction and disposal of Petroleum;

7. "Petroleum": all Crude Oil or Natural Gas, or other hydrocarbons produced or capable of being produced from Crude Oil, Natural Gas, oil rocks or tar sands;

8. "Development": the activities carried out by the holder of Exploration and Production based on either the Field Development Plan or the Main Pipeline Development Plan, which aim at Production and transportation of Petroleum;

9. "Exploration": the search for Petroleum by geological, geophysical and other means including drilling of exploration and appraisal wells;

10. "Field": an area consisting of a single Reservoir or multiple Reservoirs connected to the same individual geological structural feature or stratigraphic condition. The field name refers to the surface area, although it may refer to both the surface and the underground productive formations.

11. "Field Pipeline": a pipeline, including valve stations, pump stations, compressor stations and associated installations, collecting Crude Oil or Natural Gas from a Field or a group of Fields and delivering it to a transfer point for further transportation;

12. "Pipeline": an entity that consists of a linear pipeline accompanied with other components on the ground level including stations of pumping, valves, compression, and other accompanied accessories for gauging, supervision, telecommunications, remote control, for the purposes of transporting Crude Oil and Natural Gas from the Transfer Point to the Delivery Point.

13. "Main Pipeline": the principal pipeline, including valve stations, pump stations, compressor stations and associated installations built by the Transporter, for the transportation of Crude Oil or Natural Gas from one or several Fields or sources inside or outside Iraq;

14. "Field Development Plan": a scheduled programme and cost estimate specifying the appraisal and Development activities required to develop and produce Petroleum from a specific Field or group of Fields by the holder of an Exploration and Production contract, prepared in accordance with this law and the relevant provisions in the Regulations for Petroleum Operations and the Exploration and Production Contract covering that contract Area;

15. "Main Pipeline Development Plan": a scheme and cost estimate specifying all activities to be carried out by the transporter for the transportation of Petroleum by pipeline inside Iraq and across the territory of neighbouring States, prepared in accordance with this Law, the relevant provisions in the regulations for Petroleum Operations and the Exploration and Production Contract covering that Contract Area and any relevant bilateral agreements;

16. "Decommissioning Plan": a scheme for the closure of Petroleum Operations and restoration of the operating environment including the removal and disposal of all installations;

17. "Iraqi Person": any citizen with Iraqi nationality or any company or institution with legal personality established and registered pursuant to Iraqi legislation, with its headquarters in Iraq and having at least fifty percent (50%) of its share capital held by national citizens or by Iraqi public or private companies or institutions;

18. "Foreign Person": any non-Iraqi citizen or any company or institution with legal personality established and registered pursuant to Iraqi legislation, and having less than fifty percent (50%) of its share capital held by national citizens or by Iraqi public or private companies or institutions;

19. "Petroleum Operations": all or any of the activities related to Exploration, Development, Production, separation and treatment, storage, transportation and sale or delivery of Petroleum at the Delivery Point, Export Point or to the agreed Supply Point inside or outside Iraq, and includes Natural Gas treatment operations and the closure of all concluded activities;

20. "Natural Gas": all hydrocarbons which are in a gaseous state at atmospheric conditions of temperature and pressure, that might be associated or not with liquid hydrocarbons, as well as the residue gas remaining after the extraction of liquid hydrocarbons from the Reservoir;

21. "Associated Natural Gas": Natural Gas which under Reservoir conditions is either in solution with liquid hydrocarbons or as gas-cap gas which overlies and is in contact with Crude Oil;

22. "Non-associated Natural Gas": the free Natural Gas other than Associated Natural Gas;

23. "Operator": the entity designated by the Designated Authority, in consultation with the holder of Exploration and Production right, to conduct Petroleum Operations on behalf of the latter;

24. "Producing Governorate": any Iraqi Governorate that produces Crude Oil and natural gas continually on rates more than one hundred and fifty thousand (150,000) barrels a day;

25. "Reservoir": a separate accumulation of Petroleum in a geological unit limited by rock characteristics, structural or stratigraphic boundaries, contact surfaces between Petroleum and water in the formation; or a combination of these, so that Petroleum Production from any portion of the accumulation will affect the pressure in the accumulation as a whole;

26. "Contract Area": the area within which the holder of an Exploration and Production right is authorized to explore for, develop and produce Petroleum;

27. "Development and Production Area": a part of the Contract Area which following a Commercial Discovery has been delineated according to the terms and conditions of the Exploration and Production Contract;

28. "Crude Oil": all hydrocarbons, regardless of specific gravity, which are produced and saved from the Field in liquid state at atmospheric pressure and temperature, including asphalt, tar and the liquid hydrocarbons known as distillates or condensates obtained from Natural Gas within the Contract Area;

29. "Transporter": the entity designated by the Council of Ministers to receive Crude Oil or Natural Gas from the holder of Exploration and Production right at the Transfer Point and deliver Crude Oil for export or Natural Gas to the holder of Exploration and Production right at the Delivery Point;

30. "Production Measurement Point": the place(s) at which volumes and qualities of Crude Oil or Natural Gas to be transferred at the Transfer Point are measured;

31. "Transfer Point": the inlet flange(s) of the outgoing Pipelines from the Production Measurement Point, where the Transporter shall receive Crude Oil or Natural Gas from the holder of Exploration and Production right;

32. "Delivery Point": the point(s) of the loading facility at which Crude Oil reaches the inlet flange of the receiving tank-ship or such other point inside or outside Iraq, as agreed to under the Exploration and Production Contract. In the case of Gas it is the flange of the inlet to the receiving installation for Natural Gas;

33. "Supply Point": the place at which Crude Oil or Natural Gas is transferred from a Main Pipeline or a Field Pipeline to a different type of transport, processing or use;

34. "The Ministry": is the Ministry of Oil in the Republic of Iraq and other companies and organizations specifically authorized by it;

35. "Designated Authority": the Ministry of Oil, the Iraq National Oil Company, or the Regional Authority;

36. "Regional Authority": the authorized ministry in the Regional Government;

37. "Federal Oil and Gas Council": the Council which is formed by the Council of Ministers according to Article 5D of this law to exercise the authorities designated to it according to the provisions of this law; and

38. "Panel of Independent Advisors": the panel of experts that is appointed by the Federal Oil and Gas Council, according to the provisions of this law.

Chapter II: Management of Petroleum Resources

Article 5: Competence of Authorities

a. The Council of Representatives

First: The Council of Representatives shall enact all Federal legislation on Crude Oil and Natural Gas.

Second: The Council of Representatives shall approve all international petroleum treaties related to Petroleum Operations that Iraq signs with other countries.

b. The Council of Ministers

First: The Council of Ministers shall be responsible for recommending proposed legislation to the Council of Representatives on the development of the country's Petroleum resources.

Second: The Council of Ministers is the competent authority to formulate Federal Petroleum policy and supervise its implementation. It also administers the overall Petroleum Operations including the formulation of Federal policy on all matters within the scope of this law, including Exploration, Production, Transportation, Marketing, the proposal of Petroleum legislation, and the approval of such regulations as may be necessary from time to time on the said matters.

Third: In carrying out the above functions, the Council of Ministers shall ensure that the Federal Oil and Gas Council and the Ministry adopt appropriate and effective mechanisms for consultation and co-ordination with the Regional and Producing Governorate authorities in accordance with the provisions of this law.

c. The Federal Oil and Gas Council

First: To assist the Council of Ministers in creating Petroleum policies and related plans, arranged by the Ministry in coordination with the Regions and Producing Governorates, and to put important legislation for Exploration and Production based on Article 9 of this law the Council of Ministers shall create an entity to be named "the Federal Oil and Gas Council". The Prime Minister or his nominee shall be the president of this Council, and the Council shall include:

1. the Federal Government's Ministers of Oil, Finance, and Planning;
2. the Director of the Iraq Central Bank;
3. a Regional government minister representing each Region;
4. a representative from each Producing Governorate not included in a Region;
5. the Chief Executives of important related petroleum companies including the Iraq National Oil Company and the Oil Marketing Company; and
6. Experts in petroleum, finance, and economy, with their number not exceeding three (3), to be appointed for a period not exceeding five (5) years based on a resolution from the Council of ministers.

The formation of the Federal Oil and Gas Council shall take into consideration a fair representation of the basic components of the Iraqi society.

Second: The Federal Oil and Gas Council holds the responsibility of putting Federal Petroleum policies, Exploration plans, Development of Fields and main pipeline plans inside Iraq, and this has the right to approve any major changes in such plans and policies.

Third: The Federal Oil and Gas Council reviews and changes the Exploration and Production contracts that give the rights of Petroleum Operations according to Article 10 of this Law, and what might be relevant to the Republic of Iraq.

Fourth: The Federal Oil and Gas Council approves the types of, and changes to, model Exploration and Production contracts, according to the criteria defined in this Law, and selects appropriate model contract types according to the nature of the Field or Exploration area to provide maximum returns to the people of Iraq.

Fifth: The Federal Oil and Gas Council sets the special instructions for negotiations pertaining to granting rights or signing Development and Production contracts, and setting qualification criteria for companies.

Sixth: To assist the Federal Oil and Gas Council in reviewing Exploration and Production contracts and Petroleum Fields' Development plans, the Council relies on the assistance of a panel called the "Panel of Independent Advisors" that includes oil and gas experts, Iraqis or foreigners. The Council shall decide their number. They should be qualified and have a good reputation and long practical experience in Exploration and Production operations and in Petroleum contracts, and they should be chosen by a unanimous decision of the Council and contracted for a year, which can be extended. The Panel of Independent Advisors gives its recommendations and advice to the Federal Oil and Gas Council on issues related to contracts, Field Development plans, and any other related issues requested by the Federal Oil and Gas Council.

Seventh: The Federal Oil and Gas Council is the competent authority to approve the transfer of rights among holders of Exploration and Production rights and associated amendment of contracts provided this does not adversely affect the national content including the percentage of national participation.

Eighth: The Federal Oil and Gas Council and the Ministry are responsible for ensuring that Petroleum discovered resources are developed, and produced in an optimal manner and in the best interest of the people in accordance with legislation, regulations and contractual conditions as well as recognised international standards.

Ninth: Members of the Federal Oil and Gas Council can suggest policies and law drafts to the Federal Oil and Gas Council.

Tenth: The Federal Oil and Gas Council may create entities necessary for the implementation of its duties.

Eleventh: The Federal Oil and Gas Council shall adopt an internal procedure to regulate its internal processes to take its decisions by a two-thirds (2/3) majority on setting Petroleum policies, planning, model contracts and guidelines for negotiations of contracts.

d. The Ministry of Oil

First: The Ministry is the competent authority for proposing Federal policy, laws and plans.

Second: The Ministry creates legislation as well as issuing regulations and guidelines to implement the Federal plans.

Third: The Ministry undertakes the necessary monitoring and supervisory actions in co-ordination with the Regional Authorities and Producing Governorates, to ensure their proper, coordinated, and uniform implementation throughout Iraq.

Fourth: On the basis of policies, regulations, guidelines and requirements under Article 5D First, and 5D Second, and in accordance with the overall economic and social policies of the Federal Government, the Ministry shall in consultation with the Regional Authorities and Producing Governorates draw up Federal policies and plans on Exploration, Development and Production on an annual or as needed basis. Such policies and plans shall address both the short term as well as the long term requirements. The geographical distribution and timing of actions and projects shall comprise proposals from the Regions and Governorates in accordance to Annex Nos. 1, 2, 3 and 4. The suggestions for petroleum policies and related plans are to be submitted to the Federal Oil and Gas Council to be reviewed and decided upon.

Fifth: The Ministry is the competent authority to represent the Iraqi Republic in regional and international forums.

Sixth: The Ministry is empowered to negotiate with other countries and organizations multilateral and bilateral treaties related to Oil and Gas, subject to approval in accordance with the Constitution.

Seventh: The Ministry is responsible for monitoring Petroleum Operations to ensure adherence with the laws, regulations, and contracting terms. In addition to its administrative and technical monitoring duties, the Ministry shall carry out verification of costs and expenditures incurred by the holders of rights to ensure correct and justified cost recoveries for the purpose of determining revenues accruing to the Government. The Ministry shall through inspection, technical audits and other appropriate actions verify conformance with legislation, regulations, contractual terms and internationally recognised practices. The Ministry must coordinate with Regional Governments and Producing Governorates to create specialized entities that carry out the above responsibilities instead of the Ministry.

Eighth: The Ministry has the right to execute contracts related to Oil and Gas supply services other than those covered by Exploration and Development Contracts and according to other applicable legislation.

e. The Iraq National Oil Company

First: The Iraq National Oil Company (INOC), in accordance with Article 6 of this Law, can participate in Exploration and Production operations inside Iraq on behalf of the Government. INOC is obligated to sell its share of Crude Oil to the Oil Marketing Company based on the delivery price that covers the cost in addition to a reasonable profit that would facilitate the company's development in Exploration and Production.

Second: The tasks and scope of operation of INOC shall include carrying out Oil and Gas Exploration, Development, Production, Transportation, Storage, Marketing and sales down to the Delivery Point in accordance with the rights and obligations under this law including the necessary contracts, permits and approvals applicable to all other holders of rights.

Third: INOC shall have the right to participate as a commercial partner in international projects related to the transportation, marketing and sale of Oil and Gas. It may also participate in Exploration and Production contracts outside the Republic of Iraq subject to approval by the Council of Ministers.

Fourth: INOC shall form fully owned Subsidiary companies in selected areas in Iraq based on the location of Fields, size of Petroleum reserves, Production capacity and cost benefit analysis, or based on rearrangements and task management of existing companies based on its work capacity leading to better efficiency based on appropriate bylaws and procedures to be issued for the purpose.

Fifth: INOC shall have the right to establish in association with others affiliated companies or acquire shares in existing companies inside the Republic of Iraq. INOC may also undertake the same outside the Republic of Iraq subject to the approval of the Council of Ministers.

Sixth: INOC shall have the right to acquire tangible and intangible assets belonging to natural or legal entities for the purpose of achieving its objectives and in accordance with the law.

f. Regional Authority

The Regional Authorities shall have the following competencies:

First: The Regional Authorities shall undertake the necessary preparations in order to propose to the Federal authorities activities and plans on behalf of the Region to be included in the Federal plans for Petroleum Operations. It shall further assist the Federal Authorities in discussions leading to the finalisation of the Federal plan as required.

Second: Carry out the licensing process regarding activities within its respective Region related to Exploration and Production of discovered but undeveloped Fields mentioned in Annex No. 3 according to mechanisms mentioned in Article 9 and based on contracting types prepared by the Federal Oil and Gas Council and in accordance to regulations issued by Federal Oil and Gas Council with qualified international oil companies on the bases put forward by the Federal Oil and Gas Council.

Third: Be represented in discussions carried out by the Federal Oil and Gas Council in accordance with Article 5 of this Law.

Fourth: Collaborate with the Ministry to undertake the monitoring and supervision of Petroleum Operations to ensure adherence to legislation, regulations, guidelines and the specific terms of the relevant Exploration and Production Contracts. Such functions shall be carried out in close coordination and harmonisation with the Ministry to ensure uniform and consistent implementation throughout the Republic of Iraq.

Article 6: Creating the Iraq National Oil Company

A. The Iraq National Oil Company (INOC) is a holding company fully owned by the Iraqi Government and based in Baghdad. INOC is financially and administratively independent and runs on commercial bases.

B. Its scope of operations shall include:

First: Managing and operating existing producing Fields mentioned in Annex No. 1, and both the North Oil Company and the South Oil Company are linked to it.

Second: Participation in the Development and Production of discovered and yet not developed Fields mentioned in Annex No. 2.

Third: Carrying out for Exploration and Production operations in new areas outside its areas in adherence to this law through applying for Exploration and Production rights in the new areas on a competitive basis.

Fourth: INOC shall also own, manage and operate the Main Oil and Gas Pipeline Network and the export ports in the Republic of Iraq and enter into contracts with existing and future shippers of Oil and Gas in accordance with this Law. The company continues its responsibilities in operating the Main Oil and Gas Pipeline Network and the export ports in Iraq during a transitional period not exceeding two years until the reorganization of the companies in the Ministry is completed. Then, the Federal Oil and Gas Council shall decide the entity responsible of operating the Main Oil and Gas Pipeline Network and the export ports in Iraq based on a proposal submitted by the Ministry after coordinating with the INOC in adherence to this Law and after the approval of the Council of Ministers.

Fifth: To ensure and develop the coordination and collaboration with Regions and Producing Governorates, INOC establishes subsidiary companies which it owns in total and which will undertake the Petroleum Operations in the Regions and Producing Governorates. These subsidiary companies will be represented on the INOC board and will be paid for the cost they incur in addition to a specific reasonable profit in order that they can develop and enhance their operations.

Sixth: The board of the INOC oversees the INOC and its subsidiary companies; in accordance to the INOC law, the board includes members from the Federal Government, the Regions, and the Producing Governorates.

Article 7: Reorganising the Ministry of Oil

A. The Ministry, pursuant to a law, must create the important institutional and methodology changes to reflect its new responsibilities and duties. In particular, the Ministry shall create a new department as soon as possible specialized in planning, developing, and following up the process of obtaining rights. This new department must consist of members of the Ministry trained and specialized in the bidding process and conduct professional negotiations with oil companies to sign contracts of Exploration and Production rights in accordance with the Ministry's authorities and in accordance with Article 9 of this Law. In addition, this department must include in each and every negotiations representatives from the related Producing Governorates. It is permissible that the negotiation and rights teams include expert advisers with a distinguished international reputation and experience.

B. The law of reorganization of the Ministry of Oil must include the suggested mechanisms that will be the basis of re-structuring the relationship between the Ministry and other related companies and regulating entities in a way that guarantees a full separation between, on the one hand, the Production and oil services companies, and, on the other hand, the regulatory, monitoring, and supervisory departments in the Ministry. In addition, there must be separation yet integration between the producing units and the services departments in a way that guarantees increasing productivity and maximizing profits.

Article 8: Field Development and Oil and Gas Exploration

A. Regarding the priorities aimed at restoring and increasing Production related to existing Fields, INOC is the Operator and is authorized to directly sign services contracts or administrative contracts with appropriate oil or services companies, in case this was needed to accelerate reaching to the goals stated in this Article.

B. The Ministry, and after coordinating with Regions and Producing Governorates, and in adherence to Article 9 of this Law, is to propose to the Federal Oil and Gas Council the best methods to develop the discovered but yet not developed Fields.

C. The Ministry prepares model Exploration and Production contracts to be approved by the Federal Oil and Gas Council and to be appended to this law. These model contracts must guarantee the best levels of coordination between the Oil Ministry, INOC, and the Regions each according to their specific responsibility in relation to both this Law and the international oil companies.

D. Utmost effort must be put into ensuring speedy and efficient Development of the Fields discovered but partially or entirely not yet developed when this law is enacted, and it is permissible to develop these Fields in collaboration with reputable oil companies that have the efficient financial, administrative, technical, operational capabilities according to the contracting terms and the regulations issued by the Federal Oil and Gas Council.

E. The Federal Oil and Gas Council, the Oil Ministry, INOC, and the Regional Authorities have to carry out an exploratory program in Iraq to assess the Oil and Gas resources and to compensate Production, and to add new reserves.

F. The Ministry must provide the Federal Oil and Gas Council with a comprehensive proposal for Oil and Gas Exploration throughout the Republic of Iraq in coordination with the Regions and the Producing Governorates, sorting out the areas according to their Oil and Gas potential, implemented within a short time table in order to guarantee increasing reserves and continuing Production and Development.

Article 9: Grant of Rights

A. The rights for conducting Petroleum Operations shall be granted on the basis of an Exploration and Production contract. The contract shall be entered between the Ministry (or the Regional Authority) and an Iraqi or Foreign Person, natural or legal, which has demonstrated to the Ministry or the Regional Authority the technical competence and financial capability that are adequate for the efficient conduct of Petroleum Operations according to the guidelines of the Federal Oil and Gas Council and as mentioned in Article 5C Fifth, and in accordance with the mechanisms of negotiations and contracting stated in Article 10 of this Law.

B. The licensing process shall be based on transparent and accountable tendering and shall take into account recognized practices by the international petroleum industry. It shall adhere to the following principles and procedures:

First: Competitive licensing rounds based on clearly defined terms and terms of application as well as the criteria to be used in the selection of successful candidates.

Second: The contractual terms offered to applicants shall be specified in model contracts accompanying the letter of invitation.

Third: The form and terms of the model contract shall take account of the specific characteristics and requirements of the individual area, Field or prospect being offered, including whether the resources are discovered or not, the risks and potential rewards associated with the investments under consideration, and the technological and operational challenges presented.

Fourth: All model contracts shall be formulated to honour the following objectives and criteria:

1. National control;
2. Ownership of the resources;
3. Optimum economic return to the country;
4. An appropriate return on investment to the investor; and
5. Reasonable incentives to the investor for ensuring solutions which are optimal to the country in the long-term related to:
   a. improved and enhanced recovery,
   b. technology transfer,
   c. training and development of Iraqi personnel,
   d. optimal utilization of the infrastructure, and
   e. environmentally friendly solutions and plans.

Fifth: The Model Contracts may be based upon Service Contract, Field Development and Production Contract, or Risk Exploration Contract provided they are adapted to best meet the objectives and criteria under Article 9B above which serve the best interest of the Republic of Iraq.

Sixth: Only pre-qualified companies by the Ministry or the Regional Authority shall be considered in any licensing round. The criteria for prequalification shall be specified in the invitation to bidding according to the regulation and instructions issued by the Federal Oil and Gas Council.

Seventh: Evaluation of pre-qualified applicants shall aim at establishing a short list of successful candidates for negotiations.

Eighth: The selection and ranking of successful applicants shall be on the basis of the quality and relevance of the proposed work plan and the anticipated economic return to Iraq.

Ninth: The overall allocation of Exploration and Production rights throughout the Republic of Iraq shall aim at achieving variety among oil companies and Operators with different background, expertise, experience and approach so as to enhance efficiency through positive competition, benchmarking of performance and transparency. The possibility of using consortia of selected companies, particularly in large Fields, should be considered.

Tenth: Not later than two (2) months after the endorsement of approval of Exploration and Production contracts, the contract must be published.

C. The granting of rights for the activities referred to in Article 9A shall always respect national interests, for example those related to defense, navigation, research and development, conservation, health and safety and a high level of environmental protection.

D. The Designated Authority is to regulate the form and manner in which rights are granted under this Article in a manner consistent with this law and the regulations of the Federal Oil and Gas Council.

Article 10: Mechanisms of Negotiations and Contracting

A. The Ministry, the INOC, or the Regional Authority, based on their respective specialties and responsibilities, and after completing initial procedures for granting rights as indicated in Article 9 [will conclude] an initial signing of Exploration and Production contracts with the selected contractor.

B. The Exploration and Production contracts mentioned in Article 10A must include the following: "the contract is valid with no objection from the Federal Oil and Gas Council according to the provisions of the Oil and Gas Law No. _____ of 2007 including the contractual guidelines on negotiations and model contracts and any amendments to these that might be issued by the Federal Oil and Gas Council."

C. The initial contract mentioned in Article 10B must be submitted to the Federal Oil and Gas Council within thirty (30) days from the day of the initial signing or it is considered cancelled.

D. The Federal Oil and Gas Council must adhere to the following steps when deciding on the contracts submitted to it by Ministry, INOC, or the Regional Authority:

First: Submit the initial contract stated in Article 10C, if the Federal Oil and Gas Council finds it advisable, to the Panel of Independent Advisors for analysis on the extent of its compliance with the model contracts approved by the Federal Oil and Gas Council and its regulations pertaining to Exploration and Production rights in accordance with Article 9.

Second: In case the initial contract has serious discrepancies as compared to the model contracts and guidelines issued by the Federal Oil and Gas Council, the Federal Oil and Gas Council will make a decision on the contract relying on the opinion of the Panel of Independent Advisors, which decision shall require a two-thirds (2/3) majority of the members in attendance.

Third: The Ministry, INOC, or the Regional Authority must be informed of the objection of the initial contract in accordance to the legal reasons within sixty (60) days of receipt of the initial contract by the Federal Oil and Gas Council, and the contract remains valid in case no objection is made by the Federal Oil and Gas Council within the stated period. In case the Federal Oil and Gas Council cannot hold a meeting within sixty (60) days of receiving the initial contract due to extraordinary reasons, the Council must take a decision regarding the contract within forty five (45) days using all the possible means. The contract remains valid in case no decision is made by the Federal Oil and Gas Council within the stated period.

C. The Ministry, INOC, or the Regional Authority shall address the reasons for objection issued by the Federal Oil and Gas Council by amending the initial contract and submitting it again according to the steps mentioned in this Article.

Article 11: Petroleum Revenues

A. According to the Constitution of Iraq (Articles 106, 111, 112 and 121(3)) regarding the ownership of Oil and Gas resources, the distribution of its revenues, and the monitoring of federal revenue allocation, the Council of Ministers must submit a draft federal revenue law to the Council of Representatives regulating these matters in adherence to the sections of this Article.

B. The oil revenues include all the government revenues from Oil and Gas, royalties, signing bonuses and production bonuses of Petroleum contracts with foreign or local companies.

C. The revenues mentioned in Article 11B must be deposited in an account called "the Oil Revenue Fund" established for this purpose, and the federal revenue law shall regulate the Oil Revenue Fund and ensure its fair distribution according to the Constitution.

D. Another fund must be created under the name "The Future Fund," and a certain portion of the Oil Revenue Fund must be deposited in the Future Fund and be regulated by the law.

Article 12: State Participation

A. The Republic of Iraq shall aim at achieving real national participation in the management and Development of its Petroleum resources in adherence to Article 111 of the Constitution.

B. The Exploration and Production rights with regard to existing producing Fields are hereby given to INOC, and also the granting of additional Exploration and Production regarding not yet developed Fields to be implemented by the Federal Oil and Gas Council in accordance with Article 6 and Annex No. 2 of this Law.

C. The Main Pipeline network inside Iraqi territories is hereby assigned to INOC or any specialized company created for this purpose. The formal procedure for this assignment and necessary approvals shall be established by the Federal Oil and Gas Council in accordance with Article 21 this Law.

D. The Republic of Iraq reserves the right to participate in Petroleum Operations in any phase of Petroleum Operations on terms and conditions that are established by contract.

E. The Federal Oil and Gas Council is authorized to designate INOC to exercise the Republic of Iraq's participation share in accordance with Article 15E of this law.

Chapter III: Field Exploration and Field Development Operations

Article 13: Exploration and Production Contracts

A. An Exploration and Production Contract shall give the holder an exclusive right to conduct Petroleum Exploration and Production in the

Contract Area. In addition, the contract shall give the holder the right of transportation in accordance with Article 21A of this Law.

B. Except if additional time is needed to complete the operations to assess a Discovery, the exclusive Exploration and Production right shall be granted as follows:

1. A First Period shall be a maximum of four (4) years.
2. Subject to having fulfilled all commitments by the holder, the Designated Authority may grant a Second Period of two (2) years provided however that a substantial work program is committed to under this period.

C. A Third Period of Exploration can for special considerations of continuity be granted by the Designated Authority provided however that such extension is justified by the quality and substance of the work program and does not exceed two (2) years.

D. All extensions shall be subject to the provisions concerning the relinquishment of Contract Areas in adherence to the Petroleum regulations.

E. In the event of a Discovery, the exclusive Exploration and Production right may be retained by the holder for the purposes of completing the operations initiated within a specified area to assess or determine the commercial value of a Discovery for an additional period of two (2) years or, in the case of a non-associated Natural Gas Discovery, for an additional period not to exceed four (4) years.

F. On the basis of a Field Development Plan prepared and approved in accordance with this Law and the relevant contract, INOC and other holders of an Exploration and Production right may retain the exclusive right to develop and produce Petroleum within the limits of a Development and Production Area for a period to be determined by the Federal Oil and Gas Council varying from fifteen (15) to twenty (20) years, not exceeding twenty (20) years dating from the date of approval of the Field Development Plan, depending on considerations related to optimal oil recovery and utilisation of existing infrastructure. In cases which for technical and economic considerations warrant longer Production period, the Federal Oil and Gas Council, on newly negotiated terms, has the authority to grant an extension not exceeding five (5) years. The remaining acreage outside the Development and Production Area shall be relinquished at the end of the Exploration and Production right.

G. The appointment of an Operator shall be approved by the Designated Authority, and the procedures for such appointment are stated in the initial Contract, and according to the guidelines issued by the Federal Oil and Gas Council, and the Operator should be named in the initial Contract.

Article 14: Obligations of the Holders of Exploration and Production Rights

A holder of Exploration and Production right is obliged, *mutatis mutandis*, to:

A. Conduct Petroleum Operations in accordance with the terms of this law, the Regulations for Petroleum Operations as well as other applicable legislation and Good Oil Field Practices;

B. Promptly report any Discovery within the Contract Area to the Designated Authority;

C. Conduct the necessary delineation and evaluation of the Discovery with a view to determining its commercial potential and keep the Designated Authority fully informed of progress and results;

D. In the event of a Commercial Discovery, prepare and submit to the Designated Authority, in accordance with the Regulations for Petroleum Operations, a Field Development Plan for the Discovery:

E. Prepare and submit a revised Field Development Plan for any material amendment to the original Plan for approval by the Designated Authority;

F. Implement the Field Development Plan or the revisions thereto once these have been approved by the Designated Authority;

G. Submit a Decommissioning Plan to the Designated Authority, not later than two (2) years before the planned termination of Production;

H. Compensate the Injured parties for any losses or damages resulting from the conduct of the Petroleum Operations as provided by law;

I. When the national interest so requires, give preference to the Designated Authority in the acquisition of Petroleum produced in the Contract Area, and access to pipeline transportation, in accordance with terms and conditions to be agreed upon with the Designated Authority;

J. Provide the greatest possible support for required research and development activities in connection with Petroleum Operations and endeavor to carry out as much of these activities by Iraqi institutions;

K. Collect, organize and maintain in good condition usable data from all phases and on all aspects of Petroleum Operations in accordance with this Law and with Petroleum regulations, and

L. At no cost, supply the Ministry and affiliated companies, with all data collected and assembled from Petroleum Operations, in accordance with Article 19 of this Law.

Article 15: Competence Building and Local Content

A. The Republic of Iraq aims at the development of a competent and effective Iraqi private sector capable of substantial participation in Petroleum Operations including the acquisition, alone or together with international companies, of Exploration and Production rights. Such development shall however adhere to the objectives of professional competence in accordance with this Law. Towards this end holders of Exploration rights are encouraged to pursue cooperation and association with serious and qualified Iraqi private initiatives.

B. INOC and other holders of Exploration and Production rights shall give preference to the purchase of Iraqi products and services whenever they are competitive in terms of price, comparable in terms of quality and available on a timely basis in the quantity required.

C. INOC and other holders of Exploration and Production rights shall to the maximum reasonable extent undertake to employ Iraqi citizens having appropriate qualifications and shall undertake to train and prepare potential candidates towards this objective.

D. INOC and other holders of Exploration and Production rights shall maximize to the greatest reasonable extent, training and technology transfer opportunities for Iraqi nationals, at all levels of Petroleum Operations including management.

E. INOC and other holders of Exploration and Production rights are required to diligently seek and develop associations, affiliations, joint ventures and other forms of partnership and or co-operation in order to promote the rapid growth of an Iraqi private sector capable of assisting and enhancing Petroleum Operations to the mutual benefit of the said holders and the nation.

Article 16: Unitisation

A. A Petroleum Discovery which is located partly in one Contract Area and partly in another Contract Area shall be developed and operated jointly pursuant to a unitization agreement which shall be submitted for approval by the Federal Oil and Gas Council to be approved. Should the right-holders fail to reach agreement on the modalities of unitisation, the Federal Oil and Gas Council has the right to decide on the terms six (6) months after serving notice to the parties to this effect.

B. A Petroleum Discovery which extends from areas authorized for Production into areas not authorized for Production shall be developed only after consultation with the Federal Oil and Gas Council about the measures necessary to protect the interests of the Republic of Iraq.

C. The Council of Ministers shall adopt the necessary measures to protect the interests of the Republic of Iraq in Petroleum Discoveries extending beyond the borders of the Republic. In such cases efforts shall be made to seek joint solutions with the said neighboring countries.

Article 17: Conservation

A. The extraction of Petroleum resources shall aim at the avoidance of waste, including preventing leakages from Pipelines, and the optimal maintenance of energy in the Reservoir in accordance with Good Oilfield Practices and Good Pipeline Practices.

B. INOC and other holders of an Exploration and Production right shall diligently apply the latest technologies and oilfield practices that lead to optimum recovery from the individual Reservoir or a group of Reservoirs that are targeted under the Field Development Plan(s).

C. The Field Development Plan shall be based on thorough investigations of alternative extraction strategies in order to select a solution that combines the highest level of Petroleum recovery with acceptably high levels of Production and as low cost as possible.

D. Subsequent to the approval of a Field Development Plan, INOC and other holders of Exploration and Production right shall continue to improve Reservoir understanding through optimal data collection and Reservoir monitoring and shall accordingly seek to identify and implement actions that would improve Petroleum recovery.

Article 18: Access to Main Pipelines and Field Pipelines

A. The Main Pipelines are the property of the Federal Government.

B. INOC as the Transporter with respect to Main Pipelines and the holder of Exploration and Production right under Article 18A with respect to Field

Pipelines have the obligation to transport, without any discrimination and on reasonable commercial terms, the Petroleum of third parties, provided in general that:

1. capacity is available in the Field Pipeline;
2. there are no insurmountable technical problems that prevent such utilisation of the Field Pipeline.

C. Details shall be provided for the modalities of the system of access by third parties to Field Pipelines in regulations to be made by the Ministry in coordination with the Regions and Producing Governorates.

D. Whenever there is a dispute concerning the commercially reasonable terms for the transport of Petroleum in a Main Pipeline or a Field Pipeline for Crude Oil or for Natural Gas, the availability of uncommitted capacity in the pipeline in question or a proposed increase of its capacity, the dispute shall be first referred to the Ministry for resolution, the Ministry must work in coordination with Regions and Producing Governorates. Thereafter, resolution shall be sought according to the procedures set out in Article 30 of this Law.

Article 19: Ownership of Data

A. All data obtained pursuant to any Contract provided for under this Law is the property of the Iraqi Government, and shall not be published, reproduced or exported without the prior approval of the Ministry.

B. The terms and conditions for the exercise of rights in respect of primary, differentiated, processes, interpreted and analyzed data related to Oil and Gas in Iraq including but not limited to geological and geophysical reports, engineering data, samples, logs and well surveys, shall be established in data supply obligations in the relevant contract and by regulations.

C. The Ministry submits copies of the current available Petroleum data to the INOC and to the Regions, and the INOC and Regions must take the responsibility of supplying the Ministry with new data and updates resulted from the Petroleum Operations implemented by them in a continues and periodic fashion.

D. Anyone who has the information in his possession or sells, buys, transfers, receives, deals with any of the information or data mentioned in this article shall be considered in violation, unless the contract terms states otherwise, and shall be prosecuted under the Iraqi criminal and civil law. No one has the right to own such data and information.

E. Without prejudice to section D of this Article, it is allowed for someone to have a permission from the Designated Authorities to own, buy, sell, transfer, or receive data and information indicated in section F of this Article under the condition of supplying the Designated Authorities with copies of the data, and his permission should not be revoked without logical reasons.

F. Old Data, for the purposes of this law, mean all primary, differentiated, processes, interpreted and analyzed data and information related to Oil and Gas in the Republic of Iraq indicated in section B of this Article.

Article 20: Restrictions on Production Levels

In the event that, for national policy considerations, there is a need to introduce limitations on the national level of Petroleum Production, such limitations shall be applied in a fair and equitable manner and on a pro-rata basis for each Contract Area on the basis of approved Field Development Plans.

Chapter IV: Transportation

Article 21: Main Pipelines

A. INOC, or the specialized company created by the Ministry, shall own all Main Pipelines. Such Pipelines shall be constructed and operated by the INOC subsidiary representing Transporter for the purpose of transporting Crude Oil or Natural Gas to specified Delivery Points for Crude Oil and Natural Gas respectively. The Ministry in co-ordination with INOC and in consultation with Operators shall ensure that the Main Pipeline network is optimally designed, operated and maintained so as to serve the overall requirement for Petroleum transportation in the Republic of Iraq.

B. The construction and operation of Main Pipeline or any major modification thereof shall be subject to approval by the Ministry on the basis of a Main Pipeline Development Plan outlining the proposed work. If the proposed work is undertaken by the INOC subsidiary company specialized company representing Transporter in association with Iraqi or Foreign Persons, the agreement between the parties shall accompany the Main Pipeline Development Plan. Such agreement shall outline the terms of financing, implementation, and the modalities of utilisation and operation of the new or modified Main Pipeline.

C. INOC and other holders of Exploration and Production right shall deliver Crude Oil and Natural Gas to the Main Pipeline at appropriate Transfer Point(s) In accordance with Article 13A. The transportation of Crude Oil or Natural Gas beyond the Transfer Point shall be carried out by the Designated Authority representing Transporter on the basis of a contract.

D. All the above activities shall be carried out in accordance with Good Pipeline Practices.

E. The co-ordination of tasks related to the transport of Crude Oil through new Pipelines outside the Iraqi territories is the responsibility of the Ministry. The follow up of operations subsequent to the approval of the necessary bilateral agreements shall be the responsibility of INOC in accordance with the said bilateral agreements and any specific instructions from the Ministry.

Article 22: Rights and Obligations Regarding Pipelines

A. The Exploration and Production Contract shall provide a non-exclusive right to access Main Pipelines on reasonable commercial terms. It shall also confer the right to construct and operate Field Pipelines to deliver Crude Oil or Natural Gas from the Contract Area to the Transfer Point, for further transportation through the Main Pipeline to the Delivery Point.

B. INOC and of her holders of Exploration and Production right shall implement the Field Development Plan and construct Field Pipelines connected to the Main Pipeline or the modifications thereto following approval of such plans have been approved by the Ministry.

C. INOC and other holders of Exploration and Production right shall prepare and submit a revised Field Pipeline Development Plan for any material amendment to the original Plan for approval by the Ministry.

D. INOC and other holders of Exploration and Production right shall negotiate with INOC or the specialized company as the Transporter for the right to use the Main Pipeline. The Ministry is to be kept informed on the progress of these negotiations.

E. INOC and other holders of Exploration and Production right shall submit a Decommissioning Plan to the Ministry, not later than two (2) years before the planned termination of Production.

Chapter V: Gas

Article 23: Exploitation of Gas

A. Natural Gas is a valuable Petroleum resource of increasing importance in the economic development of the Republic of Iraq and the Middle East. It shall be utilized to generate additional revenues through optimal utilization partly through improving oil recoveries by gas injection into suitable Reservoirs; through utilization for power generation, utilization in petrochemical and chemical industries, utilization for domestic purposes, utilization in Industrial processes, utilization for export and/or through the replacement of fluid fuels. The latter will have the additional benefit of reducing the impact on the environment while at the same time maximizing revenue by freeing more crude and fuel oil for export.

B. INOC and other holders of Exploration and Production rights shall diligently pursue all alternatives for optimal utilization of surplus volumes of produced gases in accordance with the objectives of Article 23A above. Should they fail to identify commercial utilization, the volumes of surplus Natural Gas shall be offered after treatment to Government at no cost at the Field's outlet. The cost incurred by the holder of Exploration and Production rights shall be recoverable under the respective contract.

Article 24: Associated Gas

A. INOC and other holders of Exploration and Production right are entitled to use, free of charge, the quantity of Associated Natural Gas necessary for Petroleum Operations.

B. INOC and other holders of Exploration and Production rights shall in the Field Development Plan propose optimal plans for the utilization or disposal of Associated Natural Gas.

C. All Associated Natural Gas produced from a Reservoir which is neither used in Petroleum Operations, utilized or re-injected in the Field, shall be offered for delivery free of charge to the Ministry in accordance with Article 23B above.

Article 25: Flaring of Gas

A. Flaring of Natural Gas is only permitted for the purposes of commissioning, testing of installations, safety precautions or while awaiting the completion of transportation facilities provided the flared volumes are strictly kept to a minimum and the Ministry is promptly notified.

B. The flaring of Associated Natural Gas shall be kept to a minimum. It shall not be permitted beyond a maximum period of one (1) year during which measures shall be completed to utilize the gas or deliver it to a nominated government entity in accordance with Article 23B above.

Article 26: Non-associated Gas

A. The Development and Production of Natural Gas or liquid components thereof from a Non-associated Natural Gas Discovery shall be subject to the approval of the Ministry of a Field Development Plan supported by signed agreement(s) for the sale of Natural Gas from the Discovery and approved by the Council of Ministers. In the event that only liquid Petroleum is to be produced, a scheme for the re-injection of Natural Gas or other acceptable schemes for its disposal shall be presented in the Field Development Plan.

B. The flaring of Non-associated Natural Gas may only be permitted in accordance with Article 25B.

Chapter VI: Regulatory Matters

Article 27: Regulations for Petroleum Operations

The Ministry, in coordination and collaboration with the INOC, Regions, and Producing Governorates, shall approve regulations for Petroleum Operations and submit them to the Federal Oil and Gas Council to be approved.

Article 28: Use and Benefit of Land and Rights of Way

A. Land use and benefit for the purpose of conducting Petroleum Operations is regulated by the legislation on land use and benefit, without prejudice to the following provisions.

B. For the purpose of conducting Petroleum Operations, the duration of the right of use and benefit of the land shall be the same as the duration of the Contract.

C. The land where installations are located, and a strip of land, to be defined by regulation, surrounding those Installations, are considered to be a zone of partial protection in accordance with the legislation on land use and benefit.

D. INOC and other holders of a right to conduct Petroleum Operations who, by virtue of the exercise of Petroleum Operation rights in the Contract Area, causes damage to crops, soils, building and improvements or requires the relocation of the legal users or occupants of the land within the respective Contract Area, has the obligation to compensate the holders of title to the assets and the persons relocated.

E. Subject to the payment of the compensation that are due, the holder of the right to conduct Petroleum Operations may require the right of way in accordance with the legislation in force, in order to have access to the locations where Petroleum Operations are conducted.

F. In cases where lands and rights of way are owned by an Iraqi Person, the land shall be either rented or bought by the relevant state owned company, according to the applicable laws and regulations.

Article 29: Access to Zones Subject to Maritime Jurisdiction

The access to Petroleum Operations sites located in interior waters, the territorial waters, and other zones subject to maritime jurisdiction is regulated by law, and any relevant international agreements.

Article 30: Inspection

A. The Designated Authority, or its authorized representatives, has the right to inspect sites, including buildings and installations, where Petroleum Operations are being conducted, as well as all assets, records and data kept by INOC and other holders of Exploration and Production right relating to Petroleum Operations.

B. The Designated Authority may designate an independent entity or a commission created for this purpose, to any out the inspection.

C. The terms and conditions pursuant to which the Inspection is carried out shall be established by regulations.

D. In carrying out its inspections, the Designated Authority shall not unreasonably interfere with the Petroleum Operations.

Article 31: Environmental Protection and Safety

In addition to carrying out their Operations in accordance with Good Oil Field Practices, INOC and other holders of Exploration and Production rights shall conduct Petroleum Operations in accordance with environmental and other applicable legislation of the Republic of Iraq to prevent pollution of air, lands and waters. They shall also conduct Petroleum Operations so as to comply with the environmental management standards of the ISO 14000 series, as amended. In general, they shall carry out Petroleum Operations in order to:

1. Ensure that there is no ecological damage or destruction caused by Petroleum Operations, but where unavoidable, ensure that measures for protection of the environment are in accordance with internationally acceptable standards. For this purpose, INOC and other holders of a right shall prepare and submit to the relevant authorities for approval an environmental impact assessment, including environmental impact mitigation measures, for each major operation in the Contract Area;
2. Notify the Ministry and other specified authorities immediately in the event of an emergency or accident affecting the environment;

3. Control the flow and prevent the escape or loss of Petroleum discovered or produced within the Contract Area;
4. Avoid damage to Petroleum Reservoirs;
5. Avoid destruction to land, the water table, trees, crops, buildings or other Infrastructure and goods;
6. Clean up the sites after the closure of Petroleum Operations and comply with the environmental resolution requirements;
7. Ensure the health and safety of personnel in the planning and conduct of Petroleum Operations, and take preventive measures if their physical safety would be at risk;
8. Report to the competent entity within the government on the amounts of operational and accidental discharge, leakage and waste resulting from Petroleum Operations; and
9. Provide compensation for damages to State and private property in accordance with the applicable laws and regulations.

B. INOC and other holders of a right under this Law shall act in a secure and effective manner when conducting Petroleum Operations. In order to guarantee the disposal of polluted water and waste oil in accordance with approved methods, as well as the safe plugging of all boreholes and wells before these are abandoned.

Article 32: Transfer of Ownership and Decommissioning

A. On completion of the Exploration and Production Contract or Main Pipeline Contract the ownership of all works and facilities shall be transferred to the Designated Entity. The properties shall be transferred to the relevant federal state enterprise or to the Ministry in actual operating condition and in a satisfactory state of work at the time of the transfer.

B. All site relinquishment and related costs that become due at the time of transfer with regards to any works and facilities shall be payable by INOC and other holders of Exploration and Production right according to a Decommissioning Plan, submitted in accordance with Article 9F [should be 14G] of this Law.

C. An outline Decommissioning Plan shall be included in the Field Development Plan submitted by the Contractor to the Council of Ministers.

Chapter VII: Fiscal Regime

Article 33: Taxation

A. INOC and its subsidiary companies as well as other Individual and collective persons who are holders of a right to conduct Petroleum Operations are, subject to the payment of the following fiscal impositions:

1. Royalty;
2. Property Contribution and the Property Transfer Tax (SISA) as established in accordance with the law;
3. municipal and local taxes due; and
4. the taxes provided for in the Income Tax Code.

B. The appropriate monitoring authority is authorized to establish a law regulating methods of taxation, the rates, tax exemptions applicable to Petroleum Exploration, Development and Production activities.

C. The Commission of Financial Audit has the authority to audit the income derived from Petroleum Operations.

D. A Foreign Person may repatriate its exports proceeds in accordance with the foreign exchange regulations in force at the time. It may freely transfer shares in accordance with Article 5C Seven.

Article 34: Royalty

A. INOC and other holders of an Exploration and Production right shall pay a royalty on Petroleum produced from the Development and Production Area, at the rate of twelve point five percent (12.5%) of Gross Production measured at the entry flange to the Main Pipeline.

B. The collection of Royalty shall be in kind or in cash at the option of the Ministry.

C. Where the royalty is paid in cash, it shall be calculated according to the prevailing Market Price in accordance with Petroleum Regulations.

Article 35: Maintaining Records

A. Holders of Exploration and Production right can transfer any net profits from Petroleum Operations to outside Iraq after paying taxes and fees owed.

B. INOC and other holders of Exploration and Production right shall maintain proper records and books in both Arabic and English of accounts in accordance with the provisions of the Contract enabling the relevant calculations to be performed, and in compliance with the requirements of the laws relevant to the taxes referred to in Article 33. INOC and other holders shall prepare and submit to the specialized entity annually, or quarterly, a statement of accounts.

Chapter VIII: Miscellaneous Provisions

Article 36: Transparency

A. All activities related to Oil and Gas, while occurring, have to be transparent and responsible. To ensure this transparency and give the Iraqi people the chance to hold governmental entities responsible for their activities and actions, different sorts of information must be published. This information includes but is not limited to the following:

1. All the revenues, payments and receipts that are delivered to any governmental unit, or entity run by the government, from activities related to Oil or Gas. This includes but is not limited to the income of selling Oil, Gas and their products, signing and production rewards, royalties, revenue of selling assets, taxes, fees, customs and taxes, public services fees, share of profits from oil and gas cartels, commercial activities related to Oil and Gas (and their products) contracts, oil and gas revenue

investment yield, and any other payments resulted from or related to commercial Production of hydrocarbons;

2. The revenues of oil and gas usage and distribution, including distribution among governmental entities;
3. All of the financially significant contracts related to Exploration, Development, processing and marketing of oil and gas resources in Iraq;
4. All of the financially significant contracts related to importing or exporting services and goods for the Oil and Gas industry or by any governmental unit or entity controlled by the government;
5. The annual report of the Federal Oil and Gas Council;
6. The annual and quarterly reports of the INOC, the subsidiary companies, and the entities controlled by the government including the budgets audited according to international accounting standards;
7. All other information necessary for understanding the operations and activities carried out by any governmental unit or entities controlled by the government related to oil and gas;
8. Any information that must be declared in accordance to laws and regulations;
9. Any condition or secret agreement aimed at blocking or trying to block access to documents and information that must be made public in accordance to this Article in violation of the law and is considered void.

B. Publicizing the information stated in Section A of this Article does not extend to and has no effect on the Oil and Gas industry royalties that must be kept secret in accordance to the national or international laws except for financial information.

C. Any person or governmental entity obligated to publish information mentioned in Section A of this Article shall publish it in publicly accessible media.

D. The Ministry shall issue the regulations needed for implementing the laws of this Section including the legal basis covering what should be included and an exempted as mentioned in Section B of this Article.

Article 37: Implementing Anti-corruption Laws

A. Any contractual right shall be considered void if it is in violation of any of the laws of the Republic of Iraq, particularly the Iraqi anti-corruption laws.

B. The authorized person's violation of the Iraqi anti-corruption may lead to the cancellation of his rights contract, in whole or in part. Each rights contract shall include terms indicating these conditions.

C. Any person who violates the Iraqi anti-corruption laws may be prosecuted under the criminal law active in Iraq.

Article 38: Competitive Public Bidding

A. All oil companies working in the Republic of Iraq shall submit public bids on a competitive basis in order to offer any goods or services, and this should occur in accordance to the general bidding laws and the Federal Oil and Gas Council shall determine the maximum amount that can be excluded from the bidding process.

B. Bidding by the holders of Petroleum Operations rights stated in this Law shall be competitive and in accordance with the Petroleum laws and with the special terms of the related contracts.

C. All public bidding must be allowed to the public within a reasonable timeframe must declare thereafter the reasons for selecting the chosen bid, the complete results of the bidding call must also be published, and competitors must be given the opportunity to raise objections.

D. Any contract that is signed in violation of the regulations set by this Article shall be considered void and ineffective.

Article 39: Resolution of Disputes

A. Any disputes arising from the interpretation and application of this Law, the Regulations for Petroleum Operations and the terms and conditions of contracts shall in the first instance be attempted to be resolved in good faith by means of negotiation among the parties.

B. If the dispute cannot be resolved by agreement, the matter shall be referred to the Minister to resolve through discussions with senior officers of the holders of rights concerned. Failing resolution through these discussions the matter of dispute may be submitted to arbitration or to the competent judicial authority.

C. If the dispute relates to a technical, engineering, operational or accounting matter relative to Petroleum Operations and is of a kind that is readily subject to resolution by an expert in the relevant field, the parties may refer the dispute to an independent technical expert for a recommendation as to the resolution of the dispute. If a party does not accept the recommendation of the expert, it may initiate arbitration proceedings according to Article 39D below.

D. Arbitration between the State of Iraq and foreign investors shall be conducted as follows:

1. In accordance with the Rules of Procedure for Arbitration Proceedings of Paris, Geneva or Cairo for the Settlement of Disputes between States and Nationals of other States and based on the Iraqi law.
2. The rules of such other international instances of recognized standing as agreed by the parties to the contracts referred to in this law, provided that the parties have expressly defined in the contract the conditions for Implementation including the method for the designation of the arbitrators and the time limit within which the decision must be made.

Article 40: Existing Contracts

A. The Designated Authority in the Kurdistan Region will take responsibility to review all existing Exploration and Production contracts with any entity before this law enters into force to ensure harmony with the objectives and general provisions of this law to obtain maximum economic returns to the people of Iraq, taking into consideration the prevailing circumstances at the time at which those contracts were agreed, and in a period not exceeding three (3) months from the date of entry into force of this law. The Panel of Independent Advisors will take responsibility to assess the contracts referred to in this Article, and their opinion shall be binding in relation to these contracts.

B. Except for the provision of paragraph A above, the Ministry shall review all the existing Exploration and Production contracts with any entity before this law enters into force to ensure harmony with the objectives and general provisions of this Law. These contracts must then be submitted to the Federal Oil and Gas Council, to ensure and to validate the maximum economic return for the people of Iraq, in a period not exceeding three (3) months from the time the Federal Oil and Gas Council issues model contracts and related regulations. The Federal Oil and Gas Council shall take a decision on the accuracy of the review and validity of the contracts.

Article 41: Changes in Administrative Borders

In the case of changes in borders of Regions or Producing Governorates, or in the case of establishing new Regions, the new affected places shall be dealt with in accordance to the provisions of this Law regarding to granting rights and Petroleum Operations.

Article 42: Relationship to Existing Legislation

Any Article in prejudice to this Law shall cease to be effective on adoption of this Law.

Article 43: Entry into Force

This Law enters into force thirty (30) days after publication in the Official Gazette.

NOTES AND QUESTIONS

1. *Structure.* The Hydrocarbon Draft Law packaged consists of five main parts: (1) Hydrocarbon Law Framework; (2) Revenue Sharing Law with Annexes; (3) INOC (Iraqi National Oil Co.) Reconstitution; (4) a Ministry of Oil Reorganization; (5) a new tax law. The Hydrocarbon law itself covers a motley of legal issues: the organization of various public entities dealing with oil; the contracts from exploration to production and distribution; natural gas and pipelines; and royalties, anti-corruption, and dispute settlement mechanisms. How accessible to the ordinary citizen is such a complex law? Could it be otherwise?

2. *Objective.* The Hydrocarbon Law is supposed to ensure that Iraq's oil and gas are owned by all the people of Iraq; that revenues are shared fairly in proportion to population distribution; help with Iraq's oil industry and encourage foreign investment and expertise in order to jump-start 30 years of stalled progress; make sure that Iraq will not abdicate its sovereignty of control or interest in its oil resources; and allow power sharing by the regions while keeping final authority with the central government.

Is that likely to be achieved? How does the "Oil Revenue Fund" under Art. 11D compare with the Alaska Permanent Fund? Will the Iraqi citizen see an annual oil check arrive in the mail following this law?

3. *Decision-making.* The Hydrocarbon Law expands on Articles 108 to 112 of the Iraqi Constitution. The Council of Ministers is given supreme oversight via an appointed Federal Oil and Gas Council. The MoO (Ministry of Oil) will be the policy setting body. INOC and its subsidiaries will be operating entities, and it will get control of 90 percent of known reserves. Regions will be allowed to contract out exploration and development in new areas. The law will decentralize exploration and development but centralize control of revenue. It ensures transparency (compare the opacity in Iran and Arab oil-producing countries) of contracts, revenues, royalties, etc. Can such a complex arrangement work? Who decides in case of dispute?

4. *Deadlock.* By the end of 2008, the law had still not be adopted, and the Development Fund for Iraq, established in 2003 under American control, was extended another year as the extra-territorial recipient of oil revenues. See Chapter 5. The formula of revenue-sharing since the establishment of the Fund has been 17 percent for the Kurdish Regional Government and 83 percent for the central government.

So why is the proposed legislation controversial? The main disagreement is over the power to grant contracts for the development of oil and gas fields, especially new ones. But the debate over the Hydrocarbon Law taps into several hot issues facing Iraqi society today. Federalism, that is, power sharing between the central government and the regions, is an important factor across the field. Legitimacy of the GoI and its ability to govern is another important factor. Reconciliation between sects, tribes, and political rivals at odds with one another for decades, and private vs. public sector stewardship of natural resources, labor, revenues, and profits are also important variables to consider. Finally, regional disputes, most notably Kirkuk, must be taken into account, together with the urgent obvious need for economic progress and reconstruction as a whole, and the crucial role of oil in a balanced rise of the country from decades of traumas.

5. There is a lot at stake: Iraq's natural oil assets amount to about $500,000 per person. Deputy PM Barham Saleh called the Hydrocarbon Law "the most important law for Iraq after the Constitution." The troubled history of the stewardship of Iraq's oil resources leads to suspicion that these laws are part of a plan to cheat Iraqis out of their birthright. The inherent complexity of the laws invites concern that they can be abused, circumvented, or ignored. How can the hydrocarbon legislation contribute to building up the citizen's understanding and support to Iraq's political leaders?

6. There is concern that Iraq's "brain drain" leaves it without the technical expertise to carry out the law, and some legislators resent being rushed, and insist they will not bow to outside pressure. Still, critics abound on any side; some claim the Hydrocarbon law is a giveaway for big oil and foreign, chiefly U.S., interests while others claim it is too restrictive and will discourage investment. Does that appear in the law? If so, how can it be remedied?

B. WATER

1. RIVERS

The crisis over water in the Iraq is severe, despite the abundance of mountains and two major rivers and their tributaries. Dereliction of infrastructure, positioning downstream from Turkey and Syria, dwindling resources—increasingly affected by pollution, and agricultural/industrial initiatives—have elevated the strategic importance of water in the region. For Iraq, water has become an issue of national security and foreign policy as well as one of domestic stability. Given water's growing ability to redefine interstate relations, the success of future efforts to address water sharing and distribution will hinge upon political and strategic approaches to this diminishing natural resource.

AN INTRODUCTION TO IRAQ'S PROBLEMS AS RIPARIAN DOWNSTREAM STATE

Adapted from www.unesco.org

Turkey and Syria

Along the Tigris and Euphrates Rivers, Turkey, Syria, and Iraq are locked in a mute confrontation over water resources. Relations between the three countries, strained at best, have been exacerbated since the 1980s by growing tensions over water. The Euphrates River (2,815 km) and the Tigris River (1,899 km) are the two principal waterways in Iraq that have defined the country since the rise of civilization. Both rivers originate in Turkey and a substantial part of the Euphrates flows through Syria.

River	Turkey	Syria	Iraq
Euphrates	1,230 (41%)	710 (21%)	1,060 (35%)
Tigris	400 (22%)	44(2%)	1,418 (76%)

In 1980, a Joint Technical Committee on Regional Waters was created by Turkey and Iraq, on the basis of a former protocol (1946) concerning the control and management of the Euphrates and the Tigris. Syria joined the committee afterwards.

The Euphrates represents the most critical issue for Iraq's water strategy as more than 90% of its water comes from outside the country (against only 50% for the Tigris). According to an agreement between Syria and Iraq (1990), Iraq shares the Euphrates' waters with Syria on a 58% (Iraq) and 42% (Syria) basis, based on the flow received by Syria at its border with Turkey. Since Turkey has unilaterally promised to secure a minimum flow of 15.8 km^3/year at its border, this agreement would de facto represent 9 km^3/year for Iraq. This has increased tensions among the countries regarding water management due to Turkey's a major water development project, called the Southeastern Anatolia Project (GAP in Turkish). The Southeast Anatolia Project consists of 15 dams, 14 hydroelectric stations and 19 irrigation projects, therefore seriously limiting water into its neighboring countries.

Turkey disagrees over quotas to meet Syria and Iraq's minimum requirements for what would be the natural flow of the water and what would provide their people with adequate access to those resources, claiming that Syria and Iraq take more than their allotted amount of water from the rivers as compared to how much each country contributes to the rivers' flows.

Syria and Israel — Impact on Iraq

Closely tied to the disputes surrounding Iraq and Syria's water supply is the proximity of both countries to Israel. Syria faces water difficulties on its southwestern border as well in the water-rich area of the Golan Heights, occupied by Israel since 1967. The Golan Heights has important water resources which, according to some Israeli sources, would mean that Israel loses nearly one-third of its fresh water if the Golan is returned to Syria.

The GAP project in Turkey and the irrigation projects in Syria will reduce Iraqi irrigation potential unless an agreement is reached on the sharing of waters between the riparian countries. Since water shortages are forecast to occur with the development of irrigation, solutions have to be found for an integrated basin-level planning of water resources development.

Authorities

In Iraq, the Ministry of Agriculture is responsible for organizing the ownership of agricultural lands, contracts with farmers, cooperatives and agricultural companies in addition to enhancing agricultural investment activities. In particular, the Ministry is responsible for providing agricultural inputs to all farmers, and for marketing the agricultural commodities. In addition, the Ministry of Irrigation [Ministry of Water Resources] is in charge of water resources development, irrigation and drainage development, as well as its operation and maintenance. Its major functions are to assess water requirements and resources, control running water, reservoirs, wetland and marshes, underground water, the construction of dams, canals and drainage systems, soil conservation, classification, land evaluation and use, and research and studies on land and water. Substantial funding will need to be allocated to these bureaus in order for Iraq to properly address this growing crisis.

2. THE MARSHES OF SOUTHERN IRAQ— A SUCCESS STORY?

The 5,000-year-old way of life of the Marsh Arabs, celebrated by Wilfred Thesiger among others, has long been under threat. Its final disappearance is documented in "The Iraqi Marshlands" edited by Emma Nicholson and Peter Clark, and published by Politico's. As the accompanying map suggests, Saddam Hussein's aggressive drainage programme in the 1990s, which had the dual purpose or reclaiming land and pursuing rebels hiding in the waterways, turned much of the marshland into desert, depopulating the area. Some 200,000 of the inhabitants fled, many of them to refugee camps in Iran. The damage is probably irretrievable.

The Economist, Sept. 5, 2002

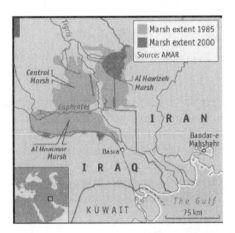

USAID, MARSHLANDS

http://www.usaid.gov/iraq/accomplishments/marsh.html

From 1991 to 2003, the Ba'athist regime nearly destroyed the Mesopotamian Marshlands, one of the largest wetland systems in the world. Massive drainage structures diverted water from 8,000 square miles of marshes. The drainage targeted the unique, 5,000-year-old Marsh Arab society, seen as disloyal and unmanageable after the Shi'a insurrection of 1991. The Ba'athists raided settlements, killed tens of thousands, burned houses, and killed livestock. Already some of the poorest people in Iraq, the Marsh Arabs were exiled or internally displaced. Many escaped to cities, but the fewer than 100,000 that remained were forced to relocate, some as many as 18 times. Currently, water supply is diminishing due to dam construction and expanding irrigation schemes in the Tigris and Euphrates headwaters in Turkey and Syria.

Restoration of the Mesopotamian Marshlands at the confluence of the Tigris and Euphrates in southeastern Iraq carries political, cultural, and economic significance beyond the ecology of the wetland areas. Evidence of the atrocities committed against the marsh dwellers is still apparent. As a consequence of the drainage and destruction, the largely displaced and widely persecuted marsh dwellers still suffer from economic loss, inadequate nutritional intake, and absence of primary health care and acceptable drinking water.

Since 2003, USAID has helped restore Iraq's marshlands and develop the local economy. Reflooding as much as 25 to 30 percent of the original marshlands has been directed by local tribes and MWR. USAID-funded activities include national level as well as local marshland level activities.

In February 2004, an Iraqi and international team, mobilized by USAID's prime contractor, convened in Basra to design an action plan for the Marshlands Restoration Program. The program, led by the Ministry of Water Resources (MOWR) in cooperation with USAID and other donors, will restore the marshland ecosystem through improved management and strategic reflooding in addition to providing social and economic assistance to Marsh Arabs including health, education, and rural development.

Accomplishments

Development of Hydrologic Model of Tigris and Euphrates River Basins. A reservoir simulation model for water allocation and flood control was completed by the U.S. Army Corps of Engineers. Hydrologic Engineering Center where MOWR engineers were trained and can train others in turn. Trainings have also been conducted on stream gauging equipment.

Equipping Ministry of Water Resources Soil and Water Laboratory. Soil testing and water quality equipment is being installed; staff will receive training on operating the equipment.

Monitoring and Development of an Integrated Marsh Management Plan. Rehabilitated the University of Basra laboratory, which monitors four marsh locations and collects data.

Livestock Improvement. Established 30 alfalfa farms in the marshes to provide livestock feed. Established a veterinary service and supply of medicine to treat livestock diseases in marsh settlements. Surveyed animal diseases and treated more than 14,000 animals.

Agriculture Development. Established 72 demonstration farms in the marshes, introducing new crops and improved management practices for sorghum, wheat, barley, and broad beans. Established eight date palm nurseries with 4,500 trees with a 90 percent survival rate.

Fish Restocking. Rehabilitated the Marine Science Center hatchery facilities. Currently breeding high value fish (bunni) to produce native species for release into the marshes.

NOTES AND QUESTIONS

1. Water is vital to the production of oil as well; one barrel of water is required to produce one barrel of oil, therefore placing the burden of Iraq's economy on oil will obviously have severe effects for the rest of country. Iraq has tremendous agriculture prospects, and shouldn't be overshadowed by its oil wealth. How can the equation be drawn between oil, water, and other resources to offer a diversified and healthier economy? Can law help? What sort of arrangements could the upstream countries, Iran, Turkey and Iraq, be prepared to accept?

2. There is much talk about water wars in the region. Professor Tony Allan of the University of London has debunked that myth by underlining the economic dimension of water and coining the concept of "virtual water," which is the amount of water included in a given agricultural crop production. See J.A. Allan, *The Middle East Water Question: Hydro-Politics and the Global Economy* (2001); Virtual Water — The Water, Food and Trade Nexus: Useful Concept or Misleading Metaphor?, 28 *Water International* 4-11 (2001). While some distance to "water wars" as an alarmist catchphrase is needed, both the decline and rise of the price of international foodstuffs directly affect the water component. Tension over water is real. In the case of Iraq, it may not have yet loomed large because of the overwhelming difficulties on other fronts. How can Iraq anticipate the water problem when violence dies down and normal life resumes?

3. Water's growing role in the emerging hydropolitics of the region underlines the need for a new approach to safeguard this diminishing resource. The integration of water into strategic cooperation frameworks that are developing among regional states could facilitate the protection and preservation of water resources. What legal framework is needed for such interaction eventually paving the way for the long-term security of Middle East water? For Iraqi and other precedents in the region, see J.A. Allan & Chibli Mallat eds., *Water in the Middle East: Legal, Political and Commercial Implications* (1995), especially Hasan Chalabi & Tarek Majzoub, *Turkey, the Waters of the Euphrates and Public International Law*, at 189-235; Murat Metin Hakki, *Turkey, Water and the Middle East*, 5 Chinese Journal of International Law 441-458 (2006); M. El-Fadel, Y. El Sayegh, A. Abou Ibrahim, D. Jamali & K. El-Fadl, *The Euphrates-Tigris Basin: A Case Study in Surface Water Conflict Resolution*, 31 Journal of Natural Resources Life Science and Education 99-110 (2002).

4. Domestically, it can be argued that the issue of water, no less than the issue of oil, is an eminently federal problem. The Constitution deals with water in Articles 110.8 and 114.7. In the first article, the federal government has exclusive powers in "[p]lanning policies relating to water sources from outside Iraq and guaranteeing the rate of water flow to Iraq and its just distribution inside Iraq in accordance with international laws and conventions." In the second article, federal and regional authorities "formulate and regulate the internal water resources policy in a way that guarantees their just distribution." This is arguably a better formula than the general one dealing with oil and gas (Art. 111, stating that oil and gas are the property of all Iraqis, and Art. 112, stating that federal and "producing" regional powers

"shall undertake the management of oil and gas" and "shall together formulate the necessary strategic policies to develop the oil and gas.") How the Ministry of Water has succeeded in staving off any major domestic and international disputes over water may have important lessons for federalism in Iraq generally, and the continuously sulfurous debate over oil and gas in particular. What "with" and "together" mean in Art. 112 represent the point of greatest disagreement. Missing in the Iraqi debate is that both oil and water issues, indeed most matters of importance to the country, can be solved only by a *process*, never in one fell swoop under some magic formula or law. The institutional process is called federalism.

5. The Marshlands of Southern Iraq have elicited significant attention in the last two decades because of their dramatic shrinking in connection with the policy of repression of the Iraqi government under Saddam Hussein. Against the dour security and economic situation, and the difficulties Iraq faces as the downstream country for its two large rivers, the reclaiming of the Marshlands may turn into a success story, and has been a focus of the work of the Ministry of Water Resources, led by Dr. Latif Rasheed, an engineer by profession. According to Curtis Richardson et al., "[n]early 20% of the original 15,000-square-kilometer marsh area was reflooded by March 2004, but the extent of marsh restoration is unknown." *The Restoration Potential of the Mesopotamian Marshes of Iraq*, 25 Science 1307-1311 (Feb. 2005). The USAID report claims that 25 to 30 percent of the Marshes had been reclaimed by 2006. For a dedicated resource on the Marshes, see http://www.iraqmarshes.org/. In several conversations with the Minister in early 2009, and in several publications of the Water Ministry, which is acknowledged across Iraq as the most efficient and fair amongst all ministries, Dr. Rasheed has pointed out that current map surveys of the Marshes suggest that 80 percent of the ecological surface that existed prior to the punishment of the Marsh inhabitants by the previous regime has been restored, but that the severe drought in the region over the past three years has allowed only 40 percent to be visible.

C. ECONOMICS IN AN IRAQI CONTEXT

1. AN ISLAMIC ECONOMY? MUHAMMAD BAQER AL-SADR

Is there an Iraqi/Islamic way to approach the economy? The following text was adapted for this book by Isaak Hurst drawing on Western and Islamic economics, respectively Adam Smith as read by former U.S. Federal Reserve Chairman Alan Greenspan in *The Age of Turbulence* (2007), and Muhammad Baqer al-Sadr (d.1980), as read by Chibli Mallat, *The Renewal of Islamic law: Muhammad Baqer as-Sadr, Najaf and the Shi'i International* (2003).

To date, Sadr's *Iqtisaduna* (Our Economy, 1959-61) stands as the most interesting and most comprehensive work written on Islamic economics. In the Muslim world, it has been used in Arab and Iranian circles, and translations in several languages of part or whole of the book have appeared, including two Persian translations, one of which was read in the Iranian *hauzas* (circles of scholars) before the Revolution.

With all its lengthy analyses of land property and the economic system, *Iqtisaduna* did not offer mechanisms that could be applied to an economy in search of precise guidelines. But the richness of the work and its scholarly thoroughness suggest that some paradigms have been established in the field along lines first elaborated in *Iqtisaduna*. The virtues of the book my reside more in these paradigms than in the application of the ideas to the economy of the "Islamic" state. For example, Sadr's "general theory of land ownership," his analysis of the concept of labor, particularly in relation to revival and constant exploitation of land, are reminiscent of the familiar "agrarian question" and its emphasis on the socialistic principle advocating the devolution of land to the peasants. This indeed constitutes an important dilemma for post-war Iraq as it did for post-revolutionary Iran.

For Sadr, revival, with its close connection with the concept of labor, is the root of the general theory of land ownership. With the waning of property rights deriving from "work by conquest," the right to the fruit of land had to be based on the principle of revival and constant exploitation, that is, the laborer who exerts his efforts on raw natural resources owns the fruit of his labor. This is the general opportunity to profit form the wealth one creates.

> The natural effort of every individual to better his own condition, when suffered to exert itself with freedom and security is so powerful a principle, that it is alone, and without an assistance . . . capable of carrying on the society to wealth and prosperity. Every man (consistent with the law) should be free to pursue his own interest his own way.

Adam Smith, *The Wealth of Nations,* quoted in Alan Greenspan, *The Age of Turbulence*, at 262. Smith's insight into the importance of self-interest was all the more revolutionary in that, throughout history in many cultures, acting in one's self-interest — indeed, seeking to accumulate wealth — had been perceived as unseemly and even illegal. Yet, in Smith's view, if government simply provides stability and freedom and otherwise stays out of the way, personal initiative will see to the common good. Or as he put it, "Little else is requisite to carry a state to the highest degree of opulence from the lowest barbarism but peace, easy taxes and a tolerable administration of justice: all the rest being brought about by the natural courts of things." Greenspan, id. at 262.

In the arguments to the advocates of land reform in post-revolutionary Iran, the concept of labor of the exploitation of land and the ownership of its fruit has also been introduced under the more general heading of "social justice." Alongside revival, Sadr also developed a number of legal concepts that put the ruler of the Islamic state, individually as well as institutionally, at the heart of a legal order which is centralized and *dirigiste*. Whenever, possible, Sadr seems to advocate the necessary intervention of the state as the owner of "strategic" resources and as the provider of the lines of economic development and redistribution of wealth. This is mainly true of his theory of land ownership, which was (and remains) a sensitive element in the discussions over the nature and function of the "Islamic state."

The question is whether the individual can own the rights of resources as private property. Here, Sadr classifies minerals based on the amount of labor to render their mineral qualities operational. There are two classifications, "external" and "internal" minerals. External minerals, oil, salt, sulphur, are considered "public property." They are publicly shared among the people, and Islam does not recognize the title of anyone to them. Only the state, or its representative, can exploit them.

> As to private property by which the individual exploit these minerals, they are absolutely forbidden. The most any individual can profit from external minerals is restricted to his personal needs. By contrast, internal minerals, such as iron and gold, are minerals, which require for the manifestation of their qualities to be worked on and developed. Many jurists consider excavation as a form of revival, but puts limits on its ownership. What is included in the property is the mineral discovered by excavation. It does not extent to the depths of the earth, to the ores of the mineral and its roots. . . . This is what is called in *fiqh* the minerals contiguous area, *harim al-ma'dan*.

Mallat, *The Renewal of Islamic Law* at 133-34. This limit once set, Sadr concludes that even with potential privatization, "this kind of property is very clearly different form the ownership of natural resources in the capitalist doctrine, because it is a kind of property which does not differ from being a type of division of labor among the people. It cannot lead to the establishment of private monopolistic enterprise, in the fashion of enterprises in capitalist society." Id.

Summing up the theory of land property, Sadr tries also to connect it to the more general scheme of the system he proposes. Property falls in this scheme with the general theory of distribution before production.

> The land, by nature, is the property of the *imam*. An individual does not possess a right of control, *ruqba*. A personal interest (security, specialization, (*ikhtisas shakhsi*) is not valid, except on the basis of the labor spent by the individual on the land to preparte it (*i'dad*) and exploit it (*istithmar*). This security, or the right gained by an individual as the result of his work does not prevent the *imam* from excising a tax (*tasq*) on the revived land, so that all of mankind can profit from it. This does not prevent [the *imam*] relieving [the laborer] from the duty of *tasq* sometimes, in exceptional circumstances.

Sadr, *Iqtisaduna*, 1977 ed. at 433, quoted by Mallat, *The Renewal of Islamic Law* at 132. In Islamic Iran, there have been in practice several attempts by the advocates of land reform to enforce redistribution of agrarian property, but they have all been systematically undermined by the Council of Guardians. In the first decade of the Revolution, no less than seven such bills, drawn first by the Revolutionary Council (1979-81), then by Parliament, have been passed, then immediately frozen as anti-constitutional. Only in 1986 was a limited bill on "temporary cultivation agricultural land" passed, which survived the opposition of the Council of Guardians. But even in this case, several constitutional hurdles were brought up in the Majlis by the opponents of the bill.

A brief survey of the land reform bills shows the extent of the controversy. As soon as the new regime came to power, the concern for "social justice" that had provided a key ideological tenet in the revolutionary process, and the combination of this theme with land property in the works of Shi'i jurists like the Iraqi Sadr, and the Iranian Taliqani and Beheshti, meant that agrarian reform was high on the agenda. However, the pro-reform advocates in Parliament had been slowly cornered into the evasive concept of necessity as the sole and weak argument for redistribution of land. From the early reforms of 1979-81, which were put to an end by Khumaini, through to 1988, when the Council of Guardians used its power as super-legislator to undermine all Parliamentary bills on land reform, a pattern was slowly established to vindicate the rules of Islamic law as safeguards to private property, however extensive (and unfair) they might seem to be. The opponents of land reform, particularly in the Council of Guardians, slowly asserted the sanctity of private property in Islamic law. Even the supporters of land reform in Parliament had fallen in the legislative grid in which the Council of Guardians ensnared them. When in 1986 they tried to salvage the de facto occupation of "temporary cultivation" land, the only argument left was the weak and unconvincing concept of necessity.

The powerful interest of land owners in Iran, who had by the time Khumaini suspended the first bill prepared by the Revolutionary Council in 1981 regrouped and organized, made certain the *dirigiste* and redistribution theories such as could be found in *Iqtisaduna* would not be applied by the Council of Guardians, which upheld effectively the torch of the sanctity of private property. Parliament was completely paralyzed in its attempt to introduce "social justice" in the countryside. Sadr's theory had been defeated, although many of the concepts discussed in *Iqtisaduna* offered the language of the background polemic and the general paradigms which will continue to impress on the debate.

Against the Iranian development in agrarian reform, *Iqtisaduna* stands as a work favoring a significant interventionist role by the state. The area of discretion of the ruler can be considered large enough to accommodate the advocacy of land reform in Sadr's theory. On the basis of the thrust of Sadr's arguments, advocates of land reform in Iran were able to find comfort in a possible land distribution by the state to landless and needed peasants in the name of social balance.

Protection of property has always been a moving target as the law continually tries to keep up with the nature of economic change. Even in the United States, where property rights are broadly protected, the claims of property owners in New London, Connecticut, whose land was taken over by city government in 2005 for commercial redevelopment, were brought to the U.S. Supreme Court. The Court's ruling in favor of city government provoked loud outcries in the Congress. So it's not surprising that different cultures have different views as to whether and to what extent property should be protected. Alan Greenspan, *The Age of Turbulence*, at 255.

2. IRAQI CIVIL LAW

The above text demonstrates a specific Iraqi-Islamic legal tradition, penned by Sadr, on key economic concepts like ownership of minerals, and the role of labor in land, as well as the role of the state. The next text consists of excerpts from an article by Dan E. Stigall on the civil law of Iraq. It offers a significant contrast in style to the legal framework in Sadr's approach, but it is also strongly rooted in the Iraqi legal tradition.

Dan E. Stigall, A Closer Look at Iraqi Property and Tort Law

68 Louisiana Law Review 766-822 (2008)

A brief outline of Iraq's legal roots is required for any complete discussion of Iraqi law, if only to set the backdrop for the discussion and provide some point of orientation. The territory of modern Iraq has a long and rich legal history that included complex, secular legal regimes such as that of the Mesopotamians and the fifth century Syro-Roman Code. In the early seventh century, however, the legal aspect of the region would be profoundly impacted by the emergence of Islamic law. Although secular legal institutions have long held sway in modern Iraq, the importance of Islam should be kept in mind when pondering contemporary legal institutions — even the most seemingly secular. This is not only because Islamic law still exists as a subsidiary source of law under the Iraqi Civil Code, but also because it allows one to better appreciate the cultural context of Iraqi law and the legal issues under consideration. As Sait and Lim note when discussing property law in the Middle East, [a] lack of engagement with the internal Islamic dialogue risks creating land systems that are bereft of authenticity and legitimacy and thereby of effectiveness and durability. Even where well-intentioned donor-driven efforts to establish modern land systems succeed, the obduracy of informal norms, practices and processes leads to unattended dualisms that undermine the prospect of integrated and unifying land policies.

In the twentieth century, Iraq blended into its legal culture many elements of the continental civil law tradition with the enactment of its modern civil code. The code was principally authored by Abd al-Razzaq Al-Sanhūrī, who was then working as the dean of the Iraqi Law College. Jwaideh notes that as Iraq approached modernity, "[t]he conditions under which [Ottoman law] had been enacted had completely changed and legislation for a new and unified civil code became a necessity." The substance of this new civil code was taken largely from Egyptian law (which mirrored the French civil code), then-existing Iraqi laws (such as those from the *Mejelle* and other Ottoman legislation), and from Islamic law. "The proposal put every effort to coordinate between its provisions which stem from two main sources: Islamic law and Western law, resulting in a synthesis in which the duality of sources and their variance is almost imperceptible."

Property Defined

Before launching into a discussion of the rules governing property, it is prudent to first ascertain the meaning of "property" in the context of Iraqi legal culture. In Islamic law, which influences and informs secular Iraqi civil law, property generally falls under three distinct rubrics of public property, state property, and private property. Property in those categories is further subject to certain land tenure arrangements, such as *mulk* (private full ownership), *miri* (state ownership), *waqf* (endowment), and *metruke* (common land). Private ownership of property is recognized, though with the understanding that everything ultimately belongs to God. Therefore, private property rights may be impinged upon when there is a compelling societal need.

Acquisitive Prescription

One of the fundamental distinctions between Islamic property law and continental civilian property law is the effect of nonuse on property. Islamic property ownership is traditionally tied to use so that nonuse can lead to the loss of ownership. Under traditional civil law principles, however, property ownership is absolute, exclusive, and perpetual so that ownership is never lost by nonuse alone. Despite this difference, some shared tenets subsist. Civil law jurists since the nineteenth century have noted that acquisitive prescription is rooted in the belief that it is in the best interest of society to have property used and maintained rather than to have it abandoned. This is different, but not wholly hostile to Islamic land law, which holds that a landowner who neglects to use land and leaves it uncultivated for three years loses ownership. The emphasis on land use is the same. . . .

In addition to the traditional civilian property rights enumerated above, there exist within the Iraqi Civil Code hosts of property rights that bear no relation to French law but that are vestiges of Iraq's past. These characteristically Middle Eastern legal institutions are blended into the Iraqi Civil Code and are a mark of Al-Sanhūrī's comparativist mastery. A review of these property rights is especially beneficial to Western lawyers and jurists who might be otherwise unfamiliar with them and, therefore, unable to fully understand the opportunities and limitations of agreements for the use of property. . . .

Conclusion

Iraqi property law is based on continental civil law but is heavily influenced by Ottoman law and, to some extent, traditional Islamic legal principles. One even sees glimpses of ancient Mesopotamian law and faintly hears the echoes of Hammurabi. That rich blend supplies Iraqi law with a regime of property law that recognizes and respects private ownership of property, provides mechanisms for protection of property rights, and discourages the forceful and fraudulent taking of property. While maintaining this respect for ownership, however, it still promotes the continued use of property by maintaining a variant of acquisitive prescription—the notion that an adverse possessor can obtain ownership through years of unforced, open, and uninterrupted possession—which is heavily influenced by Islamic property law. It also provides a broad array of property rights and legal devices to allow for full use and exploitation of property, such as lease, use, habitation, loan, and a host of rights and institutions that reflect Iraq's complex and fascinating history and culture.

Iraqi tort law has an equally rich pedigree and has evolved on its own to address the needs of contemporary Iraq. With the potential diminution in legal immunity for contractors and other entities, one may expect to see the increased application of Iraqi law in U.S. courts. Thus, understanding the contours of this magnificent legal landscape can greatly assist both governmental and non-governmental actors in making appropriate choices when operating in modern Iraq.

NOTES AND QUESTIONS

1. Could there be a specific Iraqi way to run the economy? Can either Sadr's *Iqtisaduna* or the Civil Code of Iraq offer useful categories to Iraqi law- and policy-makers? Is confluence possible between Western-style and Islamic economics (or Iraqi economics?)

2. The above excerpts give a brief taste of an expanding field. A lively debate over Islamic economics, including Islamic financial institutions and banks, has been taking place amongst lawyers and economists. See Haidar Ali Hamoudi, *You Say You Want a Revolution: Interpretive Communities and the Origins of Islamic Finance*, 48 Virginia Journal of International Law 250-306 (2008); *Muhammad's Social Justice or Muslim Cant?: Langdellianism and the Failures of Islamic Finance*, 40 Cornell International Law Journal 89-134 (2006); see also Hamoudi's blog at muslimlawprof.org. See also Ibrahim Warde, *Islamic Finance in the Global Economy* (2000); Timur Kuran, *Islam and Mammon: The Economic Predicaments of Islamism* (2004). How difficult is an Iraqi application, both as a traumatized country and an oil-based economy?

SECURITY

Introduction. American and Iraqi officials regularly contend that the situation in Iraq has progressed. Such statements elicit a valid question from reasonable people: progress relative to what? In 2008, life in Iraq is arguably better than it was at the height of the insurgency, from 2005 to 2007, or markedly worse than previous to the rise of the insurgency, from April 2003 to March 2004. One could argue that chaos cannot legitimately function as a standard for measurement. The more optimistic journalists and politicians stumble from six months to six months ("the next six months will be crucial . . ."), while countless books and articles appearing between 2005 and 2008 oscillate between considering Iraq as a new Vietnam or a failed state. On the failed state side, the most interesting works are by Peter Galbraith, *The End of Iraq* (2006), which controversially argues for the division of Iraq along ethnic and religious lines; Charles Ferguson, *No End in Sight, Iraq's Descent into Chaos* (2008), an offshoot of a 2007 PBS television program with interviews. On the replication of Vietnam, see George Packer, *The Assassins' Gate* (2008); Michael Isikoff & David Corn, *Hubris* (2006); Gwynne Dyer, *After Iraq: Anarchy and Renewal in the Middle East* (2008). And lastly, for a viewpoint from a former supporter of the war, see Fred Kaplan, *Daydream Believers: How a Few Grand Ideas Wrecked American Power* (2008), in addition to many other contributions cited elsewhere in this book. U.S. political decision-making in Afghanistan then Iraq during the Bush administration was followed carefully, with the corresponding growing disillusion, in the trilogy of Bob Woodward, *Bush at War* (2002); *Plan of Attack* (2004); and *State of Denial* (2006). A remarkable insight on the ideology and network of the so-called "neocons" is James Mann, *The Rise of the Vulcans* (2004), which shows the significant difference in outlook between six key figures in Bush's "war cabinet." With the perceived success of the 2007 surge, no doubt more books will appear on the possible or impending "victory," while former officials, still at the second level, are starting to contribute tomes drawn from their experience, including books in 2008 by Scott McClellan, former White House press secretary, and Douglas Feith, former number three at the Pentagon. A subtle book by a connoisseur of the Arab world is by Fouad Ajami, *The Foreigner's Gift: The Americans, the Arabs, and the Iraqis in Iraq* (2006). There is still too little in English (and in Arabic) from an Iraqi perspective. The former finance minister Ali Allawi (see Chapter 6), the Iraqi ambassadors to Washington, Samir Sumaidei (Sumayde') and to the UN, Hamed Bayyati, Deputy Prime Minister Barham Saleh, and former National Security Council advisor Muwaffaq Rubaei (al-Rubay'i) have all been articulate figures on the English-speaking media scene, as has naturally been the Foreign Minister, Hoshyar Zibari. One hopes they and their colleagues will find the time to put their thought and experience to paper.

Eventually, informed biographies and autobiographies will shed light on the history of important opposition leaders, many of whom held key positions in government after the fall of Saddam Hussein. A synopsis of the then Iraqi opposition can be found in Mallat, The Middle East into the 21st Century 71-125 (1996). A masterful description of the Iraqi Kurdish leadership is in Jonathan Randal, *After Such Knowledge, What Forgiveness?* (1999). An interesting, but sometimes inaccurate, biography of one of the main protagonists in the Iraqi opposition, then in government, is by Aram Roston, *The Man Who Pushed Bmerica to War: The Extraordinary Life, Adventures and Obsessions of Ahmad Chalabi* (2008). The march to Saddam's removal from power, which started in American in August 1990, is yet to be written. Of note is the passage by Congress in 1998, under the Clinton Administration, of the Iraq Liberation Act.

A. THE SECURITY SITUATION IN IRAQ

1. INSURGENCY AND COUNTERINSURGENCY

This section cannot give the security and ongoing changes in Iraq the treatment necessary; it requires an expertise in intelligence and military matters which, in an ongoing war, is elusive to the public. Emphasis is therefore on two aspects: the overall security situation with a few telling maps, and the choice of two contrastive testimonies: a unique missive intercepted in 2004, showing the pattern of sectarian strife advocated by Abu Mus'ab al-Zarqawi, probably the most lethal Islamist leader in post-Saddam Iraq, and, in counterpoint, the counter-insurgency philosophy of General David Petraeus, the key military commander in Baghdad in 2007-2008, through a manual for the army published in late 2006 under his signature.

(a) Insurgency: The Zarqawi Letter

LETTER BY ABU MUS'AB AL-ZARQAWI

Translation by the State Department, www.state.gov/p/nea/rls/31694.htm.[*]

In February 2004, an emissary of the leader of al-Qa'eda in Iraq, Jordanian Abu Mus'ab al-Zarqawi, was arrested en route to Osama bin Laden. He was (allegedly) carrying the following letter from Zarqawi to Usama ben Laden, an intimate assessment of the situation in Iraq. Zarqawi was killed on June 8, 2006.

> In the name of God, the Merciful, the Compassionate,
> From .... to the proudest of persons and leaders in the age of the servants,
> .... To the men on the mountain tops, to the hawks of glory, to the lions of [the] Shara [Mountains], to the two honorable brothers ....,
> Peace and the mercy and blessings of God be upon you.

Even if our bodies are far apart, the distance between our hearts is close.

Our solace is in the saying of the Imam Malik. I hope that both of us are well. I ask God the Most High, the Generous, [to have] this letter reach you clothed in the garments of health and savoring the winds of victory and triumph. .... Amen.

I send you an account that is appropriate to [your] position and that removes the veil and lifts the curtain from the good and bad [that are] hidden in the arena of Iraq.

---

*Also available at http://www.globalsecurity.org/wmd/library/news/iraq/2004/02/040212-al-zarqawi.htm/.

As you know, God favored the [Islamic] nation with jihad on His behalf in the land of Mesopotamia. It is known to you that the arena here is not like the rest. It has positive elements not found in others, and it also has negative elements not found in others. Among the greatest positive elements of this arena is that it is jihad in the Arab heartland. It is a stone's throw from the lands of the two Holy Precincts and the al-Aqsa [Mosque]. We know from God's religion that the true, decisive battle between infidelity and Islam is in this land, i.e., in [Greater] Syria and its surroundings. Therefore, we must spare no effort and strive urgently to establish a foothold in this land. Perhaps God may cause something to happen thereafter. The current situation, o courageous shaykhs, makes it necessary for us to examine this matter deeply, starting from our true Law and the reality in which we live. . . .

Here is the current situation as I, with my limited vision, see it. I ask God to forgive my prattle and lapses. I say, having sought help from God, that the Americans, as you know well, entered Iraq on a contractual basis and to create the State of Greater Israel from the Nile to the Euphrates and that this Zionized American Administration believes that accelerating the creation of the State of [Greater] Israel will accelerate the emergence of the Messiah. It came to Iraq with all its people, pride, and haughtiness toward God and his Prophet. It thought that the matter would be somewhat easy. Even if there were to be difficulties, it would be easy. But it collided with a completely different reality. The operations of the brother mujahidin began from the first moment, which mixed things up somewhat. Then, the pace of operations quickened. This was in the Sunni Triangle, if this is the right name for it. This forced the Americans to conclude a deal with the Shi`a, the most evil of mankind. The deal was concluded on [the basis that] the Shi`a would get two-thirds of the booty for having stood in the ranks of the Crusaders against the mujahidin.

First: The Makeup [of Iraq]

In general, Iraq is a political mosaic, an ethnic mixture, and scattered confessional and sectarian disparities that only a strong central authority and a overpowering ruler have been able to lead, beginning with Ziyad Ibn Abihi (tr. note: 7th century A.D.) and ending with Saddam. The future faces difficult choices. It is a land of great hardships and difficulties for everyone, whether he is serious or not. . . .

As for the details:

1. The Kurd

In their two Barazani and Talabani halves, these have given the bargain of their hands and the fruit of their hearts to the Americans. They have opened their land to the Jews and become their rear base and a Trojan horse for their plans. They (the Jews) infiltrate through their lands, drape themselves in their banners, and take them as a bridge over which to cross for financial control and economic hegemony, as well as for the espionage base for which they have built a large structure the length and breadth of that land. In general, Islam's voice has died out among them — the Kurds–and the glimmer of religion has weakened in their homes. The Iraqi Da`wa has intoxicated them, and the good people among them, few as they are, are oppressed and fear that birds will carry them away.

3. The Shi`a

[They are] the insurmountable obstacle, the lurking snake, the crafty and malicious scorpion, the spying enemy, and the penetrating venom. We here are entering a battle on two levels. One, evident and open, is with an attacking enemy and patent infidelity. [Another is] a difficult, fierce battle with a crafty enemy who wears the garb of a friend, manifests agreement, and calls for comradeship, but harbors ill will and twists up peaks and crests (?). Theirs is the legacy of the Batini bands that traversed the history of Islam and left scars on its face that time cannot erase. The unhurried observer and inquiring onlooker will realize that Shi`ism is the looming danger and the true challenge. "They are the enemy. Beware of them. Fight them. By God, they lie." History's message is validated by the testimony of the current situation, which informs most clearly that Shi`ism is a religion that has nothing in common with Islam except in the way that Jews have something in common with Christians under the banner of the People of the Book. From patent polytheism, worshipping at graves, and circumambulating shrines, to calling the Companions [of the Prophet] infidels and insulting the mothers of the believers and the elite of this [Islamic] nation, [they] arrive at distorting the Qur'an as a product of logic to defame those who know it well, in addition to speaking of the infallibility of the [Islamic] nation, the centrality of believing in them, affirming that revelation came down to them, and other forms of infidelity and manifestations of atheism with which their authorized books and original sources — which they continue to print, distribute, and publish — overflow. The dreamers who think that a Shi`i can forget [his] historical legacy and [his] old black hatred of the Nawasib [those who hate the Prophet's lineage], as they fancifully call them, are like someone who calls on the Christians to renounce the idea of the crucifixion of the Messiah. Would a sensible person do this? These are a people who added to their infidelity and augmented their atheism with political cunning and a feverish effort to seize upon the crisis of governance and the balance of power in the state, whose features they are trying to draw and whose new lines they are trying to establish through their political banners and organizations in cooperation with their hidden allies the Americans.

These [have been] a sect of treachery and betrayal throughout history and throughout the ages. It is a creed that aims to combat the Sunnis. When the repulsive Ba`thi regime fell, the slogan of the Shi`a was "Revenge, revenge, from Tikrit to al-Anbar." This shows the extent of their hidden rancor toward the Sunnis. However, their religious and political "ulama" have been able to control the affairs of their sect, so as not to have the battle between them and the Sunnis become an open sectarian war, because they know that they will not succeed in this way. They know that, if a sectarian war was to take place, many in the [Islamic] nation would rise to defend the Sunnis in Iraq. Since their religion is one of dissimulation, they maliciously and cunningly proceeded another way. They began by taking control of the institutions of the state and their security, military, and economic branches. As you, may God preserve you, know, the basic components of any country are security and the economy. They are deeply embedded inside these institutions and branches. I give an example that brings the matter home: the Badr Brigade, which is the military wing of the Supreme Council of the Islamic Revolution, has shed its Shi'a garb and put on the garb of the police and army in its place. They have placed cadres in these institutions, and, in the name of preserving the homeland and the citizen, have begun to settle their scores with the Sunnis. The American army has begun to disappear from some cities, and its presence is rare. An Iraqi army has begun to take its place, and this is the real problem that we face, since our combat against the Americans is something easy. The enemy is apparent, his back is exposed, and he does not know the land or the current situation of the mujahidin because his intelligence information is weak. We know for certain that these Crusader forces will disappear tomorrow or the day after. He who looks at the current situation [will] see the enemy's haste to constitute the army and the police, which have begun to carry out the missions assigned to them. This enemy, made up of the Shi'a filled out with Sunni agents, is the real danger that we face, for it is [made up of] our fellow countrymen, who know us inside and out. They are more cunning than their Crusader masters, and they have begun, as I have said, to try to take control of the security situation in Iraq. They have liquidated many Sunnis and many of their Ba'th Party enemies and others beholden to the Sunnis in an organized, studied way. They began by killing many mujahid brothers, passing to the liquidation of scientists, thinkers, doctors, engineers, and others. I believe, and God knows best, that the worst will not come to pass until most of the American army is in the rear lines and the secret Shi'i army and its military brigades are fighting as its proxy. They are infiltrating like snakes to reign over the army and police apparatus, which is the strike force and iron fist in our Third World, and to take complete control over the economy like their tutors the Jews. As the days pass, their hopes are growing that they will establish a Shi'i state stretching from Iran through Iraq, Syria, and Lebanon and ending in the Cardboard Kingdom of the Gulf. The Badr Brigade entered carrying the slogan of revenge against Tikrit and al-Anbar, but it shed its garb and then put on the emblem[s] of the army and police to oppress the Sunnis and kill the people of Islam in the name of law and order, all under cover of smooth talk. The noxiousness of falsehood rides the horse of dissimulation. Their Ghunusi religion (one based on special personal enlightenment) veils itself with lies and covers itself with hypocrisy, exploiting the naivete and good-heartedness of many Sunnis. We do not know when our [Islamic] nation will begin to learn from historical experience and build on the testimony of the empty eras. The Shi'i Safavid state was an insurmountable obstacle in the path of Islam. Indeed it was a dagger that stabbed Islam and its people in the back. One of the Orientalists spoke truth when he said that had the Safavid state not existed we in Europe would today be reading the Qur'an just as the Algerian Berber does. Yes, the hosts of the Ottoman state stopped at the gates of Vienna, and those fortifications almost collapsed before them [to permit] Islam to spread under the auspices of the sword of glory and jihad all across Europe. But these armies were forced to return and withdraw to the rear because the army of the Safavid state had occupied Baghdad, demolished its mosques, killed its people, and captured its women and wealth. The armies returned to defend the sanctuaries and people of Islam. Fierce fighting raged for about two centuries and did not end until the strength and reach of the Islamic state had waned and the [Islamic] nation had been put to sleep, then to wake up to the drums of the invading Westerner.

The Qur'an has told us that the machinations of the hypocrites, the deceit of the fifth column, and the cunning of those of our fellow countrymen whose tongues speak honeyed words but whose hearts are those of devils in the bodies of men — these are where the disease lies, these are the secret of our distress, these are the rat of the dike. "They are the enemy. Beware of them." Shaykh al-Islam Ibn Taymiyya spoke with truth and honesty when he said — after he mentioned their (Shi'a) thinking toward the people of Islam — "For this reason, with their malice and cunning, they help the infidels against the Muslim mass[es], and they are one of the greatest reasons for the eruption of Genghis Khan, the king of the infidels, into the lands of Islam, for the arrival of Hulagu in the country of Iraq, for the taking of Aleppo and the pillage of al-Salihiyya, and for other things. For this reason, they pillaged the troops of the Muslims when they passed among them going to Egypt the first time. And for this reason, they commit highway robbery against the Muslims. And for this reason, help for the Tartars and Franks appeared from among them against the Muslims. Deep sadness over the victory of Islam appeared, since they were friends with the Jews, Franks, and polytheists against the Muslims. These are among the customs of the hypocrites. . . . Their hearts are full of vinegar and ire like no others with regard to Muslims old and young, godly and ungodly.

Their greatest [act of] worship is to curse the Muslim friends of God from first to last. These are the people most anxious to divide the Muslims. Among their greatest principles are leveling charges of infidelity and damning and cursing the elite of those who have ruled matters, like the orthodox caliphs and the 'ulama' of the Muslims, because of their belief that anyone who does not believe in the infallible imam, who is not present, does not believe in God and his Prophet, may God bless him and grant him salvation. . . .

The Shi'a love the Tartars and their state because through it they achieved a glory that they did not achieve through the Muslims' state. . . . They were among the greatest helpers [of the Tartars] as they seized the countries of Islam, killing Muslims and capturing their women. The story of Ibn al-'Alqami and his like with the Caliph and their case in Aleppo is famous. All the people know it. If the Muslims defeat the Christians and polytheists, this causes distress among the Shi'a. And if the polytheists and Christians beat the Muslims, this occasions a holiday and joy among the Shi'a." — al-Fatawa, part 28, pages 478 to 527.

Praise be to God, it is as if veils had been lifted from the hidden for him (Ibn Taymiyya) and he looked at what was before him and then spoke clearly on the basis of observation and information. Our imams have traced a clear path and lifted the veil from these people. Imam al-Bukhari says, not in the house have I prayed behind a Shi'i or behind Jews or Christians. They are not to be greeted. They are not to be congratulated on holidays. They are not to be taken in marriage. They cannot bear witness. The animals they slaughter are not to be eaten. — Khalq Af'al al-'Ibad, page 125.

Imam Ahmad says — he was asked about who had cursed Abu Bakr, 'Umar, and 'A'isha, may God be pleased with them — "I do not see him within Islam."

Imam Malik says, "He who curses the Companions of the Prophet, may God bless him and grant him salvation, has no share or part in Islam." — Kitab al-Sunna of al-Khallal, number 779.

Al-Farabi says, "I do not see the Shi`a except as atheists." — al-Lalika'i, part 8, page 1545.

And when Ibn Hazm brought evidence and proofs against the Jews and Christians for distorting the Torah and the Gospel, they found no retort except to say that the Shi`a among them spoke of distortions to the Qur'an. "He said, God's mercy! When they speak of the claim of the Shi`a that substitution has occurred, the Shi`a are not Muslims. They are a sect that follows the path of the Jews and Christians in lying and infidelity." — al-Fasl, part 2, page 78.

Ibn Taymiyya said, "With this, it becomes clear that they are more evil than the sectarians and more deserving of being fought than the Kharijis. This is the reason for the general opinion that circulates that the Shi`a are people of heresy. The populace spreads around that Shi`i is the opposite of Sunni because they show resistance to the sunna of the Prophet of God, may God bless him and grant him salvation, and to the Laws of Islam." — from Sa'ir Ahl al-Ahwa', part 28, page 482.

And he said, "If the sunna and ijma` are in agreement that — if [the spirit of] the Muslim attacker could [only] come out by killing, then he should be killed, even if the property that he took was [but] a fraction of a dinar — how could it be with regard to fighting those who deviate from the Laws of Islam and fight God and His Prophet, may God bless him and grant him salvation?" — part 4, page 251.

And with all this, let the people of Islam know that we are not the first to have begun going down this road. We are not the first to have brandished the sword. These people (the Shi`a) are continuing to kill those who call for Islam and the mujahidin of the community, stabbing them in the back under cover of the silence and complicity of the whole world, and, regretfully, even of the symbolic figures beholden to the Sunnis.

Moreover, they are a bone in the throats of the mujahidin and a dagger in [the backs of] their leading personalities. People without exception know that most of the mujahidin who have fallen in war have done so at the hands of these people. The wounds are still spreading, and they are working the daggers of hatred and cunning in them assiduously, Night or day, they do not let up.

2. As regards the Sunnis

They are more wretched than orphans at the tables of the depraved. They have lost the[ir] leader and wandered in the desert of artlessness and negligence divided and fragmented, having lost the unifying head who gathered the scattered [pieces] and prevented the egg from shattering. They also are [various] kinds.

1. The Masses

These masses are the silent majority, absent even though present. "The hooligans following everyone and his brother hungered. They did not seek enlightenment from the light of science and did not take refuge in a safe corner." These, even if in general they hate the Americans, wish them to vanish and to have their black cloud dissolve. But, despite that, they look forward to a sunny tomorrow, a prosperous future, a carefree life, comfort, and favor. They look ahead to that day and are thus easy prey for cunning information [media] and political enticement whose hiss rings out. . . . In any event, they are people of Iraq.

2. The Shaykhs and "Ulama"

These are mostly Sufis doomed to perdition. Their part of religion is an anniversary in which they sing and dance to the chanting of a camel driver, with a fatty banquet at the end. In truth, these are narcotic opiate[s] and deceitful guides for an [Islamic] nation that is feeling its way on a pitch-black night. As for the spirit of jihad and the jurisprudence of martyrdom and disavowal of the infidel, they are innocent of all of that, just as the wolf was innocent of the blood of Joseph, may peace be upon him. With all the horrors and bad circumstances, not one of them ever speaks about jihad or calls for sacrifice or self-sacrifice. For these, three is too much, not to say four. They are not suited to this.

3. The [Muslim] Brothers

As you have observed, they make a profession of trading in the blood of martyrs and build their counterfeit glory on the skulls of the faithful. They have debased the horse, put aside arms, said "no jihad" . . . and lied.

Their whole effort is to extend political control and seize the posts of Sunni representation in the government cake whose creation has been decided, while taking care in secret to get control of the mujahidin groups through financial support for two purposes. The first is for propaganda and media work abroad to attract money and sympathy, exactly as they did during the events in Syria, and the second is to control the situation and dissolve these groups when the party ends and the gifts are distributed. They are now intent on creating a Sunni shura body to speak in the name of the Sunnis. It is their habit to grab the stick in the middle and change as the political climate changes. Their religion is mercurial. They have no firm principles, and they do not start from enduring legal bases. God is the one from whom we have sought help.

D. The Mujahidin

These are the quintessence of the Sunnis and the good sap of this country. In general, they belong to the Sunni doctrine and naturally to the Salafi creed. The Salafis splintered only as the bend curved, and the people of the [distant] regions fell behind the caravan. In general, these mujahidin distinguish themselves by the following:

1. Most of them have little expertise or experience, especially in organized collective work. Doubtlessly, they are the result of a repressive regime that militarized the country, spread dismay, propagated fear and dread, and destroyed confidence among the people. For this reason, most of the groups are working in isolation, with no political horizon, farsightedness, or preparation to inherit the land. Yes, the idea has begun to ripen, and a light whisper has arisen to become noisy talk about the need to band together and unite under one banner. But matters are

still in their initial stages. With God's praise, we are trying to ripen them quickly.

2. Jihad here unfortunately [takes the form of] mines planted, rockets launched, and mortars shelling from afar. The Iraqi brothers still prefer safety and returning to the arms of their wives, where nothing frightens them. Sometimes the groups have boasted among themselves that not one of them has been killed or captured. We have told them in our many sessions with them that safety and victory are incompatible, that the tree of triumph and empowerment cannot grow tall and lofty without blood and defiance of death, that the [Islamic] nation cannot live without the aroma of martyrdom and the perfume of fragrant blood spilled on behalf of God, and that people cannot awaken from their stupor unless talk of martyrdom and martyrs fills their days and nights. The matter needs more patience and conviction. [Our] hope in God is great.

E. The Immigrant Mujahidin

Their numbers continue to be negligible as compared to the enormity of the expected battle. We know that the convoys of good are many, that the march of jihad continues, and that only confusion over the banner and a muffled reality keep many of them from [answering] the call to battle. What prevents us from [calling] a general alert is that the country has no mountains in which we can take refuge and no forests in whose thickets we can hide. Our backs are exposed and our movements compromised. Eyes are everywhere. The enemy is before us and the sea is behind us. Many an Iraqi will honor you as a guest and give you shelter as a peaceable brother. As for making his house into a base for launching [operations] and a place of movement and battle, this is rarer than red sulphur. For this reason, we have worn ourselves out on many occasions sheltering and protecting the brothers. This makes training the green newcomers like wearing bonds and shackles, even though, praise be to God and with relentless effort and insistent searching, we have taken possession of growing numbers of locations, praise be to God, to be base sites for brothers who are kindling [the fire of] war and drawing the people of the country into the furnace of battle so that a real war will break out, God willing.

Second: The Current Situation and the Future

There is no doubt that the Americans' losses are very heavy because they are deployed across a wide area and among the people and because it is easy to procure weapons, all of which makes them easy and mouth-watering targets for the believers. But America did not come to leave, and it will not leave no matter how numerous its wounds become and how much of its blood is spilled. It is looking to the near future, when it hopes to disappear into its bases secure and at ease and put the battlefields of Iraq into the hands of the foundling government with an army and police that will bring the behavior of Saddam and his myrmidons back to the people. There is no doubt that the space in which we can move has begun to shrink and that the grip around the throats of the mujahidin has begun to tighten. With the deployment of soldiers and police, the future has become frightening.

Third: So Where Are We?

Despite the paucity of supporters, the desertion of friends, and the toughness of the times, God the Exalted has honored us with good harm to the enemy. Praise be to God, in terms of surveillance, preparation, and planning, we have been the keys to all of the martyrdom operations that have taken place except those in the north. Praise be to God, I have completed 25 [operations] up to now, including among the Shi`a and their symbolic figures, the Americans and their soldiers, the police and soldiers, and the coalition forces. God willing, more are to come. What has prevented us from going public is that we have been waiting until we have weight on the ground and finish preparing integrated structures capable of bearing the consequences of going public so that we appear in strength and do not suffer a reversal. We seek refuge in God. Praise be to God, we have made good strides and completed important stages. As the decisive moment approaches, we feel that [our] body has begun to spread in the security vacuum, gaining locations on the ground that will be the nucleus from which to launch and move out in a serious way, God willing.

Fourth: The Work Plan

After study and examination, we can narrow our enemy down to four groups.

1. The Americans

These, as you know, are the most cowardly of God's creatures. They are an easy quarry, praise be to God. We ask God to enable us to kill and capture them to sow panic among those behind them and to trade them for our detained shaykhs and brothers.

2. The Kurds

These are a lump [in the throat] and a thorn whose time to be clipped has yet to come. They are last on the list, even though we are making efforts to harm some of their symbolic figures, God willing.

3. Soldiers, Police, and Agents

These are the eyes, ears, and hands of the occupier, through which he sees, hears, and delivers violent blows. God willing, we are determined to target them strongly in the coming period before the situation is consolidated and they control arrest[s].

4. The Shi`a

These in our opinion are the key to change. I mean that targeting and hitting them in [their] religious, political, and military depth will provoke them to show the Sunnis their rabies ... and bare the teeth of the hidden rancor working in their breasts. If we succeed in dragging them into the arena of sectarian war, it will become possible to awaken the inattentive Sunnis as they feel imminent danger and annihilating death at the hands of these Sabeans. Despite their weakness and fragmentation, the Sunnis are the sharpest blades, the most determined, and the most loyal when they meet those

Batinis (Shi`a), who are a people of treachery and cowardice. They are arrogant only with the weak and can attack only the broken-winged. Most of the Sunnis are aware of the danger of these people, watch their sides, and fear the consequences of empowering them. Were it not for the enfeebled Sufi shaykhs and [Muslim] Brothers, people would have told a different tale.

This matter, with the anticipated awaking of the slumberer and rousing of the sleeper, also includes neutralizing these [Shi`a] people and pulling out their teeth before the inevitable battle, along with the anticipated incitement of the wrath of the people against the Americans, who brought destruction and were the reason for this miasma. The people must beware of licking the honeycomb and enjoying some of the pleasures from which they were previously deprived, lest they surrender to meekness, stay on the[ir] land, prefer safety, and turn away from the rattle of swords and the neighing of horses.

5. The Work Mechanism

Our current situation, as I have previously told you, obliges us to deal with the matter with courage and clarity and to move quickly to do so because we consider that [unless we do so] there will be no result in which religion will appear. The solution that we see, and God the Exalted knows better, is for us to drag the Shi`a into the battle because this is the only way to prolong the fighting between us and the infidels. We say that we must drag them into battle for several reasons, which are:

1 — They, i.e., the Shi`a, have declared a secret war against the people of Islam. They are the proximate, dangerous enemy of the Sunnis, even if the Americans are also an archenemy. The danger from the Shi`a, however, is greater and their damage is worse and more destructive to the [Islamic] nation than the Americans, on whom you find a quasi-consensus about killing them as an assailing enemy.

2 — They have befriended and supported the Americans and stood in their ranks against the mujahidin. They have spared and are still sparing no effort to put an end to the jihad and the mujahidin.

3 — Our fighting against the Shi`a is the way to drag the [Islamic] nation into the battle. We speak here in some detail. We have said before that the Shi`a have put on the uniforms of the Iraqi army, police, and security [forces] and have raised the banner of preserving the homeland and the citizen. Under this banner, they have begun to liquidate the Sunnis under the pretext that they are saboteurs, remnants of the Ba`th, and terrorists spreading evil in the land. With strong media guidance from the Governing Council and the Americans, they have been able to come between the Sunni masses and the mujahidin. I give an example that brings the matter close to home in the area called the Sunni Triangle — if this is the right name for it. The army and police have begun to deploy in those areas and are growing stronger day by day. They have put chiefs [drawn] from among Sunni agents and the people of the land in charge. In other words, this army and police may be linked to the inhabitants of this area by kinship, blood, and honor. In truth, this area is the base from which we set out and to which we return. When the Americans

disappear from these areas — and they have begun to do so — and these agents, who are linked by destiny to the people of the land, take their place, what will our situation be?

If we fight them [and we must fight them], we will confront one of two things. Either:

1 — We fight them, and this is difficult because of the gap that will emerge between us and the people of the land. How can we fight their cousins and their sons and under what pretext after the Americans, who hold the reins of power from their rear bases, pull back? The real sons of this land will decide the matter through experience. Democracy is coming, and there will be no excuse thereafter.

2 — We pack our bags and search for another land, as is the sad, recurrent story in the arenas of jihad, because our enemy is growing stronger and his intelligence data are increasing day by day. By the Lord of the Ka`ba, [this] is suffocation and then wearing down the roads. People follow the religion of their kings. Their hearts are with you and their swords are with Bani Umayya (the Umayyads), i.e., with power, victory, and security. God have mercy.

I come back and again say that the only solution is for us to strike the religious, military, and other cadres among the Shi`a with blow after blow until they bend to the Sunnis. Someone may say that, in this matter, we are being hasty and rash and leading the [Islamic] nation into a battle for which it is not ready, [a battle] that will be revolting and in which blood will be spilled. This is exactly what we want, since right and wrong no longer have any place in our current situation. The Shi`a have destroyed all those balances. God's religion is more precious that lives and souls. When the overwhelming majority stands in the ranks of truth, there has to be sacrifice for this religion. Let blood be spilled, and we will soothe and speed those who are good to their paradise. [As for] those who, unlike them, are evil, we will be delivered from them, since, by God, God's religion is more precious than anything and has priority over lives, wealth, and children. The best proof [of this] is the story of the Companions of the Ditch, whom God praised. [Imam] al-Nawawi said that this story contained proof that, if the city and the desert fought each other until all without exception perished unless they professed belief in the oneness of God, this would be good. Persons live, blood is saved, and honor is preserved only by sacrifice on behalf of this religion. By God, o brothers, with the Shi`a, we have rounds, attacks, and dark nights that we cannot postpone under any circumstances. Their danger is imminent, and what we and you feared is most certainly a reality. Know that those [Shi`a] are the most cowardly of God's creatures and that killing their leaders will only increase their weakness and cowardice, since with the death of one of their leaders the sect dies with him. It is not like when a Sunni leader dies. If one dies or is killed, a sayyid arises. In their fighting, they bring out courage and hearten the weak among the Sunnis. If you knew the fear [that exists] among the Sunnis and their masses, your eyes would cry over them in sadness. How many mosques have been converted into Husayniyyas (Shi`i mosques), how many houses have they demolished on the heads of their occupants, how many brothers have they killed and mutilated, and how many sisters have had their honor defiled at the hands of these depraved infidels? If we are able to strike them with one painful blow after another until they enter the battle, we will be able to [re]shuffle the cards. Then, no value or influence will remain to the Governing Council or even to the Americans, who will enter a second battle with the Shi`a. This is what we want, and, whether they like it or not, many Sunni areas will stand with the mujahidin. Then, the mujahidin will have assured themselves land from which to set forth in striking the Shi`a in their heartland, along with a clear media orientation and the creation of strategic depth and reach among the brothers outside [Iraq] and the mujahidin within.

1 — We are striving urgently and racing against time to create companies of mujahidin that will repair to secure places and strive to reconnoiter the country, hunting the enemy — Americans, police, and soldiers — on the roads and lanes. We are continuing to train and multiply them. As for the Shi`a, we will hurt them, God willing, through martyrdom operations and car bombs.

2 — We have been striving for some time to observe the arena and sift the those who work in it in search of those who are sincere and on the right path, so that we can cooperate with them for the good and coordinate some actions with them, so as to achieve solidarity and unity after testing and trying them. We hope that we have made good progress. Perhaps we will decide to go public soon, even if in a gradual way, so that we can come out into the open. We have been hiding for a long time. We are seriously preparing media material that will reveal the facts, call forth firm intentions, arouse determination, and be[come] an arena of jihad in which the pen and the sword complement each other.

3 — This will be accompanied by an effort that we hope will intensify to expose crippling doubts and explain the rules of shari`a through tapes, printed materials, study, and courses of learning [meant] to expand awareness, anchor the doctrine of the unity of God, prepare the infrastructure, and meet [our] obligation.

5 [sic] — The Timing for Implementation. It is our hope to accelerate the pace of work and that companies and battalions with expertise, experience, and endurance will be formed to await the zero hour when we will begin to appear in the open, gain control the land at night, and extend it into daylight, the One and Conquering God willing. We hope that this matter, I mean the zero hour, will [come] four months or so before the promised government is formed. As you can see, we are racing against time. If we are able, as we hope, to turn the tables on them and thwart their plan, this will be good. If the other [scenario] [happens] — and we seek refuge in God — and the government extends its control over the country, we will have to pack our bags and break camp for another land in which we can resume carrying the banner or in which God will choose us as martyrs for his sake.

6 — What About You? You, gracious brothers, are the leaders, guides, and symbolic figures of jihad and battle. We do not see ourselves as fit to challenge you, and we have never striven to achieve glory for ourselves. All that we hope is that we will be the spearhead, the enabling vanguard,

and the bridge on which the [Islamic] nation crosses over to the victory that is promised and the tomorrow to which we aspire. This is our vision, and we have explained it. This is our path, and we have made it clear. If you agree with us on it, if you adopt it as a program and road, and if you are convinced of the idea of fighting the sects of apostasy, we will be your readied soldiers, working under your banner, complying with your orders, and indeed swearing fealty to you publicly and in the news media, vexing the infidels and gladdening those who preach the oneness of God. On that day, the believers will rejoice in God's victory. If things appear otherwise to you, we are brothers, and the disagreement will not spoil [our] friendship. [This is a cause in which] we are cooperating for the good and supporting jihad. Awaiting your response, may God preserve you as keys to good and reserves for Islam and its people. Amen, amen.

Peace and the mercy and blessings of God be upon you.

(b) Counterinsurgency: The Petraeus Doctrine, FM 3-24

FM 3-24, a "Field Manual" entitled "Counterinsurgency" (COIN in abbreviation), was published by the Pentagon on December 15, 2006. It is a major strategic document for modern warfare by the most powerful army in the world. Its importance in the Iraqi context comes from the fact that its chief author, David Petraeus (with James Amos as co-author), was appointed in 2007 as the head of American military operations in Iraq. FM 3-24, a long and detailed document (282 pages), is the official U.S. military blueprint for counterinsurgency. In the following excerpts, note central departures from received military strategy in five key areas: (a) political primacy; (b) popularity of local government (Host Nation, HN) as main criterion for success of COIN; (c) initiative and adaptability in military operations; (d) importance of legal framework; (e) Iraq as a privileged testing ground, which shows in the large number of illustrations from the Iraqi theater, of which three are provided in the following excerpts.

GENERAL DAVID H. PETRAEUS, COUNTERINSURGENCY

FM 3-24

Ironically, the nature of counterinsurgency presents challenges to traditional lessons-learned systems; many nonmilitary aspects of COIN do not lend themselves to rapid tactical learning. As this publication explains, performing the many nonmilitary tasks in COIN requires knowledge of many diverse, complex subjects. These include governance, economic development, public administration, and the rule of law. Commanders with a deep-rooted knowledge of these subjects can help subordinates understand challenging, unfamiliar environments and adapt more rapidly to changing situations. Reading this publication is a first stop to developing this knowledge.

1-3. Political power is the central issue in insurgencies and counterinsurgencies; each side aims to get the people to accept its governance or authority as legitimate. Insurgents use all available tools — political (including diplomatic), informational (including appeals to religious, ethnic, or ideological beliefs), military, and economic — to overthrow the existing authority. This authority may be an established government or an interim governing body. Counterinsurgents, in turn, use all instruments of national power to sustain the established or emerging government and reduce the likelihood of another crisis emerging.

1-4.   Long-term success in COIN depends on the people taking charge of their own affairs and consenting to the government's rule. Achieving this condition requires the government to eliminate as many causes of the insurgency as feasible. This can include eliminating those extremists whose beliefs prevent them from ever reconciling with the government. Over time, counterinsurgents aim to enable a country or regime to provide the security and rule of law that allow establishment of social services and growth of economic activity. COIN thus involves the application of national power in the political, military, economic, social, information, and infrastructure fields and disciplines. Political and military leaders and planners should never underestimate its scale and complexity; moreover, they should recognize that the Armed Forces cannot succeed in COIN alone.

1-14.   Before most COIN operations begin, insurgents have seized and exploited the initiative, to some degree at the least. Therefore, counterinsurgents undertake offensive and defensive operations to regain the initiative and create a secure environment. However, killing insurgents — while necessary, especially with respect to extremists — by itself cannot defeat an insurgency. Gaining and retaining the initiative requires counterinsurgents to address the insurgency's causes through stability operations as well. This initially involves securing and controlling the local populace and providing for essential services. As security improves, military resources contribute to supporting government reforms and reconstruction projects. As counterinsurgents gain the initiative, offensive operations focus on eliminating the insurgent cadre, while defensive operations focus on protecting the populace and infrastructure from direct attacks. As counterinsurgents establish military ascendancy, stability operations expand across the area of operations (AO) and eventually predominate. Victory is achieved when the populace consents to the government's legitimacy and stops actively and passively supporting the insurgency.

1-28.   Organizations like the Irish Republican Army, certain Latin American groups, and some Islamic extremist groups in Iraq have pursued an urban approach. This approach uses terrorist tactics in urban areas to accomplish the following:

> Sow disorder.
> Incite sectarian violence.
> Weaken the government.
> Intimidate the population.
> Kill government and opposition leaders.
> Fix and intimidate police and military forces, limiting their ability to respond to attacks.
> Create government repression.

1-29. Protracted urban terrorism waged by small, independent cells requires little or no popular support. It is difficult to counter. Historically, such activities have not generated much success without wider rural support. However, as societies have become more urbanized and insurgent networks more sophisticated, this approach has become more effective. When facing adequately run internal security forces, urban insurgencies typically assume a conspiratorial cellular structure recruited along lines of close association—family, religious affiliation, political party, or social group.

1-42. In times of turmoil, political, social, security, and economic benefits can often entice people to support one side or the other. Ideology and religion are means of persuasion, especially for the elites and leadership. In this case, legitimacy derives from the consent of the governed, though leaders and led can have very different motivations. In Iraq, for example, an issue that motivated fighters in some Baghdad neighborhoods in 2004 was lack of adequate sewer, water, electricity, and trash services. Their concerns were totally disconnected from the overall Ba'athist goal of expelling U.S. forces and retaining Sunni Arab power.

1-73. Many contemporary insurgencies are identity-based. These insurgencies are often led by traditional authority figures, such as tribal sheikhs, local warlords, or religious leaders. As the Indonesian Dar 'ul Islam rebellions of 1948 and 1961 demonstrate, traditional authority figures often wield enough power to single-handedly drive an insurgency. This is especially true in rural areas. Identity-focused insurgencies can be defeated in some cases by co-opting the responsible traditional authority figure; in others, the authority figures have to be discredited or eliminated. Accurately determining whether a leader can be co-opted is crucial. Failed attempts to co-opt traditional leaders can backfire if those leaders choose to oppose the counterinsurgency. Their refusal to be co-opted can strengthen their standing as they gain power and influence among insurgents.

[Illustration 1] The Capture of Saddam Hussein (p. 210)

The capture of Saddam Hussein in December 2003 was the result of hard work along with continuous intelligence gathering and analysis. Each day another piece of the puzzle fell into place. Each led to coalition forces identifying and locating more of the key players in the insurgent network—both highly visible ones like Saddam Hussein and the lesser ones who sustained and supported the insurgency. This process produced detailed diagrams that showed the structure of Hussein's personal security apparatus and the relationships among the persons identified.

The intelligence analysts and commanders in the 4th Infantry Division spent the summer of 2003 building link diagrams showing everyone related to Hussein by blood or tribe. Those family diagrams led counterinsurgents to the lower level, but nonetheless highly trusted, relatives and clan members harboring Hussein and helping him move around the countryside. The circle of bodyguards and mid-level military officers, drivers, and gardeners protecting Hussein was described as a "Mafia organization," where access to Hussein controlled relative power within the network.

Over days and months, coalition forces tracked how the enemy operated. Analysts traced trends and patterns, examined enemy tactics, and related enemy tendencies to the names and groups on the tracking charts. This process involved making continual adjustments to the network template and constantly determining which critical data points were missing. Late in the year, a series of operations produced an abundance of new intelligence about the insurgency and Hussein's whereabouts. Commanders then designed a series of raids to capture key individuals and leaders of the former regime who could lead counterinsurgents to him. Each mission gained additional information, which shaped the next raid. This cycle continued as a number of mid-level leaders of the former regime were caught, eventually leading coalition forces into Hussein's most trusted inner circle and finally to Hussein's capture.

B-46. Figure B-10 shows a simple, social network of key individuals and relationships. The nodes in this data set are from a modified, subnetwork of the link diagram representing Saddam Hussein and his connections to various family members, former regime members, friends, and associates. The original diagram contained hundreds of names and took shape on a large 36-by-36-inch board. Each "box" in the network contained personal information on a particular individual. This information included roles and positions of certain people within the network—for example, chief of staff, chief of operations, and personal secretary. These were not necessarily positions the individuals occupied before the fall of Hussein; rather they were based on an understanding of the role they were filling in the insurgency or Saddam's underground operations. Analysts assigned these roles based on an assessment of various personalities and recent reports. Such a process helped coalition forces focus their efforts in determining those who were closest to Hussein and their importance.

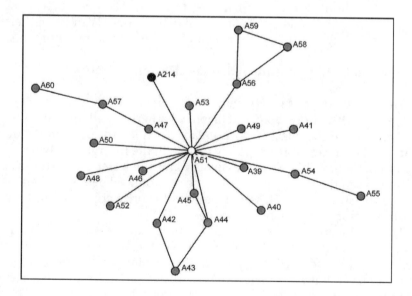

Political Factors Are Primary

1-123. General Chang Ting-chen of Mao Zedong's central committee once stated that revolutionary war was 80 percent political action and only 20 percent military. Such an assertion is arguable and certainly depends on the insurgency's stage of development; it does, however, capture the fact that political factors have primacy in COIN. At the beginning of a COIN operation, military actions may appear predominant as security forces conduct operations to secure the populace and kill or capture insurgents; however, political objectives must guide the military's approach. Commanders must, for example, consider how operations contribute to strengthening the HN [Host Nation] government's legitimacy and achieving U.S. political goals. This means that political and diplomatic leaders must actively participate throughout the conduct (planning, preparation, execution, and assessment) of COIN operations. The political and military aspects of insurgencies are so bound together as to be inseparable. Most insurgent approaches recognize that fact. Military actions executed without properly assessing their political effects at best result in reduced effectiveness and at worst are counterproductive. Resolving most insurgencies requires a political solution; it is thus imperative that counterinsurgent actions do not hinder achieving that political solution.

1-132. Illegitimate actions are those involving the use of power without authority—whether committed by government officials, security forces, or counterinsurgents. Such actions include unjustified or excessive use of force, unlawful detention, torture, and punishment without trial. Efforts to build a legitimate government though illegitimate actions are self-defeating, even against insurgents who conceal themselves amid noncombatants and flout the law. Moreover, participation in COIN operations by U.S. forces must follow United States law, including domestic laws, treaties to which the United States is party, and certain HN laws. Any human rights abuses or legal violations committed by U.S. forces quickly become known throughout the local populace and eventually around the world. Illegitimate actions undermine both long- and short-term COIN efforts.

1-134. Insurgencies are protracted by nature. Thus, COIN operations always demand considerable expenditures of time and resources. The populace may prefer the HN government to the insurgents; however, people do not actively support a government unless they are convinced that the counterinsurgents have the means, ability, stamina, and will to win. The insurgents' primary battle is against the HN government, not the United States; however, U.S. support can be crucial to building public faith in that government's viability. The populace must have confidence in the staying power of both the counterinsurgents and the HN government. Insurgents and local populations often believe that a few casualties or a few years will cause the United States to abandon a COIN effort. Constant reaffirmations of commitment, backed by deeds, can overcome that perception and bolster faith in the steadfastness of U.S. support. But even the strongest U.S. commitment will not succeed if the populace does not perceive the HN government as having similar will and stamina. U.S. forces must help create that capacity and sustain that impression.

1-136. At the strategic level, gaining and maintaining U.S. public support for a protracted deployment is critical. Only the most senior military officers are involved in this process at all. It is properly a political activity. However, military leaders typically take care to ensure that their actions and statements are forthright. They also ensure that the conduct of operations neither makes it harder for elected leaders to maintain public support nor undermines public confidence.

1-139. U.S. forces start with a built-in challenge because of their reputation for accomplishment, what some call the "man on the moon syndrome." This refers to the expressed disbelief that a nation able to put a man on the moon cannot quickly restore basic services. U.S. agencies trying to fan enthusiasm for their efforts should avoid making unrealistic promises.

1-147. U.S. forces committed to a COIN effort are there to assist a HN government. The long-term goal is to leave a government able to stand by itself. In the end, the host nation has to win on its own. Achieving this requires development of viable local leaders and institutions. U.S. forces and agencies can help, but HN elements must accept responsibilities to achieve real victory. While it may be easier for U.S. military units to conduct operations themselves, it is better to work to strengthen local forces and institutions and then assist them. HN governments have the final responsibility to solve their own problems. Eventually all foreign armies are seen as interlopers or occupiers; the sooner the main effort can transition to HN institutions, without unacceptable degradation, the better.

TABLE 1-1. Successful and Unsuccessful Counterinsurgency Operational Practices

Successful practices	*Unsuccessful practices*
• Emphasize intelligence. • Focus on the population, its needs, and its security. • Establish and expand secure areas. • Isolate insurgents from the populace (population control).	• Overemphasize killing and capturing the enemy rather than securing and engaging the populace. • Conduct large-scale operations as the norm. • Concentrate military forces in large bases for protection.

Successful practices	*Unsuccessful practices*
• Conduct effective, pervasive, and continuous information operations. • Provide amnesty and rehabilitation for those willing to support the new government. • Place host-nation police in the lead with military support as soon as the security situation permits. • Expand and diversify the host-nation police force. • Train military forces to conduct counterinsurgency operations. • Embed quality advisors and special forces with host-nation forces. • Deny sanctuary to insurgents. • Encourage strong political and military cooperation and information sharing. • Secure host-nation borders.	• Focus special forces primarily on raiding. • Place low priority on assigning quality advisors to host-nation forces. • Build and train host-nation security forces in the U.S. military's image. • Ignore peacetime government processes, including legal procedures. • Allow open borders, airspace, and coastlines.

2-5.   Durable policy success requires balancing the measured use of force with an emphasis on nonmilitary programs. Political, social, and economic programs are most commonly and appropriately associated with civilian organizations and expertise; however, effective implementation of these programs is more important than who performs the tasks. If adequate civilian capacity is not available, military forces fill the gap. COIN programs for political, social, and economic well-being are essential to developing the local capacity that commands popular support when accurately perceived. COIN is also a battle of ideas.

2-35.   When contractors or other businesses are being paid to support U.S. military or other government agencies, the principle of unity of command should apply. Commanders should be able to influence contractors' performance through U.S. Government contract supervisors. When under contract to the United States, contractors should behave as an extension of the organizations or agencies for which they work. Commanders should identify contractors operating in their AO and determine the nature of their contract, existing accountability mechanisms, and appropriate coordination relationships.

2-36.   Sovereignty issues are among the most difficult for commanders conducting COIN operations, both in regard to forces contributed by other nations and by the host nation. Often, commanders are required to lead through coordination, communication, and consensus, in addition to traditional command practices. Political sensitivities must be acknowledged. Commanders and subordinates often act as diplomats as well as warriors. Within military units, legal officers and their staffs are particularly valuable for clarifying legal arrangements with the host nation. To avoid adverse effects on operations, commanders should address all sovereignty issues through the chain of command to the U.S. Ambassador. As much as possible, sovereignty issues should be addressed before executing operations. Examples of key sovereignty issues include the following:

> Aerial ports of debarkation.
> Basing.
> Border crossings.
> Collecting and sharing information.
> Protection (tasks related to preserving the force).
> Jurisdiction over members of the U.S. and multinational forces.
> Location and access.
> Operations in the territorial waters, both sea and internal.
> Overflight rights.
> Police operations, including arrest, detention, penal, and justice
>   authority and procedures.
> Railheads.
> Seaports of debarkation.

Militias of various ethnic and political groups formed in Iraq during Operation Iraqi Freedom. If militias are outside the HN government's control, they can often be obstacles to ending an insurgency.

Militias may become more powerful than the HN government, particularly at the local level. They may also fuel the insurgency and a precipitate a downward spiral into full-scale civil war.

3-113. Militias may or may not be an immediate threat to U.S. forces; however, they constitute a long-term threat to law and order. The intelligence staff should track them just like insurgent and other armed groups. Commanders need to understand the role militias play in the insurgency, the role they play in politics, and how they can be disarmed.

3-137. Detainees and insurgent defectors are important HUMINT sources. The information they provide about the internal workings of an insurgency may be better than any other HUMINT source can provide. In addition, defectors can provide otherwise unobtainable insights into an insurgent organization's perceptions, motivations, goals, morale, organization, and tactics. Both detainees and defectors should be thoroughly questioned on all aspects of an insurgency discussed in section II. Their answers should be considered along with information obtained from captured equipment, pocket litter, and documents to build a better understanding of the insurgency. Properly trained Soldiers and Marines can conduct immediate tactical questioning of detainees or defectors. However, only trained HUMINT personnel are legally authorized to conduct interrogations. A trained debriefer should be used for questioning a defector. All questioning of detainees is conducted to comply with U.S. law and regulation, international law, execution orders and other operationally specific guidelines.

[Illustration 2] Iterative Design During Operation Iraqi Freedom II (p. 99)

During Operation Iraqi Freedom II (2004-2005), the 1st Marine Division employed an operational design similar to that used during the Philippine Insurrection (circa 1902). The commanding general, Major General James N. Mattis, USMC, began with an assessment of the people that the Marines, Soldiers, and Sailors would encounter within the division's area of operations. The area of operations was in western Iraq/Al Anbar Province, which had a considerably different demographic than the imam-led Shia areas in which the division had operated during Operation Iraqi Freedom I.

Major General Mattis classified provincial constituents into three basic groups: the tribes, former regime elements, and foreign fighters. The tribes constituted the primary identity group in western Iraq/Al Anbar Province. They had various internal tribal affiliations and looked to a diverse array of sheiks and elders for leadership. The former regime elements were a minority that included individuals with personal, political, business, and professional ties to the Ba'ath Party. These included civil servants and career military personnel with the skills needed to run government institutions. Initially, they saw little gain from a democratic Iraq. The foreign fighters were a small but dangerous minority of transnational Islamic subversives.

To be successful, U.S. forces had to apply a different approach to each of these groups within the framework of an overarching plan. As in any society, some portion of each group included a criminal element, further complicating planning and interaction. Major General Mattis's vision of resolution comprised two major elements encompassed in an overarching "bodyguard" of information operations.

The first element and main effort was diminishing support for insurgency. Guided by the maxims of "first do no harm" and "no better friend–no worse enemy," the objective was to establish a secure local environment for the indigenous population so they could pursue their economic, social, cultural, and political well-being and achieve some degree of local normalcy. Establishing a secure environment involved both offensive and defensive combat operations with a heavy emphasis on training and advising the security forces of the fledgling Iraqi government. It also included putting the populace to work. Simply put, an Iraqi with a job was less likely to succumb to ideological or economic pressure to support the insurgency. Other tasks included the delivery of essential services, economic development, and the promotion of governance. All were geared towards increasing employment opportunities and furthering the establishment of local normalcy.

Essentially, diminishing support for insurgency entailed gaining and maintaining the support of the tribes, as well as converting as many of the former regime members as possible. "Fence-sitters" were considered a winnable constituency and addressed as such. The second element involved neutralizing the bad actors, a combination of irreconcilable former regime elements and foreign fighters. Offensive combat operations were conducted to defeat recalcitrant former regime members. The task was to make those who were not killed outright see the futility of resistance and give up the fight. With respect to the hard-core extremists, who would never give up, the task was more straightforward: their complete and utter destruction. Neutralizing the bad actors supported the main effort by improving the local security environment. Neutralization had to be accomplished in a discrete and discriminate manner, however, in order to avoid unintentionally increasing support for insurgency.

5-38. Insurgents use unlawful violence to weaken the HN government, intimidate people into passive or active support, and murder those who oppose the insurgency. Measured combat operations are always required to address insurgents who cannot be co-opted into operating inside the rule of law. These operations may sometimes require overwhelming force and the killing of fanatic insurgents. However, COIN is "war amongst the people." Combat operations must therefore be executed with an appropriate level of restraint to minimize or avoid injuring innocent people. Not only is there a moral basis for the use of restraint or measured force; there are practical reasons as well. Needlessly harming innocents can turn the populace against the COIN effort. Discriminating use of fires and calculated, disciplined response should characterize COIN operations. Kindness and compassion can often be as important as killing and capturing insurgents.

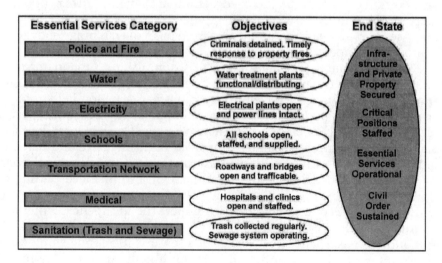

Essential Services Category	Objectives	End State
Police and Fire	Criminals detained. Timely response to property fires.	Infra-structure and Private Property Secured
Water	Water treatment plants functional/distributing.	
Electricity	Electrical plants open and power lines intact.	Critical Positions Staffed
Schools	All schools open, staffed, and supplied.	Essential Services Operational
Transportation Network	Roadways and bridges open and trafficable.	
Medical	Hospitals and clinics open and staffed.	Civil Order Sustained
Sanitation (Trash and Sewage)	Trash collected regularly. Sewage system operating.	

TABLE 5-7. Example Progress Indicators

- **Acts of violence** (numbers of attacks, friendly/host-nation casualties).
- **Dislocated civilians**. The number, population, and demographics of dislocated civilian camps or the lack thereof are a resultant indicator of overall security and stability. A drop in the number of people in the camps indicates an increasing return to normalcy. People and families exiled from or fleeing their homes and property and people returning to them are measurable and revealing.
- **Human movement and religious attendance**. In societies where the culture is dominated by religion, activities related to the predominant faith may indicate the ease of movement and confidence in security, people's use of free will and volition, and the presence of freedom of religion. Possible indicators include the following:
  - ☐ Flow of religious pilgrims or lack thereof.
  - ☐ Development and active use of places of worship.
  - ☐ Number of temples and churches closed by a government.
- **Presence and activity of small- and medium-sized businesses**. When danger or insecure conditions exist, these businesses close. Patrols can report on the number of businesses that are open and how many customers they have. Tax collections may indicate the overall amount of sales activity.
- **Level of agricultural activity**.
  - ☐ Is a region or nation self-sustaining, or must life-support type foodstuffs be imported?
  - ☐ How many acres are in cultivation? Are the fields well maintained and watered?
  - ☐ Are agricultural goods getting to market? Has the annual need increased or decreased?
- **Presence or absence of associations**. The formation and presence of multiple political parties indicates more involvement of the people in government. Meetings of independent professional associations demonstrate the viability of the middle class and professions. Trade union activity indicates worker involvement in the economy and politics.
- **Participation in elections,** especially when insurgents publicly threaten violence against participants.
- **Government services available**. Examples include the following:
  - ☐ Police stations operational and police officers present throughout the area.
  - ☐ Clinics and hospitals in full operation, and whether new facilities sponsored by the private sector are open and operational.
  - ☐ Schools and universities open and functioning.
- **Freedom of movement of people, goods, and communications**. This is a classic measure to determine if an insurgency has denied areas in the physical, electronic, or print domains.
- **Tax Revenue**. If people are paying taxes, this can be an indicator of host-nation government influence and subsequent civil stability.

- Industry exports.
- Employment/unemployment rate.
- Availability of electricity.
- Specific attacks on infrastructure.

[Illustration 3] Clear-Hold-Build in Tal Afar (p. 124-25)

In early 2005, the city of Tal Afar in northern Iraq had become a focal point for Iraqi insurgent efforts. The insurgents tried to assert control over the population. They used violence and intimidation to inflame ethnic and sectarian tensions. They took control of all schools and mosques, while destroying police stations. There were frequent abductions and executions. The insurgents achieved some success as the populace divided into communities defined by sectarian boundaries. Additionally, Tal Afar became an insurgent support base and sanctuary for launching attacks in the major regional city of Mosul and throughout Nineveh province. During the summer of 2005, the 3d Armored Cavalry Regiment (ACR) assumed the lead for military efforts in and around Tal Afar. In the months that followed, the 3d ACR applied a clear-hold-build approach to reclaim Tal Afar from the insurgents.

Destruction or Expulsion of Insurgent Forces (Clear)

In August 2005, the 3d ACR and Iraqi forces began the process of destroying the insurgency in Tal Afar. Their first step was to conduct reconnaissance to understand the enemy situation; understand the ethnic, tribal, and sectarian dynamics; and set the conditions for effective operations. Iraqi security forces and U.S. Soldiers isolated the insurgents from external support by controlling nearby border areas and creating an eight-foot-high berm around the city. The berm's purpose was to deny the enemy freedom of movement and safe haven in outlying communities. The berm prevented free movement of fighters and weapons and forced all traffic to go through security checkpoints manned by U.S. and Iraqi forces. Multinational checkpoints frequently included informants who could identify insurgents. Multinational forces supervised the movement of civilians out of contentious areas. Forces conducted house-to house searches. When they met violent resistance, they used precision fires from artillery and aviation. Targets were chosen through area reconnaissance operations, interaction with the local populace, and information from U.S. and Iraqi sources. Hundreds of insurgents were killed or captured during the encirclement and clearing of the city. Carefully controlled application of violence limited the cost to residents.

Deployment of Security Forces (Hold)

Following the defeat of enemy fighters, U.S. and Iraqi forces established security inside Tal Afar. The security forces immediately enhanced personnel screening at checkpoints based on information from the local population. To enhance police legitimacy in the people's eyes, multinational forces began recruiting Iraqi police from a more diverse, representative mix comprising city residents and residents of surrounding communities. Police recruits received extensive training in a police academy. U.S. forces and the Iraqi Army also trained Iraqi police in military skills. Concurrently, the local and provincial government dismissed or prosecuted Iraqi police involved in offenses against the populace. The government assigned new police leaders to the city from Mosul and other locations. U.S. forces assisted to ensure Iraqi Army, police, and their own forces shared common boundaries and were positioned to provide mutual support to one another. At the same time, U.S. forces continued to equip and train a border defense brigade, which increased the capability to interdict the insurgents' external support. Among its successes, the multinational force destroyed an insurgent network that included a chain of safe houses between Syria and Tal Afar.

Improving Living Conditions and Restoring Normalcy (Build)

With insurgents driven out of their city, the local population accepted guidance and projects to reestablish control by the Iraqi government. The 3d ACR commander noted, "The people of Tal Afar understood that this was an operation for them—an operation to bring back security to the city." With the assistance of the Department of State and the U.S. Agency for International Development's Office of Transition Initiatives, efforts to reestablish municipal and economic systems began in earnest. These initiatives included providing essential services (water, electricity, sewage, and trash collection), education projects, police stations, parks, and reconstruction efforts. A legal claims process and compensation program to address local grievances for damages was also established. As security and living conditions in Tal Afar improved, citizens began providing information that helped eliminate the insurgency's infrastructure. In addition to information received on the streets, multinational forces established joint coordination centers in Tal Afar and nearby communities that became multinational command posts and intelligence-sharing facilities with the Iraqi Army and the Iraqi police. Unity of effort by local Iraqi leaders, Iraqi security forces, and U.S. forces was critical to success. Success became evident when many families who had fled the area returned to the secured city.

Detention and Interrogation

7-38. Detentions and interrogations are critical components to any military operation. The nature of COIN operations sometimes makes it difficult to separate potential detainees from innocent bystanders, since insurgents lack distinctive uniforms and deliberately mingle with the local populace. Interrogators are often under extreme pressure to get information that can lead to follow-on operations or save the lives of noncombatants, Soldiers, or Marines. While enemy prisoners in conventional war are considered moral and legal equals, the moral and legal status of insurgents is ambiguous and often contested. What is not ambiguous is the legal obligation of Soldiers and Marines to treat all prisoners and detainees according to the law. All captured or detained personnel, regardless of status, shall be treated humanely, and in accordance with the Detainee Treatment Act of 2005 and DODD 2310.01E. No person in the custody or under the control of DOD, regardless of nationality or physical location, shall be subject to torture or cruel, inhuman, or degrading treatment or punishment, in accordance with, and as defined in, U.S. law. (Appendix D provides more guidance on the legal issues concerning detention and interrogation.)

Limits on Detention

7-39. Mistreatment of noncombatants, including prisoners and detainees is illegal and immoral. It will not be condoned. The Detainee Treatment Act of 2005 makes the standard clear:

> *No person in the custody or under the effective control of the Department of Defense or under detention in a Department of Defense facility shall be subject to any treatment or technique of interrogation not authorized by and listed in the United States Army Field Manual on Intelligence Interrogation [FM 2-22.3].*
>
> *No individual in the custody or under the physical control of the United States Government, regardless of nationality or physical location, shall be subject to cruel, inhuman, or degrading treatment or punishment.*

7-42. Abuse of detained persons is immoral, illegal, and unprofessional. Those who engage in cruel or inhuman treatment of prisoners betray the standards of the profession of arms and U.S. laws. They are subject to punishment under the Uniform Code of Military Justice. The Geneva Conventions, as well as the Convention against Torture and Other Cruel, Inhuman or Degrading Treatment or Punishment, agree on unacceptable interrogating techniques. Torture and cruel, inhuman, and degrading treatment is never a morally permissible option, even if lives depend on gaining information. No exceptional circumstances permit the use of torture and other cruel, inhuman, or degrading treatment. Only personnel trained and certified to interrogate can conduct interrogations. They use legal, approved methods of convincing enemy prisoners of war and detainees to give their cooperation. Interrogation sources are detainees, including enemy prisoners of war. (FM 2-22.3 provides the authoritative doctrine and policy for interrogation. Chapter 3 and appendix D of this manual also address this subject.)

NOTES AND QUESTIONS

1. Zarqawi's letter is a chilling premonition of the descent into chaos in Iraq that followed the capture of its bearer, who was allegedly taking it from

Zarqawi to Ben Laden. The author of this book was in Baghdad when the letter was intercepted causing a severe shock in society, and he discussed it with Jalal Talibani, the Iraqi Kurdish leader who was soon to become the first democratically elected president of the country. The determined attacks against the police and other "agents" were obvious, with brutal patterns already starting against waiting queues of potential recruits. While it took some time to implement them, measures could be taken to lessen the risks. But neither Jalal Talibani nor the author of this book thought that the extreme sectarianism planned in the letter would wreck the country, especially since the cold assessment of Zarqawi underlined his perception of the desperate situation of the resistance to the new order in Iraq. We were very wrong. Sectarian killings developed in the summer of 2004, and peaked in 2005-2006, leaving a trail of distrust between the Sunni and Shi'i communities the world over. Ethnic cleansing is characteristically difficult to prevent or reverse because the cycle of violence, as predicted by Zarqawi, impels a cold doomsday logic.

2. Sectarian and ethnic violence is a daunting question for the 21st century, adumbrated in a premonitory book by Daniel Patrick Moynihan, *Pandemonium, Ethnicity in International Politics* (1993), and amplified by Amy Chua, *World on Fire* (2002) who adds a layer of correlation between free capitalist markets and hardening ethnic identities. As an illustration of this dual trend, Iraq has proved to be one of the worst manifestations of the descent into this combined sectarian/ethnic mayhem. In his memoirs on the year he spent in Iraq, L. Paul Bremer noted the first massive expression of sectarian politics in the establishment of the Shi'i militia labelled by its founder, Muqtada as-Sadr, "al-Mahdi army" in reference to the millenarian Imam believed by Shi'is to rise at the end of history to save humanity. Considering the profound roots of political sectarianism in Iraq, and its ruthless logic in Saddam Hussein's Iraq (magisterially underlined in Hanna Batatu's seminal work *The Old Social Classes* (1978)): What might be done to prevent the ethnic or sectarian spiral of violence? Is there precedent in Iraq that might guide policy for dealing with future sectarian violence?

3. Bremer did not have a clear answer and he underlines in *My Year in Iraq* his frustration with the Mahdi army and the failure to arrest Sadr. See also Chapter 4 on Sadr and the assassination of Majid al-Khu'i. A troubling question arises: unlike Ben Laden, Sadr's whereabouts were generally known, and the proximity and full force of the American military and other special operations unit would make him a relatively easy target. Yet, a decisive hold on such a course of action—routinely used in contrast by the Israeli government against the Hamas leaders in Gaza and the West Bank—is clear over the five years of American military involvement in Iraq. At what level are decisions of this nature taken? Did the U.S. president himself decide that Sadr should not constitute a target?

4. Petraeus's report addresses sectarianism perfunctorily. Yet the Sunni militia supported by the Americans responds to the importance he gives to local

government, no doubt key to the improvement in security in the Western provinces in 2007-2008 compared to 2004-2005. How much, however, can a militia be considered legal? How does a Sunni militia differ from a Shi'i militia like the Mahdi army?

5. Arguably, U.S.-supported militias are temporary. The most recent discussions focus on their integration in the army. Is this realistic? Can the army hold when essentially composed of ethnic or sectarian groups? Where does this fit in a military strategy?

6. The following figures provide snapshots of security in 2008 Iraq. They should be read as "factual checks" on insurgency and counterinsurgency theories. Violence is multifarious: in Iraq, most of the violence has been sectarian, but government and coalition forces are also targets to armed resistance that sees itself as nationalistic (the Ba'th) or religious (al-Qa'eda).

(c) Security Measured

How does one "measure" security? Note the variety of sources. The first and second of the following maps and charts below appeared in a report published by the U.S. Department of Defense in March 2008, which is further excerpted below. The two other charts come from the UN and from diligent journalism.

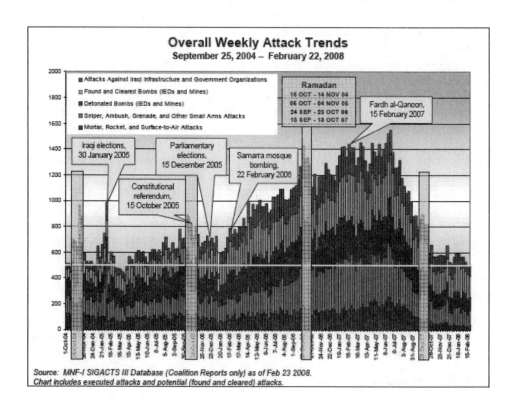

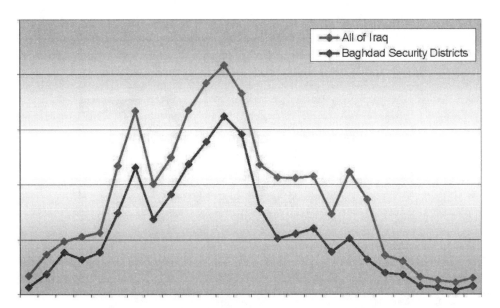

Compare the above U.S. government charts with the following map of the United Nations Office for Humanitarian Affairs, March 2008.[*]

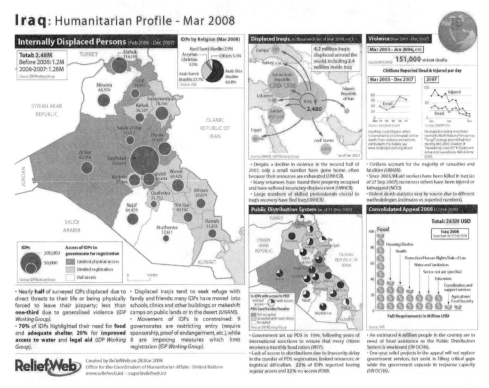

---

*Available at http://www.reliefweb.int/rw/fullMaps_Sa.nsf/luFullMap/416B56CEAD089BE68
525741A00518BE7/$File/080326_irq_hpm_part1-2.pdf?OpenElement/.

Improvement of security in Baghdad, in one criticism of the "surge," is owed to the effective ethnic cleansing of several mixed parts of the city. An expressive map on "Ethnic violence in Baghdad" shows the devastation of these neighborhoods, especially those with a strong Sunni presence.

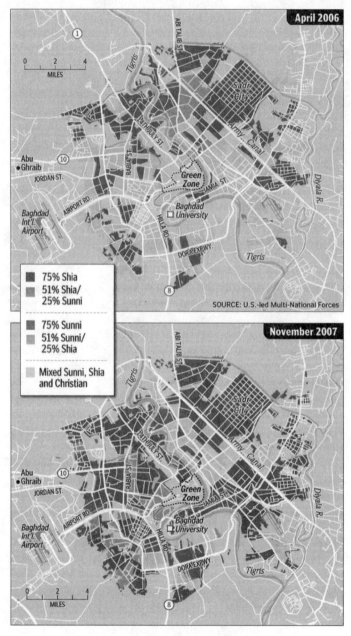

Baghdad: 2006 and 2007

Source: Gene Thorp & Dita Smith, Wash. Post, Dec. 15, 2007

2. SECURITY AND THE U.S. PRESIDENTIAL DEBATE

On March 7, 2008, the U.S. Department of Defense presented Congress with the following report, entitled "Measuring stability and security in Iraq."

This report to Congress, Measuring Stability and Security in Iraq, is submitted pursuant to Section 9010 of the Department of Defense Appropriations Act 2007, Public Law 109-289 as amended by Section 1308 of Public Law 110-28 and Section 1224 of Public Law 110-181.1 The report includes specific performance indicators and measures of progress toward political, economic, and security stability in Iraq, as directed in that legislation. This is the eleventh in a series of quarterly reports on this subject. . . .

The strategic goal of the United States in Iraq remains a unified, democratic and federal Iraq that can govern, defend and sustain itself and is an ally in the war on terror. This goal is being pursued along political, security, economic and diplomatic lines of operation . . . New strides have been taken in reconciliation at the national, provincial and local levels, and the Iraqi economy is growing. However, recent security gains remain fragile, and sustained progress over the long term will depend on Iraq's ability to address a complex set of issues associated with key political and economic objectives.

Violence levels are down throughout most of Iraq. Since the June 2007 report, deaths from ethno-sectarian violence are down nearly 90%.

Total civilian deaths and Coalition deaths have each dropped by over 70%. A number of factors have contributed to the decrease in violence in Iraq, to include a Coalition focus on securing the population, progress against Al Qaeda in Iraq (AQI), militia extremists and criminal special groups, rejection of AQI by significant portions of the population and the continued strength of the tribal Awakening movement and Sons of Iraq (formerly known as Concerned Local Citizens), limitations on malign Iranian influence, Muqtada al Sadr's order to Jaysh al-Mahdi (JAM) to suspend attacks, actions in source and transit countries against foreign fighter facilitation networks, and an increase of over 100,000 Iraqi Army, police and border forces. However, there remain a number of concerns. AQI and other extremist groups remain resilient; though they have sustained significant losses, these groups continue to pose a substantial threat and continue to carry out barbaric attacks. While their strength and influence are significantly reduced in Anbar Province, Baghdad, the belts around Baghdad and many areas of Diyala Province, AQI elements remain highly lethal in parts of the Tigris River Valley and in Ninewa Province. AQI members have, in particular, been targeting key figures in the Awakening movement and Sons of Iraq groups and have also been conducting a smaller number of less effective, high-profile attacks against the local population. Additionally, ethno-sectarian struggles over power and resources continue, and among Shi'a groups, criminal activity and infighting continue to impede progress.

The Awakening movement among the tribes of western, central and northern Iraq continues to grow. Many Sunni Arab and a growing number of Shi'a sheikhs are working with the Coalition, and their tribal members and other local citizens are fighting AQI through participation in Sons of Iraq groups. Overall, Sons of Iraq in north and central Iraq continue to complement Iraqi Army, Iraqi Police and Coalition forces and now number approximately 91,000 volunteers (71,500 Sunni, 19,500 Shi'a). To date, close to 20,000 have already transitioned to the ISF or civil employment. The Sons of Iraq program is helping to improve security at the local level by involving local citizens in the security of their communities. The program enables Iraqi and Coalition forces to interact with local residents who are trusted in their communities to obtain information on insurgents and illegal militia activity and to protect key infrastructure. The successes of Sons of Iraq groups have provoked AQI to attack their leaders.

Though the contributions of the Sons of Iraq have been important, these groups also pose challenges for the Government of Iraq (GoI) and, to a degree, for the Coalition. These include the potential for infiltration by insurgents, the possibility of distortions in the local economy if salaries are not carefully managed and the need for a comprehensive plan to transition Sons of Iraq to sustainable forms of employment in the ISF or in the private sector. In addition, the GoI is understandably concerned about the employment of a large number of former insurgents. Coalition forces are helping to address these concerns through engagement at the local, provincial, and national levels. . . .

United Nations Security Council Resolution (UNSCR) 1790, which currently authorizes the Coalition to conduct the full range of operations in Iraq, will expire at the end of 2008. In anticipation of the expiration of the UNSCR, the U.S. and Iraq are preparing for upcoming status of forces negotiations. The goal of those negotiations will be to produce an agreement that will provide the United States and its Coalition partners with authorities necessary to conduct the operations that may be required to support the GoI.

In summary, Iraq has seen important security gains in recent months. However, these security gains cannot be taken for granted and there is tough, challenging work ahead. Sustained improvements in security will remain linked to political and economic progress. On the economic front, enduring improvements are dependent on the GoI's still-tenuous ability to provide essential services and improve oil, electricity and water infrastructure. Advances in these areas are critical to keeping Iraq on the path to sustainable economic development. On the political front, much will depend on continued legislative progress and the implementation of recently passed legislation, improvements in the effectiveness of Iraq's ministries and whether Iraq's political leaders have the will and ability needed to turn nascent political accommodation at the local and national levels into lasting national reconciliation. Further progress will depend on the continued ability of Iraqi leaders to capitalize on the hard-fought gains achieved by the Coalition and Iraqi forces and other courageous members of Iraqi society who are dedicated to peace.

NOTES AND QUESTIONS

1. The DOD figures and chart can be read optimistically as "a turning point" sometime in early 2008, or more skeptically as a momentary improvement of the security situation against a catastrophic situation of over 2 million people displaced, and an ethnic cleansing which has changed the face of Baghdad, if not Iraq. In Spring 2008, Prime Minister Nuri al-Maliki suddenly emerged stronger from his martial confrontation with Shi'i militias in Karbala, then Basra and Baghdad, while Sunni militias have in the main joined the so-called Sons of Iraq (*abna' al-'iraq*). Meanwhile, public services such as garbage collection and sewage treatment are failing to meet needs, and electricity distribution has not markedly improved (see Chapter 6 on the

economy). Continued sectarian fighting and the Iraqi federal government's inability to fulfill basic needs indicate that Iraq is not yet able to stand alone. But the argument is circular: unless the Host Nation, in Petraeus's doctrine, takes responsibility, how can foreigners make the Iraqi government stand on its own feet?

2. The United Office for Humanitarian Affairs reports 4.2 million Iraqis displaced. These are internal and external refugees. The agency also mentions some 150,000 civilian reported deaths between March 2003 and December 2007. Other reports put the figures of casualties much higher. The toll on the sociological configuration of Iraq is dramatic, as per the Thorp and Smith *Washington Post* map, with 75 percent of Baghdad becoming uniformly Shi'i, against a far more mixed city before 2003. Meanwhile, the non-Muslim minorities of Iraq have disappeared, or are threatened with disappearance. Jews, who formed a third of Baghdad's population in 1900, have been the subject of repeated pogroms. Iraqi Jews all but ceased to exist as a community since 1968, when the newly established Ba'th started its repression with the hanging of several of Iraq's Jewish citizens. The Christian communities of Iraq have been facing a similar risk since 2003. See the report of Minority Rights Group, Assimilation, Exodus, Eradication: Iraq's Minority Communities Since 2003 (2007). Can this trend be stopped? Reversed? Will the displaced go back, where to? Can the diversity of the capital, also said to be "the largest Kurdish city of Iraq" before 2003, be restored? The new Iraqi Constitution mentions the state duty "to compensate all victims of terrorism." How feasible is such commitment?

3. Iraq is an important component of the domestic debate in the United States. It may not be a total coincidence that the final 2008 presidential contenders owed much of their ascendancy to their distinctive policy positions on Iraq: Barack Obama's early rise came on the strength of his firm opposition to the war in 2002 and 2003; John McCain moved from a fledgling position in the Republican primaries to being the nominee in large part as a supporter of the "surge" and "victory" in Iraq. Although their positions inevitably fluctuate, an expressive window on their respective Iraq strategy appears in the foreign policy articles contributed, like the other leading presidential candidates, in articles published in *Foreign Affairs* at the outset of the campaign. Portions of the articles relevant to Iraq follow.

JOHN MCCAIN, AN ENDURING PEACE BUILT ON FREEDOM: SECURING AMERICA'S FUTURE

Foreign Affairs 19-34 (Nov./Dec. 2007)

Defeating radical Islamist extremists is the national security challenge of our time. Iraq is this war's central front, according to our commander there, General David Petraeus, and according to our enemies, including al Qaeda's leadership. . . .

That is why I support our continuing efforts to win in Iraq. It is also why I oppose a preemptive withdrawal strategy that has no Plan B for the aftermath of its inevitable failure and the greater problems that would ensue.

Uniting the World's Democracies

Our organizations and partnerships must be as international as the challenges we confront . . . NATO has begun to fill this gap by promoting partnerships between the alliance and great democracies in Asia and elsewhere. We should go further by linking democratic nations in one common organization: a worldwide League of Democracies. . . .

This League of Democracies would not supplant the UN or other international organizations but complement them by harnessing the political and moral advantages offered by united democratic action. By taking steps such as bringing concerted pressure to bear on tyrants in Burma (renamed Myanmar by its military government in 1989) or Zimbabwe, uniting to impose sanctions on Iran, and providing support to struggling democracies in Serbia and Ukraine, the League of Democracies would serve as a unique handmaiden of freedom. If I am elected president, during my first year in office I will call a summit of the world's democracies to seek the views of my counterparts and explore the steps necessary to realize this vision just as America led in creating NATO six decades ago.

BARACK OBAMA, RENEWING AMERICAN LEADERSHIP

Foreign Affairs 2-16 (July/Aug. 2007)

. . . [A] war in Iraq that never should have been authorized and never should have been waged. In the wake of Iraq and Abu Ghraib, the world has lost trust in our purposes and our principles.

Moving Beyond Iraq

To renew American leadership in the world, we must first bring the Iraq war to a responsible end and refocus our attention on the broader Middle East. . . . [I]t is time for our civilian leaders to acknowledge a painful truth: we cannot impose a military solution on a civil war between Sunni and Shiite factions. The best chance we have to leave Iraq a better place is to pressure these warring parties to find a lasting political solution. And the only effective way to apply this pressure is to begin a phased withdrawal of U.S. forces, with the goal of removing all combat brigades from Iraq by March 31, 2008 — a date consistent with the goal set by the bipartisan Iraq Study Group. This redeployment could be temporarily suspended if the Iraqi government meets the security, political, and economic benchmarks to which it has committed. But we must recognize that, in the end, only Iraqi leaders can bring real peace and stability to their country. . . .

The morass in Iraq has made it immeasurably harder to confront and work through the many other problems in the region. . . . Changing the dynamic in Iraq will allow us to focus our attention and influence on resolving the festering conflict between the Israelis and the Palestinians. . . .

Throughout the Middle East, we must harness American power to reinvigorate American diplomacy. Tough-minded diplomacy, backed by the whole range of instruments of American power — political, economic, and military — could bring success even when dealing with long-standing adversaries such as Iran and Syria. . . .

B. U.S.-IRAQ POLITICAL AND SECURITY ARRANGEMENTS

Introduction. Opposition to a bilateral security agreement was strong both in Iraq and in the United States. Many Iraqis were unhappy with the prospect of the long-term presence of U.S. troops in Iraq. A BBC/ABC poll conducted in August 2007 revealed that 79 percent of Iraqis were opposed to such a presence. Global Policy Forum, "Should the Security Council Renew the MNF Mandate for 2008?," Nov. 15, 2007. The Iraqi Council of Representatives (CoR) asked on several occasions for Prime Minister Maliki's cabinet to seek its approval prior to petitioning the UN for a renewal of its mandate authorizing the presence of foreign troops in Iraq. In April 2007, after the CoR's request was ignored by Maliki's cabinet, 144 MPs — an absolute majority of CoR's 275 seats — signed a letter addressed to the UN Security Council in which they declared the 2006 renewal "unilateral and unconstitutional" and demanded a timetable for the withdrawal of Coalition troops. On June 5, 2007, the Iraqi CoR passed a law requiring the government to obtain parliamentary approval prior to asking the UN for any further renewal of its mandate. This law was ignored by Maliki's cabinet when, on December 5, 2007, the cabinet asked the UN to extend the mandate until December 31, 2008. Hard negotiations continued, resulting in two agreements discussed below.

The following texts illustrate some of this dynamic opposition, starting in section B.1.a with the massive revolt against the 1948 Treaty of Portsmouth, itself a reworking of Anglo-Iraqi treaties in 1922, 1926, and 1930. The two following documents at B.1.b and B.1.c emerged during the stormy debate over the proposed SOFA, and are illustrative of the ambient difficulties until SOFA became a "withdrawal and temporary presence" agreement.

Section 2 introduces the American dimension of the debate, also a stormy one because of the controversial dimension of the Iraq war. Section B.2.a presents an early legal assessment of foreign military presence in Iraq and B.2.b. provides the arguments presented to get any security agreement with Iraq vetted by the U.S. Senate as a normal treaty.

1. IRAQI OPPOSITION TO FOREIGN MILITARY PRESENCE

(a) *Al-Wathbah* — The 1948 Revolt Against the Treaty of Portsmouth

HANNA BATATU, THE OLD SOCIAL CLASSES AND THE
REVOLUTIONARY MOVEMENTS OF IRAQ

545-557 (1978)

Al-Wathbah — the Leap — was the most formidable mass insurrection in the history of the monarchy. It sprang from the same conditions of existence that had since the first years of the forties been making for the social subsoil of Baghdad in revolt against hunger and unequal burdens. It was the students and

Schalchiyyah workers braving machine guns on the Ma'mun Bridge and dying for their ideas — or, as cynics would have it, for vain illusions. It was the political representatives of the various layers of the middle class — the National Democrats, the Liberals, the Independence party — resentful of constraints or plotting for political gain. It was the privileged stratum of ex-Sharifian officer-*mallaks*, bureaucrat-*mallaks*, and sheikh-*mallaks* menaced in their political power and social interests. It was British overlordship shaken, the Anglo-Iraqi Treaty of 1930 sapped, and the Portsmouth Agreement of 1948 abolished. It was the rule of Regent 'Abd-ul-ilah momentarily supplanted by the rule of the demos. It was also the first great test of the Iraqi Communist party.

Iraq had been for some time moving toward the *Wathbah* — the restlessness of the parties, the demonstration of 28 June 1946, the "massacre" at Gawurpaghi had been so many prefatory notes or premonitory symptoms — but it was from the moment that the regent and Nuri as-Sa'id proceeded to enmesh their people in another treaty with the English that the *Wathbah* broke forth.

The old treaty — that of 1930 — which virtually reduced Iraq into an appendage of the British Empire, had become something of an anachronism. However, from the point of view of Nuri and the regent, its annulment was out of the question. Such a course was not only beyond their power, but hardly in accord with their interests. If to many of their subjects, the treaty seemed like a millstone round their necks, in their own eyes it constituted a protective shield against indigenous revolutions. But with the peoples on the move everywhere in the East, the English, Nuri, and the regent realized the necessity of redefining, sooner rather than later, their relationships in a manner that, at least in words, would be as inoffensive as possible to national sentiment.

Extending the treaty under the guise of revising it — this is really what, on close examination, the Portsmouth Agreement amounted to — was in any circumstances a risky affair, and markedly the more so when the regent and Nuri did not have both feet on the ground. In retrospect, it is clear that they had only an insufficient idea of the seriousness of their situation. But they could and did foresee trouble, even though its scale and intensity when it came, caught them completely by surprise. It was in the hope of averting it or, at least, blunting its edge, that they had months beforehand, resolved upon an unusual step: in March 1947 Nuri vacated the premiership, yielding that high office, for the first time since the founding of the monarchy, to a Shi'ite, that is, to a member of the sect that embraced a clear majority of the population. The Shi'ite chosen was Salih Jabr. . . .

Raising a Shi'i to the premiership proved eventually to be of little avail. It meant nothing to the workers without bread, the lawyers without lawsuits, the forgotten clerks, the students clandestinely propagandized, and the parties held in leash. It took now only a few incidents to precipitate the thinly disguised, long-seething ferment in which all these elements were caught.

. . . On the following morning, students from al-Karkh Secondary School took to the streets and, after crossing the river, merged with the students of al-A'dhamiyyah, who had also come out. The procession . . . moved peacefully toward the School of Law. From there it expected to advance, with swollen ranks, on the royal palace, it ultimate focal point. But as it approached the Law School, mounted policemen suddenly appeared and barred its way. Law students, who rushed out of their classrooms to join the demonstrators, were driven back, at first with clubs and then with a discharge of firearms. Several of them fell wounded. Thirty-nine others were arrested, and the Law School shut down. The reaction was swift. On 6 January, the students of all the other colleges went on strike. The authorities relented: on the eighth, the apprehended students were released and the Law School reopened. Thus came to an end what might b termed the preliminary phase of the *Wathbah*.

. . . From 8 to 15 January, the Baghdad of the opposition paused, so to say. On the surface it looked as if the spirit of protest had dissolved. But the calm was deceptive. An acute and tense watchfulness prevailed. All eyes were riveted on London, whither an official delegation headed by Jabr and including Nuri had gone for final negotiations and the signature of a new treaty. The Communists, for their part, were not exactly marking time. A letter had come from Kut prison, in which Fahd vigorously demanded that the party make serious preparation to send its forces into the street. A hasty mobilization of the party's means began. . . .

The surface stillness broke abruptly with the announcement on 16 January of the terms of the treaty signed the day before at Portsmouth. Although abundantly oiled over with the idioms of mutuality, the new agreement committed Iraqis to "a firm alliance" with Britain, to policies in foreign lands congruent with its interests, and to the recognition of Iraq's air bases as links in its "essential" communications. The agreement also pledged Iraq to "invite" British forces to its territory in time of war or of a threat of war, and to furnish them with assistance and sundry facilities, and, further, to permit the continued use of the Shu'aybah and the Habbaniyyah bases by the R.A.F. until the withdrawal of the "allied armies" from "all ex-enemy countries." In the conditions of the then unfolding "Cold War," such a withdrawal was scarcely in view and, indeed, in the case of Germany, has not come about to this very day. In brief, the Portsmouth Agreement was—except for relatively minor points, little more than the 1930 Treaty with a coating of new-fashioned terminology. Its gloss of mutuality carried as much conviction as the remark made months before by Ernest Bevin, the secretary of state for foreign affairs. Britain regarded Iraq as "a member of the family," he had said, tongue in cheek.

The publication of the agreement sparked a three-day strike and continuous demonstrations by college students. The movement bore from the beginning a grim earnestness, and developed with unaccustomed force. Behind the seething students, stimulating them, urging them on, welding them together, was the Communist-led "Student Cooperation Committee." On 16, 17, and 18 January, not only the Communist and their confederates— the Progressive Democrats, the Populists, and the Kurdish Democrats, but also students from the National Democratic and Independence parties, worked with the Committee and followed its lead. On the nineteenth, however, the Independence party, which stood farthest to the right, ordered its student elements to separate themselves from the Committee and bide their time. The National Democrats held on, and to the end would play a role by no means inconspicuous. However, from this point, the Communists emerged unmistakably as the fundamental force of the *Wathbah*, with the "Cooperation Committee" and the "Student Cooperation Committee" as their chief levers. The stormy mass march of 20 January, in which for the first time the Schalchiyyah workers and the hungry *shargawiyyas* took part, was a distinctly Communist initiative. Blood was shed that day in Baghdad. In a vain attempt to disperse the demonstrators, the police, losing its senses or acting under instructions, fired murderously into their midst. Lead, however, did not dissipate resistance. The multitudes became only bitter and more defiant. On the succeeding day passions rose higher. Student delegations who wanted to escort the bodies of some of the victims to their final resting place were fired upon by the police inside the Royal Hospital. Two fell dead and seventeen others were wounded. One of the pharmacy students, whose brains were blown out by a bullet, was carried by his companions to the dean of his school who, shuddering in horror, submitted his resignation. The faculties of Pharmacy and Medicine and the physicians at the hospital followed his example. As word of the outrage spread, resentment mounted to a fever heat. Tempestuous protests pervaded the streets. Crowds, thick with Communists, and armed with huge canes, clashed with the police, who became much like aidless flotsam in a wrathful sea. An atmosphere redolent of social revolution enveloped Baghdad. The regent overtaken by happenings more authoritarian than himself, took fright. Unsure of the army, he effected an about-face: in the night of January 21, after summoning a palace council, to which this time he invited the representatives of the parties, he openly disowned the treaty. . . .

. . . More blood was yet to flow. The demonstrators that had been halted in Amin Square became now uncontrollable. The police force that had contained them pulled back and withdrew at a run in the direction of the bridge. There the detachments that had just dealt destruction to the Karkh crowds were waiting with their armored cars and machine guns. The demonstrators advanced, seemingly determined to cross in spite of any losses. For an instant the police, losing some of their assurance, hesitated. A few minutes later, however, a volley of shots burst forth. Only a fifteen-year-old girl, 'Adawiyyah al-Falaki, who carried a banner and marched at the head of the others crossed unscathed. Her four immediate companions and others behind them had fallen. The firing had ceased. The bridge now echoed only with murmurs of pain and cries of grief.

Apparently appalled at the extent of loss of life and noticing that, far from dispersing, the crowds on both sides of the bridge were beginning to reform, having recovered from their stupefaction, the police withdrew completely from the scene.

How many fell that day cannot be determined. Numerous bodies were buried without being registered. Others drifted down the Tigris. The total figure for dead and injured is commonly set at between three and four hundred.

The sequel is already known. Late that evening Premier Salih Jabr fled for his life to the Euphrates, and eventually to England. The regent charged Muhammad as-Sadr, a Shi'i *sayyid* and man of religion, and a leader of the 1920 uprising, with forming a new government.

(b) Letter from Iraqi Parliamentarians Concerning the Multi National Forces (MNF) Renewal: April 2007[*]

In the name of God, Most Gracious, Most Merciful

To: the Presidency of the Iraqi Council of Representatives, the Iraqi Cabinet, the United Nations Secretary General, members of the UN Security Council, the Secretary General of the Arab League, the Presidency of the Organization of the Islamic Conference, and the Presidency of the European Union.

Subject: Timetable for withdrawal of the occupation forces (multinational forces [MNF]) from Iraq.

Whereas, the UN Security Council will soon review the MNF mandate on June 15th 2007.

Whereas, the Iraqi Cabinet has unilaterally requested a renewal of the UN mandate keeping the occupation troops (MNF) in Iraq.

Whereas, such a request issued by the Iraqi Cabinet without the Iraqi Parliament's approval is unconstitutional.

Whereas, the Iraqi parliament, as the elected representatives of the Iraqi people, has the exclusive right to approve and ratify international treaties and agreements including those signed with the United Nations Security Council.

Whereas, the Iraqi people have expressed their will by demonstrating in marches demanding an end to the occupation by setting a timetable for withdrawal.

Therefore, we the Iraqi members of parliament signing below demand a timetable for the withdrawal of the occupation forces (MNF) from our beloved Iraq.

[This text is then followed by the names and signatures of 144 Iraqi Members of Parliament. The Iraqi CoR has 275 seats. —Ed.]

(c) Statement by Ayatollah Kazem al-Ha'iri on the U.S. Government Agreement with the Iraqi Government[**]

The religious authority, His Eminence Grand Ayatollah Al-Sayyid Kazim al-Husayni al-Ha'iri, may his shadow lasts, has issued a statement on the US agreement with the Iraqi government:

In the name of God, the Merciful, the Compassionate praised be God, and may the peace and blessings of Allah be upon Muhammad and his good, chaste family members. "And incline not to those who do wrong, or the Fire will seize you" [Qur'an 11: 113] "Islam rises above all and none rises above it." [Prophetic *hadith*]

My dear sons in our occupied Iraq: May the peace and blessings of Allah be upon you.

You are aware that the occupiers of Iraq want to legalize their illegitimate presence on our land so that it will be possible for them to tamper with the security of the homeland and the citizen and to continue to plunder the

---

[*]This section is a reproduction of the full letter.

[**]This section is a reproduction of the full statement, which can be found in Arabic at the Shi'i News Agency website, Mount Lebanon, May 21, 2008. Reproduced at http://www.juancole.com/.

country's resources and thus increase the poverty and deprivation. They want to force the Iraqi Government to agree, under the excuse of removing Iraq from the Seventh Chapter of the UN Charter, to completely concede Iraq's independence and resources and make its presence and future go with the wind, where it will not have authority or sovereignty, and force it to agree to provisions that will stamp the stigma of humiliation and disgrace on Iraq's forehead forever.

Such enforcement on the government will not leave any dignity or sanctity to the individual. They want their dog, which is squatting on Iraq, protected from any accountability by the government or the nation. They want all Iraq's political and legal entities: The presidency, Prime Ministry, and Council of Representatives, as well as the nation to be accountable to the Americans. "If they enter a country, they despoil it, and make the noblest of its people its meanest. Thus do they behave." [Qur'an 27: 34]

Besides, the American, who has entered Iraq with the slogan of liberation, soon announced himself an occupier. He did not fulfil any promise. Therefore, is any goodness expected from such agreements?

From the position of fatherhood, I give my advice to every official in this nation not to stain himself with such an agreement. Let him fear God for what is left of his dignity.

Let everyone know also that such an agreement will not be binding to anyone, except to the one who signs it. No one should ever think that he can plot against our nation despite its preoccupation with its tragedies; the killing, destitution, starvation, and deprivation. All this is the work of the Americans and their supporters. The nation, whom Prophet Muhammad, may the peace and blessings of Allah be upon him, awakened, will not accept humiliation and disgrace. Here is his grandson, Al-Husayn, peace be upon him, crying out defiantly: "Never will we be humbled."

Our zealous sons, we are going through a difficult test. We have no other choice but to adhere to the truth together. Do not ignore what is being plotted against you and do not busy yourselves with trivial matters that lead to differences between you. This is the wish of your enemy, who is lying in wait for you.

Place your trust in Allah, close your ranks, stay alert, and watch out of your enemy.

I address the occupation from my place here by repeating the words of our Lady Zaynab, peace be upon her: "Go ahead and plot and do what you like, but by God you will never wipe out our Koran and revelation."

Dear sons: Let me tell you. The blessed religious seminary in Iraq is dearer, cleaner, higher, and nobler than the recognition of the legitimacy of such an agreement.

May the peace and blessings of Allah be upon you.

[Signed] Kazim al-Husayni al-Ha'iri, 15 Jumada al-Ula 1429 AH, 21 May 2008

NOTES AND QUESTIONS

1. The Portsmouth agreement, and the strong opposition which eventually led to its abandonment by the Iraqi government at the time, did not prevent

the emergence of the Baghdad Pact (or CENTO, Central Treaty Organization, modeled after NATO) in 1955. The U.S. was central to the Baghdad Pact emergence, but the official parties were Iran, Iraq, Pakistan, Turkey, and the UK. CENTO effectively collapsed in 1958 with the Revolution in Iraq. In all these pacts and treaties, two considerations elude us for a meaningful comparison half a century later: the heavy colonial legacy, and the opposition to the Soviet Union as matrix of international relations for half a century.

2. In a similar comparative register, one should note the difficulty of drawing models from American experience with the Nazi precedent and post–World War Japan. "Without exception, [U.S. colleagues on the military transport plane] were reading new books on the American occupation and reconstruction of Germany and Japan." Noah Feldman, What We Owe Iraq 1 (2004). Unlike the popularity of the leaders of Nazi Germany and the militarized Japanese Empire, which was palpable, the Ba'th regime was hardly popular, save with some sections of the Sunni-Takriti population. This was noted by Bremer: "[B]ut here we defeated a hated regime, not a country." My Year in Iraq 37 (2006). This did not prevent him from perceiving his job squarely as "running an occupation": "They're [the U.S. administration] interested in my being considered for the job of running the occupation of Iraq." Id. at 7. See Chapter 5 on the alternatives to US military occupation

3. Ba'thism in Iraq also lasted much longer than Nazism in Germany. Saddam Hussein was in power between 1968 and 2003, Hitler between 1933 and 1945. Also, any comparative exercise that does not take into account Iraq's unique sectarian and ethnic tripartite socio-political dimension is futile. See Chapter 3 on the Constitution.

4. The opposition to any form of security agreement with the United States is strong, and the memory of the *Wathbah* remains. Demonstrations in Baghdad by the followers of Muqtada Sadr, together with varying voices typified by a leading religious leader like Ha'iri, but also detected in the Sistani circles, are illustrative of the risks. In Najaf, Ayatollah Sistani's representative, 'Abd al-Mahdi al-Karbala'i, called on February 16, 2008 for further discussions and professional expertise before any binding agreement. Eventually, an agreement was reached and supported by the large majority of the Iraqi CoR, see below, section B.3.b, Note 2. Does that erase nationalist suspicions and opposition? Can history, past and recent, provide any tools to make the agreement "work"? Will the declared withdrawal of the Obama administration be sufficient to remove the sting? Even if a large number of "advisors" remains?

2. AMERICAN OPPOSITION TO THE PROPOSED AGREEMENT

The Bush administration has labeled the security agreement with Iraq an "executive agreement" between heads of state in order to avoid Congressional approval. The text outlines the nature of permissible military operations in the host country and addresses issues such as taxes, compensation for claims, and the exit and entry rights of foreign forces. Most importantly, Status of Forces

Agreements (SOFAs) establish the judicial authority to which foreign troops are accountable. Regarding this last aspect, the following report, by Frederic Kirgis from the American Society of International Law (ASIL), noted as early as March 2004 the complex legal aspects of foreign military presence in Iraq. "Traditionally, most SOFAs grant the host country jurisdiction over service personnel who are alleged to have violated domestic laws. There are generally two exceptions to that rule: the foreign government retains jurisdiction over its nationals when their alleged crimes are against its other service personnel or when the national's alleged offense took place in the scope of his or her official duties." More generally, international agreements pose several constitutional problems from a domestic U.S. perspective, from the president's war powers to non-treaty agreements over foreign military deployment and presence.

(a) International Agreements and U.S. Law

Frederic Kirgis, International Agreements and U.S. Law

The American Society of International Law (May 1997)[*]

There is confusion in the media and elsewhere about United States law as it relates to international agreements, including treaties. The confusion exists with respect to such matters as whether "treaty" has the same meaning in international law and in the domestic law of the United States, how treaties are ratified, how the power to enter into international agreements is allocated among the Executive Branch, the Senate and the whole Congress, whether Congress may override an existing treaty, and the extent to which international agreements are enforceable in United States courts.

Under international law a "treaty" is any international agreement concluded between states or other entities with international personality (such as public international organizations), if the agreement is intended to have international legal effect. The Vienna Convention on the Law of Treaties sets out an elaborate set of international law standards for treaties, broadly defined.

"Treaty" has a much more restricted meaning under the constitutional law of the United States. It is an international agreement that has received the "advice and consent" (in practice, just the consent) of two-thirds of the Senate and that has been ratified by the President. The Senate does not ratify treaties. When the Senate gives its consent, the President—acting as the chief diplomat of the United States—has discretion whether or not to ratify the instrument. Through the course of U.S. history, several instruments that have received the Senate's consent have nonetheless remained unratified. Those instruments are not in force for the United States, despite the Senate's consent to them.

Not all international agreements negotiated by the United States are submitted to the Senate for its consent. Sometimes the Executive Branch negotiates an agreement that is intended to be binding only if sent to the Senate, but the President for political reasons decides not to seek its consent. Often, however, the Executive Branch negotiates agreements that are intended to be binding without the consent of two-thirds of the Senate. Sometimes these agreements are entered into with the concurrence of a simple majority

---

[*]Available at http://www.asil.org/insights/insigh10.htm

of both houses of Congress ("Congressional-Executive agreements"); in these cases the concurrence may be given either before or after the Executive Branch negotiates the agreement. On other occasions the President simply enters into an agreement without the intended or actual participation of either house of Congress (a "Presidential," or "Sole Executive" agreement). The extent of the President's authority to enter into Sole Executive agreements is controversial, as will be noted below.

Although some Senators have at times taken the position that certain important international agreements must be submitted as treaties for the Senate's advice and consent, the prevailing view is that a Congressional-Executive agreement may be used whenever a treaty could be. This is the position taken in the American Law Institute's Restatement Third of Foreign Relations Law of the United States, §303, Comment e. Under the prevailing view, the converse is true as well: a treaty may be used whenever a Congressional-Executive agreement could be.

The President's authority to enter into Sole Executive agreements, however, is thought not to be so broad. Clearly, the President has some authority to do so in his capacities as commander in chief of the armed forces and as "chief diplomat." Thus, armistice agreements and certain agreements incidental to the operation of foreign embassies in the United States could be done as Sole Executive Agreements. The agreement-making scope of these two sources of Presidential authority is nevertheless somewhat vague.

Congress has attempted to curb the President's claimed authority as commander in chief to commit U. S. armed forces to positions of peril by adopted the well-known War Powers Joint Resolution in 1973, over a presidential veto. The War Powers Resolution in practice has had the effect of inducing Presidents to consult with, and report to, Congress when U.S. armed forces are used in combat situations, but it has not significantly limited the President's practical power to commit the United States to use military force.

Presidents have sometimes asserted agreement-making authority stemming directly from the basic constitutional grant to the President of executive power. If this grant includes some authority to enter into Sole Executive agreements independently from more specific grants of presidential power, it would be difficult to ascertain what limits, short of those imposed on the government itself by the Bill of Rights, there might be to it. For this reason, many members of Congress and others have disputed any claim by a President to base agreement-making authority solely on the grant of executive power.

At one time there was some doubt whether a treaty (adopted with the consent of two-thirds of the Senate) must comply with the Bill of Rights, and the Supreme Court has yet to hold a treaty unconstitutional. Nevertheless, there is very little doubt that the Court would do so today if a treaty clearly violated the Bill of Rights. Even more certainly, it would hold unconstitutional a Congressional-Executive agreement or a Sole Executive agreement that is inconsistent with the Bill of Rights.

As a matter of domestic law within the United States, Congress may override a pre-existing treaty or Congressional-Executive agreement of the United States. To do so, however, would place the United States in breach of the obligation owed under international law to its treaty partner(s) to honor the treaty or agreement in good faith. Consequently, courts in the United States are disinclined to find that Congress has actually intended to override a treaty or other internationally binding obligation. Instead, they struggle to interpret the Congressional act and/or the international instrument in such a way as to reconcile the two.

Provisions in treaties and other international agreements are given effect as law in domestic courts of the United States only if they are "self-executing" or if they have been implemented by an act (such as an act of Congress) having the effect of federal law. Courts in this country have been reluctant to find such provisions self-executing, but on several occasions they have found them so — sometimes simply by giving direct effect to the provisions without expressly saying that they are self-executing. There are varying formulations as to what tends to make a treaty provision self-executing or non-self-executing, but within constitutional constraints (such as the requirement that appropriations of money originate in the House of Representatives) the primary consideration is the intent — or lack thereof — that the provision become effective as judicially-enforceable domestic law without implementing legislation. For the most part, the more specific the provision is and the more it reads like an act of Congress, the more likely it is to be treated as self-executing. A provision in an international agreement may be self-executing in U.S. law even though it would not be so in the law of the other party or parties to the agreement. Moreover, some provisions in an agreement might be self-executing while others in the same agreement are not.

All treaties are the law of the land, but only a self-executing treaty would prevail in a domestic court over a prior, inconsistent act of Congress. A non-self-executing treaty could not supersede a prior inconsistent act of Congress in a U.S. court. A non-self-executing treaty nevertheless would be the supreme law of the land in the sense that — as long as the treaty is consistent with the Bill of Rights — the President could not constitutionally ignore or contravene it.

Even if a treaty or other international agreement is non-self-executing, it may have an indirect effect in U.S. courts. The courts' practice, mentioned above, of interpreting acts of Congress as consistent with earlier international agreements applies to earlier non-self-executing agreements as well as to self-executing ones, since in either case the agreement is binding internationally and courts are slow to place the United States in breach of its international obligations. In addition, if state or local law is inconsistent with an international agreement of the United States, the courts will not allow the law to stand. The reason, if the international agreement is a self-executing treaty, is that such a treaty has the same effect in domestic courts as an act of Congress and therefore directly supersedes any inconsistent state or local law. If the international agreement is a non-self-executing treaty, it would not supersede inconsistent state or local law in the same way a federal statute would, but the courts nevertheless would not permit a state of the union to force the United States to breach its international obligation to other countries under the agreement. The state or local law would be struck down as an interference with the federal government's power over foreign affairs.

To summarize: the Senate does not ratify treaties; the President does. Treaties, in the U.S. sense, are not the only type of binding international agreement.

Congressional-Executive agreements and Sole Executive agreements may also be binding. It is generally understood that treaties and Congressional-Executive agreements are interchangeable; Sole Executive agreements occupy a more limited space constitutionally and are linked primarily if not exclusively to the President's powers as commander in chief and head diplomat. Treaties and other international agreements are subject to the Bill of Rights. Congress may supersede a prior inconsistent treaty or Congressional-Executive agreement as a matter of U.S. law, but not as a matter of international law. Courts in the United States use their powers of interpretation to try not to let Congress place the United States in violation of its international law obligations. A self-executing treaty provision is the supreme law of the land in the same sense as a federal statute that is judicially enforceable by private parties. Even a non-self-executing provision of an international agreement represents an international obligation that courts are very much inclined to protect against encroachment by local, state or federal law.

(b) "An Agreement Without Agreement"

BRUCE ACKERMAN & OONA HATHAWAY, AN AGREEMENT
WITHOUT AGREEMENT

Wash. Post, Feb. 15, 2008

The Bush administration is so intent on securing its legacy in Iraq that it is once again ignoring the Constitution. Without seeking the consent of Congress, it is well on its way toward a long-term agreement with the Iraqi government that threatens to deepen the American commitment without the congressional support the Constitution requires. . . . Such agreements, the White House is quick to point out, are not usually subject to congressional approval. That is true. But this truth will not suffice, since the administration is still aiming for an agreement that moves far beyond the traditional scope of these limited military accords. . . .

For example, the administration plans to exempt civilian contractors from prosecution under Iraqi laws. Military personnel also enjoy this exemption, but they can be court-martialed. These military tribunals have no jurisdiction over civilian contractors. Indeed, many of them will be immune from prosecution anywhere. . . .

At the very least, Congress should not give its consent without amending existing statutes to assure that all civilians granted immunity from Iraqi law can be held criminally responsible in American courts. . . .

Sen. Joseph Biden, as chairman of the Foreign Relations Committee, is a strong critic of the administration's unilateral approach. But if the stonewalling continues, he should make it his committee's business to sponsor a congressional resolution declaring invalid any military agreement that seeks to go beyond the traditional limits of the standard Status of Forces Agreement. No president has the unilateral power to impose broad international obligations on the nation without congressional support. But it is especially wrong for a lame-duck president to make such commitments about a controversial policy that is at the very center of the debate among the candidates vying to succeed him.

NOTES AND QUESTIONS

1. The complications associated with negotiating a SOFA and the potential for adverse effects notwithstanding, the Bush administration encountered a fierce domestic opposition to its efforts to secure a bilateral agreement with Iraq. Some legal experts in the United States took umbrage with the Bush administration's characterization of the proposed agreement as a SOFA, claiming that the broad scope and potentially lengthy duration of the type of agreement suggested in a joint Bush-Maliki letter exceeded the parameters of a SOFA and was more in keeping with a parameters of a treaty. Bruce Ackerman and Oona Hathaway called on Senator Joseph Biden, Chairman of the Senate's Foreign Relations Committee, who has since become the Vice-President, to sponsor a congressional resolution that would make invalid any military agreement that exceeds the traditional limits of a SOFA. But what if the Iraqi government requests the continuation of foreign military presence? Could this just be ignored by limiting the debate to domestic constitutional matters in America?

2. Labeling is important here because SOFAs, as Executive agreements, do not have to be presented to the U.S. Senate in order to receive the Senate's advice and consent. Conversely, treaties, per the U.S. Constitution, must be approved by two-thirds of the Senate prior to ratification by the President. The Senate has repeatedly demanded to have a say in the formulation of any agreement which binds the U.S. to Iraq, for instance during the Petraeus/Crocker hearings before the Senate in April 2008. The Bush administration, given a domestic political climate increasingly opposed to the war in Iraq, proved wary of pursuing such an effort in Congress. Can one propose a different label, or an altogether new legal regime? Does the "withdrawal" and "temporary" label do the trick?

3. There is another option the Bush administration might have explored in its efforts to secure an agreement prior to leaving office. In addition to executive agreements and treaties, U.S. law provides for a third type of agreement called a Congressional-Executive agreement. In a Congressional-Executive agreement the President is permitted to enter into an arrangement with another country or countries with the concurrence of a simple majority of both houses of Congress. Frederic Kirgis claims in the article above that, though some Senators have at times demanded that certain important international agreements be submitted as treaties to the Senate, "the prevailing view is that a Congressional-Executive agreement may be used whenever a treaty could be." Would a Congressional-Executive agreement have been preferable?

4. Congress has limited options available for recourse if the President signs an Executive agreement that Congress believes to be unconstitutional. Congress may supersede an agreement as a matter of domestic law, but not as a matter of international law. U.S. courts are wary of allowing Congress to place the United States executive in violation of international law.

5. People typically say that the Senate ratifies treaties. This manner of speaking is incorrect. In fact, the Senate "consents" and the President "ratifies." Note, too, that the President is not required to ratify a treaty to which the Senate has given its consent.

6. "Obama and Biden believe it is vital that a Status of Forces Agreement (SOFA) be reached so our troops have the legal protections and immunities they need. Any SOFA should be subject to Congressional review to ensure it has bipartisan support here at home." This is the "official position" of the Obama White House, posted on its website (http://www.whitehouse.gov/agenda/iraq/, visited February 7, 2009). Would a Congressional vote on the Agreement create a precedent on SOFAs for U.S. administrations, present and future?

3. STRATEGIC FRAMEWORKS, SOFAS, WITHDRAWAL AGREEMENTS

Recognizing Iraq's continued dependency on foreign assistance, American and Iraqi officials announced in November 2007 that a bilateral agreement was in the works. After protracted negotiations, two agreements were eventually signed. The first, arguably the more durable, translated into law the joint letter signed by President Bush and Prime Minister Maliki on November 26, 2007 and entitled "A Declaration of Principles for a Long-Term Relationship of Cooperation and Friendship Between the Republic of Iraq and the United States of America" (http://www.globalpolicy.org/security/issues/iraq/election/2007/1127declarationofprinciples.htm). This became the Strategic Framework Agreement, reproduced below in section B.3.a. The second agreement, dealing with security, was far more controversial. Negotiated as the Status of Forces Agreement (SOFA), like similar arrangements between the U.S. and a large number of countries, it eventually became the "Agreement Between the United States of America and the Republic of Iraq on the Withdrawal of United States Forces from Iraq and the Organization of Their Activities during Their Temporary Presence in Iraq," reproduced below in section B.3.b. Both agreements entered into force on January 1, 2009.

(a) Strategic Framework Agreement (SFA)

Strategic Framework Agreement for a Relationship of Friendship and Cooperation Between the United States of America and the Republic of Iraq

Preamble

The United States of America and the Republic of Iraq:

1. Affirming the genuine desire of the two countries to establish a long-term relationship of cooperation and friendship, based on the principle of equality in sovereignty and the rights and principles that are enshrined in the United Nations Charter and their common interests;

2. Recognizing the major and positive developments in Iraq that have taken place subsequent to April 9, 2003; the courage of the Iraqi people in establishing a democratically elected government under a new constitution; and welcoming no later than December 31, 2008, the termination

of the Chapter VII authorization for and mandate of the multinational forces in UNSCR 1790; noting that the situation in Iraq is fundamentally different than that which existed when the UN Security Council adopted Resolution 661 in 1990, and in particular that the threat to international peace and security posed by the Government of Iraq no longer exists; and affirming in that regard that Iraq should return by December 31, 2008 to the legal and international standing that it enjoyed prior to the issuance of UNSCR 661;

3. Consistent with the Declaration of Principles for a Long-Term Relationship of Cooperation and Friendship Between the Republic of Iraq and the United States of America, which was signed on November 26, 2007;

4. Recognizing both countries' desire to establish a long-term relationship, the need to support the success of the political process, reinforce national reconciliation within the framework of a unified and federal Iraq, and to build a diversified and advanced economy that ensures the integration of Iraq into the international community; and

5. Reaffirming that such a long-term relationship in economic, diplomatic, cultural and security fields will contribute to the strengthening and development of democracy in Iraq, as well as ensuring that Iraq will assume full responsibility for its security, the safety of its people, and maintaining peace within Iraq and among the countries of the region.

Have agreed to the following:

Section I: Principles of Cooperation

This Agreement is based on a number of general principles to establish the course of the future relationship between the two countries as follows:

1. A relationship of friendship and cooperation is based on mutual respect; recognized principles and norms of international law and fulfillment of international obligations; the principle of non-interference in internal affairs; and rejection of the use of violence to settle disputes.

2. A strong Iraq capable of self-defense is essential for achieving stability in the region.

3. The temporary presence of U.S. forces in Iraq is at the request and invitation of the sovereign Government of Iraq and with full respect for the sovereignty of Iraq.

4. The United States shall not use Iraqi land, sea, and air as a launching or transit point for attacks against other countries; nor seek or request permanent bases or a permanent military presence in Iraq.

Section II: Political and Diplomatic Cooperation

The Parties share a common understanding that their mutual efforts and cooperation on political and diplomatic issues shall improve and strengthen security and stability in Iraq and the region. In this regard, the United States shall ensure maximum efforts to work with and through the democratically elected Government of Iraq to:

1. Support and strengthen Iraq's democracy and its democratic institutions as defined and established in the Iraqi Constitution, and in so doing, enhance Iraq's capability to protect these institutions against all internal and external threats.

2. Support and enhance Iraq's status in regional and international organizations and institutions so that it may play a positive and constructive role in the international community.

3. Support the Government of Iraq in establishing positive relations with the states of the region, including on issues consequent to the actions of the former regime that continue to harm Iraq, based on mutual respect and the principles of non-interference and positive dialogue among states, and the peaceful resolution of disputes, without the use of force or violence, in a manner that enhances the security and stability of the region and the prosperity of its peoples.

Section III: Defense and Security Cooperation

In order to strengthen security and stability in Iraq, and thereby contribute to international peace and stability, and to enhance the ability of the Republic of Iraq to deter all threats against its sovereignty, security, and territorial integrity, the Parties shall continue to foster close cooperation concerning defense and security arrangements without prejudice to Iraqi sovereignty over its land, sea, and air territory. Such security and defense cooperation shall be undertaken pursuant to the *Agreement Between the United States of America and the Republic of Iraq on the Withdrawal of United States Forces from Iraq and the Organization of Their Activities during Their Temporary Presence in Iraq.*

Section IV: Cultural Cooperation

The Parties share the conviction that connections between their citizens, forged through cultural exchanges, educational links and the exploration of their common archeological heritage will forge strong, long lasting bonds of friendship and mutual respect. To that end, the Parties agree to cooperate to:

1. Promote cultural and social exchanges and facilitate cultural activities, such as Citizens Exchanges, the Youth Exchange and Study Program, the Global Connections and Exchange (GCE) program, and the English Language Teaching and Learning program.

2. Promote and facilitate cooperation and coordination in the field of higher education and scientific research, as well as encouraging investment in education, including through the establishment of universities and affiliations between Iraqi and American social and academic institutions such as the U.S. Department of Agriculture's (USDA's) agricultural extension program.

3. Strengthen the development of Iraq's future leaders, through exchanges, training programs, and fellowships, such as the Fulbright program and the International Visitor Leadership Program (IVLP), in fields including science, engineering, medicine, information technology, telecommunications, public administration, and strategic planning.

4. Strengthen and facilitate the application process for U.S. visas consistent with U.S. laws and procedures, to enhance the participation of qualified Iraqi individuals in scientific, educational, and cultural activities.

5. Promote Iraq's efforts in the field of social welfare and human rights.

6. Promote Iraqi efforts and contributions to international efforts to preserve Iraqi cultural heritage and protect archeological antiquities, rehabilitate Iraqi museums, and assist Iraq in recovering and restoring its smuggled artifacts through projects such as the Future of Babylon Project, and measures taken pursuant to the U.S. Emergency Protection for Iraqi Cultural Antiquities Act of 2004.

Section V: Economic and Energy Cooperation

Building a prosperous, diversified, growing economy in Iraq, integrated in the global economic system, capable of meeting the essential service needs of the Iraqi people, as well as welcoming home Iraqi citizens currently dwelling outside of the country, will require unprecedented capital investment in reconstruction, the development of Iraq's extraordinary natural and human resources, and the integration of Iraq into the international economy and its institutions. To that end the Parties agree to cooperate to:

1. Support Iraq's efforts to invest its resources towards economic development, sustainable development and investment in projects that improve the basic services for the Iraqi people.

2. Maintain active bilateral dialogue on measures to increase Iraq's development, including through the Dialogue on Economic Cooperation (DEC) and, upon entry into force, the Trade and Investment Framework Agreement.

3. Promote expansion of bilateral trade through the U.S.-Iraq Business Dialogue, as well as bilateral exchanges, such as trade promotion activities and access to Export-Import Bank programs.

4. Support Iraq's further integration into regional and international financial and economic communities and institutions, including membership in the World Trade Organization and through continued Normal Trade Relations with the United States.

5. Reinforce international efforts to develop the Iraqi economy and Iraqi efforts to reconstruct, rehabilitate, and maintain its economic infrastructure, including continuing cooperation with the Overseas Private Investment Corporation.

6. Urge all parties to abide by commitments made under the International Compact with Iraq with the goal of rehabilitating Iraq's economic

institutions and increasing economic growth through the implementation of reforms that lay the foundation for private sector development and job creation.

7. Facilitate the flow of direct investment into Iraq to contribute to the reconstruction and development of its economy.

8. Promote Iraq's development of the Iraqi electricity, oil, and gas sector, including the rehabilitation of vital facilities and institutions and strengthening and rehabilitating Iraqi capabilities.

9. Work with the international community to help locate and reclaim illegally exported funds and properties of Saddam Hussein's family and key members of his regime, as well as its smuggled archeological artifacts and cultural heritage before and after April 9, 2003.

10. Encourage the creation of a positive investment environment to modernize Iraq's private industrial sector to enhance growth and expand industrial production including through encouraging networking with U.S. industrial institutions.

11. Encourage development in the fields of air, land, and sea transportation as well as rehabilitation of Iraqi ports and enhancement of maritime trade between the Parties, including by facilitating cooperation with the U.S. Federal Highway Administration.

12. Maintain an active dialogue on agricultural issues to help Iraq develop its domestic agricultural production and trade policies.

13. Promote access to programs that increase farm, firm, and marketing productivity to generate higher incomes and expanded employment, building on successful programs by the USDA and the USAID programs in agribusiness, agriculture extension, and policy engagement.

14. Encourage increased Iraqi agricultural exports, including through policy engagement and encouraging education of Iraqi exporters on U.S. health and safety regulations.

Section VI: Health and Environmental Cooperation

In order to improve the health of the citizens of Iraq, as well as protect and improve the extraordinary natural environment of the historic Lands of the Two Rivers, the Parties agree to cooperate to:

1. Support and strengthen Iraq's efforts to build its health infrastructure and to strengthen health systems and networks.

2. Support Iraq's efforts to train health and medical cadres and staff.

3. Maintain dialogue on health policy issues to support Iraq's long-term development. Topics may include controlling the spread of infectious diseases, preventative and mental health, tertiary care, and increasing the efficiency of Iraq's medicine procurement system.

4. Encourage Iraqi and international investment in the health field, and facilitate specialized professional exchanges in order to promote the

transfer of expertise and to help foster relationships between medical and health institutions building on existing programs with the U.S. Department of Health and Human Services, including its Centers for Disease Control and Prevention.

5. Encourage Iraqi efforts to strengthen mechanisms for protecting, preserving, improving, and developing the Iraqi environment and encouraging regional and international environmental cooperation.

Section VII: Information Technology and Communications Cooperation

Communications are the lifeblood of economic growth in the twenty-first century, as well as the foundation for the enhancement of democracy and civil society. In order to improve access to information and promote the development of a modern and state of the art communications industry in Iraq, the Parties agree to cooperate to:

1. Support the exchange of information and best practices in the fields of regulating telecommunications services and the development of information technology policies.

2. Exchange views and practices relating to liberalizing information technologies and telecommunications services markets, and the strengthening of an independent regulator.

3. Promote active Iraqi participation in the meetings and initiatives of the Internet Governance Forum, including its next global meetings.

Section VIII: Law Enforcement and Judicial Cooperation

The Parties agree to cooperate to:

1. Support the further integration and security of the Iraqi criminal justice system, including police, courts, and prisons.

2. Exchange views and best practices related to judicial capacity building and training, including on continuing professional development for judges, judicial investigators, judicial security personnel, and court administrative staff.

3. Enhance law enforcement and judicial relationships to address corruption, and common transnational criminal threats, such as terrorism, trafficking in persons, organized crime, drugs, money laundering, smuggling of archeological artifacts, and cyber crime.

Section IX: Joint Committees

1. The Parties shall establish a Higher Coordinating Committee (HCC) to monitor the overall implementation of the Agreement and develop the

agreed upon objectives. The committee shall meet periodically and may include representatives from relevant departments and ministries.

2. The Parties shall seek to establish additional Joint Coordination Committees (JCCs), as necessary, responsible for executing and overseeing this Agreement. The JCCs will report to the HCC and are to:

> a. Monitor implementation and consult regularly to promote the most effective implementation of this Agreement and to assist in dispute resolution as necessary;

> b. Propose new cooperation projects and carry out discussions and negotiations as necessary to reach an agreement about details of such cooperation; and

> c. Include other governmental departments and ministries for broader coordination from time to time, with meetings in Iraq and the United States, as appropriate.

3. Disputes that may arise under this Agreement, if not resolved within the relevant JCC, and not amenable to resolution within the HCC, are to be settled through diplomatic channels.

Section X: Implementing Agreements and Arrangements

The Parties may enter into further agreements or arrangements as necessary and appropriate to implement this Agreement.

Section XI: Final Provisions

1. This Agreement shall enter into force on January 1, 2009, following an exchange of diplomatic notes confirming that the actions by the Parties necessary to bring the Agreement into force in accordance with the respective constitutional procedures in effect in both countries have been completed.

2. This Agreement shall remain in force unless either Party provides written notice to the other of its intent to terminate this Agreement. The termination shall be effective one year after the date of such notification.

3. This Agreement may be amended with the mutual written agreement of the Parties and in accordance with the constitutional procedures in effect in both countries.

4. All cooperation under this Agreement shall be subject to the laws and regulations of both countries.

Signed in duplicate in Baghdad on this 17th day of November, 2008, in the English and Arabic language, each text being equally authentic.

(b) The SOFA/Withdrawal Agreement (SWA)

Agreement Between the United States of America and the Republic of Iraq on the Withdrawal of United States Forces from Iraq and the Organization of Their Activities during Their Temporary Presence in Iraq

Preamble

The United States of America and the Republic of Iraq, referred to hereafter as "the Parties":

Recognizing the importance of: strengthening their joint security, contributing to world peace and stability, combating terrorism in Iraq, and cooperating in the security and defense spheres, thereby deterring aggression and threats against the sovereignty, security, and territorial integrity of Iraq and against its democratic, federal, and constitutional system;

Affirming that such cooperation is based on full respect for the sovereignty of each of them in accordance with the purposes and principles of the United Nations Charter;

Out of a desire to reach a common understanding that strengthens cooperation between them;

Without prejudice to Iraqi sovereignty over its territory, waters, and airspace; and Pursuant to joint undertakings as two sovereign, independent, and coequal countries;

Have agreed to the following:

Article 1. Scope and Purpose

This Agreement shall determine the principal provisions and requirements that regulate the temporary presence, activities, and withdrawal of the United States Forces from Iraq.

Article 2. Definition of Terms

1. "Agreed facilities and areas" are those Iraqi facilities and areas owned by the Government of Iraq that are in use by the United States Forces during the period in which this Agreement is in force.

2. "United States Forces" means the entity comprising the members of the United States Armed Forces, their associated civilian component, and all property, equipment, and materiel of the United States Armed Forces present in the territory of Iraq.

3. "Member of the United States Forces" means any individual who is a member of the United States Army, Navy, Air Force, Marine Corps, or Coast Guard.

4. "Member of the civilian component" means any civilian employed by the United States Department of Defense. This term does not include individuals normally resident in Iraq.

5. "United States contractors" and "United States contractor employees" mean non-Iraqi persons or legal entities, and their employees, who are citizens

of the United States or a third country and who are in Iraq to supply goods, services, and security in Iraq to or on behalf of the United States Forces under a contract or subcontract with or for the United States Forces. However, the terms do not include persons or legal entities normally resident in the territory of Iraq.

6. "Official vehicles" means commercial vehicles that may be modified for security purposes and are basically designed for movement on various roads and designated for transportation of personnel.

7. "Military vehicles" means all types of vehicles used by the United States Forces, which were originally designated for use in combat operations and display special distinguishing numbers and symbols according to applicable United States Forces instructions and regulations.

8. "Defense equipment" means systems, weapons, supplies, equipment, munitions, and materials exclusively used in conventional warfare that are required by the United States Forces in connection with agreed activities under this Agreement and are not related, either directly or indirectly, to systems of weapons of mass destruction (chemical weapons, nuclear weapons, radiological weapons, biological weapons, and related waste of such weapons).

9. "Storage" means the keeping of defense equipment required by the United States Forces in connection with agreed activities under this Agreement.

10. "Taxes and duties" means all taxes, duties (including customs duties), fees, of whatever kind, imposed by the Government of Iraq, or its agencies, or governorates under Iraqi laws and regulations. However, the term does not include charges by the Government of Iraq, its agencies, or governorates for services requested and received by the United States Forces.

Article 3. Laws

1. While conducting military operations pursuant to this Agreement, it is the duty of members of the United States Forces and of the civilian component to respect Iraqi laws, customs, traditions, and conventions and to refrain from any activities that are inconsistent with the letter and spirit of this Agreement. It is the duty of the United States to take all necessary measures for this purpose.

2. With the exception of members of the United States Forces and of the civilian component, the United States Forces may not transfer any person into or out of Iraq on vehicles, vessels, or aircraft covered by this Agreement, unless in accordance with applicable Iraqi laws and regulations, including implementing arrangements as may be agreed to by the Government of Iraq.

Article 4. Missions

1. The Government of Iraq requests the temporary assistance of the United States Forces for the purposes of supporting Iraq in its efforts to maintain security and stability in Iraq, including cooperation in the conduct of operations against al-Qaeda and other terrorist groups, outlaw groups, and remnants of the former regime.

2. All such military operations that are carried out pursuant to this Agreement shall be conducted with the agreement of the Government of Iraq. Such operations shall be fully coordinated with Iraqi authorities. The coordination of all such military operations shall be overseen by a Joint Military Operations

Coordination Committee (JMOCC) to be established pursuant to this Agreement. Issues regarding proposed military operations that cannot be resolved by the JMOCC shall be forwarded to the Joint Ministerial Committee.

3. All such operations shall be conducted with full respect for the Iraqi Constitution and the laws of Iraq. Execution of such operations shall not infringe upon the sovereignty of Iraq and its national interests, as defined by the Government of Iraq. It is the duty of the United States Forces to respect the laws, customs, and traditions of Iraq and applicable international law.

4. The Parties shall continue their efforts to cooperate to strengthen Iraq's security capabilities including, as may be mutually agreed, on training, equipping, supporting, supplying, and establishing and upgrading logistical systems, including transportation, housing, and supplies for Iraqi Security Forces.

5. The Parties retain the right to legitimate self defense within Iraq, as defined in applicable international law.

Article 5. Property Ownership

1. Iraq owns all buildings, non-relocatable structures, and assemblies connected to the soil that exist on agreed facilities and areas, including those that are used, constructed, altered, or improved by the United States Forces.

2. Upon their withdrawal, the United States Forces shall return to the Government of Iraq all the facilities and areas provided for the use of the combat forces of the United States, based on two lists. The first list of agreed facilities and areas shall take effect upon the entry into force of the Agreement. The second list shall take effect no later than June 30, 2009, the date for the withdrawal of combat forces from the cities, villages, and localities. The Government of Iraq may agree to allow the United States Forces the use of some necessary facilities for the purposes of this Agreement on withdrawal.

3. The United States shall bear all costs for construction, alterations, or improvements in the agreed facilities and areas provided for its exclusive use. The United States Forces shall consult with the Government of Iraq regarding such construction, alterations, and improvements, and must seek approval of the Government of Iraq for major construction and alteration projects. In the event that the use of agreed facilities and areas is shared, the two Parties shall bear the costs of construction, alterations, or improvements proportionately.

4. The United States shall be responsible for paying the costs for services requested and received in the agreed facilities and areas exclusively used by it, and both Parties shall be proportionally responsible for paying the costs for services requested and received in joint agreed facilities and areas.

5. Upon the discovery of any historical or cultural site or finding any strategic resource in agreed facilities and areas, all works of construction, upgrading, or modification shall cease immediately and the Iraqi representatives at the Joint Committee shall be notified to determine appropriate steps in that regard.

6. The United States shall return agreed facilities and areas and any non-relocatable structures and assemblies on them that it had built, installed, or established during the term of this Agreement, according to mechanisms and

priorities set forth by the Joint Committee. Such facilities and areas shall be handed over to the Government of Iraq free of any debts and financial burdens.

7. The United States Forces shall return to the Government of Iraq the agreed facilities and areas that have heritage, moral, and political significance and any non-relocatable structures and assemblies on them that it had built, installed, or established, according to mechanisms, priorities, and a time period as mutually agreed by the Joint Committee, free of any debts or financial burdens.

8. The United States Forces shall return the agreed facilities and areas to the Government of Iraq upon the expiration or termination of this Agreement, or earlier as mutually agreed by the Parties, or when such facilities are no longer required as determined by the JMOCC, free of any debts or financial burdens.

9. The United States Forces and United States contractors shall retain title to all equipment, materials, supplies, relocatable structures, and other movable property that was legitimately imported into or legitimately acquired within the territory of Iraq in connection with this Agreement.

Article 6. Use of Agreed Facilities and Areas

1. With full respect for the sovereignty of Iraq, and as part of exchanging views between the Parties pursuant to this Agreement, Iraq grants access and use of agreed facilities and areas to the United States Forces, United States contractors, United States contractor employees, and other individuals or entities as agreed upon by the Parties.

2. In accordance with this Agreement, Iraq authorizes the United States Forces to exercise within the agreed facilities and areas all rights and powers that may be necessary to establish, use, maintain, and secure such agreed facilities and areas. The Parties shall coordinate and cooperate regarding exercising these rights and powers in the agreed facilities and areas of joint use.

3. The United States Forces shall assume control of entry to agreed facilities and areas that have been provided for its exclusive use. The Parties shall coordinate the control of entry into agreed facilities and areas for joint use and in accordance with mechanisms set forth by the JMOCC. The Parties shall coordinate guard duties in areas adjacent to agreed facilities and areas through the JMOCC.

Article 7. Positioning and Storage of Defense Equipment

The United States Forces may place within agreed facilities and areas and in other temporary locations agreed upon by the Parties defense equipment, supplies, and materials that are required by the United States Forces in connection with agreed activities under this Agreement. The use and storage of such equipment shall be proportionate to the temporary missions of the United States Forces in Iraq pursuant to Article 4 of this Agreement and shall not be related, either directly or indirectly, to systems of weapons of mass destruction (chemical weapons, nuclear weapons, radiological weapons, biological weapons, and related waste of such weapons). The United States Forces shall control the use and relocation of defense equipment that they own and are stored in Iraq. The United States Forces shall ensure that no storage depots for explosives or munitions are near residential areas, and they shall remove such materials stored therein. The United States shall provide the Government of Iraq with essential information on the numbers and types of such stocks.

Article 8. Protecting the Environment

Both Parties shall implement this Agreement in a manner consistent with protecting the natural environment and human health and safety. The United States reaffirms its commitment to respecting applicable Iraqi environmental laws, regulations, and standards in the course of executing its policies for the purposes of implementing this Agreement.

Article 9. Movement of Vehicles, Vessels, and Aircraft

1. With full respect for the relevant rules of land and maritime safety and movement, vessels and vehicles operated by or at the time exclusively for the United States Forces may enter, exit, and move within the territory of Iraq for the purposes of implementing this Agreement. The JMOCC shall develop appropriate procedures and rules to facilitate and regulate the movement of vehicles.

2. With full respect for relevant rules of safety in aviation and air navigation, United States Government aircraft and civil aircraft that are at the time operating exclusively under a contract with the United States Department of Defense are authorized to over-fly, conduct airborne refueling exclusively for the purposes of implementing this Agreement over, and land and take off within, the territory of Iraq for the purposes of implementing this Agreement. The Iraqi authorities shall grant the aforementioned aircraft permission every year to land in and take off from Iraqi territory exclusively for the purposes of implementing this Agreement. United States Government aircraft and civil aircraft that are at the time operating exclusively under a contract with the United States Department of Defense, vessels, and vehicles shall not have any party boarding them without the consent of the authorities of the United States Forces. The Joint Sub-Committee concerned with this matter shall take appropriate action to facilitate the regulation of such traffic.

3. Surveillance and control over Iraqi airspace shall transfer to Iraqi authority immediately upon entry into force of this Agreement.

4. Iraq may request from the United States Forces temporary support for the Iraqi authorities in the mission of surveillance and control of Iraqi air space.

5. United States Government aircraft and civil aircraft that are at the time operating exclusively under contract to the United States Department of Defense shall not be subject to payment of any taxes, duties, fees, or similar charges, including overflight or navigation fees, landing, and parking fees at government airfields. Vehicles and vessels owned or operated by or at the time exclusively for the United States Forces shall not be subject to payment of any taxes, duties, fees, or similar charges, including for vessels at government ports. Such vehicles, vessels, and aircraft shall be free from registration requirements within Iraq.

6. The United States Forces shall pay fees for services requested and received.

7. Each Party shall provide the other with maps and other available information on the location of mine fields and other obstacles that can hamper or jeopardize movement within the territory and waters of Iraq.

Article 10. Contracting Procedures

The United States Forces may select contractors and enter into contracts in accordance with United States law for the purchase of materials and services in Iraq, including services of construction and building. The United States Forces shall contract with Iraqi suppliers of materials and services to the extent feasible when their bids are competitive and constitute best value. The United States Forces shall respect Iraqi law when contracting with Iraqi suppliers and contractors and shall provide Iraqi authorities with the names of Iraqi suppliers and contractors, and the amounts of relevant contracts.

Article 11. Services and Communications

1. The United States Forces may produce and provide water, electricity, and other services to agreed facilities and areas in coordination with the Iraqi authorities through the Joint Sub-Committee concerned with this matter.

2. The Government of Iraq owns all frequencies. Pertinent Iraqi authorities shall allocate to the United States Forces such frequencies as coordinated by both Parties through the JMOCC. The United States Forces shall return frequencies allocated to them at the end of their use not later than the termination of this Agreement.

3. The United States Forces shall operate their own telecommunications systems in a manner that fully respects the Constitution and laws of Iraq and in accordance with the definition of the term "telecommunications" contained in the Constitution of the International Union of Telecommunications of 1992, including the right to use necessary means and services of their own systems to ensure the full capability to operate systems of telecommunications.

4. For the purposes of this Agreement, the United States Forces are exempt from the payment of fees to use transmission airwaves and existing and future frequencies, including any administrative fees or any other related charges.

5. The United States Forces must obtain the consent of the Government of Iraq regarding any projects of infrastructure for communications that are made outside agreed facilities and areas exclusively for the purposes of this Agreement in accordance with Article 4, except in the case of actual combat operations conducted pursuant to Article 4.

6. The United States Forces shall use telecommunications systems exclusively for the purposes of this Agreement.

Article 12. Jurisdiction

Recognizing Iraq's sovereign right to determine and enforce the rules of criminal and civil law in its territory, in light of Iraq's request for temporary assistance from the United States Forces set forth in Article 4, and consistent with the duty of the members of the United States Forces and the civilian component to respect Iraqi laws, customs, traditions, and conventions, the Parties have agreed as follows:

1. Iraq shall have the primary right to exercise jurisdiction over members of the United States Forces and of the civilian component for the grave premeditated felonies enumerated pursuant to paragraph 8, when such crimes are committed outside agreed facilities and areas and outside duty status.

2. Iraq shall have the primary right to exercise jurisdiction over United States contractors and United States contractor employees.

3. The United States shall have the primary right to exercise jurisdiction over members of the United States Forces and of the civilian component for matters arising inside agreed facilities and areas; during duty status outside agreed facilities and areas; and in circumstances not covered by paragraph 1.

4. At the request of either Party, the Parties shall assist each other in the investigation of incidents and the collection and exchange of evidence to ensure the due course of justice.

5. Members of the United States Forces and of the civilian component arrested or detained by Iraqi authorities shall be notified immediately to United States Forces authorities and handed over to them within 24 hours from the time of detention or arrest. Where Iraq exercises jurisdiction pursuant to paragraph 1 of this Article, custody of an accused member of the United States Forces or of the civilian component shall reside with United States Forces authorities. United States Forces authorities shall make such accused persons available to the Iraqi authorities for purposes of investigation and trial. The authorities of either Party may request the authorities of the other Party to waive its primary right to jurisdiction in a particular case.

6. The Government of Iraq agrees to exercise jurisdiction under paragraph 1 above, only after it has determined and notifies the United States in writing within 21 days of the discovery of an alleged offense, that it is of particular importance that such jurisdiction be exercised.

7. Where the United States exercises jurisdiction pursuant to paragraph 3 of this Article, members of the United States Forces and of the civilian component shall be entitled to due process standards and protections pursuant to the Constitution and laws of the United States. Where the offense arising under paragraph 3 of this Article may involve a victim who is not a member of the United States Forces or of the civilian component, the Parties shall establish procedures through the Joint Committee to keep such persons informed as appropriate of: the status of the investigation of the crime; the bringing of charges against a suspected offender; the scheduling of court proceedings and the results of plea negotiations; opportunity to be heard at public sentencing proceedings, and to confer with the attorney for the prosecution in the case; and, assistance with filing a claim under Article 21 of this Agreement. As mutually agreed by the Parties, United States Forces authorities shall seek to hold the trials of such cases inside Iraq. If the trial of such cases is to be conducted in the United States, efforts will be undertaken to facilitate the personal attendance of the victim at the trial.

8. Where Iraq exercises jurisdiction pursuant to paragraph 1 of this Article, members of the United States Forces and of the civilian component shall be entitled to due process standards and protections consistent with those available under United States and Iraqi law. The Joint Committee shall establish procedures and mechanisms for implementing this Article, including an enumeration of the grave premeditated felonies that are subject to paragraph 1 and procedures that meet such due process standards and protections. Any exercise of jurisdiction pursuant to paragraph 1 of this Article may proceed only in accordance with these procedures and mechanisms.

9. Pursuant to paragraphs 1 and 3 of this Article, United States Forces authorities shall certify whether an alleged offense arose during duty status. In those cases where Iraqi authorities believe the circumstances require a review of this determination, the Parties shall consult immediately through the Joint Committee, and United States Forces authorities shall take full account of the facts and circumstances and any information Iraqi authorities may present bearing on the determination by United States Forces authorities.

10. The Parties shall review the provisions of this Article every 6 months including by considering any proposed amendments to this Article taking into account the security situation in Iraq, the extent to which the United States Forces in Iraq are engaged in military operations, the growth and development of the Iraqi judicial system, and changes in United States and Iraqi law.

Article 13. Carrying Weapons and Apparel

Members of the United States Forces and of the civilian component may possess and carry weapons that are owned by the United States while in Iraq according to the authority granted to them under orders and according to their requirements and duties. Members of the United States Forces may also wear uniforms during duty in Iraq.

Article 14. Entry and Exit

1. For purposes of this Agreement, members of the United States Forces and of the civilian component may enter and leave Iraq through official places of embarkation and debarkation requiring only identification cards and travel orders issued for them by the United States. The Joint Committee shall assume the task of setting up a mechanism and a process of verification to be carried out by pertinent Iraqi authorities.

2. Iraqi authorities shall have the right to inspect and verify the lists of names of members of the United States Forces and of the civilian component entering and leaving Iraq directly through the agreed facilities and areas. Said lists shall be submitted to Iraqi authorities by the United States Forces. For purposes of this Agreement, members of the United States Forces and of the civilian component may enter and leave Iraq through agreed facilities and areas requiring only identification cards issued for them by the United States. The Joint Committee shall assume the task of setting up a mechanism and a process for inspecting and verifying the validity of these documents.

Article 15. Import and Export

1. For the exclusive purposes of implementing this Agreement, the United States Forces and United States contractors may import, export (items bought in Iraq), re-export, transport, and use in Iraq any equipment, supplies, materials, and technology, provided that the materials imported or brought in by them are not banned in Iraq as of the date this Agreement enters into force. The importation, re-exportation, transportation, and use of such items shall not be subject to any inspections, licenses, or other restrictions, taxes, customs duties, or any other charges imposed in Iraq, as defined in Article 2, paragraph 10. United States Forces authorities shall provide to relevant Iraqi authorities an appropriate certification that such items are being imported by

the United States Forces or United States contractors for use by the United States Forces exclusively for the purposes of this Agreement. Based on security information that becomes available, Iraqi authorities have the right to request the United States Forces to open in their presence any container in which such items are being imported in order to verify its contents. In making such a request, Iraqi authorities shall honor the security requirements of the United States Forces and, if requested to do so by the United States Forces, shall make such verifications in facilities used by the United States Forces. The exportation of Iraqi goods by the United States Forces and United States contractors shall not be subject to inspections or any restrictions other than licensing requirements. The Joint Committee shall work with the Iraqi Ministry of Trade to expedite license requirements consistent with Iraqi law for the export of goods purchased in Iraq by the United States Forces for the purposes of this Agreement. Iraq has the right to demand review of any issues arising out of this paragraph. The Parties shall consult immediately in such cases through the Joint Committee or, if necessary, the Joint Ministerial Committee.

2. Members of the United States Forces and of the civilian component may import into Iraq, re-export, and use personal effect materials and equipment for consumption or personal use. The import into, re-export from, transfer from, and use of such imported items in Iraq shall not be subjected to licenses, other restrictions, taxes, custom duties, or any other charges imposed in Iraq, as defined in Article 2, paragraph 10. The imported quantities shall be reasonable and proportionate to personal use. United States Forces authorities will take measures to ensure that no items or material of cultural or historic significance to Iraq are being exported.

3. Any inspections of materials pursuant to paragraph 2 by Iraqi authorities must be done urgently in an agreed upon place and according to procedures established by the Joint Committee.

4. Any material imported free of customs and fees in accordance with this Agreement shall be subjected to taxes and customs and fees as defined in Article 2, paragraph 10, or any other fees valued at the time of sale in Iraq, upon sale to individuals and entities not covered by tax exemption or special import privileges. Such taxes and fees (including custom duties) shall be paid by the transferee for the items sold.

5. Materials referred to in the paragraphs of this Article must not be imported or used for commercial purposes.

Article 16. Taxes

1. Any taxes, duties, or fees as defined in Article 2, paragraph 10, with their value determined and imposed in the territory of Iraq, shall not be imposed on goods and services purchased by or on behalf of the United States Forces in Iraq for official use or on goods and services that have been purchased in Iraq on behalf of the United States Forces.

2. Members of the United States Forces and of the civilian component shall not be responsible for payment of any tax, duty, or fee that has its value determined and imposed in the territory of Iraq, unless in return for services requested and received.

Article 17. Licenses or Permits

1. Valid driver's licenses issued by United States authorities to members of the United States Forces and of the civilian component, and to United States contractor employees, shall be deemed acceptable to Iraqi authorities. Such license holders shall not be subject to a test or fee for operating the vehicles, vessels, and aircraft belonging to the United States Forces in Iraq.

2. Valid driver's licenses issued by United States authorities to members of the United States Forces and of the civilian component, and to United States contractor employees, to operate personal cars within the territory of Iraq shall be deemed acceptable to Iraqi authorities. License holders shall not be subject to a test or fee.

3. All professional licenses issued by United States authorities to members of the United States Forces and of the civilian component, and to United States contractor employees shall be deemed valid by Iraqi authorities, provided such licenses are related to the services they provide within the framework of performing their official duties for or contracts in support of the United States Forces, members of the civilian component, United States contractors, and United States contractor employees, according to terms agreed upon by the Parties.

Article 18. Official and Military Vehicles

1. Official vehicles shall display official Iraqi license plates to be agreed upon between the Parties. Iraqi authorities shall, at the request of the authorities of the United States Forces, issue registration plates for official vehicles of the United States Forces without fees, according to procedures used for the Iraqi Armed Forces. The authorities of the United States Forces shall pay to Iraqi authorities the cost of such plates.

2. Valid registration and licenses issued by United States authorities for official vehicles of the United States Forces shall be deemed acceptable by Iraqi authorities.

3. Military vehicles exclusively used by the United States Forces will be exempted from the requirements of registration and licenses, and they shall be clearly marked with numbers on such vehicles.

Article 19. Support Activities Services

1. The United States Forces, or others acting on behalf of the United States Forces, may assume the duties of establishing and administering activities and entities inside agreed facilities and areas, through which they can provide services for members of the United States Forces, the civilian component, United States contractors, and United States contractor employees. These entities and activities include military post offices; financial services; shops selling food items, medicine, and other commodities and services; and various areas to provide entertainment and telecommunications services, including radio broadcasts. The establishment of such services does not require permits.

2. Broadcasting, media, and entertainment services that reach beyond the scope of the agreed facilities and areas shall be subject to Iraqi laws.

3. Access to the Support Activities Services shall be limited to members of the United States Forces and of the civilian component, United States contractors, United States contractor employees, and other persons and entities that are agreed upon. The authorities of the United States Forces shall take appropriate actions to prevent misuse of the services provided by the mentioned activities, and prevent the sale or resale of aforementioned goods and services to persons not authorized access to these entities or to benefit from their services. The United States Forces will determine broadcasting and television programs to authorized recipients.

4. The service support entities and activities referred to in this Article shall be granted the same financial and customs exemptions granted to the United States Forces, including exemptions guaranteed in Articles 15 and 16 of this Agreement. These entities and activities that offer services shall be operated and managed in accordance with United States regulations; these entities and activities shall not be obligated to collect nor pay taxes or other fees related to the activities in connection with their operations.

5. The mail sent through the military post service shall be certified by United States Forces authorities and shall be exempt from inspection, search, and seizure by Iraqi authorities, except for non-official mail that may be subject to electronic observation. Questions arising in the course of implementation of this paragraph shall be addressed by the concerned Joint Sub-Committee and resolved by mutual agreement. The concerned Joint Sub-Committee shall periodically inspect the mechanisms by which the United States Forces authorities certify military mail.

Article 20. Currency and Foreign Exchange

1. The United States Forces shall have the right to use any amount of cash in United States currency or financial instruments with a designated value in United States currency exclusively for the purposes of this Agreement. Use of Iraqi currency and special banks by the United States Forces shall be in accordance with Iraqi laws.

2. The United States Forces may not export Iraqi currency from Iraq, and shall take measures to ensure that members of the United States Forces, of the civilian component, and United States contractors and United States contractor employees do not export Iraqi currency from Iraq.

Article 21. Claims

1. With the exception of claims arising from contracts, each Party shall waive the right to claim compensation against the other Party for any damage, loss, or destruction of property, or compensation for injuries or deaths that could happen to members of the force or civilian component of either Party arising out of the performance of their official duties in Iraq.

2. United States Forces authorities shall pay just and reasonable compensation in settlement of meritorious third party claims arising out of acts, omissions, or negligence of members of the United States Forces and of the civilian component done in the performance of their official duties and incident to the non-combat activities of the United States Forces. United States Forces authorities may also settle meritorious claims not arising from the performance of

official duties. All claims in this paragraph shall be settled expeditiously in accordance with the laws and regulations of the United States. In settling claims, United States Forces authorities shall take into account any report of investigation or opinion regarding liability or amount of damages issued by Iraqi authorities.

3. Upon the request of either Party, the Parties shall consult immediately through the Joint Committee or, if necessary, the Joint Ministerial Committee, where issues referred to in paragraphs 1 and 2 above require review.

Article 22. Detention

1. No detention or arrest may be carried out by the United States Forces (except with respect to detention or arrest of members of the United States Forces and of the civilian component) except through an Iraqi decision issued in accordance with Iraqi law and pursuant to Article 4.

2. In the event the United States Forces detain or arrest persons as authorized by this Agreement or Iraqi law, such persons must be handed over to competent Iraqi authorities within 24 hours from the time of their detention or arrest.

3. The Iraqi authorities may request assistance from the United States Forces in detaining or arresting wanted individuals.

4. Upon entry into force of this Agreement, the United States Forces shall provide to the Government of Iraq available information on all detainees who are being held by them. Competent Iraqi authorities shall issue arrest warrants for persons who are wanted by them. The United States Forces shall act in full and effective coordination with the Government of Iraq to turn over custody of such wanted detainees to Iraqi authorities pursuant to a valid Iraqi arrest warrant and shall release all the remaining detainees in a safe and orderly manner, unless otherwise requested by the Government of Iraq and in accordance with Article 4 of this Agreement.

5. The United States Forces may not search houses or other real estate properties except by order of an Iraqi judicial warrant and in full coordination with the Government of Iraq, except in the case of actual combat operations conducted pursuant to Article 4.

Article 23. Implementation

Implementation of this Agreement and the settlement of disputes arising from the interpretation and application thereof shall be vested in the following bodies:

1. A Joint Ministerial Committee shall be established with participation at the Ministerial level determined by both Parties. The Joint Ministerial Committee shall deal with issues that are fundamental to the interpretation and implementation of this Agreement.

2. The Joint Ministerial Committee shall establish a JMOCC consisting of representatives from both Parties. The JMOCC shall be co-chaired by representatives of each Party.

3. The Joint Ministerial Committee shall also establish a Joint Committee consisting of representatives to be determined by both Parties. The Joint Committee shall be cochaired by representatives of each Party, and shall deal with

all issues related to this Agreement outside the exclusive competence of the JMOCC.

4. In accordance with paragraph 3 of this Article, the Joint Committee shall establish Joint Sub-Committees in different areas to consider the issues arising under this Agreement according to their competencies.

Article 24. Withdrawal of the United States Forces from Iraq

Recognizing the performance and increasing capacity of the Iraqi Security Forces, the assumption of full security responsibility by those Forces, and based upon the strong relationship between the Parties, an agreement on the following has been reached:

1. All the United States Forces shall withdraw from all Iraqi territory no later than December 31, 2011.

2. All United States combat forces shall withdraw from Iraqi cities, villages, and localities no later than the time at which Iraqi Security Forces assume full responsibility for security in an Iraqi province, provided that such withdrawal is completed no later than June 30, 2009.

3. United States combat forces withdrawn pursuant to paragraph 2 above shall be stationed in the agreed facilities and areas outside cities, villages, and localities to be designated by the JMOCC before the date established in paragraph 2 above.

4. The United States recognizes the sovereign right of the Government of Iraq to request the departure of the United States Forces from Iraq at any time. The Government of Iraq recognizes the sovereign right of the United States to withdraw the United States Forces from Iraq at any time.

5. The Parties agree to establish mechanisms and arrangements to reduce the number of the United States Forces during the periods of time that have been determined, and they shall agree on the locations where the United States Forces will be present.

Article 25. Measures to Terminate the Application of Chapter VII to Iraq

Acknowledging the right of the Government of Iraq not to request renewal of the Chapter VII authorization for and mandate of the multinational forces contained in United Nations Security Council Resolution 1790 (2007) that ends on December 31, 2008;

Taking note of the letters to the UN Security Council from the Prime Minister of Iraq and the Secretary of State of the United States dated December 7 and December 10, 2007, respectively, which are annexed to Resolution 1790;

Taking note of section 3 of the Declaration of Principles for a Long-Term Relationship of Cooperation and Friendship, signed by the President of the United States and the Prime Minister of Iraq on November 26, 2007, which memorialized Iraq's call for extension of the above-mentioned mandate for a final period, to end not later than December 31, 2008;

Recognizing also the dramatic and positive developments in Iraq, and noting that the situation in Iraq is fundamentally different than that which existed when the UN Security Council adopted Resolution 661 in 1990, and in particular that the threat to international peace and security posed by the

Government of Iraq no longer exists, the Parties affirm in this regard that with the termination on December 31, 2008 of the Chapter VII mandate and authorization for the multinational force contained in Resolution 1790, Iraq should return to the legal and international standing that it enjoyed prior to the adoption of UN Security Council Resolution 661 (1990), and that the United States shall use its best efforts to help Iraq take the steps necessary to achieve this by December 31, 2008.

Article 26. Iraqi Assets

1. To enable Iraq to continue to develop its national economy through the rehabilitation of its economic infrastructure, as well as providing necessary essential services to the Iraqi people, and to continue to safeguard Iraq's revenues from oil and gas and other Iraqi resources and its financial and economic assets located abroad, including the Development Fund for Iraq, the United States shall ensure maximum efforts to:

  a. Support Iraq to obtain forgiveness of international debt resulting from the policies of the former regime.
  b. Support Iraq to achieve a comprehensive and final resolution of outstanding reparation claims inherited from the previous regime, including compensation requirements imposed by the UN Security Council on Iraq.

2. Recognizing and understanding Iraq's concern with claims based on actions perpetrated by the former regime, the President of the United States has exercised his authority to protect from United States judicial process the Development Fund for Iraq and certain other property in which Iraq has an interest. The United States shall remain fully and actively engaged with the Government of Iraq with respect to continuation of such protections and with respect to such claims.

3. Consistent with a letter from the President of the United States to be sent to the Prime Minister of Iraq, the United States remains committed to assist Iraq in connection with its request that the UN Security Council extend the protections and other arrangements established in Resolution 1483 (2003) and Resolution 1546 (2003) for petroleum, petroleum products, and natural gas originating in Iraq, proceeds and obligations from sale thereof, and the Development Fund for Iraq.

Article 27. Deterrence of Security Threats

In order to strengthen security and stability in Iraq and to contribute to the maintenance of international peace and stability, the Parties shall work actively to strengthen the political and military capabilities of the Republic of Iraq to deter threats against its sovereignty, political independence, territorial integrity, and its constitutional federal democratic system.

To that end, the Parties agree as follows:

In the event of any external or internal threat or aggression against Iraq that would violate its sovereignty, political independence, or territorial integrity, waters, airspace, its democratic system or its elected institutions, and upon request by the Government of Iraq, the Parties shall immediately initiate strategic deliberations and, as may be mutually agreed, the United States shall take appropriate measures, including diplomatic, economic, or military measures, or any other measure, to deter such a threat. The Parties agree to continue close cooperation in strengthening and maintaining military and security institutions and democratic political institutions in Iraq, including, as may be mutually agreed, cooperation in training, equipping, and arming the Iraqi Security Forces, in order to combat domestic and international terrorism and outlaw groups, upon request by the Government of Iraq. Iraqi land, sea, and air shall not be used as a launching or transit point for attacks against other countries.

Article 28. The Green Zone

Upon entry into force of this Agreement the Government of Iraq shall have full responsibility for the Green Zone. The Government of Iraq may request from the United States Forces limited and temporary support for the Iraqi authorities in the mission of security for the Green Zone. Upon such request, relevant Iraqi authorities shall work jointly with the United States Forces authorities on security for the Green Zone during the period determined by the Government of Iraq.

Article 29. Implementing Mechanisms

Whenever the need arises, the Parties shall establish appropriate mechanisms for implementation of Articles of this Agreement, including those that do not contain specific implementation mechanisms.

Article 30. The Period for Which the Agreement Is Effective

1. This Agreement shall be effective for a period of three years, unless terminated sooner by either Party pursuant to paragraph 3 of this Article.

2. This Agreement shall be amended only with the official agreement of the Parties in writing and in accordance with the constitutional procedures in effect in both countries.

3. This Agreement shall terminate one year after a Party provides written notification to the other Party to that effect.

4. This Agreement shall enter into force on January 1, 2009, following an exchange of diplomatic notes confirming that the actions by the Parties necessary to bring the Agreement into force in accordance with each Party's respective constitutional procedures have been completed.

Signed in duplicate in Baghdad on this 17th day of November, 2008, in the English and Arabic languages, each text being equally authentic.

NOTES AND QUESTIONS

1. The Strategic Framework Agreement requires the United States to "[s]upport and strengthen Iraq's democracy and its democratic institutions as defined and established in the Iraqi Constitution." How achievable is such a goal? Should the U.S. prevent, for instance, a military coup in Iraq? Can it go after bombers alleged to come across the borders to undermine Iraqi democracy,

as was the case in an instance of military action against Syria on October 26, 2008?

2. Some sort of agreement was required if U.S. troops are to remain in Iraq, if just to give a continued legal basis to that presence. Multi National Forces, U.S. troops included, were operating under the auspices of UN Security Council Resolution 1790, the last such resolution since UNSCR 1511 (October 16, 2003). This mandate expired on December 31, 2008. The SOFA/Withdrawal Agreement was approved by the Iraqi CoR on November 26, 2008, by 149 out of 198 members who were present, and fulfilled Iraqi constitutional conditions when the Presidential Council confirmed it on December 5. But the Agreement was supposed to be ratified by referendum before July 30, 2009, according to Article 2 of the law enabling the SWA (http://www.parliament.iq/Iraqi_Council_of_Representatives.php?name=articles_ajsdyawqwqdjasdba46s7a98das6dasda7das4da6sd8asdsawewqeqw465e4qweq4wq6e4qw8eqwe4qw6eqwe4sadkj&file=showdetails&sid=2292). Article 3 requires the Iraqi government to abide by the results of the referendum. What is the legal situation of U.S. forces if the referendum fails, or if it is not held?

3. SOFA agreements vary with each country. There are over 100 such agreements with the U.S. in the world. Of these, most famous and controversial are those SOFAs established between the U.S. and South Korea, Japan, and, formerly, Iran. Citizens of these countries have, at different points in history, protested both the presence of U.S. troops and the agreements that authorized it. Ayatollah Khumaini repeatedly declared when he was in exile that the presence of U.S. troops on Iranian soil was a source of national shame. Protests of this kind are often instigated and motivated by what these citizens consider the inappropriate — that is, lax — handling of criminal cases by the U.S. military involving wrongful acts committed against civilians by U.S. troops. The U.S. 1960 US-Japan SOFA, 11 UST 1757 is over 100 pages long. The SOFA agreements between the U.S. and Qatar, and between the U.S. and Kuwait, have remained secret. The much shorter SOFA agreement with East Timor is provided here as an illustration. Note that "the Government of the Democratic Republic of Timor-Leste authorizes the United States Government to exercise criminal jurisdiction over such personnel," under Article VI.

STATUS OF FORCES AGREEMENT BETWEEN THE GOVERNMENT OF THE DEMOCRATIC REPUBLIC OF TIMOR-LESTE AND THE GOVERNMENT OF THE UNITED STATES OF AMERICA

http://www.laohamutuk.org/reports/UN/02US_TLSOFA.htm

Signed 1 October 2002

Preamble

The Government of the Democratic Republic of Timor-Leste and the Government of the United States of America (hereinafter referred to as the "Parties"), recognize the importance of closer cooperation between our two countries, and further recognize that the following principles and understandings are intended to enhance the cooperation between the Parties in furtherance of the objectives of this agreement:

The Parties recognize the independence and sovereignty of the Democratic Republic of Timor-Leste as matters of the highest importance;

The Parties recognize the importance of this agreement to their bilateral interests, regional peace and security, and humanitarian undertakings;

The Parties reaffirm that the principles of mutual respect, friendship, good faith, partnership and cooperation will guide the implementation of this agreement;

Therefore, the Parties have agreed as follows:

Article I

United States military and civilian personnel of the United States Department of Defense who may be present in the Democratic Republic of Timor-Leste in connection with humanitarian and civic assistance, ship visits, military training and exercises and other agreed activities shall be accorded a status equivalent to that accorded to the administrative and technical staff of the Embassy of the United States of America under the Vienna Convention on Diplomatic Relations of April 18, 1961.

Such personnel may enter and exit the Democratic Republic of Timor-Leste with United States identification and with collective movement or individual travel orders; the Democratic Republic of Timor-Leste shall accept as valid, without a driving fee or test, driving licenses or permits issued by the appropriate United States authorities to United States personnel for the operation of vehicles; such personnel, including contract security guards, be authorized to wear uniforms while performing their official duties and to carry weapons when their orders call for it.

Article II

Vehicles, vessels and aircraft owned or operated by or for the United States armed forces shall not be subject to the payment of landing, navigation, overflight or parking charges, port and pilotage fees, or overland transit fees while in the Democratic Republic of Timor-Leste; however, the United States armed forces shall pay reasonable charges for services requested and received. Aircraft, vessels and vehicles of the United States shall be free of inspections.

Article III

The Government of the United States of America, its military and civilian personnel, contractors and contractor personnel shall not be liable to pay any tax or similar charge assessed within the territory of the Democratic Republic of Timor-Leste.

The Government of the United States of America, its military and civilian personnel, contractors and contractor personnel may import into, export out of, and use in the Democratic Republic of Timor-Leste any personal property, equipment, supplies, materials, technology, training or services utilized in connection with activities covered by this agreement. Such importation, exportation and use shall be exempt from any inspection, license, other restrictions, customs duties, taxes or any other charges assessed within the territory of the Democratic Republic of Timor-Leste.

Article IV

The Government of the United States of America and the Government of the Democratic Republic of Timor-Leste shall cooperate in taking such steps as shall be necessary to ensure the security of the United States personnel and property in the territory of the Democratic Republic of Timor-Leste.

Article V

In the event that the Government of the United States of America awards contracts for the acquisition of articles and services, including construction, to implement this agreement, such contracts shall be awarded in accordance with the laws and regulations of the Government of the United States of America. Acquisition of articles and services in the Democratic Republic of Timor-Leste by or on behalf of the Government of the United States of America in connection with activities covered by this agreement shall not be subject to any taxes, customs duties or similar charges in the territory of the Democratic Republic of Timor-Leste.

Article VI

The Government of the Democratic Republic of Timor-Leste recognizes the particular importance of disciplinary control by U.S. military authorities over United States personnel and, therefore, the Government of the Democratic Republic of Timor-Leste authorizes the United States Government to exercise criminal jurisdiction over such personnel. The Government of the Democratic-Republic of Timor-Leste and the Government of the United States of America confirm that such personnel may not be surrendered to, or otherwise transferred to, the custody of an international tribunal or any other entity or state without the express consent of the Government of the United States of America.

Article VII

The Government of the Democratic Republic of Timor-Leste recognizes that it shall be necessary for U.S. personnel and systems to use the radio spectrum. The United States Government shall be allowed to operate its own telecommunication systems (as telecommunication is defined in the 1992 Constitution of the International Telecommunication Union). This shall include the right to utilize such means and services as required to assure full ability to operate telecommunication systems, and the right to use all necessary radio spectrum for this purpose. Use of radio spectrum shall be free of cost.

Article VIII

Other than contractual claims, the Parties waive any and all claims against each other for damage to, loss or destruction of property owned by each party, or death or injury to any military or civilian personnel of the armed forces of either party, arising out of activities in the Democratic Republic of Timor-Leste covered by this agreement. Claims by third parties arising out of the acts or omissions of any U.S. personnel may, at the discretion of the United States Government, be dealt with and settled by the United States Government in accordance with U.S. law.

Article IX

This Agreement shall enter into force upon signature of both Parties. After this Agreement has been in force for one year, either party may request a review of the Agreement. Such review shall begin 180 days after either party has made the request in writing.

Done at Washington this first day of October, 2002, in duplicate in the English language.

FOR THE GOVERNMENT OF THE DEMOCRATIC REPUBLIC OF TIMOR-LESTE:

/s/ J. Ramos-Horta

FOR THE GOVERNMENT OF THE UNITED STATES OF AMERICA:

/s/ Colin L. Powell

4. Central to the SOFA arrangements from the U.S. perspective is the immunity of American servicemen to the Iraqi criminal process. This is complicated in Iraq by the large presence of "contractors," many of whom provide security to American diplomats. Negotiations over the immunity of civilian contractors, as well as military personnel, were particularly difficult in the case of Iraq, see Article 12 of the SWA on Jurisdiction. Hybrid courts have developed in the international criminal field, but those tried never included American citizens. Could a two-tiered, or even a mixed system that includes hybrid U.S.-Iraqi courts, alleviate the stigma? Could the Joint Ministerial Committee established under Article 23 play such a role?

4. ALTERNATIVES: NATO, THE UN, A REGIONAL PACT...?

Any potential long-term, bilateral agreement between Iraq and the United States in which the U.S. is largely responsible for the stability and prosperity of Iraq faces a number of prominent obstacles, including the complicated, contentious nature of the agreement itself, opposition to the agreement from a significant number of both countries' constituents, and the wisdom of such an agreement historically speaking. One possible alternative is Iraq's inclusion in NATO, or some arrangement with NATO. NATO membership would secure needed military resources, primarily in the form of training and guidance, and provide Iraq with multilateral support within a tested framework, and it does so to some extent already. However, Iraq's inclusion in the NATO alliance faces a number of major obstacles, starting with the difficulty to consider Iraq "European" or "Transatlantic"; NATO members resisting the idea of Iraq's inclusion despite recent moves to expand; Iraqi and regional resistance to so close an association with a Western body; and Iraq's inability to meet NATO standards for stability, human rights, etc. in a timely manner. On the other hand, Turkey has been part of NATO since 1952, and few will doubt that its sovereignty is undermined by that membership, especially after the decision of the Turkish government not to take part in the U.S.-led military action against Iraq in 2003. As can be seen from the following documents, available on NATO's website, a significant cooperation has already taken place between the Organization and the Iraqi government. Other NATO documents, including accession and negotiations with third parties, are also included.

(a) NATO

Article 10 of the NATO Treaty, 4 April 1949

The Parties may, by unanimous agreement, invite any other European State in a position to further the principles of this Treaty and to contribute to the security of the North Atlantic area to accede to this Treaty. Any State so invited may become a Party to the Treaty by depositing its instrument of accession with the Government of the United States of America. The Government of the United States of America will inform each of the Parties of the deposit of each such instrument of accession.

NATO in Iraq

While NATO does not have a direct role in the international stabilization force that has been in Iraq since May 2003, the Alliance is helping Iraq provide for its own security by training Iraqi military personnel, supporting the development of the country's security institutions, and coordinating the delivery of equipment.

The decision to establish a NATO training mission in Iraq was made in 2004 in response to a request of the Iraqi Interim Government.

All NATO member countries are contributing to the training effort either in or outside Iraq, through financial contributions or donations of equipment.

NATO is involved in training, equipping, and technical assistance — not combat. The aim is to help Iraq build the capability of its government to address the security needs of the Iraqi people.

What This Means in Practice

NATO is training and mentoring middle and senior level personnel from the Iraqi security forces in Iraq and outside of Iraq, at NATO schools and training centers. The Alliance also plays a role in coordinating offers of equipment and training from individual NATO and partner countries. The NATO training effort currently focuses on mid-and-senior level Iraqi officers.

It aims to help the Iraqi security forces develop an officer corps trained in modern military leadership skills, as well as to inculcate the values appropriate to democratically-controlled armed forces.

Since the beginning of the mission in 2004 and as of December 2006, the NATO mission has trained over 4 000 officers in country, as well as 934 in NATO and national facilities.

In addition, the Alliance is helping to coordinate training, equipment and technical assistance provided by NATO nations on a bilateral basis, both inside and outside of Iraq, to ensure that the Allies complement each other.

This work is carried out by the NATO Training and Equipment Coordination Group, established at NATO Headquarters on 8 October 2004.

Since the beginning of the mission, NATO has delivered military equipment worth some EUR€ 110 million, including ammunition, helmets and body armour, light vehicles, 36 BMP-1 armoured infantry fighting vehicles and 77 Hungarian T-72 main battle tanks, to Iraq.

The main activities of the NATO Training Mission-Iraq are:

The National Defense University:

NATO has set up the National Defense University, based in the International Zone at the Cultural Centre Building, Baghdad.

The North Atlantic Council agreed to support the establishment of this centre on 22 September 2004 and it was officially opened by NATO Secretary General, Jaap de Hoop Scheffer, and Prime Minister Al-Jaafari on 27 September 2005.

The NDU is composed of three main entities:

- The Joint Staff College (JSC) based in Ar Rustimaya provides two courses: the Junior Staff Officer Course and the Senior Staff Officer Course, training approximately 100 officers a year;
- The Iraqi Military Academy of Ar Rustimaya (IMAR): it has the responsibility for the Basic Officer Commissioning Course, during which 120 lieutenants are trained every year (this figure is expected to rise over time);
- The National Defense College (NDC), previously known as the Higher Defense Study Course. It is based in the International Zone at the Cultural Centre Building, Baghdad and started delivering its annual course for flag officers in September 2006.

In response to a second request by Iraqi authorities in December 2005, NATO agreed to develop the professional education programmes for the Basic Officer Commissioning Course (BOCC) and the Non-Commissioned Officer (NCO) Course.

Over an estimated two years, the NDU will gradually become autonomous and Iraqi staff will eventually take leadership of these courses.

The NATO Training and Equipment Coordination Group

This group was established at NATO HQ on 8 October 2004. It works with a similar centre based in Baghdad to coordinate the requirements of the Iraqi government for training and equipment that is offered by NATO as a whole or by individual NATO member countries.

NATO Training Outside of Iraq

Training is also conducted outside Iraq in NATO schools and training centres throughout NATO member countries. In order to allow an increasing number of Iraqi personnel to take part in specialised training outside of Iraq, a language institute was opened in February 2006, with the support of NATO.

This Defense Language Institute in Baghdad is teaching civilian and military officials English. It is attached to the National Defense University. NATO played a key role in its establishment by advising on the course curriculum and assisting in the acquisition of its facilities, computers and furniture.

NATO Membership

Enlargement

NATO has an open door policy on enlargement. Any European country in a position to further the principles of the North Atlantic Treaty and contribute to security in the Euro-Atlantic area can become a member of the Alliance, when invited to do so by the existing member countries.

On 29 March 2004, seven new countries formally joined the Alliance: Bulgaria, Estonia, Latvia, Lithuania, Romania, Slovakia and Slovenia. This was the fifth, and the largest, round of enlargement in the Alliance's history.

The fifth round of NATO enlargement may not be the last. At present, three countries — Albania, Croatia and the former Yugoslav Republic of Macedonia — are members of NATO's Membership Action Plan (MAP), designed to assist aspiring partner countries meet NATO standards and prepare for possible future membership.

At the 2006 Riga Summit, NATO Heads of State and Government declared that the Alliance intends to extend further invitations to countries that meet NATO standards to join NATO at the next Summit, in 2008.

Both Georgia and Ukraine are currently engaged in an Intensified Dialogue with the Alliance focusing on their membership aspirations and related reforms.

Enlargement in Practice

Aspirant countries are expected to participate in the Membership Action Plan to prepare for potential membership and demonstrate their ability to meet the obligations and commitments of possible future membership. They must then be officially invited by NATO to begin accession talks with the Alliance.

Countries seeking NATO membership have to be able to demonstrate that they are in a position to further the principles of the 1949 Washington Treaty and contribute to security in the Euro-Atlantic area. In addition, they are also expected to meet certain political, economic and military goals, which are laid out in the 1995 Study on NATO Enlargement. These include providing evidence:

- that they each represent a functioning democratic, political system based on a market economy;
- that they treat minority populations in accordance with the guidelines of the Organization for Security and Co-operation in Europe (OSCE);
- that they have worked to resolve outstanding disputes with neighbours and have made an overall commitment to the peaceful settlement of disputes;

- have the ability and willingness to make a military contribution to the Alliance and to achieve interoperability with other members' forces;
- and are committed to democratic civil-military relations and institutional structures.

Once they are invited to begin accession talks, the major steps in the process are:

1. Accession talks with a NATO team

These talks take place at NATO headquarters in Brussels and bring together teams of NATO experts and representatives of the individual invitees. Their aim is to obtain formal confirmation from the invitees of their willingness and ability to meet the political, legal and military obligations and commitments of NATO membership, as laid out in the Washington Treaty and in the Study on NATO Enlargement.

The talks take place in two sessions with each invitee. In the first session, political and defense or military issues are discussed, essentially providing the opportunity to establish that the preconditions for membership have been met. The second session is more technical and includes discussion of resources, security, and legal issues as well as the contribution of each new member country to NATO's common budget. This is determined on a proportional basis, according to the size of their economies in relation to those of other Alliance member countries.

Invitees are also required to implement measures to ensure the protection of NATO classified information, and prepare their security and intelligence services to work with the NATO Office of Security.

The end product of these discussions is a timetable to be submitted by each invitee for the completion of necessary reforms, which may continue even after these countries have become NATO members.

2. Invitees send letters of intent to NATO, along with timetables for completion of reforms

In the second step of the accession process, each invitee country provides confirmation of its acceptance of the obligations and commitments of membership in the form of a letter of intent from each foreign minister addressed to the NATO Secretary General. Together with this letter they also formally submit their individual reform timetables.

3. Accession protocols are signed by NATO countries

NATO then prepares Accession Protocols to the Washington Treaty for each invitee. These protocols are in effect amendments or additions to the Treaty, which once signed and ratified by Allies, become an integral part of the Treaty itself and permit the invited countries to become parties to the Treaty.

4. Accession protocols are ratified by NATO countries

The governments of NATO member states ratify the protocols, according to their national requirements and procedures. The ratification procedure varies from country to country. For example, the United States requires a two-thirds majority to pass the required legislation in the Senate. Elsewhere, for example in the United Kingdom, no formal parliamentary vote is required.

5. The Secretary General invites the potential new members to accede to the North Atlantic Treaty

Once all NATO member countries notify the Government of the United States of America, the depository of the Washington Treaty, of their acceptance of the protocols to the North Atlantic Treaty on the accession of the potential new members, the Secretary General invites the new countries to accede to the Treaty.

6. Invitees accede to the North Atlantic Treaty in accordance with their national procedures.

7. Upon depositing their instruments of accession with the U.S. State Department invitees become NATO members.

1995 Study on NATO Enlargement

In 1995, the Alliance carried out and published the results of a Study on NATO Enlargement that considered the merits of admitting new members and how they should be brought in.

It concluded that the end of the Cold War provided a unique opportunity to build improved security in the entire Euro-Atlantic area and that NATO enlargement would contribute to enhanced stability and security for all.

The Study further concluded that enlargement would contribute to enhanced stability and security for all countries in the Euro-Atlantic area by encouraging and supporting democratic reforms, including the establishment of civilian and democratic control over military forces; fostering patterns and habits of cooperation, consultation and consensus-building characteristic of relations among members of the Alliance; and promoting good-neighbourly relations.

It would increase transparency in defense planning and military budgets, thereby reinforcing confidence among states, and would reinforce the overall tendency toward closer integration and cooperation in Europe. The Study also concluded that enlargement would strengthen the Alliance's ability to contribute to European and international security and strengthen and broaden the transatlantic partnership.

According to the Study, countries seeking NATO membership have to be able to demonstrate that they have fulfilled certain requirements. These include providing evidence that they each represent a functioning democratic, political system based on a market economy; that they treat minority populations in accordance with OSCE guidelines; have worked to resolve outstanding disputes with neighbours and have made an overall commitment to the peaceful settlement of disputes; have the ability and willingness to make a military contribution to the Alliance and to achieve interoperability with other members' forces; and are committed to democratic civil-military relations and institutional structures.

Once admitted, new members enjoy all the rights and assume all the obligations of membership, including acceptance at the time that they join of all the principles, policies and procedures previously adopted by Alliance members.

(b) A UN Peace-Keeping Force?

JAMES DOBBINS, THE UN's ROLE IN NATION-BUILDING:
FROM THE CONGO TO IRAQ

Rand Corporation (2005)

The U.S. and UN Ways of Nation-Building

Over the years, the United States and the United Nations have developed distinctive styles of nation-building derived from their very different natures and capabilities. The United Nations is an international organization entirely dependent on its members for the wherewithal to conduct nation building. The United States is the world's only superpower, commanding abundant resources of its own and having access to those of many other nations and institutions.

UN operations have almost always been undermanned and under resourced. This is not because UN managers believe smaller is better, although some do. It is because member states are rarely willing to commit the manpower or the money any prudent military commander would desire. As a result, small and weak UN forces are routinely deployed into what they hope, on the basis of best-case assumptions, will prove to be postconflict situations. Where such assumptions prove ill founded, UN forces have had to be reinforced, withdrawn, or, in extreme cases, rescued.

Throughout the 1990s, the United States adopted the opposite approach to sizing its nation-building deployments, basing its plans on worst-case assumptions and relying on overwhelming force to quickly establish a stable environment and deter resistance from forming. In Somalia, Haiti, Bosnia, and Kosovo, U.S.-led coalitions intervened in numbers and with capabilities that discouraged significant resistance. In Somalia, this American force was drawn down too quickly. The resultant casualties reinforced the American determination to establish and retain a substantial overmatch in any future nation-building operation. In the aftermath of the September 2001 terrorist attacks, American tolerance of military casualties significantly increased. In sizing its stabilization operations in Afghanistan and Iraq, the new American leadership abandoned the strategy of overwhelming preponderance (sometimes labeled the Powell doctrine after former Chairman of the Joint Chiefs of Staff General Colin Powell) in favor of the "small footprint" or "low profile" force posture that had previously characterized UN operations.

In both cases, these smaller American-led forces proved unable to establish a secure environment. In both cases, the original U.S. force levels have had to be significantly increased, but in neither instance has this sufficed to establish adequate levels of public security.

It would appear that the low-profile, small-footprint approach to nation building is much better suited to UN-style peacekeeping than to U.S.-style peace enforcement. The United Nations has an ability to compensate, to some degree at least, for its "hard" power deficit with "soft" power attributes of international legitimacy and local impartiality. The United States does not have such advantages in situations where America itself is a party to the conflict being terminated, or where the United States has acted without an international mandate. Military reversals also have greater consequences for the United States than for the United Nations. To the extent that the United Nations' influence depends more on moral than physical power, more on its legitimacy than its combat prowess, military rebuffs do not fatally undermine its credibility. To the extent that America leans more on "hard" than on "soft" power to achieve its objectives, military reverses strike at the very heart of its potential influence. These considerations, along with recent experience, suggest that the United States would be well advised to resume supersizing its nation-building missions and to leave the small-footprint approach to the United Nations.

The United Nations and the United States tend to enunciate their nation building objectives very differently. UN mandates are highly negotiated, densely bureaucratic documents. UN spokespersons tend toward understatement in expressing their goals. Restraint of this sort is more difficult for U.S. officials, who must build congressional and public support for costly and sometimes dangerous missions in distant and unfamiliar places. As a result, American nation-building rhetoric tends toward the grandiloquent. The United States often becomes the victim of its own rhetoric when its higher standards are not met. UN-led nation-building missions tend to be smaller than American operations, to take place in less demanding circumstances, to be more frequent and therefore more numerous, to have more circumspectly defined objectives, and — at least among the missions studied — to enjoy a higher success rate than U.S.-led efforts. By contrast, U.S.-led nation-building has taken place in more demanding circumstances, has required larger forces and more robust mandates, has received more economic support, has espoused more ambitious objectives, and — at least among the missions studied — has fallen short of those objectives more often than has the United Nations.

. . .

There are three explanations for the better UN success rate. The first is that a different selection of cases would produce a different result. The second is that the U.S. cases are intrinsically more difficult. The third is that the United Nations has done a better job of learning from its mistakes than has the United States. Throughout the 1990s, the United States became steadily better at nation-building. The Haitian operation was better managed than Somalia, Bosnia better than Haiti, and Kosovo better than Bosnia. The U.S. learning curve was not sustained into the current decade. The administration that took office in 2001 initially disdained nation-building as an unsuitable activity for U.S. forces. When compelled to engage in such missions, first in Afghanistan and then in Iraq, the administration sought to break with the strategies and institutional responses that had been honed throughout the 1990s to deal with these challenges.

The United Nations has largely avoided the institutional discontinuities that have marred U.S. performance. The UN Secretary-General, Kofi Annan, was Undersecretary-General for Peacekeeping and head of the UN peacekeeping operation in Bosnia throughout the first half of the 1990s, when UN nation-building began to burgeon. He was chosen for his current post by the United States and other member governments largely on the basis of his demonstrated skills in managing the United Nations' peacekeeping portfolio. Some of his closest associates from that period moved up with him to the UN front office while others remain in the Department of Peacekeeping Operations. As a result, UN nation-building missions have been run over the past 15 years by an increasingly experienced cadre of international civil servants. Similarly in the field, many UN peacekeeping operations are headed and staffed by veterans of earlier operations. The United States, in contrast, tends to staff each new operation as if it were its first and destined to be its last. Service in such missions has never been regarded as career enhancing for American military or Foreign Service officers. Recruitment is often a problem, terms tend to be short, and few individuals volunteer for more than one mission. . . .

Continuing Deficiencies

Even when successful, UN nation building only goes so far to fix the underlying problems of the societies it is seeking to rebuild. Francis Fukuyama has suggested that such missions can be divided into three distinct phases: (1) the initial stabilization of a war-torn society; (2) the creation of local institutions for governance; and (3) the strengthening of those institutions to the point where rapid economic growth and sustained social development can take place. Experience over the past 15 years suggests that the United Nations has achieved a fair mastery of the techniques needed to successfully complete the first two of those tasks. Success with the third has largely eluded the United Nations, as it has the international development community as whole.

Despite the United Nations' significant achievements in the field of nation building, the organization continues to exhibit weaknesses that decades of experience have yet to overcome. Most UN missions are undermanned and underfunded. UN-led military forces are often sized and deployed on the basis of unrealistic best-case assumptions. Troop quality is uneven and has even gotten worse as many rich Western nations have followed U.S. practice and become less willing to commit their armed forces to UN operations. Police and civil personnel are always of mixed competence. All components of the mission arrive late; police and civil administrators arrive even more slowly than soldiers.

These same weaknesses have been exhibited most recently in the U.S.-led operation in Iraq. There, it was an American-led stabilization force that was deployed on the basis of unrealistic, best-case assumptions and American troops that arrived in inadequate numbers and had to be progressively reinforced as new, unanticipated challenges emerged. There, it was the quality of the U.S.-led coalition's military contingents that proved distinctly variable, as has been their willingness to take orders, risks, and casualties. There, it was American civil administrators who were late to arrive, of mixed competence, and not available in adequate numbers. These weaknesses thus appear to be endemic to nation-building rather than unique to the United Nations.

Conclusions

Assuming adequate consensus among Security Council members on the purpose for any intervention, the United Nations provides the most suitable institutional framework for most nation-building missions, one with a comparatively low cost structure, a comparatively high success rate, and the greatest degree of international legitimacy. Other possible options are likely to be either more expensive (e.g., coalitions led by the United States, the European Union, NATO) or less capable organizations (e.g., the African Union, the Organization of American States, or ASEAN). The more expensive options are best suited to missions that require forced entry or employ more than 20,000 men, which so far has been the effective upper limit for UN operations. The less capable options are suited to missions where there is a regional but not a global consensus for action or where the United States simply does not care enough to foot 25 percent of the bill.

Although the U.S. and UN styles of nation-building are distinguishable, they are also highly interdependent. It is a rare operation in which both are not involved. Both UN and U.S. nation-building efforts presently stand at near historic highs. The United Nations currently has approximately 60,000 troops deployed in 17 countries. This is a modest expeditionary commitment in comparison with that of the United States, but it exceeds that of any other nation or combination of nations. Demand for UN-led peacekeeping operations nevertheless far exceeds the available supply, particularly in sub-Saharan African. American armed forces, the world's most powerful, also find themselves badly overstretched by the demands of such missions. A decade ago, in the wake of UN and U.S. setbacks in Somalia and Bosnia, nation-building became a term of opprobrium leading a significant segment of American opinion to reject the whole concept. Ten years later, nation-building appears ever more clearly as a responsibility that neither the United Nations nor the United States can escape. The United States and the United Nations bring different capabilities to the process. Neither is likely to succeed without the other. Both have much to learn not just from their own experience but also from that of each other. It is our hope that this study and its predecessor will help both to do so.

NOTES AND QUESTIONS

1. The SWA includes three important dates: withdrawal of U.S. troops out of the cities by June 30, 2009 (Art. 23.2), referendum by July 31, 2009, full withdrawal by December 31, 2011 (Art. 23.1). Considering the keenness of the Obama administration to withdraw from Iraq as soon as possible, how do the dates square with increased stability in the country? Increasing insecurity? The status quo?

2. As developed in Chapter 5, the UN has been heavily involved in Iraq, despite early tensions and the loss of leading personnel. According to the Rand report, the UN has acquired much greater expertise than the U.S. in nation-building. But its military operations have been undermined by lack of money and troops. Can a combination of UN nation-building and U.S. military support work? How would SOFAs and other agreements relate to such a mix?

3. Would the NATO alternative, with Turkey as the paradigmatic example of a country with a Muslim majority and a Muslim-Democrat government, encourage the development of such a Treaty? Would the other NATO countries agree? On NATO and Iraq, see Fred Tanner, Iraq and World

Order: A Perspective on NATO's relevance, in The Iraq Crisis and World Order 328-343 (2006). How does the Afghanistan example, where NATO operates formally, with the comfort of a stream of Security Council Resolutions, compare? How about arrangements in Qatar and in Kuwait, where the U.S. has the largest military bases outside Iraq in the Arab world? Is it possible to envisage a regional compact like the 1955 Baghdad Pact (CENTO), see Note 1 above at B.1.c? Could it include countries like Syria and Iran?

4. The fog of continuous warfare in Iraq adds confusion to military arrangements with foreign troops and bases. On the one hand, most SOFAs, NATO treaties, and other more informal arrangements, such as the coordination of intelligence matters and the conduct of "special operations," do not take place with countries facing an insurgency doubling up as civil war and foreign intervention as in Iraq. So long as the insurgency continues, which feeds at least in part on the presence of foreign troops, discussion of SOFAs and similar formal arrangements carries much passion, also feeding the opposition, military and otherwise. How can the vicious circle be broken, especially since the success of the Petraeus strategy is determined by increasing the Host Nation's self-reliance in security matters? Is self-reliance/sovereignty ultimately not primarily defined by the total absence of foreign troops?

INDEX

Surnames starting with "al-" are alphabetized by the following part of the name.